PassKey
Learning Systems

EA Review
Part 2: Businesses

Enrolled Agent Study Guide

May 1, 2021-February 28, 2022
Testing Cycle

Joel Busch, CPA, JD

Christy Pinheiro, EA, ABA®

Kolleen Wells, EA

Thomas A. Gorczynski, EA, USTCP

Executive Editor: Joel Busch, CPA, JD

This study guide is designed for exam candidates who will take their exams in the May 1, 2021, to February 28, 2022 testing cycle.

Title: PassKey Learning Systems EA Review Part 2 Businesses; Enrolled Agent Study Guide, May 1, 2021-February 28, 2022 Testing Cycle

ISBN: 978-1-935664-74-1

First Printing, March 2021.

Official website: ***www.PassKeyonline.com.***

Table of Contents

Recent Praise for the PassKey EA Review Series

(Real customers, real names, public testimonials)

Passed on First Try

Jake Bavaro

I recently passed the first part of the EA exam using just the textbook and separate practice test workbook. The textbook is very easy to read and understand. Although I have a background in accounting and tax, someone with little or no knowledge of either should be able to grasp all of the various topics covered in the book. I really do believe that it is a superior preparation resource.

I Highly recommend these materials

Tosha H. Knelangeon

Using only the [PassKey] study guide and the workbook, I passed all three EA exams on my first try. I highly recommend these materials. As long as you put in the time to read and study all the information provided, you should be well-prepared.

You can pass using just this book.

Vishnu Kali Osirion

I really rushed studying for this section. These authors make tax law relevant to your day-to-day experiences and understandable. You can pass the exam with just this as a resource. I do recommend purchasing the workbook as well, just for question exposure. The questions in the book and in the workbook are pretty indicative of what's on the exam. This is a must-buy. Cheers.

Suika Yutaka

I prefer self-study over any other type of course, and I loved this book. I have a very demanding job, and this made me greatly appreciate the concise and to-the-point style of this book. Also, note that this is the most reasonably priced full review (i.e., covering all three parts of the exam) I know of. Greatest praise!

PassKey was the only study aid that I used

Stephen J Woodard, CFP, CLU, ChFC

The guides were an invaluable resource. They were concise and covered the subject matter succinctly with spot-on, end-of-chapter questions that were very similar to what I encountered on the exams.

100% Success!

Shreejith Nair

Very easy to understand with very good examples on each topic. I cleared [the exam] on my first attempt. I would highly recommend PassKey to all folks. Best of luck.

Very useful, I passed my exams by reading only PassKey!

Shixiong Feng

Very useful, I passed the 1st and 2nd exams by only reading the PassKey EA Review. If you are willing to spend some time reading the whole book thoroughly, then this book is the only thing you need to pass the EA exams.

Amazing!

Sopio Svanishvilion

PassKey helped me pass all three parts of the Enrolled Agent exam. They are a "must-have" if you want to pass your EA exams.

A great EA review book

William Highfield (Lafayette, Colorado)

I used the Complete EA Review book as a study guide and passed all my tests the first time. Don't get the idea the tests were easy, but the book was so well-organized and inclusive that the memorization and familiarization processes went very well.

This review is the best on the market.

Yaw Asiante-Asamoah

I passed on all three parts on one attempt. The questions in the EA Review and Workbook are similar to the real exams. I got a big raise, and my bonus went up at my seasonal job. It's worth the money, trust me.

This book is worth the money.

Bridgette Holzapple

I passed Part 2 on my first try. The questions on the test were very similar to the problems in the workbook. You will pass, no doubt!

I passed all three parts on my first attempt.

Michelle D. Stroschen

I passed all three parts on my first attempt. I would definitely recommend it! These books are reasonably priced and have up-to-date information.

Introduction

Congratulations on taking the first step toward becoming an enrolled agent, a widely respected professional tax designation. The Internal Revenue Service licenses enrolled agents, known as EAs, after candidates pass a competency exam testing their knowledge of federal tax law. As an enrolled agent, you will have the same representation rights as a CPA, with the ability to represent taxpayers in IRS audits and appeals—an EA's rights are unlimited before all levels and offices of the IRS.

The PassKey study guide series is designed to help you study for the EA exam, which is formally called the *IRS Special Enrollment Examination* or "*SEE.*"

EA Exam Basics

The EA exam consists of three parts, which candidates may schedule separately and take in any order they wish. The computerized exam covers all aspects of federal tax law, with Part 1 testing the taxation of individuals; Part 2 testing the taxation of businesses; and Part 3 testing representation, practice, and procedures.

Each part of the EA exam features 100 multiple choice questions, with no written answers required. The exam will include some experimental questions that are not scored. You will not know which of the questions count toward your score and which do not.

Computerized EA Exam Format

Part 1: Individual Taxation–100 questions

Part 2: Business Taxation–100 questions

Part 3: Representation, Practice, and Procedures–100 questions

You will have 3.5 hours to complete each part of the exam. The actual seat time is four hours, which allows time for a pre-exam tutorial and a post-exam survey. An on-screen timer counts down the amount of time you have to finish.

The testing company Prometric exclusively administers the EA exam at thousands of testing centers across the United States and in certain other countries. You can find valuable information and register online at ***https:/www.prometric.com/IRS***.

Prometric Testing Center Procedures

The testing center is designed to be a secure environment. The following are procedures you will need to follow on test day:

1. Check in about a half-hour before your appointment time and bring a current, government-issued ID with a photo and signature. If you do not have a valid ID, you will be turned away and will have to pay for a new exam appointment. Refunds will not be issued by Prometric if you forget to bring a proper ID with you.

2. The EA exam is a closed-book test, so you are not allowed to bring any notes or reference materials into the testing room. The center supplies sound-blocking headphones if you want to use them.
3. No food, water, or other beverages are allowed in the testing room.
4. You will be given scratch paper and a pencil to use, which will be collected after the exam.
5. You will be able to use an on-screen calculator during the exam, or Prometric will provide you with a handheld calculator. You cannot bring your own calculator into the examination room.
6. Before entering the testing room, you will be scanned with a metal detector wand.
7. You will need to sign in and out every time you leave the testing room. Bathroom breaks are permitted, but the test timer will continue to count down.
8. You are not allowed to talk or communicate with other test-takers in the exam room. Prometric continuously monitors the testing via video, physical walk-throughs, and an observation window.

Important Note: Violation of any of these procedures may result in the disqualification of your exam. In cases of cheating, the IRS says candidates are subject to consequences that include civil and criminal penalties.

Exam-takers who require special accommodations under the Americans with Disabilities Act (ADA) must contact Prometric directly to obtain an accommodation request. The test is administered in English; a language barrier is not considered a disability.

Exam Content

Each year, using questions based on the prior calendar year's tax law, the IRS introduces multiple new versions of each part of the EA exam. If you fail a particular part of the exam and need to retake it, do not expect to see identical questions the next time.

Prometric's website includes broad content outlines for each exam part. When you study, make sure you are familiar with the items listed, which are covered in detail in your PassKey guides. Questions from older exams are available on the IRS website for review. Be aware that tax law changes every year, so be familiar with recent updates and do not rely too heavily on these earlier questions and answers.

Your PassKey study guides present an overview of all the major areas of federal taxation that enrolled agents typically encounter in their practices and are likely to appear on the exam. Although our guides are designed to be comprehensive, we suggest you also review IRS publications and try to learn as much as you can about tax law in general, so you are well-equipped to take the exam.

In addition to this study guide, we highly recommend that all exam candidates read:

- **Publication 17,** *Your Federal Income Tax* (for Part 1 of the exam), and
- **Circular 230,** *Regulations Governing the Practice of Attorneys, Certified Public Accountants, Enrolled Agents, Enrolled Actuaries, and Appraisers before the Internal Revenue Service* (for Part 3 of the exam)

You may download these publications for free from the IRS website.

Note: Some exam candidates take *Part 3: Representation, Practice, and Procedures* first rather than taking the tests in order, since the material in Part 3 is considered less complicated. However, test-takers should know that several questions pertaining to taxation of *Individuals* (Part 1) and *Businesses* (Part 2) are often included on the Part 3 exam.

Exam Strategy

Each multiple-choice question has four answer choices. There are several different question formats, and examples of each format are featured in your PassKey study guides.

During the exam, you should read each question thoroughly to understand precisely what is being asked. Be particularly careful when the problem uses language such as "not" or "except."

Format One–Direct Question

Which of the following entities are required to file Form 709, United States Gift Tax Return?

A. An individual

B. An estate or trust

C. A corporation

D. All of the above

Format Two–Incomplete Sentence

Supplemental wages do not include payments for:

A. Accumulated sick leave

B. Nondeductible moving expenses

C. Vacation pay

D. Travel reimbursements paid at the federal government's per diem rate

Format Three–All of the Following Except

Five tests must be met for you to claim an exemption for a dependent. Which of the following is *not* a requirement?

A. Citizen or Resident Test

B. Member of Household or Relationship Test

C. Disability Test

D. Joint Return Test

If you are unsure of an answer, you may mark it for review and return to it later. Try to eliminate clearly wrong answers from the four possible choices to narrow your odds of selecting the right answer. But be sure to answer every question, even if you have to guess, because all answers left incomplete will be marked as incorrect. Each question is weighted equally.

There may also be a limited number of questions that have four choices, with three incorrect statements or facts and only one with a correct statement or fact, which you would select as the right answer.

With 3.5 hours allotted for each part of the exam, you have slightly more than two minutes per question. Try to answer the questions you are sure about quickly, so you can devote more time to those that include calculations or that you are unsure about. Remember, the clock does not stop for bathroom breaks, so allocate your time wisely.

To familiarize yourself with the computerized testing format, you may take a tutorial on the Prometric website. However, the tutorial only illustrates what the test screens look like; it does not allow you to revisit questions you have left open or marked for review, as you can do during the actual exam.

Scoring Methods

The EA exam is not graded on a curve, and the IRS does not reveal either a percentage of correct answers needed to pass or a predetermined pass rate. Each question on the exam is worth one point. The IRS determines scaled scores by calculating the number of questions answered correctly from the total number of questions in the exam and converting to a scale that ranges from 40 to 130. The IRS has set the scaled passing score at 105, which corresponds to the minimum level of knowledge deemed acceptable for EAs.

After you finish your exam and submit your answers, you will exit the testing room, and a Prometric staff member will print results showing whether you passed or failed. Test results are automatically shared with the IRS, so you do not need to submit them yourself. Test scores are confidential and will be revealed only to you and the IRS. If you pass, your printed results will show a passing designation but not your actual score. The printout also will not indicate which specific questions you answered correctly or incorrectly.

If you fail, you will receive a scaled score, so you will be able to see how close you are to the minimum score of 105. You will also receive the following diagnostic information to help you know which subject areas to concentrate on when studying to retake the exam:

- Level 1: Area of weakness where additional study is necessary. You need to focus on this domain as you prepare to retake the test. You may want to consider taking a course or participating actively in a study group on this topic.
- Level 2: Might need additional study.
- Level 3: Clearly demonstrated an understanding of the subject area.

These diagnostic indicators correspond to various sections of each part of the exam.

If necessary, you may take each part of the exam up to four times during the current testing window. You will need to re-register with Prometric and pay fees each new time you take an exam part.

In general, exam-takers may carry over passing scores for individual parts of the exam up to two years from the date they take them. However, due to the global pandemic, the IRS extended the two-year period to three years.

This applies to any examination parts that had not expired as of February 29, 2020, and any examination parts passed on June 1, 2020, and later. For example, assume a candidate passed Part 1 on November 15, 2019. Subsequently, the candidate passed Part 2 on February 15, 2020. That candidate has until November 15, 2022, to pass the remaining part.

Applying for Enrollment

Once you have passed all three parts of the EA exam, you can apply to become an enrolled agent. The process includes an IRS review of your tax compliance history. Failure to timely file or pay personal income taxes can be grounds for denial of enrollment. The IRS Return Preparer Office will review the circumstances of each case and make determinations on an individual basis. You may not practice as an EA until the IRS approves your application and issues you an enrollment card, a process that takes up to 60 days or more.

Successfully passing the EA exam can launch you into a fulfilling and lucrative new career. The exam requires intense preparation and diligence, but with the help of PassKey's comprehensive *EA Review*, you will have the tools you need to learn how to become an enrolled agent.

We wish you much success.

Ten Steps for the EA Exam

STEP 1: Learn

Learn more about the enrolled agent designation, and explore the career opportunities that await you after passing your EA exam. In addition to preparing income tax returns for clients, EAs can represent individuals and businesses before the IRS, just as attorneys and CPAs do. A college degree or professional tax background is not required to take the EA exam. Many people who use the PassKey study guides have had no prior experience preparing tax returns, but go on to rewarding new professional careers.

STEP 2: Gather Information

Gather more information before you launch into your studies. The IRS publishes necessary information on its website *(www.irs.gov/Tax-Professionals/Enrolled-Agents).*

You will also find valuable information about the exam itself on the Prometric testing website at www.prometric.com/IRS. Be sure to download the official Candidate Information Bulletin, which takes you step-by-step through the registration and testing process.

STEP 3: Obtain a PTIN

PTIN stands for "Preparer Tax Identification Number." Before you can register for your EA exam, you must obtain a PTIN from the IRS. The PTIN sign-up system can be found at www.irs.gov/ptin. You will need to create an account and provide personal information. Foreign-based candidates without a Social Security number are also required to have a PTIN in order to register to take the exam; they will need to submit additional paperwork with their Form W-12 (PTIN Application and Renewal).

STEP 4: Register with Prometric

Once you have your PTIN, you may register for your exam on the Prometric website by creating an account to set up your user ID and password. You must also complete Form 2587, Application for Special Enrollment Examination.

STEP 5: Schedule Your Test

After creating an account, you can complete the registration process by clicking on "Scheduling." Your exam appointment must be scheduled within one year from the date of registration. You can choose a test site, time, and date that are convenient for you. Prometric has test centers in most major metropolitan areas of the United States, as well as in many other countries.

You may schedule as little as two days in advance—space permitting—through the website or by calling Prometric directly Monday through Friday. Be aware that the website and the phone line show different available times and dates, so you may want to check both for your preferred testing dates. The testing fee is nonrefundable. Once you've scheduled, you'll receive a confirmation number. Keep it for your records because you will need it to reschedule, cancel, or change your appointment.

STEP 6: Adopt a Study Plan

Focus on one exam part at a time, and adopt a study plan that covers each unit of your PassKey guides. You'll need to develop your own individualized study program. The period of time you'll need to prepare for each exam is truly unique to you, based on how much prior tax preparation experience you have and your current level of tax knowledge, how well you understand and retain the information you read, and how much time you have to study for each test.

For those without prior tax experience, a good rule of thumb is to study *at least* 60 hours for each of the three exam sections. Part 2: Businesses may require additional study preparation, as evidenced by the lower pass rates. One thing is true for all candidates: for each of the tests, start studying well in advance of your scheduled exam date.

STEP 7: Get Plenty of Rest and Good Nutrition

Get plenty of rest, exercise, and good nutrition prior to the EA exam. You'll want to be at your best on exam day.

STEP 8: Test Day

Be sure to arrive early at the test site. Prometric advises arriving at least 30 minutes before your scheduled exam time. If you miss your appointment and are not allowed to take the test, you'll forfeit your fee and have to pay for a new appointment. Remember to bring a government-issued ID with your name, photo, and signature. Your first and last name must exactly match the first and last name you used to register for the exam.

STEP 9: During the Exam

This is when your hard work finally pays off. Focus and don't worry if you don't know the answer to every question, but make sure you use your time well. Give your best answer to every question. All questions left blank will be marked as wrong.

STEP 10: Congratulations. You Passed!

After celebrating your success, you need to apply for your EA designation. The quickest way is by filling out Form 23, Application for Enrollment to Practice Before the Internal Revenue Service, on the IRS website. You may also pay online. Once your application is approved, you'll be issued an enrollment card, and you'll officially be a brand-new enrolled agent!

This page intentionally left blank.

Essential Tax Law Figures for Businesses

Here is a quick summary of some of the essential tax figures for the revised enrolled agent exam cycle (May 1, 2021, to February 28, 2022).

Note: The *American Rescue Plan Act (ARPA)* was signed into law on March 11, 2021. This bill includes many retroactive provisions that impact 2020 and 2021 tax returns. However, because these are retroactive changes passed *after* December 31, 2020, they will not be tested in the current testing cycle. We have added some relevant footnotes to this introductory text, but the provisions in this bill will not be covered.

Important Legislation for the 2020 Tax Year:

1. ***The Coronavirus Aid, Relief, and Economic Security (CARES) Act*** became law on March 27, 2020. This $2.2 trillion economic stimulus bill included a host of new tax credits and retroactive provisions to provide COVID-19 relief to individuals and businesses.
2. **The *Consolidated Appropriations Act of 2021 (CAA 2021)*** was signed into law on December 27, 2020, by President Donald Trump. This legislation extends and modifies many provisions of the earlier *CARES Act.* The *Consolidated Appropriations Act* included a second round of stimulus payments, a second round of PPP loan funding, and numerous tax extenders. Included in the bill:
    - *COVID-19-related Tax Relief Act of 2020,* (COVIDTRA);
    - *Coronavirus Response and Relief Supplemental Appropriations (CRRSA) Act;* and,
    - The *Taxpayer Certainty and Disaster Tax Relief Act (TCDTR).*

Normal Income Tax Return Filing Deadlines:

- **Individual filing Deadline:** April 15[1] (extended due date: October 15).
- **Estates and Trusts Income Tax Return Deadline:** April 15 (Automatic extension period of 5 ½ months; due September 30 for a calendar-year entity).
- **Estate Tax Return Deadline (Form 706):** Due within nine months after the date of the decedent's death (a 6-month extension is available).
- **Partnership Deadline:** March 15 (extended due date: September 15) or the 15th day of the 3rd month after the end of the partnership's tax year, for fiscal-year filers.
- **C Corporation Deadline:** April 15 (extended due date: October 15), or the 15th day of the fourth month following the end of the corporation's tax year, in the case of fiscal-year filers.

[1] If a due date falls on a weekend or legal holiday, the deadline is pushed to the next business day. On March 17, 2021, the Internal Revenue Service and the U.S. Department of the Treasury announced the 2021 income tax filing and payment deadline is May 17, 2021. Individual taxpayers do not need to file any forms or call the IRS to qualify for this automatic federal tax filing and payment relief.

- C Corporations with a June 30th Fiscal Year End: Due the 15th day of the 3rd month after the end of the entity's tax year. For a June 30 fiscal year entity, Form 1120 is due September 15th.

- **S Corporation Deadline:** March 15 (extended due date: September 15) or by the 15th day of the third month following the end of the tax year for fiscal year filers.
- **Exempt Entity Deadline:** May 15 (extended due date: November 15).
- **Employee benefit plan (Form 5500 series):** Last day of the 7th calendar month after the end of the plan's tax year; due July 31 for a calendar-year plan, (an extension is available to October 15 for a calendar-year plan).
- **FBAR:** The official due date for the FBAR (FinCen 114) coincides with the filing of the individual tax return (April 15). An automatic extension is allowed to October 15. The form must be filed electronically and is only available online through the BSA E-Filing System website.[2]

Estimated Tax Due Dates:

- **Individuals:** Quarterly estimated taxes are due by April 15, June 15, September 15, and January 15, of the following year.[3]
- **Farmers and Fishermen:** January 15 (if *not* filing a return by Mar. 1), or March 1 (if filing a tax return on or before Mar 1).
- **C Corporations:**[4] April 15, June 15, September 15, and December 15 (for calendar-year corporations).

Form 1099 Deadlines:

Form 1099-NEC Normal Filing Deadline

- To the Recipient by January 31[5]
- IRS Paper filing by January 31
- IRS electronic filing by January 31

Form 1099-MISC Normal Filing Deadline

- Form 1099-MISC to the recipient by January 31
- IRS Paper Filing by February 28[6]
- IRS electronic filing by March 31

---

[2] FBAR refers to Form 114, Report of Foreign Bank and Financial Accounts, that must be filed with the Financial Crimes Enforcement Network (FinCEN), which is a bureau of the Treasury Department. Although the FBAR is not filed directly with the IRS, the IRS is responsible for FBAR enforcement.

[3] For the 2020 tax year only, estimated tax payments normally due on April 15, 2020, and June 15, 2020, were treated as "timely" if the payments were made by July 15, 2020.

[4] Corporations generally must make estimated tax payments if they expect their estimated tax (income tax less credits) to be $500 or more.

[5] Because January 31, 2021 is a Sunday, the actual 2020 deadline is pushed forward one day to February 1, 2021.

[6] Because February 28, 2021, is a Sunday, the actual 2020 deadline is pushed forward one day to March 1, 2021.

Note: A 30-day extension may be requested for information returns (Form W-2 and Form 1099-MISC) but only in extraordinary circumstances, such as in the case of a natural disaster, death of the business owner, or other extraordinary events. Form 8809 is used to request an extension.

2020 Net Investment Income Tax (NIIT): The tax in 2020 is 3.8% of the *lesser* of:

- Net investment income, or
- The amount of modified adjusted gross income (MAGI) over $12,950 for Estates and trusts.

2020 "Nanny Tax" for Household Employers: The nanny tax threshold is $2,200 in 2020. A household employer is normally obligated to withhold and pay federal FICA (Social Security and Medicare) taxes for any household employee the employer pays $2,200 *or more* during the year. A household employer is required to pay FUTA taxes if they paid a household employee $1,000 or more in a calendar quarter. These thresholds are on a *per-employee* basis.

2020 Maximum Compensation Subject to FICA

- OASDI[7] maximum wage base: $137,700
- Social Security Tax Rate:
    - Employee: 6.2%
    - Self-employed: 12.4%
- Maximum Social Security Tax:
    - Employee: $8,537.40
    - Self-employed: $17,074.80
- Medicare: No limit (2.9% for self-employed, 1.45% for employees)
- Self-employed tax rate: 15.3%
- *Additional* Medicare Tax: 0.9% on earned income exceeding the following thresholds:
    - Married filing jointly: $250,000[8]
    - Married filing separately: $125,000
    - Single: $200,000
    - Head of household: $200,000
    - Qualifying widow(er) with dependent child: $200,000
- **2020 FUTA Wage Base:** The FUTA tax rate is 6% on the first $7,000 paid to each employee. Only the employer pays FUTA tax. The tax is not withheld from the employee's wages.

---

[7] "OASDI" is the official name for Social Security in the United States, and the terms are often used interchangeably. The acronym stands for "Old-Age, Survivors, and Disability Insurance".

[8] Earned income of spouses is combined towards this Additional Medicare Tax threshold for MFJ returns. Employers must withhold this tax from wages or compensation when they pay employees more than $200,000 in a calendar year, regardless of the employee's filing status.

2020 Estate and Trust *Exemption* Amounts[9]

- Estate Exemption Amount: $600
- Simple Trust: $300
- Complex Trust: $100
- Qualified disability trusts: $4,300

2020 Estate and Gift Tax *Exclusion* Amounts

- 2020 Annual Exclusion for Gifts: $15,000
- Lifetime *noncitizen* marital threshold for gift tax: $157,000[10]
- Estate and Gift Tax Unified Credit: $11,580,000
- Generation-Skipping Transfer Tax Exemption: $11,580,000
- Highest estate and gift tax rate: 40%
- The portability election (DSUE) remains effective in 2020.

2020 QSEHRA Limits (Maximum payments and reimbursements through the QSEHRA)[11]

- Self-only: $5,250
- Family: $10,600

2020 FSA Limits:

- Health Care FSA: $2,750.
- Dependent Care FSA (DCFSA): $5,000 ($2,500 if MFS).

> **Note:** As part of the disaster relief provisions implemented by the CAA 2021, employers may allow employees to carryover unused benefits or contributions remaining in an FSA from 2020 to 2021. The use of dependent FSA (DCFSA) funds is permitted up to age 14 rather than the usual age of 13. Employers can also allow employees to change their FSA contribution elections outside of open enrollment for plan years ending in 2021.

2020 HSA and HDHP Limits: To qualify to contribute to a health savings account, the taxpayer must have a high-deductible health insurance policy. The plan must also have an annual limit on out-of-pocket expenses (not including premiums).[12]

HSA contribution limits	Self-only: $3,550, Family: $7,100
HSA catch-up contributions (age 55 or older)	$1,000
HDHP minimum deductible	Self-only: 1,400, Family: $2,800
HDHP maximum out-of-pocket amounts (not including insurance premiums)	Self-only: $6,900, Family: $13,800

---

[9] For estates and trusts, the exemption amount is not allowed in the entity's final tax year (the year of dissolution).
[10] There is no limit on the amount that a U.S. citizen can transfer to another U.S. citizen spouse in a calendar year. This limitation only applies to noncitizen spouses.
[11] Employees have three months after the end of the calendar year to submit expenses for reimbursement through a QSEHRA, so they can submit the prior year's expenses for reimbursement until March 31, 2021.
[12] An HSA can be combined with a qualified high-deductible health plan and offers the opportunity to save for health care on a pre-tax basis. Another name for an HDHP is an "HSA-Eligible" Plan.

2020 Contribution Limits – Retirement Plans

- **Roth and traditional IRAs:** $6,000 (additional catch-up contribution of $1,000 for taxpayers age 50 or older)[13]
- **Roth IRA contribution limit phaseout (MAGI):**
    - $196,000–$206,000: MFJ/QW
    - $124,000–$139,000: Single and HOH
    - $0 to $10,000: MFS[14]
- **SIMPLE IRA elective deferral limits:**
    - Under age 50: $13,500
    - Age 50 and over: $16,500
- **Profit Sharing/SEP-IRA contribution limits (employee + employer):**
    - Up to 25% of compensation, up to a maximum of $57,000
    - Age 50 and over $63,500
- **Qualified plan contribution Limits:**
    - 401(k)/403(b) plan deferral limits: $19,500 (50 and over $26,000)
    - Defined contribution plan limits (employee + employer):
        - Up to $57,000
        - If age 50 or older: $63,500
        - Employee compensation limit for calculating contributions: $285,000
        - Total contributions cannot exceed 100% of compensation.
    - Defined Benefit Plan Limits:[15]
        - Annual compensation maximum limit: $285,000
        - Normal maximum annual retirement benefit limit: Lesser of (1) $230,000, or (2) the average of the three highest years of compensation
    - Key employee threshold for nondiscrimination testing: $185,000
    - Highly compensated employee threshold for nondiscrimination testing: $130,000

Note: IRA *conversions* from traditional IRAs to Roth IRAs are still allowed after enactment of the Tax Cuts and Jobs Act; however, later *recharacterizations* or "unwinding" is no longer allowed.[16] The TCJA also prohibits recharacterizing amounts that were rolled over to a Roth IRA from other types of retirement plans, such as 401(k) or 403(b) plans.

[13] The 2020 Traditional and Roth IRA Contribution Deadline is April 15, 2021. The "catch-up" contribution limit for participants age 50 or older applies from the start of the year for those turning 50 at any time during the year.

[14] With regards to the Roth contribution limit, if the taxpayer is "married filing separately" but did not live with their spouse at any time during the year, the taxpayer may use the higher phaseout threshold for single taxpayers.

[15] A defined benefit plan is also called a "traditional pension" and these retirement plans are solely funded by the employer, not the employee. Actuarial assumptions and computations are required to figure these contributions.

[16] An IRA "recharacterization" is a reversal of a previous conversion. For example, if a taxpayer converts to a Roth IRA and then later changes his mind, he would use a process known as "recharacterization" to convert the funds *back* to his traditional IRA.

2020 Section 179 Expense:

- Maximum deduction amount: $1,040,000.
- Beginning phaseout limitation: $2,590,000.
- Heavy SUV Limit: $25,900

2020 Bonus Depreciation:

The 100% bonus depreciation amount remains in effect through January 1, 2023. Bonus depreciation also applies to used property. Assets that qualify for bonus depreciation include:

- MACRS property with a recovery period of 20 years or less
- Computer software
- Water utility property
- Qualified film or television production (excluding pornographic films)
- Qualified live theatrical production, as defined in section 181(e)
- Fruit and nut-bearing trees[17]

2020 QBI deduction Limits

In 2020, the QBI deduction is up to 20% of QBI from a pass-through entity conducting a trade or business in the U.S. It also includes up to 20% of qualified real estate investment trust dividends (REIT) and qualified publicly traded partnership income (PTP). The 199A SSTB phaseouts are as follows:[18]

- Married filing jointly: $326,600-$426,600
- Head of Household/Single: $163,300-$213,300
- Married filing Separately: $163,300-$213,300

2020 Standard Mileage Rates:

- Business: 57.5¢ per mile[19]
- Charitable purposes: 14¢ per mile
- Medical and moving: 17¢ per mile[20]

2020 Qualified Transportation Benefits[21]

- Commuter benefits/transit passes: $270 per month.
- Parking: $270 per month.

---

[17] This includes grapevines, orange trees, almonds and olive orchards, etc. In the past, fruit and nut bearing trees would not be "placed in service" for several years, because the trees would not be "placed in service" until they bear fruit. Now, farmers are allowed to take bonus depreciation at the time of planting. This is an election for bonus depreciation only. These plants and trees would not be eligible for Section 179 in their pre-productive period. A farmer may also choose to wait, and when the trees begin bearing fruit or nuts, then the farmer may claim section 179 or regular MACRS depreciation.

[18] If the taxpayer's income is above this threshold, or if the taxpayer uses Form 1099-PATR (to report distributions they received from a farm or cooperative), the QBI deduction will be calculated on Form 8995-A. If the taxpayer's income is below the threshold the deduction is calculated on Form 8995.

[19] Business mileage is no longer deductible as an unreimbursed employee business expense, except for U.S. armed forces reservists, state or local government officials paid on a fee basis, and certain performing artists.

[20] Moving mileage is deductible *only* by U.S. armed forces members on active duty who move pursuant to a military order and incident to a permanent change of station.

[21] The transportation benefits are excluded from W-2 wages, but the employer is no longer allowed a deduction for the expense.

Tax Law Updates for Businesses

Taxpayer First Act of 2019

On July 1, 2019, the **Taxpayer First Act of 2019 (TFA)** was signed into law. The TFA makes the most significant changes to IRS administrative procedures since the IRS Restructuring and Reform Act of 1998. The most important aspects of this bill that apply to tax year 2020 are:

- **Expansion of efile Requirements for Businesses Filing Information Returns:** The Act) expanded requirements for certain entities that file information returns to file electronically. This is a separate mandate from the existing requirement for partnerships with more than 100 partners to file electronically.[22]
- **Expansion of efile requirements for Form 990:** The TFA now requires efiling for tax-exempt organizations that file Form 990. Forms 990 and 990-PF with tax years ending July 31, 2020, and later MUST be filed electronically. Form 990 and 990-PF filings for tax years ending on or before June 30, 2020, may still be paper-filed.[23]
- **Applications for nonprofit exemption:** Form 1023, *application for exemption under Internal Revenue Code Section 501(c)(3),* must now be submitted electronically. After April 30, 2020, the IRS will only accept electronic filing of the form and online payment of the user fee. Beginning January 5, 2021, the IRS allows exempt entities to now file an electronic version of Form 1024-A, for organizations seeking to be exempt under Section 501(c)(4). The IRS provides a 90-day grace period during which it will continue to accept paper versions of Form 1024-A; however, after April 5, 2021, paper applications will no longer be permitted.

Families First Coronavirus Response Act (FFCRA)

The Families First Coronavirus Response Act (FFCRA), signed into law on March 18, 2020. The FFCRA:

- **FFCRA Sick and Medical Leave:** Required certain employers to provide employees with paid sick leave[24] or expanded family and medical leave[25] for specified reasons related to COVID-19. This is also sometimes called "FFCRA paid leave" or "COVID-19 sick leave."
- **FFCRA Self-Employed Credits:** The FFCRA extended equivalent refundable credits to self-employed individuals and household employers (taxpayers who file Schedule H). Form 7202 is used by self-employed taxpayers to figure the amount to claim for qualified sick and family leave equivalent credits.

---

[22] Prior law prohibited any requirement that businesses who file fewer than 250 returns during a calendar year do so electronically. Under the Taxpayer First Act, the 250 is reduced to 100 in calendar year 2021 (for 2020 tax filings), and from 100 to 10 after 2021. In the case of a partnership, the number will be 50 for calendar year 2021 (for 2020 tax filings).

[23] For small tax-exempt organizations, the legislation specifically allows transitional relief. For tax years ending before July 31, 2021, the IRS will accept either paper or electronic filing of Form 990-EZ. For tax years ending July 31, 2021 or later, Forms 990-EZ must be filed electronically. Source: https://www.irs.gov/newsroom/irs-recent-legislation-requires-tax-exempt-organizations-to-e-file-forms

[24] "Paid sick leave" – means paid leave under the Emergency Paid Sick Leave Act.

[25] "Expanded family and medical leave" – means paid leave under the Emergency Family and Medical Leave Expansion Act. See full definitions at: https://www.dol.gov/agencies/whd/pandemic/ffcra-questions

- **Extended, but not mandatory:** The *mandatory* FFCRA leave requirements expired on December 31, 2020, but were modified and extended by the *Consolidated Appropriations Act of 2021*.[26] Employers can choose to provide FFCRA leave on a voluntary basis after December 31, 2020, and continue to take available tax credits through September 30, 2021.[27]

Coronavirus Aid, Relief, and Economic Security (CARES) Act:

The *CARES Act* was passed on March 27, 2020, and made many tax law changes that apply to the 2020 tax year.

- **Net Operating Losses (NOLs):** The TCJA eliminated the net operating loss (NOL) carryback for most losses occurring after 2017. Under the TCJA, NOL carrybacks were unavailable to all taxpayers except farmers and casualty insurance companies, who were allowed a two-year carryback. The CARES Act temporarily suspended these TCJA changes.
    - **NOLS under the CARES Act:** The CARES Act allows the return of the carryback for losses in 2018, 2019, and 2020.[28] For most taxpayers, NOLs that arose in 2018-2020 can be carried back five years. This means that an NOL that arose in 2020 can be carried back to 2015. The taxpayer may also elect out of the carryback period.
    - **NOL 80% Limit Repealed:** For 2020, the CARES Act repeals the 80% limitation on the deductibility of NOL carryovers, making the limitation equal to 100% of taxable income before the NOL deduction.
    - **NOLS for Farmers:** The CARES Act allows farmers who elected a two-year NOL carryback to retain the two-year carryback rather than claim the five-year carryback provided in the CARES Act. Farmers who previously waived an election to carry back an NOL may also revoke the waiver.
- **QIP Technical Correction:** The CARES Act includes a much-awaited technical correction that assigns a 15-year recovery period to qualified improvement property (QIP) placed in service after 2017. Without the technical correction, a 39-year recovery period applied, and as a result, QIP did not meet the requirements for bonus depreciation. This error has now been fixed. Businesses that invested in QIP may amend their 2018 and 2019 tax returns to claim the additional depreciation expense.
- **Acceleration of Corporate AMT Credits:** The Tax Cuts and Jobs Act repealed the corporate AMT for corporations. The TCJA allowed any unused AMT credits to be claimed over four years (2018-2021). The CARES Act *accelerates* the recovery period of corporate AMT credits to two years (2018-2019) or just one year (2018) if the corporation elects to do so.

---

[26] A further extension was implemented by the American Rescue Plan of 2021, which was passed on March 11, 2021.

[27] The paid sick and family leave refundable tax credits enacted as part of the FFCRA were extended through September 30, 2021, by the American Rescue Plan of 2021, however, employers are no longer required to provide *mandatory* FFCRA leave after December 31, 2020.

[28] Revenue Procedure 2020-24 provides guidance to taxpayers with net operating losses that are carried back under the CARES Act.

- **Charitable Gifts for Corporate Taxpayers:**
    - **25% of AGI Limit:** The CARES Act increased the limit for charitable contributions to 25% of taxable income for corporations for 2020 for most cash contributions. This provision applies to C-corporations only. The limitation on deductions for contributions of food inventory is also increased to 25%.
    - **100% of AGI Limit for "Qualified Disaster" Contributions:** Corporations can deduct qualified disaster relief contributions up to 100% of taxable income paid between January 1, 2020, until 60 days after the enactment of the CAA-2021 (February 25, 2021).
- **Business Interest Expense:** The TCJA enacted a limitation on business interest expense that limited a business's ability to deduct interest expense to 30% of adjusted taxable income. The CARES Act modifies this limitation and temporarily increases the deductibility to 50% of adjusted taxable income for tax years 2019 and 2020. Additionally, businesses may elect to use their 2019 adjusted taxable income rather than their 2020 adjusted taxable income for purposes of computing the 50% limitation. The increase is effective for tax years 2019 and 2020 (but only applies to 2020 for partnerships).[29]
- **Deferral Social Security Tax:** The CARES Act permits employers, self-employed individuals, and household employers who file Schedule H to defer 50% of the social security tax imposed for the period beginning on March 27, 2020, and ending December 31, 2020. These taxes must be repaid.[30]
- **Paycheck Protection Plan (PPP) loans (first round):** Taxpayers may exclude from gross income any covered loan forgiveness. Congress expanded the Paycheck Protection Program (PPP) and clarified that debt forgiven under the PPP is not includible in gross income. Business expenses paid with forgiven PPP funds are tax-deductible. Congress authorized a second round of PPP funding at the end of 2020. The IRS refers to first-round PPP Loans as "First Draw PPP Loans" and this second round as "Second Draw PPP Loans."
- **The Employee Retention Tax Credit (ERTC):** The ERTC is a refundable tax credit designed to encourage businesses to retain and compensate employees during periods in which businesses are not fully operational. This credit was later expanded by the *Consolidated Appropriations Act of 2021* (changes covered next).

---

[29] Taxpayers filing as partnerships are still required to use the 30% limitation. However, in 2020, partners in partnerships subject to the business interest expense limitation rules will be able to deduct 50% of any excess business interest expense that was allocated to them in 2019. The remaining 50% would remain suspended until the partnership allocates excess taxable income to the partners.

[30] The CAA 2021 extended the repayment period for these deferred payroll taxes. If an employer voluntarily deferred payment of their employees' share of Social Security taxes on applicable wages between September 1, 2020 and December 31, 2020, they now have until December 31, 2021 to have affected employees repay these amounts. Penalties and interest will not begin to accrue on the deferred amounts until January 1, 2022.

The Consolidated Appropriations Act of 2021 (CAA 2021)

The *CAA 2021* was signed into law on December 27, 2020. Included in the bill:

- *COVID-19-related Tax Relief Act of 2020, (COVIDTRA);*
- *The Coronavirus Response and Relief Supplemental Appropriations (CRRSA) Act; and*
- *The Taxpayer Certainty and Disaster Tax Relief Act (TCDTR).*

Expansion and Extension of Employee Retention Credit (ERTC): The CAA 2021 and the ARPA of 2021 expands and extends the employee retention credit introduced as part of the CARES Act, allowing employers to remain eligible up for the credit until December 31, 2021. This expansion[31] provides eligible employers who were impacted by COVID-19 with a refundable payroll tax credit for a percentage of "qualified wages." The changes are as follows:

Provisions	CARES Act: 3/13/20 - 12/31/20	New Law (for 2020): 3/13/20 - 12/31/20	New Law (for 2021): 1/1/21-12/31/21
If the business received a PPP loan	No ERTC if received a PPP loan[32]	Taxpayers that receive a PPP loan can claim the ERTC, but double-dipping is not allowed	Taxpayers that receive a PPP loan can claim the ERTC, but double-dipping is not allowed
Maximum Creditable Wages per Employee	$10,000 per year	$10,000 per year	$10,000 *per quarter*
Maximum credit	50% of eligible wages, up to $5,000 per employee	50% of eligible wages, up to $5,000 per employee	70% of eligible wages, up to $7,000 per quarter
Large Employer threshold	More than 100 employees	More than 100 employees	More than 500 employees

[31] For wages paid between March 12, 2020 and December 31, 2020, the ERTC can be applied to 50% of qualifying wages up to $10,000 for all 2020 quarters. Employers with 100 or fewer full-time employees (this threshold increases to 500 beginning in 2021) can use all employee wages (whether the employee is working or not). The Consolidated Appropriations Act of 2021 and the American Rescue Plan Act of 2021 extended this credit to December 31, 2021. For employers who qualify in 2021, the Act allows them to claim a credit against 70% of qualified wages paid. Additionally, the amount of wages that qualifies for the credit in 2021 is $10,000 per employee *per quarter*.

[32] Under the CARES Act, businesses could take advantage of either the PPP or the ERTC, but not both. The *CAA- 2021* and *ARPA 2021* retroactively eliminated this limitation and extends and enhances the ERTC through December 31, 2021.

Extension and Expansion of the PPP in the CAA 2021

Expanded PPP loans: The CAA 2021 provides for a second round of payments under the Paycheck Protection Program (PPP). This second round of loan funding is referred to as "Second Draw PPP Loans." The legislation also provides a simplified forgiveness procedure for PPP loans up to $150,000. The Act extends the repayment term of any portions of PPP loan proceeds that are *not* forgiven from 2 years to 5 years.

Requirements	First Draw PPP Loans	Second Draw PPP Loans
Eligibility	No more than 500 employees	No more than 300 employees
Maximum loan amount	$10 million	$2 million
Tax treatment	Loan forgiveness is not taxable; business expenses paid with PPP loans are tax-deductible	Loan forgiveness is not taxable; business expenses paid with PPP loans are tax-deductible
Forgiveness requirements	60%/40% allocation between payroll and other business costs	60%/40% allocation between payroll and other business costs
For businesses without employees or payroll (sole-proprietorships without employees), the PPP loan amounts are calculated based on profit. Forgiveness is based on "owner compensation replacement" rather than payroll, as well as spending incurred on qualifying business expenses.		

Economic Injury Disaster Assistance (EIDL) Loans and Advances: The CAA-2021 Act allows Economic Injury Disaster Assistance (EIDL) Advances provided as emergency grants under the CARES Act to be excluded from gross income while the corresponding expenses would remain deductible. Before the passing of the CAA 2021, a business that received both a PPP loan and an EIDL grant was required to reduce the amount of the PPP loan available for forgiveness by the EIDL Advance. The CAA-2021 clarifies that any loan forgiveness granted to an EIDL loan recipient under discretionary powers provided by the CARES Act does not result in gross income or a denial of deductions for allocable expenses.[33]

[33] The CAA 2021 repeals Section 1110(e)(6) of the CARES Act that required PPP loan forgiveness to be reduced by any EIDL advances (up to $10,000). This retroactive provision will allow any PPP borrowers who had forgiveness reduced by EIDL advances to have it forgiven.

Disaster Tax Relief for Businesses

As part of the CAA 2021, the Taxpayer Certainty and Disaster Tax Relief Act (TCDTR) also implemented special disaster relief provisions for disasters other than COVID-19,[34] also called "Qualified Disasters."

- **Qualified Disaster Area Distributions (non-COVID related):** Residents of qualified disaster areas may take qualified distributions of up to $100,000 from a retirement plan or an IRA without penalty. The tax on the withdrawals may be paid over a three-year period, or the amounts may be recontributed to the plan.
- **Employee Retention Credit for Employers Affected by Qualified Disasters:** This is a separate credit from the one in the CARES Act. This is a tax credit of 40% of wages (up to $6,000 per employee) to employers in FEMA disaster zones other than COVID-19. This provision specifically denies businesses' use of the same wages in qualifying for the ERC under the CARES Act or other potential credits (no double-dipping).

Extended Business Credits and Deductions:

The Consolidated Appropriations Act of 2021 extended the following deductions and credits:

Permanent Extenders

- **Energy-Efficient Commercial Buildings Deduction:** The deduction for energy efficiency improvements to lighting, heating, cooling, ventilation, and hot water systems of commercial buildings is made permanent with the new law. The Act also added an inflation adjustment for tax years beginning after 2020.
- **Railroad Track Maintenance Credit.** The credit for qualified railroad track maintenance expenditures was made permanent. A 50% credit will be allowed for any qualified expenditures incurred before January 1, 2023. The credit is reduced down to 40% for any expenditures incurred after January 1, 2023.
- **Tax breaks for Beer, Wine, and Distilled Spirits:** The bill includes numerous tax breaks for distillers and wine producers. Federal excise tax rates on beer were reduced. Certain tax credits were enacted for wine.

Extended through 2025

- **New Markets Tax Credit:** The New Markets Tax Credit was extended through 2025. This credit provides incentives for businesses to invest in low-income communities.
- **Work Opportunity Tax Credit:** The WOTC provides a credit on qualified first-year wages paid to individuals who are members of certain targeted groups (for certain employees, the employer is eligible for the credit for up to two years of wages). The credit was set to expire at the end of 2020, but has now been extended through 2025.

[34] In this case, "qualified disaster zones" does not refer to any area that was declared a disaster zone only because of the effect of COVID-19. In other words, this relief is for *other* presidentially declared disasters.

- **Employer Credit for Paid Family and Medical Leave:** The employer credit for paid family and medical leave (FMLA leave)[35] can be claimed by employers providing paid family leave. If paid leave is 50% of wages normally paid to an employee, the tax credit is 12.5% of wages paid. If paid leave is 100% of wages normally paid to an employee, the tax credit is 25% of wages paid. Employers claim the tax credit on Form 8994. This credit has been extended from 2025.

Note: That this is a completely different credit than the sick and family leave credit implemented by the FFCRA! This was an existing employer credit that allows eligible employers who provide *voluntary* paid family and medical leave to claim a general business credit equal to as much as 25% of the benefit they pay to workers who take time off for reasons which would qualify for leave under the federal *Family and Medical Leave Act (FMLA).* Many owners with fewer than 50 employees are exempt from providing ten weeks of paid expanded paid family medical leave act (FMLA).

- **Motorsports Entertainment Complex Cost Recovery:** The allowance for a 7-year cost recovery period for motorsports entertainment complexes.
- **Empowerment Zone credits:** Empowerment Zone tax incentives are available to businesses that hire individuals in economically depressed areas that are designated as "empowerment zones." These credits were also set to expire in 2020. They have now been extended through 2025.

Centralized Partnership Audit Regime

The Bipartisan Budget Act of 2015 (BBA) repealed the prior audit rules under the Tax Equity and Fiscal Responsibility Act of 1982 (TEFRA) and replaced them with the centralized partnership audit regime (CPAR). On February 22, 2019, the IRS issued final regulations (T.D. 9844) that implement the Centralized Partnership Audit Regime that now governs partnership audit procedures. Under the new centralized audit regime (CPAR), tax is generally determined, assessed, and collected at the partnership level as a result of an audit. The new "centralized partnership audit" regime is *mandatory*, unless the partnership qualifies to **elect-out.** Certain partnerships with 100 or fewer partners to elect out of this new regime.

Eligible partnerships can elect out of the CPAR on Schedule B-2 of a timely filed tax return (Form 1065). When the entity elects out, IRS proceedings and adjustments will be assessed at the partner level under the general audit rules applicable to individuals instead of at the entity level. To elect out of the new partnership rules, in addition to the maximum 100-partner requirement, the partnership must only have "eligible" partners, which are:

- Individuals.
- C corporations (and any foreign entity that would be treated as a C corporation if it were a domestic corporation).

[35] The Taxpayer Certainty and Disaster Tax Relief Act of 2019 extended the FMLA credit until December 31, 2020, and the credit was extended again by the CAA 2021 to tax year 2025. FMLA provisions apply to all public agencies, all public and private elementary and secondary schools, and companies with 50 or more employees. See detailed FAQ on this credit here: https://www.irs.gov/newsroom/section-45s-employer-credit-for-paid-family-and-medical-leave-faqs

- S corporations (if an S corporation as a partner, the number of shareholders in that S corporation counts towards the 100-partner threshold),
- Estates of deceased partners only (NOT bankruptcy estates).

> **Note:** An "eligible partner" does not include a disregarded single-member LLC, trust, grantor trust, or a bankruptcy estate, even if the disregarded entity is wholly owned by an eligible partner. Partnerships with non-qualified partners cannot opt-out of the centralized audit regime, even if the partnership has fewer than 100 partners.

Unit 1: Business Entities and Requirements

More Reading:
Publication 334, Tax Guide for Small Business
Publication 583, Starting a Business and Keeping Records
Publication 1635, Understanding Your EIN
Publication 505, Tax Withholding and Estimated Tax
Publication 1544, Reporting Cash Payments of Over $10,000

For Part 2 of the enrolled agent exam, you will be expected to know a broad range of information about tax provisions that affect various types of businesses.

You will need to understand the different types of businesses, including sole proprietorships, partnerships, limited liability companies, corporations, and farming businesses, as well as trusts and estates, retirement plans, tax-exempt organizations, and the special tax laws that apply to each.

Note: Congress approved a massive COVID-relief bill on March 27, 2020, *Coronavirus Aid, Relief, and Economic Security (CARES) Act.* This legislation affected both individuals and businesses, and included retroactive changes that affected 2020 as well as prior years. The *Consolidated Appropriations Act of 2021 (CAA 2021)* was signed into law on December 27, 2020. The *CAA 2021* extended and modified many provisions of the earlier CARES Act.

For examinations delivered between May 1, 2021, and February 28, 2022, Part 2 of the exam is broken down into the following sections and corresponding percentages of questions:

1. **Business Entities – 30 questions**
2. **Business Financial Information – 37 questions**
3. **Specialized Returns and Taxpayers – 18 questions**[36]

We start with an overview of the different types of business entities. Each has its own drawbacks, risks, and benefits. Which entity a business should use is primarily a legal and financial decision, although there are other factors to consider, especially after the enactment of the TCJA. We briefly review each entity type in this chapter and will examine more complex entities in greater depth in later units.

Sole Proprietorships

A sole proprietorship is not a separate legal entity. It is an unincorporated business that is owned and controlled by one person. A sole proprietorship may be a single-person business, or it may have several employees, but there is only one owner who accepts all the risk and liability of the business. It is the simplest business type and also the easiest to start. An estimated 70% of businesses in the United States are sole proprietorships. A sole proprietorship cannot be passed on to a new owner as the same business entity because, by definition, a sole proprietorship is owned and operated by a single, specific individual. If a business operated as a sole

[36] These specifications are listed in the current Special Enrollment Examination Candidate Information Bulletin, which is available for download on the Prometric website, here: https://www.prometric.com/test-takers/search/irs

proprietorship is sold, it must be operated by the new owner as either a different sole proprietorship or as a different type of business entity through a sale of assets of the business.

A taxpayer does not have to conduct full-time business activities to be considered self-employed. Operating a part-time business in addition to having a regular job or business may also be self-employment, and may also constitute a sole proprietorship. An activity qualifies as a business if its primary purpose is for profit, and if the taxpayer is involved in the activity with continuity and regularity. A hobby, which is not conducted for profit, does not qualify as a business.

Sole proprietors often receive Form 1099-NEC from their business customers showing income they were paid for services.[37] The amounts reported on Forms 1099-NEC, along with any other business income, are reported and taxed on the taxpayer's personal income tax return. Income and expenses from the sole proprietorship are reported on Schedule C, *Profit or Loss from Business,* of Form 1040. A self-employed individual with net earnings of $400 or more from self-employment is required to pay self-employment tax by filing Schedule SE, *Self-Employment Tax*, with his Form 1040.

Example: Boyd works as an independent plumbing contractor for Texas Construction, Inc. Texas Construction sends Boyd a Form 1099-NEC that shows he received $25,000 for contract work in 2020. He also received payments of $7,000 from several individuals for contract work he completed on their homes. Although Boyd did not receive Forms 1099-NEC for the $7,000, he must include the payments as self-employment income, along with the $25,000 from Texas Construction, on his Schedule C.

Partnerships

A partnership is a relationship that exists between two or more taxpayers who join together to carry on a trade or business. Each person contributes money, property, labor, or skill and expects to share in the profits and losses of the business.

A partnership must file an annual information return to report the income, deductions, gains, and losses from its operations, but the partnership itself does not pay income tax. Instead, any profits or losses "pass-through" to its partners, who are then responsible for reporting their respective shares of the partnership's income or loss on their individual returns.

Example: Brett and Leia Haas are father and daughter who co-own and operate Haas Accounting, LLP. Each is active in the business, and each has an equal share in partnership interests and profits. The partnership must file Form 1065 to report its income and loss for the year. The partnership must also issue a Schedule K-1 to each partner. In 2020, Haas Accounting had $80,000 of net ordinary income. Since they share profits and losses equally, Brett and Leia will each report $40,000 of self-employment income on their individual tax returns. A partner's share of partnership income is reported on page 2 of Schedule E, *Supplemental Income and Loss.*

However, in the event a partnership tax return is audited, by default, the partnership itself will be subject to paying income tax in the event it is determined that it had originally

[37] For the 2020 tax year, the IRS revived the Form 1099-NEC, an older form which had been previously retired. The 1099-NEC will be used to report nonemployee compensation payments for 2020 and onward. The Form 1099-MISC will still be used to report other types of payments, such as rent and royalties.

underreported its taxable income on the return. This is referred to as the "centralized audit regime." However, if eligible, the partnership can elect out of the centralized audit regime on its tax return. An "eligible" partnership that can elect out of the centralized audit regime:

- Must have 100 or fewer partners during the year, and
- Has only eligible partners which include:
    - Individuals (natural persons only, not LLCs, and not grantor trusts!)
    - C Corporations or foreign entities classified as corporations
    - S corporations
    - Estates of deceased partners (but not bankruptcy estates!)

Partnerships with non-qualified partners cannot opt-out of the centralized audit regime, even if the partnership has fewer than 100 partners.

An unincorporated organization with two or more owners is generally classified as a partnership for federal tax purposes if its members carry on a business and divide its profits. A partnership can look very different depending on how it is structured - it can be anything from a small business run by a married couple to a complex business organization with thousands of general partners and limited partners. A partnership can have an unlimited number of partners, and can have partners that are foreign or domestic. A partnership must always have at least one general partner whose actions legally bind the business and who is legally responsible for a partnership's debts and liabilities. The default legal classification for a partnership is a *general partnership* where all partners are *general* partners with each partner jointly and severally liable for the debts and obligations of the partnership.

However, a "joint undertaking" merely to share expenses is not automatically a partnership. For example, co-ownership of rental property is usually not considered a formal partnership unless the co-owners provide substantial services to the tenants.

Example: Cornell and Dolan are cousins who own a residential rental property together. Each owns a 50% interest in the rental. Cornell takes care of any repairs, and Dolan collects and divides the rent. They do not have any other business with each other. The co-ownership of the rental property is not considered a partnership for tax purposes. Instead, they would divide the income and expenses based on their ownership percentages, and each would report his respective share on Schedule E on his individual return.

The IRS defines "substantial services" as services that are primarily for the tenant's convenience, such as regular cleaning, changing linen, or maid service. This would be something like a hotel or bed-and-breakfast. In that case, the rental activity could not be classified as a joint undertaking. Instead, it would be reported on Schedule C, or, if the rental was owned and operated by more than one person, it would be classified as a partnership.

Example: Orlando and Suzanne are siblings. In 2020, they purchase a Victorian home in downtown New Orleans. They spend a substantial sum to divide the home into four separate units, which they then advertise as a bed-and-breakfast. They offer maid service and daily breakfast to all their guests. The IRS would classify their business as a hotel. Therefore, Orlando and Suzanne would be required to file a partnership return in order to report their earnings and profits.

A partnership's annual tax return is filed on Form 1065, *U.S. Return of Partnership Income.* Partners are not employees of the business, and they should not be issued a Form W-2. Instead, the partnership must furnish a copy of Schedule K-1 to each of its partners, showing the income and losses allocated to him. A partnership return must show the name and address of each partner and the partner's share of taxable income. The return must be signed by a general partner.

A **limited partnership (LP)** is a partnership that has at least one limited partner in addition to its general partner(s). A limited partnership allows an investor (the limited partner) to own an interest in a business without assuming personal liability or risk beyond the amount of his investment in the partnership.

Note: A Limited Partnership (LP) is a state-level entity. Unlike a general partnership (GP), which can be formed merely with a handshake between two persons, in many states, in order to form an LP, a Certificate of Limited Partnership or Certificate of Formation must generally be filed with the Secretary of State in which the partnership chooses to do business. For example, in order to form an LP in California, a Certificate of Limited Partnership (Form LP–1) must be filed with the California Secretary of State, and the applicable filing fees must be paid.

A *limited partner* generally has no obligation to contribute additional capital to the partnership and, therefore, does not have an economic risk of loss for partnership liabilities. A limited partner may not sign the partnership return or represent the business before the IRS in their capacity as a limited partner. In most states, a limited partner is restricted regarding how active they can be in the management of the partnership.

Example: Carter wants to open a dance club. He approaches his aunt, Marisol, for the funds. Marisol agrees to invest in her nephew's business, but she does not want to be involved in the day-to-day running of the club. After consulting with a legal advisor, Carter and his aunt form a limited partnership (LP). Per their partnership agreement, Marisol is a limited partner. She is an investor in the club and contributes $250,000 to establish the club. Carter is an experienced restaurateur and nightlife expert, so he runs the club. Carter is the general partner.

A **Limited Liability Partnership (LLP)** is an entity that is formed under state law and is generally used for specific professional services, such as those offered by a law firm or CPA firm. Some professionals form an LLP because the option of an LLC is prohibited in their state for their particular business type.[38]

For example, in California and New York, LLCs cannot provide certain professional services. Doctors, CPAs, attorneys, veterinarians, and other similar, licensed professionals cannot form an LLC for those particular business activities, but they *are* allowed to form an LLP and offer these professional services.

Typically, an LLP allows each partner to actively participate in management affairs but still provides limited liability protection to each partner. A partner in an LLP generally would not be personally liable for the partnership debts or the malpractice of other partners (or the

[38] With regards to limited partnerships and limited liability partnerships, different states often have significantly different requirements for formation and legal liability.

employees under the management of other partners) and would only be at risk for his own malpractice and his interest in the partnership's assets.[39]

Example: Dylan and Farad are licensed attorneys in California who decide to go into business with each other. They form an LLP by registering their business with California's Secretary of State. Once they complete their registration, they open an office and begin accepting new clients. For tax purposes, their business will be taxed as a partnership, and they will be required to file a Form 1065 every year. In a limited liability partnership, the partners enjoy some protection against personal legal liability.

Married Couple Businesses and Qualified Joint Ventures

Often, a small business is operated by spouses without incorporating or creating a formal partnership agreement. The business is usually considered a partnership, whether or not there is a formal partnership agreement.

Note: Federal tax law makes many references to laws specific to a "husband and wife." These laws also now apply to same-sex spouses who are legally married. However, couples that are in civil unions or registered domestic partnerships are not considered "married" for tax purposes. Therefore, these couples cannot claim a "qualified joint venture." They would be required to file a partnership tax return (Form 1065).

If both spouses materially participate as the only members of a jointly owned and operated business, the business may be treated as a *qualified joint venture*, or QJV. This allows them to avoid the complexity of filing a partnership return but still allows each spouse to take credit for self-employment earnings from the business for Social Security purposes. Items of business income, gain, loss, deduction, and credit are split between the spouses in accordance with their respective interests in the business. The spouses then file separate Schedules C and separate Schedules SE. This option is available only to married couples who file joint tax returns.

A qualified joint venture is available only to businesses owned and operated by spouses as co-owners and not in the name of a state law entity; spousal owners of a limited liability company or a limited partnership generally do not qualify.

The IRS specifically excludes state-approved entities (such as LLCs) from electing to file as a qualified joint venture. There is a narrow exception in the law for married couples who live in a community property state. Married couples who co-own and operate an LLC in a community property state may still file on two Schedules C, as long as they agree to file a joint return.[40]

Example: Uther and Johanna live in Hawaii, where they operate a small business together as husband and wife. They qualify for and treat their business as a qualified joint venture and file on two Schedule Cs. Later in the year, they decide to form an LLC. They must file a partnership return (Form 1065) for their business, starting with the date of formation of the LLC. They can no longer treat their business activity as a qualified joint venture.

---

[39] The laws regarding LPs, LLPs and LLCs vary greatly from state-to-state. Information is generally available online through a state's Secretary of State's office or the governor's office.

[40] There are currently nine community property states: Louisiana, Arizona, California, Texas, Washington, Idaho, Nevada, New Mexico, and Wisconsin. See Rev. Proc. 2002-69, 2002-2 CB 831, for special rules applicable to married couple state law entities in community property states.

Example: Grant and Natalie are married and file jointly. They live in Texas and run a small grocery store together as a qualified joint venture. During the year, they form an LLC for liability protection. Since Texas is a community property state, they are allowed to continue reporting their income and loss on two Schedule Cs.

Example: Martina and Alejandro are married and co-own and operate a retail business together in California. California is a community property state, so even if the couple forms an MMLLC, they would generally be able to avoid filing a partnership return, and continue to report their business activity on two Schedule Cs. However, in 2020, the couple separates. Although they continue to run the business together, Martina does not want to file a joint return with Alejandro. They are forced to file a partnership return in 2020 to report the business activity, because the qualified joint venture election can only be made by married spouses that file jointly.

C Corporations

When forming a corporation, prospective shareholders provide money, property, or both in exchange for the issuance of the corporation's capital stock. A corporation is considered an entity separate from its shareholders and must elect a board of directors who are responsible for oversight of the company. A corporation conducts business, realizes net income or loss, and distributes profits to shareholders.

Most major companies are organized as C corporations. C corporations and S corporations (discussed next) are differentiated for tax purposes only. Legally, they are both simply corporations. For tax purposes, however, they are treated much differently.

A C corporation may have an unlimited number of shareholders and may be either foreign or domestic. A C corporation must file annual income tax returns on Form 1120, *U.S. Corporation Income Tax Return,* to report its net income and losses, and pay tax on its income. Its after-tax profits may also be taxable income to its shareholders when distributed as dividends, resulting in double taxation.

The corporation does not receive a tax deduction when it distributes dividends to shareholders, and shareholders cannot deduct any losses of the corporation.

A corporation deducts its ordinary and necessary business expenses like any other business, but it is also allowed certain special deductions. C corporations are taxed at a flat rate.

Note: The Tax Cuts and Jobs Act permanently eliminated the graduated rates for C Corporations. All C corporations are now taxed at a flat rate of 21%. There is no longer a separate tax rate for personal service corporations (PSC)—all C corporations are taxed at a 21% flat rate, regardless of their size or business activity. The TCJA also permanently repealed the corporate alternative minimum tax (AMT).

S Corporations

An S corporation is a distinct form of entity, organized as a corporation for *legal* purposes, but *elected* with the IRS for tax purposes. For federal income tax purposes, an S corporation is generally not subject to tax; instead, its income, losses, deductions, and credits are passed through directly to its shareholders in a manner similar to a partnership. However, while not common, the S corporation itself may be responsible for income tax on certain built-in gains and passive investment income. We will cover these special taxes that apply to S corporations in a later chapter.

An S corporation is required to file an annual income tax return to report its income or loss using Form 1120-S, *U.S. Tax Return for an S Corporation.* It also reports each shareholder's applicable share of income or losses on Schedules K-1. The shareholders report the pass-through income or loss on their individual tax returns. As a result, the shareholders of S corporations are generally able to avoid double federal taxation on their corporate income. S corporations must meet the following requirements:

- Be a domestic corporation.
- Have only "permitted" shareholders (partnerships, C corporations,[41] and nonresident aliens are not eligible).
- Have no more than 100 shareholders.
- Have only one class of stock (voting and nonvoting stock are not considered to be separate classes of stock, as long as they have identical rights to distribution and liquidation proceeds).
- Not be an ineligible type of corporation (certain financial institutions, insurance companies, and domestic international sales corporations are not eligible for S corporation status).

Limited Liability Companies (LLCs)

A **limited liability company (LLC)** is another type of business entity that may be formed under state law. Depending upon whether it has a single owner or multiple owners, an LLC will be treated for federal tax purposes either as:

- A "disregarded entity," (as described later)
- A corporation; if the entity elects to be treated as a corporation, or
- As a partnership.

Most LLCs in the United States are taxed as partnerships. Like the owners of S corporations and partnerships, the members of an LLC can avoid double taxation.

An LLC can provide the liability protection of a corporation with the tax benefits of a partnership. Unlike a partnership, none of the members of an LLC are personally liable for its debts. If a multi-member limited liability company (MMLLC) is treated as a partnership for tax purposes, it must file Form 1065 annually, and one of its owners/members must sign the return.

A **Professional Service Limited Liability Company**, or **PLLC** is a type of limited liability company that is owned and operated by licensed professionals, such as doctors, lawyers, engineers, and CPAs. PLLCs are not available in every state, and have ownership restrictions and can generally only offer services related to its profession.

[41] There is an exception for S corporations who own 100% of another S corporation under certain circumstances, as well as an exception for 501(C)(3) organizations that are organized as corporations. An exempt entity is allowed to own S corporation stock without jeopardizing the S corporation's status.

Farmers and Fishermen

Farming businesses are primarily engaged in crop production, animal production, or forestry and logging. They may include stock, dairy, poultry, fish, fruit, and tree farms, as well as plantations, ranches, timber farms, and orchards. It is the nature of the activity, and not the entity type that determines whether a business qualifies as a farming business.

Congress has enacted many tax laws specific to farming. These laws provide special tax treatment and reflect the highly unpredictable nature of the business. For example, farmers have a different schedule for paying estimated taxes; they may postpone gain or income in certain cases that other businesses cannot; they can deduct a higher percentage of mileage expenses than other businesses, and they are given special tax considerations when disaster strikes.

Farming and fishing businesses operating as sole proprietorships report income and loss on Schedule F, *Profit or Loss from Farming*, of Form 1040. A farmer is typically self-employed if he operates his own farm or rents farmland from others to engage in the business of farming.

Self-employed farmers and fishermen must also complete Schedule SE to determine self-employment taxes due. A farming business may also be organized as a partnership or a corporation. Even if a farming business is organized as a partnership or corporation, there are many rules that apply to farm businesses that do not apply to any other entity type. Farmers are unique in that respect, and we have dedicated an entire unit to discussing many of the rules that apply specifically to farming activities.

Tax-Exempt Organizations (Nonprofit Entities)

The Internal Revenue Code (IRC Section 501(c)) outlines the requirements for tax-exempt organizations. They must be organized and operated exclusively for an exempt purpose, and none of their earnings may be used to benefit any private shareholder or individual. Nonprofit organizations may be created as corporations, trusts, or unincorporated associations, but never as partnerships or sole proprietorships.

Most charitable organizations must request tax-exempt status by filing Form 1023, *Application for Recognition of Exemption.* However, churches, including synagogues, temples, and mosques, are treated as tax-exempt by default and do not have to apply for formal exemption, although many do.

Most tax-exempt organizations must annually file Form 990, *Return of Organization Exempt from Income Tax,* to report its income and losses. Many small tax-exempt organizations can file either a Form 990-EZ or the 990-N (e-Postcard) in lieu of Form 990. Form 990 is an informational return only, but a nonprofit organization may be taxed on activities outside the scope of its tax-exempt status on a separate form (Form 990-T)

Entity Classification Election Rules

Certain business entities may choose how they will be classified for tax purposes by filing Form 8832, *Entity Classification Election*. An LLC with a single member is classified as a "disregarded entity," or as not being separate from its owner for income tax purposes, unless the owner files Form 8832 and elects to be taxed as a corporation. Thus, a single-owner LLC owned by an individual is treated as a sole proprietorship, and the owner is subject to the tax on net earnings from self-employment if the LLC conducts a trade or business activity.

Because it is a disregarded entity, a single-member LLC that is owned by a corporation or a partnership is included on the entity's tax return as if it were a division of the corporation or partnership.

A *single*-member LLC cannot be classified as a partnership, because a partnership must have at least two owners. An LLC with at least two members is classified as a partnership by default unless it files Form 8832 and elects to be treated as a corporation (an LLC that wishes to be taxed as an S corporation would file Form 2553, rather than Form 8832).

In general, an election to change an LLC's classification cannot take effect more than 75 days prior to the date the election is filed; nor can it take effect later than 12 months after the date the election is filed (although late elections are possible in some cases).

Once a business entity makes an election to change its classification, it generally cannot change the election again within five years (60 months). The 60-month limitation does not apply if the previous election was made by a newly formed eligible entity and was effective on the date of formation.

Example: Kiana and Garrick are siblings and own their own business, K&G LLC, which is treated as a partnership for tax purposes. A year after they began business operations, they decide to change the classification and be taxed as a C corporation, so they file Form 8832. At this point, if Kiana and Garrick change their minds and want their business to go *back* to being classified as a partnership again, they would have to wait at least 60 months (five years).

Recordkeeping for Businesses

Adequate records help a taxpayer to monitor business operations, verify his income and expenses, and support expenses on his tax return. Except in a few cases, the law does not require a business to keep any specific kind of records or to use a particular recordkeeping system, so long as the system clearly shows a business's income and expenses.

The taxpayer's recordkeeping system should include a summary of business transactions, which is usually made in the taxpayer's books, such as accounting journals and ledgers. The books must show the business's gross income, as well as its deductions and credits.

Additional documents must be kept to support these entries. These include sales slips, paid bills, invoices, receipts, deposit slips, canceled checks, credit card charge slips, cash register tapes, invoices, mileage logs, and phone records.

Electronic records are acceptable so long as they provide a complete and accurate record of data that is accessible to the IRS in a legible format. They are subject to the same controls and retention guidelines as those used for the taxpayer's original hard copy books and records.

Taxpayers must keep records as long as they are needed for the administration of any provision of the Internal Revenue Code. Usually, this means the business must keep records long enough to support income and deductions until the statute of limitations for a related tax return has expired.

Definition: A "**statute of limitation**" is a time period to review and analyze tax-related issues by the IRS. The Internal Revenue Code requires that the IRS must assess, refund, credit, and collect taxes within specific time limits known as the statute of limitations. When they expire, the IRS can no longer assess additional tax, allow a claim for refund by the taxpayer, or take collection action.

Generally, a business must keep records for at least three years from when a tax return was due or was filed, whichever is later. If a business has employees, it must keep all employment tax records for at least four years.

Taxpayers must keep records relating to property until the statute of limitations expires for the year in which the property is sold or otherwise disposed of. These records are needed to figure any depreciation, amortization, or depletion deductions, and to figure basis for computing gain or loss. A taxpayer may need to keep records relating to the basis of property even longer since they may be important in determining the basis of replacement property.

Business funds should be kept separate from personal funds. The IRS is more likely to audit a business and deny deductions and losses if there is no clear separation between business and personal expenses. A separate bank account for business-related transactions is advisable, with business-related bills paid from it rather than from a personal account.

Financial Statements

Financial statements are the formal records of a business's financial activities. There are many types of financial statements, but the two most common ones used for tax reporting purposes are the income statement and the balance sheet.

Income Statement: The income statement is also called the "profit and loss" statement. It indicates the business's revenue, expenses, and net income or loss during a period, such as a month, quarter, or fiscal or calendar year.

Balance Sheet: The balance sheet is a summary of a business's assets, liabilities, and equity on a specific date, such as at the end of its fiscal year. A balance sheet provides a "snapshot" of the business's financial condition. Balance sheet accounts are carried forward from year to year, unlike income statement accounts, which are closed out at year-end and only reflect business operations within a specified period.

Employer Identification Number (EIN)

An employer identification number is used for reporting purposes. Unlike Social Security numbers that are assigned to individuals, EINs are assigned to business entities.

If a sole proprietor has no employees, the business owner is normally not required to obtain an EIN. However, an EIN can be requested by a sole proprietor who simply wishes to protect his Social Security number for privacy reasons. This way, a sole proprietor can provide his EIN rather than his SSN to companies that need to issue him a Form 1099-NEC for independent contractor payments. If a sole proprietor decides to form a business entity such as a partnership or corporation, he will be required to request an EIN for each separate entity. A business must apply for an EIN if any of the following apply:

- The business pays employees,

- The business operates as a corporation, exempt organization, trust, estate, or partnership for tax purposes,
- The business files any of these tax returns:
    - Employment taxes (payroll taxes)
    - Excise tax[42]
    - Alcohol, Tobacco, and Firearms
- The business withholds taxes paid to a nonresident alien
- The business establishes a pension, profit-sharing, or retirement plan

A *new* EIN is required for any of the following changes:

- When a sole proprietor or partnership decides to incorporate, or when a sole proprietor takes on a partner and becomes a partnership
- When a partnership becomes a sole proprietorship (for example, when one partner dies)
- When a sole proprietor files for bankruptcy under Chapter 7 or Chapter 11
- When a taxpayer terminates one partnership and begins another partnership
- When a business establishes a pension, profit-sharing, or retirement plan
- The individual owner dies, and the business is taken over by the estate (in this case, the new EIN would be the EIN of the estate).

New EIN Not Required

A business does not need to apply for a new EIN in any of the following instances:

- Merely to change the name of a business
- To change the location or add more business locations (e.g., additional stores, or branches of the same entity)
- If a sole proprietor operates multiple businesses (including stores or branches of the same business)

Further, a single-member limited liability company (LLC) classified as a disregarded entity may use the owner's SSN or EIN and does not need a separate EIN, *unless* the business is required to file employment or excise tax returns. Most taxpayers can apply for an EIN online or paper-file Form SS-4, *Application for Employer Identification Number.*

Specific Reporting Requirements

Businesses are subject to a number of reporting requirements, including the following:

Form W-2: A business must complete and file with the Social Security Administration Forms W-2, *Wage, and Tax Statement,* showing the wages paid and taxes withheld for the year for each employee. A copy of the W-2 must be given to each current and former employee who received

[42] Excise taxes are taxes paid when purchases are made on a specific good, such as gasoline. Excise taxes are often included in the price of the product. There are also excise taxes on certain activities, such as on gambling, indoor tanning, or on highway usage by trucks. Excise taxes are reported on Form 720, *Quarterly Federal Excise Tax Return.*

taxable wages or salaries during the year by no later than January 31[43] of the following year. Businesses have a single filing deadline for all Form W-2s (January 31). This is true for both employee and IRS copies, or whether filing on paper or electronically. Large employers are typically required to use e-file, and failing to do so may incur a penalty.

Note: Prior law required that businesses who file more than 250 returns (W-2s, and/or 1099 Forms) during a calendar year do so electronically. Under a new efile mandate implemented by the Taxpayer First Act, the 250 is reduced to 100 in the calendar year 2021 (for 2020 tax year filings), and from 100 to 10 after 2021. For partnerships, the threshold is lower, and 50 for calendar-year 2021 (for 2020 tax year filings) and lowered to 10 in any future tax years. This is a separate e-file mandate from the existing requirement for partnerships with more than 100 partners to file electronically.

Form W-9: A taxpayer uses this form to provide his correct taxpayer identification number (TIN) to any individual or entity who is required to file an information return with the IRS.

Form 1099-NEC: A business must report nonemployee compensation paid during the year to certain independent contractors that provided services by providing a Form 1099-NEC by January 31 of the following year.

Form 1099-MISC: This form was redesigned for 2020 to remove the box for nonemployee compensation. Amounts that are reported on the 1099-MISC include:

- Payments of $600 or more for rents, prizes and awards, crop insurance proceeds, and certain medical and health care payments,
- Royalties over $10,
- Gross proceeds paid to an attorney's office, when the total amount is $600 or more.[44]

Except for attorneys, payments to corporations are generally exempt from Form 1099 reporting requirements. Forms 1099 should only be used for payments that are made in the course of a trade or business. Personal payments are not reportable.

Example: Stephanie hires a painter to paint the exterior of her home. The job costs $3,500. Stephanie is not required to report the payment to the painter because it is for her personal residence. Since it was a personal payment, she cannot deduct the cost on her income tax return. However, the painter is still required to report the income on his income tax return. The following year, Stephanie calls the same painter to paint the interior of her business office, which she owns. The painting job costs $2,000. Since the cost is a business expense, Stephanie is required to issue a Form 1099-NEC to the contractor.

A business should only include payments made by cash, check, ACH transfer, or other direct means on Form 1099-MISC or 1099-NEC. Credit card payments, including third-party network

[43] The deadline for Form W-2 and 1099-NEC forms is generally Jan. 31. However, tax year 2020 forms (that are filed in 2021) the deadline is Feb. 1, 2021, because Jan. 31 is a Sunday. If a business is using Forms 1099-MISC to report amounts in box 8, *Substitute Payments in Lieu of Dividends or Interest,* or box 10, *Gross Proceeds Paid to An Attorney,* there is an exception to the normal due date. Those forms are due to recipients by February 16, 2021.

[44] An attorney's office is subject to the 1099 reporting requirements, even when the attorney / law firm is an incorporated entity. This is contrary to the normal 1099 rules, as corporations are generally exempt. This exception has been tested on prior exams.

transactions, must be reported on Form 1099-K by the payment settlement entity and are not subject to reporting on Form 1099-MISC or 1099-NEC.

Form 1099-K: The Form 1099-K, *Payment Card and Third Party Network Transactions,* is an IRS information return used by payment settlement entities (like Paypal and Stripe) to report online payment transactions.

Note: Rideshare drivers, like those that work for Uber and Lyft, generally receive a Form 1099-K for their driving services, since the payments made to them are processed by a third-party network. The 1099-K includes a breakdown of the driver's annual gross earnings. Not every driver receives a 1099-K. The current 1099-K reporting threshold is either (1) $20,000 in gross earnings and (2) 200 transactions. A driver would typically receive a 1099-K if they earned more than $20,000 in fees and provided more than 200 rides to passengers.

Form 1099-INT: A business that is not in a line of business that pays interest as part of its regular activities (such as a bank or a credit union) must generally report interest paid to any single individual taxpayer when the total is $600 or more for the year. For banks and similar institutions, the reporting requirement threshold is $10 or more per year.

Form W-4: When a business hires an employee, it must have the employee complete a Form W-4, *Employee's Withholding Certificate.* Form W-4 tells the employer the employee's marital status and the number and type of dependents (qualifying children under 17 or other dependents). In addition, at the option of the employee, the employee can inform the employer of taxable income they expect to have outside of their job, (if applicable) the expected amount of their itemized deductions, and any requested additional withholding. If an employee fails to complete a Form W-4, the employer must withhold federal income taxes from his wages as if he were single and taking the standard deduction.

Form 8300, Report of Cash Transactions over $10,000: When a business receives a cash payment of more than $10,000 from one transaction (or two or more related transactions), it must file Form 8300, *Report of Cash Payments Over $10,000 Received in a Trade or Business* within 15 days after they receive the cash.[45] This type of transaction is also called a "designated reporting transaction."[46]

A business must also provide a written statement to each person or customer named on any Form 8300 that is filed. The statement must be provided to the customer no later than January 31 of the following year.

Example: Adam's Used Autos, LLC is a small, family-owned car dealership. On January 6, 2020, Jennifer Jones buys a used car from Adam's Used Autos and pays $17,000 in cash. The dealership asks Jennifer for her driver's license and verifies her identification, in order to get the necessary information to complete Form 8300. Adam's Used Autos must file Form 8300 *no later* than January 21, 2020 (15 days later). The dealership must also send a statement to Jennifer by January 31, 2021 (the following year).

---

[45] For the purposes of this rule, "cash" includes the coins and currency of the United States, cashier's checks, bank drafts, traveler's checks, as well as cash in a foreign currency. "Cash" does not include bank wire transfers, credit card transactions, ACH transactions, or amounts paid with personal checks.

[46] The information contained on the form assists law enforcement in its anti-money laundering efforts.

If a business receives over $10,000 in cash during two or more "related" transactions, the business must also treat the transactions as a single transaction and report the payments on Form 8300.

Note that the Form 8300 reporting requirement *only* applies to business transactions. Sales of personal-use property that is sold in a private sale are typically not subject to reporting.

Example: Sheena is an elementary school teacher. She decides to sell her personal vehicle. She places an ad in her local newspaper listing her car for $12,500. She finds a buyer for the car, who pays her $12,500 in cash a week later. Sheena does not have to report the sale on Form 8300 because she is not a professional car dealer, and the transaction was not a business transaction.

Employee and Worker Classification

Because businesses are responsible for withholding and paying income, employment, and FUTA taxes, as well as reporting payments to independent contractors, they must accurately determine whether a person they pay is an independent contractor or an employee.

A business is generally not required to withhold or pay taxes in connection with payments to independent contractors. However, it must understand the relationship that exists with each person it pays to perform services. A person performing services for a business may be:

- **An independent contractor**
- **An employee**
- **A statutory employee**
- **A statutory nonemployee**

The IRS evaluates three primary characteristics to determine the relationship between a business and workers it pays for services:

- **Behavioral Control:** Covers whether the business has a right to direct or control how the work is done.
- **Financial Control:** Covers whether the business has a right to direct or control the financial and business aspects of the worker's job. Factors include how the worker is paid, whether expenses are reimbursed, and whether tools and supplies are provided.
- **Type of Relationship:** Relates to how the worker and the business owner perceive their relationship, such as whether there are written contracts or employee-type benefits, such as vacation pay or a retirement plan.

Whether a person is classified as an employee or an independent contractor depends on the facts and circumstances of each individual case. If the determination of whether a worker is an employee or independent contractor is still unclear after weighing the various facts and circumstances of an individual case, Form SS-8, *Determination of Worker Status for Purposes of Federal Employment Taxes and Income Tax Withholding,* can be filed with the IRS.

The Form SS-8 may be filed by either the business or the worker. The IRS will review the case to officially determine the worker's status. Employers who misclassify workers as independent contractors rather than employees may face substantial tax penalties for failing to pay employment taxes and failing to file payroll tax forms.

An independent contractor that is considered self-employed pays self-employment tax if net earnings from self-employment are $400 or more. He reports self-employment income on Schedule C (Form 1040). There is generally no tax withholding on income received as a self-employed individual, as long as he has provided his tax identification number to the payer. However, an independent contractor may be required to make quarterly estimated tax payments.

Note: Some states may have more stringent rules regarding how a worker is classified as an employee. Please note the EA exam tests *federal* tax law rules only.

Note: If a business does not request a Social Security number or a taxpayer identification number for a payee, such as an independent contractor, it must withhold federal income taxes at a 24% rate in 2020. U.S. source income received by a foreign person (a nonresident alien) is subject to a withholding rate of 30%, unless a lower tax treaty rate applies.

Example: Ivan, a licensed electrician, submits a job estimate to a housing complex for electrical work at $26 per hour for 400 hours. He is to receive milestone payments every two weeks for the next ten weeks. Ivan will receive $10,400, regardless of whether he works more or less than 400 hours to complete the work. He also performs electrical installations under contracts with other companies that he obtains through ads placed online. Ivan would likely be classified as an independent contractor.

Example: Katrina is a salesperson employed full-time by an auto dealership. She is on duty in the showroom on certain assigned days and times. She uses lists of prospective customers that belong to the dealership. She develops leads and reports results to the sales manager. Because of her experience, she requires minimal assistance in closing and financing sales. She is paid a commission and is eligible for bonuses offered by the dealership. The business also pays the cost of her health and group-term life insurance. Katrina is classified as an employee.

Statutory Employees

Some workers are classified as statutory employees. Statutory employees are unique, because they are issued Forms W-2 by their employers, but report their wages, income, and allowable expenses on Schedule C, just like self-employed taxpayers. Statutory employees are usually salespeople or other employees who work on commission. The difference is that statutory employees are not required to pay self-employment tax, because their employers must treat them as employees for Social Security tax purposes. Examples of statutory employees include:

- Full-time life insurance salespeople,
- Traveling salespeople,
- Certain commissioned truck drivers,
- Directors (board members) of corporations and officers of nonprofit organizations,
- Certain home workers who perform work on materials or goods furnished by the employer.

If a person is a statutory employee, the "statutory employee" in box 13 of Form W-2 should be checked.

Statutory Nonemployees

There are two main categories of statutory nonemployees: direct sellers and licensed real estate agents. They are treated as self-employed for federal tax purposes, including income and employment taxes, if:

- Payments for their services are directly related to sales, rather than to the number of hours worked, and
- Services are performed under a written contract providing that they will not be treated as employees for federal tax purposes.

In 2020, compensation for a statutory nonemployee is reported on Form 1099-NEC. The taxpayer then reports the income on Schedule C.

> **Example:** Eugenia works as a full-time real estate agent for Trusty Realty Services. She visits the realty office at least once a day to check her mail and her messages. She manages dozens of listings and splits her real estate commissions with Trusty Realty. She does not work for any other real estate company. Eugenia is classified as a statutory *non*employee. Trusty Realty issues Eugenia a Form 1099-NEC for commissions, and she files Schedule C to report her income and expenses from her realty business.

> **Example:** Alana sells cosmetics, perfumes and personal products as an independent sales representative of Mary Kare. Alana's customers pick products directly out of catalogs. Alana then orders the products and delivers them to her customers personally. Sometimes she will host Mary Kare parties at her home, where customers can socialize and try different products. Alana earns a 40% commission on her product sales. She is not an employee of Mary Kare. She will file a Schedule C to report her income and expenses.

Employing Family Members

The tax requirements for a business that employs family members may differ from those applicable to other employees. The rules vary depending on the family relationship and the type of business entity.

A child working for a parent: Normally, there are no special rules (as compared to other employees) when a child is an employee of a business owned by a parent, assuming the amounts paid to the child are ordinary, necessary and reasonable in amount. If the parent's business is a sole proprietorship or a partnership in which each partner is the child's parent, payments for the child's services are subject to income tax withholding (regardless of age).

However, if the child is under 18, wage payments are *not* subject to Social Security and Medicare taxes (also called FICA taxes, or "payroll taxes"). If the child is under 21, payments are not subject to FUTA tax. This special rule for employee children does not apply if the business is organized as a corporation.

> **Example:** Kendra is 17 and works for her father's company, ABC Sporting Goods, Inc. Her father is the sole shareholder and owner. Since the company is organized as a C corporation, Kendra's wages are subject to all payroll taxes, including Social Security tax, Medicare tax, and FUTA.

Example: Deborah and Richard are married partners in the Sandwich Shoppe, a small restaurant that they co-own and operate. Their daughter, Angie, age 15, works as a hostess on the weekends. Her parents pay her $14 an hour, which is a reasonable wage in their locality. Deborah and Richard must withhold income tax on Angie's earnings. However, because of her age, and because she is working directly for her parents, her wages are not subject to Social Security, Medicare, and FUTA (federal unemployment taxes).

Spouse employed by a spouse: The wages for the services of a spouse are subject to income tax, Social Security, and Medicare taxes, but not FUTA tax. However, FUTA tax is applicable if the spouse works for a corporation or a partnership in which the employing spouse is a partner.

Example: Jefferson Veterinary Services is a PLLC (a Professional Service Limited Liability Company). The business is taxed as a sole proprietorship for federal tax purposes. Dr. Rene Jefferson is the sole owner of the business. His wife, Anastasia, works full-time in the business as an office manager. Anastasia's wages are subject to Social Security, Medicare, and income tax withholding, but they are not subject to FUTA tax.

Employment Taxes and Self-Employment Tax

An employer uses information from the employee's Form W-4, as well as the IRS withholding tables, to calculate how much to withhold from each wage payment. The employer must also withhold the employee's share of Social Security and Medicare taxes from wages, and pay the corresponding employer's share of each tax.

Employers must report federal income taxes withheld and employment taxes on Form 941, *Employer's Quarterly Federal Tax Return*, or Form 944, *Employer's Annual Federal Tax Return.* Businesses must also make federal tax deposits of income and employment taxes electronically, generally by using the Electronic Federal Tax Payment System (EFTPS).

In 2020, only the first $137,700 of an individual's employee compensation and/or net earnings from self-employment is subject to the Social Security tax. The maximum amount of Social Security tax is $8,537.40 in 2020 for employees and $17,074.80 for self-employed individuals. There is **no cap** on the Medicare tax.

Social Security and Medicare Taxes: 2020 Rates	
Social Security tax rate	
Employer's portion/Employee's portion	6.2% each
Total for a self-employed taxpayer	12.4%
Maximum earnings subject to Social Security taxes	$137,700
Regular Medicare Tax Rate	
Employer's portion/Employee's portion	1.45% each
Total for a self-employed individual	2.9%
Maximum earnings subject to Medicare taxes	No limit

CARES Act Payroll Tax Deferral

For tax year 2020, the CARES Act provides a temporary payroll tax deferral. This applies to wages paid between March 27, 2020, and December 31, 2020. This is only a deferral, not forgiveness of the tax owed. All employers (including self-employed taxpayers) may defer the deposit and payment of the *employer's* share of Social Security tax.

If elected, this means the business could defer the 6.2% "employer portion" of the Social Security tax. Self-employed individuals may also choose to defer the employer portion of their self-employment taxes and defer payments that would otherwise be required to be made for the period beginning on March 27, 2020, and ending December 31, 2020. If the business chooses to defer these taxes, 50% of the deferred taxes must be paid by December 31, 2021 and the remaining 50% must be paid by December 31, 2022.[47]

Federal Unemployment (FUTA) Tax

The Federal Unemployment Tax Act (FUTA), provides for payments of unemployment compensation to workers who have lost their jobs. A business reports and pays FUTA tax separately from federal income tax, and Social Security and Medicare taxes. FUTA tax is paid *only* by the employer, never by the employee. The current FUTA tax rate is 6% on the first $7,000 of each employee's wages. Most employers receive a maximum credit of up to 5.4% against this FUTA tax for any unemployment tax paid to the state. The tax is reported on Form 940, Employer's Annual Federal Unemployment (FUTA) Tax Return.

Once an employee earns $7,000 in gross wages for the year, that is the maximum amount of wages that are subject to FUTA. This means that the business no longer has to pay FUTA for that particular employee. However, if an employee quits, and a new employee is hired, then the FUTA tax must be collected on the new employee's wages, as well, up to the $7,000 limit.

Example: Pathway Brokers, Inc. hires a new receptionist on January 10. The receptionist only works a month before quitting. She had earned $2,300 in wages in January before she quit. Pathway Brokers must pay $138 in FUTA tax on her wages ($2,300 x 6% = $138). If the company hires another employee to replace her, it will be required to pay FUTA tax on the new employee's wages as well, up to the $7,000 threshold.

Additional Medicare Tax

An **Additional Medicare Tax** of 0.9% (.009) applies to an individual taxpayer's earned income that exceeds the following thresholds:

2020 Additional Medicare Tax Thresholds	
Filing Status	**Threshold Amount**
MFJ	$250,000
MFS	$125,000
Single, HOH, or QW	$200,000

[47] The CARES Act payroll tax deferral is not on the test specifications for the current testing cycle, so it is unlikely that you will be tested on this topic.

A taxpayer's earned income (including wages, taxable fringe benefits, bonuses, tips, commissions, and self-employment income) that is subject to Medicare tax is also subject to the Additional Medicare Tax to the extent it exceeds the applicable threshold amount for his filing status.

An employer is required to withhold the Additional Medicare tax if an employee is paid more than $200,000, regardless of an employee's filing status or whether the employee has wages paid by another employer.

There is no "employer's share" of the Additional Medicare Tax like there is for the "regular" Medicare tax. An employee may be subject to the Additional Medicare tax even if amounts are not withheld from his wages.

Example: Patricia and Durante are married and file jointly. Patricia makes $40,000 working as a teacher. Durante makes $230,000 as a physician for Mercy General Hospital. They have no other earned income during the year. Because Durante's salary exceeds $200,000, Mercy General is required to withhold and remit an additional 0.9% Medicare tax on the excess wages over the threshold of $200,000 (i.e., the applicable tax is on $30,000, his excess wages over the threshold). The total *Additional* Medicare tax withheld by the employer is $270 ($30,000 × 0.9%). Patricia and Durante file jointly, and their combined AGI on their joint income tax return is $270,000, which is $20,000 over the threshold for joint filers (AGI $270,000 - $250,000 MFJ threshold). Therefore, their actual Additional Medicare Tax is $180 ($20,000 X 0.9%). Assuming they do not owe any other federal income taxes, interest, or penalties to which the withholding could be applied, they will receive a $90 ($270 amount withheld - $180 actual tax) refund of the additional 0.9% Medicare tax withholding.

Self-employed taxpayers can deduct half of their SE tax in figuring their adjusted gross income. Self-employed taxpayers *cannot* deduct one-half of the 0.9% Additional Medicare tax as an adjustment to income or as a business expense.

An individual general partner in a partnership is considered to be self-employed, and his income is subject to self-employment tax and Additional Medicare tax, just like a sole proprietor. Income reported by the partnership to limited partners is considered passive activity income and is generally not subject to self-employment tax or the Additional Medicare tax).

Example: Deacon is unmarried. He earns $195,000 a year working as an employee for a software company. He also does some web design on the side. He earns $35,000 in net self-employment income from his side-jobs. Therefore, his gross income for the year would be $230,000. Deacon must pay the Additional Medicare Tax on $30,000, the amount that exceeds the threshold for his filing status ($230,000 - $200,000 threshold for single filers). His Additional Medicare Tax is $270 ($30,000 X 0.9%).

Example: Bailey is unmarried. She earns $180,000 a year working as a financial planner for an investment firm. She also has $45,000 in income from a limited partnership investment. She is not a general partner; she is only an investor. Therefore, even though her income is above the threshold for her filing status ($225,000 = $180,000 + $45,000), she will not be subject to the Additional Medicare Tax, because her "earned income" (her wages) are still below the $200,000 threshold.

Trust Fund Recovery Penalty (TFRP)

Trust fund taxes refer to amounts withheld from employees' wages (Social Security, Medicare, and income tax) by employers and held in trust until they are remitted to the Treasury. This penalty is also called the "100% penalty." If a business does not deposit its trust fund taxes in a timely manner, the IRS may assess a trust fund recovery penalty (TFRP). The amount of the penalty is equal to the unpaid balance of the trust fund taxes.

The TFRP may be assessed against any person who:

- Is **responsible** for collecting or paying withheld income and employment taxes, or for paying collected excise taxes, and
- **Willfully fails** to collect or pay them.

Once the IRS asserts the penalty, it can take collection action against the personal assets of anyone who is deemed a "responsible person." It is not only the executives of businesses or the top finance and accounting personnel who may be held responsible for the TFRP. A responsible person may also include a person who signs checks for the company or who otherwise has the authority to spend business funds, such as a bookkeeper. For the IRS to determine that an individual willfully failed to pay the required taxes, the responsible person:

- Must have, or should have, been aware of the outstanding taxes, and
- Intentionally disregarded the law or been plainly indifferent to its requirements (no evil intent or bad motive is required).

Using available funds to pay other creditors when the business fails to pay employment taxes is an indication of willfulness.

Example: Clorinda ran her own tax preparation business and also processed the payroll for her local church. The church had four employees. Clorinda prepared and signed the payroll tax returns and all the checks and then gave them to the pastor to mail. The pastor did not mail the payroll tax reports or remit the payments to the IRS. Instead, he used the money to purchase a new piano for the church. Clorinda knew the pastor was misusing the funds but did not report the information to authorities. The IRS assessed the TFRP against the pastor, the church, and Clorinda. Even though Clorinda was just the bookkeeper, she knew that the pastor was improperly handling the payroll tax funds, and she did nothing about it, so the IRS can assess 100% of the penalty against Clorinda.

Business Entities Snapshot				
Business type	**Sole Proprietorship**	**C Corporation**	**S Corporation**	**General Partnership**
Formation	No state filing required.	State filing required.	State filing required.	No state filing required.
Existence	Automatically dissolved upon death.	Perpetual life.	Perpetual life.	Varies from state to state.
Liability	A sole proprietor has unlimited liability because the sole proprietorship is not a separate legal entity.	Shareholders are not responsible for the debts of the corporation.	Shareholders are not responsible for the debts of the corporation.	General partners are liable for the debts of the partnership.
Operational Requirements	None.	Board of directors, annual meetings, and annual reporting required.	Board of directors, annual meetings, and annual reporting required.	No formal requirements.
Management	A sole proprietor has full control of management and operations.	Management reports to the directors, who are elected by the shareholders.	Management reports to the directors, who are elected by the shareholders.	Partners may have an oral or written operating agreement.
Taxation	Not a separate taxable entity. A sole proprietor pays all taxes on his/her individual return.	Taxed at the entity level. Dividends paid to owners are also taxable income for them.	Generally, no tax at the entity level. Income and losses are passed through to shareholders.	Generally, no tax at the entity level. Income and losses are passed through to partners.
Pass-Through	Yes	No	Yes	Yes
Double Taxation	No	Yes	No	No
Transferability	No	Yes	Yes	Yes

Unit 1: Study Questions

(Test yourself and then check the correct answers at the end of this section.)

1. Caden, age 16, works the counter of a juice bar owned by his mother, a sole proprietor. Which of the following taxes, if any, should be withheld from his paycheck?

A. Income tax.
B. Income tax, Social Security and Medicare taxes.
C. Income tax, Social Security and Medicare taxes, and FUTA tax.
D. None of the above.

2. Sunset Funeral Services, Inc. provides burial and funerary services to its customers. Thomas recently paid $11,000 in cash to Sunset Funeral Services for payment of a burial insurance policy. What form is Sunset Funeral Services required to file for this transaction?

A. Form 1099-K.
B. Form 1099-MISC.
C. Form 8300.
D. Form 1099-NEC.

3. Which of the following entities does *not* require an EIN?

A. An estate.
B. A C corporation.
C. Nonprofit organization.
D. A sole proprietorship with no employees.

4. Which of the following is considered a drawback of the C corporation entity?

A. It may have many different types of shareholders.
B. It may have investors who are nonresident aliens.
C. Its profits are potentially subject to double taxation.
D. It is run by a board of directors.

5. Kramer is a single sole proprietor who runs a cabinet-making business as a sole-proprietor. He is required to file Schedule SE if his net earnings from self-employment were at least:

A. $5
B. $108
C. $400
D. $600

6. Mandy and her cousin, Tammy, work together, making beaded necklaces and selling them at craft shows. They run their business jointly and attempt to make a profit, but they do not have any type of formal business agreement. Instead, they just shook hands and agreed to share profits and losses equally. They received $24,900 in 2020 from selling necklaces, and they had $2,900 of expenses. What is the correct way for Mandy and Tammy to report their income?

A. Mandy and Tammy must split the income and report the gross income as "other income" on each taxpayer's individual Form 1040.
B. Mandy and Tammy must report each person's own income and expenses on Schedule C.
C. Mandy and Tammy should calculate income and subtract expenses, and each should report the net amount as "other income" on her individual Form 1040.
D. Mandy and Tammy are working as a partnership and should report their income on Form 1065.

7. Julian is self-employed and has a small business selling used video games and comic books online. He has a profit motive in the activity. His gross sales were $29,000 for the year, and his expenses total $9,500. Which schedule should Julian complete to report his income and expenses?

A. Schedule A.
B. Schedule C.
C. Schedule D.
D. Schedule F.

8. All of the statements are correct about the following business entities *except:*

A. S corporations may have an unlimited number of shareholders.
B. A multi-member LLC typically provides the liability protection of a corporation but the tax benefits of a partnership.
C. "Pass-through" entities include LLCs, LLPs, S corporations, and general partnerships.
D. An owner of a sole proprietorship bears all the liabilities and risks of the business.

9. Aubert is a sole proprietor with no employees. Aubert uses his Social Security number to run his business and also to file information returns. In which scenario would be *required* to obtain an EIN for his sole proprietorship?

A. If he is required to file excise tax returns.
B. If he changes the name of his business.
C. If he changes the physical location of his business.
D. If he operates more than one sole proprietorship.

10. A C corporation is taxed at a flat rate of:

A. 15%
B. 20%
C. 21%
D. 35%

11. Federal law requires businesses to provide a Form 1099-NEC for each independent contractor paid at least _______ for services during a year.

A. $400
B. $500
C. $600
D. $700

12. Ellsworth is a full-time life insurance salesman and a statutory employee. He receives a Form W-2 for his earnings. How should he report his income?

A. On Form 1040 as regular wages.
B. On Schedule C, not subject to self-employment tax.
C. On Schedule C, subject to self-employment tax.
D. On Schedule E, not subject to self-employment tax.

13. The IRS evaluates all of the following characteristics to assess the relationship between a business and its workers except:

A. Type of relationship.
B. Financial control.
C. Income level.
D. Behavioral control.

14. In which of the following instances is a partnership not required to obtain a new EIN?

A. The partners decide to incorporate.
B. The partnership is taken over by one of the partners and is subsequently operated as a sole proprietorship.
C. The general partner ends the old partnership and begins a new one.
D. The partnership adds additional business locations.

15. Donald and Selma are married and run a small pet grooming business together. They want to treat their business as a qualified joint venture. They live in Virginia, a non-community property state, and they each materially participate in the business. Their business is not an LLC or other state-level entity. Which of the following statements is correct?

A. They may choose to report their qualified joint venture on two separate Schedules C, so long as they file jointly.
B. They may choose to report their qualified joint venture on two separate Schedules C, so long as they file separate tax returns (MFS).
C. They are required to file a partnership tax return for their business activity.
D. They may file a single Schedule C, listing Donald as the sole proprietor one year and Selma as the sole proprietor the following year.

16. A business that fails to pay required payroll taxes to the IRS may be subject to:

A. Underpayment of estimated tax penalty.
B. Substantial valuation misstatement penalty.
C. Gross understatement of income penalty.
D. Trust fund recovery penalty.

17. A domestic LLC with at least two members that does not file Form 8832 will be automatically classified as ________ for federal income tax purposes.

A. An S corporation.
B. A partnership.
C. A qualified joint venture.
D. A domestic trust.

18. Precision Auto Sales is a used car dealership and auto body shop. Which of the following customer transactions would require filing Form 8300, *Report of Cash Payments Over $10,000 Received in a Trade or Business?*

A. A customer wired $7,000 from his bank account to the dealership's bank account and also presented a $4,000 cashier's check to purchase a used car.
B. A payment of $10,000 made with a cashier's check for a custom paint job on a car.
C. A payment of $12,000 made with a personal check to purchase a used car.
D. The dealership receives monthly ACH payments (automatic payments from a customer's bank account) totaling over $15,000 during 2020.

Unit 1: Quiz Answers

1. The answer is A. Only income tax would be withheld from Caden's wages. In certain situations, family members who work for other family members are subject to different tax requirements. Only income tax is withheld from the paycheck of a child under age 18 who is working for a parent who is a sole proprietor.

2. The answer is C. The receipt of the cash by Sunset Funeral Home is a transaction that must be reported on Form 8300. When a business receives cash for more than $10,000 from a single transaction, it is required to file Form 8300, *Report of Cash Payments Over $10,000 Received in a Trade or Business.*

3. The answer is D. A sole proprietorship without employees does not require an employer identification number. The other choices listed all require an EIN.

4. The answer is C. C corporations are subject to double taxation (a corporate-level tax and dividends distributed to shareholders are taxable to the shareholders without a corresponding deduction by the corporation. The other statements are simply facts about C corporations, but are not considered drawbacks.

5. The answer is C. Kramer is required to file an income tax return if his net earnings from self-employment are *$400 or more.* If net earnings from self-employment are less than $400, a taxpayer is normally not required to file Schedule SE.

6. The answer is D. Mandy and Tammy are working as a partnership and should report their income and expenses on Form 1065, *U.S. Return of Partnership Income.* Each partner should receive a Schedule K-1 to report her individual share of the partnership's income on her Form 1040.

7. The answer is B. Julian should complete Schedule C to report his business income and expenses.

8. The answer is A. An S corporation cannot have an unlimited number of shareholders. Only a C corporation may have an unlimited number of shareholders. An S corporation is generally limited to no more than 100 shareholders.

9. The answer is A. Aubert must request an EIN if he files excise tax returns. A tax ID number (EIN) is normally not required if a taxpayer operates a sole proprietorship with no employees. However, a sole proprietor who is required to file excise tax returns must obtain an EIN (he cannot use his social security number). A sole proprietorship is not required to obtain a new EIN when it changes location or its business name. An individual may operate multiple businesses using the same EIN, so long as all the businesses are sole proprietorships.

10. The answer is C. The TCJA permanently lowered the corporate tax rate to a flat 21% of taxable income. This applies to all C corporations.

11. The answer is C. Federal law requires businesses to provide a Form 1099-NEC for each independent contractor paid at least $600 for services during a year. If a business makes payments directly to a corporation (rather than an individual), it is generally not required to issue a Form 1099-NEC.

12. The answer is B. Ellsworth would report his income on Schedule C, *not* subject to self-employment tax. Statutory employees are unique because they report their wages, income, and allowable expenses on Schedule C, like self-employed taxpayers. However, statutory employees are not required to pay self-employment tax because their employers treat them as employees for Social Security tax purposes.

13. The answer is C. Income level is not a factor in determining a worker's status. The main issue involves whether the employer or the worker has the right to direct or control how the work is done and to control the financial and business aspects of the job. This helps determine whether a worker should be classified as an employee or an independent contractor.

14. The answer is D. A partnership is not required to obtain a new EIN simply to add business locations. In all of the other circumstances, the entity would need to obtain a new EIN.

15. The answer is A. Their business is not incorporated, and it is not an LLC or another state-level entity, so Donald and Selma may choose to report their qualified joint venture on two separate Schedules C, as long as they file jointly. An **unincorporated** business jointly owned by a married couple can be treated as a qualified joint venture (QJV). A business qualifies as a QJV if spouses file jointly, are the business' only owners, and both materially participate in the business.

16. The answer is D. The trust fund recovery penalty applies to any person who is responsible for collecting or paying income and employment taxes, or for paying excise taxes collected, and who willfully fails to collect or pay these taxes. The amount of the penalty is equal to the unpaid balance of the trust fund taxes.

17. The answer is B. A domestic LLC with at least two members that does not file Form 8832 is classified automatically as a partnership for federal tax purposes.

18. The answer is B. Precision Auto Sales must file Form 8300 to report the transaction made with a cashier's check, because it was $10,000. Answer "A" is incorrect because a bank wire transfer is not considered "cash" for Form 8300 reporting. Since the remaining cash remitted ($4,000) was below $10,000, the dealer has no 8300 filing requirement. Answer "C" is incorrect because personal checks are not considered "cash" for the purposes of this rule (although cashier's checks *are*). Answer "D" is incorrect because ACH payments are not considered cash for the purpose of reporting on Form 8300.[48]

[48] Source: See the IRS Form 8300 Reference Guide: https://www.irs.gov/businesses/small-businesses-self-employed/irs-form-8300-reference-guide

Unit 2: Accounting Periods and Methods

More Reading:
Publication 334, Tax Guide for Small Business
Publication 538, Accounting Periods and Methods

Tax Years and Accounting Periods

The tax year is an annual accounting period for reporting income and expenses. Individuals file their tax returns on a calendar-year basis. Certain businesses have the option to file their tax returns on either a calendar-year or a fiscal-year basis.

- **Calendar Tax Year:** A calendar tax year is always twelve consecutive months beginning January 1 and ending December 31.
- **Fiscal Tax Year:** Generally, a fiscal tax year covers twelve consecutive months ending on the last day of any month *except* December. However, one variation of a fiscal year-end does not fall on the same date each year.

A **52/53-week** tax year is a fiscal tax year that varies from 52 to 53 weeks but does not necessarily end on the last day of the month. For example, some businesses choose to end their fiscal year on a particular day of the week, such as the last Friday in June or the Saturday that falls closest to January 31.

Example: Sandra works for the state of New York as an accountant. The state's budget follows a fiscal year that begins April 1 and ends on March 31. This is an example of a 12-month period not ending in December. Most federal and state governments operate on a fiscal-year basis, as do most large corporations.

Short Tax Year: This is a tax year of fewer than 12 months. A short tax year may result in the first or last year of an entity's existence, or when an entity changes its accounting period (for example, from a fiscal year to a calendar year, or vice versa). Even if a business is not in existence for a full year, the requirements for filing the return and paying any tax liability are generally the same as if a full 12-month tax year had ended on the last day of the short tax year.

Example: Ballard and Nathan are friends who started a business partnership five years ago, each sharing equally in the profits and losses. Ballard died on November 1, 2020, and his partnership interest transferred to Nathan under their pre-existing partnership agreement. Therefore, the partnership is no longer in existence following his death (since there is now only one owner). Nathan decides to continue the business as a sole proprietor. Nathan must request a new employer identification number since his business structure has changed. The partnership is dissolved, and a final partnership tax return must be filed for the short tax year from January 1, 2020, to November 1, 2020 (the date of Ballard's death).

Example: Christa formed Redding Textbooks, Inc. on February 1, 2020 to sell used textbooks. She immediately started having financial troubles and dissolved her corporation on October 31, 2020. Christa must file a corporate return for a short tax year covering the nine-month period that Redding Textbooks was in existence.

A business adopts a tax year when it *files its first income tax return*. Any form of business entity may potentially adopt the calendar year as its tax year. However, not every business can choose a fiscal year, with the exception of a new C corporation, which may generally elect to use any fiscal year it chooses. Form 1128, *Application to Adopt, Change, or Retain a Tax Year*, is used to request a change in the tax year. The IRS requires the use of the calendar year in the following instances:

- If the business keeps no books or records.
- There is no annual accounting period.
- The Internal Revenue Code or income tax regulations require the use of a calendar year.

If a business files its first tax return using the calendar tax year and later changes its business structure (such as moving from a sole proprietorship to a partnership), the business must continue to use the calendar year unless it receives IRS approval or is otherwise forced to change in order to comply with the IRC.

An estate is unique. A taxpayer's death marks the end of his final tax year as an individual taxpayer, and the following day is the beginning of the first tax year for his estate.

The executor or personal representative of the estate is responsible for filing the individual's final income tax return (Form 1040), income tax returns for the estate (Form 1041), and possibly an estate tax return (Form 706), assuming the estate has a filing requirement.

The executor chooses the estate's tax period when he files its first income tax return. Generally, the estate's first tax year is any period of 12 months or less that ends on the last day of a month. If the executor selects the last day of any month other than December, the estate has adopted a fiscal tax year.

Example: Marshall is an unmarried physician. He dies on July 1, 2020, and his adult daughter, Heidi, is named the executor of his estate. Heidi is responsible for filing Marshall's final individual tax return (Form 1040). The final Form 1040 covers the period from January 1 through July 1 (the period that Marshall was still alive). In addition, Heidi must file income tax returns for the estate for each year with the first tax return beginning on July 2, and these fiduciary returns will normally be required to be filed every year until the estate's assets have been fully distributed. Heidi must request an EIN for her father's estate, which is considered a separate entity for tax purposes. Marshall's assets are valued at approximately $15 million on the date of his death. Therefore, in addition to the income tax returns, an *estate tax* return (Form 706) must also be filed.

The due date for Form 1041 is the fifteenth day of the fourth month following the end of the entity's tax year. The Form 1041 extended due date is now September 30 (for a calendar year filer) – 5½ months after the original due date.

Note: Unlike other entity types, the extended due date for estate and trust *income tax* returns (Form 1041) is not the 15th of the month – it is the *last* day of the month (September 30th).

Required Tax Year

Partnerships and S corporations generally must use a "required" tax year. For partnerships, this means that, unless the partnership can establish a legitimate business purpose for a different tax year, a partnership's "required" tax year must conform to its partners' tax years. If one or more partners with the same tax year own a majority (more than 50%) interest in the partnership's capital and profits, the tax year of those partners is the required tax year for the partnership.

If there is no majority interest tax year, the partnership must use the tax year if all of the principal partners (those who have an interest of 5% or more in the partnership's capital and profits) have the exact same tax year. If there is no majority interest tax year and all of the principal partners do not have the same tax year, the partnership must use the tax year that would result in the least aggregate deferral of income to its partners. An entity does not have to use a required tax year if it receives permission from the IRS to use another permitted tax year or if it files an election under section 444 (as described further in the next section).

A business is always allowed to use a year other than a "required" tax year if it can establish a "substantial business purpose" for using a different tax year. For example, a seasonal business, such as a ski resort or a Christmas tree farm, may use a tax year that follows the natural cycle of the business itself. This is sometimes called a "natural tax year." A "natural tax year" is a fiscal year in which the last two months of the year provide over 25% of the business's gross receipts for the entire year.

A partnership or S corporation may establish a bona-fide "business purpose" for a tax year by filing Form 1128, *Application to Adopt, Change, or Retain a Tax Year*. Unless it can establish a business purpose for using a fiscal year, an S corporation or partnership must generally use the calendar year. However, an S corporation can automatically adopt a fiscal year under the "business purpose test" if the fiscal year conforms to the tax year of a majority of its shareholders.

Example: Polar Partnership has two partners, both of which are C corporations. Corporation ABA owns a 30% partnership interest in Polar Partnership and operates on a calendar year. Corporation BEX owns the remaining 70% of the partnership interest and operates on a fiscal year ending March 31.

Partners	Ownership Interest	Tax Year
Corporation ABA	30%	Calendar year (December 31)
Corporation BEX	70%	March 31 (fiscal year-end)

Since Corporation BEX owns a majority interest in Polar Partnership, the partnership must file on the same tax year as Corporation BEX. Therefore, the tax year for the partnership will end on March 31, the same tax year as the majority-interest partner.

A business may normally elect a fiscal year based on a genuine business purpose; however, it is not considered a "legitimate" business purpose to elect a particular fiscal tax year just so that partners or shareholders may defer income recognition.

Example: Evangeline and Farhan are clothing designers. They decide to form a 50/50 partnership in order to sell designer swimwear for men and women. Although Evangeline and Farhan are both individuals who report their personal income on a calendar year, they file Form 1128 in order to request a natural business year for their partnership. Their natural business year would end in September, after the summer is over, when most swimsuits for the year are sold. Their request for a natural business year is granted. They will file their partnership return with a fiscal year-end of September 30.

Section 444 Election

A partnership, S corporation, or Personal Service Corporation (PSC) can also request to use a tax year other than its required tax year by filing Form 8716, *Election to Have a Tax Year Other Than a Required Tax Year*. This is known as a section 444 election, and it does not apply to any business that establishes a genuine business purpose for using a different tax year.

A partnership, S corporation, or PSC that makes this election must generally make certain required payments based upon the value of the tax deferral the owners receive by using a tax year different from the required tax year. A business can request a section 444 election if it meets all of the following requirements:

- It is not a member of a tiered structure.
- It has not previously had a section 444 election in effect.
- It elects a year that meets the deferral period requirement.

The deferral period depends on whether the entity is using the election to retain its tax year or to adopt or change its tax year. If it intends to retain its tax year, it may only do so if the deferral period is three months or less. The deferral period is the number of months between the beginning of the retained year and the end of the first required tax year. If the entity is requesting adoption or a change to a tax year other than the required tax year, the deferral period is the number of months from the end of the new tax year to the end of the required tax year. Generally, the IRS will allow a section 444 election only if the deferral period is less than the shorter of:

- Three months, or
- The deferral period of the tax year being changed.

Example: Century Education, LLC is a newly formed partnership owned by two individual partners. The partnership began business operations on December 1, 2020. Century Education wants to make a section 444 election to adopt a September 30 tax year. The partnership's deferral period for the tax year beginning December 1, 2020, is three months, the number of months between September 30 and December 31.

The section 444 election remains in effect until it is terminated. If the election is terminated, another section 444 election cannot be made for the same tax year. The election also ends automatically when any of the following occurs:

- The entity changes to its required tax year.
- The entity liquidates.
- The entity becomes a member of a tiered structure.

- The IRS determines that the entity willfully failed to comply with the required payments or distributions.
- The entity is an S corporation, and the S election is terminated.

Filing Due Dates for Entities

Partnership and S corporation returns are due on the fifteenth day of the third month following the end of the year. For calendar-year partnerships and S corporations, returns are due March 15.

For C corporations using a calendar year, its tax returns are due on April 15 of the following year. If the corporation is on a fiscal year, the tax return is normally due on the fifteenth day of the fourth month following the end of the tax year.

However, a corporation with a fiscal tax year ending **June 30** must file by the 15th day of the *3rd* month after the end of its tax year, resulting in a September 15 due date. A corporation with a short tax year ending anytime in June will be treated as if the short year ended on June 30, and must file by the 15th day of the 3rd month after the end of its tax year.

C corporations with fiscal tax years ending on June 30 will continue to have a due date of September 15 until 2025. After Dec. 31, 2025, the regular due date for corporations with a June 30 fiscal year-end will be October 15. For these and other entities' returns, if the due date falls on a Saturday, Sunday, or legal holiday, it is delayed until the next business day. Dissolving entities must file short-year tax returns. In this case, the due date would be based on the date of final dissolution.

Example: A calendar-year C corporation dissolved on July 22, 2020, and ceased all operations. Its final return is due by November 15, 2020 (the fifteenth day of the fourth month following the close of its short tax year). The return will cover the period from January 1, 2020, through July 22, 2020.

Example: Velvet Bakery Inc. is a C corporation with a June 30 fiscal year-end. This means that the corporation's 2020 tax year begins on July 1, 2020, and ends on June 30, 2021. Velvet Bakery must file its 2020 Form 1120 by the due date of September 15, 2021, unless the business files for an extension.

Nonprofit entities using the calendar year must file their information returns (Form 990) by May 15. For nonprofit entities using a fiscal year, returns are due on the fifteenth day of the fifth month following the end of their tax year.

Example: Forgotten Feline, Inc. is an animal rescue organization organized as a corporation for legal purposes. The entity has formal recognition as a 501(c)3 entity. Forgotten Feline operates on a calendar year. The organization must file its information return (Form 990) by May 15.

Entities and individuals may request extensions of time to file their federal income tax returns. An extension does not grant the entity additional time to pay the tax due. The tax due must be paid by the filing deadline, or the entity will be subject to interest and penalties on the amount of unpaid tax.

Entity Type (Calendar-Year entities)[49]	Due Date/Extended Due Date
Sole Proprietorships (Form 1040)	April 15/October 15
Partnerships	March 15/September 15
C Corporations (except June 30 fiscal years)	April 15/October 15[50]
S Corporations	March 15/September 15
Exempt Organizations (Form 990)	May 15/November 15
Form 1041 (trust and fiduciary returns)	April 15/September 30[51]
FBAR	April 15/October 15[52]
Retirement Plans (Form 5500)	July 31/October 15
Estate Tax Return (Form 706)	Nine months after death, six-month extension

Accounting Methods

An accounting method is a set of rules used to determine when and how income and expenses are reported. No single accounting method is required of all taxpayers. However, the taxpayer must use a system that properly reflects income and expenses, and it must be used consistently from year to year. Businesses generally report taxable income under one of the following accounting methods:

- **Cash method**
- **Accrual method**
- **Special methods of accounting for certain items of income and expenses**
- **Hybrid method (using elements of the methods above)**

The special methods include, for example, those related to accounting for long-term contracts, farming businesses, and installment sales. Different rules apply to each accounting method.

A business owner may use different accounting methods if he has two separate and distinct businesses. Two businesses will not be considered "separate and distinct" unless a separate set of books and records is maintained for each business.

[49] Study Note: For Part 2 of the EA exam, you must memorize filing deadlines for partnerships, C corporations, and the other entities covered in this study guide.

[50] As a reminder, a C Corporation tax return is due on the 15th day of the 4th month after the end of the corporation's tax year. However, a corporation with a fiscal tax year ending June 30 must file by the 15th day of the 3rd month after the end of its tax year. A corporation with a short tax year ending anytime in June will be treated as if the short year ended on June 30, and must file by the 15th day of the 3rd month after the end of its tax year. C corporations with tax years ending on June 30 will continue to have a due date of September 15 until tax year 2025. After Dec. 31, 2025, the regular due date for these returns will be October 15.

[51] Remember, the extension for Form 1041 is for a 5½ month extension, not 6 months.

[52] An automatic extension allows the FBAR to be filed by October 15, without the need to request the extension.

Example: Cardan is a self-employed enrolled agent. He prepares tax returns from January through April every year. He is also a motivational speaker who is booked for many paid engagements. He reports his tax preparation business using the accrual method and his speaking business using the cash method. He keeps separate books and records for each business and files a separate Schedule C for each business. Cardan may use different accounting methods because he has two separate and distinct businesses with separate sets of records for each.

Rules for the Cash Method

The cash method of accounting is the simplest method to use, but some businesses cannot use the cash method. The cash method may be used by taxpayers (other than tax shelters) with less than $26 million in annual gross receipts in 2020 (see "small business taxpayers" below), regardless of the taxpayer's industry, or whether or not the business produces inventory.

Taxpayers are permitted to file a Form 3115, *Application for Change in Accounting Method,* if they want to switch from the accrual method to the cash method. The *Tax Cuts and Jobs Act* allows:

- "Small business taxpayers" with average annual gross receipts of $26 million or less in the prior three-year period to use the cash method of accounting.
- Exempts small business taxpayers from certain accounting rules for inventories, cost capitalization, and long-term contracts.
- More small business taxpayers to use this cash method going forward.

Note: The most common accounting method is the **cash method**, which is used by most small businesses. The **accrual method** is used by most large corporations and is considered a more accurate method of recognizing income and expenses, because it reflects when taxable income is actually earned. The accrual method is required for publicly-traded corporations (such as Coke, Nike, Sears, and Ford).

Note: Large nonprofit entities are often required to use the accrual method because many of them receive government funding (such as federal grants) and must have audited financial statements.

Some businesses are required by law to use the accrual method, regardless of their size or gross receipts. The following businesses are required to use the accrual method:

- A business with average annual gross receipts exceeding $26 million
- Any tax shelter, regardless of its size

Gross receipts for a short tax year are annualized. An entity that fails to meet the applicable gross receipts test for any tax year is prohibited from using the cash method and must change to the accrual method, effective for the tax year in which the entity fails to meet the test.

Example: Angelo and Phillip Shelby are brothers. They form Shelby Software Development, Inc., a C corporation. In 2020, the corporation's annualized gross receipts for the year are $14 million. The corporation may use the cash method because it has applicable gross receipts under the threshold.

Note: Under the TCJA, all businesses (except tax shelters) are permitted to use the cash method of accounting if they meet the annual gross receipts test, even if the business produces, manufactures, or sells inventory. Average annual gross receipts are determined by adding the gross receipts for the three preceding tax years and dividing the total by three. If the business has been in existence for less than three years, then the applicable average gross receipts will be determined based on the applicable number of years in existence.

Study note: You should memorize the basic rules of which entities can and cannot use the cash method and the accrual method for the EA exam.

Under the cash method, a taxpayer generally deducts expenses when they are paid. However, a business generally cannot attempt to lower its taxable income by paying expenses applicable to future years. In other words, a business cannot pay an expense several years in advance in order to take a current deduction. The business would instead be required to capitalize costs paid in advance and deduct them in the years to which they apply.

The 12-Month-Rule for Certain Prepaid Expenses

There is an exception to the timing of the deductibility on prepaid expenses under the "12-month rule" under which the cash-basis taxpayer is not required to capitalize amounts paid for periods that do not extend beyond the earlier of the following:

- 12 months after the benefit begins, or
- The end of the tax year *after* the tax year in which payment is made.

Example: Lizbeth is a sole proprietor who rents retail space for her eyebrow threading business. She pays two years of rent in advance in order to receive a substantial discount from her landlord. She cannot use the 12-month rule because the benefit from her advance payment exceeds the 12-month time period. She must recognize the rent expense over the two-year period, regardless of which method of accounting she uses.

Example: Wallace Partnership is a calendar-year business. It pays $15,000 on July 1, 2020, for a business insurance liability policy that is effective for one year beginning on that date. The 12-month rule applies, and the full $15,000 is deductible in 2020.

Example: Paulo is a sole proprietor and pays $3,000 in 2020 for a business liability insurance policy that is effective for three years (36 months), beginning on July 1, 2020. This payment does not qualify for the 12-month rule. Therefore, only $500 (6/36 × $3,000) is deductible in 2020, $1,000 (12/36 × $3,000) is deductible in 2021, $1,000 (12/36 × $3,000) is deductible in 2022, and the remaining $500 is deductible in 2023, when the policy expires.

Constructive Receipt of Income

Under the cash method, taxpayers report income when it is actually or "constructively" received during the tax year. Income is constructively received when the amount is credited to the taxpayer's account or made available without substantial restriction so that the taxpayer or his agent has access to the funds.

The taxpayer does not need to have physical possession of the payment. However, income is not considered to be "constructively" received if control or use of it is substantially restricted.

Example: BBQ Rotisserie, LLC operates on the cash method. Interest income was credited to BBQ Rotisserie's bank account on December 31, 2020, but the owners did not withdraw it until January 10, 2021. The business must include the interest income in its gross income for 2020, not 2021. The owners had ownership and control of the income in 2020, so it is taxable in the year received.

Example: Lucky Fox Bail Bonds, LLP is a cash-basis partnership that bills a customer on December 10, 2020. The customer sends the company a post-dated check. The check is received on December 31, 2020, but cannot be deposited until the following year because it was postdated to January 15, 2021. Lucky Fox Bail Bonds would include this income in gross income for 2021 since constructive receipt did not occur until January 15, 2021, the date that the check could be legally deposited.

Accrual Method

Under the accrual method of accounting, a business generally records income when a sale occurs, or income is earned, regardless of when the business gets paid. Under the accrual method, an expense is deducted when "all events" have occurred to fix the liability with reasonable accuracy and economic performance has occurred with respect to the liability. This is also called the "all-events" test.

A business that uses the accrual method must also report costs when they are incurred, either as expenses or as capitalized assets. It does not matter when the business actually *pays* for the expenses. Under the accrual method, income is generally reported when one or more of the following occurs:

- Payment is received.
- The taxpayer earns the income.
- The income is due to the taxpayer.
- When the title (ownership) of products sold has passed.

Under TCJA, a business must recognize income on the accrual method no later than the time it is recognized on their applicable financial statement, (if the business has one). The accrual method gives a more accurate assessment of a business's financial situation than the cash method. Income earned in each period is more accurately matched against the expenses for that period, so a business gets a better picture of net profit or loss.

Example: Porta-Products, Inc. is an accrual-basis corporation that manufactures products and sells them to retailers nationwide. Porta-Products recognizes gross income from sales of products when it ships the product to retailers. On November 31, 2020, a retailer orders 1,000 cases of product at a price of $15 per case. On December 3, 2020, Porta-Products ships 1,000 cases and sends the retailer an invoice for $15,000. On January 10, 2021, the retailer pays the invoice. Porta-Products would recognize the income in 2020, because all the events that fix the right to receive income occurred when Porta-Products shipped the products.

Example: Rocket Computer, Inc. is a calendar-year, accrual-basis corporation. The business sold a computer on December 28, 2020, for $2,500 and provided the customer with a bill that same day, but did not receive payment until February 2, 2021. Rocket Computer must include the $2,500 in its 2020 income, the year the company actually earned the income, even though the related payment did not occur until the following year.

Hybrid Accounting Method

Businesses may also use a hybrid accounting method that is a combination of the cash, accrual, and perhaps other special methods, so long as the hybrid method clearly reflects income and is used consistently. However, the following restrictions apply:

- If inventory is necessary to account for income, and the business does not qualify as a "small business" (as detailed earlier under "Rules for the Cash Method"), the business must use the accrual method for purchases and sales. The cash method can be used for other income and expense items.
- If an entity uses the cash method for reporting income, it must use the cash method for reporting expenses.
- If an entity uses the accrual method for reporting expenses, it must use the accrual method for reporting income.

Changing Accounting Methods

When a business files its first tax return, it may choose any permitted accounting method. Subsequent changes, either in the overall accounting method or the treatment of a material item, generally require that the taxpayer obtain IRS approval. Prior approval is needed for:

- Changes from cash to accrual or vice versa, unless the change is required by law.
- Changes in the method used to value inventory, (see discussion of inventory methods later).
- Changes in the method of depreciation or amortization: this includes situations where a taxpayer changes from an "impermissible method" of depreciation or misses depreciation on an asset altogether.

The taxpayer must file Form 3115, *Application for Change in Accounting Method*, to request a change in either an overall accounting method or the accounting treatment for an individual item. However, IRS consent is not required for the following:

- Making an adjustment in the useful life of a depreciable or amortizable asset (but a taxpayer cannot change the recovery period for MACRS or ACRS property)
- Correcting a math error or an error in figuring tax liability
- A change in accounting method when the change is required by tax law, such as when a business's average gross receipts exceed $26 million in 2020.

Note: Unclaimed depreciation, for closed as well as open years, is allowed through a Section 481(a) adjustment that reduces income in the year of change. If the entire adjustment is less than $25,000, a *de minimis* rule permits taxpayers to take 100% of the amount into account in the year of change (see IRS Rev. Proc. 96-31 for more information).

Example: Five years ago, Alexandra bought a residential rental condominium for $97,500. The land value was $15,000, and the building's depreciable basis was $82,500. Alexandra self-prepared her own returns for several years and did not claim any depreciation on the rental. Alexandra visits an enrolled agent, Gordon, in 2020 and he discovers the missed depreciation deductions that went on for many years. Gordon tells Alexandra that she can claim her missed depreciation by filing Form 3115. The unclaimed depreciation of $14,500 is treated as a negative adjustment on Schedule E, with the annotation of "§481(a) adjustment".

Example: Russel is a general partner in Fitness Planet, LLC. Russel reviews the tax return for the prior year and discovers a mathematical error in the depreciation of an asset. The asset should have been depreciated over 15 years rather than five. Fitness Planet, LLC does not have to ask the IRS for permission merely to correct the depreciation error. Fitness Planet can file an amended return to correct the amount of depreciation claimed in the prior year.

Accounting for Inventory

The TCJA exempts certain businesses from the requirement to track and keep inventories. Specifically, taxpayers that meet the $26 million gross receipts test in 2020 are not required to account for inventories, but rather may use a method of accounting for inventories that either:

- Treats inventories as non-incidental materials and supplies, or
- Conforms to the taxpayer's financial accounting treatment of inventories.

However, even with these changes, a cash-basis taxpayer may still not deduct items for sale to customers until the *later* of (1) when they are sold or (2) when they are paid for.

The uniform capitalization rules (commonly referred to as UNICAP) provide detailed guidance regarding the direct costs and certain indirect costs related to the production of goods or the purchase of merchandise for resale that businesses must capitalize as part of the cost of inventory. UNICAP rules apply to producers of tangible and intangible personal property, and producers of real property, as well as a business that acquires wholesale inventory for resale.

In general, only large businesses are subject to the uniform capitalization rules. A business that wishes to change its accounting treatment of inventory must file Form 3115 and request a change to its accounting method.

Note: The Tax Cuts and Jobs Act modified the UNICAP rules for small and mid-sized businesses. Businesses that meet the $26 million gross receipts test in 2020 (based on average gross receipts for the prior three tax years) will no longer be required to apply the uniform capitalization (UNICAP) rules. However, this new exemption does not apply to businesses that are engaged in the production of real property (for example, a real estate developer). The TCJA retains the exemptions from the uniform capitalization rules that are not based on a taxpayer's gross receipts (covered next).

If a business is subject to the UNICAP rules, the taxpayer's inventory should include all of the following, if applicable:

- Merchandise or stock in trade
- Raw materials, work in process, finished products

- Supplies that physically become a part of items for sale (labels, stickers, boxes, exterior packaging, etc.)

A taxpayer's inventory may also include:

- Purchased merchandise if the title has passed to the taxpayer, even if the merchandise is still in transit or the business does not have physical possession of it for another reason
- Goods under contract for sale that have not yet been applied to the contract
- Goods out on consignment
- Goods held for sale in display rooms or booths located away from the taxpayer's place of business
- Intangible costs (examples include film or video production)

The following items are *never* included in inventory:

- Goods the business has sold if legal title (ownership) has passed to the buyer,
- Goods consigned to the business (but not owned by the business),
- Goods ordered for future delivery, if the business does not yet have the legal title; or
- Land, buildings, and depreciable equipment that are used in the business are never included in the calculation of inventory.

Example: Digital-X Studios is a professional film studio with average gross receipts of $170 million per year. Digital-X Studios produces cartoons and movies for Hollywood. Even though the company does not produce any tangible products, film production is subject to the UNICAP rules, so Digital-X Studios must capitalize all of its costs, including set design, costumes, special effects, film editing, and salaries for actors and production workers. When a film is finally completed and distributed, Digital-X Studios is allowed to deduct the production costs as COGS.

Businesses often make a full physical inventory count at the end of each tax year, as well as at other reasonable intervals. The recorded inventory balances are then adjusted to agree with the actual counts. Physical inventory counts may identify irregularities such as theft, as well as damaged goods and obsolete products.

Example: Big Bargains Grocery, Inc. has six store locations, and has $35 million in average gross receipts. Big Bargains Grocery employees take a physical inventory of each store at least once a month. During the physical inventory, store employees are required to record any damaged goods such as dented cans and ripped packaging. When the physical inventory is completed, each store manager does a final reconciliation, adjusting the books to reflect adjustments for expired food and damaged merchandise. If the business did not track its inventory, it would never know when products were stolen, damaged, or expired.

Example: Heritage Emporium, Inc. manufactures historical and theatre costumes. During the month of October, Heritage Emporium purchases extra raw materials to produce additional costumes for the Halloween holiday. All the materials and shipping costs associated with the inventory are capitalized rather than expensed. As the costumes are sold, Heritage Emporium expenses the costs associated with the inventory as *cost of goods sold*. At the end of each month, Heritage Emporium does a physical inventory count and adjusts COGS for any damaged or stolen inventory.

Certain *types* of businesses are not subject to UNICAP, regardless of their gross receipts. Regardless of a business' size, the following expenditures and entity types are not subject to UNICAP:

- Small businesses with average annual gross receipts of $26 million or less in 2020.
- Sellers of personal-use or nonbusiness property (such as a hobby activity that produces occasional income, but is not a business).
- Research and experimental expenditures, and marketing or advertising costs, regardless of business size. This includes software research and development costs.
- Intangible drilling and development costs of oil and gas or geothermal wells.
- Timber raised, harvested, or grown, and the underlying land.
- Qualified creative expenses incurred as self-employed writers, photographers, musicians, or artists.
- Loan originations,
- Warranty costs and product liability costs,
- Property provided to customers in connection with providing services. It must be *de minimis* and not be included in inventory in the hands of the service provider. An example would be a veterinarian who primarily provides veterinary services, but carries a small amount of pet food and flea medication for sale to customers.

Example: Earnest Brownwood is a self-employed writer that reports his business activity on Schedule C. His last novel became a blockbuster bestseller and was optioned for a Hollywood picture. As a result, Earnest's income from writing was over $30 million dollars in the prior year. Earnest writes novels about real historical figures. He often travels to foreign locations to do his research. Although it often takes him several years to write a novel, all his research expenses are deductible when they are incurred. His qualified creative expenses do not have to be capitalized because self-employed writers are exempt from UNICAP.

Cost of Goods Sold (COGS)

Cost of goods sold (COGS) is deducted from a business's gross receipts to determine its gross profit. COGS is calculated by adding up the cost of goods available *minus* any ending inventory. COGS is also referred to as "cost of sales." The following expenses related to inventory sold are included in the calculation of COGS:

- **The cost of products or raw materials, including freight**
- **Storage costs of raw materials and finished products**
- **Labor costs to produce the goods**
- **Factory overhead**

The equation for cost of goods sold is as follows:

Beginning Inventory +

Inventory Purchases and Production Costs - Ending Inventory

= Cost of Goods Sold (COGS)

Cost of goods sold is the direct costs attributable to the production (or purchase) of the goods (and sometimes services) sold by a business. In a manufacturing business, labor costs allocable to the cost of goods sold include both the direct and indirect labor used in fabricating the raw material into a finished, saleable product.

Other labor costs not associated with the manufacturing process, such as selling or administrative expenses, are not included in the COGS equation.

Example: In calculating COGS, Nathan's Custom Shoes includes the cost of leather and thread in the shoes it manufactures, as well as wages for the workers who produce and assemble the shoes. Inventory does not include the cost of advertising for the finished shoes. COGS is recorded as an expense when the company sells its finished goods.

Shipping Terms and Transfer of Ownership

Certain shipping terms dictate when a taxpayer must take an item out of its inventory and recognize income from a sale. The terms indicate the point at which title (ownership) of goods transfers from seller to buyer. The three most common terms are:

1. **FOB Destination:** Title passes to the buyer at the point of destination (when the goods arrive at the buyer's location).
2. **FOB Shipping Point:** Title passes to the buyer at the point of shipment (when the goods leave the seller's premises). FOB shipping point is also called "FOB origin."
3. **C.O.D.** ("cash on delivery" or "collect on delivery"): Payment is made upon delivery and title passes at that time. For a business that sells by mail on a C.O.D basis, the merchandise is generally included in the seller's closing inventory until the buyer pays for it.

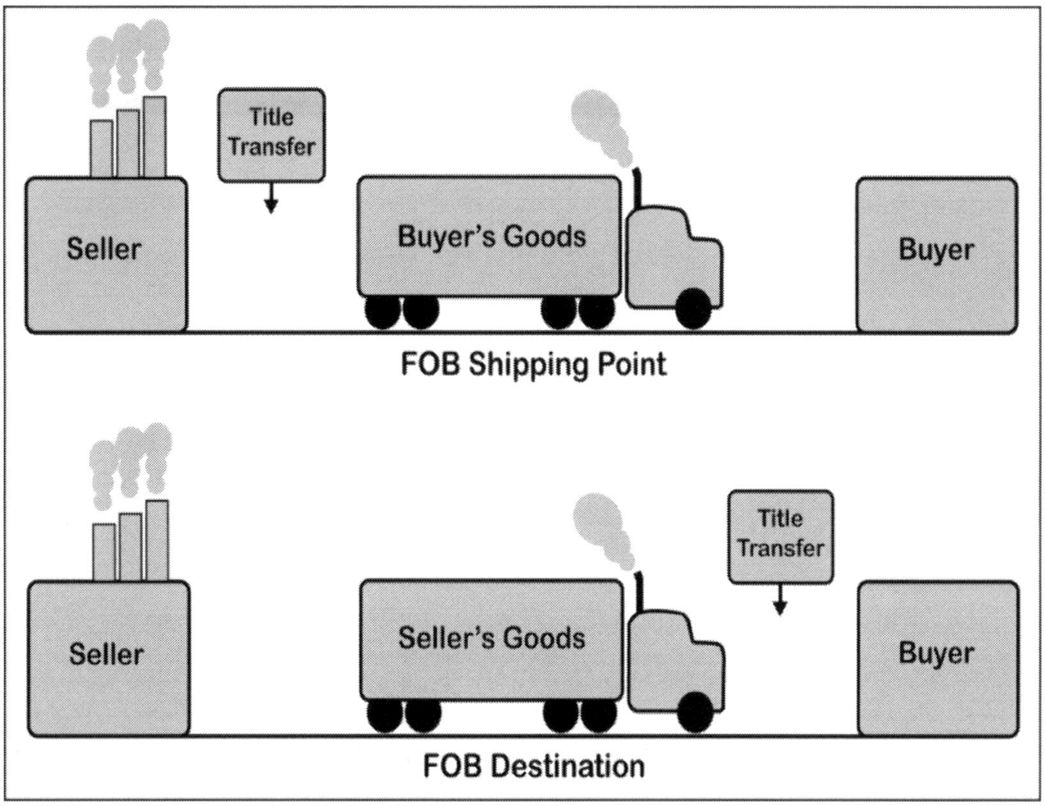

Example: Furniture Mart, Inc. is a calendar-year, accrual-basis corporation that manufactures custom household furniture. It does not accrue income until the products have been delivered and accepted by the buyer. In 2020, the company received an order for furniture to be custom manufactured for a total price of $32,000. Furniture Mart ships the furniture FOB destination to the customer on December 26, 2020, but it is not delivered and accepted by the customer until January 3, 2021. Furniture Mart will bill its customer for the $32,000 contract price and recognize the income from this sale in 2021, because the furniture had not been accepted, and title had not passed to the buyer until 2021. In this case, the method of shipping is important, because it determines in which year the business will recognize the income.

Common Inventory Methods

The value of a business's inventory is a major factor in figuring taxable income. Several common methods are used to assign costs to the items in inventory. They include the specific identification method, the average cost method, FIFO, and LIFO. LIFO and FIFO are the two most commonly used inventory accounting methods in the U.S., but all of the inventory methods listed are acceptable for IRS purposes. Some inventory methods are suited for specific types of businesses, while others are ideal for larger or smaller businesses.

The IRS does not require a business to use any specific inventory method, but the IRS does require businesses to request permission if the business later decides to switch from one inventory method to another. To change an inventory method, businesses must generally obtain IRS consent by filing Form 3115.

Specific Identification Method

This method is used when it is possible to identify and match the actual cost to specific items in inventory. It is most useful with an inventory that includes a limited number of highly specific and high-dollar items, such as custom goods or rare items like artwork or gemstones. Specific identification inventory valuation is also used for larger items such as furniture or vehicles.

This method is used when individual items can be clearly identified, such as with a serial number. The business simply accounts for each individual item as it is sold. This method requires a detailed physical count so that the business knows exactly how many goods remained in year-end inventory.

Specific Identification Example: Texarkana Classic Cars, Inc. is an auto dealership that sells rare, collectible cars. Each car is tracked individually by its vehicle identification number (VIN number), and its actual cost is tracked on a spreadsheet. When a car is sold, the cost is taken out of inventory, and the spreadsheet is retired. This is an example of specific identification inventory valuation.

Average Cost Method

This method is commonly used when a business has quantities of items that are largely interchangeable rather than individually unique. The average cost method is basically the opposite of the "specific identification" method, because none of the goods are unique or counted individually.

The formula for figuring average inventory cost is:

Average Unit Cost = (Cost of Units Purchased or Manufactured)/(Total Quantity of Units)

Aggregate Inventory Cost = (Average Unit Cost) × (Units in Current Inventory)

This method allows the business to calculate an average cost per unit without tracking the individual units as they are purchased, manufactured, or sold.

Average Cost Method Example: Gracie owns a t-shirt store. She does not track the cost of the individual t-shirts, since they are all similar in style and cheaply made. She purchases 500 plain white t-shirts at $1 apiece. The following week, the price of cotton fabric goes up, and she purchases 500 more t-shirts at $2 apiece. Gracie then sells 500 t-shirts the following week. The weighted average cost of Gracie's inventory is calculated as follows:

Total cost of t-shirts:

(500 shirts at $1 each) = $500

(500 shirts at $2 each) = $1,000

Total number of units = 1,000 t-shirts

Weighted average: $1,500 total cost/ 1,000 t-shirts = **$1.50 average cost per shirt**

The average cost per shirt for the 1,000 shirts Gracie has purchased is $1.50 each. If she applies this average cost to the 500 t-shirts that are left unsold at the end of the week, the calculated cost of the t-shirts remaining in her inventory would be $750 ($1.50 × 500 remaining t-shirts).

FIFO (First-in, First-out)

The first-in, first-out (FIFO) method is a variation of the average cost method in which it is assumed that inventory items are sold in the order they are acquired or produced, with the oldest goods sold first and the newest goods sold last. This assumption would mirror the actual flow of inventory items in certain businesses, such as rotating stock in a grocery store.

The actual quantities in inventory at the end of the tax year are assigned costs based upon the cost of items of the same type that the business most recently purchased or produced. The formula for figuring inventory based on the FIFO method is as follows:

Unit Cost Per Item = (Cost/Quantity) of most recent lot of items purchased/produced

Aggregate Inventory Cost = (Unit Cost Per Item × Quantity) for each item

FIFO expenses the **oldest** inventories **first**. As a result, in an economy with rising prices (inflation), the use of FIFO will typically assign a higher value to ending inventory than other methods and thus result in reporting a lower cost of sales and higher taxable income. This is because the oldest and lowest costs are allocated to cost of goods sold.

Specifically, for stock sales, the IRS requires the use of the FIFO method if the business acquired the shares at different times or at different prices, and the business cannot identify which shares they sold. What this means is that if the taxpayer uses the FIFO method, then a sale of stock will be allocated to the shares that were purchased earliest.

Example: Tabitha purchased 150 shares of Crown Soda, Inc. for $10 per share in 2018 and another 150 shares of Crown Soda stock for $15 per share in 2019. Tabitha had 300 shares at the beginning of 2020. She sold 200 shares on June 1, 2020 for $35 per share. Under the FIFO method, Tabitha would treat the sale as 150 shares with a cost of $10 (the earliest block purchased) and 50 shares with a cost of $15.

Example: Walton Electronics, a cash-basis, calendar-year taxpayer, sells car audio equipment. Beginning inventory on January 1 included 300 car stereos with a cost per unit of $20. On January 10, the business purchased 600 more stereos at $20.10; on January 16, it purchased 400 stereos at $20.20; and on January 25, it purchased 500 stereos at $20.30. In the month of January, the business sold a total of 1,200 car stereos. Under FIFO, it is assumed that the **oldest** merchandise is sold **first**. Walton Electronics had a beginning inventory of 300 stereos. Those units are assumed to have been sold first, followed by the units purchased on January 10 and January 16. Thus, the cost assigned to the units on hand at the end of January is determined as follows:

Beginning inventory	300 units
January 10 purchases	600 units
January 16 purchases	400 units
January 25 purchases	500 units
Total units available	1,800 units
Units sold	(1,200 units)
Units left in inventory at the end of January	**600 units**

Solution based upon FIFO Calculation:

January 25 purchases	500 @ $20.30 =	$10,150
Unsold portion of January 16 purchases	100 @ $20.20 =	$2,020
Total inventory at the end of January	600 units	**$12,170**

LIFO (Last-in, First-out)

The last-in, first-out (LIFO) method assumes that the **newest inventory** purchased or produced is sold **first**, and the oldest inventory is sold last. Since the prices of goods, labor, and materials generally rise over time, this method will typically result in assigning a lower aggregate value to inventory on hand, higher amounts being recorded as the cost of sales, and lower taxable income. The LIFO Method is preferred by many U.S. companies because it has the common effect of reducing a company's taxable income when more recent items have a higher cost than older inventory items.

As a result, the use of the LIFO method is subject to highly complex rules governing its calculation and close scrutiny by the IRS. Once a business has adopted the LIFO method, it must obtain permission from the IRS to change from the LIFO method to another method of inventory valuation.

The formula for figuring inventory using the LIFO method is as follows:

Unit Cost Per Item = (Cost/Quantity) for the oldest lot of the item that was purchased or produced

Aggregate Inventory Cost = (Unit Cost Per Item × Quantity) for each item

LIFO Example: Using the same background information for Walton Electronics outlined previously, but using a **LIFO** assumption, rather than FIFO, the 300 units on hand at January 1 are assumed to have a LIFO cost per unit of only $10 because Walton has been in business for 10 years, and the unit costs of its purchases have approximately doubled during that period due to inflation. Therefore, the cost assigned to the units on hand at the end of January is determined as follows:

January 10 purchases	600 units
January 16 purchases	400 units
January 25 purchases	500 units
Total units available	1,800 units
Units sold	(1,200 units)
Units left in inventory at the end of January	**600 units**

Solution based upon LIFO Calculation:

Beginning inventory	300 @ $10.00 =	$3,000
Unsold portion of January 10 purchases	300 @ $20.10 =	$6,030
Total inventory at the end of January	600 units	**$9,030**

In comparison to the earlier FIFO example, the aggregate cost assigned to ending inventory using LIFO would be lower. Since the income generated by Walton in January from selling 1,200 units would be the same using either inventory method, its taxable income would be **higher** using FIFO instead of LIFO.

Differences between FIFO and LIFO

Each method produces different income results, depending on the trend of price levels at the time. In times of inflation, when prices are rising, LIFO will produce a higher cost of goods sold and a lower closing inventory. Under FIFO, the cost of goods sold will be lower, and the closing inventory will be higher. However, in times of falling prices, the opposite will hold.

Economic Climate	FIFO	LIFO
Periods of rising prices (Inflation)	(+) Higher value of inventory	(-) Lower value of inventory
	(-) Lower cost of goods sold	(+) Higher cost of goods sold
Periods of falling prices (Deflation)	(-) Lower value of inventory	(-) Higher value of inventory
	(+) Higher cost of goods sold	(+) Lower cost of goods sold

Other Inventory Valuation Methods

In addition to the inventory accounting and identification methods already described, the following valuation methods, or *conventions*, are commonly used to assign a value to inventory: the cost method, lower-of-cost or market, and the retail method. These methods are commonly used in industries where inventory loses value quickly. This is especially important for retailers of fashion goods, seasonal goods, or technological goods where products are constantly written down and replaced.

The Cost Method

Under the cost method, all direct and indirect costs of producing and purchasing the inventory are included in the valuation of the inventory.

- For merchandise on hand at the beginning of the tax year, cost means the ending inventory cost of the goods at the end of the preceding year.
- For merchandise *purchased* during the year, cost means the invoice price minus appropriate discounts, plus transportation or other charges incurred in acquiring the goods. It may also include other costs that must be capitalized under the uniform capitalization rules.
- For merchandise *produced* during the year, cost means all direct and indirect costs, including those that have to be capitalized under the uniform capitalization rules.

A trade discount is sometimes given for volume or quantity purchases. The cost of the actual value of inventory must be reduced by trade discounts. When using the cost method of inventory valuation, it is important that the business take into account damaged or obsolete goods.

Changes in market prices and damaged inventory may lower the value of the businesses' inventory below their cost, so it is important to take frequent physical inventory counts in order to account for this issue.

Example: Doggie Fashions, Inc. is an accrual-basis corporation that manufactures dog sweaters. The cost basis of the company's sweater inventory was $2,500 on December 31, and is $3,500 on January 31. In January, Doggie Fashions has $20,000 of sales. In the same month, the corporation also has a number of expenses, including wages for the sweater designers ($5,000) and the cost of raw materials such as yarn, appliqué, and rhinestones ($3,000). The wages and the cost of the raw materials are directly related to the production of the inventory (the sweaters) and are included in the cost of goods sold calculation. Other costs not directly related to the manufacture of the sweaters, which might include items like a receptionist's salary ($1,500), telephone charges ($130), and advertising ($1,200) are also deductible expenses, but are not part of COGS. The income statement for January would look like this:

Gross income from dog sweater sales:	$20,000
COGS: ($2,500 + $5,000 + $3,000 - $3,500)	-7,000
Gross Profit	13,000
Other expenses: ($1,500 + $130 + $1,200)	-2,830
Income for January	**$10,170**

The "Lower-of-Cost or Market" Method

The "lower-of-cost or market" method is commonly used for inventory that tends to lose value quickly, such as seasonal clothing. The market value of each item on hand is compared with its cost, and the lower of the two is used as its inventory value. Market value is typically based upon the normal selling price at the date the inventory is being valued.

If inventory is offered for sale below market in the normal course of business, inventory can be valued at the lower price, less the direct cost of disposition. This method may also be used for items that cannot be sold at normal prices or are unusable because of damage, imperfections, changes of style, odd or broken lots, or other similar causes.

In these cases, items should be valued at their actual selling price minus the direct cost of disposition, even if another method is used to value the rest of the entity's inventory. However, the lower-of-cost or market method cannot be used in conjunction with the LIFO method. The lower-of-cost or market method applies to the following:

- Goods purchased and on hand
- The basic elements of cost (direct materials, direct labor, and certain indirect costs) of goods being manufactured and finished goods on hand.

Example: Joseph makes custom motorcycle accessories at his machine shop. Some of the items in his shop were damaged by customers, and are now worth less than their original cost.

Inventory Item	Cost	Market	Lower
Chrome Air Cleaners	$300	$500	$300
Custom Foot Pegs	$200	$100	$100
Chrome Drag Bars	$450	$200	$200
Total	**$950**	**$800**	**$600**

Under the lower-of-cost or market method, the following items would be valued at $600 in closing inventory. Joseph must value each item in the inventory separately. He cannot value the entire inventory at cost ($950) and at market ($800) and then use the lower of the two figures.

The Retail Inventory Method

Under the retail method, the total retail selling price of goods on hand at the end of the tax year in each department or for each class of goods is reduced to approximate cost by using an average markup expressed as a percentage of the total retail selling price (cost ÷ retail price). This method is also known as the Retail Inventory Estimation Method, and it is typically used by businesses that resell merchandise to estimate their ending inventory balances.

This inventory valuation method assumes that all the inventory of the business has a consistent markup. For example, if a store marks up all its merchandise by 35%, that percentage would be used as a basis for estimating the cost of its current inventory.

The retail inventory method only provides an estimate, it is not wholly accurate. A business would still need to do a physical inventory count at reasonable intervals to account for damaged and missing inventory.

The retail inventory is useful for certain business types; for example, multi-store retailers who want a quick estimate of their stock across multiple locations.

Example (Retail Method): Quick-N-Mart is a convenience store chain with 4 different locations. Quick-N-Mart purchases packaged food, snacks, and other high-turnover products. The markup on their merchandise is 50% in all their locations. On Jan 1, Quick-N-Mart's beginning inventory cost is $110,000 (in aggregate across all locations). The company also paid an additional $190,000 for inventory purchases in January and had gross sales of $210,000. The calculation of its ending inventory on January 31 is:

Jan 1. Starting inventory	$110,000
Purchases in Jan.	$190,000
Goods available for sale	= $300,000
Inventory sold in Jan.	– $105,000 (Sales of $210,000 x 50% markup)
Ending inventory (estimated)	**$195,000**

Casualty Loss or Theft of Inventory

Inventory "shrinkage" is a general term for lost, stolen, or damaged inventory. "Shrinkage" reduces a businesses' ending inventory and thus increases COGS. The discrepancy may occur due to shoplifting, goods being damaged or lost, supplier fraud, or even a natural disaster. Sales do not affect the shrinkage calculation.

When a business incurs a casualty or theft loss of inventory, it has **two options** to record the loss. The business can:

1. Adjust its cost of goods sold, or
2. It can record the loss separately as a casualty or theft loss.

If the business deducts the loss separately, it must eliminate the affected inventory items from the cost of goods sold by making a downward adjustment to opening inventory or purchases. The business must avoid counting the loss twice. If the business expects an insurance reimbursement for the loss, it should not claim a loss to the extent it has a reasonable prospect of recovery.

Example: Cornerstone Computers, Inc. is a wholesale computer and electronics retailer. The business uses a point-of-sale inventory tracking system, but also does a periodic manual count. At the end of the year, the business has inventory records showing 20,000 computer laptop units on hand, but a physical count of the inventory shows only 19,850 units. Cornerstone Computers has an inventory discrepancy 150 (20,000 – 19,850). This is an example of inventory shrinkage, and might be due to shoplifting, inventory errors, or even employee theft. Cornerstone Computers will adjust its cost of goods sold, increasing the cost of goods sold to reflect the lost or stolen items.

Extended Example: Texas Trailers, Inc. is a U.S. manufacturer of livestock trailers. Texas Trailers uses the "lower-of-cost" method of valuing its inventory, which it produces and manufactures using a small team of 4 employees. All the direct and indirect costs of producing the trailers are included in the valuation of the inventory. The market values of the inventory exceed the manufacturing costs. It costs Texas Trailers approximately $10,000 to produce a horse trailer. At the end of the year, Texas Trailers does an inventory valuation to figure its inventory.

Beginning inventory: 14 trailers in stock as of 12/31/2020 at a cost of $10,000 each = $140,000
Plus 8 trailers produced during the year (8 x $10,000 each) = $80,000 additional inventory
Minus 10 trailers sold in 2020 (10 trailers X $10,000) = $100,000 sold
Calculation: ($140,000 + $80,000 - $100,000) = **$120,000 ending inventory**

Right after the inventory valuation is completed, Texas Trailers discovers that three of the trailers remaining in inventory have faulty rear axles as well as other manufacturing defects that prevent the trailers from being sold. The defective trailers are a legal and safety risk, so they are worthless and must be destroyed. Texas trailers does not have insurance to cover losses from defective merchandise, so the business decides to adjust its COGS calculation to account for the defective trailers.

Ending inventory before adjustment of defective merchandise= $120,000
Minus the cost of 3 defective trailers (3 x $10,000) = $30,000 inventory write-down
$120,000 - $30,000 defective merchandise= **$90,000 corrected ending inventory**

In this way, Texas Trailers adjusts its cost of goods sold to reflect the defective merchandise that was taken out of inventory.

Unit 2: Study Questions

(Test yourself first, then check the correct answers at the end of this quiz.)

1. A business must adopt its first tax year by:

A. The due date (including extensions) for filing a return.
B. The due date (not including extensions) for filing a return.
C. The date the EIN is established.
D. The first time the business makes estimated tax payments.

2. When determining whether or not a business can use the cash method, normally how many years are used to determine average annual gross receipts?

A. One year.
B. Two years.
C. Three years.
D. Four years.

3. Which of the following changes in accounting method does **not** require prior approval from the IRS?

A. A change from FIFO to LIFO inventory valuation.
B. A change from the accrual method to the cash method.
C. A change in the overall method of figuring depreciation.
D. Correction of a math error in depreciating an asset.

4. Which of the following entities *cannot* use the cash method of accounting?

A. A family farming corporation with average gross receipts of $22 million.
B. A C corporation with average gross receipts of $10 million.
C. A tax shelter with average gross receipts of $1.5 million.
D. A partnership that produces inventory and has $15 million in average gross receipts.

5. Which of the following date ranges would be a permissible fiscal tax year?

A. January 1, 2020, to December 31, 2021.
B. February 2, 2020, to February 2, 2021.
C. July 1, 2020, to June 30, 2021.
D. May 1, 2020, to May 31, 2021.

6. Under the "lower-of-cost or market" method of valuing inventory, what is the value of the inventory as a whole, based on the table below?

Item	Cost	Market
Shirts	$200	$500
Shoes	$300	$200
Shorts	$225	$150
Total	**$725**	**$850**

A. $550
B. $725
C. $750
D. $850

7. Which would not be considered the end of an acceptable tax year?

A. January 31.
B. April 15.
C. December 31.
D. The last Friday in February.

8. Raymond operates a retail clothing store using the accrual method and reports income on Schedule C, *Net Profit or Loss from Business.* He also runs a lawn care service that he operates only in the summer months. Which of the following statements is correct?

A. The lawn care business is required to use the accrual method of accounting because Raymond has already elected this method for his other business, and all businesses operated by one individual must use the same method of accounting.
B. Raymond must combine the income for both businesses and keep one set of books and records for both.
C. Raymond may keep one set of books and records for the two businesses and use different methods of accounting for them.
D. The lawn care business may use either the cash or accrual method, so long as both businesses have separate and distinct books and records.

9. Vargas Surgical Group, Inc., a C corporation, was organized on May 1, 2020. It elected the calendar year as its tax year. When is the first tax return due for Vargas Surgical for this short tax year?

A. March 15, 2021.
B. April 15, 2021.
C. June 30, 2021.
D. September 15, 2021.

10. Which of the following activities would make a business potentially subject to the uniform capitalization (UNICAP) rules?

A. An individual who produces paintings as a hobby and occasionally sells them at a profit.
B. A corporation that produces clothing for distribution to wholesale customers.
C. A real estate professional who acquires land and holds it for investment.
D. A bestselling author who is self-employed.

11. Barnaby owns a jewelry store. All of the following transactions are examples of constructive receipt of income in 2020 *except*:

A. Barnaby receives a check payment in his mailbox on December 31, 2020, but does not pick-up the check from the mailbox and deposit the check in the bank until January 2, 2021.
B. Barnaby receives a direct deposit of funds to his bank account on December 15, 2020, but does not withdraw any of the funds until February 1, 2021.
C. Barnaby receives a signed IOU from a delinquent account on November 10, 2020. He receives payment on this account on January 10, 2021.
D. An escrow agent receives a payment on Barnaby's behalf that is restricted for his use. It is an advance payment for a custom ring, but he cannot access any of the funds until the ring is delivered and inspected by the buyer. On December 28, 2020, the ring is delivered, and the restriction is lifted. Barnaby picks up the cash on January 9, 2021.

12. When a business is subject to the uniform capitalization rules, all of the following costs must be included in inventory *except*:

A. The cost of shipping raw materials to the seller's factory.
B. The cost of shipping a finished product to a customer.
C. Raw materials.
D. Direct labor costs.

13. Soft Sleeper, Inc., a mattress manufacturer, had the following expenses during the tax year:

Beginning inventory	$80,000
Ending inventory	52,500
Raw materials purchased	12,000
Manufacturing costs	80,000
Freight-in costs	550
Freight-out to customers	750

Calculate Soft Sleeper's cost of goods sold (COGS) for the year:

A. $67,050
B. $120,050
C. $120,800
D. $670,800

14. Deluxe Coffee, Inc. is a cash-basis, calendar-year corporation. On October 1, 2020, Deluxe Coffee pays $3,600 for a business liability insurance policy covering three years. The policy coverage begins October 1, 2020, and ends September 30, 2023. How must Deluxe Coffee treat the expense for its insurance policy?

A. The entire $3,600 may be deducted in 2020.
B. 2020 deduction of $1,200; 2021 deduction of $1,200; 2022 deduction of $1,200.
C. 2020 deduction of $1,500; 2021 deduction of $1,200; 2022 deduction of $900.
D. 2020 deduction $300; 2021 deduction $1,200; 2022 deduction $1,200; 2023 deduction $900.

Unit 2: Quiz Answers

1. The answer is B. A business must adopt its first tax year by the due date (not including extensions) for filing a return for that year. A business adopts a tax year when it files its first income tax return. An extension can only be requested when the adopted tax year has been determined.

2. The answer is C. The gross receipts test requires having average annual gross receipts in the *three prior years*. If a business was not in existence for the entire three years prior, then gross receipts are averaged over the period that the business has been in existence.

3. The answer is D. The correction of a math error does not require prior approval from the IRS. Consent from the IRS is not required for the following changes:

- Correction of a math error for computing tax liability or other mathematical error.
- A correction in depreciable life or correction of a depreciation error.
- An adjustment to an asset's useful life.

4. The answer is C. A tax shelter must *always* use the accrual method, regardless of its size, entity type, or its gross receipts. The other companies have average gross receipts under $26 million and are allowed to use the cash method in 2020.

5. The answer is C. July 1 through June 30 would be a permissible tax year. A fiscal tax year is any tax year that is 12 consecutive months and ends on the last day of any month except December. Answer "A" is incorrect because this is a <u>calendar</u> tax year, not a fiscal tax year. Answer "B" is incorrect because a fiscal year, (other than a 52-53 week year or a short tax year), must end on the <u>last day</u> of the month. Answer "D" is incorrect because it is more than a year (May 1, 2020, through May 31, 2021, is exactly 12 months and 30 days, or 395 days total).

6. The answer is A. To value inventory using the lower of cost or market method, compare the cost and the fair market value (FMV) of *each* of the items in inventory, and choose the lower of the two to obtain the inventory's value. The answer is calculated as follows: ($200 for shirts + $200 for shoes + $150 for shorts) = **$550 inventory valuation**.

7. The answer is B. April 15 is the IRS due date for individual tax returns but would not be the end of an entity's tax year, except in a rare instance in which an entity's existence terminates in the middle of a month. Answer "A" is incorrect because January 31 is the last day of the month, which qualifies as a fiscal tax year-end. Answer "C" is incorrect because December 31 is a calendar year-end. Answer "D" is incorrect because a tax year that ends on the same day of the week every year is a 52/53-week tax year, which is a legitimate type of fiscal year.

8. The answer is D. Raymond may use two different methods of accounting for two distinct and separate businesses. Separate accounting records must be kept for each business.

9. The answer is B. Since Vargas Surgical Group chose a calendar year, its first tax return is due April 15, 2021. This short period return will cover the period from May 1, 2020 (the date of formation), through December 31, 2020. Tax returns for C corporations are normally due on the fifteenth day of the fourth month after the end of the corporation's tax year.

10. The answer is B. A corporation that produces clothing for distribution to wholesale customers would likely be subject to the uniform capitalization rules. A business may be subject to the uniform capitalization rules if the business produces real property or personal property for sale to customers. Answer "A" is incorrect because producing items as a hobby would not be subject to the UNICAP rules. Answer "C" is incorrect because the purchase of land for investment would not be subject to UNICAP. Answer "D" is incorrect because self-employed authors, writers, and artists are exempt from the rules.

11. The answer is C. The amount promised to Barnaby as an IOU does not have to be included in income for 2020. According to the doctrine of constructive receipt, income is included in gross income when a person has an unqualified right to the funds. Constructive receipt must be more than just a billing, an offer, or a mere promise to pay.

12. The answer is B. Shipping finished products to customers is not an expense that should be included in inventory. This cost is a current expense and would be deductible when incurred, rather than capitalized as a cost of the inventory. In general, the business would deduct the expense of shipping finished goods to customers as simply delivery or postage expense.

13. The answer is B. Soft Sleeper's cost of goods sold is calculated as follows:

Beginning inventory	$80,000
Raw materials purchased	12,000
Freight-in	550
Manufacturing costs	80,000
Ending inventory	(52,500)
COGS	**$120,050**

The cost of freight-out to customers is not included in the calculation of inventory or capitalized as COGS. It is instead deductible as a business expense (this cost is usually expensed out as postage and delivery).

14. The answer is D. Since the advance payment covers more than 12 months (the policy is for 36 months), the $3,600 must be deducted ratably over the three-year policy period. To figure the monthly premium amount, the policy cost is divided by the coverage period: ($3,600 ÷ 36 = $100). The number of months of coverage in each tax year is then multiplied by the monthly premium:

- 2020: Deduction of **$300** ($3,600 ÷ 36 × 3)
- 2021: Deduction of **$1,200** ($3,600 ÷ 36 × 12)
- 2020: Deduction of **$1,200** ($3,600 ÷ 36 × 12)
- 2023: Deduction of **$900** ($3,600 ÷ 36 × 9)

Unit 3: Business Income

More Reading:
Publication 525, Taxable and Nontaxable Income
Publication 334, Tax Guide for Small Business
Publication 925, Passive Activity and At-Risk Rules

In this unit, we review the details of various types and treatments of business income. Gross income reportable by a business for tax purposes includes all types of income received, unless specifically exempt from taxation, in the form of money, property, or services. Sources of income for a business may include the following:

- Income received for professional services
- Income received for manufacturing or selling products
- Gains from the sale of a business or investment property
- Income from the discharge of indebtedness (debt cancellation income)
- Income from an interest in an estate or trust
- Portfolio income from investments
- The fair market value of property or services received through bartering
- Rental activities and royalties

Although most income that a business receives is taxable, there are certain exceptions where income is deferred, or not subject to tax at all.

For example, a corporation or partnership may choose to invest in tax-exempt muni bonds, just like an individual taxpayer. The interest income received from the muni bonds would retain its character as tax-exempt income to the business. Businesses may also engage in "tax-deferred" transactions, where the taxation of income is deferred to a later date. An example is a section 1031 exchange, which allows for the deferral of income on the exchange of business or investment real estate.

Advance Payments for Services

Advance payments for services to be performed after the tax year is generally taxable in the year it is received, even by an accrual-basis taxpayer. However, an accrual-basis taxpayer can elect to accrue income for advanced payments for the year of receipt of the advanced payment using the same figure used for financial accounting purposes, with the remainder of the advanced payment reported as taxable income in the following year - regardless of the number of years of services that are required to be provided. The taxpayer cannot postpone the recognition of income beyond the year following the year of the advanced payment.

Example: The Champion Tennis Club is a calendar-year, accrual-based business that offers instructional tennis courses for new players. On November 1, the club receives payment for a 12-month contract for 24 one-hour courses beginning on that date. The club gave six tennis classes in 2020. The club must include (6/24) of the payment in income for 2020 and the remainder, (18/24) of the payment in 2021, even if the club does not finish giving all of the courses by the end of 2021.

Service Agreement: If a business receives an advance payment for a service agreement on property it sells, leases, builds, installs, or constructs, the business can postpone reporting income, but only if it offers the property without a service agreement in the normal course of business. This includes an agreement providing for incidental replacement of parts or materials, should the parts break during normal use. A postponement is not allowed if:

- The taxpayer will perform any part of the service after the end of the tax year immediately following the year he receives the advance payment.
- The taxpayer will perform any part of the service at any unspecified future date that may be after the end of the tax year immediately following the year he receives the advance payment.

Guarantee or Warranty: Many companies provide or sell additional warranties or service repair contracts on their products. Cash-basis taxpayers would recognize income at the time of the sale. Generally, an accrual-basis taxpayer normally cannot postpone reporting income received under a guarantee or warranty contract.

However, IRC Section 451(c) provides a rule for a taxpayer using an *accrual method* of accounting to elect to defer certain advance payments in gross income, recognizing income in the year of receipt only to the extent income is effectively earned in that first year (i.e., a properly accrued amount in the year of the advance payment) and recognize all of the remaining gross income in the next tax year.

Example: Ervin is an accrual-based, calendar-year taxpayer who owns a computer repair shop called Ervin's PC Repair. On July 1, 2020, he receives payments for one-year contracts that specify he will repair or replace certain computer components that break. Ervin may choose to include each payment evenly in gross income over the current and following tax years as it is earned, rather than recognizing all the income for the contract at once. He cannot delay recognition of the income beyond the next tax year.

Advance Payment for Sales of Goods

Special rules apply to advance payments on agreements for the future sale of goods to customers—including gift certificates or gift cards that can be redeemed later for goods. The advance payment is generally included in income in the year it is received, even by a taxpayer reporting under the accrual method.

However, there is an alternative method, if elected, in which the advance payment can be included in gross receipts under the method of accounting the taxpayer uses for financial reporting.

Example: Pitaya Specialty Foods uses the accrual method of accounting for tax and financial reporting purposes. The company accounts for the sale of goods when it ships purchased goods to a customer. A customer purchases a $100 gift card from Pitaya's website on December 28, 2020, using a credit card. Pitaya ships the gift card to the customer on January 3, 2021. Under the alternative method of reporting income for advance payment of sales, if elected, Pitaya may recognize the $100 of gross receipts in either 2020 (the tax year in which it received the payment), or 2021 (the tax year in which it actually shipped the gift card) *if* they report the $100 as income for financial accounting purposes in 2021.

Passive Activities - In General

Certain types of business activities are considered passive activities and are subject to passive activity limits on the deductibility of losses. These "passive activity loss rules" are designed to prevent investors from using losses incurred from income-producing activities in which they do not materially participate.

The passive activity rules apply to individuals, estates, trusts (other than grantor trusts), personal service corporations, and closely held corporations. The rules also apply to *owners* of grantor trusts, partners in a partnership, and shareholders of an S corporation (but not to the entities themselves).

Before applying the passive activity limits, a taxpayer must determine the effects of at-risk limits,[53] which apply to individuals (including partners in a partnership and S corporation shareholders), estates, trusts, and certain closely held corporations. There are **two kinds** of passive activities:

1. **Passive business activities:** Trade or business activities in which the taxpayer does not materially participate during the year. The taxpayer "materially participates" in an activity if he is involved in the operations of the activity on a regular, continuous, and substantial basis.
2. **Rental real estate activities:** Rental of real estate is generally passive, even if the taxpayer participates in the activity, except for bona fide real estate professionals.[54]

Note: *"Active"* participation isn't the same as *"material"* participation (defined in the next section). Active participation is a less stringent standard than material participation.

Example: Riddick owns two residential rental properties. He also has a full-time job as a postal worker. He "actively" participates in the rental activity by personally collecting rents from his tenants and checking on the properties on a regular basis. He reports income and loss from his rentals on Schedule E. His rental activity is still considered a passive activity.

Study Note: There are additional exceptions related to limits on the deductibility of passive losses from real estate rental activities. Rental activities are primarily covered in Part 1, although they are also listed on the test specification for Part 2.

The determination of whether a taxpayer "materially participated" in a business activity is based upon satisfaction of at least one of seven tests. The taxpayer will be treated as "materially participating" in an activity if they satisfy *any* one of the following seven tests:

1. They participated in the activity for more than 500 hours during the year.
2. The taxpayer's participation was substantially *all* the participation in the activity of *all* individuals for the tax year.
3. The taxpayer participated in the activity for more than 100 hours during the tax year, and participated no less than any other individual.

[53] At-risk limits are explained in detail in later units pertaining to the specific types of entities that may be affected.

[54] Only individuals can actively participate in rental real estate activities. However, a decedent's estate is treated as actively participating for its tax years ending less than 2 years after the decedent's death. Limited partners aren't treated as actively participating in a partnership's rental real estate activities.

4. The activity is a significant participation activity, and the taxpayer participated in all significant participation activities for more than 500 hours. A significant participation activity is a business in which the taxpayer participates, (without qualifying for any of the other tests), for more than 100 hours.
5. The taxpayer materially participated in the activity during any 5 of the preceding 10 taxable years.
6. The activity is a personal service activity[55] in which the taxpayer materially participated for any 3 preceding tax years.
7. Based on all the facts and circumstances, the taxpayer participated in the activity on a regular, continuous, and substantial basis during the year.

If a taxpayer owns a portion of a business as a limited partner, he is generally not treated as materially participating in the activity. However, a limited partner *may* be treated as materially participating if he met test (1), (4), or (5) above. Further, he would not be treated as a limited partner if he were also a general partner in the partnership during the partnership's tax year.

This can happen with married couples, because a taxpayer's participation in an activity also includes their spouse's participation. This is true even if the taxpayer's spouse does not own an interest in the activity, and regardless of whether the married couple files jointly or separately.

Example: Sunshine Surf Shop, LLC is a retail business with 4 individual partners. Each partner owns 25% of the business and shares profits and losses from the business equally. Cynthia is the only general partner, and she works as the full-time business manager in the daily operations of the shop. Cynthia is married to Thomas, who is one of the limited partners in the business. Thomas also owns 25% of the partnership, but he does not work in the business at all—he is merely an investor. However, because of Cynthia's participation in the business, Thomas is also considered to have materially participated in the activity. This is true whether they file MFS or MFJ.

Example: Jeanine is a limited partner in Venture Funding, LP, a real estate development company. She does not participate in the business at all; she is merely an investor. Her partnership interest is considered a passive activity and is subject to the passive activity rules.

A closely-held corporation or a personal service corporation is treated as "materially participating" in a rental activity only if one or more shareholders who own more than 50% of the corporation materially participate in the activity.

Activities That Are NOT Passive Activities

Nonpassive activities are businesses in which the taxpayer works on a regular, continuous, and substantial basis. The following are not passive activities:

- A trade or business activity in which the taxpayer has materially participated by meeting one of the seven material participation tests.

[55] An activity is a personal service activity if it involves the performance of personal services in the fields of health (including veterinary services), law, engineering, architecture, accounting, actuarial science, performing arts, consulting, or any other trade or business in which capital isn't a material income-producing factor.

- A "working interest" in an oil or gas well, which the taxpayer holds directly, or through an entity that doesn't limit the taxpayer's liability (such as a general partner in a partnership).
- Rental real estate activities in which the taxpayer materially participated as a real estate professional. A taxpayer qualifies as a "real estate professional" if:
    - **More-than-50% Rule:** More than one-half of the personal services the taxpayer performs in trades or businesses during the tax year are in real property trades or businesses in which the taxpayer materially participates, **and**
    - **More-than-750 Hour Rule:** Hours spent providing personal services in real property trades or businesses in which the taxpayer materially participates total more than 750 during the tax year.

Example: Nilda is a licensed real estate agent that owns a four-plex and ten residential rentals. She materially participated in each rental activity by spending more than 1,000 hours per year on her real estate property activities. She personally manages the properties by collecting rents and hiring professionals to perform any necessary repairs. All her income comes from her real estate business. She is considered a bona-fide real estate professional. Her real estate activities are not treated as passive activities.

In addition, a "real estate professional" must **materially participate** in each real estate rental activity in order for that activity to be considered *nonpassive*.

Example: Gannon is a licensed real estate agent who works in California for BeMAX, a well-known real estate company. Gannon works full-time as a real estate agent, and works over 750 hours during the year, so he meets the requirements to be considered a real estate professional. Gannon also owns two condos in Florida that he rents to long-term tenants. Since the condos are so far away, he hires a management company to manage the rentals for him. He doesn't visit the rentals or approve any of the tenants—he lets the management company deal with all of that. Although he may meet the qualifications of a "real estate professional" he is not considered to materially participate in the Florida rental activity.

Note: One major benefit of being classified as a "real estate professional" is that the taxpayer is not subject to the 3.8% Net Investment Income tax (NIIT) on income from rental real estate activities in which they materially participate. By definition, "passive activity income" also does not include:

- **Portfolio income:** Such as interest, dividends, annuities, and royalties not derived in the ordinary course of a trade or business, or gain or loss from the disposition of property that produces these types of income or that is held for investment.
- **Personal service income:** This includes salaries, wages, commissions, self-employment income from a business, deferred compensation, taxable Social Security and other retirement benefits, and payments from partnerships to partners for personal services (i.e., guaranteed payments).
- **Income from intangible property:** income from a patent, copyright, or literary, musical, or artistic composition, if the taxpayer's personal efforts significantly contributed to the creation of the property.

- **State, local, and foreign income tax refunds.**
- **Income from a covenant not to compete.** A "covenant not to compete" is a type of legal agreement between two parties. Sometimes a business will pay another business or individual for agreeing not to enter into direct competition.[56]
- **Alaska Permanent Fund dividends.**
- **Cancellation of debt income:** if at the time the debt is discharged, the debt is not allocated to passive activities; it is not considered passive activity income.

Study Note: The three main categories of income to remember for the EA exam are: (1) **active income, (2) passive activity income,** and (3) **portfolio income**. "Portfolio income" includes interest, dividends, etc. Do *not confuse* the widely-used term "passive income" with "passive-activity income." They are not the same thing. Although some of the items listed above seem "passive" in nature, they are, by definition, excluded from treatment as passive activities. This categorization of income is important because passive activity losses generally cannot be offset against active income or portfolio income (with a few exceptions).

Example: Pasquale has a job working full-time as a firefighter. The income that he earns from his job is classified as wages, (*earned* income). He also owns several CDs (certificates of deposit) through his local credit union. He earns interest on the CDs when they mature. The interest from the CDs is classified as *portfolio* income. None of Pasquale's income is classified as passive activity income.

Passive Activity Loss Limitations (PAL rules)

Losses from passive activities that exceed the income from passive activities in a given year are generally disallowed as deductions for the current year. Passive activity losses are deductible only to the extent that the taxpayer has income from other passive activities to offset the losses, or when the taxpayer completely disposes of the activity.

Suspended losses can be carried forward to the following year, subject to the same passive loss rules and limitations. The taxpayer uses Form 8582, *Passive Activity Loss Limitations,* to summarize income and losses from passive activities and compute deductible losses.

Example: Delilah owns a 25% interest in a partnership that runs a Miami nightclub and a 10% interest in an S corporation that runs an organic farming business. She has no involvement in the day-to-day operation of either business; therefore, her interest in each business is considered a passive activity. In 2020, the nightclub incurred an ordinary loss of $40,000, of which $10,000 is allocated to Delilah because of her 25% ownership. The farming business has ordinary income of $75,000, of which $7,500 is allocated to Delilah because of her 10% ownership. As Delilah's losses from passive activities for the year exceed her income from passive activities by $2,500 ($10,000 of loss minus $7,500 of income), deduction of the excess loss is disallowed in the current year. Delilah may carry forward the $2,500 excess losses to the following year.

[56] Courts also call these contracts "restrictive covenants." The payment allocable to the contract is recognizable as ordinary income to the receiver, and the payor is entitled to amortize the cost of the covenant over a 15-year period.

Example: Brandon is an investor in a limited partnership, Skadden Mining, LP. He does not participate in the businesses at all; he is merely an investor. Brandon has $80,000 in wages for the year, as well as $12,000 in losses from his limited partnership investment. He has no other income or loss for the year. Brandon's $12,000 passive activity loss is disallowed in the current year. He can carry forward the losses indefinitely until he has passive income to offset, or he disposes of the activity.

Generally, the taxpayer can deduct in full any previously disallowed passive activity losses in the year he disposes of his entire interest in the activity in a fully taxable transaction. When an entire interest in a passive activity is sold to an unrelated party, current and suspended losses related to the activity are "released" and may be used to offset gain from the sale. In other words, upon complete disposition of the activity, all passive carryovers are allowed.

Example: Lyle is a 5% limited partner in a Florida resort. For the last three years, the resort business has incurred losses, for a total passive loss of $150,000. These passive losses were suspended and carried over on Lyle's individual tax returns because of passive activity loss limitations. In 2020, Lyle decides that the resort will never be profitable. On June 30, 2020, Lyle disposes of his entire partnership interest by selling it to an unrelated person. The full $150,000 in suspended losses are deductible in 2020, the year that Lyle completely disposes of the activity.

Sometimes an activity will be passive in one year, and not passive in the next. A "former" passive activity is an activity that was a passive activity in an earlier tax year, but is not a passive activity in the current tax year; for example, a business investor who decides to take an active role in business operations in the current year. A prior year's disallowed loss from the activity can be deducted up to the amount of current year income from the activity if the taxpayer is now materially participating in the business. This means that the suspended losses from the converted activity may be offset against the income from this activity after the taxpayer becomes a material participant.

Example: Suzanne is a partner in Chewy Treats, LLC, a partnership that makes organic dog treats. In prior years, Suzanne did not materially participate in the business, so her $4,000 loss from the partnership was suspended and carried forward to 2020. In 2020, Suzanne decided to become involved in the business operations and materially participated in the business. Chewy Treats became profitable in 2020, and her share of partnership income was $10,000. Suzanne can use the $4,000 carryover losses against the $10,000 of income in 2020, for a net income of $6,000 in 2020 on the partnership activity.

Example: Noriko is a 30% partner in Sandal Source, LLC, a retail shoe store. She is only an investor, and has never participated in the business for many years—her cousin, Emiko, who is a general partner, completely ran the business. As such, this activity is treated as a passive activity to Noriko. For 2020, the store had a net operating loss. The distributive share of loss received by Noriko was $20,000. Noriko did not have passive income from any other sources during the year, so her loss was not deductible in 2020 and was carried forward to 2021. Effective January 1, 2021, Noriko begins working full-time at the store in order to save on employee wages and also to help her cousin with the daily management. As such, for 2021, Noriko would be considered to be materially participating in the activity, and any profits generated during the year can be offset from the prior-year loss when it was a passive activity.

Grouping Business Activities

A taxpayer may make an election to "group" multiple business activities or multiple rentals as a single activity for purposes of the passive loss restrictions. If two activities are grouped into one larger activity, a taxpayer needs only to show material participation in the activity as a whole. If the two activities are separate, the taxpayer must show material participation in each one. This type of election is called a "Section 469" election. This election is irrevocable.

A Section 469 grouping election can be made by individuals, C Corporations, S Corporations, partnerships, trusts and estates. The election to group activities is made by filing a statement with the business's original income tax return for the taxable year.

Example: Lindsey is a partner in Reuven Skin LLC, which manufactures and sells skincare products to drugstores and other retail outlets. She is also a partner in Bridge Trucking, LLC. Reuven Skin and Bridge Trucking are under common ownership and control. Bridge Trucking's main business is transporting finished skincare products for Reuven Skin, and it is the only trucking business Lindsey is involved in. Lindsey groups Reuven Skin's wholesale activity and Bridge Trucking as a single activity.

Example: Chandler owns a bagel shop and a clothing store in Cincinnati and a bagel shop and a clothing store in Milwaukee. There may be more than one reasonable method for grouping Chandler's activities, including the following: 1) the clothing stores and the bagel shops into one activity; 2) a separate clothing store activity and a separate bagel shop activity; 3) a Cincinnati activity and a Milwaukee activity; or 4) four separate business activities in four different cities. Chandler decides that he wants to group the bagel shops together as a single business and the clothing stores together as a single business. He reports the income from both bagel shops on one Schedule C, and the income from the clothing stores on another Schedule C.

Generally, when activities are grouped into appropriate economic units, they may not be regrouped in a later tax year. However, if any of the activities resulting from a grouping is not an appropriate economic unit and one of the primary purposes of the grouping is to avoid the passive activity rules, the IRS may regroup the activities.

If one component of a grouping is disposed of in a fully taxable transaction, then the suspended passive losses from that activity are not released until the entire grouping is disposed of in a fully taxable transaction.

In general, a rental activity cannot be grouped with a trade or business activity. However, they can be grouped together if the activities form an appropriate economic unit and:

- The rental activity is insubstantial in relation to the trade or business activity,
- The trade or business activity is insubstantial in relation to the rental activity, or
- Each owner of the trade or business activity has the same ownership interest in the rental activity, in which case the part of the rental activity that involves the rental of items of property for use in the trade or business activity may be grouped with the business activity.

Example: Dax and Esme are married and file jointly. Dax is the only shareholder of Eco-Dry Cleaners, an S corporation. Esme is the only shareholder of Campus Realty, an S corporation that owns a commercial office building, part of which is rented to Eco-Dry Cleaners (her husband's business). Esme's rental business and Dax's dry-cleaning business are not insubstantial in relation to each other. Since Dax and Esme file a joint return, they are treated as one taxpayer for purposes of the passive activity rules. Common ownership applies (Dax and Esme, who are a married couple) to both businesses, with the same ownership interest (100% in each). Dax and Esme may conclude that Campus Realty's rental activity and Eco-Dry Cleaners form an appropriate economic unit and group them as a single business activity, if they wish.

Rental Income

Note: Passive activity income (and losses) and the treatment of rental income may be tested on Part 1 or Part 2, these concepts are now listed on the Prometric testing specifications on both parts of the EA exam for the current exam cycle.

A business may have income from rental activity for any amounts received or accrued as payment for the use of property. Rental income also includes advance payments and nonrefundable deposits from renters. Rental income earned by a sole proprietor, and related expenses, are generally reported on the following forms:

- **Schedule E**, ***Supplemental Income and Loss,*** is used by taxpayers who are not professional real estate dealers or do not provide substantial services.
- **Schedule C, *Profit or Loss from Business***: Used for professional real estate dealers, and by owners of hotels and boarding houses who provide "substantial services" for tenants or guests. The services must be substantial and not simply those normally provided with the mere rental or lease of property for occupancy only. Normally services such as daily maid service will be considered a substantial service, (for example, a hotel, motel, or boarding house would typically be reported on Schedule C).

Example: Denny owns a cabin in Lake Tahoe that he occasionally uses for ski trips. This year, Denny decides to list the cottage for short-term tenants through AirWeb, a popular vacation rental website. Denny rents the cottage for $150 per night, and the average customer stay is 7 days or less. Denny provides fresh linens, blankets, and he hires a maid service to provide daily cleaning. The income from the short-term rental activity will be reported on Schedule C. It is not treated as passive income. He will owe self-employment tax on his profits.

A person can qualify as a "real estate professional" and still have passive income from a rental activity, or even a mix of both. In that case, the income reported on Schedule E would not be subject to SE tax, while the income reported on Schedule C would be subject to SE tax.

Example: Allyson is a licensed real estate agent who works for Coconut Realty. She earns $75,000 a year in commissions as a realtor. She also owns a small office building that she rents to business tenants. She manages the building herself and collects rents, but spends less than ten hours a month on the activity. Allyson would report her real estate agent income on Schedule C. Her realtor income would be subject to self-employment tax. The rental income from the office building would be reported on Schedule E, and would *not* be subject to self-employment tax.

Example: Keith owns a duplex that he rents to long-term tenants. He does not offer substantial services to the tenants in his duplex; they are merely monthly renters. Keith also owns a small hotel outside the Las Vegas strip. The hotel offers daily maid service, continental breakfast, and fresh linens and towels. The rental income from the duplex would be reported on Schedule E. It is considered passive activity income and not subject to self-employment tax. The income from the hotel would be reported on Schedule C, because the occupancy is short-term and the hotel provides "substantial services" to its guests. The income from the hotel would be subject to self-employment tax, just like any other Schedule C business.

Lease cancellation payments received from a tenant are reported as income in the year received. Advance rental payments received under a lease must be recognized in the year received, regardless of which accounting method is used.

However, a security deposit is not considered income upon initial receipt, if the deposit is refundable to the tenant at the end of the lease. If the taxpayer keeps the security deposit because the tenant did not live up to the terms of the lease or because he damaged property, the deposit amount is recognized as income in the year it is forfeited by the tenant.

Special $25,000 "Loss Allowance" for Real Estate Rental Activities

When a taxpayer *actively participates* in a rental real estate activity, the taxpayer may be able to deduct up to $25,000 of losses against his nonpassive income. This is a special rule that applies only to real estate activities and no other "passive" business type.

Note: "Active participation" is not the same standard as "material participation." Material participation is a much higher standard. For example, the owner of a rental property will generally be treated as *actively* participating if he makes management decisions such as approving new tenants, deciding rental contracts, approving repairs, and other similar management decisions.

To be considered "actively participating" in a rental activity, a taxpayer must own at least 10% of the rental property and must make management decisions in a significant and bona fide way, such as approving new tenants and establishing the rental terms. In this case, active participation can also include participation by the taxpayer's spouse.

The full $25,000 loss allowance is available for taxpayers, whether single or MFJ, whose modified adjusted gross income (MAGI) is $100,000 or less.

If a taxpayer is married and files a separate return, but lived apart from his spouse for the entire tax year, the taxpayer's special allowance for rental losses cannot exceed $12,500; this full allowance would be available if his MAGI is $50,000 or less. However, if the taxpayer *lived* with his spouse at any time during the year and is filing MFS, the taxpayer cannot use any of his passive rental losses to offset nonpassive income. Only rental activities qualify for this "special loss allowance," and certain taxpayers do not qualify. The following taxpayers are not allowed to claim the "special loss allowance:

- A limited partner in an activity,
- A taxpayer who has less than 10% ownership in a rental activity,

- A trust or corporation (The $25,000 special allowance is available only to natural persons, although grantor trusts are permitted.)

Rental losses that cannot be deducted due to the limitations described above can be carried forward indefinitely and used in subsequent years, subject to the same limitations.

Note: If the IRS determines a taxpayer has not actively participated, rental losses are not currently deductible, and he is not eligible for the special $25,000 loss allowance.

Example: Gibson lives and works in Florida. He earns $95,000 in wages working for an accounting firm. He also owns a rental condo in Las Vegas, Nevada. Gibson does not manage the rental condo himself; he has a friend who handles the collection of rents and any issues that may arise with the tenants. It has been several years since Gibson has visited the property. The rental has a ($22,000) loss for the year. Gibson did not actively participate in the rental activity. His losses cannot offset his wage income. He must carryover his losses to the following year, to offset other passive income. He must continue to carry over his losses until he either (1) actively participates in the activity or (2) until he disposes of the rental in a sale.

Example: Tristen owns a residential rental property in San Diego, California. He lives in San Diego and has a regular job that he works full-time, earning $80,000 in wages. Tristen actively manages his rental by choosing his own tenants, hiring workers to do any required repairs, and personally collecting the rent. He visits the property frequently and checks on his tenants. Tristen is *actively* participating in this rental activity. The rental activity has a ($15,000) loss for the year. Since he is actively participating in the rental, he may deduct the losses from his wage income ($80,000 - $15,000 loss), which will bring his income down to $65,000 for the year.

If a taxpayer has income and losses from a mix of passive activities, then passive rental losses can offset income from other passive activities.

Example: Alannah has income from several sources during the year. She earned $70,000 in wages, $15,000 income from her investment in a limited partnership, and a ($26,000) loss from a residential rental. She actively participated in the rental activity. She can use the passive income from her limited partnership interest to offset part of her rental loss. Then use the remaining rental real estate loss to offset her nonpassive income (her wages), which would bring her income down to $59,000. The calculations are figured as follows:

Limited Partnership income	$15,000
Residential rental loss	($26,000)
Passive losses remaining	($11,000)
Wages	$70,000
Wages MINUS remaining passive rental loss: ($70,000 - $11,000)	$59,000

Personal Property Rentals

The rental of personal property (such as vehicles, equipment, or formal wear) is not reported on Schedule E. Instead, it is reported on Schedule C, if the activity is a trade or business.[57] If a taxpayer is "not in the business" of renting personal property, (but still has a profit motive) then they should report their income on line 8 and expenses on line 22 of Schedule 1 (Form 1040). For example, if a taxpayer only rents out their boat occasionally to friends and family. Advance payments for renting personal property must be reported in the year received.

Note that the IRS publications do not specifically address the treatment of personal property rentals, nor do they define at which point a personal property rental activity becomes a "trade or business."

Example: Laurel owns Sunbelt Party Rentals, LLC which rents out catering equipment, tents, and tables for weddings and other celebrations. Laurel has a profit motive in the activity and works in the business full-time. She should report her personal property rental activity on Schedule C, not Schedule E.

Example: Ralph owns an RV that he rents out sporadically during the summertime to family and friends. He rents his RV for $30 a day, which is much less than other car rental companies charge. He doesn't advertise, and only rents to people he knows. His rental activity does not rise to the level of a trade or business, but he does have a profit motive in the activity. He should report his rental income on line 8 of Schedule 1 (Form 1040), and any expenses associated with the personal property rental activities may be entered as an adjustment to income on Schedule 1, Line 22. The expenses would be limited to his income from the activity.

Note: Personal property is not the same as "personal-use" property that a taxpayer uses for personal purposes. "Personal property" is an accounting term that is used to describe any tangible asset other than real estate. In civil law, personal property is sometimes called "movable property." Examples of personal property include appliances, furniture, vehicles, and collectibles. The distinguishing factor between personal property and real property is that personal property is movable, while real property, such as land or buildings, remains in one location.

Real Estate Dealers and Developers

A "real estate developer" (or real estate "dealer") is someone primarily engaged in the business of purchasing land or real estate for development, managing the construction process, and selling real estate to customers. For a real estate developer, the real estate is treated as inventory. Note that this is not the same thing as a "real estate professional."

Income earned by a real estate developer is reported on Schedule C, if the taxpayer is self-employed. The income is subject to self-employment tax.

Example: Hester purchases distressed homes at auction and fixes them up, then later resells the properties to buyers. She does not attempt to rent the properties at all. House flipping is her business, so she would report the activity on Schedule C. Her net profits are subject to SE tax.

[57] See IRS Tax Topic No. 414 Rental Income and Expenses, for more information. https://www.irs.gov/taxtopics/tc414.

Example: Blaze is a real estate developer. He purchases land, subdivides and constructs houses and condominiums for resale. Occasionally he will sell off individual parcels to other developers or private buyers. Blaze is a professional real estate *dealer*. The land he purchases is *inventory*, because he is buying it specifically for resale. He would report his income on Schedule C, and all his profits would be subject to SE tax.

Investment Income

A business may earn interest or dividend income from investments or from lending money to others. A common example is when a C corporation owns stock in another corporation.

For most sole proprietors, dividend income is considered nonbusiness income and is reported directly on Form 1040. However, dividends are treated as business income by professional stockbrokers and securities dealers.

Bartering Income

Bartering occurs when a taxpayer exchanges goods or services without exchanging money. An example of bartering is a plumber doing repair work for a dentist in exchange for dental services. The fair market value of goods and services received in a barter exchange must be included in income by each party in the year received. If the parties agree in advance on the fair market value of goods and services exchanged, it may be used, absent conflicting evidence.

Definition: The IRS defines **fair market value** (FMV) as the price at which a property would change hands between a buyer and a seller when both have reasonable knowledge of all the necessary facts, and neither is being forced to buy or sell.

Example: Quaid is a self-employed web designer. Frank is a house painter. Quaid and Frank are members of a barter club where members contact each other directly and bargain. In return for Quaid's web design services, Frank paints Quaid's business office. Quaid must report the exchange as income on Schedule C. Frank must also include in his income the fair market value of the web services Quaid provided.

Business-Related Court Awards and Damages

Court awards and settlements that grant compensation for physical injuries or illness are generally excluded from taxation (except for any punitive damages, which are always taxable). Most other types of court awards and settlements are taxable income, such as damages for:

- Patent or copyright infringement,
- Breach of contract, or interference with business operations.
- Compensation for lost profits.
- Compensatory damages for other financial losses.
- Interest earned on any type of court award.
- Punitive damages related to business income or business activity.

Note: With respect to court awards, punitive damages may be awarded in addition to compensatory damages for actual monetary losses. Punitive damages are generally meant to "punish" the defendant for a willful or malicious act. Punitive damages are subject to income tax but are not subject to self-employment tax.

Example: Geoffrey is a professional trucker. He was in a serious car accident during one of his long hauls. He sustained physical injuries and permanent damage to his foot, which was crushed during the accident. Geoffrey sued the truck manufacturer when it was discovered that the brakes on his semi-truck were faulty. During the trial, it was discovered that the manufacturer knew about the defect for several years, but chose not to warn customers. Geoffrey wins his case. The jury awards him $500,000 in compensatory damages for his injuries, and $2 million in punitive damages. Even though Geoffrey is self-employed, the $500,000 in compensatory damages are not taxable to Geoffrey and do not need to be reported as business income, because they are compensation for his injury. The $2 million in punitive damages are taxable, but the award is not considered self-employment income and therefore, not subject to self-employment tax, even though the income is somewhat related to his trucking activity.

Income from Canceled Debt

If a business-related debt is canceled or forgiven, other than as a gift or bequest, the business generally includes in income the amount of the cancellation of debt (COD). However, a cash-basis business is not required to realize income from a canceled debt to the extent that the payment of the debt would have led to a business deduction.

Example: Leeward Ranch, LLC, is a cash-basis partnership. Leeward Ranch arranges computer repair services on credit but later has trouble paying its debts. The computer repair company forgives Leeward Ranch's repair bill. Leeward Ranch is not required to recognize the canceled debt as income because payment of the computer repair bill would have been deductible as a business expense anyway.

In the example above, the canceled debt of an accrual-basis business would be considered income, because a deduction for the repair expense already would have been recorded. If a taxpayer owes a debt to a seller for property he bought and the seller reduces the amount owed, the taxpayer generally does not have income from the reduction.

If the taxpayer is bankrupt or insolvent, the amount of the canceled debt may be excluded from taxable income (for insolvency, up to the extent of the insolvency). If the taxpayer is not bankrupt or insolvent, the amount of the reduction is treated as a purchase price adjustment, and the buyer's basis in the property is reduced.

Additional exclusions may apply to the discharge of qualified farm indebtedness. Taxpayers who use these exclusions are required to reduce specified tax attributes, including loss and credit carryforwards and the bases of assets, by corresponding amounts.

Amounts Not Considered Business Income

Just as with individual taxpayers, certain types of business-related income and property transfers are not taxable or reportable. Others may be partially taxable, and in some instances, the recognition of income is delayed until a later date. Examples include:

- Issuances of stock, including the sale of Treasury stock
- Most business loans (loans create debt, not income)
- State and local taxes that are collected in connection with sales or the provision of services and remitted to state or local governments if the taxes are imposed on a

customer of the taxpayer (sales tax collected are not included in the company's revenues, and the amounts are also not treated as a business expense if imposed on the customer)

- Like-kind exchanges of property (section 1031 exchanges)
- Gain from an involuntary conversion, if the gain is reinvested properly.
- **Paycheck Protection Program (PPP) Loan Forgiveness:** Normally, loan forgiveness results in taxable income to the debtor. However, the CARES Act provided for forgiveness of PPP loans that were used to cover payroll and other enumerated expenses. A forgiven PPP loan is not taxable income if the loan amounts were used for qualifying expenses. Forgiveness is not automatic—a business must apply for PPP loan forgiveness. Once the loan is forgiven, it is moved from the business' balance sheet and is treated as tax-exempt income for partnership and S corporation basis purposes only.[58]

Example: Bloomer's Floral Shop sells floral arrangements for weddings and special events in a state that imposes sales tax on the buyer. Each bouquet that is sold is subject to sales tax, which the shop collects from its customers at the time of purchase. The sales tax is not included in the gross receipts of the business. Instead, the amount collected is treated as a liability, and listed on the company's balance sheet. At the end of each month, Bloomer's Floral Shop prepares a sales tax return and remits all the collected sales tax to the state. The sales tax collected is neither income nor an expense, and it is not included in the company's sales revenues.

[58] The PPP Loan program and other provisions of the Paycheck Protection Program are not listed on the Prometric EA exam specifications for the current testing cycle, so it is unlikely that you will encounter a question about this topic.

Unit 3: Study Questions

(Test yourself and then check the correct answers at the end of this section.)

1. What is the definition of "personal property" for tax purposes?

A. Personal assets of an individual taxpayer.
B. Real property owned by a business or individual.
C. Assets that are moveable and tangible, whether owned by a business or an individual.
D. Real property owned by a business taxpayer.

2. When is a business <u>not</u> required to recognize income from a canceled debt?

A. Canceled debt is always taxable to a business.
B. Canceled debt is never taxable income to a business.
C. A business does not have to recognize canceled debt income to the extent that the payment of the debt would have led to a business deduction.
D. Canceled debt is taxable income for a sole proprietorship or partnership, but not for a C corporation or an S corporation.

3. Ginny has several sources of income during the year. Which of the following would be considered "passive activity" income?

A. Income from a limited partnership in which she does not materially participate.
B. Interest income earned on a certificate of deposit.
C. Unemployment compensation.
D. Income from a court award for breach of contract.

4. For tax purposes, which of the following would not be considered business income?

A. Damages received in a lawsuit or a settlement for personal physical injuries.
B. Interest earned on a court award for breach of contract.
C. Barter income from consulting services.
D. Legal damages awarded for copyright infringement.

5. Happy Pet Store, a cash-basis business, purchases $1,000 worth of newspaper advertising services on credit in 2020. The pet store is struggling financially and is unable to pay the bill. The advertiser forgives the bill on January 30, 2021. What is the correct statement about how Happy Pet Store should handle the canceled debt?

A. Happy Pet Store must recognize the canceled debt income in 2020.
B. Happy Pet Store must recognize the canceled debt income in 2021.
C. Happy Pet Store must recognize ½ the canceled debt income in 2020 and ½ in 2021.
D. Happy Pet Store does not have to recognize the canceled debt as income because payment of the advertising would have been deductible as a business expense.

6. Sean has an ownership stake in several limited partnerships. He is only a passive investor and did not materially participate in any of the businesses. In 2020, he had the following results from these activities:

- Appliance repair store: ($20,000) net loss.
- Ice cream parlor: $31,000 net income.
- Specialty bakery: ($17,500) net loss.

He had no other income or loss during the year. What is the tax treatment of Sean's ownership of these businesses?

A. Taxable income of $31,000 and deductible losses of $37,500.
B. Deductible capital loss of $6,500.
C. No net taxable income in 2020; carryover of passive loss of $6,500 to the following year.
D. Taxable income of $31,000 in 2020. No carryover of losses.

7. Losses from passive activities are generally deductible only up to the amount of _________ in a given year.

A. Non-passive income.
B. Debt basis.
C. Capital gains.
D. Passive income.

8. Palm Apartments LLC, a cash-basis partnership, owns a residential rental complex with 10 units. On December 31, 2020, one tenant, Marie, pays two months of rent in advance (for January and February of the following year), because she is leaving town on an extended vacation. When are these advance rental payments taxable to Palm Apartments?

A. In the year received.
B. In the year in which they are accrued.
C. They are not taxable.
D. The payments are taxable when the checks are cashed.

9. Which of the following transactions generates taxable business income?

A. Like-kind exchanges of property.
B. Business loans.
C. The sale of treasury stock.
D. A barter exchange of services between two sole proprietors.

10. Nickel Tools, Inc. rents large tools and machinery for use in construction projects. The company always charges a refundable security deposit and a nonrefundable cleaning deposit when someone rents a machine. Nickel Tools received the following amounts during the current tax year:

- Rental income: $500,000
- Refundable security deposits: $40,050
- Cleaning deposits: $10,500

What amount should be included in the corporation's gross income?

A. $500,000
B. $510,500
C. $540,050
D. $550,550

Unit 3: Quiz Answers

1. The answer is C. In a broad definition, "personal property" includes any asset other than real estate. Personal property is *movable*, unlike land and buildings that remain in one location. "Personal property" should not be confused with "personal-use" property that a taxpayer uses for personal purposes rather than for business purposes.

2. The answer is C. Canceled debt is not taxable income for a business to the extent that payment of the debt would have led to a business deduction.

3. The answer is A. Income from a limited partnership in which Ginny does not materially participate would be considered passive activity income. Portfolio income, such as interest, dividends, annuities, and royalties not derived in the ordinary course of a trade or business, or gain or loss from the disposition of property that produces these types of income or that is held for investment, is not passive activity income. Unemployment compensation and income from court awards is not considered "passive activity" income.

4. The answer is A. Gross income does *not include* most types of compensation for physical injuries. All of the other choices would be reportable as business income.

5. The answer is D. As a cash-basis taxpayer, Happy Pet Store would have been able to deduct the cost of the advertising services as a business expense. It is therefore not required to recognize the canceled debt as taxable income.

6. The answer is C. Under the passive activity limitation rules, Sean would not be able to deduct the full amount of his losses. Since he had passive activity income of $31,000 in 2020, he can offset losses up to that amount with his losses. He can carry over the remaining losses of **$6,500** to the following year.

7. The answer is D. Losses from passive activities that exceed the income from passive activities in a given year are generally disallowed. The losses may be carried forward to the next year. Only when a taxpayer materially participates (for example, a bona-fide real estate professional) in a business activity would his losses not be limited.

8. The answer is A. Palm Apartments, LLC must recognize the advance rental payments in the year the partnership receives them. Advance rental payments received under a lease must be recognized in the year received, regardless of which accounting method is used. This means that a taxpayer who owns rental properties and receives rent in advance cannot delay recognizing the income. This is true even if the taxpayer is on the accrual basis.

9. The answer is D. A barter exchange of services between two sole proprietors would be business income to both parties involved in the transaction. The fair market value of goods and services received in a barter exchange must be included in income by each party in the year received. If the two parties agree in advance to the fair market value of the goods or services being exchanged, the IRS will generally accept that amount as the FMV.

10. The answer is B. The refundable security deposits are not taxable income to Nickel Tools, Inc., because those amounts are returned to the customer if the items rented are returned in good condition. The amounts included in gross income would be the rental income and the nonrefundable cleaning deposits ($500,000 + $10,500 = **$510,500**).

Unit 4: Business Expenses

More Reading:
Publication 535, Business Expenses
Publication 587, Business Use of Your Home
Publication 463, Travel, Gift, and Car Expenses

Business expenses are the costs of carrying on a trade or business, and are usually deductible if the business operates to make a profit. However, some costs must be capitalized and depreciated or amortized.

This unit addresses general concepts and discusses common business expenses and explains what kinds of expenses are deductible and which expenses are not. A cash-basis business generally claims deductible business expenses in the period they are paid. Accrual businesses claim business expenses when they are incurred.

Deductible Business Expenses

To be deductible, a business expense must be both *ordinary* and *necessary*. An *ordinary* expense is one that is common and accepted in the taxpayer's industry. A *necessary* expense is one that is helpful and appropriate for the particular trade or business. However, an expense does not have to be indispensable to be considered necessary.

Example #1: Eunice is an enrolled agent who mails cards and newsletters to clients with year-end tax-saving tips. The newsletters are a marketing tool for her business and would be considered ordinary and necessary. She can deduct the printing and mailing costs as a business expense.

Example #2: Eunice renovates her home office and spends $8,000 on silk designer curtains for the windows. As she does not meet with clients in her home office, an expenditure of this size would likely not be considered reasonable, and therefore would not be deductible as a business expense.

In addition to being ordinary and necessary, the following rules apply to business expenses:

- Some costs must be *capitalized* rather than deducted currently as business expenses. Certain costs that would otherwise be currently deductible are allocated to the cost of producing inventory or holding it for resale. If a cost is included in inventory, it may later be deductible as a component of cost of goods sold. Other costs must be capitalized and either amortized ratably to expense or added to the basis of an asset and recovered when the asset is disposed of.
- Personal expenses and living expenses generally cannot be deducted as business expenses. However, if a taxpayer incurs an expense for something that is used *partly* for business and *partly* for personal use, the taxpayer may divide the total cost between the business and personal use. The business part is deductible.

Expenses under the Accrual Method

Under the accrual method of accounting, a taxpayer generally deducts or capitalizes business expenses when both of the following apply:

- "All events" have occurred that fix the fact of liability, and the liability can be determined with reasonable accuracy.
- Economic performance has occurred: the property or services are provided, or the property is used.

Exception for Recurring Items: Expenses for certain recurring items may be treated as incurred during the tax year even though economic performance has not occurred. For example, frequently-used office supplies may qualify as a recurring item. If so, the taxpayer can deduct them in 2020, even if the supplies are not delivered until 2021, when economic performance occurs. The exception for recurring items applies if all of the following requirements are met:

- The all-events test described above has been met.
- Economic performance occurs by the earlier of the following dates:
    - 8½ months after the close of the year, or
    - The date the taxpayer files a timely return, including extensions, for the year.
- The item is recurring, and the taxpayer consistently treats similar items as incurred in the tax year in which the all-events test is met.
- And either:
    - The item is not material, or
    - Accruing the item in the year in which the all-events test is met results in a better match against income than accruing the item in the year of economic performance.

A new expense or an expense that is not incurred every year can be treated as recurring if the taxpayer reasonably expects to incur it regularly in the future. The exception does not apply to workers' compensation or tort liabilities.

Example: Retail Concepts, Inc. is an *accrual-based*, calendar-year corporation. The company orders office supplies on December 20, 2020, and receives them two days later. Retail Concepts does not pay the bill for the supplies until January 10, 2021. As an accrual-based taxpayer, the corporation can deduct the expense in 2020 because all events have occurred to fix the liability, the amount of the liability can be determined, and economic performance occurred in 2020.

Business Start-up and Organizational Costs

Business start-up costs include investigating whether to open a business, legal costs to purchase an existing business, and training new employees before the business actually opens. Start-up costs are amounts paid or incurred for: (a) creating an active trade or business; or (b) investigating the creation or acquisition of an active trade or business.

Start-up costs include amounts paid or incurred in connection with an existing activity engaged in for profit, and for the production of income in anticipation of the activity becoming an active trade or business. Common start-up costs include:

- An analysis or survey of potential markets
- Advertisements to announce the opening of a business (before it actually opens)
- Salaries and wages for employees who are being trained and their instructors
- Travel costs for securing prospective distributors, suppliers, or customers
- Salaries and fees for executives and consultants, or for similar professional services.

Note: By definition, business start-up costs are incurred *before* a business actually begins operations. Start-up costs generally do not include deductible interest, taxes, or research and experimental costs.

Costs associated with starting a business generally must be treated as capital expenditures and may not be deducted currently, subject to the exceptions described below. The following costs related to a new business may be deductible as current expenses, without the need for amortization, in 2020:

- Up to $5,000 to organize a corporation, partnership, or LLC, and
- Up to $5,000 of start-up costs.

In order to currently deduct start-up expenditures, the taxpayer must elect to deduct these expenditures, and they cannot be deducted until the year the business begins.

If organizational or start-up costs incurred **exceed $50,000**, there is a dollar-for-dollar reduction in the available immediate deduction until the current deduction for either item is eliminated.

Organizational costs or start-up costs that are not currently deductible may be amortized ratably over 180 months (15 years) on Form 4562, *Depreciation and Amortization*. The amortization period starts with the month the taxpayer opens the business for regular operations.

Example: Supply Village, Inc. has corporate start-up expenses of $51,000 in 2020. Supply Village is $1,000 over the $50,000 threshold, so it must reduce its deduction for start-up expenses by the amount that it is over the threshold. Supply Village can deduct $4,000 of its start-up expenses ($5,000 allowable deduction minus the excess $1,000). The remaining amount of start-up expenses, $47,000 ($51,000 - $4,000 allowable deduction), must be amortized over 180 months.

Example: Fresh-Water Inc. opened for business on November 1, 2020. Prior to opening, the company incurred $21,200 of start-up expenses for advertising and new employee training. Since Fresh-Water had less than $50,000 of start-up costs, the company can deduct the full $5,000 on its 2020 tax return, and can also claim $180 of amortization ([$21,200 - $5,000]/180 = $90 per month × 2 [two months, November and December]) for a total of $5,180 for 2020.

All amounts paid to "investigate" a business before actually creating the business are treated as amortizable start-up costs. Amortizable start-up costs for purchasing a business include only investigative costs incurred in the course of a general search for or preliminary investigation of the business. These are costs that help someone decide whether or not to purchase a business.

Example: Paula is interested in purchasing a dog grooming business from a friend who is about to retire. Paula hires an attorney to investigate the business and make sure there are no legal claims against the business. The attorney charges Paula $7,700 for this investigative service. Paula purchases the business on December 1, 2020, and decides to run it as a sole proprietorship. $5,000 of Paula's legal fees would be deductible immediately as start-up costs. The remaining $2,700 would be amortized ratably over 180 months starting on December 1. Therefore, for 2020, the business can deduct $5,000 on its tax return, and can also claim an additional $15 of amortization ([$7,700 - $5,000]/180 = $15 per month × 1 [one month (December)]. The total deductible start-up costs on her Schedule C would be $5,015. The remaining start-up costs will be deducted in future years through amortization.

Example: Burger Wagon Inc. received its corporate charter on September 12, 2020. During the remainder of 2020, the company paid $5,500 for advertising; $12,000 for the training of new employees; and $4,000 of legal and accounting costs. Burger Wagon officially opened its doors the following year, on January 8, 2021. The company can elect to deduct $5,000 as start-up costs in the 2021 tax year (the year the business actually begins operations). It will then amortize the remaining $16,500 over 180 months starting in January 2021.

Qualifying Organizational Costs

Organizational costs are classified somewhat differently than start-up costs. Organizational costs are costs that are incurred that directly relate to a business's formation. These include costs to create and file articles of incorporation or articles of organization with the Secretary of State. Organizational costs also include any legal costs to create contracts, such as a formal partnership agreement. Organizational costs also include any other type of filing fees that are required by state governments.

A corporation or partnership can elect to deduct up to $5,000 of its initial organizational expenditures and amortize the remainder over a period of 180 months. If organizational costs exceed $50,000, there is a dollar-for-dollar reduction until the current deduction is eliminated. Qualifying organizational costs must be:

- Directly related to the creation or formation of the business.
- Chargeable to a capital account
- For a partnership, the costs must have been incurred by the due date of the tax return (excluding extensions) for the year in which business begins
- For a corporation, incurred before the end of the first tax year in which the corporation begins business operations.

Examples of qualifying organizational costs include:

- The cost of temporary directors
- The cost of organizational meetings
- Organization and filing fees for a corporation, limited partnership, or any other legal entity, (such as the costs of forming an LLC or LLP)
- Legal and accounting fees for setting up the business

Example: Ariana and Piper are both licensed dentists. They decide to form a Limited Liability Partnership (an LLP). The state filing fees for the LLP and the legal fees to draft their partnership agreement totaled $6,500. On June 1, 2020, they officially open their doors and start offering their medical services to the public. The partnership may immediately deduct $5,000 of the organizational costs. The remainder ($1,500) must be amortized over a period of 180 months, starting in June (the month the business commences operations).

If a taxpayer completely disposes of a business before the end of the amortization period, the taxpayer can deduct any remaining unamortized start-up costs or organizational costs. However, the business can deduct these deferred only to the extent they qualify as a loss.

Example: Oakbrook Eatery is a restaurant that began operations five years ago. Oakbrook began having cash-flow difficulties and officially closed its doors on November 1, 2020. Oakbrook had $65,000 of unamortized start-up costs on the books when it ceased operations. The entire $65,000 would be deductible on Oakbrook's final tax return, because unamortized startup costs are deductible as a business loss in the year the business is terminated.

Costs incurred in expanding an already-existing business are generally deductible as ordinary and necessary business expenses. In other words, the amounts do not have to be amortized if the business is already in operations and just adding new locations or expanding an existing location.

Example: Lean Fitness, Inc. operates a chain of personal fitness gyms. Lean Fitness decides to expand its operations by adding another location outside of its current geographical area. Lean Fitness incurs costs to advertise and prepare the new location, as well as train employees. These costs are deductible as ordinary business expenses and do not have to be amortized as start-up costs, since it is merely an expansion of its existing business operations.

Failed Business Purchases and Failed Start-Ups

If an individual taxpayer *attempts* to go into business and is ultimately unsuccessful (i.e., the business is never actually created, started, or purchased), the costs incurred may fall into one of two categories:

- Costs incurred before making a decision to purchase or start a specific business, which are considered personal and thus nondeductible.
- Costs incurred in a bona-fide attempt to purchase (or start) a specific business, which are capital costs that may be claimed as a capital loss on Schedule D, Form 1040. Doing this, the taxpayer is limited to a "capital loss limit" of $3,000 per year over any capital gains they might have.

Example: Dayna wants to purchase a local bakery. She incurs $5,400 in legal fees as well as contract costs during the negotiation process. However, just before the final contract is signed, one of the owners of the bakery changes his mind and decides that he doesn't want to sell. Dayna may deduct the costs that she incurred in connection with her bona-fide attempt to purchase the bakery as a capital loss on Schedule D.

The cost of assets acquired in connection with an unsuccessful attempt to go into business must be capitalized and cannot be deducted or recovered until the assets are later disposed of or sold. Only losses from a genuine, failed business venture are deductible. Hobby losses are not deductible as capital losses.

If a corporation incurs costs related to an unsuccessful attempt to acquire or start a new business, it can deduct all of its investigatory costs as a business loss.

Deductible Taxes

Businesses generally can deduct taxes in the year paid, regardless of which method of accounting the business uses. Under the accrual method, a taxpayer may choose to ratably accrue real estate taxes.

Real Estate Taxes: In order for real estate taxes to be deductible, the taxing authority must calculate the tax based on the assessed value of the real estate. If a property is sold, the deductible portion of the real estate taxes must be allocated between the buyer and the seller according to the number of days in the property tax year that each owned the property. The seller is treated as paying the taxes up to, but not including, the date of sale. The buyer is treated as paying the taxes beginning with the date of sale.

Businesses cannot deduct taxes charged for local benefits and improvements that tend to increase the value of the property. These include assessments for streets, sidewalks, water mains, sewer lines, and public parking facilities. A business must instead increase the basis of its property by the amount of the assessment.

However, a business can deduct taxes that are actually for local benefits such as maintenance, repairs, or interest charges related to capital improvements.

Example: Emmett owns a business office on Main Street. During the year, the city charged an assessment of $4,000 to each business on Main Street to improve the sidewalks. Emmett cannot deduct this assessment as a current business expense. Instead, he must increase the basis of his property by the amount of the assessment.

Example: Waterfront City converts a downtown area into an enclosed pedestrian mall. The city assesses the full cost of construction, financed with 10-year bonds, against the affected properties. The city pays the principal and interest with the annual payments made by the property owners. The assessments for construction costs are not deductible as taxes or as business expenses but are depreciable capital expenses. The part of each payment used to pay the interest on the bonds is deductible as taxes.

Personal Property Taxes: Every U.S. state imposes some type of tax on real property (land and structures). Personal property taxes are usually assessed as a percentage of the value of an item. Not all states impose personal property taxes, but many states do. Taxes imposed by a state or local government on personal property used in a taxpayer's trade or business are deductible as a business expense.

Some states impose a tax on "tangible personal property," which includes furniture or other belongings. Some states also impose taxes on the value of business inventory.

Example: Good Sports, Inc. is a popular sporting goods store located in West Virginia. West Virginia imposes an inventory tax on all businesses that operate in the state. The tax is based on the value of a business's inventory and assets at the end of the year. The inventory tax would be deductible on Good Sports, Inc.'s corporate tax return as a business expense.

State Income Taxes: Federal income taxes are never deductible. However, corporations and partnerships can deduct state and local income taxes, as well as franchise taxes. A self-employed individual who reports income on Schedule C can deduct state and local income taxes only as an itemized deduction on Schedule A.

Example: Baker Tools, Inc. is a calendar-year C corporation incorporated in New Mexico. New Mexico imposes a gross receipts tax as well as an income tax on corporate earnings. During the tax year, Baker Tools pays $42,000 of combined state income tax and gross receipts tax. These taxes would be deductible as a business expense on the corporation's federal tax return.

Business Excise Taxes: Excise taxes that are ordinary and necessary expenses of carrying on a trade or business are deductible. A "gross-receipts" tax[59] is a type of excise tax on the gross receipts of a business. A gross receipts tax is similar to a sales tax, but it is levied on the seller of goods and services, rather than the consumer. A business will report the full amount of its income before the deduction of the gross receipts tax, then the business should deduct the gross receipts tax as a business expense.

Excise taxes are taxes paid when purchases are made on a specific item, such as gasoline, or on a certain type of business activity, such as highway usage by semi-trucks. When paid in connection with the purchase of a specific item, an excise tax is considered part of the cost of that item. Therefore, it may be deductible currently or as the item is used, or be subject to capitalization, such as when the item is used in manufacturing inventory.

For example, indoor tanning salons are subject to a 10% Federal excise tax, which is a deductible business expense.

Sales and Use Taxes: Sales and use taxes collected by a business in connection with the sale of goods or services to its customers are remitted to the taxing authorities, and are excluded from the business's gross receipts and its deductible expenses if the sales or use tax is imposed on the customer, as the seller is simply acting as an agent on behalf of the customer as it relates to the remittance of the tax to the tax authority. However, if the sales or use tax is imposed on the seller, and the seller then bills the customer for the tax, the sales/use tax is (1) reported as gross income by the seller and then, separately, (2) deducted as an ordinary business expense by the seller.

When a business pays sales tax in connection with the purchase of goods or services, the tax is considered a component of the cost of the item purchased. Thus, if the item is depreciable property, the sales/use tax is added to its depreciable basis.

If the item is merchandise for resale or to be used in the production of inventory, the tax is capitalized as a component of inventory. If the tax is related to a currently deductible business expense, it is likewise considered part of that expense.

---

[59] Currently, six states impose a broad-based gross receipts tax: Delaware, Nevada, Ohio, Oregon, Texas, and Washington. Sometimes, this is called a "commerce tax" or a "commercial activity tax."

Example: Stephen is the sole proprietor of a popular comic bookstore. His store is located in Washington, a state that imposes sales tax on the buyer of goods. The applicable tax rate in his area is 8.75%. Stephen is required to collect sales tax on all the items that he sells. He does not include the sales tax that he collects in his gross receipts. For accounting purposes, the amounts he collects in sales tax is not revenue to his company. Stephen is simply collecting this amount on behalf of the state to be remitted to the state tax authority at some future date.

Business Bad Debts

Most business bad debts are a result of credit sales of goods or services to customers for which payment has not been received. These are recorded in a business's books as either accounts receivable or notes receivable. If, after a reasonable period of time, a business has tried to collect the amount due, but is unable to do so, the uncollectible part becomes a business "bad debt."

A debt becomes uncollectible or worthless when there is no longer any chance the amount owed will be paid. A debt's "worthlessness" is often presumed to result from an identifiable event, such as bankruptcy, liquidation, or termination of a business's activities, but a business does not have to wait for the debt to be due or to obtain a court judgment to show the debt is uncollectible. A business "bad debt" is a loss from the worthlessness of a debt that was either:

- Created or acquired in a taxpayer's trade or business, or
- Closely related to the trade or business when it became partly or totally worthless.

To be considered "closely related" to a taxpayer's trade or business, the primary motive for incurring the debt must be business-related.

A taxpayer can claim a business bad debt deduction only if the amount owed was previously included in his gross income. Thus, unlike an accrual-basis taxpayer, a cash-basis business does not report income until payment is actually or constructively received from a customer. Since a cash-basis business does not report any income on sales made on credit (until paid), cash-basis businesses will not have deductible business bad debts.

When a business loans money to a client, supplier, employee, or distributor for a business reason and the balance due later becomes worthless, the business can deduct the balance as a bad debt. However, the loan must have a genuine business purpose in order for this treatment to qualify.

Example: Allure Eyewear, Inc. is an accrual-based corporation that manufactures sunglasses. One of the company's salesmen, Claude, loses all his sunglass samples and asks his employer for a loan to replace them. Allure Eyewear loans Claude $3,000 to replace his sunglass samples and sample bags. Claude later quits his job without repaying the debt. Allure Eyewear has a business-related bad debt that it can deduct as a business expense.

If a business receives property in partial settlement of a debt, the debt should be reduced by the property's FMV, which becomes the taxpayer's basis in the property. The remaining unpaid balance of the debt can be deducted as a bad debt when and if it becomes worthless.

An entity may later recover a debt that was previously written off as a bad debt deduction. If a business recovers a bad debt that was deducted in a prior year, the recovered portion must be reported as income on the entity's current-year tax return. There is no need to amend the prior-year tax return on which the bad debt deduction was claimed.

Example: The Food Depot is an accrual-based restaurant supply company. One of the restaurants that it does business with, Garden Café, defaults on several invoices and then files for bankruptcy. The Food Depot writes off the bad debt, believing that the invoices were uncollectible. A year later, the owners of the Garden Café approach the Food Depot, attempting to do business again. The Food Depot tells the Garden Café that it will not deliver any products or do business with them again unless all the delinquent invoices are paid. The Garden Café pays the old debt in order to have its customer account reactivated. The Food Depot would recognize the recovery of the previously deducted bad debt on its current-year tax return. It does not need to amend its prior-year tax return.

Insurance Expenses

The IRS allows businesses to deduct insurance costs when calculating business income. The following types of insurance premiums are deductible:

- Business property insurance, malpractice insurance, and casualty insurance (that covers fire, storm, theft, accident, or similar losses)
- Business interruption insurance (that reimburses a business if it is temporarily shut down due to a fire or similar disaster)
- Credit insurance that covers losses from business bad debts
- Contributions to a state unemployment insurance fund (these contributions are also deductible as taxes)
- Vehicle insurance that covers business vehicles (not deductible if a business uses the standard mileage rate to figure vehicle expenses)
- Group-term life insurance for employees
- Group accident, health, long-term care, and workers' compensation insurance for employees

As described earlier, if a cash-basis business pays insurance premiums in advance, it may rely upon a 12-month rule and deduct amounts paid that do not extend beyond the earlier of the following: (1) 12 months after the benefit begins, or (2) the end of the tax year after the tax year in which payment is made.

Self-Employed Health Insurance Deduction

A self-employed individual may be able to deduct premiums paid for medical and dental insurance and qualified long-term care insurance for himself, his spouse, and his dependents as an adjustment to income, instead of a medical expense on Schedule A.

To qualify, a taxpayer must have a net profit reported on his Schedule C (Form 1040), or Schedule F; be a partner with net earnings from self-employment reported on Schedule K-1; or be a more-than-2% shareholder in an S corporation who had premiums paid or reimbursed by the corporation and reported to him as wages on Form W-2.

However, these additional wages are not subject to Social Security, Medicare, or Unemployment (FUTA) taxes. A sole proprietor, partner or more-than-2% S corporation shareholder claims the self-employed health insurance deduction on Schedule 1 (Form 1040).

He cannot take the deduction for any month he was eligible to participate in any employer-subsidized health plan (including one that his spouse was eligible for), even if he or his spouse did not actually participate in the plan. The self-employed health insurance deduction is only available to a business that has net income for the year. If the business earns no money or incurs a loss, the taxpayer does not get a deduction.

Example: Carlton is a sole proprietor who reports income and loss on Schedule C. In 2020, he pays $12,000 for his health insurance. He had a net loss of $3,000 for the year because of a fire in his warehouse. He had no other sources of income. Since he does not have any net earnings for the year, his health insurance is not deductible, because he does not have any income to offset. The deduction does not get carried over and is essentially lost.

This is not the case for C corporations, however. A C corporation may fully deduct its employee health insurance premiums, even if the corporation has a net business loss for the year.

Note: The IRS prescribes a different tax treatment for health insurance premiums for every entity type. If a **sole proprietor** pays accident or health insurance premiums, the amount is not deductible on Schedule C; it is deductible only as an adjustment to income on the individual taxpayer's Schedule 1 of Form 1040. If a **partnership** pays accident or health insurance premiums for its partners, it generally can deduct them as guaranteed payments to the partners. If an **S corporation** pays accident or health insurance premiums for its more-than-2% shareholder-employees, it generally can deduct them and must also include them in the shareholders' wages subject to federal income tax withholding. A **C corporation** can deduct employee health premiums dollar-for-dollar as a regular business expense, even if the expense creates a business loss for the year.

Business Interest Expense

A business can deduct interest paid or accrued during the tax year on debts related to a trade or business for which it is legally liable. It does not matter what type of property secures the loan. A business deducts business-related interest as follows:

- **Cash Method:** A business can deduct interest paid during the tax year. It cannot deduct a promissory note given in payment of interest because it is a promise to pay and not an actual payment.
- **Accrual Method:** A business can deduct interest that has accrued during the tax year.

A taxpayer cannot accelerate a tax deduction by paying interest in advance of when it is due. If a business uses the accrual method, it cannot deduct interest owed to a related person who uses the cash method until payment is made, and the interest is includable in the gross income of that person.

If the proceeds of a loan are used for more than one purpose, the related interest must be allocated based upon the use of the proceeds, among the following:

- Personal interest
- Investment interest
- Portfolio interest
- Interest related to a trade or business

Example: Geffen is the sole proprietor of a small retail shop, Geffen's Trinkets. He takes out a business loan in order to upgrade the shelving and interior of his store. He also takes out a loan to purchase more inventory for his shop. The interest he pays on both loans would be classified as business interest expense. The interest is tax-deductible, dollar-for-dollar, on his Schedule C.

Note: Do not confuse *business* interest expense with *investment* interest expense. They are not the same thing. *Business* interest expense is the cost of interest that is charged on business loans used to maintain operations, purchase business assets, or purchase inventory. *Investment* interest expense is the interest paid on money borrowed to purchase taxable investments.

Example: Ginny likes to invest in stocks and cryptocurrency. She is not a professional stockbroker or securities trader. During the year, Ginny takes out a $20,000 loan and uses the proceeds to buy various stocks and Bitcoin. The interest is classified as investment interest, not business interest. Ginny can only deduct her investment interest expense as an itemized deduction on Schedule A. The amount that she can deduct in a given year is limited to her net taxable investment income for the year.

Interest charged on income tax assessed on an individual's income tax returns is not a business deduction, even if the tax is related to income from a trade or business. This interest should be treated as a business deduction only in figuring a net operating loss deduction. Penalties on underpaid deficiencies and underpaid estimated tax are not "interest" and are not deductible.

Interest Expense Limitation for Large Businesses

The Tax Cuts and Jobs Act imposed a limitation on deductible business interest on certain large businesses. The interest expense limitation affects large businesses with average annual gross receipts (for the prior three tax years) in excess of $26 million in 2020. Originally, the TCJA imposed a limitation for business interest expense based on 30% of a business's adjusted taxable income (ATI).[60]

The CARES Act *increased* the ceiling for business interest deductions from 30% to 50% of adjusted taxable income for tax years 2019 and 2020. The CARES Act also allows businesses to use 2019 adjusted taxable income to calculate its business interest limitation for 2020. Any disallowed business interest may be carried forward to subsequent years.

Note: Most small and mid-sized businesses are not affected by this limitation. It only applies to large businesses that have average annual gross receipts of $26 million or more in 2020. The business interest expense deduction limitation also does not apply to certain electing real property trades or businesses, electing farming businesses, and certain regulated public utilities.

The CARES Act changes are temporary. In 2021, the limit will revert back to the 30% level.

[60] A business's "ATI" represents a business's total earnings before interest, taxes, depreciation, amortization and depletion are factored in.

Example: Baker Cosmetics, Inc. is a C corporation with average annual gross receipts of $50 million. In 2020, the corporation incurs $20 million of business interest expense. Baker Cosmetics has adjusted taxable income (ATI) of $18 million for the year. The company can only deduct $9 million of its business interest expense in 2020. The corporation's business interest expense is limited to 50% of its ATI ($18 million x 50% = $9 million). The disallowed interest expense must be carried forward to future tax years.

Rent Expense

A business can deduct expenses for renting property, including real estate, machinery, and other items used to conduct business. However, the cost of acquiring a lease is not considered rent and must be amortized over the term of the lease. Generally, rent paid in a trade or business is deductible in the year paid or accrued. However, if a taxpayer pays rent in advance, he can deduct only the amount that applies to his use of the rented property during the tax year. The rest of the payment can be deducted only over the period to which it applies.

If a taxpayer has both business and personal use of rented property, he may only deduct the amount actually used for business. To compute the business percentage, the taxpayer must compare the portion of the property used for business to the entire property. The resulting percentage is used to figure the business portion of the rent expense.

Example: Bertha rents an office to use both as a painting studio and as a site to run her math tutoring business. Her painting is merely a hobby and does not produce any business income. Her total rental payments for the space are $11,000 for the year. The office is 1,000 square feet; she uses 800 square feet for the math tutoring business and the remaining 200 square feet for her personal art studio. Therefore, she uses the office 80% for her business and 20% for personal purposes. The deductible portion of the rent expense is $8,800 (80% × $11,000).

Home Office Deduction

A self-employed taxpayer may be able to deduct certain expenses related to part of his home if the space is used "regularly and exclusively" for business and it is:

- The taxpayer's principal place of business, and/or
- The place used to meet with patients, clients, or customers in the normal course of business; or
- A separate structure not attached to the home that is used in connection with the business.

A taxpayer can use any reasonable method to calculate the percentage of the home that is used for business. Typically, the square footage of the home used for business is divided by the home's total square footage.

Because of the exclusive use rule, a taxpayer is not allowed to deduct business expenses for any part of the home that is used for both personal and business purposes. A self-employed taxpayer must complete Form 8829, *Expenses for Business Use of Your Home,* and then transfer the total to his Schedule C (Form 1040).

Simplified Home Office Deduction: A taxpayer may also choose to compute his home office deduction using a simplified calculation formula: a deduction of $5 per square foot is allowed for the space in the home that is used for business, up to a maximum allowable square footage of 300 square feet (for a maximum deduction of $1,500).

> **Example:** Alfred is a self-employed insurance broker with a home office he uses exclusively for business. The office measures 15 × 15, or 225 square feet. Alfred deducts $1,125 ($5 × 225) using the simplified option. He does not have to calculate depreciation or prorate his utilities under the simplified method.

Under this option, a taxpayer can claim the full amount of allowable mortgage interest, real estate taxes, and casualty losses on his home as itemized deductions on Schedule A.

These deductions do not need to be allocated between personal and business use, as is required under the regular method. The simplified option does not include a deduction for depreciation. Each year, a taxpayer may use either the simplified method or the regular method to calculate the home office deduction. If he chooses the regular method after having used the simplified method in an earlier year, depreciation is calculated using an optional depreciation table for the property.

Business-Related Meals and Entertainment

The TCJA eliminated the deduction for *most* entertainment expenses. However, there are some narrow exceptions. The TCJA does not affect expenses that are typically not considered entertainment, depending on the taxpayer's business activity.

> **Example:** Evander is a clothing designer. He attends a fashion show to introduce his new designs to potential buyers. The costs for attending the fashion show would *not* be classified as "entertainment" because the fashion show is directly related to his business as a designer. Any expenses he incurred during the show would be deductible as normal business expenses.

The disallowance for deducting entertainment also does not apply to businesses that provide entertainment to the general public. Entertainment that is provided to customers, as well as food and drinks, are also not subject to the 50% limit and are fully deductible. For example, the owner of a nightclub can hire a nightly entertainer, and that would be a normal business expense of the nightclub

> **Example**: Mango's Nightclub is a salsa-themed dance club. Mango's offers live music Thursday through Saturday night. The club also serves free appetizers and chips to its bar patrons during happy hour. All of the costs, including the cost of the food for patrons, would be 100% deductible as a business expense for the nightclub.

> **Example:** Five Star Realty, Inc. hosts open houses once a month. These events are advertised in the local newspaper and on the radio. During the open house, food and drinks are provided, as well as a presentation explaining the property management services that Five Star Realty offers. The events are open to the general public and used primarily as a marketing ploy to find new business customers. All the costs, including the food and drinks provided during the events, are 100% deductible by Five Star Realty.

Exceptions also exist for company-wide events. In this case, the entertainment, as well as the meals, would be 100% deductible (there is no 50% limit to the meals in this case). Examples include: team-building activities, holiday parties, and company picnics. In order to be fully deductible, the events cannot discriminate in favor of highly-compensated employees. In other words, all the employees must be able to participate, not just highly-paid executives or company officers.

Example: Edison owns an auto repair shop with twenty employees. Every year, Edison organizes a holiday party at Christmastime. All of the employees and their spouses are invited to the holiday party. The party includes professional catering and a music DJ. The cost of the holiday party, including the cost of meals, is 100% deductible as a business expense, because it is a team-building event for the benefit of all the employees.

Business Meals

Businesses normally deduct 50%[61] of the cost of business meals if the taxpayer (or an employee of the taxpayer) is present and the food or beverages are not considered lavish or extravagant. The meals may be provided to a current or potential business customer, client, consultant, or similar business contact. The following meal-related expenses are also subject to the 50% limit:

- Any taxes and tips on a business meal
- Any subsidized meals provided by employers to employees at an employer-operated eating facility (such as an employee cafeteria) are now subject to the 50% rule.

The cost of transportation to a business meal is *not* subject to the 50% limit.

Example: Caressa is a self-employed realtor who takes a client to lunch to celebrate the closing of a home sale. The total restaurant bill is $88. She also pays $10 in taxi fare to get to the restaurant.

Deductible meal expense	$88 × 50% =	$44
Deductible travel expense		$10
Total deductible business expense		**$54**

Caressa's deductible expense for travel is $10. Her allowable deduction for meals is $44. So, the total allowable expense on her Schedule C is $54.

Business meals are deductible if they are incurred while:

- Traveling away from home (whether eating alone or with others) on business,
- Taking customers or clients to a restaurant or other eatery,
- Attending a business convention or reception, business meeting, or business luncheon,
- Obtaining deductible educational expenses, such as meals during a continuing education seminar.

---

[61] The Consolidated Appropriations Act, 2021, raises the deductible meal limit for tax years 2021 and 2022 for food and beverages provided by a restaurant. These meals will be 100% deductible, but not until tax years 2021-2022.

Food and beverages that are provided during entertainment events (such as a baseball game) will not be considered entertainment if purchased separately from the entertainment, if the cost is stated separately from the entertainment on invoices or receipts.

Example: Tamara is an attorney. She takes her best client to a baseball game. She has skybox seats. During the game, a catered meal is delivered to their skybox. The sports tickets cost $200 each. The meal inside the skybox costs $60, and she receives a separate receipt. Tamara may deduct $30 of the meal ($60 cost x 50% limit). The cost of the baseball tickets would be a nondeductible entertainment expense, even if some type of business activity was conducted during the game.

If a taxpayer is subject to the Department of Transportation (DOT)[62] hours of service limits, the allowable deductible percentage is increased to 80% for business meals. DOT regulations apply to truck drivers, commercial bus drivers, pilots, and certain other workers in the transportation industry.

Travel Expenses

Travel expenses are among the most common business expense deductions. To be deductible for tax purposes, business expenses for travel must be incurred while carrying on a genuine business activity while traveling away from home. The taxpayer must be able to prove that the travel is directly related to the conduct of business.

Adequate records must be retained to support these expenses, including receipts, bills, credit card statements, or canceled checks. An exception is made for smaller expenses, (other than lodging), that cost less than $75.[63]

Travel costs for a business purpose are 100% deductible, and not subject to a 50% limitation. If the travel includes an element of personal travel, the personal portion of the expense is not deductible. Commuting costs are considered personal and not deductible.

In some instances, the personal portion may be incremental costs related to a spouse's travel. In other cases, a business must determine the nondeductible portion of an expense by multiplying it by a fraction. The numerator of the fraction is the number of personal days during the travel period, and the denominator is the total number of days spent traveling.

Example: Blake flies to New Orleans on business and takes his wife with him so she can vacation there. Blake pays $190 for each airline ticket and $200 for a double hotel room. The cost of a single hotel room is normally $150. Blake can deduct the cost of his own plane ticket, $190, and $150 for the hotel room. His wife's travel expenses are not deductible as a business expense.

Taxpayers are considered "traveling away from home" if their duties require them to be away from home substantially longer than an ordinary day's work, and they need to sleep or rest to meet the demands of their work.

---

[62] A business is allowed to deduct 80% of employees' meal costs when DOT hours of service limits apply to the following: air transportation workers such as pilots, crew, and mechanics regulated by the Federal Aviation Administration, interstate truck operators, railroad employees such as engineers and conductors regulated by the Federal Railroad Administration, certain merchant mariners regulated by the Coast Guard.

[63] Receipts are required to substantiate expenses only where those expenses exceed $75 for a specific expenditure. Receipts do not have to be retained for non-lodging expenses that are less than $75. See IRM 1.32.1, *Official IRS Travel Guide,* and IRM 1.32.11, *Official IRS City-to-City Travel Guide*, for references.

Per Diem Rates for Business Travel (M&IE)

"Per diem" is a daily allowance paid by a business to its employees for expenses incurred when traveling. To ease recordkeeping requirements, a business may elect to use a federal per diem rate as an alternative to keeping track of employees' actual expenses during business travel away from home. The allowance is *in lieu* of tracking *actual* travel expenses.

A per diem rate can be used for the combined costs of lodging and M&IE (meals and incidental expenses), as well as a per diem rate for meal costs alone.[64] An employer may also use the *per diem* method for reimbursing employee expenses. However, a self-employed person can only use a per diem rate for meal costs.

Per diem payments are not included in an employee's taxable wages, if an employee submits an expense report to their employer, which includes the business purpose of the trip, as well as the dates and place of the trip. The employee must file the expense report with the employer within a reasonable period of time (the IRS prescribes a safe harbor of 60 days). If any of these requirements are not met, the payment is taxable to the employee.

Example: Wilson is a sales representative of Solar Sales, Inc. a company that manufactures and installs solar panels. Wilson travels to many different locations in order to sell solar panels. When Wilson submits his monthly expense report to his employer, his report only includes the total cost of his expenses with no details or other substantiation. If Solar Sales reimburses Wilson, the payment will be taxable to him, because Wilson has not properly substantiated the amount, time, date, place and business purpose of the expenses.

The applicable per diem rates vary based on whether the travel is domestic or foreign, and also by location. For example, the per diem rate in large cities like Los Angeles and New York is higher than for smaller cities.

Example: Abbot & Abbot, LLP. is a CPA firm that employs dozens of auditors. The company's main office is located in Texas, but twice a year all the auditors travel to Florida to a different regional office for mandatory employee training. They typically train there for several days. Abbot & Abbot allows the employees to use federal per diem rates when they submit their expense reports for reimbursement. The employees are pleased because they do not have to save receipts for every meal purchase.

Claiming the *per diem* is not mandatory for any business. The IRS allows businesses to use per diems as an *alternative* to actual meals and travel expenses paid.

Example: Kaufman Consulting, Inc. is a financial services firm with twenty employees. The company reimburses its employees for meals and incidental expenses when the employees are traveling on work-related business. Instead of using the federal per diem rates, Kaufman Consulting requires all of its employees to submit actual receipts for all their meals and travel costs in order to obtain reimbursement. This is their company policy.

[64] Publication 1542, Per Diem Rates provides the rates for all continental U.S. areas.

Deductible Transportation Expenses

Ordinarily, expenses related to the use of a vehicle for business can be deducted as transportation expenses. To claim a deduction for business use of a car or truck, business-related costs must have been incurred for one or more of the following:

- Traveling from one work location to another within the taxpayer's tax home area (generally, the tax home is the entire city or general area where the taxpayer's main place of business is located, regardless of where he actually lives).
- Visiting customers.
- Attending a business meeting away from the regular workplace.
- Traveling from home to a temporary workplace. A temporary workplace can be either within or outside the taxpayer's tax home area.

Self-employed individuals may choose to use either the standard mileage rate or actual car expenses in order to figure the deduction for vehicle expenses. Corporations generally cannot use the standard mileage rate. However, businesses, including corporations, may reimburse an employee under an accountable plan for business-related use of his car using the standard mileage rate.

Any amounts reimbursed in excess of the standard mileage rate are reportable on the employee's Form W-2 as wages. Whether using the standard mileage rate or claiming actual expenses, a taxpayer must keep records that identify the vehicle and provide evidence of ownership or a lease.

Note: The TCJA made substantial changes to the tax treatment of transportation fringe benefits that are offered to employees. Transportation fringe benefits are covered later.

A business owner should maintain a daily log showing miles traveled, destination, and business purpose to support the total business miles claimed or the business use percentage to be applied to allocate actual expenses. "Actual expenses" include the following costs:

- Depreciation
- Lease payments
- Registration
- Garage rent
- Repairs and maintenance
- Gas, oil, and tires
- Car insurance
- Parking fees and tolls

If the business use of a vehicle is less than 100%, expenses must be allocated between business and personal use, and only the business-use portion is deductible.

A *self-employed* taxpayer filing Schedule C or Schedule F can deduct interest on a loan relating to the purchase of an automobile that is used for work. A corporation or partnership may also deduct these costs on a vehicle that the business owns directly. However, an *employee* cannot deduct the interest on a loan relating to an automobile purchase.

Example: Darius uses a delivery van in his landscaping business. He has no other car, so the van is used for his personal transportation on the weekends. Darius chooses to deduct actual costs, rather than using the standard mileage rate. Based on his records, Darius' total vehicle expenses are $6,252, which includes the cost of diesel fuel, oil changes, tire replacement, and repairs. Darius uses the vehicle 75% for business, so his allowable auto expense deduction using the actual expense method is $4,689 ($6,252 × 75%).

Example: Coldwell Dairy Farms, Inc. is a C corporation with twenty-five employees. The corporation has an accountable plan for reimbursing employees for business mileage based on current IRS mileage rates. At the end of each month, each employee submits a detailed spreadsheet that lists their business-related mileage. Coldwell Dairy Farms issues a reimbursement check to each employee on a monthly basis. The reimbursements are not taxable to the employee, and they are fully deductible by the corporation as transportation expenses.

For 2020, the standard mileage rate for business use of a vehicle is 57.5¢ per mile. A taxpayer who elects to use the standard rate cannot deduct actual expenses of operating a vehicle, such as gas, oil, and insurance. However, parking fees and tolls may be deducted *in addition* to the standard mileage rate.

Example: Dr. Marianna Clarkson is a self-employed business coach as well as a popular motivational speaker. She travels frequently for speaking events, and she has a dedicated utility van that she uses for most of her business trips. The van is a qualified nonpersonal-use vehicle, because it has been modified to hold her audiovisual equipment and projection screens. Occasionally she flies, if the speaking engagement is out-of-state. In 2020, she incurs 11,200 business miles on her utility van. The 2020 mileage rate is 57.5¢ per mile, so her deduction for mileage on Schedule C is $6,440. She also incurred an additional $200 in bridge tolls and $54 in parking fees at the airport. The tolls and parking amounts are deductible in addition to her mileage on Schedule C. She would also be able to deduct any airline tickets as a separate travel expense.

A business is prohibited from using the standard mileage rate if it:

- Operates five or more cars at the same time (this is considered a "fleet")
- Claimed a depreciation deduction using any method other than straight-line
- Claimed a section 179 deduction or the special "bonus depreciation" allowance on the car
- Claimed actual car expenses for a car that was leased

In order to claim the section 179 deduction on a vehicle, the taxpayer must use the vehicle more than 50% for business. If the taxpayer used the vehicle more than 50% for business, they can multiply the cost of the vehicle by the percentage of business use (section 179 and bonus depreciation are covered in more detail later).

Example: Braydon purchased a new heavy-duty truck in April 2020 for $24,500 and used it 60% for his farming business. Based on his business usage, the total cost of Braydon's car that qualifies for the section 179 deduction is $14,700 ($24,500 cost × 60% business use).

Example: Perfect Shuttle, LLC is an airport shuttle service that operates out of southern California. Perfect Shuttle provides airport transportation as well as luxury car service. The company employs 10 full-time drivers and operates a fleet of 15 shuttles and limousines. The business cannot use the standard mileage rate, because it operates more than five cars at the same time. The business can deduct the actual costs of maintaining and operating the vehicles.

Business Gifts

A business can deduct business-related gifts to clients and customers. The deductible amount is limited to $25 for amounts given to any person during the year. If a taxpayer and a spouse *both* give gifts, they are treated as one taxpayer for this limit, even if they have separate businesses. A gift to the spouse of a business customer or client is generally considered an indirect gift to the customer or client.

The $25 limit for business gifts does not include incidental costs such as packaging, insurance, and mailing costs, or the cost of engraving jewelry, which may be deducted separately. Related costs are considered incidental only if they do not add substantial value to a gift.

Example: Wholesale Produce Inc. gives a large fruit basket to its best customer, Princess Grocery. The fruit basket costs $57, and the shipping and mailing of the basket cost $17. Wholesale Produce Inc. can deduct $25 for the basket and $17 for the cost of mailing, for a total deduction of $42.

Example: Deborah sells custom greeting cards in a local boutique. Deborah gives three gourmet candy boxes to each of the store's owners to thank them for their patronage. Deborah pays $45 for each candy package, or $135 total. She can deduct a maximum of $75 ($25 gift limit × 3 gifts) on her Schedule C for the gifts.

Promotional Gift Exceptions: The following items are considered promotional in nature and not subject to the $25 gift limit:

- An item with the business name clearly imprinted on it that costs $4 or less (examples include imprinted pens, desk sets, and plastic bags)
- Signs, display racks, or other promotional materials to be used on the business premises of the recipient

A business may also deduct gifts to employees. Noncash gifts of nominal value that are distributed to employees to promote goodwill may be excluded from taxable compensation. Gifts of greater value and of cash or cash-equivalent items such as gift cards are considered compensation and must be included in an employees' wages.

Example: Buzzard Poultry, Inc. gives each of its 75 employees a $25 holiday turkey during Thanksgiving each year. The company can deduct the cost of the turkeys ($1,875 = $25 × 75). This noncash gift is not taxable to the employee, and the fair market value of the gift is not included in the employee's wages.

Note: The TCJA clarifies that employee awards or gifts don't include cash, cash equivalents, gift cards, gift coupons, certain gift certificates, tickets to theater or sporting events, vacations, meals, lodging, stocks, bonds, securities, and other similar items. These would be taxable to the employee as compensation and includable in the employee's wages.

Recordkeeping Requirements for Business Expenses				
Expense	**Amount**	**Date**	**Description**	**Business Purpose**
Travel	Record of each expense for travel, lodging, and meals.	Dates for each trip and the number of days spent on business.	Destination (name of city, town, etc.)	The business purpose for the expense.
Meals	Cost of each separate expense.	Date of the meal.	Name and address or location of the place of the meal.	The business purpose for the expense or the business benefit gained or expected to be gained.
Gifts	Cost of the gift.	Date of the gift.	Description of the gift.	Business relationship.
Transportation	Cost of each separate expense.	Date of the expense.	The business destination.	The business purpose for the expense.

Charitable Contributions as Business Expenses

Among business entities, only C corporations are permitted to deduct charitable contributions on their income tax returns. In 2020, the deduction is generally limited to 25% of modified taxable income for most cash contributions (with lower limits for other forms of contributions), and is explained later in the dedicated units for C Corporations.

Self-employed taxpayers cannot deduct charitable contributions as business expenses, but can claim deductions on Schedule A if they itemize deductions. Contributions made by partnerships and S corporations are reported on their respective returns as separately stated items, and may be deductible by their partners and shareholders.

An exception to this general rule exists for expenses bears a "direct relationship" to the taxpayer's trade or business, in which a reasonable expectation of financial return may constitute an allowable deduction as a business expense, rather than a charitable contribution.

Example: Friedrich is a sole proprietor who manufactures handmade flutes and sells them through his business, Friedrich's Fine Flutes. Friedrich makes a $1,000 payment to a local church (which is a qualified charitable organization) for a half-page advertisement in the church's program for its annual Spring Concert. In the program, the church thanks its concert supporters, including Friedrich's Fine Flutes. The advertisement includes the URL for Friedrich's business website, where he sells his instruments. Friedrich reasonably expects that the advertisement will attract new customers to his website and will help him to sell more musical instruments. Friedrich may deduct the $1,000 payment as a normal advertising expense (§1.162-15).

Deducted or Capitalized Costs

There are certain costs that businesses may choose to either deduct currently or capitalize as an addition to the basis of a related asset. There are specific rules about the circumstances in which each type of item may be deducted, or if capitalized, how its cost may be recovered through depreciation or amortization. Examples of costs that are generally capital in nature, but which a business may elect to deduct currently include research and experimental costs; certain intangible drilling costs; and circulation costs for publishers of newspapers and magazines.

Miscellaneous Business Expenses

Additional expenses that may be deductible by a business include the following:

- Advertising
- Credit card convenience fees
- Certain franchise or trademark fees
- Education and training for employees
- Internet-related expenses, such as annual domain registration fees
- Interview expense allowances for job candidates
- Outplacement services provided to employees
- Legal and accounting fees directly related to operating the business[65] and tax preparation fees for business returns
- License and regulatory fees paid annually to state or local governments
- Penalties paid for late performance or nonperformance of a contract
- Repairs to business and rental property, including the cost of labor and supplies
- Subscriptions and memberships to trade magazines and professional organizations
- Supplies and materials used during the year
- Utilities for a business office, including heat, lights, power, telephone service, and water and sewage

Nondeductible Expenses

The following expenses are not allowed as business deductions:

- Political contributions, including indirect contributions such as advertising in a convention program of a political party
- Lobbying expenses for Federal, state, or local legislation[66]
- Dues for country clubs, golf clubs, and athletic clubs, hotel and airline clubs, even if the club is used for business activity
- Penalties and fines paid to any governmental agency for breaking the law, such as parking tickets or fines for violating local zoning codes
- Legal and professional fees for work of a personal nature

---

[65] Although most business-related legal fees are deductible, under the Tax Cuts and Jobs Act, no deduction is allowed for any legal settlement or legal fees related to sexual harassment or sexual abuse if the payments are subject to a nondisclosure agreement.

[66] In prior years, some limited lobbying expenses were deductible, if the lobbying was for local or regional legislation. The Tax Cuts and Jobs Act disallows any business deduction for *any* lobbying expenses.

Unit 4: Study Questions

(Test yourself and then check the correct answers at the end of this section.)

1. Drexel operates a computer service repair business. He has four employees who also service customers' computers in the field. Drexel drives a sedan when he visits clients, and each of his four technicians drives their own van assigned to them to make their repair visits. Which of the following methods can Drexel use to claim deductions for the cost of these vehicles?

A. He can use standard mileage for the sedan, but must use actual costs for the vans.
B. He must use actual expenses for all of the vehicles.
C. He must use standard mileage for the vans and the sedan.
D. He can choose to use either method.

2. Savannah is a self-employed tax preparer who reports income and loss on Schedule C. She goes to a continuing education seminar out-of-state and incurs the following expenses:

Tax seminar	$400
Train ticket	$35
Restaurant meal expense	$26
Taxi fare to the restaurant	$10

What is her deductible expense for this event?

A. $400
B. $435
C. $458
D. $465

3. Marian operates a shoe repair shop as a sole-proprietorship in a small building that she owns. In 2020, she had the following income and expenses:

Repair cracks in the shop's floor	$1,000
Property tax on business assets	$2,000
County assessment for upgrading sidewalks	$6,800
Utility expenses for her shop	$1,800

What is the tax treatment of the above expenditures?

A. Marian may deduct the repairs, property tax, and utilities on Schedule C. The assessment must be added to the basis of the property and depreciated.
B. All of the expenses are deductible on Schedule C.
C. The property tax must be deducted on Schedule A, and the rest of the expenses may be deducted on Schedule C.
D. Only the utilities and repairs may be deducted on Schedule C.

4. Norman is an interstate truck driver subject to the Department of Transportation (DOT) rules for hours of service. During 2020, he incurs $3,064 in meal expenses while on the job. He is self-employed and files his income and loss on Schedule C. What is his deductible expense for business meals?

A. $1,532
B. $2,298
C. $2,451
D. $3,064

5. Super-Sweets Inc. is a confectionary company that makes chocolates. The company gives the following business gifts to its best customer:

Rotating glass display for Super-Sweets	$500
Coffee and tea gift basket	$50
Twenty pens imprinted with the Super-Sweets name and logo	$35
Postage for the gift basket	$20

How much can Super-Sweets Inc. deduct on its business tax return?

A. $25
B. $525
C. $580
D. $605

6. Which of the following costs qualify as business start-up costs?

A. State and local taxes.
B. Research and experimental costs.
C. A survey of potential markets.
D. Inventory purchases.

7. Rainbow Fabrics, LLC made a business loan to Gold's Warehouse, one of its wholesalers, in the amount of $10,000. After paying $2,000, Gold's Warehouse defaults on the loan. Rainbow Fabrics makes a good faith attempt to collect the loan, but Gold's Warehouse files for bankruptcy. How much of this bad debt may Rainbow Fabrics deduct as a business expense?

A. $0
B. $2,000
C. $8,000
D. $10,000

8. The Hughes Partnership paid the following penalties in 2020. Which of these is deductible?

A. A penalty paid to the county for violating construction regulations.
B. A penalty imposed by the IRS for late filing of a Form 1065 partnership return.
C. A penalty paid to the city for violating its sign ordinance.
D. A penalty for late performance of a contract.

9. Hannah, a self-employed realtor, traveled to a business convention by ferry and incurred the following expenses:

- Ferry ticket: $100
- Meals: $80
- Hotel room: $90
- Computer game purchased during the convention: $50

How much is deductible as a current business expense?

A. $190
B. $230
C. $280
D. $320

10. Bobby owns Jackpot Pawn Shop. He makes a business loan to a client in the amount of $5,000. Bobby also loans his brother, Keith, $1,000 so he can buy a car. His brother, Keith, used to work sporadically at the shop as an employee. Both of the loans become uncollectible in 2020. How much can Bobby deduct as a business bad debt expense?

A. $1,000
B. $4,000
C. $5,000
D. $6,000

11. Lilly owns a dress shop. Several years ago, Lilly properly deducted a $10,000 business bad debt after a textile supplier defaulted on a loan. In 2020, the textile supplier wishes to do business with Lilly again and repays $9,000 of the loan. How must Lilly report this repayment?

A. She must amend her prior-year tax return to correct the previously reported bad debt.
B. She must reflect this recovery of $9,000 as income in 2020.
C. She can deduct a loss of $1,000 on her current-year tax return.
D. She is not required to report the $9,000 loan repayment if she is on the cash basis.

12. Devina is a sole proprietor who owns a public relations business. She has a nine-year-old son she claims as a dependent. In 2020, she paid $7,400 of premiums for medical and dental health insurance for herself and her son, who is her dependent. She reported a net profit of $23,000 on her Schedule C for the year. Which of the following statements is correct?

A. She can deduct 100% of the health insurance premiums as an adjustment to income.
B. She can deduct 50% of the health insurance premiums on Schedule C.
C. She can deduct 50% of the health insurance premiums on Schedule A.
D. She can deduct 100% of the health insurance premiums on Schedule C.

13. Maddie rents a small storage unit to store her business records on February 1, 2020. She is given a discount if she pays the full amount of the lease upfront, which is $1,620 for a three-year lease. What is the amount of Maddie's 2020 deductible expense for leasing the storage unit?

A. $495
B. $540
C. $560
D. $1,620

14. Garrett operates his printing business out of a rented business office. He does not have a home office. He uses his own truck to deliver completed print jobs to his customers. Which of the following statements is correct?

A. Garrett can deduct the cost of round-trip transportation between customers and his shop.
B. Garrett can deduct all his commuting costs from home to his office space.
C. Garrett cannot deduct costs related to the use of a personal truck.
D. Garrett can only deduct the costs to travel to his customers who are disabled and cannot come to his shop.

15. Quentin requested a $100,000 business loan to purchase a machine for his business. The machine cost $90,000. The rest of the money went into Quentin's bank account, and he purchased a jet ski with the money later in the year. However, the entire loan was secured by his business assets. Which of the following statements is correct?

A. Quentin cannot purchase personal items with a business loan; therefore, none of the interest is deductible.
B. All of the interest is deductible, because it is secured by his business assets.
C. Only the amount of interest allocable to the purchase of the business machine is deductible.
D. None of the answers is correct.

16. Discount Dollar, LLC is a retail store located in Las Vegas, NV. It pays a combined 8.25% sales tax to local and state taxing authorities when a customer purchases its merchandise. Nevada imposes sales tax on the buyer of the goods. How should Discount Dollar treat the sales tax it collects from its customers?

A. Include the amount in its gross receipts and its deductible expenses.
B. Add the amount to the depreciable basis of the items sold.
C. Capitalize the cost as a component of inventory of the items sold.
D. Exclude from its gross receipts and deductible expenses the sales taxes it collects and remits them to local and state taxing authorities.

Unit 4: Quiz Answers

1. The answer is B. Drexel is forced to use actual costs for his business-related automobile expenses. Many businesses, including self-employed individuals, (but not corporations) can choose to use either the standard mileage rate or actual vehicle expenses in order to claim deductions for the cost of vehicles used in the business. However, a business is prohibited from using the standard mileage rate if it operates five or more vehicles at the same time. Since he has four employees, plus himself, and each has their own company-provided vehicle, he has reached the five-vehicle threshold that requires the use of the actual cost method.

2. The answer is C. The answer is **$458** ($400 + $35 + $10 + [26 × 50%]). Savannah's deductible meal expenses are subject to a 50% limit, but the taxi fare, the train ticket, and the tax seminar are 100% deductible.

3. The answer is A. Marian may deduct the repairs, property tax, and utilities as business expenses. The assessment must be added to the basis of the property and depreciated. Note that the property tax is deductible as a business expense on Schedule C (rather than on Schedule A) because it is assessed on business property. Assessments for streets, sidewalks, sewer lines, and other public services generally add value to the property and must be added to the basis of the property, rather than deducted currently.

4. The answer is C. A taxpayer who is subject to the Department of Transportation's (DOT) hours of service can deduct a larger percentage of his meal expenses when traveling away from his tax home. Norman would multiply his meal expenses incurred while away from home on business by the DOT hours of service limit of 80% ($3,064 × .80 = **$2,451**).

5. The answer is C. There is a $25 limit per person per tax year for business gifts; however, the cost of packaging, insuring, and mailing are not included in determining the cost of a gift for purposes of the $25 limit. Promotional items such as the display rack are also not included in the cost. Therefore, Super-Sweets can deduct the following:

Glass display: $500	$500
Coffee and tea basket: (only $25 is deductible as a gift expense)	$25
20 imprinted pens: $35	$35
Postage for the gift basket: $20	$20
($500 + $25 + $35 + $20) = allowable deduction	**$580**

6. The answer is C. Start-up costs are costs incurred in creating an active trade or business or investigating the creation or acquisition of an active trade or business. A survey of potential markets would be a deductible start-up cost.

7. The answer is C. A loan to a client, customer, employee, or distributor for a business reason can be deducted as a business bad debt if it becomes worthless. Worthlessness is often presumed to result from an identifiable event, such as bankruptcy, liquidation, or termination of a business's activities. The amount of the loan, minus what was repaid, is the deduction that would be allowable on Rainbow Fabrics' tax return: $10,000 loan - $2,000 recovery/payments on the loan = **$8,000 deductible bad debt expense.**

8. The answer is D. The Hughes Partnership can deduct only the penalties paid for the late performance of a contract. That would be an allowable business expense. The other fines and penalties are not deductible, because penalties or fines paid to any government entity because of a violation of laws or regulations are not allowable as business expenses.

9. The answer is B. Hannah can deduct the cost of her hotel room, one-half of her meal expense, and her ferry ticket to attend the convention ($100 + $90 + [$80 × 50% meal limitation] = **$230**). The cost of a computer game is a personal expense and not deductible.

10. The answer is C. Only the loan to the client ($5,000) would be deductible as a business bad debt expense. A loss related to a loan to a client, customer, employee, or distributor for a business reason can be deducted as a business bad debt. Since Keith is a related person and not a regular employee and the loan was for personal reasons, Bobby cannot deduct his loss on the loan to his brother as a business bad debt.

11. The answer is B. Lilly is not required to amend her prior-year return to report the recovery of the bad debt. Since Lilly recovered a bad debt that was deducted properly in a prior year, she should include the recovered portion as income on her current year tax return.

12. The answer is A. The self-employed health insurance deduction is a tax deduction that covers medical, dental, and long-term care insurance premiums for those who are self-employed. Devina can deduct 100% of the health insurance premiums as an adjustment to income, because she has business profits for the year. The amounts cannot be deducted on Schedule C as a business expense. A self-employed individual with a net profit for the year can deduct premiums paid for medical and dental insurance for herself, her spouse (if married), and her dependents.

13. The answer is A. Maddie must capitalize the deduction. If a taxpayer pays rent in advance, only the amount that applies to the current year is deductible, *unless* the expense qualifies for the 12-month rule. Since Maddie paid the storage rent three years in advance, the balance must be deducted over the period to which it applies. Calculation: $1,620/36 (months) = **$45 per month**/$45 × 11 months (February to December) = **$495**

14. The answer is A. Garrett can deduct the cost of round-trip transportation between customers and his print shop. A taxpayer cannot deduct the costs of driving a car between his home and his main workplace. These costs are personal commuting expenses. The costs of driving to meet with clients or do other business-related errands are deductible, whether Garrett uses his own truck or not.

15. The answer is C. Generally, interest on a business loan is fully deductible. However, debt incurred for personal reasons is not deductible as a business expense. This is true even if the loan is secured by business assets. The amount of interest attributable to the portion of loan proceeds used to purchase the business machine is deductible, but not the amount for Quentin's purchase of the jet ski, which is a personal expense.

16. The answer is D. As a retailer, Discount Dollar acts as a collection agent for the state taxing authorities. The amounts of sales tax it collects and remits to them should be excluded from its taxable gross income and deductible expenses. A business should not deduct state and local sales taxes imposed on the buyer that the business must collect and pay over to the state or local government. Also, the business should not include these sales taxes in gross receipts or sales. For more information, see IRS Publication 535, *Business Expenses.*

Unit 5: Employee Compensation & Fringe Benefits

More Reading:
Publication 535, Business Expenses
Publication 15-A, Employer's Tax Guide
Publication 15-B, Employer's Tax Guide to Fringe Benefits

Employee Compensation

Employee compensation can take many different forms. Compensation usually refers to wages, but it can also include other incentives, such as fringe benefits, stock options, and other company benefits. An employer can deduct the compensation it provides its employees if all of the following tests are met:

- The payments must be ordinary and necessary expenses directly related to the trade or business.
- The amounts must be reasonable. Reasonable pay is the amount that similar businesses would normally pay for the same services. If the IRS determines pay is excessive, it can disallow the deduction of the excess amount.
- There must be proof that services were actually performed (unless the compensation qualifies as supplemental wages, such as maternity leave, sick pay, or vacation pay).
- The expenses must have been paid or incurred during the tax year.

The term "supplemental wages" refers to compensation paid in *addition* to an employee's regular salary or wages. Supplemental wages also may include the following:

- Bonuses, commissions, overtime pay, and severance pay
- Taxable awards
- Taxable employee awards and prizes
- Back pay
- Retroactive pay increases
- Payments for nondeductible moving expenses

Supplemental wages are taxable to the employee just like regular wages and deductible as a wage expense by the employer. Supplemental wages are subject to income tax withholding, FICA, and may be subject to backup withholding.

Example: Elvin is a full-time salesman for Dent Appliances, Inc., an appliance store. In 2020, Elvin earns wages of $20,000; commissions of $12,000; overtime of $5,000; and an end-of-the-year bonus of $1,000. All of the amounts are taxable compensation to Elvin and deductible by his employer as wages. Elvin also receives $575 in mileage reimbursements from his employer, because he used his own car to pick up supplies for the store every week. Elvin always submits his mileage reimbursement reports in a timely manner. The reimbursements are not taxable to Elvin, and fully deductible by his employer as a business expense.

Transfers of property to an employee can also be considered compensation. If an employer transfers property (for example, a vehicle, equipment, or other property) to an employee, the employee must recognize taxable compensation on the date of the transfer. Wages paid in any medium other than cash is computed on the basis of the fair market value of such items at the time of payment.

In other words, the fair market value of the property transferred to the employee. The business would recognize a gain or loss on the transfer equal to the difference between the fair market value and its basis in the property.

Example: Varne Manufacturing is having cash flow difficulties. The company offers one of its employees a used motorcycle in lieu of his weekly salary. The employee gladly accepts the motorcycle. The amount that must be recognized by the employee is the FMV of the motorcycle on the date of transfer. The company, on the other hand, must treat the transfer as a sale.

Note: If an employee's wages are paid in *property* rather than *money*, the employer must ensure that the amount of the payroll tax required to be withheld is available for payment in money (Rev. Rul. 2004-37).

In addition to deducting compensation payments to employees, a business can deduct amounts paid to independent contractors.

Employment Taxes: A business's deduction for compensation paid to employees is not reduced by the Social Security, Medicare, and income taxes it is required to withhold from them. Further, a business can deduct the amounts paid as the *employer's* share of Social Security and Medicare taxes, as well as state and federal unemployment and disability fund taxes.

Example: Shogun Medical Partnership pays its part-time secretary $18,000 a year. The partnership also pays an additional $1,500 of state-related employment taxes on the secretary's wages. The full $18,000 in wages can be deducted on the partnership's tax return. The Shogun Partnership can also deduct the $1,500 in additional employment taxes.

A self-employed individual can deduct one-half of his self-employment tax as a business expense in figuring adjusted gross income. This deduction only affects *income* tax. It does not affect net earnings from self-employment or self-employment tax.

Fringe Benefits for Employees

For businesses that have employees, there are many fringe benefits and a new tax credit for employers that offer paid family and medical leave to their employees. All these changes can affect a business's bottom line.

Study Note: For Part 1 of the EA exam, you must understand fringe benefits from the employee's perspective. For Part 2, you must know how these benefits are treated from the employer's perspective.

A fringe benefit is an extra benefit supplementing an employee's salary. It is a type of non-cash compensation that may be offered by a business to make positions more desirable for employees. There are many types of fringe benefits that employers are allowed to offer their employees on a tax-free basis.

Examples include: medical and dental insurance, use of a company car for business-related errands, subsidized meals, and employee discounts. Some fringe benefits may be partially taxable. Examples of *taxable* fringe benefits include:

- Off-site athletic facilities and health club memberships,
- Concert and athletic event tickets,
- Intangible property such as vacations, stocks, or securities,
- The value of employer-provided life insurance over $50,000,
- Any cash benefit or benefits in the form of a credit card or gift card (an exception applies for occasional meal money or transportation fare to allow an employee to work beyond normal hours),
- Transportation benefits, if the value of a benefit for any month is more than a specified nontaxable limit,[67]
- Employer-provided vehicles, if they are used for personal purposes or commuting.

Note: Because of the Tax Cuts and Jobs Act, *most* entertainment expenses are no longer deductible. Therefore, the cost of entertainment provided to an employee is no longer a non-taxable fringe benefit. There is an exception for entertainment expenses that are directly for the benefit of employees, (i.e., occasional office parties or company picnics that include all the staff).

Generally, nontaxable benefits are not subject to income tax withholding, Social Security and Medicare taxes, or unemployment (FUTA) tax. However, there are exceptions for certain items. For example, an S corporation shareholder with company ownership of more than 2% is not considered an "employee" for purposes of excluding certain fringe benefits, such as accident insurance and health insurance benefits.

Health and accident insurance premiums paid on behalf of a greater-than-2% shareholder of an S corporation are deductible by the S corporation as wages and subject to income tax withholding. In other words, the premiums are included in the shareholder-employee's salary and reported on the individual's Form W-2. However, these additional wages are not subject to Social Security, or Medicare, or unemployment (FUTA) taxes.

The S Corporation is allowed a tax deduction for the wages paid, and the shareholder is allowed a deduction on his or her personal tax return for the health insurance premiums included in their wages. Health insurance paid on behalf of employees that are not shareholders in the S corporation would merely be deducted as a business expense by the company.

Example: Audio Acoustics, Inc. is an S Corporation with two owner-shareholders and fifteen employees. Raymond is a 50% owner-shareholder who also works full-time as a sales manager for Audio Acoustics. The company pays Raymond's salary as well as his health insurance. The cost of Raymond's health insurance is reported as wages on his Form W-2 and subject to income tax. The wages are then deductible by Audio Acoustics as wage expense. Carmella is also a full-time employee of Audio Acoustics, but she is not a shareholder or an owner of the business. Audio Acoustics deducts Carmella's health insurance premiums simply as a business expense, and Carmella does not have to include the value of the health insurance in her wages or taxable income.

---

[67] The nontaxable benefit for both mass transit and parking for 2019 was $265 per month, although the amounts are no longer deductible by the employer, they are still non-taxable to the employee if the employer continues to provide the benefit. Any expense over that amount is included in the employee's taxable income as wages. An employee can receive both parking and transit benefits in the same month.

The tax treatment is very different for C corporations. One big advantage of C corporations is that shareholders and employees can receive many nontaxable fringe benefits. C corporations may deduct the entire cost of health insurance provided to their employees, regardless of whether or not the employee is an owner of the company. Shareholder-employees of a C corporation can receive fringe benefits such as health insurance and accident premiums tax-free, regardless of their ownership stake in the business.

Example: Jordy is a software developer and the sole owner and shareholder of Moonbeam Developers, Inc. Jordy's company is organized and operated as a C Corporation. Jordy is 42 years old and has a chronic health condition. Consequently, his health insurance costs are very high. His health insurance costs $22,000 per year, his long-term care insurance costs $10,000 per year, and his disability insurance costs $5,000 per year. The entire $37,000 is deductible as a business expense ($22,000 + $10,000 + $5,000). The amounts do not have to be added to Jordy's Form W-2 as wages.

Cafeteria Plans (Section 125 Plans)

A "cafeteria plan"[68] is a written benefit plan that provides employees an opportunity to choose between receiving at least one taxable benefit, such as cash, and one qualified (nontaxable) benefit. It is called a "cafeteria plan" because employees are allowed to choose between different types of benefits, or elect to receive an amount in cash. A cafeteria plan is the only way an employer can offer employees a choice between taxable and nontaxable benefits without the choice causing all the benefits to become taxable. A plan offering only a choice between taxable benefits is not a cafeteria plan.

Employees generally contribute a portion of their salaries on a pre-tax basis to pay for a portion of the qualified benefits. Having a salary reduction option is typically deemed sufficient to satisfy the requirement to provide a taxable option, even though the amounts are withheld on a pre-tax basis. The plan may make benefits available to employees, their spouses, and their dependents. Qualified benefits may include:

- Accident and health benefits (but not Archer medical savings accounts or long-term care insurance)
- Adoption assistance
- Group-term life insurance
- Health savings accounts (HSAs), including distributions to pay long-term care services
- Flexible spending arrangements (FSAs), including Dependent Care FSAs (DCFSA) and Health Care FSAs (HCFSA)

A cafeteria plan cannot include certain types of fringe benefits, which may nevertheless be deductible by the employer and non-taxable to the employee. Some of these additional items are addressed later in this unit under the heading "Other Types of Employee Fringe Benefits."

---

[68] A cafeteria plan is also called a "Section 125 Plan" if it meets the specific requirements of and regulations of section 125 of the Internal Revenue Code.

Nondiscrimination Rules for Cafeteria Plans

If a cafeteria plan favors either "highly compensated employees" (HCEs) or "key employees" as to eligibility to participate, contributions, or benefits, the employer must include in their taxable income the value of taxable benefits they could have selected.

This is intended to discourage employers from offering tax-free benefits to their owners or highly compensated executives while ignoring lower-paid employees. Highly compensated employees are usually limited in the amount of money they can set aside in their 401(k) plans and other retirement plans.

Nondiscrimination testing was put into place to ensure all employees benefit from the company retirement plans and cafeteria plans, not just highly-paid executives. The IRS requires employers to make sure their cafeteria plans do not favor highly compensated employees over the rest of the company's employees.

If a cafeteria plan or a retirement plan fails to pass IRS nondiscrimination testing, highly compensated employees and key employees may lose the tax benefits of participating in the plan. If this happens, then the plans can lose their tax-favored status, and the HCEs or key employees must include the value of these benefits as taxable compensation. These types of "corrections" often take the form of taxable distributions to plan participants.

In order to qualify for tax-favored status, an employee benefit plan or a cafeteria plan must not discriminate in favor of (1) highly compensated employees (HCEs) or (2) key employees.[69]

In 2020, the "key employees" compensation threshold for nondiscrimination testing is normally $185,000 (for officers). However, for employees that own at least one-percent of the employer, the compensation threshold to be considered a key employee is $150,000. Also, a key employee also includes those that more than 5% of the company (regardless of salary). The "highly compensated employees" threshold for nondiscrimination testing is $130,000 in 2020.

"Highly compensated" employees and "key employees" have similar-sounding names, but the rules for defining key employees are slightly different. The compensation salary threshold is lower for HCEs. There could be situations where an employee is identified as an HCE but not a key employee and vice versa. However, it is possible for an employee to be both an HCE and a key employee for the year.

Those who own more than 5% of the company are also considered both highly compensated employees as well as key employees. Therefore, ownership is just as important as salary. For example, even if an employee's salary is $30,000, if the employee owns more than 5% of the company, then that person would still be classified as both an HCE and a key employee by default.

Note: There is no compensation threshold to be an HCE or key employee under the 5% ownership test. That means someone who owns *more than* 5% of the business is automatically classified as an HCE or key employee, even if that person does not draw a salary or draws only a nominal salary.

[69] Highly compensated employees and key employees are described in IRC Section 125(e)(1) and IRC Sect 416(i).

Example: Quincy and Margot are cousins. They are equal shareholders (50/50) of Aquitaine Vineyards, Inc. The business has 40 other employees that are unrelated to Quincy and Margot. Quincy works full-time in the business and is paid a $199,000 salary. Quincy is classified as an HCE and key employee. Margot also works in the business, but only a few hours a week. She is only paid $27,400 for the year. Despite the relatively small amount of wages during the year, Margot is also an HCE and key employee by default, because she owns more than 5% of the company's stock. This means that Aquitaine Vineyards, Inc. cannot set up a benefit plan that discriminates in favor of Margot or Quincy, the owners of the company.

With small businesses, key employees and highly compensated employees will often overlap. But with large corporations, the two will not necessarily be the same.

Example: Fergus is the vice-president of Grainger Insulation, Inc., a nationwide manufacturing firm. Grainger Insulation is a large company with hundreds of employees. Fergus is a corporate officer, but he is not an owner of the company. His salary is $226,000 in 2020, and was $198,000 in the previous year. Because of his high salary, Fergus is classified as a "key employee," despite the fact that he does not have an ownership stake in the company.

The IRS uses a process called "family attribution" in order to make the determination of who qualifies as either an HCE or a key employee, which means that an employee can be determined to be an HCE or key employee merely by familial relationship. An employee who is a spouse, child, grandparent, or parent of someone who is a greater-than 5% owner of the business, is also *automatically* considered an owner under the family attribution rules. In this case, family members include the spouse, parents, children, and grandparents. "Family members" for this purpose do not include grandchildren, siblings, aunts, uncles, or in-laws.

Example: Harvey and Nathalie are husband and wife. They are each 50% owners of Health Information Systems, Inc. an S corporation. The company has 40 employees and offers a cafeteria plan. Harvey earns a salary of $186,000 a year. Nathalie only works sporadically in the business and earns only $48,000 during the year. Nathalie's uncle, Morton, works full-time for the company, earning $62,900 during the year. Morton is not an owner. Both Harvey and Natalie are automatically considered "Highly Compensated Employees" as well as key employees regardless of their compensation, because they own more than 5% of the company's stock. However, Morton is not considered an HCE or a key employee, because his salary is under the threshold amounts, he is not an owner of the company, and "uncles" are not considered close family members under the family attribution rules.

HCEs hired in the middle of the year will not receive HCE status until the start of the *following* year when they are eligible to collect the entirety of their salary. For example, an HCE hired in April 2020 does not qualify as an HCE until January 1, 2021, regardless of their salary level.

Note: The main difference between "Key Employees" and HCEs is that HCEs can be any employee that earns more than a certain dollar amount in the prior year. An HCE can also be a family member of one of the owners, even without any compensation. All other employees are referred to as "non-key" employees.

A plan is considered to have improperly "favored" HCEs and key employees if more than 25% of all the benefits are given to those highly-paid employees. If a cafeteria plan fails discrimination testing, then the highly compensated employees and key employees will lose the favorable tax treatment for all their benefits. Non-key employees, however, are not affected.

Example: McCarthy Construction, Inc. sponsors a cafeteria plan. The company has 200 employees, including 20 executives which are considered highly compensated employees. During the year, the president of McCarthy Construction decides to change their cafeteria plan and only offer their health care FSA to the executives, excluding all the lower-paid workers. A health care FSA cannot discriminate in favor of highly-compensated employees (HCEs) as to eligibility to participate. Therefore, the company's plan fails discrimination testing. Unless corrections are made, all the health benefits offered to the executives will become taxable to them as wages.

Types of Allowable Fringe Benefits

Accident and Health Benefits: Nontaxable accident or health benefits may include the following:

- Accident or health insurance, including long-term care insurance. This would also include employer contributions to a separate trust or fund that directly or through insurance provides accident or health benefits,
- Flexible spending accounts (FSAs) or health savings accounts (HSAs)

Adoption Assistance Programs: An adoption assistance program provides payments or reimbursements for qualifying expenses related to adopting a child, with up to $14,300 excludable in 2020.

Group Term Life Insurance: Group-term life insurance is a nontaxable fringe benefit, but only up to a certain amount. The cost of the first $50,000 of group-term life insurance coverage a company pays on behalf of an employee is excludable from the employee's taxable income. If the company pays for more than $50,000 of coverage, the excess benefit must be included in the employee's taxable income.

Some employers only pay for the first $50,000 of group-term life insurance coverage and then offer *additional* coverage at the employee's expense. If the *employee* pays for the additional life insurance coverage after $50,000, the amounts that the employee pays are not counted as taxable income to the employee.

Group term life insurance on an employee's dependents can be offered as a *de minimis* fringe benefit if the coverage offered is $2,000 or less. If the dependent or spousal life insurance benefit is greater than $2,000, then the Fair Market Value of the entire benefit must be included in the employee's income.

Example: Walsh Timber Company is a corporation with 45 employees. Walsh Timber offers group term life insurance coverage to every employee as a fringe benefit. Employees are allowed up to $75,000 of personal life insurance coverage, as well as $2,000 of spousal coverage. Since the first $50,000 in coverage on the employee can be excluded, only the value of $25,000 of life insurance coverage on the employee is taxable. The $2,000 of spousal life insurance coverage is excludable from the employee's taxable income.

Health Savings Accounts (HSAs)

An HSA is a type of health savings account that is owned by the company's employee. This means that the employee has control over the funds, and any contributions an employer makes to an HSA become the employee's property and cannot be withdrawn by the employer. Contributions to an HSA are typically used to pay current or future medical expenses of the account owner, his spouse, and any qualified dependent. The medical expenses must not be reimbursable by insurance or other sources.

Although an employee may withdraw from their HSA at any time (and for any reason), if the amounts withdrawn are not used for qualifying medical expenses, there will be a 20% penalty. This penalty applies if the taxpayer uses the HSA funds for non-medical expenses before age 65. Once the taxpayer turns 65, they may use the HSA withdrawals for non-medical expenses without facing the 20% penalty, but they will still owe income taxes on the amount.

Example: Brandon is 40 and single. He has an HSA through his employer. In 2020, he saves $2,000 in his HSA. He withdraws the entire amount on December 31, 2020. During the year, Brandon incurs $1,200 in qualifying medical expenses from a dental procedure. Since he only has $1,200 in qualifying expenses, but he withdrew $2,000 from his HSA, he will owe a 20% penalty on $800 ($2,000 - $1,200), plus additional income tax on the amount withdrawn.

In order to qualify for an HSA, the employee must be covered by a high-deductible health plan (HDHP) at work. A self-employed taxpayer is also eligible to have an HSA account.

Note: An FSA and an HSA are not the same thing! Flexible spending accounts (FSA) and health savings accounts (HSA) are both fringe benefits that can reduce an employee's income tax liability. However, an HSA is always paired with a high-deductible health plan, and the funds in an HSA are immediately vested, meaning, that the HSA funds belong to the *employee*, not the employer. An HSA is also "portable." It stays with the employee if they change employers or leave the workforce.

No contributions can be made to an individual's HSA after he becomes enrolled in Medicare. Any excess contributions to an HSA are subject to a 6% penalty tax unless corrected by the deadline (generally the HSA owner's filing due date, plus extensions).

Example: Hillary, who is single with no dependents, has always participated in an HSA offered by her employer. Hillary turns age 65 on January 10, 2020, and promptly enrolls in Medicare. She ceases to be an eligible individual for HSA purposes when she becomes enrolled in Medicare. Therefore, she is no longer eligible to participate in the HSA. Hillary is unaware of this rule, so she accidentally contributes $3,000 to her HSA in 2020, meaning to use the amounts for medical expenses later in the year. Hillary must withdraw the excess HSA contribution before the due date of her tax return, or she will be subject to an excise tax of 6%.

An employer's contribution amount to an employee's HSA must be comparable for all employees who have comparable coverage during the same period, or there will be an excise tax equal to 35% of the amount the employer contributed to all employees' HSAs (i.e., the plan cannot discriminate *in favor* of highly compensated employees).

However, an employer is allowed to make *larger* HSA contributions for a non-highly compensated employee than for a highly compensated employee (i.e., the plan may discriminate *against* highly compensated employees).

2020 Plan Limits for HSAs and High-Deductible Health Plans	
HSA contribution limit (employer + employee)	Self-only: $3,550 Family: $7,100
HSA catch-up contributions (age 55 or older) *	$1,000
HDHP minimum deductibles	Self-only: $1,400, Family: $2,800
HDHP maximum out-of-pocket amounts (this amount includes deductibles, co-payments and other amounts, but *not* insurance premiums)	Self-only: $6,900, Family: $13,800
* Catch-up contributions of $1,000 for qualified individuals can be made any time during the year in which the HSA participant turns 55.	

Flexible Spending Arrangements (FSA)

An FSA is a form of cafeteria plan benefit that reimburses employees for expenses incurred for certain qualified benefits. Through the use of FSAs, participants can pay their out-of-pocket costs using pre-tax dollars. The employee must substantiate the expenses, and the distributions from the FSA to the employee are tax-free.

There are several different types of Flexible Spending Accounts, but the most common are dependent care FSAs (DCFSA), and health care FSAs (HCFSA).

Dependent Care FSA: A Dependent Care FSA is limited to $5,000 per calendar year, per family ($2,500 if MFS). The FSA must be provided for a qualifying person's care to allow the employee to work. The exclusion cannot exceed the smaller of the earned income of either the employee or, if married, the employee's spouse. DCFSA funds are tax-free if the amounts are used for qualifying daycare expenses. A "qualifying dependent" is generally a child under age 13 (although the CAA-2021 increased this age limit to 14 for 2020 only), a disabled spouse, or a dependent parent in eldercare.

Health Care FSA: Health FSAs are commonly funded by employees through voluntary salary reduction contributions, and employers may also contribute. Contributions to an FSA are not includible in the employee's wages, and reimbursements from an FSA that are used to pay qualified medical expenses are not taxed. For tax year 2020, the contribution limit for health flexible spending accounts (FSAs) is $2,750.

An FSA generally cannot provide a cumulative benefit to the employee beyond the plan year. FSAs are sometimes referred to as having a "use-it-or-lose-it" rule. Employers may allow plan participants to carry over up to $550[70] of their unused health FSA balances remaining at the end of a plan year. Or, a company may also choose to allow an employee a grace period of up to two-and-a-half months from the end of the plan year to use his balance. At the end of the grace period, all unspent funds would be forfeited back to the employer.

[70] Per IRS Notice 2020-33, employers have the option to allow employees to carryover $550 for the end of the 2020 plan year (assuming the employer chooses *not* to implement the CAA-2021 carryover changes, which are optional).

Example: Yetta has a Flexible Spending Account at work. At the end of 2020, she still has $350 in her FSA. Her company allows a grace period of two-and-a-half months to use the funds, so Yetta goes to her eye doctor and purchases a new set of eyeglasses on January 15, 2021. She spends $350 on the eyeglasses, so her funds will not be forfeited. She submits the optometrist's receipt to her benefits department and gets a full reimbursement. The reimbursement is tax-free.

Note: An FSA cannot have *both* a carryover and a grace period: it can have one or the other or neither. This option is solely at the employer's discretion. However, for tax year 2020 and 2021, the Consolidated Appropriations Act (CAA) of 2021 eliminates the health FSA carryover limit, allowing employees to carry over any unused amounts from the 2020 or 2021 plan year to the next plan year, and also permits dependent care FSA carryovers for those years. These changes are optional, and employers may choose **not** to implement them. If an employer does choose to implement a change, employees must be notified as soon as the employer decides to adopt any of these temporary changes. Also, dependent care FSAs will generally allow DCFSA funds to be used for daycare for children up to age 13. For tax year 2020, the age limit was temporarily raised to up to age 14. In 2021, an employee who is a participant in the FSA may receive reimbursement for a child up to age 14 if they had unused funds remaining in their 2020 dependent care FSA account.

Qualified Small Employer Health Reimbursement Arrangements

The 21st Century Cures Act (Cures Act) provides a method for small employers to reimburse individual health coverage premiums up to a dollar limit through a "Qualified Small Employer Health Reimbursement Arrangement" (QSEHRA).

A QSEHRA is not a group health plan. Employers with fewer than 50 full-time employees that do not offer a group health plan are able to offer a QSEHRA. A QSEHRA can only be funded by the employer, and no employee contributions are permitted. The arrangement provides for reimbursement of the medical expenses incurred by the employee or the employee's family members. The employee's coverage does not need to be provided by the employer.

In 2020, the maximum amount of payments and reimbursements cannot exceed $5,250 for self-only coverage or $10,600 for family coverage. Employers are permitted to set a lower QSEHRA limit, as long as the limit is consistent for all eligible employees.

Example: Successful Sports, LLC is a retail sports memorabilia shop. The business has 15 full-time employees. Rather than offering a group health plan, the business owners decide to set up a QSEHRA, and offer to reimburse the employee's out-of-pocket health insurance premiums instead. Successful Sports selects a flat, $400 monthly reimbursement amount for all the employees, and limits the reimbursement to health insurance premiums. The reimbursements are deductible by Successful Sports as a business expense, and not taxable to the employees.

Working Condition Fringe Benefits

This exclusion from wages applies to property and services an employer provides so that the employee can perform his job. There are many different types of "working condition" fringe benefits that are deductible to the employer and not taxable to the employee.

Example: Heaton is employed as a CPA. His accounting firm provides all the CPAs with a yearly subscription to an accounting trade journal. The subscription's cost is not included in Heaton's income, and fully deductible by his employer as a business expense.

A common working condition benefit is an employee's use of a company car for business purposes. A company car may be partially taxable if the employee uses it for commuting or other personal use. However, there is an exception for "qualified nonpersonal-use" vehicles. These are vehicles that an employee is unlikely to use more than minimally for personal purposes because of its design. Examples include fire trucks, police cars, hearses, school buses, cement mixers, and tractors.

Example: Officer Samuel Jones is a police officer in a small town. Each officer in the district has an assigned car. Officer Jones is required to take his police car home. In the case of an emergency, he uses the car to respond to the scene and support his department. The police car is clearly marked as a police vehicle. Therefore, Officer Samuel's limited personal use of the vehicle is not a taxable benefit.

Note: Any vehicle designed to carry cargo of over 14,000 pounds is automatically qualified as a "nonpersonal-use" vehicle. Pickup trucks and vans of 14,000 pounds or less are also considered qualified nonpersonal vehicles if they have been specially modified for business purposes and are likely to be used only minimally for personal purposes. Modifications include being marked with permanent decals or painted with advertising logos and being fitted with certain equipment specific to the business. An example of this would be a modified utility van used by an electrician. Even if the van does not meet the 14,000-pound requirement, if the van has been modified specifically to carry specific electrical tools and equipment, then it may be considered a nonpersonal-use vehicle.

An employer-provided cell phone is another common working condition benefit. There must be a substantial business reason to provide the employee a cell phone; it cannot simply be used to boost an employee's morale, to attract a prospective worker, or as a means of providing additional compensation to an employee.

Example: Janelle is an executive for TrenchCoat Media, Inc., an advertising firm in New York. Janelle frequently visits clients at their business locations. She uses her employer-paid cell phone to keep in touch with clients and her employer while she is out of her office. Her company-provided cell phone is a non-taxable fringe benefit.

Accountable Plans

A business can reimburse employees for business-related expenses on a tax-free basis. The requirements of an accountable plan are applied on an employee-by-employee basis. There are two types of reimbursement plans:

- **Accountable Plans**: Amounts paid under an accountable plan are deductible by the employer, but they are not taxable wages and are not subject to income tax withholding or payment of Social Security, Medicare, and FUTA taxes.
- **Nonaccountable Plans**: Amounts paid under a nonaccountable plan are taxable to employees as wages and are subject to all employment taxes and withholding. Generally, there are no substantiation requirements for a nonaccountable plan.

For expenses to qualify under an accountable plan, the employee must follow strict guidelines in order to have the expenses reimbursed. An accountable plan requires employees to:

- Have incurred the expenses while performing services as employees.
- Adequately account for the expenses within a reasonable period of time.
- Provide documentary evidence of travel, mileage, and other employee business expenses.
- Return any excess reimbursement or allowance to the employer within a reasonable period of time, if paid in advance. A cash advance must be reasonably calculated to equal the anticipated expense, and the employer must make the advance within a reasonable period of time.

If the reimbursement policy does not meet all criteria for an accountable plan, then the reimbursements become taxable to the employee as wages.

Example: Brigitta is a loan agent who goes to various locations to sign mortgage paperwork. In April, Brigitta's employer gives her a $1,000 advance to cover her flight, hotel, and transportation on a business trip to Alaska to close a large commercial loan. Brigitta spends $940 on her travel expenses during the trip. When she returns, she submits her receipts to substantiate the expenses. She also pays back the excess advance to her employer. She has met the requirements of an accountable plan, and the advanced funds are not included in her taxable wages.

Example: Lenore is a full-time employee for Abacus Technology, Inc. She takes two potential clients out to dinner and pays for the meal. She keeps track of her business mileage on a spreadsheet. The following week, Lenore submits her receipts to Abacus Technology for reimbursement. Abacus Technology reimburses Lenore for the out-of-pocket expenses she incurred. This arrangement is considered an accountable plan. The reimbursement is not taxable to Lenore and is deductible by her employer, Abacus Technology, as a regular business expense (subject to the 50% limitation on deductibility of meal costs).

Example: Electra is a sales representative who works for Soma Pharmaceuticals, Inc. Electra uses her own vehicle to travel to doctor's offices and hospitals while making sales calls. Soma Pharmaceuticals gives Electra a $500 auto allowance per month ($6,000 total for the year) to cover her automobile expenses. Electra does not have to provide any proof of her expenses to her employer. Electra is being reimbursed under a nonaccountable plan. Her employer must include the $6,000 on Electra's Form W-2 as if it were wages.

Other Types of Employee Fringe Benefits

Special rules allow employers to grant "employee achievement awards" that are excludable from an employee's wages if the awards are tangible personal property (i.e., the awards cannot be made in cash or gift cards, or any cash equivalents), subject to certain deduction limits. Employers may generally exclude the value of awards given for length of service or safety achievement.

"Qualified plan awards" are employee achievement awards under a written plan that does not discriminate in favor of highly compensated employees. In addition, the TCJA clarified that for the purposes of employee awards, "tangible personal property" doesn't include: cash, cash equivalents, gift cards, gift coupons, certain gift certificates, tickets to theater or sporting events, vacations, meals, lodging, stocks, bonds, securities, and other similar items. An employer's deduction and the tax-free amount for each employee are limited each year to the following:

- $400 for awards that are not "qualified plan" awards.
- $1,600 for all awards, if an employee receives both qualified and non-qualified awards during the year.

Example: White Mountain Lumber Company gives a set of golf clubs to a highly-paid executive as an employee award for outstanding sales achievement. The fair market value of the golf clubs is $750. Only the company's top executives are allowed to receive sales awards. Because the sales awards are only available to the highest-paid employees, the award is treated as a "nonqualified plan" award. The amount of the award that must be included in taxable wages to the employee is $350 ($750 - $400). White Mountain Lumber Company can deduct $400 as a business expense. If the award had been available to all the company's employees, then the entire amount would have been deductible as a business expense, and the executive would not have to report any taxable amount.

Example: Sellers Motors, Inc. is an auto manufacturer. Sellers Motors offers each employee a nice silver watch when they reach 10 years of service with the company. All the employees are eligible for length-of-service awards, even the lowest-paid workers. Each watch is worth $650, and the same watch is given to all employees that have been with the company for 10 years. Osmund has worked for Sellers Motors for the required 10 years, and he receives a silver watch in 2020. The watch is not taxable to Osmund, and it is deductible as a business expense to Sellers Motors.

Athletic Facilities: The value of an employee's use of a health club or athletic facilities may be excluded from wages, but only if the facility is on premises that the employer owns or leases. If the employer pays for a gym membership or a fitness program provided to the employee at an off-site location, the value must be included in the employee's compensation.

De Minimis (Minimal) Benefits: An employer may exclude the value of a de minimis benefit provided to an employee from the employee's wages. This is something an employer provides that has so little value that accounting for it would be impractical, such as coffee or doughnuts provided in an employee break room, or occasional personal use of the company photocopier.

Cash and cash equivalent items, such as gift cards or the use of a credit or debit card, are not excludable as de minimis benefits, except for occasional meal money or transportation fare.

Note: The 50% limit on meals now applies to food or beverage expenses excludable from employee income as a de minimis fringe benefit. The meals are still not taxable to the employee, but only 50% deductible by the employer.

Example: Summit Property Management, Inc. employs fifteen full-time employees. The company pays for soda, coffee, and snacks for the employee breakroom. These foods and beverages are considered a de minimis benefit, and not taxable to the employees.

Employer-Provided Educational Assistance

An educational assistance program is a separate written plan that allows an employer to provide educational assistance to employees for the cost of tuition, fees, books, supplies, and equipment. In general, there are two types of tax-free educational assistance:

- **Job-related education** (under IRC section 132) and
- **Non job-related** education (under IRC Sec. 127)

1. Job-related education can be a "working condition benefit" if the education maintains or improves job-related skills needed in the employee's present job. The amounts would be non-taxable to the employee, and fully deductible by the employer if the education:

- Maintains or improves skills required by the individual's current employment, trade or business, or
- Meets the express requirements of the employer, or the requirements of applicable law or regulations, imposed as a condition to the individual's retention of salary, status or employment.

Examples would include: continuing education courses for an enrolled agent or a CPA to maintain their license. Or a notary course for a bookkeeper who is employed at a tax preparation firm.

Example: Judith is a full-time employee of Chessmore Advisory, Inc., an investment advisory firm. With her employer's permission, Judith enrolls in an online program at her local college to earn a certificate in Financial Services Management. The certificate is directly related to her job and will improve her skills as an employee. Judith submits her receipts for her tuition and required textbooks to her employer, totaling $6,200. Chessmore Advisory reimburses the full amount of her educational costs. The amounts are not taxable to Judith and not subject to any limits. Chessmore Advisory may deduct the costs as a regular business expense.

2. Non job-related education is also called an "educational assistance plan" or an "employer educational program" (EAP). In this case, the education does *not* need to be job-related in order to be deductible. However, this type of assistance requires a written plan, it must meet non-discrimination requirements, and the amounts are limited to $5,250 per year. If an employer pays more than $5,250, the excess is taxed as wages to the employee.

An educational assistance plan can cover tuition, fees, and the cost of books, supplies and tools. The cost of meals, lodging, or transportation are not qualifying expenses.

Note: The CARES Act, as extended by the Consolidated Appropriations Act, 2021, allows payments toward an employee's *student loan* as an eligible educational assistance plan expense through tax year 2025. Both federal student loans and private student loans are eligible. The $5,250 annual cap applies to both the student loan repayments as well as other educational assistance.

Tuition Reduction Benefits: An educational organization (such as a college) can exclude the value of a qualified *undergraduate* tuition reduction it provides to an employee, his or her spouse, or a dependent child. A tuition reduction benefit reduces an employee's tuition bill; it does not create a refundable benefit. *Graduate* education only qualifies if it is for the education of a graduate student who performs teaching or research activities for the educational organization.

Example: Meghan is a graduate teaching assistant at the University of Alaska. Meghan is eligible for tuition reduction benefits. Meghan works directly for the college, assisting the professors teach undergraduate courses. Meghan receives a 70% reduction on her tuition and fees. The tuition reduction benefits are not taxable to Meghan, and are applied directly to her tuition bill.

Employee Discounts: Employers can exclude from wages the price reductions they give to employees on services or property they offer to customers in the normal course of business, up to the following limits:

- For a discount on services, 20% of the price charged nonemployee customers for the service.
- For a discount on merchandise or property, the company's gross profit percentage multiplied by the price nonemployee customers pay.

In order to be an excluded benefit, the discount has to be offered to all employees, regardless of compensation. Employee discounts do not apply to discounts on real property or discounts on investment property, (such as company stock).

Example: Surat Clothiers is a clothing boutique that sells fine men's suits. The business offers all their employees a 20% discount on all the clothing in the store. The employee discount is an excludable benefit and is not taxable to the employees.

Employee Stock Options

A corporation may grant stock options to its employees, as compensation for past service or an incentive for retention. An "employee stock option" is a type of taxable fringe benefit that allows the employee the legal right to buy a certain amount of company shares at a predetermined price for a specific period of time.

If an employee receives stock options, he may have income when the options are granted, when he exercises them (to buy the company's stock), or when he sells or otherwise disposes of the options or the stock. The nature, timing, and amount of the employee's taxable income and the employer's deduction for compensation expense depend on whether the options are considered to be statutory or nonstatutory options. There are two types of statutory stock options:

- **Incentive stock options (ISOs):** ISOs allow employees to purchase stock at a pre-established price (exercise price) that may be below the market price on the date of exercise.
- **ESPPs:** These are options granted under employee stock purchase plans (ESPPs). A stock purchase plan enables employees to purchase their own company's common stock, often at a discount from the regular market price.

The tax advantage of a statutory stock option for the employee is that income is not reported when the option is granted or when it is exercised. However, the drawback is that a corporation cannot take a deduction for compensation expenses when it issues a stock option to an employee.

The employee must report income only when he ultimately sells the stock. If he satisfies certain holding period requirements, the income is treated as capital gain. If not, it is treated as ordinary income, and the employer is entitled to a compensation deduction at that time.

Nonstatutory or "nonqualified" stock options (NSOs) also allow employees to purchase stock at a pre-established exercise price. The employee must recognize compensation income, typically on the exercise date of the option, and the employer is entitled to a corresponding compensation expense deduction at the same time.

Meals and Lodging for Employees

Meals and lodging may be provided tax-free to an employee, but the expense must be directly related to or associated with the business or have a legitimate business purpose. An employer may exclude from taxable wages the value of meals and lodging it provides to employees if they are provided:

- On the employer's business premises, such as in an employer's cafeteria, and/or
- For the employer's convenience.

Under the TCJA, meals provided to an employee by the employer (for example, food and beverages provided at no charge through a cafeteria operated by the employer) on the employer's property are not taxable to the employee, but the employer only receives a 50% deduction.

Example: Sacred Heart Hospital provides all its full-time hospital workers one free meal in the hospital cafeteria during their shift. The cost of running the hospital cafeteria is deductible by the employer, but the meals are subject to the 50% limit. The meal benefit is not taxable to the employees.

Situations in which meals may be provided tax-free to employees for the convenience of the employer on the employer's business premises include the following:

- Safety workers such as police officers, firefighters, and other emergency personnel need to be on call for emergencies during the meal period,
- The nature of the business requires short meal periods,
- Eating facilities are not available in areas near the workplace,
- Meals are furnished to all employees on a regular basis, as long as meals are furnished to more than half of the employees for the convenience of the employer,
- Meals are furnished immediately after working hours because the employee's duties prevented him from obtaining a meal during working hours.

Employer-provided lodging is generally 100% deductible by the employer and not taxable to the employee. Lodging can be provided to the employee, the employee's spouse, and the employee's dependents, and still not be taxable. However, for lodging, there is an additional rule: it must be required as a condition of employment. The exclusion from taxation does not apply if the employee can choose to receive additional pay or a cash allowance *instead* of free lodging.

Example: Alaskan Drilling, Inc. employs several employees at a remote drilling site. Due to the inaccessibility of facilities for the employees who are working at the job site to obtain lodging and the prevailing weather conditions, Alaskan Drilling furnishes lodging to all its employees at the site in order to carry on the drilling project. The company may exclude the value of the lodging that it provides to its employees from their wages. The costs associated with the lodging facilities would be fully deductible by the company.

Moving Expense Reimbursements

Under the TCJA, moving expenses are no longer deductible as a business expense. Employers who reimburse employees for their moving expenses must now include the moving expense reimbursements in employees' wages, subject to income and employment taxes.[71] This is true even if the expenses are substantiated and reimbursed under an accountable plan.

Example: Bright Star Estates wants to hire Dustin to lead its new marketing department. Dustin lives in another state, and only agrees to accept the position if Bright Star pays for all his moving expenses. The company agrees to pay Dustin's moving expenses as a condition of his employment contract. Dustin incurs $7,000 in moving expenses, consisting of $6,000 for moving his household goods, $800 for airfare at the time of the move, and $200 in meals while he is in transit. The employer reimburses Dustin for all these expenses. Bright Star must include the entire reimbursement as wages on Dustin's Form W-2. The amounts are deductible to Bright Star, but the entire amount is subject to payroll tax and income tax withholding, just like any other wage expense.

No-Additional-Cost Services

An employer can exclude from an employee's taxable income the value of a service provided to the employee if it does not create a substantial additional cost for the business.

Typically, no-additional-cost services are excess capacity services, such as airline, bus, or train tickets; hotel rooms; or telephone services provided free or at a reduced price to employees working in those lines of business. The exclusion for a no-additional-cost service applies whether the service is provided at no charge or at a reduced price.

Example: Pablo works as a full-time personal trainer for Gorilla Gym. Since Pablo is an employee, Gorilla Gym offers Pablo a free gym membership and an employee discount at their apparel store inside the gym. These benefits would be tax-free to Pablo because they do not create any substantial additional costs for Gorilla Gym.

Example: Gretel works as a flight attendant for Northbound Airlines. The airline allows all its current employees to fly for free by using a standby travel program. When a regularly scheduled flight has empty seats, airline employees are allowed to fly at no charge. Gretel flies for free to Cancun, Mexico. The value of the airline ticket may be excluded from her wages.

Services that are not eligible for treatment as no-additional-cost services are non-excess capacity services, such as the facilitation by a stock brokerage firm of the purchase of stock by employees,

[71] Members of the U.S. Armed Forces can still exclude qualified moving expense reimbursements from their income.

but these services may be eligible for a qualified employee discount of up to 20% of the value of the service provided.

Employee Transportation Benefits

The Tax Cuts and Jobs Act eliminated the employer's deduction for employee transportation fringe benefits (parking benefits and mass transit). Although the deduction is not allowed to employers, the exclusion from income for employees continues. In other words, a company can still offer tax-free transportation and parking benefits to its employees, but the company cannot deduct the expense.[72] In 2020, employees can exclude the following amounts (but an employer cannot deduct them):

- $270 per month in combined commuter highway vehicle transportation and transit passes, and
- $270 per month in parking benefits. Employees can receive both transit passes and parking benefits during the same month; they are not mutually exclusive.

Example: Paramount Brokers is a professional brokerage firm in Los Angeles, CA. As a condition of employment, all employees are offered free transit passes, which are valued at $270 per month. The transit passes are not taxable to the employee. However, Paramount Brokers cannot deduct the cost of the transit passes as a business expense.

Qualified transportation benefits include transit passes, qualified parking, rides in a commuter highway vehicle between the employee's home and workplace, but NOT bicycle commuting reimbursements. The TCJA repealed the provision of bicycle commuting benefits through December 31, 2025. So, if a company offers bicycle commuting reimbursement to its employees, the amount is taxable to the employee as wages.

Use of Employer-Provided Vehicles

If an employer allows an employee to use a company vehicle for commuting or other personal use, the value of the vehicle's use is generally taxable to the employee. There is an exception for situations in which the employer is ensuring the employee's safety, or when the employee is required to use a company vehicle for commuting because the employee works in a public safety profession.

Example: Connolly is a bus driver for Smallville Elementary School. Connolly is required to use the school bus during work hours, including his lunch breaks, because sometimes he is required to pick up and drop off sick students during the day. Connolly takes the bus to the sandwich shop during his scheduled lunch hour, as required by his employer. Connolly's minimal personal use of the vehicle is not considered a taxable benefit.

Example: Brentwood City has a pickup truck that is marked with the town's name. The pick-up is not a police, fire, or public safety vehicle. A city employee is allowed to take the pick-up home because he is "on-call" during the weekends. The vehicle is not a qualified nonpersonal use vehicle; thus, the commuting is a non-cash taxable fringe benefit.

[72] An exception exists for reimbursements for transportation fringe benefits when the transportation benefits are necessary to ensure the safety of the employee.

Affordable Care Act for Employers (ACA)

The Affordable Care Act mandates that certain employers provide health insurance for full-time workers. All employers that are ALEs (or "applicable large employers") are subject to the employer-shared responsibility provisions. This includes for-profit entities, most nonprofit organizations, and government entities. The IRS commonly uses these acronyms:

- **ACA:** Affordable Care Act
- **ALE:** Applicable Large Employer: an employer with 50 full-time employees (or a combination of full-time and part-time employees that is the hourly equivalent to 50 full-time employees).
- **FTE:** Full-time employee
- **MEC:** Minimum Essential Coverage

Note: The ACA employer provisions remain in full effect for 2020. Only the individual mandate was repealed by the TCJA. The employer penalty has been increased to $2,570 in 2020 per full-time employee for Applicable Large Employers who do not offer minimum essential coverage to their employees. An ALE will also face additional penalties if one or more full-time employees obtain a subsidy through the Marketplace. Unlike the *individual* shared responsibility payment, the *employer* shared responsibility penalty is subject to IRS lien and levy enforcement actions.

Employers with 50 or more employees are subject to the "Employer Shared Responsibility" provisions. In other words, the Affordable Care Act[73] penalizes employers with a monetary penalty if the employer does not offer coverage which meets minimum value and affordability standards.

For ACA purposes, a "full-time employee" is an individual employed on average at least 30 hours per week, or at least 130 hours in a calendar month. An employer that meets the 50 full-time employee threshold is referred to as an "Applicable Large Employer" or ALE. Employers with fewer than 50 full-time employees are not subject to the Affordable Care Act's employer shared responsibility provision.

The general rule is that if an employer offers group health coverage to any full-time employees, the employer must offer coverage to *all* full-time employees.[74] The employer has the option to offer coverage to part-time employees, but is not required to do so. If an employer offers coverage to any part-time employees, then *all* the part-time employees must be offered the same coverage. Employers must treat all employees who average 30 hours a week as full-time employees.

The ACA "employer mandate" is a requirement that all businesses with 50 or more full-time equivalent employees (FTE) offer and/or provide health insurance to at least 95% of their full-time employees and dependents up to age 26. "Dependents" include children up to age 26, excluding stepchildren and foster children. If the employer does not offer health coverage, and is required to, the company may be subject to penalties. These penalties are officially referred to

---

[73] IRC section 6056 requires all applicable large employers to file an annual report that ensures compliance with the employer mandate.

[74] An employer may exclude employees who are covered by TRICARE or certain health programs for veterans.

as "Employer Shared Responsibility Payments." There are **two types** of ACA penalties that apply to large employers:

4980H(a) Penalty: Failure to Offer Minimum Essential Coverage: This is the penalty for NOT OFFERING health insurance. An employer may be liable for this penalty if they are classified as an applicable large employer and do not offer minimum essential coverage to at least 95% of their full-time employees (and their dependents) and at least one employee receives the Premium Tax Credit. For calendar year 2020, the penalty amount is $2,570 for each full-time employee (without regard to whether each employee received a Premium Tax Credit), after excluding the first 30 full-time employees from the calculation.

4980H(b) Penalty: Failure to Offer Coverage that Provides Minimum Value: An ALE may be liable for this penalty if the employer DOES offer health insurance, but at least one full-time employee receives the Premium Tax Credit because that coverage is not affordable to the employee, doesn't provide minimum value, or that employee did not receive an offer of coverage. This penalty is based *solely* on the number of full-time employees who receive the Premium Tax Credit. The penalty in 2020 is $3,860 for each full-time employee who received the Premium Tax Credit. To be liable for the 4980H(b) penalty, at least one of the employers' full-time employees must receive a Premium Tax Credit.

Minimum Essential Coverage

For ACA purposes, an employer health plan meets the "minimum value" standard if both of the following apply:

- The insurance is designed to pay at least 60% of the total cost of medical services,
- The insurance benefits include substantial coverage of physician and inpatient hospital services.

Employers may not impose enrollment waiting periods that exceed 90 days for health plans. Employers are not required to offer dental or vision coverage, although they can voluntarily do so, if they wish. If the employer *offers* health coverage, and the employee subsequently *declines* the coverage, then the employer will not be subject to an ACA penalty. In other words, the ACA does not penalize an employer for employees who decline an offer of coverage.

Example: Pearland Mortgage Company has 650 full-time employees. Pearland offers health coverage to all of its full-time employees and their dependents. The coverage offers minimum value. Only 540 of Pearland's employees actually enroll in coverage. The rest of the company's employees decline the coverage. The company is compliant with ACA provisions.

Remember, the ACA employer responsibility provisions only apply to employers with at least 50 or more full-time employees. Small employers with 49 (or fewer) employees are not subject to the ACA mandate. However, small employers, generally those with fewer than 50 full-time employees, may be eligible for credits and other benefits. This includes the Small Business Health Care Tax Credit to help employers cover the cost of providing coverage.

Unit 5: Study Questions

(Test yourself and then check the correct answers at the end of this section.)

1. Zenith Advisors, LLC provides the following benefits to its employees. Which of these is fully taxable to the employee?

A. Qualified group term life insurance of $50,000.
B. Educational assistance program of up to $5,250.
C. Membership at a local fitness club with an annual value of $500.
D. Free transit passes costing $200.

2. If an employer offers moving expense reimbursements as an enticement for new employees, how should these reimbursements be treated, for tax purposes?

A. Moving expense reimbursements are disallowed in all circumstances.
B. Moving expense reimbursements are taxable to the employee as "other income" and nondeductible by the employer.
C. Moving expense reimbursements are nontaxable to the employee and deductible by the employer.
D. Moving expense reimbursements are taxable as wages to the employee, and deductible to the employer.

3. All of the following are fringe benefits that may be excluded from an employee's pay except:

A. Dependent care assistance.
B. $25 gift card for the holidays.
C. Cafeteria plan.
D. Adoption assistance benefits.

4. Heart Ambulance Services provides meals and lodging for ten paramedics at the workplace as a condition of employment because they are not allowed to leave the premises when they are on a shift. The employees eat and sleep on the premises for free. Which of the following statements is correct?

A. All the costs of meals and lodging can be excluded from the employees' wages and deductible as an expense by the employer.
B. The meals and lodging are not taxable to the employee. The employer can deduct 50% of the meal expense, and 100% of the lodging.
C. The meals and lodging are taxable to the employees and deductible by the employer. The employee may then deduct the costs as employee business expenses.
D. The meals and lodging can be deducted by both the employees and the employer as business expenses.

5. All of the following are excludable from an employee's wages and deductible by the employer *except*:

A. A non-cash employee achievement award valued at $300.
B. Occasional snacks provided by the employer in the employee break room.
C. Employer-provided vehicles that employees use for commuting purposes.
D. Meals furnished during work hours for the convenience of the employer.

6. Renee is a full-time employee of Right Angles Engineering, which offers its employees reimbursement through an education assistance program (EAP). In 2020, she takes graduate accounting courses and has $5,900 of tuition expenses and $300 of expenses for required books. Right Angles reimburses Renee for all the expenses. How should this reimbursement be treated?

A. All of the amounts are excluded from Renee's income, and the amounts are deductible by Right Angles as a qualified fringe benefit.
B. The first $5,250 of the educational expenses is excluded from Renee's wages as a qualified fringe benefit, and the remaining amount is taxable as wage income to her.
C. Only $5,900 (the tuition costs) of the educational expenses are excluded from Renee's wages as a qualified fringe benefit, and the remaining amount is taxable as wage income to her.
D. All of the reimbursement is taxable as wages to Renee because graduate courses do not qualify for reimbursement under a fringe benefit plan.

7. Superior Foods, Inc. reimburses employees for their business-related expenses. Which of the following is taxable to the employee?

A. Travel reimbursements made under an accountable plan.
B. Transit pass valued at $265 per month.
C. Travel reimbursements using the federal per diem rate.
D. Qualified bicycle commuting reimbursement of $20 per month.

8. Which of the following benefits must be included in an employee's income?

A. Childcare reimbursed under a qualified flexible spending plan.
B. Employee discounts on products.
C. A holiday gift of a $50 gas card.
D. A holiday gift of a $25 canned ham.

9. The ACA "employer mandate" applies to businesses with _______ full-time equivalent employees.

A. 25 or more.
B. 30 or more.
C. 50 or more.
D. 100 or more.

10. Encore Delivery Services is having cash-flow difficulties, so it transfers a pickup truck to Bonnie, an employee, in lieu of wages. The company owes Bonnie $7,000 of wages at the time of the transfer. At the time of the transfer, the truck had a fair market value of $7,000 and an adjusted basis to Encore Delivery of $5,500. How should the company report this transaction?

A. Wage expense of $7,000; loss of $1,500
B. Wage expense of $5,500; no gain or loss.
C. Wage expense of $1,500; no gain or loss.
D. Wage expense of $7,000; gain of $1,500.

Unit 5: Quiz Answers

1. The answer is C. Employer-paid memberships at athletic facilities and country clubs are taxable benefits. The rest of the choices are excludable from an employee's wages. In 2020, the transit passes would be excludable from the employee's wages, but not deductible by the employer as a business expense.

2. The answer is D. Moving expense reimbursements are taxable compensation to the employee, and deductible to the employer as wages. Employers who reimburse employees for their moving expenses must now include the moving expense reimbursements in employees' wages, subject to income and employment taxes. An exception to this rule applies to U.S. servicemembers only.

3. The answer is B. The value of the gift card would always be treated as *cash* and would be taxable to the employee.

4. The answer is B. Heart Ambulance Services may exclude the value of meals and on-site lodging from an employee's wages if they are provided for the convenience of the employer. Meals provided to employees are 50% deductible by the employer, and the cost of the lodging would be 100% deductible.

5. The answer is C. The value of a vehicle for personal use by an employee is a generally taxable benefit. If an employer provides a car for an employee's use, the amount that can be excluded as a working condition benefit is the amount that would be allowed as a deductible business expense if the employee paid for its use. There are exceptions for emergency personnel, such as police officers who are required to use their emergency vehicles. Certain employee achievement awards may be exempt up to $1,600. Meals are exempt if either furnished for the employer's convenience or if considered de minimis, such as occasional snacks.

6. The answer is B. Although all of the expenses are qualified educational expenses, only the first $5,250 is excluded from Renee's wages as a nontaxable fringe benefit, and the remaining amount is taxable as wage income to her. If an employer pays more than $5,250 for educational benefits for an employee during the year, the excess is taxed as wages.

7. The answer is D. A qualified bicycle commuting reimbursement of $20 per month would be a taxable benefit. All of the other choices would be nontaxable to the employee and classified as a fringe benefit.

8. The answer is C. A holiday gift of a $50 gas card would be taxable to the employee. Gifts of cash or cash equivalents such as gift cards must be included in income. Fringe benefits that may be excluded from income include employee discounts, amounts reimbursed through a qualified flexible spending plan, and *de minimis* holiday gifts.

9. The answer is C. The ACA "employer mandate" is a requirement that all businesses with 50 or more full-time equivalent employees (FTE) provide health insurance to at least 95% of their full-time employees and dependents up to age 26.

10. The answer is D. When property is transferred in lieu of wages, the employer is entitled to deduct its fair market value at the time of the transfer. A gain or loss is realized if there is a difference between the fair market value and the adjusted basis of the property. The transfer is treated as a sale, so Encore Delivery Services would have to report a gain. Encore Delivery Services should deduct $7,000 as wage expense and report the gain on the sale of the truck, figured as follows: $7,000 - $5,500 = **$1,500.**

Unit 6: Other Business Deductions & Credits

More Reading:
Instructions for Form 3800, General Business Credit
Publication 334, Tax Guide for Small Business
Publication 535, Business Expenses
Publication 536, Net Operating Losses for Individuals, Estates, and Trusts

In addition to the deductions already covered, businesses can reduce their taxable income through various deductions and business credits, including the new Section 199A Qualified Business Income Deduction. We start with a look at the net operating loss, which can allow a business with losses for the year to recover past tax payments or reduce future tax payments.

Net Operating Losses (NOLs)

A net operating loss (NOL) occurs when a business has tax deductions that exceed its income, resulting in "negative" business income for a tax year. The CARES Act made significant changes to NOLs for the 2020 tax year, as well as prior-year NOLs earned in 2018 and 2019. These changes are not permanent. The CARES Act effectively *delays* the application of the TCJA amendments until January 1, 2021.[75]

- **Five-year carryback:** The CARES Act provides a five-year carryback for losses earned in 2018, 2019, or 2020, which allows most businesses[76] to amend tax returns up to five years prior to offset taxable income. That means an NOL that arises in 2020 can be carried back to 2015. An NOL that arose in 2019 can be carried back to 2014, and so on.
- **Special rule for Farmers:** An exception to the five-year carryback rule for farmers was implemented by the *Consolidated Appropriations Act of 2021* in late December 2020. For **farmers** only, the CAA-2021 allows them to:
    - Carry back a farm NOL five years, or
    - Elect to carry back a farm NOL two years, or
    - Waive the carryback entirely, and carryforward a 2018, 2019, or 2020 NOL.
- **Repeal of the 80%-of-taxable-income limit:** The CARES Act repeals the 80% income limitation for NOL carryovers for 2018, 2019 and 2020. This means that firms may deduct their NOLs to eliminate all of their taxable income in a given year, instead of having to carry forward any NOL beyond 80% of taxable income.
- **Repeal of the excess business loss limitation:** Pass-through business owners may use business losses to offset their non-business income above the previous limit of $250,000 (single) or $500,000 (married filing jointly) for 2018, 2019, and 2020.

[75] At the time of this book's printing, the five-year CARES Act carryback provisions will expire in 2021.
[76] The CARES Act prevents real estate investment trusts (REITs) from carrying back an NOL to any preceding tax year.

NOL Tax Law Changes - 2020		
TCJA/Pre-CARES Act	**CARES Act**	**CAA-2021**
1. NOLs could only be carried forward to succeeding tax years (with the exception of farmers and casualty insurance companies, who were allowed a 2-year carryback). 2. NOL deduction limited to 80% of taxable income.	1. NOLs originating in 2018, 2019, 2020 may be carried back up to 5 preceding tax years. 2. Businesses can take an NOL deduction equal to 100% of taxable income.	1. Farmers may choose to carryback a farm NOL 5 years, or elect a 2-year carryback. 2. Farmers may also elect to forego any carryback and elect to carryforward all their net operating losses.

Under the CARES Act, businesses that carryback their NOLs **must use** the entire five-year carryback period (with the exception of farmers). In other words, a business must carry their losses back to the earliest year in the five-year carryback period. However, businesses that do not wish to carryback an NOL may make an irrevocable election to waive the carryback period for an NOL for any tax year. The elections for tax years 2018, 2019, and 2020 must be made no later than the due date of the 2020 tax return, (including extensions). NOLs can be carried forward indefinitely until the loss is fully recovered.

Partnerships and S corporations generally cannot use NOLs, but their partners and shareholders may have an NOL due to the pass-through business loss; the loss flows through to the partners or shareholders, who may use the losses to offset other income on their individual tax returns. If the taxpayer is self-employed, a net operating loss does not change the amount of self-employment tax to any of the years it is carried forward or carried back to. Also, if the taxpayer owes interest and penalties in a prior year, the NOL carryback will not abate them.

A taxpayer may choose to carryback an NOL by filing an amended tax return, or by filing a special form. A C corporation may apply for a refund by filing Form 1139, *Corporation Application for Tentative Refund.* Individuals, estates, and trusts may apply for a refund by filing Form 1045, *Application for Tentative Refund.*

Note: If a business currently has an NOL carryforward that was generated in a tax year *prior* to 2018, that is being carried forward, the pre-TCJA tax law still applies. So NOLs that arose in tax years *prior* to 2018 will not be subject to any income limitations, and the 2-year carryback and 20-year carryforward rule still applies to those old NOLs.

Example: Wendell operates a farming business as a sole proprietor and files his return on Schedule F. In 2020, he has a net operating loss of $35,000. He had taxable income of $45,000 in the prior year (which was the first year in business). Wendell can carry back his NOL in order to receive a refund of the income tax he paid in the prior year by filing Form 1045. Wendell also owed self-employment taxes and an early withdrawal penalty from an IRA in the prior year, but his farming NOL will not offset his self-employment tax or his early withdrawal penalty. The NOL *only* reduces the income tax liability.

Example: Agri-Feedlot Farms is a qualified farming business. Polly and Janice operate the farm as a 50/50 partnership and share income and losses equally. In 2020, Agri-Feedlot Farms has $30,000 in ordinary business losses. The losses are allocated to the individual partners on Schedule K-1 (Form 1065). In this case, since they have an equal partnership, Polly and Janice will each have $15,000 in partnership losses that they can potentially deduct on their individual returns. Since Agri-Feedlot Farms is a farming business, Polly and Janice may choose to: (1) carry back their losses for five years, (2) carry back their losses for two years or (3) waive the carryback period and carry all their losses forward to future years.

Example: Fresh Growers, Inc. is a qualified farming business that began business operations two years ago. The company had taxable income of $30,000 in 2019. In 2020, business slowed, and Fresh Growers has a net operating loss of $4,000 in 2020. As a farming business, Farm-Fresh is allowed to carryback its net operating loss for 2 prior years or 5 prior years, or waive the carryback period altogether. Rather than deal with filing paperwork or amended returns for such a small loss, Fresh Growers, Inc. decides to waive the NOL carryback and just carry its losses forward. Fresh Growers must attach a statement to its timely-filed return, in order to make an election to forego the carryback.

Example: Vinet Distillery, Inc. is a C Corporation that uses the cash basis of accounting. The company made $200,000 in profits every year for five years. However, the business had a $100,000 net operating loss in 2020. Vinet Distillery, Inc. may carryback its 2020 NOL to 2015 (5 year carryback), which would generate a refund if it had taxable income on its originally filed 2015 tax return. Vinet Distillery files Form 1139 to receive to apply for a refund of taxes from the carryback of their 2020 net operating loss.

Most NOLs are caused by losses in a trade or business, but NOLs can arise from other causes. For an individual, estate, or trust to have an NOL, the loss must be caused by:

- A trade or business that results in an overall loss,
- Casualty or theft losses (personal[77] casualty losses or business-related),
- Losses from rental property,
- Moving expenses,[78]
- Farming losses.

The following items are not allowed when figuring an NOL:

- Capital losses in excess of capital gains.
- The exclusion of gain from the sale of qualified small business stock.
- A net operating loss from another year (a carryback or a carryforward).
- A self-employed taxpayer's contribution to a retirement plan.

Income from other sources may eliminate or reduce a net operating loss for the year. For example, if a taxpayer has income from wages, as well as a loss from a small business, the wage income and the loss will offset taxable income.

[77] Due to the TCJA, only personal casualty losses incurred in a presidentially declared disaster area are deductible.
[78] Due to the TCJA, only moving expenses incurred by U.S. Armed Forces servicemembers are deductible.

Example: Zheng runs an auto detailing business as a sole proprietor. In 2020, he had an ($8,000) loss from his Schedule C business. Zheng files jointly with his wife, Mei. Mei has $23,000 of taxable income from wages. On their jointly filed return, Zheng's business loss is absorbed by Mei's $23,000 of wages, making their joint AGI $15,000 ($23,000 - $8,000 loss). In this scenario, there would be no loss carryover for Zheng.

Section 199A Qualified Business Income Deduction

The Qualified Business Income deduction, (also known as the QBI deduction or 199A deduction), allows a deduction of up to 20% of qualified business income, along with a special 20% deduction for certain investment income. The deduction is available regardless of whether an individual itemizes their deductions on Schedule A or takes the standard deduction.

Note: This deduction is taken "below the line." In other words, it will reduce taxable income but not a taxpayer's adjusted gross income. The section 199A deduction does not reduce self-employment taxes, excise taxes, or penalties. The section 199A deduction is only an income tax deduction. This deduction expires after 2025, unless Congress decides to extend it.

The deduction *only* applies to income from pass-through entities. Sole proprietors, partners in a partnership, members in an LLC, beneficial owners of trusts, estates, and shareholders in S corporations may be eligible for this deduction. Income earned through a C corporation is not eligible for the 199A deduction.

The QBI deduction only applies to *domestic* income, so the deduction is generally available only to U.S. businesses. For businesses with both U.S. and foreign operations, the income must be allocated properly between foreign activity and domestic activity in order to calculate the QBI deduction.

Example: Sirloin Ranch, Inc. is a meat processor that has various slaughtering plants in the United States as well as two locations in Mexico. Although this type of production activity is qualified for QBI deduction, only the U.S.-based production qualifies for the deduction. Sirloin Ranch must allocate its gross receipts and deductions between the factory production in the United States and the production in Mexico to calculate its QBI.

In order to claim the QBI deduction, taxpayers will need to fill out either Form 8995, *Qualified Business Income Deduction Simplified Computation,* or Form 8995-A, *Qualified Business Income Deduction.*

The deduction allows owners of eligible businesses to deduct up to 20% of their qualified business income (QBI),[79] along with a special 20% deduction for certain investment income. Only *taxable* income is counted. The 199A deduction has *two components:*

1. **QBI Component:** This component of the deduction equals 20% of qualifying business income from a domestic business operated as a sole proprietorship, or through a partnership, S corporation, trust, or estate.

[79] Section 199A(g) provides a deduction for agricultural and horticultural cooperatives and their patrons similar to the deduction under the former section 199, which was known as the domestic production activities deduction. A *patron* of a Specified Cooperative could potentially be entitled to two deductions under section 199A. A patron (farmer) may receive a section 199A(a) 20% QBI deduction and a section 199A(g) DPAD deduction in the same year (see Provision 11011 Section 199A - Qualified Business Income Deduction FAQs).

2. **REIT / PTP Component.** This component of the deduction equals 20% of the combined qualified REIT dividends and qualified PTP income (covered later).

Once a taxpayer adds the two components above together, the taxpayer's Section 199A deduction is subject to an overall limit of 20% of taxable income less net capital gain. Net capital gain includes net long-term capital gain and qualified dividend income.

Qualified Business Income

"Qualified Business Income" includes items of income, gain, deduction, and loss from any *domestic* trade or business activity, including rental activities that rise to the level of a trade or business. Qualified items of income, gain, deduction, and loss include:

- Only items effectively connected with the conduct of a trade or business within the United States (including Puerto Rico)[80]
- Only items included or allowed in determining taxable income for the year.

Qualified Business Income, or QBI, does *not* include:

- Employee wages,[81]
- Capital gains,
- Interest and dividend income,
- Hobby income,
- Non-taxable income, (such as muni bond interest)
- Rental income where the owner is not engaged in a bona-fide real estate "trade or business." The rental of real property may constitute a trade or business, even if the rental activity is reported on Schedule E.
- Any guaranteed payment from a partnership for services rendered with respect to the trade or business.
- Reasonable compensation paid to an S corporation shareholder.
- Income earned by a C Corporation

> **Note:** "Material participation" under section 469 is not required for the QBI deduction. Eligible taxpayers with income from a trade or business may be entitled to the QBI deduction regardless of their involvement in the trade or business.

The determination of QBI includes deductions attributable to the trade or business, including, but not limited to, the deductible portion of the self-employment tax, the deduction for self-employed health insurance, and contributions to qualified retirement plans. A qualified business loss results in no QBI deduction for the taxable year.

The QBI loss carries over to subsequent years and reduces the section 199A deduction for QBI for those future years. The section 199A loss carryover is solely for purposes of section 199A computations.

[80] *Overview of Deduction for Qualified Business Income: Section 199A,* the Joint Committee on Taxation, Congress of the United States.

[81] There is an exception for statutory employees. Items of income, gain, deduction, and loss from performance of services as a statutory employee are considered QBI and are eligible for the 199A deduction.

Note: With regards to partnerships and S corporations, the Schedule K-1s for these entities have codes for the QBI deduction items. The entity is responsible for providing each partner or shareholder with their share of QBI items, W-2 wages, UBIA of qualified property, and other information necessary for partners and shareholders to compute their deduction. If the entity fails to provide this information, final regulations provide that QBI will be presumed to be zero.

Safe Harbor Rule for Rental Activities

The IRS provides a safe harbor[82] under which a rental real estate activity will constitute a "trade or business" for the purposes of the QBI deduction. For the taxpayer to qualify for the safe harbor, 250 or more hours of service must be provided per year to each rental real estate enterprise, in any three of the five consecutive taxable years. For the purposes of meeting the safe harbor, taxpayers can treat each rental activity as a stand-alone enterprise or group together similar properties and treat each "grouping" as an enterprise. The safe harbor applies if the following three tests are met:

- The taxpayer maintained separate books and records for each enterprise;
- At least 250 hours of rental services are performed per year by owners, employees, contractors, or agents for the enterprise; and
- The taxpayer maintains sufficient, contemporaneous records, including time reports, logs, or similar documents, regarding the following: hours of all services performed; description of all services performed; dates on which such services were performed; and who performed the services.

If the taxpayer uses the safe harbor, a statement must be attached to their return, stating that the taxpayer is relying on the safe harbor provision. The safe harbor is not required if the rental satisfies the usual tests for a qualified business, including the §162 "active conduct of a trade or business" test.

Note: This safe harbor does not apply to triple-net leases (also called NNN leases), where the tenant pays for property taxes, insurance, and maintenance. In addition, the safe harbor does not apply to properties in which the owner also uses a portion of the property as their personal residence.

REIT Dividends and PTP Income

Eligible taxpayers may also be entitled to a special deduction of up to 20% of their combined qualified real estate investment trust (REIT) dividends and qualified publicly traded partnership (PTP) income. This component is not limited by W-2 wages or the UBIA of qualified property.

The deduction is claimed by individuals, so S corporations and partnerships cannot take the deduction at the entity level. However, all S corporations and partnerships report each shareholder's or partner's share of QBI on Schedule K-1, so the shareholders or partners may determine their deduction.

---

[82] IRS Revenue Procedure 2019-38 provides a safe harbor under which rental real estate activity will be treated as a trade or business for purposes of the QBI deduction.

199A Deduction Limitation Threshold

In general, the 199A deduction is available to eligible taxpayers whose pre-QBI deduction taxable income falls below certain amounts. The 2020 Qualified Business Income (QBI) threshold and phase-in range are as follows:

- **Married filing jointly: $326,600-$426,600**
- **Head of Household/Single: $163,300-$213,300**
- **Married filing Separately: $163,300-$213,300**

When a taxpayer falls below the taxable income threshold, the taxpayer is generally allowed to take the deduction without regard to any limitations that are discussed next.

Example: Felix is unmarried. He operates the Capital City Pawn Shop as a sole proprietorship in Oregon. All of his income is generated in the United States. Felix's shop has $100,000 of qualified business income (QBI) during the taxable year. His pre-QBI deduction taxable income is $130,000, which includes $30,000 in interest income. The interest income would not be qualifying business income. Felix has no long-term capital gains or qualified dividends for the year. Since Felix's taxable income is below the threshold, and he has sufficient pre-QBI taxable income, his tentative section 199A deduction is $20,000 ($100,000 QBI x 20%).

The 199A deduction for taxpayers *above* the taxable income threshold is partially subject to various limitations and may be limited or eliminated altogether. For taxpayers with taxable income that *exceeds* the phase-in range, the deduction is subject to limitations based on:

- **SSTB Limitation:** This limitation is based on the type of trade or business activity, (also called the "Specified Service Trade or Business" or "SSTB" limitation)
- **Wage and Property Limitation:** For a non-SSTB business whose income exceeds the phaseout ranges, the 20% deduction against QBI is limited to the *greater* of:
    - 50% of allocable W-2 wages paid by the business, or
    - 25% of W-2 wages, plus 2.5% of the unadjusted basis immediately after acquisition (UBIA) of all qualified property.

Specified Service Trade or Business (SSTBs) Limitation

We will discuss the "SSTB Limitation" first. If a taxpayer's income is *below* the income thresholds listed above, then the business will generally qualify for the 199A deduction. However, if a taxpayer's income is *above* this threshold, then limitations may apply. The "SSTB limitation" is a limitation that applies to certain business types only (covered in the table in the next section). If the taxpayer's taxable income is *above* the phase-in range (listed previously) and the business income is from a "specified service business" then the deduction is completely disallowed.

Example: Francesca is a self-employed attorney. Therefore, her business is an SSTB. In 2020, her QBI income from her legal practice was $170,000. She also has substantial income from various investments. Her pre-QBI deduction taxable income from all other sources is $275,000 for the year. She is single. Since her taxable income is above phase-in for single filers, and her business is a specified service business (attorney), she cannot take the QBI deduction.

Example: Abel is a plastic surgeon and a shareholder in Plastic Surgery Associates, Inc., an S corporation. Abel is married and files jointly with his wife, Bernardine. His wife, Bernardine, does not work and has no taxable income for the year. Abel has $305,000 of qualified business income from the S corporation during the year. In 2020, after adding their income from all sources, Abel and Bernardine have a joint pre-QBI deduction taxable income of $325,000. Even though Abel 's business income is from a specified service business (health services), they are below the threshold for joint filers, so they are eligible for the QBI deduction on their individual return.

A "specified service trade or business" (SSTB), includes the performance of services in the fields on the following table:

Specified Field	Includes:	Does NOT Include:
Health	Doctors, nurses, veterinarians, dentists, psychologists, and similar health care professionals	Services not directly related to a medical field, such as health clubs or gyms, or the sale of pharmaceuticals or medical devices.
Law	Attorneys, paralegals, mediators	Services by printers, delivery services, document retrieval and process servers, or stenography services.
Accounting	CPAs, enrolled agents, financial auditors, tax preparers	Payment processing and billing analysis.
Actuarial science	Actuarial services	Services by analysts, economists, mathematicians, and statisticians not engaged in analyzing or assessing the financial costs of risk.
Performing arts	Actors, singers, musicians, entertainers, directors, playwrights	Broadcasters of the performing arts, or maintenance of equipment or facilities used in the performing arts.
Consulting	Those who provide professional advice and counsel to help clients achieve goals and solve problems	Training or educational courses or consulting services that are ancillary to the sale of goods.
Athletics	Professional athletes, coaches, and team managers	Maintenance and operation of equipment or facilities for use in athletic events, or broadcasters of athletic events
Financial services	Financial advisors, investment bankers, wealth planners, and retirement advisors	Does not include taking deposits, or loan origination (i.e., banking or lending services)
Brokerage services	Stockbrokers, securities dealers, day traders, commodities traders	Services provided by real estate agents and real estate brokers, or insurance agents.
"Reputation or skill"	This provision is not as broad as it sounds. It relates mostly to a taxpayer who (1) receives income for endorsing products or services, (2) licensing or receiving income for the use of an individual's image, likeness, name, signature, voice, or trademark. Basically, it would apply to famous people, celebrity personalities, etc. that lend their name and image to licensing products.	
Note: A SSTB specifically excludes architecture and engineering.		

In some scenarios, a married couple may benefit from filing separately to avoid the SSTB limit, if both spouses have taxable income and one spouse would qualify separately.

Example: Philippe and Bethany are married. They do not live in a community property state. Philippe is an employee of a pharmaceutical company and earns $395,000 in wages during the year. Bethany is an enrolled agent and has $159,000 in self-employment income from her tax preparation business. Philippe is not eligible for the QBI deduction, because he only has wage income. Bethany cannot claim the QBI deduction if they file jointly, because her business is an SSTB, and their taxable income is over the phase-in range for joint filers. However, if Bethany and Philippe file *separate* returns (MFS), Bethany's business income is under the $163,300 threshold for MFS filers in 2020, so she would be entitled to the full QBI deduction on her separately-filed return. They can choose to file using whichever method will give them the best tax result.

Wage and Property Limitation

If the taxpayer's income is *above* the phase-in range, and the business is *not* a specified service business, the deduction is subject to the wage and property limitation. This limits the QBI deduction to 50% of qualified wages paid by the business, or, (if greater) 25% of qualified wages plus 2.5% of the unadjusted tax basis of certain depreciable business property.

Note: The taxpayer does not have to calculate *any* wage limitation if the taxpayer's taxable income is less than the income thresholds or "phase-in-range" figures. This is true even if the taxpayer has income from a specified service trade or business (SSTB).

For the purposes of this limitation, **"qualifying wages"** refers to taxable wages the business has paid to its employees, *plus* any amounts paid into a tax-deferred retirement plan.

"Qualified property" includes the original unadjusted basis of depreciable, tangible property that:

- Is held by the business and available for use at the close of the taxable year (i.e., the asset is not sold or disposed of during the year),
- Has a remaining depreciable period. The term "depreciable period" means that (1) its regular depreciable life has not ended prior to the end of the tax year of the business or (2) if it has not been more than 10 years since it was first placed in service.
- Note that **land** and **intangible assets** are not included in the definition of qualified property.

This is commonly called "UBIA" which stands for "unadjusted basis immediately after acquisition" of qualified property. The unadjusted basis of qualified property is determined *before* any bonus depreciation or Section 179 expensing.

In simplified terms, this means that taxpayers with QBI who have taxable income above the phaseout threshold must be owners of a business that either (1) pays wages to employees or (2) own qualifying depreciable property, otherwise the QBI deduction will not be permitted.

Note: The unadjusted basis calculation is based on the original capitalized cost immediately after the asset's acquisition (UBIA), ***not*** the adjusted depreciated basis of the qualified property.

Example: Kadence is a sole-proprietor with no employees. She is the owner of FunTime Land Holdings, LLC. Her business leases out large tracts of land for various purposes, including seasonal events such as hayrides, corn mazes, and petting zoos. In 2020, a Hollywood studio approaches her in order to lease her land to film a blockbuster movie. Kadence accepts the lucrative contract, and her business earns $900,000 in net self-employment income in a single year. This amount puts her well over the threshold amounts. Her business is not an SSTB, but she does not pay any wages during the year (because she has no employees). And she does not have any qualified property, because the business' only valuable assets are plots of land. Since land is not depreciable, she does not have any UBIA, either. Kadence cannot claim the QBI deduction, because her income is above the threshold amounts, and (1) she does not have any qualified wages, and (2) she does not have any qualifying depreciable property.

Example: Darian is married and owns a retail shop which he runs as a sole proprietorship. He has one employee. The shop generates $160,000 of qualifying business income. Darian paid $28,000 in wages to his sole employee. The shop has $50,000 of qualified depreciable property, mostly retail shelving and computer equipment. Darian's qualified business income is $160,000. His QBI deduction would normally be $160,000 x 20% = $32,000. Darian's business is not an SSTB, but he cannot automatically claim the "normal" 20% QBI deduction. This is because he files with his wife, and she earns high wages as a physician. Their joint pre-QBI taxable income is $450,000, which exceeds the income phase-out limits for MFJ filers. He is required to calculate his limitation using the wages or wages plus qualifying property of the business. He calculates both tests to find the greater allowable deduction.

Wage test # 1: 50% of wages $28,000 x 50% **= <u>$14,000</u>**

Wage & UBIA (Property) test # 2: Sum of 25% of W-2 wages + 2.5% of the unadjusted basis of all qualified property ($28,000 wages x 25% = **$7,000**) + ($50,000 qualified property x 2.5% = **$1,250**) **= <u>$8,250</u>**

Since the "wages-only" test is the *higher* of the two tests above, and the $14,000 wages-only limitation figure is less than the $32,000 "normal" QBI deduction amount (20% of the $160,000 of QBI) but more than 20% of Darian's adjusted taxable income ($450,000 x 20% = $90,000), Darian's allowable QBI deduction from his business is **$14,000.**

De Minimis Exceptions for SSTB Activities

There are some instances where a business may have SSTB income, but still not be subject to the SSTB limitations. These are called "de minimis" exceptions. These exceptions apply even if the business itself is operated by a taxpayer that would normally be classified as an "SSTB" (such as a doctor, lawyer, or professional athlete). If the business has SSTB income in excess of the following rules, however, then the entire business is considered an SSTB.

SSTB De minimis rule #1

If a business' gross receipts are *less* than $25 million, and less than 10% of the gross receipts are from the performance of services in a specified service trade or business, then the trade or business is not considered specified service trade or business, and thus the owner(s) of the business are not subject to the SSTB limitation.

Example: Vision Medical Group, Inc. is an optometrist's office organized as an S corporation. Vision Medical offers eye exams and also sells prescription eyeglasses, designer sunglasses, and contact lenses. In 2020, Vision Medical generated $400,000 in gross receipts. Only $38,000 of that revenue was from eye exams and other medical services. The remainder was from the sale of eyeglasses and contact lenses. Since only 9.5% of Vision Medical's income was generated by health services ($38,000 SSTB income ÷ $400,000 gross receipts) the business is not considered a "Specified Service Business" and the potential SSTB-related limitations to the QBI deduction will not apply, even though the business is a medical practice.

Example: Loving Animal Care, LLC provides veterinary services and also sells pet food and other pet products. The veterinarian services are considered to be the performance of services in the field of health. Loving Animal Care separately invoices for its veterinarian services and the sale of its pet products. The business maintains completely separate books and records each activity, as well as separate cash registers. The business chooses to treat its veterinary practice and the sales of pet products as separate businesses for purposes of Section 162 and the 199A deduction. Loving Animal Care has gross receipts of $3 million during the year. $1 million of the gross receipts is attributable to the veterinary services, an SSTB. Although the gross receipts from the veterinary services exceed 10% of the businesses' gross receipts, the sales of pet products is not considered an SSTB due to the fact that the veterinary practice and the product sales are treated as separate businesses (Treas. Reg.(§1.199A-5(c)(1)-based on Example 2, page 232).

SSTB De minimis rule #2

If a business' gross receipts are *more* than $25 million, and less than 5% of the gross receipts are from the performance of services in a specified service trade or business, then the trade or business is not considered specified service trade or business, and owner(s) of the business are not subject to the SSTB limitation.

Example: Wealth Advisors, Inc. is an S corporation with 10 shareholder-employees. The company specializes in financial planning services. In 2020, the company published several wealth management books that became international bestsellers. The gross receipts for Wealth Advisors were $40 million dollars. Only $1.5 million came from financial consulting services. The remaining $38.5 million was publishing income from the book series. Since only 3.75% of the company's income was generated by financial consulting services ($1.5 million SSTB income ÷ $40 million gross income) the business is not considered a "SSTB" and the potential SSTB-related limitations to the QBI deduction will not apply.

Example: Julie Bellamy is a famous television actress. All her business activity is done under the umbrella of her S Corporation: Bellamy Enterprises, Inc., in which she is the sole owner and shareholder. In 2020, Julie performed a starring role in a TV miniseries, earning $1.5 million for the role. The rest of the year, she worked on launching a chain of Hollywood-themed restaurants called "Julie's Famous Burgers." The restaurants are a big hit, and the activity earns $39 million during the year. Although the "acting" income is considered performing arts and, therefore an SSTB activity, the restaurant activity is not. Since less than 5% of the business income that Bellamy Enterprises, Inc. earned in 2020 was from performing arts, then the corporation is not considered an SSTB for the purposes of the 199A deduction.

FFCRA Sick and Medical Leave Credits

The Families First Coronavirus Response Act (FFCRA) was signed into law on March 18, 2020. The FFCRA provides businesses with tax credits to cover the costs of providing employees with mandatory paid sick leave and expanded family and medical leave for reasons related to COVID-19, for periods of leave from April 1, 2020, through September 30, 2021.[83] Full-time employees are eligible for 80 hours of paid leave. Wages paid to an employee are "qualified leave wages" if the employee is unable to work or telework due to COVID-19 or needs to care for his or her child whose place of care is closed for reasons related to COVID-19.

- **Qualified sick leave wages if an employee is unable to work due to their own health needs:** An employee who is unable to work or telework due to their *own health needs* (related to COVID-19) may receive paid sick leave for up to two weeks (up to 80 hours) at the employee's regular rate of pay, or up to $511 per day and $5,110 in aggregate.
- **Qualified sick leave wages if an employee is unable to work because he or she needs to care for others:** An employee who is unable to work or telework due to *caring for others* may receive paid sick leave for up to two weeks (up to 80 hours) at 2/3 the employee's regular rate of pay or up to $200 per day and $2,000 in aggregate.[84]

Eligible Employers that are entitled to claim the refundable tax credits are businesses and tax-exempt organizations that: (1) have fewer than 500 employees, and (2) pay "qualified sick leave wages" and/or "qualified family leave wages". An Eligible Employer may claim a fully refundable tax credit equal to 100% of the qualified family leave wages (and allocable qualified health plan expenses and the Eligible Employer's share of Medicare tax on the qualified family leave wages) it pays.

Eligible Employers may claim the credits on their federal employment tax returns (Form 941, *Employer's Quarterly Federal Tax Return*). An employer may request an advance payment of the credits from the IRS by submitting a Form 7200, *Advance Payment of Employer Credits Due to COVID-19.* The FFCRA also provides a comparable credit for self-employed individuals.

Note: The FFCRA Sick and Family Leave Credits are not listed on the IRS test specifications for the current exam cycle. It is unlikely that the IRS will test on these credits.

Employee Retention Credit (ERC)

The Employee Retention Credit (ERC) is a refundable tax credit against certain employment taxes equal to 50% of the qualified wages an eligible employer pays to employees after March 12, 2020, and before December 31, 2021.[85] The ERC was designed to encourage businesses to retain and compensate employees during periods in which businesses are not fully operational. Employers, including tax-exempt organizations, are eligible for the ERC if they experience either:

---

83 Under the Consolidated Appropriations Act, 2021, employers are not *required* to provide FFCRA leave after December 31, 2020. However, employers who voluntarily choose to provide leave in 2021 will be eligible for tax credits through September 30, 2021 (per the ARPA of 2021).

84 To see a full overview of the FFCRA sick and family leave credits related to COVID-19, see the IRS FAQ page here: https://www.irs.gov/newsroom/covid-19-related-tax-credits-for-paid-leave-provided-by-small-and-midsize-businesses-faqs.

85 The ERC was originally set to expire at the end of 2020, but the CAA 2021 and ARPA 2021 expanded and extended the employee retention credit introduced as part of the CARES Act, allowing employers to remain eligible up for the credit until December 31, 2021.

- A full or partial suspension of operations because of governmental orders limiting commerce, travel, or group meetings due to COVID-19, or
- A significant decline in gross receipts.

For each employee, wages (including health insurance costs) up to $10,000 during all 2020 quarters can be counted to determine the amount of the 50% credit.[86]

Note: The Employee Retention Credit is not specifically listed on the IRS test specifications for the current exam cycle. It is unlikely that the IRS will test on this credit.

The General Business Credit and Other Business Credits

A variety of tax credits are available for businesses. Credits are generally more valuable than deductions of the same amount because they are subtracted directly from a business's tax liability, dollar-for-dollar based on the amount of the applicable credit. However, most business tax credits are available in limited situations, applying only to certain industries or to very specific activities.

Most business credits fall under the umbrella of the **General Business Credit (GBC).** The GBC is not a single credit, but is instead a combination of various individual credits, combined together. Each business credit is first claimed on a separate form; the credits are then reported in aggregate on Form 3800, *General Business Credit.* The general business credit is nonrefundable. The GBC is subtracted directly from tax, reducing an entity's tax liability dollar for dollar. Further, the GBC may not offset any of a business's employment tax (or payroll tax) liabilities.

If a business is unable to use its entire GBC in the year it was earned, the credit can be carried back to the prior year and forward for up to 20 years. General business credits are treated as used on a first-in, first-out basis by offsetting the earliest-earned credits first. Therefore, the order in which the credits are used in any tax year is:

- Carryforwards to that year, using the ones that were generated the earliest;
- The general business credit earned in that year; and
- The carryback to that year.

A business's GBC consists of its carryforward of business credits from prior years, the total of its current year-generated business credits, plus any GBC's carried back from the subsequent year. The following section includes an overview of the more widely-claimed business credits.

Study Note: In addition to eligibility for and deduction of the general business credit as a whole, Prometric's online exam specifications reference the R&D Credit, the Disabled Access Credit, the Foreign Tax Credit, and Small Business Healthcare Tax Credit, suggesting they are the most likely to be tested on the EA exam. The IRS has also stated in the most recent version of the official Candidate Information that candidates should not take into account any legislation or court decisions made after December 31, 2020. We will cover the most commonly-tested credits in this chapter.

---

[86] To see more IRS guidance on the Employee Retention Credit, see the official FAQ detail page at: https://www.irs.gov/coronavirus/employee-retention-credit.

Investment Credit

The Investment Credit is actually the sum of multiple credits. The investment credit is available to businesses that engage in specific types of projects on their property. It consists of the:

- **Rehabilitation Credit:** This credit is designed to encourage businesses to restore or preserve an older building or one that qualifies for historic status. A 20% credit for qualified expenditures applies to rehabilitation costs incurred on certified historic structures.[87] The credit must be claimed ratably over a 5-year period beginning when the structure is placed in service.
- **Energy Credit:** This credit is designed for businesses that use certain types of alternative energy, such as solar, wind, or geothermal energy.
- **Qualifying Advanced Coal Project Credit, Qualifying Gasification Project Credit,** and **Qualifying Advanced Energy Project Credit:** for projects that generate electricity using coal, while also reducing carbon dioxide emissions. These credits are designed to reduce greenhouse emissions by retrofitting existing technology to make it cleaner or spurring investment in alternative energy.

The investment credit allows businesses to take a deduction for a percentage of certain investment costs from their tax liability in addition to the normal allowances for depreciation. In general, a business cannot claim the Investment Credit for property that is:

- Used mainly outside the United States;
- Used by a governmental unit or foreign entity;
- Used by a tax-exempt organization;
- Used for lodging or in the furnishing of lodging; or
- Any property that has already been expensed under section 179.

The credit is claimed on Form 3468, *Investment Credit.*

Note: The Investment Tax Credit has been modified by Congress a number of times over the years. The details regarding this credit are listed in the 2020 Instructions for Form 3468.

Work Opportunity Tax Credit

The WOTC provides a credit for businesses that hire qualified veterans and members of certain targeted employee groups. The tax credit is based on first-year wages paid to newly hired members of 10 targeted groups:

- Unemployed Veterans (including disabled veterans)
- Temporary assistance for needy families (TANF) recipients
- Food stamp recipients
- Designated community residents (those living in Empowerment Zones)
- Vocational rehabilitation referred individuals
- Ex-felons
- Supplemental security income recipients

[87] A "certified historic structure" is a building listed in the National Register of Historic Places or located in a registered historic district certified by the Secretary of the Interior.

- Summer youth employees (living in empowerment zones)
- Qualified long-term unemployment recipient

This credit was set to expire, but the *Consolidated Appropriations Act of 2021* extended the Work Opportunity Credit through 2025. The WOTC amount is calculated on Form 5884, Work Opportunity Credit, and reported on Form 3800, General Business Credit. Tax-exempt organizations claim the credit on Form 5884-C, Work Opportunity Credit for Qualified Tax-Exempt Organizations Hiring Qualified Veterans, as a credit against the employer's share of Social Security tax. The amount of the credit varies depending on the targeted group that an employee belongs to (for example, a veteran who receives food stamps or an ex-felon).

Disabled Access Credit

This is a nonrefundable tax credit for an eligible small business that incurs expenses to provide access to persons who have disabilities. The expenses must be incurred for the business to comply with the *Americans with Disabilities Act.* The credit equals 50% of eligible expenses up to a maximum credit of $5,000 per year. If the Disabled Access Credit is claimed, the deduction for eligible expenditures must be reduced by the amount of the credit.

The credit is calculated at 50% of expenditures over $250, not to exceed $10,250, for a maximum benefit of $5,000. The credit amount is subtracted from the total tax liability. To be eligible, a business must have had gross receipts of $1 million or less or had no more than 30 full-time employees during the preceding tax year.

Example: Madeline owns a small roadside diner that was originally built in 1920. To comply with current ADA regulations, she retrofitted the diner's restroom to allow wheelchair access. Qualified expenses totaled $12,000. Madeline can claim the full $5,000 of the Disabled Access Credit (50% of a maximum of $10,000 of qualified expenses).

Note: If Madeline had only incurred $5,250 of qualified expenses, the first $250 of the expenses would not qualify for the credit, but the remainder *would* – resulting in a credit of $2,500 ([$5,250 - $250] x 50% = $2,500)

Example: Willow Property Services, Inc. incurs $18,000 in expenses to install a wheelchair ramp outside its main company office. Willow Property Services had $2 million in gross receipts and $500,000 in taxable income (after subtracting business deductions) in 2020. Willow Property Services is not eligible for the Disabled Access Credit, because it has more than $1 million in gross receipts for the year. It can still claim the cost of the wheelchair ramp as a business expense, but it cannot take the Disabled Access Credit.

Credit for Employer Social Security and Medicare Taxes on Employee Tips

This is an extremely common credit in the restaurant industry. It is also called the "FICA Tip Tax Credit." Restaurants and other food and beverage establishments can claim a credit for Social Security and Medicare taxes paid or incurred by the employer on certain employees' tips. This credit is equal to the employer's portion of Social Security and Medicare taxes paid on tips received by employees of restaurants where tipping is customary. The credit applies regardless of whether the food is consumed on or off the business premises.

An employer must meet the following requirements to qualify for the credit:

- Have employees who received tips from customers for serving food or beverages, and
- Have paid employer Social Security and Medicare taxes on these tips.

The credit is claimed on IRS Form 8846, *Credit for Employer Social Security and Medicare Taxes Paid on Certain Employee Tips.* The credit equals the amount of employer Social Security and Medicare taxes paid or incurred by the employer on tips received by the employee, minus tips used to meet the federal minimum wage. The applicable federal minimum wage rate is $5.15 per hour.[88]

Example: Dagwood's Diner is a small breakfast eatery located in Wyoming. Dagwood is the owner and files a Schedule C. Dagwood does most of the cooking and cleaning. His sole employee, Isabelle, takes breakfast orders and waits on tables in the diner's small dining area. Isabelle worked 100 hours and received $450 in tips for the month of October. Isabelle also received $375 in wages (excluding tips) at the rate of $3.75 an hour. For the purposes of the Tip Credit, the $450 in tips is reduced by $140 (the difference between $5.15 and $3.75), and only $310 of the employee's tips for October 2020 are taken into account.

Note: This credit is only available to food or beverage establishments where tipping is customary for providing food or beverages (bars, restaurants, cafeterias, etc.). This credit does *not* apply to other service businesses that have tipped employees, (such as hair salons, limo services, or car washes).

Employer Credit for Paid Family and Medical Leave

Eligible employers may claim the Credit for Paid Family and Medical Leave, which is equal to a percentage of wages they pay to employees while the employees are on family and medical leave (FMLA leave).

Note: This is **not** the same credit as the FFCRA Sick and Medical Leave credits that were implemented by the *Families First Coronavirus Response Act (FFCRA)*, which was signed into law on March 18, 2020. This credit is for employers who specifically offer paid family and medical leave under the *Family and Medical Leave Act (FMLA)*, which was signed into law in 1993.

The FMLA entitles eligible employees of covered employers to take unpaid, job-protected leave for specified family and medical reasons. Employers who offer *paid* FMLA may be entitled to a tax credit for those wages. Employers must have a written policy in place that meets certain requirements, including providing:

- At least two weeks of paid family and medical leave (annually) to all qualifying employees who work full time (or prorated for employees who work part-time), and
- The policy must require a rate of payment of at least 50% of the employee's normal wages.

88 Per Sect. 45B, while the current Federal minimum wage is currently $7.25 per hour, specifically for purposes of the *Credit for Employer Social Security and Medicare Taxes on Employee Tips*, the "minimum wage" is essentially frozen at the 2007 rate of $5.15 per hour.

A qualifying employee is any employee who has been employed by the employer for one year or more and who, for the preceding year, and whose compensation for the *previous year* does not exceed 60% of the compensation threshold for "highly compensated employees."

This credit has a "lookback provision" with regards to wage compensation. For 2019, the applicable amount of compensation was $125,000. This means that in order to be a qualifying employee in **2020,** an employee must have earned no more than $75,000 (60% of $125,000) in compensation in the preceding year (2019).

For 2020, the applicable amount of compensation is $130,000. This means that, in order to be a qualifying employee in **2021**, an employee must have earned no more than $78,000 (60% of $130,000) in compensation in the preceding year (2020).

The amount of the credit varies based on the percentage of wages that are paid to the employee. In 2020, the credit amounts are as follows:

- An employer can claim a credit of 12.5% if the rate of payment is 50% of normal wages
- An employer can claim a credit of 25% if the rate of payment is 100% of normal wages.

Example: Arroyo Insurance, Inc. offers family and medical leave to workers who qualify for it. In 2020, two employees requested FMLA leave due to the birth of a child. Danny, an insurance broker, earned $102,000 in wages the prior year. Victoria, a secretary, earned $38,000 in the prior year. Arroyo Insurance, Inc. pays 50% of normal wages to employees during their qualified leave. The FMLA wages paid to Victoria would qualify for the *Credit for Paid Family and Medical Leave.* The wages paid to Danny would not qualify for the credit, because he earned more than $75,000 in the prior year.

Employers must reduce the amount of any deduction claimed for wages paid during the year by the amount of the family and medical leave credit claimed on the business' return. Employers claim the credit by filing Form 8994, *Employer Credit for Paid Family and Medical Leave*, and Form 3800, *General Business Credit,* with their tax return.[89]

Credit for Small Employer Health Insurance Premiums

The Credit for Small Employer Health Insurance Premiums (also called the "Small Business Healthcare Tax Credit") is a *refundable* credit that is designed to encourage small employers to offer health insurance to their employees. The maximum credit is up to 50% of the employer's contribution toward the employees' premium costs (35% for tax-exempt employers).

The credit is specifically targeted toward employers with low and moderate-income workers and phases out as average annual wages increase. To be eligible for the credit, all of the following must apply:

- The employer must have fewer than 25 full-time equivalent (FTE) employees.
- Average annual wages of qualifying employees must be less than $56,000 in 2020.
- The employer must pay at least 50% of the employees' premium costs.
- The employer must offer coverage through the SHOP Marketplace in order to qualify.

[89] The *Taxpayer Certainty and Disaster Tax Relief Act of 2019* extended this credit until December 31, 2020, and the credit was extended again by the CAA 2021 to tax year 2025. See the IRS FAQ page here: https://www.irs.gov/newsroom/section-45s-employer-credit-for-paid-family-and-medical-leave-faqs.

The credit is phased out completely for employers with 25 or more full-time employees or those paying annual average wages of $56,000 or more in 2020.

The employer must pay premiums on behalf of employees enrolled in a qualified health plan offered through a Small Business Health Options Program (SHOP) Marketplace, or qualify for an exception to this requirement. The credit can be claimed for a maximum of two consecutive years.[90] The credit is claimed on Form 8941, Credit for Small Employer Health Insurance Premiums.

Example: Nikolai is the owner of a small auto repair business. He has twelve full-time employees and pays a total of $50,000 a year toward their health care premiums for coverage purchased through the SHOP marketplace. Based on the average wages of his employees, Nikolai qualifies for a 15% credit, so he can claim a credit of $7,500.

Note: The amount of the Credit for Small Employer Health Insurance Premiums is calculated on a sliding scale. The credit is higher for smaller employers, and lower for larger businesses. Unlike most other business credits, the Credit for Small Employer Health Insurance Premiums is *refundable*. An employer must reduce its health insurance premium expense deduction by the amount of the credit. Because the credit is refundable, even if an employer has no taxable income, the business may be eligible to receive the credit as a refund.

Research and Development Credit (R&D Credit)

The R&D credit (also called the "Credit for Increasing Research Activities") is available to businesses that invest in qualified research and development activities to develop, design, or improve products, processes, formulas, or software. "Qualified research activities" include:

- Technological research to develop new or improved business processes, or improve product reliability or quality.
- Development of commercial software in connection with the taxpayer's trade or business activity.
- Research incurred by a pharmaceutical company to introduce a new drug or develop a new piece of technology.

The credit is designed to incentivize domestic innovation and growth, so only research and development costs performed within the United States will qualify for this credit. The research credit is an incremental credit that equals 20% of a businesses' excess qualifying research expenses for the taxable year over their base amount.

Example: Mesquite Rideshare, Inc. is a growing rideshare company that pays a software company to develop a proprietary mobile application for its rideshare services. The cost of the software development may qualify for the R&D credit.

Businesses use Form 6765, Credit for Increasing Research Activities, to figure and claim the credit, to elect the reduced credit under section 280C, and to elect to claim a certain amount of

[90] The SHOP Marketplace is a federal government website designed for small employers who want to provide health coverage to their employees. To use the SHOP Marketplace, the business must have 50 or *fewer* full-time equivalent employees (FTEs).

the credit as a payroll tax credit against the employer portion of social security taxes. The credit amount is then transferred to Form 3800, General Business Credit.

Credit for Employer-Provided Child Care Facilities and Services

Employers may claim a credit for qualified childcare facilities, as well as resource and referral expenditures. The credit is 25% of the qualified childcare facility expenditures plus 10% of the qualified child care resource and referral expenditures paid or incurred during the tax year.

The child care facility may not discriminate in favor of highly compensated employees. The maximum credit is limited to $150,000 per tax year. The credit is claimed on Form 8882, *Credit for Employer-Provided Childcare Facilities and Services.*

Example: Whitlock Tile, Inc. provides an on-site childcare center for use by its employees. The qualified child care facility is housed in an adjacent building to the factory where the employees work. The annual cost of running the child care facility is $275,000, including the cost of the three full-time workers that staff the facility. Based on this figure, Whitlock Tile, Inc. may take a $68,750 business credit ($275,000 costs x 25% = $68,750) by filing Form 8882.

Credit for Small Employer Pension Plan Startup Costs

Eligible small employers can claim a credit for qualified startup costs incurred in establishing or administering an eligible retirement plan (including a SEP, SIMPLE IRA or qualified plan). The credit is 50% of the qualified startup costs paid or incurred during the tax year. The credit is limited to $500 per year for the first credit year and each of the following two tax years. No credit is allowed for any other tax year. Eligible employers may be eligible for this credit if:

- The business had 100 or fewer employees who received at least $5,000 in compensation in the preceding year; and
- The business had at least one plan participant who was a non-highly compensated employee.

The credit is part of the general business credit and the business may carry it back or forward to other tax years if the business cannot use the credit in the current year. The credit is claimed on Form 8881, *Credit for Small Employer Pension Plan Startup Costs.*

Empowerment Zone Employment Credit

The Empowerment Zone Employment tax credit is available to businesses who employ current residents in areas deemed to be empowerment zones. Although this credit had expired, the *Taxpayer Certainty and Disaster Tax Relief Act of 2019* provided for a retroactive extension of the credit until the end of 2020.

Taxpayers use Form 8844 to claim the credit. The credit is 20% of the employer's qualified zone wages (up to $15,000) paid or incurred during the calendar year for services performed by an employee while the employee is a qualified zone employee.

Foreign Tax Credit for Corporations

U.S. corporations may claim the foreign tax credit for certain taxes paid or accrued to foreign countries. The credit is claimed on Form 1118, *Foreign Tax Credit – Corporations*. This form is submitted with the corporate return. Generally, a U.S. corporation may claim a foreign tax credit for the following foreign taxes paid or accrued:

- Income tax, war profits tax, and excess profits taxes
- Taxes paid in lieu of income taxes

Certain taxes, like sales taxes or the VAT (value-added tax), would not qualify. The corporation must first separate their business income into passive and active categories. In general, dividends, interest, rents, and royalties are treated as passive category income.

This credit is nonrefundable. If the allowable foreign taxes exceed the foreign tax credit limitation for the tax year the excess may be carried back or carried forward:

- First, carried back 1 year to offset taxes imposed in the same category, then
- Carried forward 10 years to offset taxes imposed in the same category.

In lieu of taking the foreign tax credit, a corporation may choose to deduct foreign taxes paid or accrued. A corporation may not claim a foreign tax credit for foreign taxes paid to a foreign country that the corporation does not legally owe, including amounts eligible for a refund by the foreign country.

Other Business Credits

This chapter is not comprehensive. There are dozens of obscure business credits that are not specifically listed on Prometric's EA exam specifications. To review these additional credits, see the IRS instructions for Form 3800, *General Business Credit.*

Unit 6: Study Questions

(Test yourself and then check the correct answers at the end of this section.)

1. Tatiana owns a small clothing shop as a sole-proprietorship. The shop has a net business loss of $18,000 in 2020. The business has always had profits in prior years. She has no other income for the year. How should the net operating loss be treated for tax purposes?

A. No carryback, forward indefinitely.
B. Carryback five years, or she can choose to waive the carryback with an irrevocable election.
C. Carryback two years, or she can choose to waive the carryback with an irrevocable election.
D. Carryback two years, or carryforward five years.

2. Which of the following business activities does NOT qualify for the 199A Qualified Business Deduction?

A. Rental activity that is not a §162 trade or business.
B. Manufacturing products.
C. Construction of homes.
D. Architectural services.

3. USA Management, Inc. qualified for several business credits in 2020. After applying the credits, its taxable income was reduced to zero, so the business could not use all of its business credits in the current tax year. What is the *carryover period* for the GBC?

A. The GBC may be carried back two years and carried forward five years.
B. The GBC may be carried back five years and carried forward 10 years.
C. The unused GBC cannot be carried over to another tax year.
D. The GBC may be carried back one year and carried forward for 20 years.

4. Lorelei is a sole proprietor who designs and sells gold and silver jewelry directly to customers. She has three full-time employees whose wages average $21,000 in 2020. She paid the health insurance premiums for her employees who are enrolled in coverage through the SHOP marketplace during the year. Which of the following statements is correct?

A. She does not qualify for the Credit for Small Employer Health Insurance Premiums.
B. She may qualify for a credit of up to 50% of the premiums she paid for her employees.
C. She may qualify for a credit of up to 35% of the premiums she paid for her employees.
D. She may qualify for the Small Business Health Care Tax Credit for up to three years.

5. Aroma Candles, Inc. is a small candle-making company. In 2020, Aroma Candles renovated their retail shop to comply with the Americans with Disabilities Act, adding a wheelchair ramp to their main entrance. Aroma Candles had gross receipts of $750,000 and spent $15,000 on disabled access upgrades. What is Aroma Candles' current-year Disabled Access Credit?

A. $2,500
B. $5,000
C. $7,500
D. $15,000

6. The Work Opportunity Tax Credit provides a credit for businesses that:

A. Provide job training for out-of-work veterans and other individuals in targeted groups.
B. Give severance to laid-off workers.
C. Invest in federal empowerment zones.
D. Hire unemployed veterans and other individuals from targeted groups.

7. Which event would *not* create a net operating loss?

A. Rental losses from a real estate activity.
B. Casualty losses incurred by a business.
C. Losses from the sale of stock.
D. Farming losses.

8. Which of the following is NOT considered a "Specified Service Trade or Business" for the purposes of calculating the 199A Qualified Business Income Deduction?

A. Doctor.
B. Certified Public Accountant.
C. Professional athlete.
D. Architect.

9. Which of the following is not part of the Investment Credit in 2020?

A. Qualifying Advanced Coal Project Credit.
B. Credit for Small Employer Pension Plan Startup Costs.
C. Rehabilitation Credit.
D. Energy Investment Credit.

10. Which of the following items is allowed when calculating a net operating loss?

A. Capital losses in excess of capital gains.
B. A net operating loss from another year (a carryback or a carryforward).
C. A self-employed taxpayer's contribution to his own qualified retirement plan.
D. A loss from the theft of business property.

11. The Disabled Access Credit conforms to the applicable standards of the:

A. Architectural Standards Act.
B. U.S. Department of Labor.
C. Americans with Disabilities Act.
D. National Organization on Disability.

12. Which of the following business credits is a *refundable* credit?

A. Credit for Small Employer Health Insurance Premiums.
B. Employer Credit for Paid Family and Medical Leave.
C. Investment Credit.
D. Work Opportunity Tax Credit.

Unit 6: Quiz Answers

1. The answer is B. Tatiana may carryback her losses five years, or she can choose to waive the net operating loss carryback with an irrevocable election in her 2020 tax return.

Note: The CARES Act put in place a default 5 year carryback for all net operating losses (NOLs). However, taxpayers may elect to waive the carryback period entirely for those losses on a timely filed return. The election is irrevocable. Net operating losses have an unlimited carryforward period. The Consolidated Appropriations Act of 2021 allows farming businesses only to choose either a five-year carryback or a two-year carryback option (or waive the carryback period entirely, on a timely-filed return).

2. The answer is A. Rental income where the owner is not engaged in a bona-fide real estate "trade or business" is not qualifying income for the 199A QBI deduction. This does not mean that the taxpayer has to be a "real estate professional" in order to get the QBI deduction. The rental of real property may constitute a trade or business, even if the rental activity is reported on Schedule E. The IRS also provides an optional safe harbor under which rental real estate activity will be treated as a trade or business for purposes of the QBI deduction.

3. The answer is D. The General Business Credit (GBC) may be carried back one year and carried forward for 20 years.

4. The answer is B. Based on the information provided; Lorelei may qualify for a credit of up to 50% of the premiums she paid for her employees. The actual percentage credit is determined by the number of full-time equivalent employees and their average annual wages. Small tax-exempt employers can qualify for a credit of up to 35% of the health insurance premiums paid for their employees. The Credit for Small Employer Health Insurance Premiums (also known as the "Small Business Health Care Tax Credit") is refundable, is designed for small business employers with fewer than 25 low-to-moderate income workers, and may be claimed for two consecutive years.

5. The answer is B. Aroma Candles' maximum credit would be $5,000. The amount of the Disabled Access Credit is 50% of the qualified expenses in excess of $250, but the maximum credit per year is limited to **$5,000**.

6. The answer is D. The WOTC offers credits to businesses that hire unemployed veterans, as well as other individuals from other targeted groups.

7. The answer is C. Losses from the sale of stock are capital losses and cannot be used to create an NOL. All of the other answers listed could potentially create an NOL, depending on the circumstances.

8. The answer is D. For the purposes of calculating the 199A Qualified Business Income Deduction, the fields of *architecture and engineering* are specifically excluded as "Specified Service Businesses." Specified Service Businesses include: medical professionals, law, accounting, actuarial science, performing arts, consulting, athletics, financial services, brokerage services, or endorsement-related services. Architecture and engineering are specifically not included on the list.

9. The answer is B. The *Credit for Small Employer Pension Plan Startup Costs* is not part of the Investment Credit. The Investment Credit is the sum of five credits that are designed to spur investment in activity that reduces greenhouse emissions and rehabilitates historic property. In 2020, the Investment Credit consists of the following five credits:

- The Rehabilitation Credit,
- Energy Investment Credit,
- Qualifying Advanced Coal Project Credit,
- Qualifying Gasification Project Credit, and
- Qualifying Advanced Energy Project Credit.

10. The answer is D. A casualty loss from the theft of business property would be allowed in figuring a net operating loss.

11. The answer is C. The *Disabled Access Credit* is a nonrefundable tax credit for an eligible small business that pays expenses to provide access to disabled persons. The taxpayer must pay or incur the expenses to enable the business to comply with the Americans with Disabilities Act.

12. The answer is A. Unlike most other business credits, the *Credit for Small Employer Health Insurance Premiums* is refundable. Because the credit is refundable, even if an employer has no taxable income, the business may be eligible to receive the credit as a refund.

Unit 7: Basis of Business Assets

More Reading:
Publication 551, Basis of Assets
Publication 547, Casualties, Disasters, and Thefts
Instructions for Form 3115, Application for Change in Accounting Method

A business asset is any type of property used in the conduct of a trade or business: land, buildings, machinery, furniture, trucks, patents, and franchise rights are examples. Some assets are tangible, and others are intangible.

Taxpayers generally must capitalize the cost of business assets, rather than deduct them in the year the cost is incurred. In order to compute gain or loss on the sale or other disposition of an asset, a business must be able to determine its basis.

Definition: "Basis" is the amount of a taxpayer's investment in an asset or property for tax purposes. Understanding how to calculate basis in various contexts, including for business entities such as corporations and partnerships, is critical to an individual's success in passing *Part 2: Businesses* of the EA Exam.

The basis of property is also used to determine tax deductions for depreciation, amortization, depletion, and casualty losses. If a business cannot determine the basis of an asset, the IRS will deem it to be zero.

The initial basis of property is usually its cost: the amount a business pays for the asset. The cost is the amount paid in cash, notes, other property, or services. Both cash-basis and accrual-basis businesses can charge expenses on a credit card and deduct them in the year the charge is incurred, regardless of when the credit card is paid. An asset's cost basis also may include amounts paid for the following items:

- Sales or use tax on the purchase
- Freight to obtain the property
- Installation and testing costs
- Excise taxes
- Legal and accounting fees for obtaining property, and legal fees for defending and perfecting a property's title.
- Revenue stamps
- Recording fees
- Real estate taxes (if assumed by the buyer)
- Settlement costs for the purchase of real estate
- The assumption of any liabilities on the property

If a business produces real or tangible personal property for use in a trade or business, it may be subject to the uniform capitalization rules. Note that the calculation of basis generally does not include interest payments.

Note: Certain events that occur during the period of ownership may increase or decrease basis, resulting in an ***adjusted basis***. For example, the basis of property is ***increased*** by the cost of improvements that add to the value of the property. The basis of property is ***decreased*** by depreciation deductions, insurance reimbursements for casualty and theft losses, and certain other items such as rebates.

Example: Griselda pays $4,000 for a new commercial dryer for her laundromat. Griselda also pays an additional $505 for shipping and sales tax. The installation cost for the dryer is $250. These costs are all added to the purchase price, resulting in an adjusted basis of $4,755. This is her basis for depreciation on her business tax return.

Example: Cygnet Homes, Inc. is a property development company. In 2020, the company purchased a 50-acre tract of land for development for $900,000. After the close of the sale, Cygnet Homes is immediately sued by one of the former property owners, claiming that the property sale was invalid. Cygnet Homes hires an attorney to represent them in the title dispute. Cygnet Homes eventually prevails in the dispute, but only after spending $50,000 in legal fees. Legal fees paid or incurred to defend or protect title must be added to the basis, so the company's adjusted basis of the land is now $950,000 ($900,000 original cost + $50,000 legal fees).

Example: Fort Worth Delivery, Inc. is a package delivery business. On January 5, Fort Worth Delivery purchases a cargo van for $55,000. The van had to be shipped from an out-of-state dealership, and the shipping cost was an additional $750. Before the van is placed in service, Fort Worth Delivery adds commercial shelving and wall liners to the interior, which costs an additional $1,020. All of these costs must be added to the van's basis, so the basis is increased to $56,770 ($55,000 + $750 + $1,020).

The Basis of Real Property

Real property, (also called real estate), includes land and anything built on it. Real property also includes anything growing on, or attached to land (such as trees or an existing foundation). When a taxpayer buys real property, certain fees and other expenses become part of the cost basis in the property.

Settlement Costs: Certain settlement fees and closing costs related to buying a property are added to its basis. These include abstract fees; charges for installing utility services; legal fees, including title search and preparation of the sales contract and deed; recording fees; surveys; transfer taxes; owner's title insurance; and any amounts the seller owes that the taxpayer agrees to pay, such as charges for improvements or repairs and sales commissions. However, the following settlement fees and closing costs cannot be included in the basis of a property:

- Casualty insurance premiums.
- Rent or utility costs related to occupancy of the property before closing the sale.
- Any charges for acquiring a loan, such as mortgage insurance premiums, loan assumption fees, cost of a credit report, fees for appraisal reports, fees for refinancing a mortgage, and points.
- Points are prepaid interest on a loan and are generally deducted as interest over the life of the loan.

Real Estate Taxes: If a buyer of a property pays delinquent real estate taxes that the seller owed, those taxes are added to the basis and cannot be deducted currently.

Assumption of a Mortgage: If a taxpayer buys property with an existing mortgage, the basis includes the amount paid in cash for the property plus the amount of the mortgage assumed.

Example: The Silverlake Partnership purchases a commercial building for $200,000 of cash and assumes an existing mortgage on the building of $800,000. The partnership also pays $5,500 of legal fees to a real estate attorney to handle the purchase. Silverlake's basis in the building is $1,005,500 ($200,000 + $800,000 + $5,500).

Constructing Assets: If a taxpayer builds property or has assets built, the costs of construction are included in the basis. In addition to the cost of land, these may include other costs, such as:

- Construction labor and materials;
- Architect's fees;
- Building permit charges and inspection costs;
- Payments to contractors;
- Rental of construction equipment;
- Employee wages paid for the construction work; and
- The cost of building supplies and materials used in the construction.

The value of the owner's labor (if a sole proprietor rather than an employee-owner of a corporation) or any other labor for which payment is not made is not included in the basis.

Demolition Costs: Demolition costs *increase* an asset's basis because they are necessary to prepare the property for use. As such, costs incurred to demolish a building are added to the basis of the land on which the building was located. The costs of clearing land for construction also must be added to the basis of the land, not to any future building that may be constructed later.

Example: Paxton buys a lot with a badly damaged building on it for $25,000. He demolishes the building and prepares the land for a new structure. The demolition costs $13,000. Paxton's adjusted basis in the land is now $38,000 ($25,000 + $13,000).

Rehabilitation Costs: Rehabilitation costs increase basis. However, any rehabilitation credits allowed for the expenses must be subtracted. Among the items that increase the basis of property are the following:

- The cost of extending service lines to the property
- Impact fees
- Legal fees, such as the costs of defending and perfecting title
- Zoning costs

Government assessments for items such as paving roads and sidewalks increase the value of a property, and therefore must be added to the property's basis.

A business cannot deduct assessments as taxes, but can deduct charges for maintenance, repairs, or interest charges related to the improvements. A business must decrease the basis of property by amounts that represent a recovery of the business's cost of the property.

For example, rebates are among the items that *decrease* an asset's basis. Items that reduce a property's basis also include the following:

- Deductions for amortization, depreciation, section 179, and depletion
- Nontaxable corporate distributions
- Exclusion of subsidies for energy conservation measures
- Residential energy credits, vehicle credits, and the Investment Credit
- Certain canceled debt excluded from income
- Amounts received for easements

Example: Shelley buys a color copier that costs $2,300 to use in her business. The cashier at the store gave her a rebate form when she purchased the copy machine. She sends in a rebate receipt and receives a $100 rebate from the manufacturer. The correct way to account for this rebate is to reduce the basis of the asset to $2,200 ($2,300 - $100).

IRS Tangible Property Regulations

The IRS's final **tangible property regulations** took effect on January 1, 2014, but the IRS is still issuing guidance for them. The regulations are hundreds of pages long, extremely complex, and affect virtually every business taxpayer.[91] Before the issuance of the final tangible property regulations, taxpayer decisions on whether to expense or capitalize an expense were guided by decades of often conflicting case law, as well as administrative rulings on specific factual situations. The regulations establish the rules governing the capitalization and expensing of physical assets that a taxpayer purchases, repairs, maintains, improves, or disposes of.

Study Note: Given the complexity of the rules and their specificity to various types of property and how it is used, it is unlikely an EA test taker would be expected to be familiar with all the details of the tangible property regulations. For the EA exam, it should be sufficient to have a basic grasp of the underlying concepts of expensing repairs as current deductions vs. capitalization through depreciation deductions. In this unit, we look at how improvements are categorized and at the safe harbors that the regulations carve out for expensing property. Later in the book, we discuss concepts of depreciation and amortization.

The tax code allows a taxpayer to write off **repairs** to business property. These are fixes that keep the property in working condition. **Improvements**, on the other hand, cannot be immediately expensed. The cost of improvements that *add value* to a business or rental property or *extend its useful life* must instead be capitalized and depreciated. Improvements increase the value of an asset. A taxpayer is required to capitalize the cost of improvements, thus increasing the property's basis, and claim depreciation deductions over a period of years.

Examples of *improvements* include the installation of new electric wiring, the addition of a new room, adding central air conditioning, or a complete renovation of a kitchen. In contrast, a *repair* keeps a property in operating condition but does not add to its value or substantially prolong its life. Examples include repainting a property or replacing broken windows. Unlike

[91] The rules may require businesses to make internal changes to accounting practices and procedures for financial and tax accounting purposes. Many taxpayers will be required to file Form 3115, *Request for an Accounting Method Change,* to comply with the regulations.

improvements, the costs of repairs can be deducted immediately and do not have to be capitalized.

Example: Rogelio replaces a cracked toilet in a residential rental that he owns, which costs $750. The cost of the repair is deductible as an expense. The following year, Rogelio replaces the entire plumbing system in the rental with new pipes and bathroom fixtures, which costs $19,000. The new plumbing system is an improvement that increases the value of the property. Rogelio must capitalize the cost of the new plumbing, increasing the property's basis, and depreciate the cost of this improvement over its useful life.

The tangible property regulations apply to C corporations, S corporations, partnerships, LLCs, and individuals filing a Form 1040 with Schedule C, Schedule E, or Schedule F. Under these regulations, an "improvement" is classified as a cost involving:

- The **betterment** of property, or
- The **restoration** of property,
- The **adaptation** of a property to a new or different use.

The regulations divide a building into nine different structural components called "building systems," such as those for plumbing, heating, and air conditioning, and electrical, each of which may be a separate unit of property, in addition to the building itself. Under the new, narrower definition of an "*improvement*," costs must be evaluated for a specific building system and not just for the building as a whole. For example, the cost to refurbish an elevator may "improve" the elevator, but would not be significant to the building as a whole, so under the prior rules, the cost could have been deducted as a repair. Under the new rules, the cost may be significant enough to the elevator system as a unit of property and, therefore, must be capitalized.

Example: Steven owns a small apartment building with an adjusted basis of $950,000. During the year, he spent $18,000 to fix damaged wiring in the electrical system. Under the old rules, the $18,000 cost likely would be considered a repair because it is relatively small compared to the overall cost of the building. Under the new rules, the electrical system is a separate structural component or building system. This means that the $18,000 must be compared with the cost of the electrical system alone, not the cost of the whole building. The cost is more significant in this context and thus is more likely to be deemed an "improvement" that must be capitalized and depreciated, rather than currently expensed.

A "restoration" would include amounts paid to return the unit of property to its ordinarily efficient operating condition, if the unit of property has deteriorated to a state of disrepair and is no longer functional for its intended use.

Example: Trail Ridge Farms is a farm. There is a large out-building on the farm's property that has fallen into disrepair, such that the building could no longer be used. In 2020, Trail Ridge Farms decides to restore the building by shoring the walls and replacing the leaky roof. The total cost was $45,000. These costs are considered restorations, and therefore improvements, because the building was returned to operating condition after it had deteriorated to a state of disrepair and were no longer functional for its intended use. Trail Ridge Farms cannot deduct the cost of the restoration as a current expense. The entire $45,000 cost must be capitalized and depreciated.

Safe Harbor Rules

As the previous example illustrates, in some instances, the regulations make it more difficult to classify certain costs as "repairs" and deduct them as current expenses. The tangible property regulations include several safe harbor rules that allow expensing in specific instances:

- **De Minimis Expensing Safe Harbor Election #1:** Businesses with an applicable financial statement (AFS) may use this safe harbor to deduct amounts paid for tangible property up to $5,000 per invoice or item. The rule applies as long as the business has a written capitalization policy or procedure that provides for expensing items that cost less than specified amounts. The amount deductible under the de minimis safe harbor is limited to the threshold set by the policy. A business that elects to use this safe harbor will need to attach a statement to the return.[92]
- **De Minimis Expensing Safe Harbor Election #2:** If the business does not have qualifying financial statements, it may be permitted to deduct items that cost up to $2,500 *per invoice* or *per item.* A business that elects to use this safe harbor will need to attach a statement to the return.
- **Small Taxpayer Safe Harbor for Real Property:** Taxpayers with gross receipts of $10 million or less can expense as repairs, rather than capitalize as improvements, amounts up to the lesser of $10,000 or 2% of the unadjusted basis of a building property, as long as the unadjusted basis is $1 million or less. This is an election the taxpayer must make on his tax return. Once made, the election is irrevocable.
- **Routine Maintenance Safe Harbor:** This allows for the deduction of routine maintenance costs that are required more than once within a ten-year period for buildings, or more than once within the applicable class life period for non-building properties.
- **De minimis Election for Materials and Supplies:** In addition to the safe harbor rules listed, materials and supplies may be deducted in the year the item is used or consumed in the business. No statement is required for this election. "Material and supplies" are classified as:
    - **$200 Property:** Any unit of property that costs $200 or less.
    - **12 month property:** Any unit of property that has a useful life of 12 months or less, regardless of cost.
    - **Acquired components:** This includes things like spare parts, air filters, or other components acquired to maintain or repair a unit of property.
    - **Incidental materials and supplies:** items that are not part of inventory, used in the business, and generally not tracked (e.g., pens, paper, staplers, toner, trash baskets).
    - **Consumables:** Costs of fuel, lubricants, water, and similar items that are reasonably expected to be consumed in 12 months or less, beginning when used in operations.

The *de minimis* safe harbor election does not include costs for the purchase of inventory or land.

---

[92] An "AFS" is a financial statement required to be filed with the Securities Exchange Commission (SEC), as well as other types of certified audited financial statements accompanied by a CPA report, including a financial statement provided for a loan, reporting to shareholders, or for other non-tax purposes. An AFS also includes a financial statement required to be provided to a federal or state government or agency other than the IRS or the SEC.

Example #1: Lantern Advertising Co. purchases 10 boxes of copy paper every month to use in its secretarial offices. The cost of the copy paper is approximately $420 per invoice. Even though the amount exceeds the $200 de minimis threshold, it is still deductible as a current expense, because the supplies are reordered every month, and used up on a frequent basis. Thus, the copy paper has a useful life of 12 months or less, and is therefore deductible as a supplies expense. A statement does not have to be attached to the return.

Example #2: Mikah is an enrolled agent. In 2020, Mikah purchases 10 new laptops at a discount. The laptops cost $399 each, and they are for use by employees in her tax business. Each laptop is treated as a separate unit of property. During the year, 5 laptops are used, and the remaining 5 laptops are placed in storage for future use. The 5 laptops that were actually placed in service are deductible in 2020, and the remaining 5 will be deductible in the year they are placed in service.

Example #3: Penny pays $1,200 for a box of 10 toner cartridges to use as needed for laser printers in her business. The toner cartridges represent 10 units of property for $120 each; therefore, each cartridge is deductible as materials and supplies. Penny does not have qualifying financial statements. However, she makes the *de minimis* safe harbor election to deduct items that cost up to $2,500 per invoice or per item, so she deducts the full $1,200 in the year of purchase. A statement must be attached to her return.

Example #4: Zula purchases a custom ceramic mold to create widgets for her business. The mold costs $9,500, but it is expected to be useful for only eight months, after which, a new mold must be purchased. Even though the mold is expensive, it is deductible when consumed in her business, because its useful life is less than one year. A statement does not need to be attached to her return.

Note: Remember that businesses that have an AFS may use the safe harbor to deduct amounts paid for tangible property up to $5,000 per invoice or item as an expense. Taxpayers *without* an AFS can only deduct amounts up to $2,500 per invoice or item as an expense.

Example #5: Spire Lending Services, Inc. is a C corporation with applicable financial statements (AFS). The company purchases a copier that costs $3,500. The company has a written policy in place that any tangible property purchases under $5,000 may be deducted in the current year. Spire Lending deducts the cost of the copier as an expense by electing the de minimis expensing safe harbor. A statement must be attached to the business' corporate return.

Casualty and Theft Losses of Business Property

Deductible casualty and theft losses and related insurance reimbursements reduce the basis of property. A casualty is defined as the damage, destruction, or loss of property resulting from an identifiable event that is sudden, unexpected, or unusual.

Casualty losses are generally deductible only in the tax year during which the casualty occurred, even if a business does not repair or replace the damaged property until a later year. Theft losses can be deducted only in the year the business discovers the property was stolen (in the case of embezzlement, the losses are deductible the year the theft is discovered).

If an entity has business property that is stolen or completely destroyed, the deductible loss is figured as follows:

The taxpayer's adjusted basis in the property
MINUS
Any scrap or remaining value
MINUS
Any insurance or other reimbursement received

Theft may involve taking money or property by the following means: blackmail, burglary, embezzlement, extortion, kidnapping for ransom, larceny, and robbery. The taking of property must be illegal under the state law where it happened, and it must have been done with criminal intent.

Deductible losses related to business and income-producing property (such as rental property) are reported on Form 4684, *Casualties and Thefts*.[93] Casualty losses are deductible up to the basis. If the basis is zero, then the business will not be able to deduct a loss.

Example: Andrew is a self-employed paralegal. A fire at Andrew's apartment complex destroys his couch, personal TV, and coffee table, which are personal-use property, for a total loss of $5,000. This personal casualty loss is not deductible. The same fire also damages a business asset, a laptop computer that he had brought home that day in order to catch up on his work. The computer is destroyed, resulting in a business casualty loss of $3,000 that is fully deductible on his Schedule C.

Example: Bjorn owns a shop that sells sports memorabilia. Two years ago, Bjorn purchased a signed David Ortiz baseball jersey for display for $150 at an estate sale. The jersey was stolen from his sports shop in 2020. The FMV of the jersey was $2,800 just before it was stolen, and Bjorn did not have insurance to cover the loss. Bjorn's deductible theft loss is $150, equal to his basis in the jersey.

Insurance Reimbursements: If a business has insurance coverage for property that is lost or damaged, it must file a claim for reimbursement, or it will not be able to deduct the loss. The portion of the loss that is not reimbursable by insurance, such as a deductible, is not subject to this rule. If an insurance reimbursement is later denied, or is less than the taxpayer's expected recovery, the taxpayer can amend a prior-year return in order to deduct a casualty loss that was not properly reported in the previous year. A casualty loss cannot be claimed if, during the year, there is a pending insurance claim, and it is expected that the insurance policy will fully cover the loss.

Study Note: A business that has a casualty loss must *decrease* its adjusted basis in the property by any insurance or another reimbursement it receives and by any deductible loss. A business *increases* its basis in the property by the amounts spent, whether with proceeds of insurance reimbursement or otherwise, on repairs that restore the property to its pre-casualty condition.

[93] The TCJA changed the treatment of *personal* casualty losses. Personal casualty and theft loss deductions are now only available for taxpayers with property damaged in a federally declared disaster area.

Example: Cornelius and Marshall are partners and have a gourmet food truck that is used for business purposes. Cornelius has an automobile accident that causes $3,350 in damage to the truck. He and Marshall pay the repair bill out-of-pocket so their business insurance costs will not increase. The insurance policy has a $1,500 deductible. Because the insurance would not cover the first $1,500 of the loss, this amount is their deductible casualty loss. The amount of their loss in excess of $1,500 is not deductible because they did not file an insurance claim.

Example: Dominic owns a residential rental property. On January 20, 2020, the property is flooded, and the rental incurs $35,000 of damage. Dominic files his return on February 3, 2021. He does not report the casualty loss on his tax return because he expects to get fully reimbursed by his insurance company. The insurance company denies his claim because the policy did not cover flood damage. Dominic may amend his tax return using Form 1040-X to claim the casualty loss on Schedule E.

A "total loss" occurs within the context of a casualty event when a business property is completely destroyed. Business casualty losses are fully deductible without limitations, but any insurance reimbursements must be deducted from the allowable loss.

Example: Southwest Stallions, LLC is a horse-breeding business located in Texas. On February 1, 2020, a gas explosion completely destroys a tractor on the farm. The tractor had a fair market value of $52,000 immediately before the fire. Its adjusted basis was $40,000. The tractor has no market value (i.e., no salvage value) after the fire. The insurance company only reimburses Southwest Stallions $4,000 for the tractor. The calculation for this business casualty loss is: ($40,000 adjusted basis – $0 salvage value – $4,000 insurance proceeds) = $36,000 casualty loss.

Sometimes a business will have a "partial loss." This occurs when a business property is only partially destroyed. In a partial destruction, the deductible loss is the decrease in fair market value of the property or the adjusted basis of the property, whichever is less. This amount is further reduced by the amount of any insurance reimbursement.

Example: Cabernet Vineyards has a storage warehouse that was damaged by fire but not completely destroyed. The business carried no insurance on the property. The adjusted basis for depreciation of the building at the time of the fire was $65,000 and the FMV at the time of the fire was $80,000. The value of the building after the fire was only $3,000. The business' deductible casualty loss is $62,000, (the adjusted basis of $65,000 less the salvage value of $3,000).

Basis of Securities

The basis of stocks, bonds, and other securities is the purchase price plus any costs of purchase, such as commissions and recording or transfer fees. A taxpayer must keep track of the basis per share of all stock purchases and sales.

Example: Prime Investments, LLC purchases 2,000 shares of All-Mart Corporation stock. The cost of the stock is $24,000, and Prime Investments pays a stockbroker's fee of $550 on the purchase and transfer. Therefore, the basis of the stock is $24,550 ($24,000 + $550 broker's fee).

Events that occur after the purchase of the stock can require adjustments to the basis per share of stock. The original basis per share can be changed by events such as stock dividends, stock splits, and DRIP (dividend reinvestment plan) activity.

- **Stock dividends** involve the issuance of additional shares to current shareholders. The shareholder's total basis is unchanged but is spread over more shares, which decreases the basis per share.
- A **stock split** is similar to a stock dividend. For example, a two-for-one stock split increases the number of outstanding shares two-fold and decreases the value and the basis per share by half.

As with a stock dividend, the total basis remains the same after a stock split. For example, if a taxpayer has 100 shares with a cost of $50 per share, his basis is $5,000. Assuming a two-for-one stock split, the taxpayer now has 200 shares with a basis per share of $25, which still equals a total basis of $5,000.

Example: Sunstone Partnership purchases 100 shares of Quasi Electronics, Inc. for $11,000. There is an additional $200 in broker's commissions, so the original basis per share is $112 ([$11,000 + $200] ÷ 100). Later in the year, Sunstone Partnership receives 40 additional shares of Quasi Electronics' stock as a nontaxable stock dividend. The $11,200 basis must now be spread over 140 shares (100 original shares plus the 40-share stock dividend). The adjusted stock basis is $80 per share ($11,200 ÷ 140).

Basis Other Than Cost

There are times when the cost of an asset cannot be used as its basis. In certain cases, the adjusted basis of an asset is determined using other methods. For example:

- **Property Received for Services:** If a taxpayer receives property for his services, he must include the property's FMV in income. The amount included in income is the taxpayer's basis in the property. If the services were performed for a price agreed on beforehand, this price may be used as the fair market value of the property, as long as there is no evidence to the contrary.
- **Property in Lieu of Wages:** When property is transferred in lieu of wages, the employer is entitled to deduct the property's fair market value at the time of the transfer, and the same amount is taxable compensation for the employee. A gain or loss is realized if there is a difference between the fair market value and the adjusted basis of the property.
- **Bargain Purchases:** A bargain purchase is a purchase of an item for less than its fair market value. If, as compensation for services, a taxpayer buys goods or other property at less than the FMV, the difference between the purchase price and the property's FMV must be included in his income. His basis in the property is its fair market value (the purchase price plus the amount included in income).

Unit 7: Study Questions

(Test yourself and then check the correct answers at the end of this section.)

1. All of the following items *decrease* the basis of property except:

A. Casualty or theft loss deductions.
B. The cost of defending a title.
C. Depreciation.
D. Amortization.

2. How does a stock split affect the basis of the stock?

A. There is no effect on the basis of the stock.
B. It increases the basis of the stock.
C. It decreases the basis of the stock.
D. It decreases the basis per share of the stock.

3. Wheatland Realty, LLC buys an office building. The business pays the seller $15,000 in cash. Wheatland Realty also assumes a mortgage of $180,000 on it and pays $1,000 of title fees and $2,000 of points to close the sale. What is Wheatland Realty's basis in the building after the close of the sale?

A. $15,000
B. $195,000
C. $196,000
D. $198,000

4. Funhouse Catering, Inc. purchases a small warehouse and its underlying land for its catering business, but it is in such bad condition that the company decides to demolish it and build a new one. The demolition costs $15,600. How must Funhouse Catering report this cost on its corporate tax return?

A. The demolition cost is added to the basis of the land.
B. The demolition cost may be deducted on its corporate tax return.
C. The demolition cost may be deducted on the corporate tax return as a casualty loss.
D. The demolition cost must be amortized over 180 months.

5. What item would *not* be included in an asset's basis?

A. Sales tax.
B. Installation charges.
C. Recording fees.
D. Interest paid on a loan to purchase the asset.

6. Alexander is having financial difficulties, so he sells his duplex to Cheryl, a real estate investor, who plans to use it as a rental property. Alexander was liable for $5,000 in delinquent real estate taxes on the property, which Cheryl agrees to pay. How should Cheryl treat this transaction on her business tax return?

A. Cheryl cannot deduct these taxes as an expense; she adds them to the property basis.
B. Cheryl can deduct these taxes as a current expense on her Schedule A.
C. Cheryl can deduct these taxes as a current expense on her Schedule E.
D. Cheryl can deduct these taxes as a current expense on her Schedule C.

7. Brenda purchases an industrial blender for her smoothie shop. The blender costs $800. The shop's blenders have to be frequently replaced, and she expects it to have a useful life of less than twelve months. Under the tangible property regulations, she:

A. Must capitalize the cost of the blender.
B. Can deduct the expense during the current tax year.
C. Can deduct the expense in the next tax year.
D. Must file Form 3115 if she wishes to expense the blender in the current year.

8. Irina owns a fabric store. On December 1, 2020, she has a loss of $14,000 of inventory due to water damage from a storm. The loss is completely covered by insurance. However, Irina will not be reimbursed by her insurance company until the following year. How should she treat this loss?

A. She should claim the entire loss as a casualty loss in 2020 and then claim the income from the insurance company reimbursement in 2021.
B. She must reduce the amount of her inventory loss in 2020. She must include the insurance reimbursement as income in the year that she receives it.
C. She does not report this loss on her 2020 tax return since there is a reasonable expectation of full recovery through insurance at the time of the casualty event.
D. She must reduce her cost of goods sold in 2020 to reflect the loss and then claim the reimbursement as income in 2021.

9. Action Law Group, Inc. provides legal services to Silver-Nuggets Pawn Shop. Silver-Nuggets Pawn then becomes insolvent and has trouble paying its bills. In lieu of payment, Action Law Group accepts a set of gold coins with a fair market value of $5,000 and an electric scooter with a fair market value of $2,000 and an adjusted basis of $1,000. What amount of business income must Action Law Group report for this transaction?

A. $5,000
B. $6,000
C. $7,000
D. $8,000

10. Franco purchases 50 shares of Red Granite, Inc. stock for $3,500 on January 1, 2020. He pays a broker's fee of $100. On March 30, 2020, he receives an additional 40 shares of Red Granite, Inc. stock as a nontaxable stock dividend. On December 31, 2020, the company declares a two-for-one stock split, doubling the number of his shares. Calculate the total basis of Franco's stock and his per-share basis at the end of the year:

A. Stock basis: $3,500; per-share basis: $38.88.
B. Stock basis: $3,500; per-share basis: $19.44.
C. Stock basis: $3,600; per-share basis: $20.
D. Stock basis: $3,600; per-share basis: $40.

11. Under the tangible property regulations, what are the three categories for determining what constitutes an "improvement" to property rather than a repair?

A. Betterment, restoration, or adaptation.
B. Prolonging life, creating value, or increasing profits.
C. Renovation, amelioration, or restoration.
D. Enhancement, renovation, or increasing profits.

12. Priscilla's Pastries is a popular bakery that operates as a sole proprietorship. In order to expand, the business bought a building for $250,000 on January 10, 2020. Priscilla, the business owner, paid the title company $13,000 in settlement fees to purchase the property. She also assumed an existing mortgage of $35,000 on the property. Legal fees of $9,500 were incurred in a title dispute with a neighbor in April 2020. The clear title was finally transferred to Priscilla on November 1, 2020. Property taxes in the amount of $2,600 were incurred on the property after ownership was transferred. What is Priscilla's overall basis in the building at the end of the year?

A. $250,000
B. $285,000
C. $307,500
D. $310,100

13. Micro Manufacturing Inc. does not have qualifying financial statements. Under the de minimis expensing safe harbor rule, Micro Manufacturing can deduct items that cost up to ________ per invoice or item.

A. $200
B. $500
C. $2,500
D. $5,000

14. A hailstorm damages a work van owned by Dr. Marjorie, a sole proprietor who offers mobile chiropractic services. The van's basis is $25,000, and her insurance company reimburses her $4,000 for the hail damage. Marjorie decides to replace the cracked windshield at a cost of $500 and pockets the rest of the insurance money. What is the adjusted basis of her van?

A. $19,500
B. $21,500
C. $28,500
D. $29,000

15. Vegas Burgers, Inc. is a popular restaurant. During the year, Vegas Burgers repaired a water leak in their kitchen roof. No structural changes were made. The repair cost $4,000. Vegas Burgers owns the building. How should this cost be treated on the business' tax return?

A. The $4,000 cost must be capitalized as an improvement and depreciated.
B. The $4,000 cost must be added to the basis of the building.
C. $2,500 of the repair can be expensed in the current year under the safe harbor regulations. The remainder ($1,500) can be carried over as a business loss.
D. The full amount ($4,000) can be deducted as a repair.

Unit 7: Quiz Answers

1. The answer is B. The cost of legal fees, including the cost of defending title to a property *increases* its basis. All the other answers listed will *decrease* an asset's basis.

2. The answer is D. A stock split increases the number of outstanding shares, which decreases the basis *per share,* but it does not change the basis of the stock as a whole.

3. The answer is C. Wheatland Realty's basis is **$196,000.** The title fees, mortgage amount, and the down payment are added to figure the cost basis of the building. The points are not included in the basis, because they are considered interest.

4. The answer is A. Funhouse Catering, Inc. must add the demolition costs to the basis of the land. The demolition costs cannot be deducted as a current expense. Demolition costs or other losses related to the demolition of any building are added to the basis of the land.

5. The answer is D. Interest charges are not added to an asset's basis. Interest is a potential currently deductible expense.

6. The answer is A. Cheryl cannot deduct the taxes as a current expense, since they are delinquent real estate taxes, and the person who is legally liable for the debt is Alexander. However, the taxes may be added to the property's basis and depreciated as part of her purchase price.

7. The answer is B. Brenda can expense the cost of the blender, because she expects it to have a useful life of less than one year. Under the materials and supplies rules of the tangible property regulations, a unit of property with a useful life of a year or less may be deducted rather than capitalized.

8. The answer is C. Irina expects to be fully reimbursed for her loss, so reporting it on her 2020 return is not allowed. However, if Irina's insurance company reimbursement is ultimately either more or less than her loss, she may realize an additional gain or a loss. Whether a gain would be taxable will depend on how she uses the insurance proceeds.

9. The answer is C. Action Law Group, Inc. must include the FMV of the coins and the FMV of the scooter as income ($5,000 + $2,000 = **$7,000 total**). Property exchanged for services must be included as income at its fair market value.

10. The answer is C. Franco's basis is the stock's purchase price plus the broker's fee ($3,500 + $100 = **$3,600**). After the stock split, Franco has 180 shares of stock ([50 shares + 40 additional shares] × 2 = 180). The stock split reduces his per-share basis by half to **$20** ($3,600 ÷ 180 shares of stock).

11. The answer is A. Under the tangible property regulations, an "improvement" is officially defined as a cost involving a *betterment* of the unit of property, a *restoration* of the unit of property, or an *adaptation* of the unit of property to a new or different use.

12. The answer is C. The basis is **$307,500** ($250,000 + $13,000 + $35,000 + $9,500). The settlement fees, the mortgage assumed by the buyer, and the legal fees for defending the title are all included in the basis of the property. The property taxes are not included in the basis of the building because they were incurred when Priscilla was already the legal owner. Instead, the property taxes may be deducted as a business expense on her Schedule C.

13. The answer is C. If a business does not have qualifying financial statements, it may be permitted to deduct items that cost up to **$2,500** per invoice or per item. A business that has a written capitalization policy or procedure for expensing items can deduct amounts expensed in its financial statements that cost up to $5,000.

14. The answer is B. Dr. Marjorie must reduce the basis of her van by the portion of any insurance proceeds that are not used for repairs. Since she uses $500 of the proceeds to repair the windshield, the adjusted basis is **$21,500** ($25,000 - $4,000 + $500 = $21,500).

15. The answer is D. Vegas Burgers can deduct the full cost of the repair ($4,000) in the current tax year. The expense was merely a repair to keep the building in good working order. The expenditure did not "increase or improve" the useful life of the property. Property owners can deduct expenses for repairs or routine maintenance in the year that the business incurs the costs.

Unit 8: Depreciation and Amortization

More Reading:

Publication 946, How to Depreciate Property

Publication 527, Residential Rental Property (Including Rental of Vacation Homes)

Depreciation is an income tax deduction that allows a business to recover the cost or other basis of certain property. It is an annual allowance for the wear and tear, deterioration, or obsolescence of the property. Most types of tangible property, such as buildings, machinery, vehicles, furniture, and equipment, are depreciable. Likewise, certain intangible property, such as patents, copyrights, and computer software are depreciable or amortizable.

The costs of business assets and improvements generally must be capitalized. The capitalized cost of these asset purchases may be expensed over time using depreciation or amortization over the asset's estimated "useful life" unless the asset qualifies for the section 179 deduction, bonus depreciation, or certain specified safe harbor exceptions.

Definition of Useful life: In general, an asset's "useful life" is usually the period of time for which the asset will be economically useful in a business. This can vary based on a number of factors, but the IRS has established asset classes for most types of property and equipment and assigns a useful life (also called a recovery period) to each asset class. This concept will be covered later in this unit.

Definition: In accounting terms, "depreciation" is an annual allowance for the wear and tear, deterioration, or obsolescence of an asset. Simply put, depreciation is a way of allocating a portion of the cost of an asset over the estimated period that the asset will be in service and used to earn revenues. For tax purposes, depreciation is based on the original, historical cost of the asset and is not indexed for inflation.

Basic Depreciation Rules

The cost of land cannot be depreciated. Most other types of tangible property, such as buildings, machinery, vehicles, furniture, and equipment, are depreciable. Likewise, certain intangible property, such as patents, copyrights, and certain computer software, is amortizable. In order to be depreciated or amortized, an asset must meet all the following requirements:

- The taxpayer generally must own the property. However, taxpayers may depreciate capital improvements for a property they lease (for example, a fence that is built on property that the business leases from another party). These are called "leasehold improvements" (see example, later).
- The taxpayer must use the property in business or in an income-producing activity. If a taxpayer uses the property for both business and personal-use, he can only deduct an amount of depreciation based on the business-use percentage.
- The property must have a determinable useful life of more than one year.

The property ceases to be depreciable when the business has fully recovered its cost or when it sells or retires the property from service, whichever happens first.

Example: Pomegranate Produce, Inc. is a bottling company that processes tropical fruit juice. In 2020, an older juicing machine ceases to function properly. Pomegranate Produce has the option to purchase a new machine for $500,000, or completely rebuild its old machine, which will extend its useful life for another five years. Pomegranate Produce chooses to rebuild the old machine at a cost of $125,000. Since the cost of the rebuild extended the useful life of the machine for several more years, the $125,000 cost must be capitalized and depreciated over its useful life, which is now an additional five years.

Example: Dr. Ahmed is a dentist that leases his medical office inside a larger office building. With the property owner's permission, Dr. Ahmed decides to construct two small interior spaces for his dental hygienist and his bookkeeper. These are leasehold improvements,[94] and they are "qualified improvement property." The construction costs are depreciable, even though Dr. Ahmed does not own the building itself.

Example: Brilliant Bridal, LLC is a clothing store that specializes in bridal fashions. The owners of the shop do not own the building in which the shop is located. During the year, Brilliant Bridal renovates the interior of the store, partitioning the space into smaller, more private areas, so shoppers can try on multiple gowns in private rooms. The total cost of the renovation is $32,000, and is treated as a leasehold improvement. The cost of the improvements can be depreciated by Brilliant Bridal, even though the business does not own the building.

In order to properly depreciate an asset, a taxpayer must determine the following:

- The depreciable basis of the property
- The depreciation method for the property
- The class life (which is representative of the asset's useful life)
- Whether the asset is listed property
- Whether the taxpayer elects to expense any portion of the asset
- Whether the taxpayer qualifies for any bonus depreciation

Modified Accelerated Cost Recovery System (MACRS)

The Modified Accelerated Cost Recovery System (MACRS) is the current tax depreciation system in the United States. Under MACRS, depreciable assets are divided into separate classes that dictate the number of years over which their cost will be recovered. Each MACRS class has a schedule that specifies the percentage of the asset's cost that is depreciated each year. For example, computers are depreciated over five years, and office furniture is depreciated over seven years.

The modified accelerated cost recovery system (MACRS) is the default depreciation method generally used for most tangible property. Real property is depreciated using the straight-line method, with an equal amount of expense each year. Nonresidential real property, such as office buildings, shopping malls, and factories, is depreciated over a 39-year recovery period. Residential buildings, such as apartment complexes and residential rentals, are depreciated over a 27.5-year period.

---

[94] Under IRC Section 168, Qualified Improvement Property (QIP) encompasses any non-structural improvements (e.g., retail improvements or office leasehold improvements) made to the interior of a commercial real property.

The depreciation calculations allocate deductions of the asset's cost over a recovery period roughly consistent with the asset's estimated useful economic life. These are general estimates that the IRS has assigned to certain types of assets, and the true economic life of an asset might differ.

MACRS Class Life Table

Class Life	Asset Type
3-year property	Certain tractor units; racehorses over two years old when placed into service; qualified rent-to-own property.
5-year property	Computers; office machinery; small aircraft, automobiles, taxis, buses, and trucks; breeding cattle and dairy cattle; appliances, carpets, and furniture used in residential rental activity; certain geothermal, solar, and wind property. NEW agricultural machinery and equipment.[95]
7-year property	Office furniture and fixtures; grain bins, cotton ginning equipment, USED agricultural machinery and equipment, and any other property that does not have a designated class life.
10-year property	Vessels and water transportation equipment; trees or vines bearing fruit or nuts; single purpose agricultural or horticultural structures (such as a grain silo).
15-year property	Land improvements such as fences, roads, and bridges; municipal wastewater treatment plants; qualified restaurant and retail improvement property; qualified leasehold improvement property.
20-year property	Certain farm buildings, such as a horse stable or an animal barn (does not include single purpose agricultural or horticultural structures).
25-year property	Certain municipal sewers; water utility property, including property integral to the gathering, treatment or commercial distribution of water.
27.5-year property	Residential rental property, if more than 80% of its gross rental income is from dwelling units. It also includes escalators, elevators, if installed inside the residential buildings.
39-year property	Any nonresidential real property, such as office buildings, stores, commercial malls, factory buildings, and warehouses (section 1250 property). It also includes escalators, elevators, if installed inside nonresidential buildings.

[95] The Tax Cuts and Jobs Act shortened the MACRS depreciation period for NEW farming equipment and machinery from seven years to five years. *Used* farming equipment remains seven-year property. The shorter recovery period does not apply to grain bins, cotton ginning equipment, fences, and other land improvements. The TCJA also repealed the required use of the 150% declining balance method for property used in a farming business. Special rules for farmers are covered in a later unit dedicated specifically to farming businesses.

Reporting Depreciation: A taxpayer must use Form 4562, *Depreciation and Amortization* to:

- Claim deductions for depreciation and amortization;
- Make an election under section 179 to currently expense certain depreciable property;
- To claim Bonus Depreciation for qualified property; and
- Provide information on the business use of automobiles and other listed property.

Depreciation begins when a taxpayer places the property in service of a trade or business or for the production of income.

Example: On June 23, 2020, Kendra bought a home to use as residential rental property. She made several repairs and had it ready for rent on September 1, 2020. At that time, she began to advertise the home for rent in the local newspaper. Kendra did not find a tenant until November 10, 2020. She can begin to depreciate the rental property in September and start taking other rental expenses because the property is considered "placed in service" when it is ready and available for rent.

Nondepreciable Assets

Certain property cannot be depreciated, including:

- Raw land (although land improvements, such as fences, landscaping, bridges and roads, can be depreciated)
- Property placed in service and disposed of in the same year, or property with a useful life of one year or less
- Property used only for personal use
- Inventory or any other property held for sale for customers
- Section 197 intangibles such as copyrights, patents, franchises, non-compete agreements, and goodwill. These intangible assets must be *amortized*, not depreciated.

Example: Lilly is a self-employed bookkeeper who offers payroll services. She must purchase new payroll software every year. Lilly should not depreciate the software, but may instead deduct its entire cost as a business expense since the software has a useful life of only one year.

If an asset, such as a home or motor vehicle, is both personal use and business use, only the business portion of its cost may be depreciated as a business expense.

Example: Kenton is a part-time videographer. He advertises his video services online and does wedding videography. He also uses his videography equipment to record various family functions, including his own son's wedding and a family reunion. He uses the equipment approximately 60% of the time for business, and the rest (40%) for personal-use. The cost of the equipment must be allocated between business and personal-use based on these percentages.

Example: Auto Dismantlers, Inc. buys an industrial car-crushing machine. The machine is delivered on December 20, 2020. However, the machine is not installed and operational until January 12, 2021. It is not considered "placed in service" until 2021, and the first depreciation expense deduction can be claimed in 2021. If the machine had been ready and available for use when it was delivered, it would have been considered "placed in service" in 2020, even if it were not actually used until the following year.

Depreciation Methods in General

Once a business chooses a depreciation method for an asset, the business must generally use the same method for the life of the asset. A business that wishes to switch depreciation methods may do so, but the business must ask for permission first, by filing Form 3115, *Application for Change in Accounting Method,* before switching the depreciation method on a fixed asset.

Note: A business is allowed to switch to the straight-line method without prior IRS consent. The most common switch is from the double-declining balance method to the straight-line method.

Straight-Line Depreciation: This is the simplest depreciation method and the default for residential and nonresidential real property. This method lets a business deduct the same amount of depreciation each year over the useful life of the property. It is the most conservative depreciation method. To use the straight-line method, a business must first determine the asset's basis and estimated useful life. The balance is the total depreciation expense deduction the business can take over the useful life of the property.

If an asset originally cost $200 and a five-year recovery period, the straight-line depreciation allowance would be $40 ($200 ÷ 5) each year for five years.

Straight-line Depreciation = Cost ÷ Useful Life

A business may switch to the straight-line method at any time during the useful life of the property without IRS consent. However, after a business switches to straight-line depreciation for a particular asset, it cannot change *back* to any other method for a period of ten years without written permission from the IRS.

Example: On April 1, 2020, Greystone Software Corporation purchases an advanced computer system for $40,000. The business chooses not to take any accelerated depreciation and elects to take straight-line depreciation instead. The system has a five-year life. Depreciation under the straight-line method is calculated as follows:

Depreciation for 2020 = ($40,000 ÷ 5 years) × (9 months ÷ 12) = **$6,000.**

Depreciation for 2021 = ($40,000 ÷ 5 years) × (12 ÷ 12) = **$8,000.**

The Double-Declining Balance Method: This method is also known as the "200% declining-balance method of depreciation". It uses a flat percentage depreciation rate over the life of the asset. For example, if five years is the asset's life, the double-declining balance method has a depreciation rate of (2 ÷ 5), or twice the straight-line depreciation rate. Instead of spreading the cost of the asset evenly over its life, this method expenses the asset by applying a constant rate to the declining balance of the asset, which results in declining depreciation expense each successive period.

The logic for the double-declining balance method is that there should be a greater deduction in the earlier years when the asset is more productive.

Example: Marblewood Farms purchases a tractor for $20,000 on January 1, 2020. The tractor has a five-year life. Using the double-declining balance method, the first year depreciation is $8,000 = ([2 ÷ 5] × $20,000) in the first year; $4,800 = ([2 ÷ 5] × [$20,000 - $8,000]) in the second year; $2,880 = ([2 ÷ 5] × [$20,000 - $8,000 - $4,800]) in the third year; and so on.

The Section 179 Deduction

The section 179 deduction is a special allowance that allows a business to elect to take a full deduction for the cost of new or used property in the first year it is placed in service, rather than depreciating it over its useful life. The section 179 deduction may be elected on an item by item basis, so the business does not have to claim it on all eligible property bought during the year. The Section 179 deduction is adjusted for inflation every year.

In 2020, businesses can expense up to $1,040,000 in qualified asset purchases under section 179. A reduction of the maximum 179 deduction is based on section 179 eligible assets placed in service during the year and the phaseout threshold is $2,590,000 in 2020. What this means is that the maximum 179 deduction is decreased by $1 for each $1 of section 179 *eligible* property placed in service in excess of $2,590,000 million. No section 179 deduction is permitted once the total section 179-eligible property placed in service for the year exceeds $3,630,000 (in 2020). This limit is often called the section 179 "spending cap."

Example: Arcade Manufacturing, Inc. is a company that manufactures pinball machines. In 2020, the company invests in new manufacturing equipment and places it all into service in 2020. The total cost of the manufacturing equipment is $4 million. Arcade Manufacturing is not eligible for the Section 179 deduction, because the cost of the property exceeds the spending cap. The business may still depreciate the cost of the equipment using regular depreciation, or bonus depreciation, if the business chooses to do so.

To qualify for the section 179 deduction, the property must meet all the following requirements:

- It must be eligible property.
- It must be acquired for business use (and used more than 50% for business).
- It must have been acquired by purchase (not by inheritance or as a gift).
- It must not have been purchased from a related party. For the purposes of this rule, "related parties" only includes a spouse, ancestors, or lineal descendants (the family attribution rules do not apply to siblings for purposes of section 179).

The section 179 deduction is not eligible for land, intangible assets (except off-the-shelf computer software), inventory, or property used outside the United States. The section 179 deduction applies to eligible property when it is "placed in service." This may be different than the date of purchase. Property is considered "placed in service" when it is ready and available to use, even if the item is not being currently used.

Eligible Property

Eligible section 179 property includes the following:

- Section 1245 property (i.e., tangible personal property used in a business, such as machinery, office furniture, and equipment)
  - Gasoline storage tanks and pumps at retail service stations.
  - Livestock, including horses, cattle, hogs, sheep, goats, and mink and other furbearing animals (not including livestock inventory or livestock that is held for sale to customers)

    - Certain property used predominantly to furnish lodging or in connection with the furnishing of lodging.
- Off-the-shelf computer software
- Qualified section 179 real property[96]
    - Qualified improvement property (QIP) under IRC Sec. 168(e)(6)
    - Certain property used in *nonresidential* buildings:
        - Roofs
        - Heating, ventilation, and air conditioning property
        - Fire protection systems
        - Alarm systems and security systems
- Single-purpose agricultural or horticultural property (includes grain silos, hog houses, poultry barns, livestock sheds, etc.)
- Storage facilities used in connection with distributing petroleum or any primary product of petroleum.

Note: The TCJA expanded the definition of Section 179 property to include depreciable property used in connection with furnishing lodging. This includes: furniture, refrigerators, ranges, and other equipment used in the living quarters of a lodging facility such as a dormitory where sleeping accommodations are provided. This does not include residential rentals, however.

Example: Redwood Recovery, Inc. is an inpatient alcohol and drug recovery facility. Redwood Recovery offers dormitory housing for patients who are recovering from addiction. In 2020, Redwood Recovery purchases new beds and mattresses for all the dormitory rooms, at a total cost of $23,000. The company can deduct the entire cost under section 179, under the expanded rules for qualifying property.

Example: Academy Developers, LLP owns and manages a commercial office building. The building is rented out exclusively to business tenants, so the building qualifies as nonresidential real property. In 2020, Academy Developers purchases and installs a new security system at the cost of $19,500. The cost of the security system is eligible for expensing under section 179.

Example: Hiroto owns a factory building that is used for manufacturing operations. On January 10, 2020, he purchases a new industrial ventilation system for the building at the cost of $1.5 million. He did not purchase any other qualifying business assets during the year. He claims $1,040,000 of the ventilation system's cost as a section 179 deduction, which is the maximum section 179 deduction that he can take on the purchase. In this way, the majority of the system's cost can be expensed in its first year rather than depreciated over a 39-year period. The remaining cost of $460,000 he can depreciate over the asset's useful life.

Qualified Improvement Property *does not* include the following real property improvements:

- Any enlargement of the building,
- Any elevator or escalator, or
- The expansion of the internal structural framework of the building.

---

[96] The TCJA expanded the definition of section 179 qualified property to include the following improvements to nonresidential real property: Roofs, HVAC systems, fire protection and alarm systems, and security systems and security alarms.

Example: Summerwood Property Brokers, Inc. owns a shopping center that is rented out to independent retailers. In 2020, Summerwood Brokers installs a new escalator inside the interior of the building. The cost of the new escalator is $152,000. The escalator is not "qualified improvement property," so it is not eligible for section 179 expensing. Summerwood Brokers cannot claim accelerated depreciation for the escalator, but it can depreciate the cost of the escalator using MACRS over its useful life.

The section 179 deduction for the current year may *not* exceed taxable business income for the year, calculated without regard to the section 179 deduction itself and certain other items. In other words, the section 179 deduction cannot be used to generate a business loss. However, an amount disallowed due to the taxable income limitation may be carried over for an unlimited number of years. Section 179 is more flexible than bonus depreciation. With Section 179, a business may choose to claim Section 179 on some assets, and not on others.

Example: Samantha is a self-employed enrolled agent. She opened her tax preparation business on January 15, 2020. She purchases tax-preparation software for $900, a computer system for $6,700, and a multi-telephone line system for $4,400 during the year. All of the property is Section 179 eligible. After applying her other business expenses, her net income for the year is $10,000. She could claim Section 179 on all her asset purchases, and bring her income down to zero. However, she doesn't want to do that, because she wants to make an IRA contribution for the year. She claims Section 179 only on the software, leaving plenty of taxable income on her Schedule C to make a maximum IRS contribution.

Note: The section 179 deduction is *not automatic*—it is an election that a business may choose to take each year, assuming the business has qualifying property. A business must "elect in" to take section 179 on an asset. Bonus Depreciation is the opposite—a business must "elect out" of Bonus Depreciation, otherwise it will automatically apply.

For partnerships, the section 179 limits described above apply to both the partnership and to each individual partner. The partnership determines its deduction subject to these limits, and then allocates the deduction among the partners. The partner considers the amounts allocated based upon his interest in the partnership and from any other sources in relation to the same limits.

Trade-in Property: If a business buys qualifying property with cash and a trade-in, its depreciable basis for purposes of the section 179 deduction includes only the cash portion of the purchase price.

Luxury Sports Utility Vehicle Exception: A taxpayer cannot elect to expense under section 179 more than $25,900 in 2020 of the cost of any heavy sport-utility vehicle (SUV) and certain other vehicles placed in service during the tax year. This rule applies to most vehicles weighing between 6,000 and 14,000 pounds.

This rule does not apply to certain types of "nonpersonal-use" vehicles, including ambulances, hearses, taxis, transport vans, shuttle vans, clearly marked emergency vehicles and other qualified nonpersonal use vehicles, regardless of the vehicle's weight.

Example: Airport Shuttle Service purchased a $75,000 shuttle bus in 2020. The shuttle weighs 7,900 pounds, seats 10 passengers, and is 100% business-use. Since this vehicle qualifies for an exception as a nonpersonal-use vehicle, the entire $75,000 would be fully deductible under section 179.

Bonus Depreciation (Special Depreciation Allowance)

Bonus depreciation is sometimes called the "special depreciation allowance" or just "special allowance."[97] Before the Tax Cuts and Jobs Act, businesses were allowed to deduct 50% of the cost of most new tangible property (used property was not eligible for bonus depreciation in prior years). Unlike section 179, bonus depreciation is not limited to the business's taxable income, so bonus depreciation can be used to generate a net operating loss.

Under the TCJA, a 100% first-year bonus depreciation deduction is allowed for qualified property, whether the property is new or used, as long as the property is *acquired* and *placed in service* after September 27, 2017. Qualifying property cannot be acquired from a related party unless the property is new. The definition of "qualified property" for bonus depreciation purposes is slightly different than for section 179. Qualified property for bonus depreciation includes the following assets:

- Tangible personal property with an applicable MACRS recovery period of 20 years or less,
- Water utility property,
- Purchased computer software,
- Costs incurred for qualified film, television and live theatrical productions[98]
- Fruit or nut-bearing trees and vines
- Qualified Improvement Property (QIP).[99]

Example: Interweave Music Group, Inc. purchased $10 million in sound equipment for use in its sound production business. The equipment was installed and ready for use on March 15, 2020. Chamber Music Group cannot claim section 179 on the purchase because $10 million dollars is above the section 179 "spending cap." However, the business can use bonus depreciation to fully expense the cost of the equipment in 2020.

Non-Qualifying Property

Certain types of property are not eligible for bonus depreciation. One such exclusion from qualified property is for property primarily used in the trade or business of the furnishing or sale of:

- Electrical energy, water or sewage disposal services,
- Gas or steam through a local distribution system or
- Transportation of gas or steam by pipeline.

---

97 The applicable code section is IRC §168(k), special allowance for certain property. The IRS uses both terms in the official publications and the IRS website. The IRS uses the term "bonus depreciation" in the official Prometric EA exam testing specs, but IRS Publication 946 calls it the "special depreciation allowance"

98 The TCJA added qualified film, television and live theatrical productions as types of qualified property that may be eligible for 100% bonus depreciation. For IRS purposes, a film or production is considered "placed in service" at the time of initial release, broadcast, or live performance.

99 The CARES Act included a technical correction that assigns a 15-year recovery period to qualified improvement property (QIP). The technical correction is retroactive and takes effect for qualifying property acquired and placed into service beginning January 1, 2018.

The TCJA also added an exclusion for any property used in a trade or business that has had floor-plan financing indebtedness. Floor-plan financing indebtedness is secured by motor vehicle inventory in a business that sells or leases motor vehicles to retail customers.

The bonus depreciation allowance does not apply to most real property (such as the purchase of raw land or the purchase of an entire building) or any intangible assets, such as patents, franchises, or copyrights.

There is an "ordering rule" for accelerated depreciation, but only if a taxpayer claims section 179 and bonus depreciation in the same year. The section 179 deduction is considered first (because it cannot produce a loss), followed by bonus depreciation (which can produce a loss), and then by regular depreciation. After applying bonus depreciation, normally there will be no basis remaining for regular depreciation after any bonus depreciation has been taken on the asset. If a business does not qualify to take the section 179 deduction for whatever reason, then the ordering rules do not apply, and any qualifying property will be subject to bonus depreciation, unless the taxpayer elects out. A taxpayer is never required to take *any* accelerated depreciation if they do not want to, but they have to *elect out* of bonus depreciation, and it has to be done on a timely-filed return.

Note: Bonus depreciation is not subject to the same phase-outs as the section 179 deduction, so bonus depreciation is available to much larger businesses, while section 179 is generally only available to small and mid-sized businesses.

Example: Leonard purchases an industrial excavator for his quarrying business on November 30, 2020. The cost of the excavator is $4.5 million. The cost of the excavator exceeds the section 179 spending cap, so he cannot claim section 179 on the purchase of the excavator. However, he may deduct 100% of the asset's cost by taking bonus depreciation.

Example: Persephone purchases a patent and a factory building for use in her manufacturing business. She spends $73,000 on the patent and $450,000 on the factory building. Neither asset qualifies for bonus depreciation or section 179 (the building is real property, and the patent is an intangible asset). She may depreciate the building using straight-line depreciation over 39 years, and she may amortize the patent over 15 years (to be discussed later under *amortization*).

Keep in mind that a business cannot *delay* claiming bonus depreciation to a future tax year. The business has to claim bonus depreciation in the year the asset is first placed in service.

Unlike section 179, bonus depreciation does not have a dollar limitation or a spending cap. A business can deduct any amount of bonus depreciation, and if the deduction creates a net operating loss, the business can carry any unused loss forward to deduct against future income.

Electing Out of Bonus Depreciation

If a business fails to properly "elect out" of bonus depreciation, depreciation deductions on the qualifying property must be computed as if the bonus deduction had been claimed on the return, even if the taxpayer did not claim a bonus depreciation deduction for the year the property was placed in service. In other words, a taxpayer can choose to "opt-out" of bonus depreciation, but the election to opt-out must be made on a timely-filed return (including extensions). If the taxpayer files a delinquent tax return, then the option to elect out of bonus depreciation is not available.

The election is made for each asset class the taxpayer for which the taxpayers does not want bonus depreciation (i.e., 3-year, 5-year). In other words, if an election is made, it applies to all qualified property that is in the same class of property and placed in service by the taxpayer in the same taxable year.

Example: Clearview Farms, Inc. purchases several large business assets during the year. It purchases livestock fencing for $695,000 (15-year property), a steel grain silo for $500,000 (10-year property), and industrial farming machinery for $2.5 million (7-year property). Clearview farms cannot take Section 179, because the business has exceeded the "spending cap" for the year. However, the business does qualify for bonus depreciation. All of these assets are different asset classes, which means that Clearview Farms may choose to elect out of bonus for any of these assets separately, or take bonus for all of them.

A taxpayer may *revoke* a prior election to opt-out of bonus depreciation by filing an amended return for the applicable tax year. This only applies if the original return was filed on a timely basis, however.

Note: Taxpayers who *elect out* of bonus depreciation must do so *every year*, on a timely-filed return. Taxpayers who have already timely filed their current-year return and did not elect out but still wish to do so, have six months from the original filing deadline, without an extension, to file an amended return in order to **elect out** of bonus depreciation.

There are many times that businesses may wish to elect out of accelerated depreciation. Examples of these scenarios would be companies that already have a net operating loss for the year, companies with expiring net operating loss carryforwards, the current year's marginal tax rate is expected to be lower than the marginal tax rates for the taxpayer in future years, or companies that wish to use, for a variety of other reasons, a slower method of depreciation in order to retain more of their depreciation deductions for future tax years.

Example: Bayside Advisors, LLC is a business operated as a sole proprietorship. In 2020, the owner of Bayside Advisors, Randy Shines, is in the 10% marginal tax bracket. On December 30, 2020, Bayside Advisors purchases and places into service an expensive computer system at a cost of $30,000. Since the computer system was placed into service in 2020, it is eligible for the 100% depreciation allowance under the bonus depreciation rules. Not including any potential social security or Medicare tax savings, this would result in a $3,000 income tax savings in 2020 for Randy, given his current tax rate bracket of 10%. However, Randy's business is doing so well that he expects to be in the 35% marginal tax rate bracket in future years. As such, by electing out of bonus depreciation for the computer system in 2020, most of the depreciation deduction over the class life of the computer (for depreciation taken after the current tax year), will result in a much higher 35% income tax savings to Randy than the relatively low 10% savings in the current year. Randy elects out of bonus depreciation and decides to depreciate the computer using the straight-line method. This allows him to allocate the depreciation deductions ratably to future tax years, which will save him more tax dollars in the future, when he anticipates his income will be higher.

Example: Alessandra operates a small coffee kiosk as a sole proprietor. She also owns a residential rental property that she reports on Schedule E. Alessandra purchased a new commercial espresso machine for her business that cost $4,000. Before applying her allowable depreciation for the year, she has $7,800 in taxable income on Schedule C from her coffee kiosk business. She also has rental income of $39,000 from her residential rental. Alessandra elects out of bonus depreciation for the year because she wants to be able to contribute to a traditional retirement plan. Only the income from her Schedule C is "qualifying income" for retirement contribution purposes, so she chooses straight-line depreciation on the espresso machine instead. This leaves her enough qualifying self-employment income on her return to make a full retirement plan contribution.

Note: The election *out* of bonus depreciation is made by attaching a statement to the return indicating the property for which you do not want to apply this special depreciation. Taxpayers may elect out of bonus depreciation for any class of property for any tax year.

Listed Property

Listed property is certain property that is used by taxpayers in a business which is also frequently used for personal purposes. In order to avoid the abuse of depreciation deductions for certain property, Congress enacted the "listed property" rules. Deductions for listed property are subject to special rules for depreciation, and more stringent recordkeeping rules. The IRS includes the following as **listed property:**

- Any passenger vehicle used for transportation. A "passenger automobile" is any four-wheeled vehicle and rated at 6,000 pounds or less of unloaded gross vehicle weight. However, the following vehicles are not considered "passenger automobiles" for listed property purposes, (regardless of their vehicle weight):
  - An ambulance, hearse, or a clearly-marked police or fire vehicle
  - A vehicle used directly in the trade or business of transporting persons or property for pay or hire (such as a shuttle bus, moving van, or school bus)
  - Any vehicle with a *loaded* gross vehicle weight of over 14,000 pounds that is specifically designed to carry cargo
  - Tractors and other special-purpose farm vehicles
  - A truck or van that has been specially modified into a qualified nonpersonal use vehicle.[100]
- Property used for entertainment, recreation, or amusement; such as photographic or video recording equipment

Note: The Tax Cuts and Jobs Act removed computers and peripheral equipment from the definition of listed property. Computer equipment used exclusively at a business location is never considered listed property.

If an item is used for both business and personal purposes, deductions for depreciation and section 179 are limited to the percentage of business use. Further, if the taxpayer's business use

[100] Qualified nonpersonal use vehicles are vehicles that by their nature are not likely to be used more than a minimal amount for personal purposes. They also include trucks and vans that have been specially modified, such as an electrician's van that had been permanently modified with interior shelving and painting the vehicle to display the company's name.

percentage is not more than 50%, section 179 deductions and bonus depreciation allowances are not allowed, and depreciation must be calculated using the straight-line method.

Example: In 2020, Gillian buys and places in service new videography equipment that costs $4,000. She uses the equipment 80% for her film business and 20% for personal purposes. She can deduct $3,200 under section 179 for the business portion of the cost (80% × $4,000).

Amortization

Amortization is used to deduct the cost or basis of an intangible asset over its estimated life. With the exception of off-the-shelf computer software, most intangible assets are not eligible for section 179 deductions. The basis of an intangible asset is the cost to purchase or create it.

Definition: Intangible property is property that has value, but it cannot be seen or touched. Examples of intangible assets include goodwill, patents, copyrights, trademarks, trade names, franchises, intellectual property, customer mailing lists, and favorable relationships with customers or suppliers that are carried over from an acquired business.

A taxpayer may amortize certain start-up costs for purchasing an active trade or business. These include only the investigative costs that help the taxpayer decide whether to purchase the business. Costs incurred in an attempt to purchase a specific business are capital costs that cannot be amortized.

Certain intangible assets, including the preceding examples, are designated by law as Section 197 intangibles and must be amortized, straight-line, over a 15-year period (180 months). In the case of franchise rights, non-contingent costs related to a franchise must be capitalized and amortized over 180 months. If the franchise agreement does not last for 180 months, any remaining basis in the franchise can be deducted in the year the franchise agreement ends.

Example: Roxanne wants to open her own tax preparation business. She wants to have name recognition for her business, so she decides to purchase a franchise, K&H Block. As the franchisee, Roxanne is granted the right to own and operate a business based in the franchisor's name. Roxanne pays an initial (non-contingent) franchise fee of $40,000 to the franchisor (K&H Block). The length of the franchise term is five years. Roxanne must amortize the franchise fee over 15 years (180 months). She cannot deduct the amount as a current expense. The franchise right is considered an "intangible asset" and is not eligible for section 179 or bonus depreciation. If she does not renew or extend the franchise after five years, any remaining balance can be deducted in the year the franchise agreement ends.

The valuation and classification of Section 197 intangibles is often used in the evaluation of a business for sale.

Example: Dr. Elisha is an optometrist. Another optometrist is retiring, so Dr. Elisha is purchasing his business for $1 million. The practice has $750,000 of tangible assets, including medical equipment and office furnishings. The remainder of the purchase price ($250,000) is attributed to goodwill, which Dr. Elisha must amortize over 15 years. Her goodwill amortization deduction is $16,667 a year ($250,000 ÷ 15).

Another example is the cost of a covenant not to compete executed in connection with the acquisition of a trade or business. As a section 197 intangible asset, this cost would be amortized over 15 years, even though the covenant agreement may be in place for a shorter period.

Example: Francis is a CPA who lives in Chicago, Illinois. He purchases a profitable accounting practice from another tax practitioner, Janice. Janice is selling her accounting business because she plans to retire and move overseas. Francis pays $1.8 million for Janice's CPA practice. Their contractual agreement includes a standard non-compete clause which prohibits Janice from soliciting clients and engaging in competing business activities within the city of Chicago for seven years. A professional appraiser values the covenant agreement at $240,000 of the purchase price. Francis must amortize the covenant not-to-compete over 15 years, even though the actual covenant period is seven years.

Depletion

Depletion is similar in concept to depreciation, and is the method of cost recovery for mining and agricultural activities. Depletion refers to the exhaustion of a natural resource as a result of production, such as by mining, quarrying, or cutting (of timber). Mineral property, timber, and natural gas are all examples of natural resources that are subject to the deduction for depletion. There are two ways of figuring depletion:

- **Cost depletion**
- **Percentage depletion**

Some businesses employ cost depletion at the outset of operations when a large number of units of the deposit are extracted and sold, and then convert to percentage depletion later when percentage depletion yields a more sizable deduction.

Cost Depletion: This method allocates the cost of a natural resource over the total anticipated volume to yield cost depletion per unit (expressed in tons, barrels, etc.) A depletion deduction is then allowed each year based on the units exploited. After a business determines the property's basis, estimates the total recoverable units, and knows the number of units sold during the tax year, it can calculate the cost depletion deduction as follows:

Divide the property's basis for depletion by estimated total recoverable units =

Rate per unit

Multiply the rate per unit by actual units sold =

Cost depletion deduction

Example: In 2020, Elroy buys a timber farm, and he estimates the timber can produce 300,000 lumber units when cut. At the time of purchase, the adjusted basis of the timber is $24,000. Elroy cuts and sells 27,000 lumber units during the year. Elroy's depletion rate for each unit is $.08 ($24,000 ÷ 300,000). His deduction for depletion in 2020 is $2,160 (27,000 × $.08).

Percentage Depletion: Under this method, a flat percentage of gross income from the property is taken as the depletion deduction. Percentage depletion is a tax benefit available to oil and gas investors as an incentive to develop domestic mineral and energy production.

Percentage depletion may not be used for timber, and its use for oil and gas properties is subject to strict limits. For many oil and gas investors, the percentage depletion deduction is the only deduction they take on their mineral royalty income. To figure percentage depletion, the business or investor multiplies a certain percentage, specified for each mineral, by gross income from the property during the year. The percentage is set by law and varies depending on the type of mineral property. There are different percentages for oil reserves, coal deposits, gravel pits, uranium, and so on. For example, the depletion set by the IRS for oil and gas wells is 15%.

Example: Veritas Energy, LLC purchases land for investment. Oil reserves are discovered on the land. In the first year, Veritas Energy extracts 1 million barrels of oil from the well. This results in a percentage depletion deduction of $150,000 ($1 million barrels x 15% depletion charge).

Section 179 and Bonus Depreciation

Provision	Section 179	Bonus Depreciation
First use	Property may be used or new	Property may be used or new
Annual limits	$1.04 million in 2020 (adjusted for inflation).	No dollar limit
Related party rules	Cannot be acquired from a related party	Cannot be acquired from a related party unless **new** property
Election	Must elect in. May elect Section 179 on individual asset purchases.	The election is automatic—a taxpayer must *elect out* if they do not want to claim bonus depreciation on the return. Electing out is handled on a class-by-class basis.
Delinquent filers	Allowable on a delinquent return. Never mandatory.	Mandatory unless the taxpayer opts-out on a timely-filed return.
Statutory end date	None, section 179 is permanent.	Phases down to 80% in 2023, 60% in 2024, 40% in 2025, and 20% in 2026.
Revocations	Revocations are allowable until the statute of limitations on the return has passed	Election out of bonus depreciation must be made on a timely filed return.[101]
Property cap	The phaseout threshold begins at $2.59 million.. No deduction once eligible property exceeds $3.63 million in 2020.	None. Bonus depreciation is available to most business types, regardless of size or gross receipts.
Qualified property	1. Tangible personal property 2. Qualified improvement property 3. Roofs, HVAC, fire protection systems, alarm systems, and security systems 4. Off-the-shelf software 5. Single-purpose agricultural or horticultural structures	1. Tangible personal property with a MACRS recovery period of 20 years or less, including machinery and equipment. 2. Qualified film, television, and live theatrical productions 3. Trees bearing fruits and nuts 4. Off-the-shelf software

[101] Rev. Proc. 2019-33, that provides guidance for taxpayers to make a late election (or to revoke a prior election) under section 168(k). This means that a taxpayer may revoke a prior election out of bonus depreciation by either filing an amended return or filing a Form 3115, Application for Change in Accounting Method, to make a late election, or taxpayers may revoke a prior election. This option is only available to taxpayers who filed timely returns.

Unit 8: Study Questions

(Test yourself and then check the correct answers at the end of this section.)

1. Friendship Dentistry bought out Cavity Busters Dentistry. The sale included dental supplies, furniture, fixtures, dental equipment, and goodwill of the existing practice. The contract also included a do-not-compete clause. The contract details of the sale are listed below.

Contract Purchase Details	
Dental Supplies	$4,000
Furniture	$16,500
Fixtures	$10,800
Dental equipment	$15,500
Goodwill and customer list	$60,000
A covenant not to compete	$40,000
Gross Sales Price	**$146,800**

Based on this information, what is the total dollar amount of the assets that must be amortized? How long is the required amortization period?

A. The goodwill ($60,000) must be amortized over 60 months (5 years).
B. The goodwill and equipment ($75,500) must be amortized over 60 months (5 years).
C. The goodwill and the covenant not to compete ($100,000) must be amortized over 180 months (15 years).
D. The entire purchase ($146,800) would be amortized as a single asset and classified as an installment sale.

2. If a taxpayer elects section 179 and does not elect out of bonus depreciation in the same year, bonus depreciation is taken:

A. After a section 179 deduction is taken.
B. Before a section 179 deduction is taken.
C. Before section 179 and regular MACRS deductions are taken.
D. After section 179 and regular MACRS deductions are taken.

3. Which of the following would not qualify for a depletion deduction?

A. Oil well.
B. Timber.
C. Diamond mine.
D. Dairy farm.

4. Matthew owns a pizza restaurant by becoming a franchise owner of Papa's Yummy Pizza, a popular Italian food chain. After being in business for six months, Matthew purchases new kitchen equipment costing $190,000. He also purchases a new POS computer system for use in his restaurant at a cost of $15,000. The initial cost of franchise rights, payable to Papa's Yummy Pizza was $25,000. Therefore, Matthew has the following outlays for the year:

New computer system	$15,000
New kitchen equipment	$190,000
Franchise asset	$25,000
Total asset purchases	**$230,000**

He wants to take section 179 for all his qualifying asset purchases. What is his allowable section 179 deduction?

A. $15,000
B. $190,000
C. $205,000
D. $230,000

5. Colton owns a construction company. He purchases used construction equipment from his grandfather and places it in service in 2020 as part of a bona fide business transaction. The equipment costs $5,500. Which of the following statements is correct?

A. Colton can claim a section 179 deduction for the equipment.
B. Colton can claim regular MACRS depreciation on the equipment.
C. Colton is not allowed to depreciate the equipment since it was purchased from a related party.
D. Colton may expense the machinery as supplies.

6. Zehra is a licensed therapist that works out of her home. She purchases a new computer for $1,100. She uses the computer 75% for her business and 25% for personal purposes. What is Zehra's section 179 deduction?

A. $0
B. $275
C. $825
D. $1,100

7. Louis is a sole proprietor who buys a new cell phone for $720. Based on his phone records, Louis uses the cell phone 45% for business use and 55% for personal use. What is his section 179 deduction?

A. $0
B. $324
C. $396
D. $720

8. Harper Construction, Inc. is a calendar-year, accrual-basis corporation that specializes in constructing office buildings. Harper Construction purchased a diesel truck on November 1, 2020, that had to be substantially modified for use in the business. Harper Construction accepted delivery of the modified truck on January 10, 2021. The truck was first used on a construction site on February 3, 2021. The truck is 100% business-use. What month can the company start depreciating the truck?

A. November 2020.
B. December 2020.
C. January 2021.
D. February 2021.

9. Which of the following vehicles is considered "listed property" for tax purposes?

A. An ambulance.
B. A hearse.
C. A compact passenger automobile.
D. A marked police car.

10. Which of the following properties is a business not allowed to depreciate?

A. Land.
B. Fruit trees.
C. Livestock.
D. Land improvements.

11. Which of the following types of business property qualifies for the section 179 deduction?

A. A delivery truck.
B. A business building.
C. A residential rental property.
D. A patent.

12. Using MACRS, what is the recovery period for depreciating a commercial office building?

A. 20 years.
B. 25 years.
C. 27.5 years.
D. 39 years.

13. On March 7, 2020, Super Star Construction, Inc. purchased a tower crane for their business. The crane cost $1,700,000. There were no other asset purchases for the year. Super Star Construction elected to take the maximum section 179 deduction on the crane. After applying the allowable section 179 deduction, what is the amount of *bonus depreciation* that the company can take on this asset purchased?

A. $0
B. $400,000
√C. $660,000
D. $1,020,000

14. None of the following assets are eligible for Bonus Depreciation, *except:*

√A. Factory building.
B. Qualified film production.
C. Goodwill.
D. Patent.

15. On April 1, 2020, Woodrow buys a medical office building that he plans to rent out to business tenants. He made several repairs to the building and had it ready for rent on August 1, 2020. He advertised the property in the newspaper, but did not get his first tenant until November 1, 2020. The tenant signed the lease on December 1, 2020 and finally moved in on that date. Which month can he begin depreciating the property?

A. April 2020.
√B. August 2020.
C. November 2020.
D. December 2020.

Unit 8: Quiz Answers

1. The answer is C. The cost of the goodwill and a covenant not-to-compete are both Section 197 intangible assets. These two assets total $100,000 of the contract price. These assets must be amortized over 15 years (180 months). The other assets listed are depreciable assets. Friendship Dentistry would depreciate the remaining assets using MACRS.

2. The answer is A. When figuring depreciation, applicable section 179 deductions are used first, followed by bonus depreciation, followed by MACRS depreciation (if any). This ordering rule only applies if a taxpayer elects section 179 and also takes bonus depreciation on the same asset in the same year.

3. The answer is D. A dairy farming business would not qualify since its activity does not involve the depletion of a natural resource. Depletion is the exhaustion of natural resources, such as mines, wells, quarries, and timber, as a result of production.

4. The answer is C. Matthew may expense the full cost of the kitchen equipment and the computer system. The cost of the franchise is not deductible under section 179. Therefore, Matthew's *allowable* section 179 deduction is **$205,000** ($15,000 + $190,000). Franchise rights are not eligible for section 179 or bonus depreciation. He may amortize the franchise asset over 15 years.

5. The answer is B. The equipment does not qualify as section 179 property because Colton and his grandfather are related persons, meaning Colton cannot claim a section 179 deduction. However, Colton may still depreciate the asset using the MACRS depreciation schedule.

6. The answer is C. The business part of the cost of the property is **$825** (75% × $1,100). Zehra may take a section 179 deduction only for the portion of the asset that is business-use.

7. The answer is A. Louis cannot claim section 179 on the cellphone purchase. When a taxpayer uses property for both business and nonbusiness purposes, he can elect the section 179 deduction only if he uses the property *more* than 50% for business in the year the asset is placed into service. Louis may nevertheless claim depreciation deductions for the business portion of the phone.

8. The answer is C. Harper Construction may consider the truck to have been placed in service when it is ready for its intended purpose, which was on January 10, 2021. Harper Construction does not actually need to use it for that purpose in order to begin depreciation, but the asset needs to be "ready and available" for business use.

9. The answer is C. Regular passenger automobiles weighing 6,000 pounds or less are treated as listed property for tax purposes.

10. The answer is A. The cost of land is not depreciable. Similarly, the costs of general grading or shaping of land are not depreciable because the land preparation is inextricably associated with the land. Land improvements, on the other hand, are depreciable. Examples of land improvements include: sidewalks, roads, canals, waterways, drainage facilities, sewers, wharves and docks, bridges, fences, landscaping, shrubbery, or radio and television transmitting towers (examples from Rev. Rul. 2001-60). All of the other assets listed would be depreciable.

11. The answer is A. A delivery truck may qualify for the section 179 deduction. Tangible personal property, including vehicles, generally qualifies for the section 179 deduction. Except for certain qualified real property (QRP), most real estate generally does not qualify for section 179 treatment. Intangible assets do not qualify for section 179 treatment.

12. The answer is D. Commercial real property is depreciated over a 39-year recovery period.

13. The answer is C. The section 179 deduction limit is $1,040,000 for 2020. Super Star Construction can take the maximum section 179 deduction, which reduces the asset's basis to **$660,000** ($1,700,000- $1,040,000). Therefore, the allowable bonus depreciation on the crane would be $660,000. After applying both section 179 and bonus depreciation, the asset's basis would be zero.

14. The answer is B. Qualified film, television, and live theatrical productions are qualified property that may be eligible for 100% bonus depreciation. None of the other assets listed would be eligible for Bonus Depreciation.

15. The answer is B. The building is considered "placed in service" in August when Woodrow had it "ready and available" for rent. He can begin to depreciate it in August, even though he didn't get his first tenant until months later.

Unit 9: Disposition of Business Assets

More Reading:
Publication 544, Sales and Other Dispositions of Assets
Publication 537, Installment Sales
Publication 547, Casualties, Disasters, and Thefts

There are many different ways a business can "dispose" of an asset. For example, an asset can be sold, traded, exchanged, abandoned, involuntarily converted, gifted, or destroyed. The tax treatment will vary based on the type of asset and the disposition method. Businesses treat the disposition of assets differently than individual taxpayers. A business may recognize a gain or loss for tax purposes if it:

- Sells an asset for cash
- Exchanges property for another property (a section 1031 exchange)
- Receives payment from a tenant for the cancellation of a lease
- Receives property to satisfy a debt
- Abandons property
- Loses property or has damaged property as a result of casualty or theft (and if it receives a subsequent insurance reimbursement)

A business may fully depreciate an asset until its adjusted basis is zero, but continue to use the asset thereafter. If the same asset is later sold or otherwise disposed of, its adjusted basis is compared to any amounts received to determine whether there is a taxable gain or loss. Any gain or loss from the disposition of a business asset is measured from the asset's adjusted basis on the date of disposition.

The treatment of gains or losses reportable for tax purposes is dependent upon whether the losses/gains are classified as capital gains and losses or as ordinary income (and whether the capital gains and losses are long-term or short-term).

Related Party Dispositions: There are also special rules for sales to related parties (such as a sale between related corporations, or a sale between a father and son). In general, no deduction is allowed for losses resulting from a sale or exchange of property between related parties. The loss disallowance is not affected by the fact that the related party transaction is a bona fide business transaction. In this case, related parties would include close family members, such as spouses, siblings, ancestors and lineal descendants, and closely-related businesses, such as two corporations under common control.

For individual taxpayers, long-term capital gains may be subject to more favorable tax rates. Unlike individuals, C corporations do not get preferential tax treatment for long-term capital gains. Corporate capital gains are simply added to the corporation's ordinary income and taxed at the corporation's regular tax rate. Corporate capital gains are covered in more detail later.

To properly report the disposition of an asset, a business must determine whether it is a capital asset, a noncapital asset, or a section 1231 asset. Gains and losses on dispositions of business assets are generally reported on Form 4797, *Sales of Business Property.*

Capital Assets

Capital assets include "personal-use" assets, collectibles,[102] and investment property such as stocks, bonds, and other securities (unless held by a professional securities dealer). Tax law divides investment profits into different classes determined by the holding period and the type of asset. Capital losses from the sale of *stock* are generally deductible (up to a certain limit), but losses from the sale of personal-use property are not deductible. We will discuss the differences in reporting and recognition of gain or loss on capital assets throughout this chapter.

Example: Alastair owns 25 mechanical toy banks, which he collects as a hobby. He is not a professional dealer of collectibles. Alastair's mechanical banks are considered capital assets. During the year, he sells one of his toy banks to a co-worker for $1,500. Alastair purchased the toy over five years ago, paying $900. Alastair must report a long-term capital gain of $600 on the sale. The sale of the toy bank would be reported on Schedule D (Form 1040).

Example: Osanna owns a pawn shop. She buys and sells collectible items. Osanna also carries mechanical banks, but they are part of her shop's inventory, so they are not capital assets. In 2020, she sells a toy bank for $1,800 to one of her regular customers. She originally paid $500 for the toy. She has had the toy bank in her inventory for over a year, but her holding period doesn't matter, because the toy is treated as inventory. Her income on the sale is ordinary income, and must be reported on Schedule C. The cost of the toy ($500) would be expensed as Cost of Goods Sold. She will pay income tax as well as self-employment tax on her profits.

Noncapital Assets

A noncapital asset is any property that is *not* a capital asset. Assets that are used in a trade or business or as rental property are called "noncapital assets." Noncapital assets include the following:

- Inventory, (including market livestock),
- Depreciable property used in a business, even if the asset is fully depreciated,
- Real property used in a trade or business, such as a commercial building or a residential rental property,
- **Self-produced** copyrights, transcripts, manuscripts, drawings, photographs, or artistic compositions,
- Accounts receivable or notes receivable acquired by a business,
- Stocks and bonds held by professional securities dealers,
- Collectibles held by a professional dealer (such as a pawn shop or comic book store),[103]
- Business supplies,
- Commodities and derivative financial instruments held by a professional stockbroker or securities broker.

---

[102] The term "collectibles" includes art, rugs, antiques, metals, gems, stamps, memorabilia, comic books, baseball cards, wine and spirits, and coins. The tax rate on the long-term gain from the sale of a collectible capital asset in 2020 is the taxpayer's ordinary tax rate, but no higher than 28%. This is only if the owner of the collectible is not a professional dealer, in which the collectibles would then be treated as inventory.

[103] When an individual taxpayer sells collectibles, the special tax rates on long-term capital gains do not apply. Instead, the taxpayer will owe tax at their ordinary marginal tax rate, with a cap of 28%. This rule does not apply to professional dealers, where the collectibles would be treated as regular inventory.

Example: In February 2020, Cheri purchases a black-and-white copy machine for use in her business for $5,500. In November 2020, she decides she needs a color copier instead. Cheri sells the used black-and-white copier for $3,000. The copier is a depreciable business asset, so it is treated as a noncapital asset. The loss on the sale of the copier would be deductible as a business expense.

Example: Calvin is a sole proprietor who files a Schedule C. Calvin owns a motorcycle shop that sells expensive custom motorcycles. In 2020, his motorcycle shop burns down. The fire completely destroys ten custom motorcycles that he has in inventory. He doesn't carry any business insurance to cover the loss. Since these motorcycles are business inventory (*noncapital* assets), his losses are fully deductible as a business loss. Calvin also lost his personal motorcycle in the fire, which was parked in the shop overnight. Calvin's motorcycle is a personal-use asset; therefore, this loss would not be deductible as a business expense.

Example: Yusef sells an office building to his daughter, Elif, in a bona-fide business transaction. The FMV of the building is $950,000 on the date of the sale, and they have a qualified appraisal on the property. Yusef's adjusted basis in the building is $1 million. He has a $50,000 loss on the sale ($950,000 sale price – $1 million adjusted basis). However, Yusef's loss is disallowed because Yusef and his daughter are related parties. Elif's basis for depreciation is $950,000, the amount she actually paid for the building. If, at a later date, Elif sells the building to an unrelated party, the $50,000 loss that was disallowed to her father will be allowed to reduce her own gain on the sale (but it cannot be used to create or increase her losses if she sells the building at an additional loss at a later date).[104]

Section 1231 Assets

Section 1231 property, as defined by section 1231 of the U.S. Internal Revenue Code, is real property or depreciable or amortizable business property that is held for *over one year* and used in a trade or business activity. Examples of Section 1231 assets include:

- Depreciable or amortizable business assets that have been held for more than one year,
- Real estate, buildings, or farmland used in a business,
- Natural resources, such as timber, coal, domestic iron ore;
- Most livestock held long-term for draft, breeding, dairy, or sporting purposes (examples include a stallion that is used for horseracing or a pedigree bull that is held for breeding and insemination).
- Unharvested crops of a farming business.

The tax code gives favorable tax treatment to transactions involving the disposition of section 1231 assets. If a taxpayer has a *net loss* from all section 1231 transactions, the loss is treated as ordinary loss. If the section 1231 transactions result in a *net gain*, the gain is generally treated as a long-term capital gain. This is a more favorable tax treatment since ordinary losses are not limited, and the long-term capital gain tax rates are more favorable than the rates for ordinary income.

[104] The use of the previously disallowed loss applies only to the recognition of gain (IRC §267). The loss disallowance restriction does not apply in the case of a distribution in complete liquidation of a corporation. (IRC §267(a)(1).)

However, this is not the case with depreciation recapture, or with any unrecaptured section 1231 losses that had been claimed in the prior five years (also known as the "five-year lookback rule"). Both are taxed as ordinary income, as discussed later. Gain or loss on the following transactions is subject to section 1231 treatment:

1. **Sale of cattle and horses:** They must be used for draft, breeding, dairy, or sporting purposes and held for **24 months** or longer.
2. **Sale of other livestock:** Other livestock includes hogs, mules, sheep, goats, donkeys, and other fur-bearing animals. They must be used for draft, breeding, dairy, or sporting purposes and held for **12 months** or longer. This does not include poultry.
3. **Sale of depreciable or amortizable property:** Business property and equipment that is held for more than one year is Section 1231 property. Examples include machinery and trucks, as well as amortizable section 197 intangibles, such as patents or copyrights.[105]
4. **Sale or exchange of business real estate:** The property must be used in a business activity and held for more than one year. Examples include barns, factory buildings, and office buildings.
5. **Sale of unharvested crops:** The crops and land must be sold or involuntarily converted, and the underlying land must have been held longer than one year. Growing crops sold with a leasehold on the land, even if sold to the same person in a single transaction, are not included.

Example: Barclay owns an antique vase that he purchased at auction two years ago. He also owns a residential rental property that he purchased eight years ago and two vehicles. One vehicle is a pizza delivery van he bought several years ago, which he uses exclusively in his pizza business. The second is his personal-use SUV that he uses for commuting and everyday errands. Barclay's assets are categorized as follows:

1. **Antique vase:** A capital asset (because it is a collectible, and he is not a dealer)
2. **Residential rental property:** Section 1231 (rental property held over one year)
3. **Pizza delivery van:** Section 1231 (business property held over one year)
4. **SUV:** A personal-use capital asset (because it is a personal-use vehicle)

Once again, examples of section 1231 property includes: commercial buildings, depreciable business machinery and equipment, land, depletable natural resources (such as timber, coal, and domestic iron ore), unharvested crops, and livestock that is held for draft, breeding or dairy purposes (except poultry). The property must be held and used in a trade or business for *more than* one year.[106]

Note: "Market livestock" are animals held for sale in the ordinary course of the taxpayer's business. These are treated as regular inventory for a farming business. Once the livestock is selected or held for breeding, dairy, or draft purposes, the livestock is considered a section 1231 asset.

---

105 Self-created intangibles, however, are *not* Section 1231 assets. For example, a self-created copyright or musical composition would not be a Section 1231 asset. This would also apply if the asset was gifted to another party.

106 Gains and losses from section 1231 property used in farming are reported on Form 4797, Sales of Business Property, which is then attached to the taxpayer's Schedule F.

Example: Isaiah owns a small farm where he raises goats for sale. Isaiah has three highly-prized and pedigreed male goats that are held for breeding purposes only (as studs). His remaining goats are raised for sale and eventual slaughter. In 2020, Isaiah is offered $7,900 for the sale of one of his pedigreed billy goats. Isaiah accepts the offer, and reports the sale of the stud goat on Form 4797, *Sales of Business Property*. Also during the year, he sells 15 of his other goats, which he sells for $250 each, for a gross of $3,750. The other 15 goats are treated as inventory, so that sale must be reported on Schedule F as an ordinary sale.

Example: Sports Town Hobbies is a retail shop that sells sports memorabilia. Sports memorabilia is usually classified as a collectible, and therefore, a capital asset. However, in this case, the sports memorabilia owned by the business would be noncapital assets, and simply treated as inventory. The income from the sale of the memorabilia would be treated as ordinary income. In 2020, Sports Town Hobbies also sells a piece of older display furniture that was used in the business to display merchandise. The display furniture was purchased seven years ago, and the owner decided it was time to upgrade it. The furniture display is a Section 1231 asset, because it was a depreciable asset used in the business and held for more than one year.

Example: Four years ago, Shred-X Corporation purchased an industrial shredder for $10,000. The company sells the used shredder in 2020 for $700. Shred-X had depreciated the asset down to $1,000, its remaining basis. The company has a loss of $300 on the sale of the shredder ($1,000 remaining basis - $700 sale price). The shredder is a section 1231 asset, and the loss is an ordinary loss.

The Five-Year Lookback Rule for Section 1231 Assets

Normally any net gains on all section 1231 transactions for the year are treated as long-term capital gains, giving these types of transactions a favorable tax treatment. However, there is one exception to this treatment, which is the five-year "look-back" recapture. This recapture rule states that, if there are any net 1231 *losses* in the prior five tax years, these prior five-year 1231 losses *change the character* of the 1231 gains in the current year from long-term capital gain to ordinary income. See the extended example, next.

Extended Example: Prairieland Dairy Farms, Inc. sold farm machinery and had $45,000 of section 1231 gains in 2020. In the five years prior to 2020, there was one year (2017) in which the corporation had net 1231 losses. In 2017, Prairieland Dairy had $12,000 of net 1231 losses from the sale of a farm building, which the corporation deducted as an ordinary loss in that tax year. Prairieland Dairy Farms did not sell any section 1231 assets in 2018 or 2019. Because the $12,000 of net section 1231 loss in 2017 was within the five-year lookback period prior to 2020 (in which it had a net 1231 gain of $45,000), and the 2017 losses were not already used in a five-year lookback recharacterization prior to 2020, for 2020, $12,000 of the $45,000 1231 gain will be treated as ordinary income (under the five-year lookback rule) and the remaining $33,000 will be classified as a long-term capital gain.

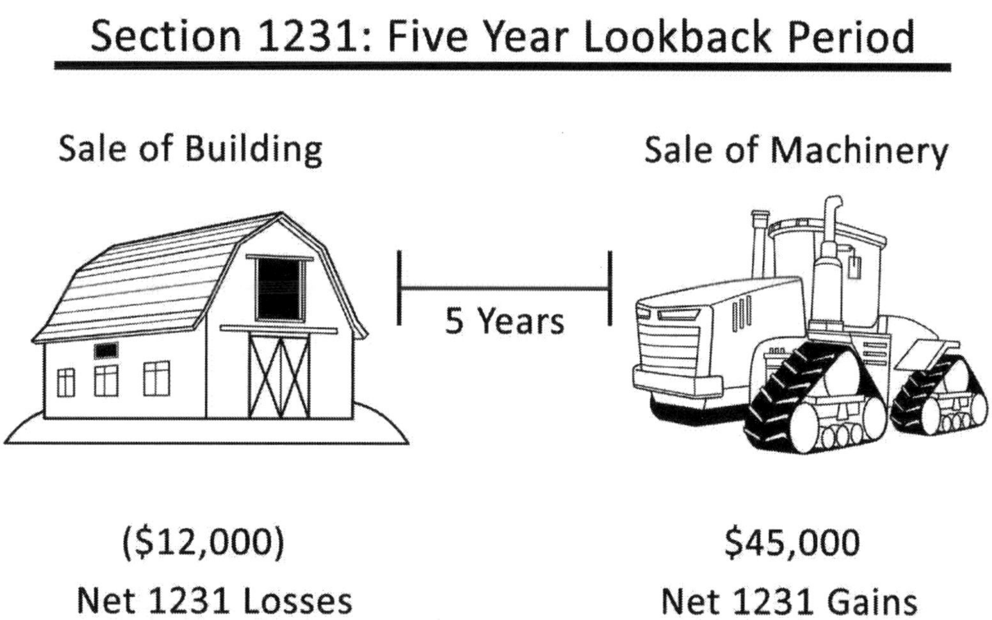

Note: Because all of the $12,000 of net 1231 losses from 2017 were recaptured (treated as ordinary income) in 2020 under the five-year lookback rule, none of the $12,000 net 1231 loss from 2017 will have to be included in any potential five-year lookback recharacterization analysis for either the 2021 or 2022 tax years. However, had the net 1231 losses from 2017 not been fully recaptured in 2020, the remaining unrecaptured 1231 losses from 2017 would have been potentially included in the five-year lookback analysis for the 2021 and 2022 tax years.

Example #2: Using the same facts as the previous example, except that if the 2017 net 1231 losses had been $60,000 instead of $12,000, then $45,000 of the $60,000 of net 1231 losses from 2017 would have recharacterized the net 1231 gains in 2020, from long-term capital gain to ordinary income. The remaining $15,000 of unrecaptured 1231 losses from 2017 would be included in the five-year lookback for 2021 (and potentially 2021 as well).

Example: Direct Aircraft Services, Inc. is a private jet charter service. In 2019, Direct Aircraft Services sold a used jet for a $50,000 loss. The jet was used in business operations for several years, so it was a section 1231 business asset. In 2020, Direct Aircraft Services sold another used jet and had a $100,000 Section 1231 gain. Applying the 5-year lookback rule, $50,000 of the 2020 gain would be **ordinary** and $50,000 would be treated as a **long-term capital gain**.

Study Note: Remember, section 1231 assets do NOT include: inventory, **self-created** copyrighted works, literary and musical compositions, and other types of artistic creations held by their creator, accounts receivable of a business, and U.S. government publications. In the case of livestock, only *poultry* would *not* be classified as a Section 1231 asset. This is because poultry, like chickens or turkeys, are typically short-lived.

Depreciation Recapture

Depreciation recapture may occur when a business sells previously depreciated or amortized property at a gain. All or a portion of the gain attributable to depreciation that would otherwise be treated as capital gain may need to be recaptured as ordinary income. The balance of the gain in excess of the recaptured depreciation is treated as capital gain.

Example: Oregon Timber, LLC is a calendar-year sole proprietorship. In 2018, Oregon Timber buys a heavy-duty truck (five-year property) that costs $10,000. The company decides to take MACRS depreciation instead of section 179 or bonus. MACRS depreciation deductions for the truck are $1,500 in 2018 and $2,550 in 2019 (based upon MACRS table for 150% declining balance depreciation using a half-year convention). Oregon Timber decides to sell the truck May 1, 2020, for $7,000. The MACRS deduction in 2020 until the date of the sale is $893 (½ of $1,785). The gain on the sale that must be treated as ordinary income is figured as follows:

Original purchase price	$10,000
MACRS depreciation deductions ($1,500 + $2,550 + $893)	(4,943)
Adjusted basis on the date of the sale	5,057
Amount received on the sale	7,000
Gain realized ($7,000 - $5,057)	**$1,943**

The realized gain on the sale of the truck is less than the amount of depreciation subject to recapture, so the entire amount is treated as ordinary income.

Section 1245 vs. Section 1250

In determining depreciable recapture for property sold at a gain, there is a critical distinction between two types of property: **section 1245** and **section 1250.** For section 1245 property, any gain attributable to previous depreciation deductions is taxed as ordinary income, subject to income tax; however, this gain amount escapes self-employment tax, which is a notable tax benefit. For section 1250 property, the ordinary income depreciation recapture is limited to the portion of previously deducted depreciation in excess of deductions that would have been taken if computed using the straight-line method. Because straight-line depreciation is normally required on buildings and other depreciable improvements, section 1250 recapture is very uncommon. As such, the focus on sales of depreciable real property at a gain should be on unrecaptured section 1250 gains.

Straight-line depreciation is taken as **unrecaptured section 1250 gain,** which is subject to a 25% maximum rate, which is also beneficial if the taxpayer is in a higher tax bracket than the 25% bracket. In other words, unrecaptured Section 1250 gain is the portion of a capital gain related to the amount a property has already been depreciated and which there is no section 1250 recapture (i.e., depreciation taken over straight-line). Unrecaptured Section 1250 gain generally only applies to depreciable real property, such as commercial buildings and residential rental properties. The next several sections will cover the difference between section 1250 property and section 1245 property.

Section 1245 Property

This type of property includes tangible personal property, (such as office furniture and equipment) that is subject to depreciation. Section 1245 property does not include buildings and structural components. Section 1245 property includes:

- Personal (tangible or intangible) property that is subject to depreciation,
- Intangible property, such as a patent, trademark, or franchise license, that is subject to amortization, or
- Other tangible property (not including buildings) that is depreciable, and that is:
  - Used as an integral part of certain specified activities (the manufacturing, production, extraction, or communication of electrical energy, gas, water, or sewage disposal services), or
  - A facility used for the bulk storage of fungible commodities.
  - Tenant improvements or leasehold improvements made by a lessee[107]

Definition: A "fungible good" or "fungible asset" is one that is essentially interchangeable with other goods or assets of the same type, such as a specific grade of a particular commodity. Examples of highly fungible commodities are crude oil, soybeans, and wheat.

A grain silo is considered section 1245 property rather than section 1250 property, even if it is attached permanently to the land. Storage structures for oil and gas and other minerals are also considered section 1245 property. In other words, they are not considered "buildings."

With the exception of real estate, most business assets will lose value as they age. Therefore, it is unusual for a business to sell depreciated assets at a large gain. However, it is possible, and when it happens, the net gain is given favorable tax treatment. The next examples will explain some scenarios where this might occur.

[107] Leasehold improvements or tenant improvements are enhancements to a leased space that are paid for by a tenant. For example, exterior fencing added by a lessee, built in cabinets, or interior wall partitions, such as those inside a medical office or dental office. A distinguishing factor here is that the lessee is not the owner of the building.

Example: Mallory publishes cookbooks on Cajun and Creole cooking. Several years ago, Mallory purchased a used book-binding machine for $9,000 for her cookbook publishing business. She has claimed $4,000 of depreciation on the machine. In 2020, Mallory paints and fixes up the machine, and is able to sell it for $11,000, which is more than she paid for it when she first bought it. Her gain is calculated as follows:

The sale price of the machine	$11,000
Minus adjusted basis ($9,000 - $4,000)	$5,000
Mallory's gain on the sale of the machine	**$6,000**

A portion of the gain is ordinary income ($4,000 of depreciation recapture), and the remainder of the gain ($2,000) is treated as long-term capital gain under section 1231 and given preferential tax treatment.

Example: Emmanuel owns a construction business. He is also very good at fixing things. Several years ago, he purchased a damaged bandsaw for $150. The bandsaw was nonfunctional, but Emmanuel fixed it up himself and got it running again. He used it in his business for several years. In 2020, a client offers Emmanuel $1,900 for the used bandsaw, which Emmanuel gladly accepts. He had depreciated the bandsaw's basis down to zero. The gain on the sale of the bandsaw is figured as follows:

Original purchase price	$150
MACRS depreciation deductions ($150)	($150)
Adjusted basis	$0
Amount received in the sale	$1,900
Gain realized ($150 depreciation recapture, $1,750 capital gain)	**$1,900**

Since he paid so little for the bandsaw to begin with, only a small portion of the gain is taxed as ordinary income ($150) from depreciation recapture, and the remainder of $1,750 gain is treated as long-term capital gain under section 1231 and given preferential tax treatment.

With regards to sales of livestock, in order to be treated as Section 1231 property, cattle or horses (specifically) must be held for draft, breeding, dairy, or sporting purposes and held for 2 years or longer.

Example: Dixie Farms breeds and sells horses for racing. Dixie Farms owns a champion stallion that is used for insemination and breeding purposes. The business originally paid $150,000 for the stallion five years ago. The stallion is properly depreciated as a business asset. In 2020, Dixie Equine Farms receives an offer to sell the stallion for $175,000, which is $25,000 more than the business originally paid for the horse. The stallion has been fully depreciated in 2020, and the current adjusted basis is zero. Dixie Farms accepts the buyer's offer and sells the stallion and reports the sale on Form 4797, *Sales of Business Property.* The gain on the sale is given favorable tax treatment because the stallion is considered a Section 1231 asset. The depreciation recapture portion of the gain ($150,000) is treated as ordinary income, but the gain that exceeds depreciation recapture ($25,000) is treated as a long-term capital gain.

Section 1250 Property

Section 1250 property usually consists of permanent structures and land improvements of general use and purpose. Common examples of section 1250 property include residential rental property, factory buildings, barns, warehouses, and office buildings. It also includes all types of commercial property, including medical centers, hotels and motels, malls, retail stores, multifamily apartment buildings, and parking garages.

Section 1250 includes the building, as well as a building's structural components, such as a deck, girders, and gutters. Section 1250 property must be used for business or held for investment, and not for personal use. As mentioned earlier in the chapter, the sale of Section 1250 property can result in **unrecaptured Section 1250 gain**, which is taxed at a maximum of 25%.

Example: Stavros is a real estate investor. He owns several apartment buildings and one factory building. He has owned all the buildings for several years. In 2020, he sells the factory building for $360,000. He originally purchased the building for $200,000 and had taken $50,000 in straight-line depreciation deductions, making his adjusted basis in the building $150,000 on the date of the sale. He has a total capital gain of $210,000 ($360,000 sales price - $150,000 basis). Of that amount, $50,000 of that gain is unrecaptured Section 1250 gain, and will be taxed at a maximum 25% capital gains tax rate, while the remaining gain ($160,000) is taxed at long-term capital gain rates.

Original purchase price of the factory building	$200,000
Depreciation	($50,000)
Adjusted basis before the sale	$150,000
Sale price of the building	$360,000
Total gain realized upon the sale	**$210,000**
Unrecaptured Section 1250 gain (taxed at a maximum of 25%)	$50,000
Long term capital gain (taxed at a maximum of 20%)	**$160,000**

Installment Sales

An installment sale involves a disposition of property in which the seller receives at least a portion of the sales proceeds during a year subsequent to the year of the sale. The resulting gain is typically reported using the installment method. The most common type of installment sale is the sale of real estate. If a business *elects out* of using the installment method, it must report the entire gain in the year of the sale, even if it does not receive the remaining proceeds until later years. Each payment received on an installment sale transaction may include the following components:

- Return of the seller's adjusted basis in the property
- Gain on the sale
- Interest income (attributable to financing the sale over a period of time)

The taxpayer must calculate a gross profit percentage, representing the ratio of the gain on the sale (numerator) to the total proceeds to be paid minus any interest income (denominator).

The denominator will also equal the total of the gain and the return of the seller's adjusted basis in the property. Each year, including the year of sale, the total payments received minus the portion attributable to interest is multiplied by the gross profit percentage to determine the portion of the gain that must be recognized.

Note: A taxpayer's gain, or gross profit, is the amount by which the selling price exceeds the adjusted basis in the property sold. The gross profit percentage is generally calculated by dividing the gross profit from the sale by the selling price. You may be required to understand how to calculate gross profit percentage for both Parts 1 and 2 of the EA exam.

Example: White Ridge Partners, LLP sells a plot of land for a price of $6,000, with a gross profit of $1,500, and it will receive payments totaling $6,000 plus interest over four years. The gross profit percentage is 25% ($1,500 ÷ $6,000). After subtracting the applicable interest portion from each payment, the business will apply the gross profit percentage to each installment, including any down payment, and report the resulting amount as installment sale income for each tax year in which it receives payments. The remainder of each payment is the tax-free return of the land's adjusted basis.

The taxpayer's gain from an installment sale is reported on Form 6252, *Installment Sale Income.* If the arrangement is modified at a later date or the full amount of the sale price is not paid, the resulting gross profit on the sale may also change.

In certain circumstances, a business may be treated as having received a payment, even though it has not received cash. For example, the receipt of property or the assumption of a mortgage by the buyer may be treated as a payment. If the buyer assumes or pays off a mortgage or other debt on the property sold, the calculation of gross profit percentage is affected.

The mortgage assumption is subtracted before calculating the gross profit percentage, except to the extent that it exceeds the adjusted basis of the property for installment sale purposes. In contrast, if the property is sold to a buyer who holds a mortgage on it and the mortgage is canceled rather than assumed, the cancellation is treated as a payment received in the year of the sale and is not subtracted in calculating the gross profit percentage.

If a business reports the sale of property under the installment method, any applicable depreciation recapture under section 1245 or 1250 is taxable in the year of sale, even if no payments are received in that year. If the gain is more than the depreciation recapture amount, the remainder of the gain would be recognized using the installment method rules.

An installment sale does not apply to:

- The sale of inventory, even if the business receives payment after the year of sale
- Dealer sales of real or personal property in the normal course of business
- A sale that results in a loss
- The sale of stock or securities traded on an established market

Installment sales to related persons are allowed. However, if a taxpayer sells property to a related person who then sells or disposes of the property within two years of the original sale, the taxpayer will lose the benefit of installment sale reporting.

Example: Regal Properties, Inc. sells a motel to a 51% shareholder of the corporation, Armand. The sale price of the motel is $2 million, and Regal Properties, Inc. realizes a profit on the sale of $250,000. Armand agrees to pay the note in five installments of $400,000. Eighteen months later, Armand sells the motel to another unrelated party. Regal Properties must report the entire profit of $250,000 on the sale, even though it has not received all of the installment payments. The installment sale method is disallowed on the related party sale, because the property was disposed of before the end of the two-year holding period.

Like-Kind Exchanges (Section 1031)

A section 1031 "like-kind" exchange occurs when a business or individual exchanges business or investment property for similar property. If an exchange qualifies under section 1031, the taxpayer does not pay tax currently on a resulting gain and cannot deduct a loss until the acquired property is later sold or otherwise disposed of.

To qualify under section 1031, an exchange must involve like-kind property. The Tax Cuts and Jobs Act now only allows section 1031 exchanges of real property. Personal property exchanges will no longer qualify. IRS regulations define "real property" for Section 1031 purposes as:

- Land and improvements to land (such as buildings, concrete parking lots, foundations),
- Unsevered natural products of land,
- Water and air space superjacent to land,
- Certain intangible interests in real property (such as leaseholds and options), and
- Property that is real property under state or local law.

Any "exchange" of personal property will be treated as a sale and will not qualify for nonrecognition treatment. This provision is permanent. To qualify for nonrecognition treatment, an exchange must meet all of the following conditions:

- The property must be held for investment or for productive use in a business.
- The property must not be "held primarily for sale" (i.e., *not* inventory)
- There must be an actual exchange of two or more assets or properties. The exchange of cash for property is treated as a sale, not as an exchange.
- In most cases, a qualified intermediary is used to facilitate a Section 1031 exchange. While a qualified intermediary is not required for all exchanges, a qualified intermediary is required for a delayed exchange.

In essence, most exchanges of real estate will qualify for Section 1031 exchange treatment, if the real estate is either held for investment or used in a business.

The most common type of 1031 exchange is a "simultaneous swap" of one rental property for another. However, taxpayers may exchange many different types of real property, even undeveloped land. The property can be improved or unimproved. For example, the exchange of a factory building for farmland would qualify, as would the exchange of a parking lot for an apartment complex.

As long as the real estate is domestic real estate (located in the United States) and not inventory or personal-use, the exchange will generally qualify. In contrast, simply selling a property and using the proceeds to purchase another similar property is a taxable transaction.

Example: Evergreen Medical Services, Inc. purchases a medical office building for $300,000. After four years, the fair market value of the building is $350,000. If the corporation were to sell the property, it would be forced to recognize a gain of $50,000. If Evergreen Medical Services instead arranges a like-kind exchange and either receives a similar property in exchange or invests the proceeds from the exchange of the building in a similar property, the taxable gain could be deferred.

Example: Goldfinch Realty Group is a professional realty company. Goldfinch Realty purchases distressed apartment homes and restores them, then sells them to investors. Goldfinch Realty does not rent out the properties; it merely flips them and re-sells them. Since the apartment homes are inventory, Goldfinch Realty cannot use section 1031 to escape recognition of gain on the transfer or sale of the properties.

A taxpayer who transfers property in a like-kind exchange must file Form 8824, *Like-Kind Exchanges*, with his tax return for the year of the exchange. If the exchange involves a related-party exchange, the form must also be filed for each of the following two years.

Deadlines for a Qualifying Exchange

In a section 1031 exchange, the property to be received must be identified in writing (or actually received) within 45 days after the date of transfer of the property given up. Further, the replacement property in a deferred exchange must be received by the earlier of:

- The 180th day after the date on which the property given up was transferred, or
- The due date, including extensions, of the tax return for the year in which the transfer of that property occurs.

These deadlines are based on calendar days; there are no exceptions for weekends or holidays. These deadlines are unwavering, except in the event of a natural disaster when the IRS may grant an extension.

Note: In 2020, the IRS provided a limited deadline extension for Section 1031 exchanges in response to the COVID-19 pandemic. IRS Notice 2020-23 stated that taxpayers in a current exchange with original 45 day or 180 day deadlines that fell between April 1 and July 15, 2020, that their 1031 deadline was extended to July 15, 2020. Note that these types of extensions are extremely rare.

In order for a section 1031 exchange to be valid, a qualified intermediary is generally used to facilitate the transaction. A "qualified intermediary" is an independent party who acquires the relinquished property and transfers it to a buyer.

The intermediary holds the sales proceeds to prevent the taxpayer from having actual or constructive receipt of the funds. The intermediary then acquires the replacement property and transfers it to the taxpayer to complete the exchange within the allowable time limits.

Example: Voland owns a piece of land in Texas he wants to exchange, and he arranges a 1031 exchange transaction by hiring a qualified intermediary first. When the land sale closes, his escrow company holds the proceeds. Within 45 days, Voland identifies an apartment building he wants to buy in Oregon and negotiates a contract to buy the building. Within the required 180 days, the escrow company releases the funds he needs to close the purchase, and the exchange transaction is complete. By using a qualified intermediary, Voland has successfully postponed recognition of any gain related to the disposition of the original property.

Qualifying Nontaxable Exchanges

An exchange of real property generally qualifies as like-kind, regardless of how each property is used or whether each property is improved or unimproved. For instance, the exchange of a building for farmland would qualify, as would the exchange of an apartment building for an office building.

The exchange of property *within* the United States for property *outside* the United States would not be considered an exchange of qualifying like-kind property.

Nonqualifying Exchanges: Personal-use realty is not eligible for section 1031 treatment, so the exchange of a personal residence for another personal residence does not qualify. Foreign realty is not eligible for nonrecognition treatment. And remember, inventory is never eligible for like-kind treatment.

Example: Claudia wants to do a Section 1031 exchange. She exchanges a residential rental property in Los Angeles for a beachfront condo in Maui. However, she does not intend to rent the condo in Maui, she simply wants to use it as a vacation home for herself. This is not a qualifying exchange. Later, Claudia's tax return is selected for audit. The like-kind exchange treatment is disallowed, and she is forced to recognize all the gain on the sale of her residential rental, in addition to paying penalties and interest.

Example: Sondra exchanges a residential rental in Hawaii with an adjusted basis of $100,000 with a vacation rental in Cancun, Mexico. The Cancun property has a fair market value of $145,000. The exchange of foreign realty for real property in the United States does not qualify for section 1031 treatment. Instead, the transaction is treated as a sale. Since the exchange does not qualify for nonrecognition treatment, Sondra must recognize $45,000 of capital gain on the transaction. Her basis in the Cancun property is $145,000, which would be the same treatment if the property had been purchased with cash.

Partially-Taxable 1031 Exchanges

If a taxpayer receives, in addition to like-kind property, property in exchange for other property that is not similar or related in use to the property exchanged, the taxpayer may need to recognize gain if the fair market value of the property received is greater than the adjusted basis of the property exchanged. His basis in the non-like-kind property ("boot") received is generally its FMV at the time of the exchange.

The taxable gain cannot exceed the amount of gain that would have been recognized if the property had been sold in a taxable transaction (i.e., the realized gain). The amount considered boot would be reduced by qualified costs paid in connection with the transaction.

Definition: "Boot" is a term used to describe cash or other non-like-kind property that is included in an exchange to compensate for a difference in the values of the like-kind properties traded. Cash boot is very common; it is usually given by one party in an exchange when one property is more valuable than the other. Cash boot will not invalidate a 1031 exchange, unless the exchange itself is not a valid exchange.

Example: Merrick owns a plot of farmland with a FMV of $300,000 and a basis of $100,000. He wants to exchange the farmland for an apartment building, which is owned by Annabelle. The apartment building is worth less than the farmland, with an approximate FMV of $275,000. In order to make up the difference in the value of the properties, Annabelle offers Merrick a used SUV with a fair market value of $20,000. Merrick accepts the SUV in lieu of cash and the exchange is completed. Since the SUV is "unlike" property, it is considered "boot" and the value is taxable. Although the exchange is still a qualifying exchange, Merrick will be forced to recognize $20,000 in taxable gain (the value of the vehicle).

When an exchange involves property that is subject to a liability, the assumption of the liability is treated as a transfer of cash and thus considered boot for the party who is relieved of the liability. If each property in an exchange is transferred subject to a liability, a taxpayer is treated as having received boot only if he is relieved of a greater liability than the liability he assumes. This is called "debt reduction boot," and it occurs most often when a taxpayer is acquiring a less expensive or less valuable property.

Although a taxpayer may have to recognize gain on a partially taxable like-kind exchange, the taxpayer would never recognize a loss. If a taxpayer receives boot in connection with an exchange and recognizes gain, the basis of the property received is equal to the basis of the property given up plus the amount of gain recognized.

The Basis of Property Received in a Like-Kind Exchange

The basis of the property received is generally the adjusted basis of the property transferred. If a taxpayer trades property and also pays money as part of the exchange, the basis of the property received is the basis of the property given up, increased by any additional money paid.

Example: Lockhart Realty, Inc. owns a small office building with an adjusted basis of $70,000 and a FMV of $145,000. During the year, Lockhart Realty trades the office building for an undeveloped plot of land with a FMV of $150,000. The company's basis in the land is $70,000, equal to the adjusted basis of the property she exchanged. The FMV of either property is irrelevant in the scenario.

Example: Alpine Assets, LLC trades a plot of farmland (adjusted basis $300,000) for a strip mall in another city (FMV $700,500). The company pays an additional $40,000 in cash to complete the exchange. Alpine Assets' basis in the strip mall is $340,000; its $300,000 basis in the farmland, plus the additional $40,000 cash paid to complete the transaction.

Related Party Exchanges

Like-kind exchanges are permitted between related parties, including between close family members. However, if either party disposes of the property within two years after a 1031 exchange, the exchange is usually disqualified from nonrecognition treatment; any gain or loss that was deferred in the original transaction must be recognized in the year the disposition occurs. The mandatory two year "holding period" begins on the date of the transfer of the last property involved in the exchange. However, there are some exceptions to the "two-year" rule. The two-year holding period rule does not apply:

- If one of the parties involved in the original exchange dies
- If the property is converted in an involuntary exchange (such as a fire or a flood)
- If it can be established to the satisfaction of the IRS that the exchange and subsequent disposition were not done for tax avoidance purposes

Example: Jarvis and Warrick are brothers. Jarvis owns a residential rental property, and Warrick owns an undeveloped tract of land. On January 10, 2020, they exchange their properties. Since they are related parties, each must hold the property he acquired for at least two years or the exchange may be disallowed and treated as a sale. On March 1, 2020, Warrick dies, and the rental property passes to his son, who promptly sells it. In this case, the original 1031 exchange is still valid, because the holding period rule does not apply if one of the parties in a related exchange dies before the two-year holding period expires.

Example: Bridget and Noel are sisters, and therefore related parties. Bridget and Noel exchange residential rental properties on July 1, 2020. The exchange qualifies as a section 1031 exchange. Bridget's rental property is completely destroyed by fire on November 1, 2020. Bridget receives insurance proceeds and reinvests the amounts in a parcel of farmland in another city. Since Bridget's disposition of the rental property was due to an involuntary conversion (a fire), it does not invalidate the earlier exchange that she made with her sister. No gain would have to be recognized by either Bridget or Noel because of the second disposition.

For purposes of this rule, a "related person" includes:

- A close family member. This includes a spouse, a child, siblings, ancestors and lineal descendants (such as parents and grandparents).
- An entity (corporation or partnership) in which the taxpayer owns either directly or indirectly more than a 50% interest. This includes ownership by a spouse or another close family member.
- Two entities in which the same taxpayer owns directly or indirectly more than 50% of each.
- An executor and a beneficiary of an estate.
- A trust for which the taxpayer is the fiduciary and the related party is a beneficiary either of that same trust or a related trust, or is a fiduciary of a related trust.

The IRS gives close scrutiny to exchanges between related parties because they can be used by taxpayers to evade taxes on gains.

Study Note: for the purposes of this rule, "related parties" does not include: step-parents, step-siblings, ex-spouses, uncles, aunts, nephews, nieces, in-laws, or cousins. Remember, half-siblings ARE related parties. Step-siblings are NOT related parties. Corporations or partnerships in which *more than* 50% of the stock or partnership interests, or *more than* 50% of the capital interests or profit interests, is owned by the taxpayer are also treated as related parties.

Example: Liliana and Marcel legally divorced on April 25, 2020. They have three children together. Their divorce was amicable. Three months after their divorce is finalized, Liliana and Marcel exchange rental properties in a Section 1031 transaction. Marcel sells his rental property ninety days later. Since their divorce was already final on the date of the exchange, then the exchange is valid. The related party transaction rules do not include ex-spouses.

Example: Justus exchanges rental properties with his step-sister, Marian. Six months after the exchange, Marian decides to sell the rental property and buy a boat. Since step-siblings are not considered related parties for the purposes of this rule, the original exchange is still valid.

Involuntary Conversions (Section 1033)

An involuntary conversion occurs when a taxpayer's property is lost, damaged, or destroyed, for which the taxpayer may receive an award, insurance reimbursement, or some other type of payment, as a result of:

- Theft, fire, flood, or another disaster,
- Condemnation, or
- Threat of condemnation

A taxpayer typically reports a gain or deducts a loss in the year the gain or loss is realized. However, under section 1033, a taxpayer can defer reporting gain on an involuntary conversion if he receives proceeds from insurance or another source and invests in property similar to the converted property. The gain on the involuntary conversion is then deferred until a taxable sale or exchange of the replacement property occurs at a later date.

Replacement Periods for Involuntary Conversions

While a section 1031 exchange only has a 180-day exchange period, a section 1033 exchange has a much longer time for completion. Unlike a Section 1031 exchange, there is no requirement that a qualified intermediary be employed to hold the escrow funds or conversion proceeds. However, *unlike* a section 1031 exchange, the replacement property cannot be purchased from a "related" party for an involuntary conversion to qualify for nonrecognition treatment.

The replacement period for an involuntary conversion generally ends two years after the end of the first tax year in which any part of the gain is realized. A three-year replacement period is allowed for real property that is held for investment (not including property held primarily for sale), such as office buildings or residential rentals.

The replacement period is four years for livestock that is involuntarily converted because of weather-related conditions. If the property is subject to an involuntary conversion in certain federally-declared disaster areas, the replacement period can be up to five years, depending on IRS guidance.

The replacement property must be purchased before the end of the tax year in which the replacement deadline applies. If the involuntary conversion property is not replaced within the allowed time period, an amended tax return would have to be filed for the year the involuntary conversion occurred, reporting a taxable transaction.

Property Type	Replacement Period
Most property except those noted below.	Two years
Real property (real estate) that is held for investment or business use, such as residential rentals and office buildings	Three years
Sale of livestock due to weather-related conditions	Four years
Main home in a federally declared disaster area	Four to five years

Basis Calculation on Converted Property

If a taxpayer reinvests in replacement property similar to the converted property, the replacement property's basis is the same as the converted property's basis on the date of the conversion, subject to the following adjustments: The basis is **decreased** by the following:

- Any loss a taxpayer recognizes on the involuntary conversion
- Any money a taxpayer receives that he does not spend on similar property

The basis is **increased** by the following:

- Any gain a taxpayer recognizes on the involuntary conversion
- Any additional costs of acquiring the replacement property

Usually, the taxpayer's basis in the new property will be its cost, reduced by any gain realized on the old property that was not recognized. However, the basis may be increased by any gain the taxpayer recognizes on the involuntary conversion and decreased by the following:

- Any loss the taxpayer recognizes on the involuntary conversion
- Any reimbursement he receives and does not reinvest in similar property

Example: A hurricane destroys Marissa's residential rental property that has an adjusted basis of $50,000. Marissa receives insurance reimbursement for $115,000, which was the fair market value of the property on the date the property was destroyed. Marissa buys a replacement rental property six months later for $115,000. Her gain on the involuntary conversion is $65,000 ($115,000 insurance settlement minus her $50,000 basis). However, Marissa does not have to recognize any taxable gain because she reinvested all the insurance proceeds in another, similar property. Her depreciable basis in the new rental property is $50,000 (the same basis as her old property).

Example: Angus Ranch, Inc. owns a livestock barn that is destroyed by a fire. The adjusted basis of the building was $40,000 before the fire. Angus Ranch files a claim with its insurance company, and receives an insurance settlement of $55,000. Six months later, Angus Ranch uses all the insurance money to rebuild the barn, paying an additional $20,000 to complete the construction. The depreciable basis in the new barn is $60,000 ($40,000 basis of the old barn $20,000 additional out-of-pocket costs). Angus Ranch does not have to be reported as a taxable transaction because it is a qualified involuntary conversion of business property.

Condemnations and Eminent Domain

A "condemnation" is a specific type of involuntary conversion. If a building is dangerous to public health and safety, the property may also be legally condemned. Condemnation is also a legal process by which private property is taken from its owner for public use. Sometimes this process is called "eminent domain."

Eminent domain allows the government to take private property in exchange for compensation. A property may be condemned by a state or local government or by a private organization that has the legal power to seize it.

The owner generally receives a condemnation award (money or property) in exchange for the property that is taken. A condemnation is a *forced sale,* with the owner being the seller and the government or other third party being the buyer.

Amounts taken out of a condemnation award to pay debts on the property are considered paid to the taxpayer and are included in the amount of the award.

Example: A local government informs Arnold that his farmland is being condemned to create a public highway. Although Arnold does not want to sell his land, the government forces the sale and issues a condemnation award to Arnold, paying him the property's fair market value of $400,000. Arnold's basis in the farmland was $80,000. Arnold decides not to purchase replacement farmland. Therefore, he has a taxable event, and he must recognize $320,000 as income ($400,000 - $80,000 = $320,000). However, if Arnold were to purchase replacement property with the condemnation award, he would have a nontaxable section 1033 exchange. He would have three years to replace the property with the condemnation proceeds, if he decided that he did not want to recognize any gain.

Example: Zion Realty, Inc. owns a large plot of land. The state government condemns the property in order to build a football stadium. The land had a basis of $260,000. The state pays Zion Realty $310,000 (the fair market value of the land at the time of the condemnation). Zion Realty has a gain of $50,000 on the condemnation ($310,000 - $260,000). Zion Realty purchases replacement land twelve months later for $290,000. The company puts the rest of the condemnation award into the bank. Zion Realty must recognize a gain of $20,000, which is the unspent part of the payment from the state ($310,000 award - $290,000 cost of the new property). The basis in the new land is as follows:[108]

Cost of replacement land: $290,000

Minus: Gain not recognized: ($30,000)

Basis of the replacement property: **$260,000**

The time period for replacing condemned property is the same as other qualified section 1033 exchanges, two years *after the end* of the first tax year in which any part of the gain on the condemnation is realized. For real property held for business use or investment, the replacement period is three years instead of two.

[108] Condemnation scenario based directly on an example in Publication 551, Basis of Assets.

Example: Macon Investments, Inc. paid $148,000 for a rental property many years ago. After factoring in depreciation deductions, the adjusted basis in the property is $75,000 at the beginning of 2020. The property is insured for $300,000 and is destroyed by a fire on June 1, 2020. On December 15, 2020, Macon Investments receives a $300,000 settlement from its insurance company. The business reinvests all the insurance proceeds, plus $5,000 in additional cash into a new rental property. Macon Investments qualifies to defer all the gain. The basis in the new property is $80,000 ($75,000 original basis + $5,000 additional cash investment).

Example: Mammoth Manufacturing owns a factory building. On October 2, 2020, the building was condemned by the state in order to build a railway. Mammoth Manufacturing receives a condemnation award from the state on March 1, 2021 (the following year). The business has until December 31, 2024 (three years *after the end* of the tax year in which it received the award), to replace the condemned factory with a similar building. This is because the factory is business-related real estate, so Mammoth Manufacturing has three full years to reinvest the proceeds in a similar property.

Unit 9: Study Questions

(Please test yourself and check the correct answers at the end of this section.)

1. On January 10, 2020, an office building owned by Agro Manufacturing burns down. The property had an adjusted basis of $190,000, and Agro Manufacturing receives an insurance reimbursement of $340,000. Agro Manufacturing buys another office property for $295,000 on November 8, 2020. What is the company's reportable gain as a result of this transaction?

A. $20,000
B. $30,000
C. $45,000
D. $150,000

2. Which of the following dispositions of depreciable property can trigger depreciation recapture?

A. Installment sale.
B. Gift.
C. Transfer at death.
D. Section 1031 exchange where no boot is received.

3. Caraway Carwash paid $200,000 for business equipment on January 5, 2020. They find that the equipment does not meet their needs, and Caraway decides to sell the equipment for $180,000 on October 10, 2020. They owned the equipment for less than 12 months, so Caraway had not taken any depreciation on the equipment yet. How should this transaction be reported?

A. Caraway has a section 1231 loss of $20,000 on the sale of the equipment. This is treated as an ordinary loss.
B. Caraway has a section 1231 loss of $20,000 on the sale of the equipment. This is treated as a capital loss.
C. This is an installment sale, with a loss of $20,000 that is treated as an ordinary loss.
D. Caraway has an ordinary loss.

4. Which of the following is *not* section 1245 property?

A. Office building.
B. Business computer.
C. Leasehold improvements made by a lessee.
D. Grain silo.

5. Arboreal Acres is a farming corporation. In 2020, Arboreal Acres sells a used tractor for $25,000. Arboreal Acres purchased the tractor seven years ago and has used it continuously on the farm. The original cost of the tractor was $20,000 because the business owner got a great deal on the tractor from a friend. The tractor is fully depreciated on the date of the sale. What is the tax treatment for Arboreal's sale of the tractor?

A. There is no gain or loss on the sale of the tractor.
B. Arboreal has a gain of $25,000. The first $20,000 is considered section 1245 recapture and is taxed as ordinary income. The remaining $5,000 is considered section 1231 gain.
C. Arboreal Acres has a gain of $25,000. The first $15,000 is considered section 1245 recapture and is taxed as ordinary income. The remaining $10,000 is considered section 1231 gain.
D. The entire gain is considered section 1245 recapture and will be taxed as ordinary income.

6. Eastwood Auto Painting, LLC is a partnership that does custom auto painting. The business owns a classic automobile, which was originally purchased for $20,000. It uses the automobile exclusively in its showroom to display its paint designs to potential customers. The car is only used as a show-piece and is not considered inventory. The automobile had been depreciated by $12,000, so the partnership's adjusted basis in it was $8,000 in 2020. A local museum asks to purchase the car in 2020, and Eastwood Auto Painting agrees to the sale, selling the car for $25,000. What is the nature of the tax treatment resulting from this sale?

A. Section 1231 gain of $17,000.
B. Ordinary income of $12,000 and a Section 1231 gain of $5,000.
C. Ordinary income of $17,000.
D. Section 1231 gain of $12,000 and ordinary income of $5,000.

7. Which of the following assets is *not* section 1231 property?

A. Office building held and used by a business for ten years.
B. Unharvested crops held for thirteen months.
C. Office equipment held for nine months.
D. A racehorse held for three years.

8. Jennifer operates Wavy Hair Salon, a sole proprietorship. In 2020, she sells all of her old salon chairs for $3,500 in order to buy new ones. She had purchased the chairs seven years ago for $15,000, and they were fully depreciated. Therefore, her basis in the chairs is zero at the time of the sale. How should she report this transaction?

A. She reports a loss of $11,500 on Schedule C.
B. She reports a gain of $3,500 on Form 4797 and Schedule C. The entire $3,500 is treated as depreciation recapture, which is subject to ordinary income tax rates.
C. She reports a gain of $3,500 on Form 4797 and Schedule C. The entire $3,500 is taxed as a long-term capital gain.
D. She is not required to report this sale.

9. Which of the following property types qualifies for section 1031 like-kind exchange?

A. A personal residence.
B. Inventory.
C. Corporation common stock.
D. Undeveloped land held for investment.

10. Which of the following property exchanges does *not* qualify as a like-kind exchange?

A. Exchange of an apartment building for an office building.
B. Exchange of timberland for a residential rental property.
C. Exchange of undeveloped farmland for a factory building.
D. Exchange of livestock for other livestock.

11. Turley Accountancy, LLP exchanges an office building with an adjusted basis of $125,000 for a strip mall building. The fair market value of the office building is $525,000. The fair market value of the strip mall is $519,000. Turley Accountancy pays an additional $4,000 to the seller to complete the exchange. After the exchange is completed, what is Turley Accountancy's basis in the strip mall?

A. $125,000
B. $129,000
C. $519,000
D. $525,000

12. Sergio owns several residential rental properties. He is not a real estate professional. He trades a condo in Mississippi (adjusted basis $30,000, FMV $50,000) for a duplex in Nevada (FMV $75,000) and pays an additional $19,000 cash to the seller in a qualified 1031 exchange. What is Sergio's basis in the Nevada duplex after the exchange?

A. $30,000
B. $49,000
C. $50,000
D. $75,000

13. Calgary Foods, Inc. trades an empty lot with an adjusted basis of $11,000 and pays additional cash of $6,000 for a parcel of farmland with a fair market value of $25,000. How much gain must Calgary Foods recognize in this Section 1031 exchange, and what is its new basis in the farmland?

<u>Gain</u>	<u>Basis of farmland</u>
A. $0	$17,000
B. $0	$25,000
C. $6,000	$17,000
D. $8,000	$25,000

14. Francine and Zachary are mother and son who complete a section 1031 exchange on January 21, 2020, properly exchanging two residential rentals. On June 29, 2020, Francine dies, and her rental property is inherited by her husband, who promptly sells it. Which of the following statements is correct?

A. Since one of the properties in the exchange has been sold before the two-year time limit for related parties, the section 1031 exchange is disallowed, and both parties (Zachary and Francine's Estate) must pay tax on the transaction.
B. The section 1031 exchange is still valid.
C. Since this was a related party exchange, the section 1031 exchange is still valid for Zachary, but Francine's estate must pay tax on the exchange because her husband disposed of the property before the two-year waiting period ended.
D. The nonrecognition treatment is lost for both parties, but Francine's husband is liable for the tax on the exchange, since he was the owner of the property when it was sold.

15. Sadie owns a small fitness gym as a sole proprietor. She sells some used fitness machines in 2020 for $65,000. She had purchased the equipment for $90,000 several years ago. She has taken $50,000 of depreciation deductions, and a section 179 deduction of $10,000. How should Sadie report the sale of these business assets?

A. Ordinary loss of $25,000.
B. Long-term capital gain of $35,000.
C. Ordinary income of $35,000.
D. Ordinary income of $10,000 and a long-term capital gain of $25,000.

16. Which of the following trades potentially qualifies as a tax-deferred like-kind exchange?

A. The exchange of a hotel in Houston, TX, for a hotel in Vancouver, Canada.
B. The exchange of a copyright for a patent.
C. The exchange of 100 shares of stock for 100 units of bonds.
D. The exchange of a parking lot for undeveloped farmland.

17. Cecil operates an auto salvage yard as a sole proprietorship. During the year, Cecil sold heavy equipment that was used in the business for $100,000. The original cost of the equipment was $120,000, and Cecil had claimed depreciation deductions totaling $47,000. Based on the information provided, what is the nature and amount of taxable income that will result from the sale of the equipment?

A. Capital gain of $27,000.
B. Ordinary income of $27,000.
C. Capital gain of $47,000 and an ordinary loss of $20,000.
D. Ordinary income of $47,000 and a capital loss of $20,000.

18. Boland Realty, LLC sells a rental duplex with an adjusted basis of $150,000. The property had been a residential rental for many years. The buyer of the duplex agrees to pay Boland Realty $300,000, with a cash down payment of $100,000 and $20,000 (plus 5% interest) in each of the next ten years. What is Boland Realty's gross profit and gross profit percentage on the installment sale?

A. The gross profit is $5,000, and the gross profit percentage is 50%.
B. The gross profit is $10,000, and the gross profit percentage is 100%.
C. The gross profit is $150,000, and the gross profit percentage is 50%.
D. The gross profit is $5,000, and the gross profit percentage is 100%.

Unit 9: Quiz Answers

1. The answer is C. Agro Manufacturing must recognize a taxable gain of **$45,000** ($340,000 - $295,000), equal to the portion of the insurance reimbursement that was not reinvested in replacement property.

2. The answer is A. An installment sale can trigger recapture. If a business reports the sale of previously depreciated property using the installment method, any applicable depreciation recapture under section 1245 or 1250 is taxable as ordinary income in the year of sale.

3. The answer is D. Because the business asset was held for less than one year, Caraway Carwash has an ordinary loss. Assets that are purchased and disposed of in the same year are not depreciated. The business simply treats the loss as a business expense.

4. The answer is A. Section 1245 property does not include real estate; such as buildings and structural components. Storage structures such as oil and gas storage tanks, grain storage bins, and silos are not treated as buildings, but as section 1245 property.

5. The answer is B. Arboreal Acres has a gain of **$25,000.** The first $20,000 is considered section 1245 recapture and is taxed as ordinary income. The remaining $5,000 is considered section 1231 gain, and is usually taxed at preferential capital gains rates.

6. The answer is B. Eastwood Auto Painting, LLC has a total gain on the sale of $17,000 ($25,000 sale price - $8,000 adjusted basis). Because the automobile is section 1245 property, the business must recognize ordinary income of **$12,000** (to recapture depreciation deductions taken on the car), and the remaining **$5,000** ($17,000 - $12,000) is treated as Section 1231 gain, and given favorable tax treatment.

7. The answer is C. Office equipment held for nine months is not a Section 1231 asset, because a business asset held for *less than* one year would not qualify. In order to qualify as section 1231 property, the property must have been held by the business for *more than* one year (at least a year and a day).

8. The answer is B. Since the amount realized from the sale is less than Jennifer's original cost for the chairs, the entire gain of $3,500 is treated as depreciation recapture, which is subject to ordinary income tax rates. She reports the sale of the chairs on Form 4797 and Schedule C.

9. The answer is D. Real property held for investment qualifies for like-kind exchange treatment. A personal residence, inventory, and common stock do not qualify under section 1031.

10. The answer is D. The exchange of livestock does not qualify. The exchange of real estate for real estate and the exchange of business property for similar business property are exchanges of like-kind property. Only exchanges of real property (real estate) qualify for 1031 exchange treatment.

11. The answer is B. Turley Accountancy's basis in the strip mall is the same as the basis of the old property, plus the additional cash boot that paid to complete the transaction ($125,000 + $4,000 = **$129,000**). Generally, an exchange of real property qualifies as a nontaxable exchange under section 1031. In a nontaxable exchange situation, the FMV of the properties exchanged may have no bearing on the basis of the property received.

12. The answer is B. Sergio's basis in the Nevada duplex is **$49,000**, (the $30,000 basis of the old condo plus the additional $19,000 cash paid).

13. The answer is A. This exchange qualifies as a nontaxable exchange for Calgary Foods. Any gain on the exchange is deferred until the farmland is later sold or disposed of. The $6,000 of cash is added to the basis of the old property to determine the basis of the new property ($11,000 + $6,000) = **$17,000** basis of farmland after the exchange.

14. The answer is B. In a related-party exchange, the nonrecognition treatment will generally be lost if either property in the exchange is disposed of within two years. However, the section 1031 exchange will still be valid if either party in the transaction dies, or if the property is subject to an involuntary conversion. In this case, Francine and Zachary's 1031 exchange is still valid, because the original owner of the property (Francine) died.

15. The answer is C. Sadie has a gain of **$35,000**, equal to the difference between her sales proceeds of $65,000 and her adjusted basis of $30,000 (cost of $90,000 minus the accumulated depreciation of $60,000 [$50,000 + $10,000]). Although she has had the property for more than one year, it is personal property classified as section 1245 property and therefore is subject to depreciation recapture to the extent of the entire amount of depreciation (and section 179 deductions) taken. Since this amount exceeds her gain, the entire amount of her gain will be taxed as ordinary income.

16. The answer is D. The exchange of a parking lot for farmland potentially qualifies for like-kind exchange treatment. Properties are like-kind if they are of the same nature or character, even if they differ in grade or quality. Real estate is typically acceptable as like-kind, even if one property is developed and the other is not. Whether the land is vacant, improved, or unimproved is not relevant as long as it is business or investment property. However, exchanges of U.S. property with property in a foreign country are not qualifying exchanges.

17. The answer is B. The disposition of the property results in a gain of **$27,000**, equal to the proceeds of $100,000 minus the adjusted basis of $73,000 (purchase price of $120,000 minus depreciation of $47,000). Because this was section 1245 property, the gain is characterized as ordinary income to the lesser of the actual gain or the amount of depreciation recaptured ($47,000).

Purchase price	$120,000
Minus depreciation deductions	($47,000)
Adjusted basis on the date of sale	$73,000
Proceeds	$100,000
Gain on sale	**$27,000**
Potential depreciation recapture (as ordinary income)	$47,000

18. The answer is C. This is an installment sale. Boland Realty's gross profit is **$150,000** ($300,000 selling price - $150,000 adjusted basis), and the gross profit percentage is **50%** ($150,000 ÷ $300,000). Boland Realty must report half of each payment received as gain from the sale. The business must also report all interest received as ordinary income.

Unit 10: Partnerships in General

More Reading:
Publication 541, Partnerships
Instructions for Form 1065

An unincorporated business with two or more owners is generally classified as a partnership for federal tax purposes. A partnership is a pass-through entity that is generally not directly taxed on its income. Instead, income and loss are determined at the partnership level and are taxable to the individual partners. In this respect, a partnership is similar to a sole proprietorship, except that it is run by more than one person. A partnership must have at least two partners, and at least one of them must be a general partner.

Unlike corporations, general partnerships do not require any formal legal documents in order to form. Partnerships that have some form of liability protections for some of the partners (such as limited partnerships and limited liability partnerships) do require formal documents – including those filed with the state.

A joint undertaking merely to share expenses is not a partnership. For example, a rental property owned by two people would generally not be classified as a business or a partnership.

Certain entities with different legal structures may be classified as partnerships for tax purposes, either based upon their election by filing Form 8832, *Entity Classification Election*, or by default, as in the case of a domestic limited liability company (LLC) with at least two members that is classified as a partnership unless it files Form 8832 and elects to be treated as a corporation (or a Form 2553, in order to be treated as an S corporation). However, the following organizations are *prohibited* from being classified as partnerships:

- A corporation (although a corporation can be a partner in a partnership)
- A joint-stock company or joint-stock association
- An insurance company
- Certain banks
- A government entity
- An organization required to be taxed as a corporation by the IRS
- Certain foreign organizations
- Any tax-exempt (non-profit) organization
- Any real estate investment trust (REIT)
- Any organization classified as a trust or estate
- Any other organization that elects to be classified as a corporation by filing Form 8832

Partnership Filing Requirements

A partnership must file a tax return unless it has neither any income nor any expenditures that would be treated as a deduction or credit for the year. A partnership reports its income or loss on Form 1065, *U.S. Return of Partnership Income*, which is due on the fifteenth day of the third month following the close of the tax year. For the 2020 tax year, the filing deadline for calendar-year partnerships is March 15, 2021. A six-month extension is allowed, so most partnerships have an extended due date of September 15.

The extension is requested on Form 7004, *Automatic Extension of Time to File Certain Business Income Tax, Information, and Other Returns* and must be filed prior to the original due date.

The partnership return must show the name and address of each partner and the partner's distributive share of taxable income (or loss) on Schedule K-1. The partnership is also required to furnish a copy of each partner's Schedule K-1 to the partner by the due date (including extensions) of the partnership tax return. The individual partner then reports his share of partnership income on Schedule E of Form 1040.

Example: Sempra Partnership is a calendar-year, cash-basis partnership that is required to file Form 1065 every year. The partnership has five partners, and each partner receives a Schedule K-1 for his share of partnership income and losses, which are then reportable on the partners' individual tax returns. Each partner must receive his Schedule K-1 by the due date of the partnership return (or by the extended due date, if the partnership requests an extension).

The IRS requires partnerships with more than 100 partners (Schedules K-1) to file their returns electronically. If a partnership fails to do so, it may be subject to penalty unless it was unable to file electronically (e.g., because the e-filing was rejected, the return required paper attachments, etc.). Each partnership return must be signed by a general partner.

Example: The Burse Partnership only has two general partners. However, the partnership has 95 independent contractors, and all of them must receive a Form 1099-NEC. Since the business must file over 50 information returns for tax year 2020, it is required to e-file (in 2021). It cannot submit the 1099 forms to the IRS on paper, or else the partnership may be subject to penalties.

The late filing penalty for Form 1065 in 2020 tax year[109] is $210 per month, per partner, for a maximum of 12 months. For purposes of this penalty, a fraction of a month is subject to a full month's late filing penalty. For even a small partnership, the late filing penalties can be very severe. Separate from and in addition to the late filing of a Form 1065, for each failure to furnish Schedule K-1 to a partner when due, in 2020, a $280 penalty per each late-filed K-1 may be imposed.

Example: The Walden partnership has four partners. The partnership accidentally files its tax return two months[110] late with the IRS, but issues each partner their Schedule K-1 by the due date. The partnership is liable for a late filing penalty for Form 1065 of $1,680 ($210 × 2 months × 4 partners). If the partnership had provided each partner with their Schedule K-1 two months late as well, the separate Schedule K-1 late filing penalty would have been $2,240 ($280 x 2 months x 4 partners).

Additional penalties may apply if the partnership fails to supply a tax identification number or fails to furnish information on tax shelters. These penalties may not be imposed if the partnership can show reasonable cause for its failure.

---

109 For the 2020 tax year, the $210 (per partner) late filing penalty applies for the 2020 tax year (those 1065 returns filed in 2021).

110 A "month" means the same day of the month that the return was due, but in the following month. For example, a partnership return filed on May 15, 2021 will be considered two months late (March 15 to May 15), but a partnership return filed just one day later, on May 16, 2021 will be considered three months late.

Partners who work in a partnership are not employees and generally do not receive wages or Forms W-2. General partners are considered **self-employed** and therefore, must pay estimated payments just like other self-employed individuals. Limited partners are subject to self-employment tax only on guaranteed payments, such as salaries and professional fees for services rendered.

The Partnership Agreement

The term *partnership agreement* refers to any written document or oral agreement that bears on the underlying economic arrangement of the partners, including allocations of income, gain, loss, deductions, and credits. Examples of such documents include:

- Loan and credit agreements
- Assumption agreements
- Indemnification agreements
- Subordination agreements
- Correspondence with a lender concerning terms of a loan
- Loan guarantees

A partnership agreement can be modified during the tax year and even after the tax year has closed to include items and elections pertaining to that year's tax return. However, the partnership agreement cannot be modified after the due date for filing the partnership return for the year, not including extensions.

Example: Pierre and Rodney are friends who run a cash-basis, calendar-year partnership together. They split the partnership's proceeds equally. In 2020, they decide to alter their partnership agreement in order to include an accountable plan for reimbursements. They have until the due date of the partnership return (March 15, 2021) to change the partnership agreement. Filing for an extension does not give them additional time to change their partnership agreement.

General Partnership vs. Limited Partnership

The two most common types of partnerships are general partnerships and limited partnerships. In a general partnership, all of the partners have unlimited liability for partnership debts. In a limited partnership, there must be at least one general partner and at least one limited partner.

Limited partners have no obligation to contribute additional capital to the partnership under state law and therefore do not have an economic risk of loss related to partnership liabilities. In this respect, a limited partner is like an investor in a corporation. Limited partners generally cannot participate in the management or the day-to-day administration of the partnership.

A limited partnership (LP), and other types of partnerships with some form of liability protections, such as a limited liability partnership (LLP) and, in some states, a limited liability limited partnership (LLLP), is formed under state limited liability law.

However, an LLP is more similar to a general partnership, in that all the partners can take an active role in managing the day-to-day affairs of the business, but partners can still have liability protections (similar to the liability protection that a limited partner might receive). An LLP type protects individual partners from liability for the malpractice of other partners. Most often, the owners of limited liability partnerships offer professional services (e.g., attorneys, engineers, architects, and doctors).

For example, LLP ownership in the State of California is limited to persons licensed to practice in the fields of public accountancy, law, engineering, or architecture. In order to form an LLP in California, the business must first register with the California Secretary of State.

Example: Casper and Barron are licensed architects. They form C&B Architects, LLP to offer architectural services to the public. They file articles of organization with the Secretary of State and form their LLP on July 1, 2020. The LLP allows Casper and Barron to actively participate in the partnership's management affairs, while still providing limited liability protection to each partner. Their first partnership return (Form 1065) will be due on March 15, 2021.

Note: A general partnership is composed of *only* general partners. In other words, a general partnership cannot have limited partners. In order for a partner to have limited liability, formal documents have to be filed with the state, and a state-level entity **must be formed.**

Family Partnerships

Family members can form a partnership together, and frequently do. However, family members will be recognized as partners only if **one** of the following requirements is met:

- If capital is a material income-producing factor, the family members must have acquired their capital interests in a bona fide transaction (even if by gift or purchase from another family member), actually own the partnership interests, and actually control the interests. This means that a family member who acquires a partnership interest from another family member needs to treat the activity as a bona fide business activity.
- If capital is not a material income-producing factor, the family members must have joined together in good faith to conduct a business. They must have agreed that contributions from each entitle them to a share in the profits and that some capital or service is provided by each partner.

Capital (investment) is a material income-producing factor if a substantial part of the gross income of the business comes from the use of capital. For example, this would apply if the operation of the business requires substantial inventories or investment in a plant, machinery, or equipment. In general, capital is not a material income-producing factor if the income of the business consists principally of fees, commissions, or other compensation for personal services performed by members or employees of the partnership.

If a family member (or any other person) receives a gift of a capital interest in a partnership in which capital is a material income-producing factor, the donee's distributive share of partnership income is subject to both of the following restrictions:

- It must be figured by reducing the partnership income by reasonable compensation for services the donor provides the partnership.
- The share attributable to donated capital must not be proportionately greater than the donor's distributive share attributable to the donor's capital.

Example: Sanford sold 50% of his business to his daughter, Noreen. The resulting partnership had a profit of $60,000. Capital is a material income-producing factor. Sanford performed services worth $24,000, which is reasonable compensation, and Noreen performed no services for the partnership. The $24,000 must be allocated to Sanford as compensation. Of the remaining $36,000 of profit due to capital, at least 50%, or $18,000, must be allocated to Sanford since he owns a 50% capital interest. Noreen's share of partnership profit cannot be more than $18,000.

For purposes of determining a partner's distributive share, an interest purchased by one family member from another family member is considered a gift from the seller.

The fair market value of the purchased interest is considered donated capital. For this purpose, "members of a family" include only spouses, ancestors, and lineal descendants (grandchild, grandparent, daughter, son, etc.).

Qualified Joint Ventures

In general, if spouses jointly own and operate an unincorporated business and share the profits and losses, they are partners in a partnership and must file Form 1065. A Qualified Joint Venture (QJV) is a joint venture that conducts a trade or business where:

- The only owners of the joint venture are a married couple who file a joint return,
- Both spouses materially participate in the trade or business, and
- Both spouses elect not to be treated as a partnership.

Spouses make the election on a jointly filed Form 1040 by dividing all items of income, gain, loss, deduction, and credit between them in accordance with each spouse's respective interest in the joint venture, and each spouse filing separate Schedule C forms.

If the spouses later form an LLC or an LLP, they generally cannot make the election to treat the activity as a qualified joint venture, although there are exceptions for spousal-owned businesses in community property states.

Costs of Organizing and Starting a Partnership

The costs to organize a partnership and to start up a business are treated much like similar costs incurred by other types of businesses. As discussed previously, start-up and organizational costs can be deductible. Up to $5,000 of *organizational* costs **and** up to $5,000 of *start-up* costs can be deducted immediately in the year the partnership's active trade or business begins. Amounts that are not deducted as a current expense can be amortized ratably over a period of 180 months (15 years) starting in the month the business begins.

Businesses start losing the immediate $5,000 up-front deduction when their organizational and/or start-up costs exceed $50,000, and then must reduce the deduction dollar-for-dollar by the amount exceeding the $50,000 threshold.

Therefore, if a business has more than $55,000 in either organizational or start-up costs, all of the organizational and start-up expenses (testing separately for each type) must be amortized over a 180-month period. The election to either deduct these costs currently or to capitalize and amortize them is irrevocable and applies to all organizational and start-up costs related to the trade or business. The partnership must file Form 4562, Depreciation and Amortization, with its tax return to claim these deductions.

Example: Ajax and Luther are business partners. They opened up the Yummy Taco Diner, LLC in Texas on February 2, 2020. One month before they opened for business, they paid $5,900 in radio advertising to promote it. The business can deduct $5,000 on the first-year partnership return as start-up expenses. The remaining start-up costs, $900 ($5,900 - $5,000) must be amortized over 180 months. If the business closes before the amortization period is over, the company can deduct any remaining expenses on the business's final tax return. They also incurred $3,000 in organizational costs to form the LLC, because they paid an attorney to file the organizational documents for their LLC with the Secretary of State. The $3,000 in legal fees are fully deductible as organizational costs in the year in which they opened for business.

Special Partnership Allocations

Unlike S corporations, which must report all income and expenses in proportion to stock ownership, partnerships have much more flexibility. Partnership agreements can be written to reflect special allocations of income, gain, loss, or deductions, as long as the allocations have substantial economic effect, which is defined in IRS regulations.

For example, the partnership agreement may, with certain restrictions, allocate all of the depreciation deductions to one partner or specify that the partners share capital, profits, and losses in different ratios.

Example: Maryam, who has design and sewing skills, forms a partnership with Cortney, who has the money to invest in developing a clothing line. Cortney contributes $100,000 of cash to the partnership. Maryam and Cortney agree to split the business profits 20/80 until Cortney recovers her entire investment; thereafter, profits will be split 50/50. These special allocations are written into their partnership agreement.

Example: Sanji and Katherine form a partnership and open a sandwich shop. Sanji contributes only $1,000, and Katherine contributes $99,000. Due to Sanji's previous expertise in restaurant management and his daily participation in the business, the partnership agreement provides that Sanji will be allocated 20% of the restaurant's business income and 2% of the partnership's losses. Thus, although Sanji owns only 1% in partnership capital, his profit-sharing ratio is 20%. This income/loss allocation between Sanji and Katherine is permissible because it correctly reflects their underlying economic arrangement.

Example: Adelaide and Bessie form a partnership to run a bridal cake bakery. The bakery is opened during the year, and the partnership has ordinary income of $10,000. The partnership agreement states they will share income and losses equally (50/50). Adelaide and Bessie agree that the $10,000 of income will be distributed equally between them. However, for tax purposes, they want the income to be allocated as $7,500 to Adelaide and $2,500 to Bessie. The tax allocation (75/25) is not consistent with the underlying economic arrangement in their partnership agreement (50/50). Unless the partnership agreement contains other provisions that justify this allocation, it has no economic effect and must be reallocated to the partners based on their economic sharing ratio.

Guaranteed Payments

A partnership may be required by the terms of its partnership agreement to make guaranteed payments to one or more partners without regard to whether the partnership has income or loss for the year. Guaranteed payments are not the same as partnership distributions. They may compensate the partner for services or for the use of capital, as if they were made to a person who is not a partner. Guaranteed payments are generally deducted by the partnership on Form 1065 as a business expense and reported to the partner receiving the guaranteed payment on their Schedule K-1.

The partner who receives a guaranteed payment reports the amount of the payment as ordinary income on Schedule E (Form 1040) of his individual tax return for the tax year in which the partnership's tax year ends, and also reports his distributive share of the partnership's ordinary income or loss. Guaranteed payments are not subject to income tax withholding by the partnership.

Example: Irvin is a general partner in the Brandenburg Partnership. Under the terms of his partnership agreement, he is entitled to a guaranteed payment of $10,000 per year, regardless of how profitable the partnership is. In 2020, Irvin's distributive share of partnership income is 10%. Brandenburg Partnership has $50,000 of ordinary income *after* deducting Irvin's guaranteed payment. He includes $15,000 of ordinary income ($10,000 guaranteed payment + $5,000 [$50,000 × 10%] for his distributive share) on his individual income tax return.

With regards to the new Section 199A Qualified Business Income deduction, §199A excludes guaranteed payments made to a partner from qualified business income. This means that a partner cannot take a 199A deduction directly on their guaranteed payments (similar to how most employees cannot claim a 199A deduction on their wages). In other words, any amounts that are paid to a partner as guaranteed payments will reduce the amount of qualifying business income otherwise eligible for the QBI deduction.

Separately Stated Items

Many of the individual components of a partnership's income or loss are calculated similarly to those of an individual. However, some deductions are not allowed at the partnership level, and certain items of income and loss must be separately stated on the tax return. For the EA exam, you must be able to distinguish the items that are separately stated on a partnership's tax return.

These separately stated items flow through to the partners with a specific character. For example, a partnership that makes charitable contributions must list them as a separately stated item. Each individual partner then reports his share of the charitable contributions on his Schedule A. Each year, a partnership provides Schedules K-1 to each of its partners, indicating their respective shares of:

- **Ordinary income or loss, and**
- **Separately stated items.**

The following items must be **separately stated** on a partnership's return:

- Net short-term capital gains and losses
- Net long-term capital gains and losses
- Charitable contributions

- Dividends received from a corporation eligible for a dividends-received deduction
- Foreign income taxes (paid or accrued)
- Taxes paid to a U.S. possession (Guam, American Samoa, Puerto Rico, etc.)
- Section 1231 gains and losses
- Section 1250 depreciation recapture
- Section 179 deductions and bonus depreciation
- Any tax-exempt income and expenses related to the tax-exempt income
- Investment income and related investment expenses
- Rental income and any related expenses
- Any recovery items, such as bad debts and tax refunds
- Distributions of unrealized receivables or inventory that may have substantially appreciated
- Qualifying section 199A wages paid by the partnership (to employees)
- Unadjusted Basis of assets immediately after acquisition (UBIA): Reporting UBIA on the partnership return is necessary for purposes of each partner calculating the 20% pass-through QBI deduction on their personal returns.

Example: Sudsy Auto Wash, LLC operates as partnership. The partnership carries on multiple activities, including the operation of a car wash and the rental of an adjacent office building that is rented to retail tenants. The business's gross receipts for 2020 were $250,000. In addition, it had the following income and expenses:

Liability insurance	($5,000)
Charitable contributions	(2,000)
Advertising expenses	(9,000)
Rental income	25,000
Guaranteed payments to partners	(15,000)

Ordinary income for Sudsy Auto Wash, LLC is figured as follows:

Gross Receipts from the car wash	$250,000
Liability insurance	(5,000)
Advertising expenses	(9,000)
Guaranteed payments to partners	(15,000)
Ordinary partnership income:	**$221,000**

The rental income and charitable contributions are not considered in determining "ordinary" income of the partnership. Instead, these are separately stated items that pass through to the partners and retain their character, just as they would for a sole proprietorship. Each individual partner receives a Schedule K-1 from the partnership, reporting his share of ordinary income or loss and each separately stated item. The partners report these amounts on their tax returns. Guaranteed payments are deductible by the partnership because they are treated like wages and are taxable to the partners who receive them.

Example: Foster is a 25% partner in Jourdain Architects, LLP, a partnership with three other individual partners. Jourdain Architects makes $20,000 of charitable contributions in 2020 that are reported on the partnership tax return, Form 1065. As Jourdain Architects is a pass-through entity, it does not receive a tax benefit from deductible contributions. Instead, Foster's Schedule K-1 shows $5,000 as his share of the partnership's charitable contributions, which he can potentially claim on his individual tax return.

Contributions to a Partnership

When a partnership is formed, or new partners are added, the partners contribute property or cash in exchange for their partnership interests. Generally, neither the partner nor the partnership recognizes gain or loss in connection with contributions, whether made in connection with the partnership's formation or after it is operating.

When a partner contributes *property* (rather than money) to a partnership, the partner's basis in his partnership interest as well as the partnership's basis in the property is generally the same as the adjusted basis of the property contributed by the partner, including any gain recognized by the partner in connection with the contribution.

For example, if a partner contributes a building with an FMV of $175,000 and a basis of $65,000, with no debt, the basis of the building in the hands of the partnership would also be $65,000. This amount would also be the partner's basis in his own partnership interest. The partner's holding period for the property is also carried over.

Example: Floyd and Hamlin are both Certified Financial Planners. They come together to form Zenith Financial, LLC, an equal partnership to offer financial services. Floyd contributes an office building to the partnership that has an adjusted basis of $145,000 and an FMV of $300,000. Hamlin contributes $125,000 in cash. The basis of Floyd's partnership interest is $145,000, and the basis of Hamlin's interest is $125,000.

However, a partner's contribution can result in gain or loss recognition in the following situations:

- When property is contributed to a partnership that would be treated as an **investment company** if it were incorporated. A partnership is treated as an investment company if over 80% of the value of its assets is held for investment in cash or readily marketable items ("readily marketable items" include currency, stocks, and interests in regulated investment companies and real estate investment trusts).
- When contributed property is distributed to a different partner within seven years of the original contribution date. The contributing partner would recognize gain on the difference between the fair market value and the adjusted basis of the property as of the contribution date. The character of the gain or loss will be the same as would have resulted if the partnership had sold the property to the distributee partner.
- When a partner contributes cash or property to a partnership and then receives an immediate distribution of different property. In this case, the transaction may be considered a "disguised sale." A "disguised sale" is not treated as a contribution and a subsequent distribution but as a sale of property, if:

- The distribution would not have been made if the initial contribution had not occurred, and
- The partner's right to the distribution does not depend on the success of partnership operations.

Example: Benjamin transfers a factory building to Leeds Partnership and then, two months later, Leeds Partnership distributes $3,000,000 in cash to Benjamin. The factory building has a fair market value of $4,000,000 and a basis of $1,200,000. This transfer would likely be treated as a "disguised sale," rather than a distribution. In this case, the transaction would not qualify for nonrecognition treatment, and Benjamin would be required to recognize income on the "sale" of the building to the partnership.

If a contribution and distribution occur within two years of each other, the transfers are presumed to be a "disguised sale" unless the facts clearly indicate they are not. If the contribution and distribution occur more than two years apart, the transfers are presumed not to be a sale unless the facts clearly indicate they are.

Example: Crystal transfers a tract of undeveloped farmland to Avant Partnership in exchange for a 20% partnership interest. The farmland has a FMV of $700,000 and an adjusted basis to $230,000 on the date that Crystal contributes the property. Four weeks later, Avant Partnership distributes $700,000 in cash to Crystal. The contribution and distribution will likely be treated as a "disguised sale" (rather than as a contribution of property by Crystal) and a distribution of cash by Avant Partnership.

Example: Yoko contributes farmland with a fair market value of $150,000 and a basis of $90,000 to the Gleason Partnership, in which Yoko is a 20% owner. Six months later, the partnership distributes $90,000 of cash and marketable securities worth $50,000 to Yoko. This transaction would likely be considered a "disguised sale" rather than a tax-free contribution and distribution of property.

The Contribution of Services to a Partnership

A partner can acquire an interest in a partnership as compensation for services performed. The tax treatment depends upon whether the partner receives a capital interest or a profits interest. If a partner receives a capital interest as compensation for services, the partner must recognize ordinary income equal to the fair market value of a partnership interest that is transferred in exchange for services. The amount is treated as a guaranteed payment and is included in the partner's gross income in the first tax year during which the partner can transfer the interest. If a partner receives only a profits interest as compensation for services, the receipt may not be taxable to the partner or the partnership, except in certain circumstances.

Example: Estelle is an attorney who contributes her legal services to a partnership in exchange for a 5% partnership interest. It is deemed a capital interest, as the partnership agreement provides for the distribution of assets to Estelle in the event she withdraws from the partnership or the partnership liquidates. The fair market value of the partnership interest is $8,000. Estelle is required to recognize $8,000 of ordinary income, and her basis in the partnership is $8,000. The payment is deducted by the partnership as a guaranteed payment and is taxable to Estelle as ordinary income.

The Basis of a Partner's Interest

A partner's basis in his partnership interest may be referred to as **outside basis.** This is in contrast to the partnership's basis in its assets, which is known as **inside basis.**

Note: Be familiar with these two terms (i.e., "inside basis" and "outside basis"), as the EA exam may use them in questions when test takers are asked to determine a partner's or a partnership's basis.

Inside basis and **outside basis** may initially be equal in a newly-formed partnership, but certain distributions of property from the partnership, transfers of partnership interests, and other basis adjustment items may disrupt this equality. The partnership's tax basis in an asset, is called the *inside basis*. It is the same as the contributing person's basis in the asset.

Example: Beltway Farms, LLC is a farming partnership that was formed by two brothers, Rami and Valerian. Rami contributes 25 acres of farmland with an adjusted basis of $300,000 and a FMV of $1 million. Valerian contributes cash in the amount of $300,000. They both have the same partnership tax basis ($300,000 for each partner). The partnership's basis in the land is the same as Rami's basis ($300,000). Rami and Valerian both have the same "outside basis" in their partnership interests.

Example: Keagan and Anika form Whitewall Accounting, LLP in 2020. Keagan contributes an office building to the partnership with a tax basis of $100,000 and a fair market value of $500,000. Anika contributes $500,000 in cash. Keagan and Anika have equal equity in the partnership. Anika's "outside basis" is $500,000 because she contributed $500,000 in cash. Keagan's "outside basis" is $100,000 (based on the adjusted basis of the contributed office building). If Keagan sells his partnership interest shortly thereafter for $500,000, Keagan would have to recognize a gain, but if Anika were to sell her partnership interest for $500,000, she would not recognize a gain (because she contributed cash).

The initial basis of a partnership interest is generally equal to the cash plus the adjusted basis of any property the partner contributed to the partnership solely in exchange for a partnership interest under section 721.

The adjusted basis of a partner's partnership interest is ordinarily determined at the end of the partnership's tax year. However, if there is a sale or exchange of all or part of a partner's interest or a liquidation of his entire interest in a partnership, the adjusted basis must also be determined on the date of the transaction. The following items *increase* a partner's (outside) basis in the partnership:

- The partner's additional cash and the adjusted basis of non-cash contributions to the partnership
- The partner's increased share (or assumption of) partnership liabilities
- The partner's distributive share of taxable and nontaxable partnership income
- The partner's distributive share of the excess of the deductions for depletion over the basis of the depletable property

In addition, if a partner must recognize a gain as a result of his partnership contribution, (under section 721(b) related to investment company contributions), the gain is added to the basis of his partnership interest.

Partner Capital Account

A capital account is a measure of a partner's financial interest in the partnership. A partnership must maintain capital accounts for all the partners. Beginning in calendar year 2020, a partnership must use the "tax basis" to compute partner capital accounts; prior to this change, a partnership could have used either GAAP or the section 704(b) method.

Tax-basis capital accounts are computed in a similar way to the partner's basis in the partnership interest, except that liabilities do not impact the capital account and the capital account can be reduced below $0.

Partnership Liabilities

Any increase in a partner's liabilities because of his assumption of partnership liabilities is treated as if it were a contribution of cash or property to the partnership by the partner. If a partner's share of partnership liabilities *increases*, this increase is treated as if the partner contributed cash or property to the partnership. A partner's (outside) basis in the partnership is *decreased* by the following items:

- The money and the adjusted basis of property distributed to the partner by the partnership.
- The partner's distributive share of the partnership's losses (including capital losses) and the partner's distributive share of nondeductible partnership expenses (but not capital expenditures). This includes the partner's share of any section 179 expenses, even if the partner cannot deduct the entire amount on his individual income tax return.
- The partner's deduction for depletion for any partnership oil and gas wells, up to the proportionate share of the adjusted basis of the wells allocated to the partner.

If a partner's share of partnership liabilities decreases or the partnership assumes any of the partner's individual liabilities, the amounts are treated as distributions to the partner by the partnership.

For example, if a partner contributes property to a partnership and the property is subject to an existing debt, and the debt is assumed by the partnership, the basis of the contributing partner's interest is reduced (but not below zero) by the portion of the liability assumed by the other partners. The partner must reduce his basis because the assumption of the liability is treated as a distribution to him. The other partners' assumption of the liability is treated as a contribution by them to the partnership.

Example: Ivette acquired a 20% interest in the Bayside Movers partnership by contributing a moving truck that had an adjusted basis to her of $80,000 and a related $40,000 auto loan balance. Bayside Movers assumed the auto loan on the vehicle and will use it in its business operations. The basis of Ivette's partnership interest is:

Adjusted basis of the moving truck	$80,000
Minus loan assumed by the other partners (80% × $40,000 liability)	($32,000)
The basis of Ivette's partnership interest	**$48,000**

A partner's basis can never go below zero. To avoid this, a partner must recognize gain equal to the amount by which cash distributions or a decrease in his share of partnership liabilities exceeds his basis.

Example: Dewey acquired a 20% interest in Tremblay Engineering, LLP by contributing an office building that had an adjusted basis of $80,000 and a related $120,000 mortgage loan. The partnership assumes the loan and plans to use the building in its business operations. Since Dewey's basis in the building is *less* than the loan balance, the $16,000 difference between the portion of the loan assumed by the *other* partners, $96,000 (80% × $120,000 debt), and his basis of $80,000 is treated as capital gain from the sale or exchange of a partnership interest. He must recognize $16,000 in capital gain and Dewey's partnership basis is zero.

Partnership Loss Limitations

The amount of a partnership's loss that a partner is potentially allowed to deduct on his tax return is normally dependent on (1) the partner's basis in the partnership (i.e., the "outside basis" limitation), and (2) the amount the partner has at-risk in the partnership (i.e., the "at-risk" limitation).

The "Outside Basis" Limitation

In general, a partner cannot deduct losses that exceed his partnership basis. Losses disallowed due to insufficient basis are carried forward until the partner can deduct them in a later year, typically when there is sufficient basis in the partnership. Debts incurred on behalf of the partnership can increase a partner's individual basis.

For example, if a partner takes out a $50,000 loan to finance partnership operations and he personally guarantees the debt, the debt is considered part of his basis in the partnership for purposes of deducting partnership losses.

Example: Josephine invests $1,000 in Network Solutions, LLP in return for a 10% general partnership interest. After she becomes a partner, Network Solutions takes out a $500,000 mortgage and incurs $100,000 of operating losses during the first year. Josephine's share of partnership liabilities would increase her basis to $51,000 ($1,000 cash investment + [$500,000 mortgage loan × 10%]). Josephine's share of the loss is $10,000 ($100,000 × 10%), reducing her basis to $41,000. Josephine is allowed to deduct the entire loss on her individual return because her partnership basis included her share of the partnership's debt.

If the partner does not have any personal liability to satisfy the debt of a partnership, deductible losses may be limited by the at-risk rules.

The At-Risk Limitation

The at-risk rule limits the deductibility of losses to the partner's basis, not including his share of most nonrecourse debt.[111] This means that a partner is prohibited from taking losses based on partnership liabilities unless the partner would be forced to satisfy the debt with his personal assets. This is intended to prevent abusive deductions from tax shelter activities.

[111] An exception to nonrecourse debt not counting towards the amount of the partner's amount "at-risk" is qualified nonrecourse debt, which is primarily mortgage debt on real property.

A partner (or related person) is considered to have assumed a partnership liability when he is personally liable for it, and:

- The creditor knows that the liability was assumed by the partner or related person,
- The creditor can demand payment from the partner or related person, and
- No other partner or person related to a partner will bear the economic risk of loss on that liability immediately after the assumption.

Example: Jayson and Kenny form a general partnership, with cash contributions of $2,000 each. Under the partnership agreement, they share all partnership profits and losses equally. The partnership borrows an additional $14,000 using a bank loan, and uses the funds to purchase equipment. Both partners are personally liable for the debt in the event it is not paid by the partnership. This debt is included in the partners' basis in the partnership. Each partner's basis would include his allocated share of the liability, or $7,000 each. Therefore, each partner's basis is $9,000 (initial $2,000 contribution + $7,000 share of the liability), and each of their amounts at-risk in the partnership is $9,000.

Example: Gabin and Danica are two friends who form a 50/50 partnership during the year, called West Lake Winery, LLC. Gabin invests $10,000 in cash. Danica also invests $10,000 in cash, and she also personally guarantees a business loan of $80,000 on behalf of the partnership to purchase wine-making equipment. Danica is the only signatory on the loan because Gabin's credit is poor. In 2020, West Lake Winery has a net loss of $24,000, which is allocated equally to the partners ($12,000 in losses each). The at-risk limitations limit Gabin's deduction to $10,000, the amount of his investment, as he is not personally liable for the note. Danica's losses are not limited, because her basis includes the debt basis of the loan ($80,000), for which she is personally liable. She is allowed to deduct her $12,000 loss in full. Gabin's disallowed losses must be carried over to the following year.

The effect of liabilities on an individual partner's basis depends mainly on two factors:

- Whether or not the liability is recourse or nonrecourse, and/or
- Whether or not the partner is a general or limited partner.

A nonrecourse liability is usually secured by an asset or property, and its terms provide that the creditor has no claim against the owner of the property. At most, the creditor may have a claim against the property. In the context of a partnership business, this determination is based on whether a particular partner bears any economic risk of loss with respect to the repayment of the liability. An example of this would be a loan where the lender's only recourse in case of default is to repossess the property. A partnership liability is considered a nonrecourse liability if no partner has an economic risk of loss for that liability.

Example: Marcelino and Kaliko run a partnership together. The partnership purchases a small office building for use in the business, but the partnership is unable to make the mortgage payments. The mortgage loan is a nonrecourse loan because the only action the lender can take is to repossess the building. The loan goes into default, and the lender repossesses the building while there is still a balance on the loan. However, the lender cannot seek payment from Marcelino or Kaliko for the balance of the loan. Since neither partner had an economic risk of loss, the debt does not affect their basis.

A partner's share of nonrecourse liabilities is generally proportionate to his share of partnership profits. A partner's basis in a partnership interest includes the partner's share of a partnership liability only if, and to the extent, the liability:

- Creates or increases the partnership's basis in any of its assets,
- Gives rise to a current deduction to the partnership, or
- Is a nondeductible, noncapital expense of the partnership.

A partnership liability is a **recourse** liability when the individual partners have an economic risk of loss. A partner has an economic risk of loss to the extent that he or a related person would be obligated to make payments to a creditor in the event of a constructive liquidation.

Partners generally share recourse liabilities based on their ratios for sharing losses. A limited partner has no obligation to contribute additional capital to the partnership, and therefore does not have an economic risk of loss in the partnership's recourse liabilities. Thus, unless a limited partner guarantees a partnership liability or makes a loan to the partnership, his basis will generally not be affected by the partnership's recourse liabilities.

Unit 10: Study Questions

(Please test yourself and check the correct answers at the end of this section.)

1. What is the latest that a partnership agreement can be modified, and its terms be applicable to the partnership tax return during a taxable year?

A. No later than the close of the taxable year.
B. No later than the partnership return due date (without extensions).
C. No later than the first day of the taxable year.
D. No later than the date for filing the partnership return due date (with extensions).

2. When payments are made by a partnership to partners without regard to partnership income, these payments are called:

A. Capital gains.
B. Ordinary distributions.
C. Passive income.
D. Guaranteed payments.

3. Carolyn and Jerome form a partnership in 2020. Each contributes $5,000 in cash for an equal partnership interest. Their partnership agreement states that they will share income and losses equally. However, Carolyn is a licensed CPA who will provide accounting services to the partnership and receive a guaranteed payment each year of $21,000, regardless of the partnership's income or loss. The partnership earns $50,000 during the year, before deducting the guaranteed payment. What is Jerome's distributive share of partnership profits for the year?

A. $0
B. $14,500
C. $22,500
D. $25,000

4. Which of the following statements is correct regarding limited partners in a partnership?

A. A limited partner has an economic liability for damages and an economic risk of loss.
B. A limited partner does not have an economic risk of loss in the partnership's recourse liabilities.
C. A limited partner does not have an economic risk of loss in the partnership's recourse liabilities; however, a limited partner may be required to contribute additional capital.
D. A limited partner is treated just like a general partner when it comes to the partnership's recourse liabilities.

5. The G&H Partnership has two partners, Gilbert and Hassid, who share profits and losses equally (50/50). The partnership has the following activity during the year:

Gross income from business operations	$200,000
Business expenses	($30,000)
Tax-exempt interest income from muni bonds	$10,000
Rental income	$120,000
Charitable contributions	($4,000)

What is Hassid's share of the partnership's ordinary business income in box 1 of Schedule K-1?

A. $85,000
B. $91,000
C. $100,000
D. $105,000

6. Cameron and Vincent form a partnership. Each contributes $20,000 during the initial formation of the partnership. Their partnership agreement states that Cameron will receive 35% of the distributive income, and Vincent will receive 65%. In 2020, the partnership has net ordinary income of $200,000. What is each partner's distributive share of the partnership profits?

A. Cameron: $77,000, Vincent $143,000.
B. Cameron: $100,000, Vincent: $100,000.
C. Cameron: $35,000, Vincent $65,000.
D. Cameron: $70,000, Vincent: $130,000.

7. Polly and Diane form P&D Partnership. Polly contributes $16,000 cash and Diane contributes manufacturing equipment with a fair market value of $15,000 and an adjusted basis of $5,000. What amount should Diane report as a gain as a result of this transaction?

A. $0
B. $3,000
C. $5,000
D. $8,000

8. If a partnership requests additional time to file its return, how long will the filing deadline be extended?

A. Three months.
B. Five months.
C. Six months.
D. Nine months.

9. Johnathan, Robin, Shanette, and Theresa form an equal partnership. Each partner contributes $10,000 and receives an equal ownership interest in the partnership (25%). Under the partnership agreement, they share partnership profits and losses equally. The partnership borrows $135,000 and purchases business equipment using a business line of credit. All of the partners *except* for Theresa personally guarantee the loan. What is each partner's basis after this transaction?

A. Theresa's basis is zero, and the other partners each have a basis of $58,333.
B. Theresa's basis is $10,000, and the other partners each have a basis of $43,750.
C. Theresa's basis is $10,000, and the other partners each have a basis of $55,000.
D. Each partner has a basis of $43,750.

10. Which of the following is NOT a separately stated item on a partnership tax return?

A. Net long-term capital gains.
B. Interest income.
C. Section 179 deduction.
D. Cost of goods sold.

11. Tasty Sandwiches, LLC operates as an accrual-based partnership and files Form 1065. In addition to receipts from sandwich and beverage sales of $250,000, the partnership has the following items of income and expenses for the year:

Wages paid to employees	$50,000
Insurance expense	$5,000
Charitable contributions	$2,000
Business Licenses	$5,000
Rental income from the rental of an office above the shop	$25,000
Guaranteed payments to Elvis, the shop's founder	$75,000

What is the ordinary business income that Tasty Sandwiches should report on its Form 1065?

A. $85,000
B. $115,000
C. $190,000
D. $210,000

12. Which of the following increases the basis of a partner's interest in a partnership?

A. A partner's share of tax-exempt interest.
B. A decrease in the partner's share of liabilities.
C. A distribution of $2,000 of cash to the partner.
D. A property distribution to a partner with an FMV of $5,000.

13. West Ridge Partnership generated income and expenses as stated below. What is the amount of ordinary business income that West Ridge should report for the year on its Form 1065?

- Employee wages: $15,000
- Rental real estate income: $20,000
- Charitable contributions: $500
- Cost of goods sold: $10,000
- Income from sales: $75,000

A. $65,000
B. $69,500
C. $50,000
D. $30,000

14. Austin is a general partner in the Kerner Partnership. During the year, Austin personally assumes $100,000 of the partnership's liabilities. Which of the following statements regarding partnership liabilities is correct?

A. The assumption of partnership debt by Austin is treated as a distribution of cash to Austin, and it decreases Austin's partnership basis.
B. The assumption of partnership debt by Austin increases his basis.
C. Austin cannot assume partnership liabilities.
D. Only limited partners are allowed to assume partnership liabilities.

15. Monica contributes farmland to a partnership in exchange for a 40% partnership interest. The farmland has a fair market value of $70,000, an adjusted basis of $40,000, and a related mortgage of $10,000 that the partnership assumes. What is Monica's basis in her partnership interest after the contribution of the land?

A. $10,000
B. $30,000
C. $34,000
D. $60,000

16. Xavier is a 10% partner in Hartville Partnership. According to the partnership agreement, Xavier is entitled to a fixed annual guaranteed payment of $5,000. During the year, the Hartville Partnership has $55,000 of net ordinary income *before* deducting the guaranteed payment. How much partnership income should Xavier report on his individual return for this year?

A. $5,000
B. $10,000
C. $11,500
D. $16,000

17. A partner is not considered "at-risk" for which of the following amounts?

A. The money and adjusted basis of any property the partner contributed to a partnership's activity.
B. The partner's share of income retained by the partnership.
C. A partnership's nonrecourse liability on personal property.
D. Certain amounts borrowed by the partnership if the partner is personally liable for repayment.

18. Genevieve acquired a 30% interest in a partnership by contributing a building in which she had an adjusted basis of $25,000. The building's fair market value was $50,000, and it had a $40,000 mortgage that was assumed by the partnership. What is Genevieve's gain or loss on the contribution of her property to the partnership?

A. $0
B. $3,000 gain.
C. $10,000 loss.
D. $25,000 gain.

19. Hatta Restaurant operates as a calendar-year partnership. Hatta's two partners, Assad and Dominic, share profits and losses 60% and 40%, respectively. Hatta Restaurant had the following income and expenses for the year:

- Gross sales: $270,000
- Cost of goods sold: $80,000
- Bank interest income: $2,500
- Wages paid: $50,000
- Short-term capital loss: $5,000

Compute the partnership's ordinary business income and flow-through amounts to the partners and choose the correct outcome.

	Assad		Dominic	
A.	Ordinary income: Short-term capital loss:	$85,000 $3,000	Ordinary income: Short-term capital loss:	$57,000 $2,000
B.	Ordinary income:	$82,500	Ordinary income:	$55,000
C.	Ordinary income: Interest income: Short-term capital loss:	$81,000 $1,500 $3,000	Ordinary income: Interest income: Short-term capital loss:	$54,000 $1,000 $2,000
D.	Ordinary income: Interest income: Short-term capital loss:	$84,000 $1,500 $3,000	Ordinary income: Interest income: Short-term capital loss:	$56,000 $1,000 $2,000

20. Lucy and Jessica are equal (50%) partners in a pizzeria restaurant. In 2020, they purchase a new $30,000 pizza oven for the restaurant and want to take the section 179 deduction for the full cost of the oven. The partnership's ordinary income before the section 179 deduction is $25,000. There were no other qualifying section 179 purchases during the year. What is the amount of section 179 deduction that Lucy can potentially deduct on her *individual* tax return?

A. $0
B. $6,000
C. $12,500
D. $15,000

21. Todd and Charlotte form an equal partnership with cash contributions of $20,000 each. Under the partnership agreement, they share all partnership profits and losses equally. They borrow $60,000 and purchase depreciable business equipment. However, Todd has poor credit, so Charlotte is the only signer on the loan. Charlotte is the only one required to pay the creditor if the partnership defaults, so she has an economic risk of loss related to the loan. The payments on the loan are made out of the partnership bank account. What is Charlotte's basis in the partnership, and what is Todd's basis?

A. Charlotte: $80,000, Todd: $20,000.
B. Charlotte: $60,000, Todd: $20,000.
C. Charlotte: $20,000, Todd: $20,000.
D. Charlotte: $60,000, Todd: $60,000.

Unit 10: Quiz Answers

1. The answer is B. Partners can modify their partnership agreement after the close of the tax year, but no later than the due date (without extensions) for filing the partnership return.

2. The answer is D. Guaranteed payments are made by a partnership to a partner and determined without regard to the partnership's income. A partnership treats guaranteed payments for services, or for the use of capital, as a business expense, just as if they were made to a person who is not a partner.

3. The answer is B. The guaranteed payment to Carolyn must be deducted *before* figuring each partner's distributive share. The answer is figured as follows:

$50,000 - $21,000 guaranteed payment = 29,000

$29,000 × 50% = **$14,500**

Guaranteed payments are deducted from partnership income before determining the distributive share of income or loss for each partner.

4. The answer is B. A limited partner generally has no obligation to contribute additional capital to the partnership. Therefore, absent some other factor, such as the guarantee of a partnership liability by the limited partner or the limited partner making a loan to the partnership, a limited partner generally does not have an economic risk of loss in connection with the partnership's recourse liabilities.

5. The answer is A. The rental income, tax-exempt income, and charitable contributions are all separately stated items that do not affect the calculation of the partnership's ordinary income. Instead, each partner's share of the separately stated items is passed through to him. The partnership's ordinary income is split evenly, so Hassid's portion is as follows:

($200,000 - $30,000) = $170,000 of ordinary income

$170,000 × 50% = **$85,000**

6. The answer is D. The profits are allocated according to the partnership agreement. Cameron's distributive share is calculated as follows: 35% × $200,000 = **$70,000.** Vincent's share is calculated as follows: 65% × $200,000 = **$130,000.**

7. The answer is A. Diane does not have a taxable gain as a result of this transaction. Usually, neither the partner nor the partnership recognizes a gain or loss when property is contributed to the partnership in exchange for a partnership interest. This applies whether a partnership is being formed or is already operating. However, if an asset is encumbered by a liability, such as a mortgage, there is a possibility that the partner will recognize a gain in connection with the contribution.

8. The answer is C. Form 7004, *Automatic Extension of Time to File Certain Business Income Tax, Information, and Other Returns*, is used by partnerships to extend their filing deadline for **six months.**

9. The answer is C. If a partner's share of partnership liabilities increases, this increase is treated as a contribution of money by the partner to the partnership. The debt is included in the bases of the three partners who signed the personal guarantees. Since Theresa does not have an economic risk of loss for this liability, the liability does not increase her basis, so her basis is based only on the cash she contributed ($10,000). The basis for each of the other partners would include his or her share of the liability, or **$55,000 each** ([$135,000 loan/liability ÷ 3 partners] = $45,000 + $10,000 original cash investment).

10. The answer is D. Cost of goods sold are a reduction of a partnership's ordinary (non-separately stated) income. The other items are separately stated on the partnership's Form 1065. Each individual partner receives a Schedule K-1 from the partnership, reporting his share of ordinary income or loss and each separately stated item. Separately stated items pass through to the partners and retain their character as the partners report these amounts on their individual tax returns.

11. The answer is B. All of the items listed are included in the calculation of ordinary income except the charitable contributions and the rental income, both of which must be separately stated on Form 1065. Thus, ordinary income for Tasty Sandwiches will be **$115,000** ($250,000 - $50,000 - $5,000 - $5,000 - $75,000). Like the other deductions listed, guaranteed payments to partners are treated as a deduction in determining ordinary income or loss.

12. The answer is A. Partnership income, including tax-exempt interest, increases a partner's basis in his partnership interest. All of the other items will *decrease* a partner's interest in a partnership.

13. The answer is C. West Ridge Partnership's ordinary income for the year is equal to its sales income minus the cost of goods sold and wages ($75,000 - $10,000 - $15,000 = **$50,000**). The income from rental real estate and the charitable contribution expense must be separately stated on the partnership's tax return, and would not figure into the calculation of ordinary income.

14. The answer is B. The assumption of partnership debt by Austin *increases* his basis. If a partner's share of partnership liabilities increases, or a partner's individual liabilities increase because he assumes partnership liabilities, it is treated as if the partner made a contribution to the partnership.

15. The answer is C. The basis of Monica's partnership interest is the adjusted basis of the farmland she contributes to the partnership ($40,000) minus the portion of the related mortgage liability assumed by the other partners (60% × $10,000 debt = $6,000), or **$34,000.**

16. The answer is B. Xavier must include $10,000 of ordinary income from the partnership on his tax return. The answer is figured as follows:

1. $55,000 - $5,000 guaranteed payment = $50,000 of ordinary income.
2. $50,000 × 10% = $5,000 (Xavier's share of the partnership's ordinary income).
3. ($5,000 guaranteed payment + $5,000 [$50,000 × 10%] distributive share) = **$10,000.**

Guaranteed payments are determined without regard to the partnership's income. They are deducted as a business expense when figuring the partnership's ordinary income. The individual partner who receives the guaranteed payments reports the payments on Schedule E (Form 1040) as ordinary income, along with his distributive share of the partnership's ordinary income.

17. The answer is C. The "at-risk rules" limit the deductibility of losses to the partner's basis, not including his share of any of the partnership's nonrecourse debt, unless the nonrecourse debt relates to a mortgage on real property.

18. The answer is B. The basis of Genevieve's partnership interest should be the adjusted basis of the property contributed ($25,000) minus the portion of the mortgage liability assumed by the other partners (70% × $40,000 = $28,000). Genevieve must recognize a gain of $3,000, since that is the amount by which the deemed distribution exceeds her basis in the partnership interest.

19. The answer is D. Interest income and short-term capital losses are separately stated items that flow through to each partner and retain their character. The other items listed are components of ordinary income, determined as follows: gross sales of $270,000, minus the cost of goods sold of $80,000 and wages of $50,000 = ordinary income of **$140,000.** Absent any provisions in the partnership agreement to the contrary, both ordinary income and the separately stated items would be allocated according to the partners' 60%/40% profit-sharing arrangement (as shown below).

Assad	60%	Dominic	40%
Ordinary income:	$84,000	Ordinary income:	$56,000
Interest income:	$1,500	Interest income:	$1,000
Short-term capital loss:	$3,000	Short-term capital loss:	$2,000

20. The answer is C. The partnership's section 179 deduction for the $30,000 oven is limited to the partnership's income of $25,000. The deduction is further split between the two partners ($25,000 × 50%) = **$12,500.** Section 179 is a separately stated item on a partnership tax return. Assuming she has no section 179 deductions from other sources, Lucy's section 179 deduction would be $12,500. The partnership could also choose to depreciate the remainder of the cost of the oven using bonus depreciation.

21. The answer is A. This loan amount is included in Charlotte's basis in the partnership because she has an economic risk of loss related to this liability. An additional $60,000 of basis in the partnership's depreciable property was created as a result of incurring this debt. Her basis in the partnership would be **$80,000** ($20,000 + $60,000), while Todd's basis would be only **$20,000,** the amount of his original investment.

Unit 11: Partnership Distributions & Liquidations

More Reading:
Publication 541, Partnerships
Instructions for Form 1065

A partnership is not a taxable entity; its income and losses flow through and are reported on the partners' individual tax returns. Each partner is taxed on his or her distributive share of income, whether or not it is actually distributed. Partnership distributions may include the following:

- Distributions of the partnership's earnings for the current or prior years.
- A withdrawal by a partner in anticipation of the current year's earnings.
- A complete or partial liquidation of a partner's interest.
- A distribution to all partners in complete liquidation of the partnership.

The tax treatment of a distribution depends on whether it is a current distribution or a *liquidating* distribution. A *current* distribution is one that does not terminate the partner's interest in the partnership. The opposite of a current distribution is a liquidating distribution, which terminates a partner's entire interest in the partnership.

A partnership distribution is not taken into account in determining the partner's distributive share of the partnership's income or loss.

If a gain or loss from the distribution is recognized by the partner, it must be reported on the partner's return for the tax year in which the distribution is received. Cash or property withdrawn by a partner in anticipation of the current year's earnings is treated as a distribution received on the last day of the partnership's tax year. A partner's adjusted basis in his partnership interest is decreased (but not below zero) by the cash and adjusted basis of property distributed to the partner.

If the amount of a cash (or the cash portion of mixed cash and property) distribution exceeds a partner's basis in the partnership, then the excess of the cash distribution over the partner's pre-distribution outside basis will normally result in capital gain to the partner. If a property distribution exceeds a partner's outside basis in the partnership, this will not normally result in taxable gain, but the partner's outside basis will be transferred into the asset(s) received in the distribution.

Example: The adjusted basis of Wilda's partnership interest is $140,000 on January 1. She receives a distribution of $80,000 cash and land that has an adjusted basis to the partnership of $20,000 and a fair market value of $30,000. The distribution decreases the basis of her partnership interest to $40,000 based on the amount of the cash and the basis of the asset (land) distributed ($140,000 – [$80,000 + $20,000]). Because the cash portion of the distribution does not exceed the basis of her partnership interest, Wilda does not recognize gain. Any gain related to the excess of the land's fair market value over its adjusted basis will be recognized when she later disposes of it.

The basis of property (other than cash) distributed to the partner is generally its adjusted basis to the partnership immediately before the distribution, unless the amount of the property distribution (based on the partnership's inside basis in the property right before the distribution) exceeds the partner's outside basis (in which case, as mentioned earlier, the partner's outside basis is transferred to the assets received from the partnership).

Example: Right-Type Printing, LLC is taxed as a partnership. Patricia is a 20% partner in the business. The adjusted basis of Patricia's partnership interest is $45,000 at the beginning of the year. She receives a distribution of a printing machine that has an adjusted basis of $23,000 to the partnership plus an additional $6,000 in cash. Her basis in the partnership is first reduced by the cash portion of the distribution ($6,000) and with a $39,000 remaining basis, her basis in the printing machine is $23,000. After this distribution, her partnership basis would be $16,000 ($45,000-$6,000-$23,000).

However, a partner cannot have a *negative* partnership basis. Therefore, the basis of property distributed to a partner cannot be more than the adjusted basis of his interest in the partnership, reduced by any cash received in the same transaction.

Example: Hedrick is a 10% partner in Broadway Realty, LLC. The basis of Hedrick's partnership interest is $100,000. He receives a distribution of $40,000 cash and a parcel of farmland that has an adjusted basis to the partnership of $80,000. Hedrick's basis in the farmland is limited to $60,000 ($100,000 basis - $40,000, the cash he receives) since the total amount cannot exceed his partnership interest. After this distribution, his partnership basis would be zero, but he recognizes no gain on the distribution as the amount of the cash received is not in excess of his outside basis in the partnership. Later, if Hedrick decides to sell the farmland, then his basis for determining gain will be $60,000. Any gain on the rental will be recognized when he sells it.

A partnership does not recognize any gain or loss because of distributions it makes to partners. The partnership may be able to elect to adjust the basis of its undistributed property. However, when a partnership distributes the following items, the distribution may be treated as a sale or exchange of property rather than a distribution:

- Unrealized receivables or substantially appreciated inventory items distributed in exchange for any part of the partner's interest in other partnership property, including cash.
- Other property, including cash, distributed in exchange for any part of a partner's interest in unrealized receivables or substantially appreciated inventory items.

This treatment does not apply to the following distributions:

- A distribution of property to the partner who contributed the same property to the partnership.
- Payments made to a retiring partner or successor in interest of a deceased partner that are the partner's distributive share of partnership income or guaranteed payments.

Special Rules for Distributed Partnership Inventory

A gain or loss on a sale or exchange of unrealized receivables or inventory items a partner received in a distribution is generally treated as ordinary income or loss. However, if a partner holds the inventory (in the hands of the partnership) for at least 5 years, then sells it, the gain would be treated as a capital gain if the assets were capital assets in the hands of the partner.

Example: Zinnia was a general partner in Totem Jewelers, a retail business that sold gold and silver jewelry. On January 3, 2020, Totem Jewelers distributed 20 pieces of jewelry to Zinnia. The jewelry had a basis of $19,000 to the partnership. Zinnia used the jewelry for her own personal use, wearing several pieces to parties and other private functions. She sold all of the jewelry for $24,000 on December 31, 2020. The $5,000 gain is taxed as ordinary income to Zinnia, even though the jewelry was a capital asset in her hands. This is because the jewelry was *inventory* to the partnership, and she sold it less than a year after it was distributed to her. If she had held the inventory for more than 5 years after the distribution and sold it at a gain, her gain would have been a long-term capital gain and taxed at a much lower rate.

If a partnership acquires a partner's debt and extinguishes the debt by distributing it to the partner, the partner will recognize capital gain or loss to the extent the fair market value of the debt differs from the basis of the debt.

The partner is treated as having satisfied the debt for its fair market value. If the issue price of the debt exceeds its FMV when distributed, the partner may have to include the excess amount in income as canceled debt.

Sale of a Partnership Interest

A partnership interest is a capital asset. As a result, a gain or loss on the sale or exchange of a partnership interest is normally treated as a capital gain or loss. However, if the partnership holds certain section 751 "hot assets", some or all of the gain or loss may be recharacterized as ordinary. Inventory and unrealized receivables are the most common section 751 assets.[112]

Gain or loss is calculated as the difference between the amount realized and the adjusted basis of the partner's interest in the partnership. If the selling partner is relieved of partnership liabilities, he must include the liability relief as part of the amount realized for his interest.

Example: Benicia became a 10% partner in the Rincon Partnership by contributing cash to the formation of the partnership. The adjusted basis of her partnership interest at the end of 2020 is $20,000, which includes her $15,000 share of partnership liabilities. Benicia feels that the partnership is not well managed, and she wants to get out of the business. She sells her interest in the partnership to an unrelated party for $10,000 in cash on December 31, 2020. At the time of the sale, she had been credited for her share of the partnership's income for the tax year. Benicia realizes $25,000 from the sale of her partnership interest ($10,000 cash payment + $15,000 liability relief). She must report $5,000 ($25,000 realized – $20,000 basis) as a capital gain.

Related Party Transactions

A partnership cannot deduct a loss on the sale or trade of property if the transaction is directly or indirectly between related parties. Under the related party transaction rules, an individual is considered to be the owner of a partnership interest directly or indirectly owned by his family members. Members of a family, for this purpose, include only siblings, half-siblings, spouses, ancestors, parents, and lineal descendants (children, grandchildren). For the purposes

[112] If the partnership has any cash-basis unrealized receivables or inventory with a built-in-gain (otherwise known as "hot assets") at the time of the partnership sale or exchange, then in accordance with IRC §751, some of the gain or loss could be classified as an ordinary gain or loss instead of entirely a capital gain or loss.

of this rule, "related parties" does *not* include: ex-spouses, in-laws, step-siblings, cousins, or step-parents.

Example: Danaher Partnership is owned by two brothers, Dwayne and Enzo. OBM Partnership is owned by two sisters, Eartha and Gretchen. Eartha and Gretchen are step-sisters to Dwayne and Enzo. During the year, Danaher Partnership sells a factory building to OBM Partnership. Danaher Partnership recognizes a capital loss on the sale of the building. The loss is allowable because step-siblings are not considered related parties.

Losses are not allowed from a sale or exchange of property (other than an interest in the partnership) directly or indirectly between a partnership and a person whose direct or indirect interest in the capital or profits of the partnership is more than 50%. If a sale or exchange is between two partnerships in which the same persons directly or indirectly own more than 50% of the capital or profits interests in each partnership, no loss is allowed.

Example: Mason and Adalyn are siblings. Adalyn is a 60% partner in the Crown Partnership, and Mason is a 55% partner in the Belkin Partnership. If one partnership sells property to the other at a loss, the loss will not be allowed because the partnerships are considered related parties, because the majority ownership in both partnerships is held by two closely-related family members (Mason and Adalyn). Losses will instead be suspended until the property is eventually disposed of in a non-related party transaction.

The basis of each partner's interest in the partnership is decreased (but not below zero) by the partner's share of a disallowed loss. If the purchaser later sells the property, only the gain realized that is greater than the loss not allowed will be taxable. If a gain from the sale of the property is not recognized because of this rule, the basis of each partner's interest in the partnership is increased by the partner's share of that gain.

Liquidation of a Partnership and Terminating Distributions

When a partnership dissolves or stops doing business, it is called a *partnership liquidation*, and the partnership will normally pay off existing debts and liabilities and distribute to the partners any remaining assets. A dissolution (or liquidation) marks the official ending of a partnership. A partnership may dissolve when a partner dies, or when one partner drops out of the business. The basis of property received in complete liquidation of a partner's interest is the adjusted basis of the partner's interest in the partnership reduced by any cash distributed to the partner in the same transaction. A partner's holding period for property distributed to him includes the period held by the partnership. If the property was contributed to the partnership by a partner in a section 721 transaction,[113] the holding period includes the period held by that partner prior to the original contribution.

Payments made by the partnership to a retiring partner or a deceased partner's estate or in liquidation of the interest of a retiring or deceased partner in exchange for his interest in partnership property are considered a *distribution*, not a guaranteed payment that could give rise to a deduction for the partnership. A retiring or deceased partner is treated as a partner until his interest in the partnership has been completely liquidated.

[113] Section 721(a) generally provides that no gain or loss shall be recognized to a partnership or to any of its partners in the case of a contribution of property to the partnership in exchange for an interest in the partnership.

The death of a partner will close the partnership's tax year for that partner, but it generally does not close the partnership's tax year for the remaining partners. A final Schedule K-1 will generally be issued to the deceased partner.

Example: Ameer was a 5% partner in Boston Consulting, LLP, a cash-basis, calendar-year partnership. Ameer died on August 1. The distributive share of ordinary partnership income allocable to Ameer through the date of his death was $40,000. For the entire year, 5% of the partnership's income was $55,000. Ameer's daughter, Noor, inherits her late father's partnership interest and takes over his role in the business effective on August 1. $40,000 of ordinary partnership income would be reported on Ameer's final income tax return (Form 1040) via the final K-1 issued to him by the partnership, and the remaining $15,000 of partnership income would be allocated to Noor on her Schedule K-1 from the partnership.

A buy-sell agreement is a legal contract that binds the partnership to buy out the interest of a deceased partner; this type of agreement helps to ensure that the business will continue uninterrupted. When other partners (themselves, and not the partnership), directly purchase a retired or deceased partner's interest, this is called a cross-purchase agreement, as opposed to a buy-sell agreement.

Example: Global Attorneys, LLP is a calendar year, cash-basis partnership law firm. When the partnership was formed, each partner signed a buy-sell agreement that stated in the event of one partner's death, the deceased partner's estate would receive $400,000 in full payment for the partnership interest, based on the deceased partner's share of the partnership's property. In 2020, Kristopher, a 20% partner, dies. Kristopher's estate was paid $400,000 by Global Attorneys, LLP in accordance with the buyout agreement. The entire $400,000 will be treated as a distribution. With the 20% partnership now no longer in existence, the remaining partners' interests will increase proportionately as a result.

In a partnership liquidation, the liquidating distributions are similar to regular distributions except that the partner may recognize a loss if the total of cash and the basis of certain qualifying property received is less than his basis in the partnership. If the basis of property received is the adjusted basis of the partner's interest in the partnership (reduced by money received in the same transaction), it must be divided among the properties distributed to the partner.

Example: Abby Farms, LLC is closing down its operations. Dean's basis in his partnership interest is $20,000. In a distribution to liquidate his entire interest, Abby Farms distributes a compact tractor and a bale wrapper to Dean. The compact tractor has an adjusted basis to the partnership of $15,000 and an FMV of $15,000. The bale wrapper has an adjusted basis to the partnership of $15,000, but it is in disrepair, so its FMV is only $5,000. To figure his basis in each property, Dean first assigns a basis of $15,000 to the compact tractor and $15,000 to the bale wrapper (their adjusted bases to the partnership). This leaves a $10,000 basis decrease (the $30,000 total of the assigned basis [$15K + $15K] minus his $20,000 allocable partnership basis). Dean allocates the entire $10,000 to the bale wrapper (its unrealized depreciation). Dean's basis in the compact tractor is $15,000, and his basis in the bale wrapper is $5,000 ($15,000 - $10,000). If he later sells either asset, he will use these assigned bases to figure his gain or loss on the sale (example from Publication 541).

Recognizing a loss on a liquidating distribution: A *loss* on a distribution occurs when the amount a partner receives as a liquidating distribution is *lower* than the partner's investment in the partnership. However, a partner cannot recognize a loss on a partnership distribution unless all of the following requirements are met:

- The adjusted basis of the partner's interest in the partnership exceeds the distribution.
- The partner's entire interest in the partnership is liquidated.
- The distribution is in cash, unrealized receivables, or inventory items (qualifying property).

Example: Andrea is a 25% partner in Park Slope Partnership. Andrea decides to retire from the partnership at the end of the year. Andrea's partnership basis is $150,000 on December 31. Park Slope Partnership makes a liquidating distribution to Andrea of cash of $90,000 and inventory with a basis of $30,000 and FMV of $30,000. Andrea would recognize a capital loss of $30,000 on the liquidating distribution ($150,000 basis - $90,000 cash -$30,000 inventory).

Example: The Hempstead Partnership is liquidating. Ernie's adjusted basis in the partnership is $80,000. He receives a liquidating cash distribution of $60,000. As Ernie's adjusted basis of his partnership interest exceeds the distribution, he has a capital loss of $20,000 ($80,000 - $60,000).

If a partnership is liquidated or dissolved with unamortized organizational or start-up expenses, the unamortized amounts can be deducted on the partnership's final tax return.

Example: The Emerson Partnership is liquidating five years after it formed. It had been amortizing $36,000 of organizational and start-up costs over 180 months. After five years, the partnership had amortized $12,000 ($36,000 ÷ 60 months). Emerson Partnership can deduct the remaining unamortized amount of $24,000 ($36,000 - $12,000) on its final partnership tax return.

Partnership Termination

A partnership terminates when all its operations are discontinued and no part of any business, financial operation, or venture is continued by any of the partners in a partnership. The partnership's tax year ends on the date of termination.

If the partnership is terminated before the end of its regular tax year, Form 1065 must be filed for the short tax year from the beginning of the tax year through the date of termination. The return is due on the fifteenth day of the third month following the date of termination.

Note: The Tax Cuts and Jobs Act repealed the 50% partnership "technical termination" rule. In prior years, partnerships experienced a "technical termination" if, within any 12-month period, there was a sale or exchange of at least 50% of the total interest in partnership capital and profits. If an existing general partnership is later converted into an LLC classified as a partnership, the conversion does not terminate the partnership, and there is no sale, exchange, or termination of partnership interests. The partnership's tax year does not close, and the LLC can continue to use the partnership's existing employer identification number.

Example: Lundgren Partnership is a calendar-year partnership. The partnership terminates and stops doing business on May 3, 2020. Its final Form 1065 for the short tax year period of January 1 through May 3 is due on August 15, 2020, the fifteenth day of the third month following the end of the month of termination.

Example: Allied Capital is a calendar-year general partnership, run by two individuals, Gideon and Conrad. In 2020, the partners decide to convert their partnership to an LLC for liability purposes. Gideon and Conrad file Articles of Organization with their Secretary of State. Allied Capital, LLC is formed on March 1, 2020. The formation of the LLC has no tax effect. Gideon and Conrad can continue to use the same EIN for their partnership, and the partnership can file its tax return as normal.

Cancellation of Another Partner's Debt

If a partnership terminates and one of the former partners is insolvent and cannot pay his share of the partnership's debts, the other partners may be forced to pay more than their share of the liabilities. If another partner pays any part of an insolvent partner's share of the debts, the partner that actually pays the debt can take a bad debt deduction on their individual tax return.

Example: Chester and Dayna are 50/50 partners in Diamond Tutoring, LLC a company that provides online tutoring services. The company is struggling, and Chester and Dayna decide to discontinue the business. The partnership is terminated, and it has $50,000 of liabilities to creditors after liquidating all of its assets. However, Chester has filed for personal bankruptcy and the court has declared him insolvent. Even though Dayna is a 50% partner, she assumes responsibility for the entire $50,000 of partnership debt, which she pays herself out of her own personal savings. She can claim a bad debt deduction on her Form 1040, in the amount of $25,000, equal to Chester's share of the debt that she personally assumed.

The cancellation of debt exclusions are applied at the partner level rather than at the partnership level. Thus, for example, an individual partner would need to be insolvent to utilize the insolvency exclusion for his share of COD income passed through from an insolvent partnership. If a partner is able to use the exclusion, he would be required to reduce specified tax attributes, including loss and credit carryforwards and the basis of assets.

Unit 11: Study Questions

(Please test yourself and check the correct answers at the end of this section.)

1. Shannon is a 10% partner in the Barker Partnership. Under the terms of a partnership agreement, she is entitled to a fixed guaranteed payment of $10,000 without regard to the income of the partnership. Her distributive share of the partnership income is 10%. The partnership has $200,000 of ordinary income *after* deducting Shannon's guaranteed payment. How much ordinary income from the partnership would Shannon report on her individual tax return?

A. $10,000
B. $20,000
C. $30,000
D. $50,000

2. The adjusted basis of Allison's partnership interest is $24,000. She receives a distribution of $9,000 cash and machinery that has an adjusted basis of $1,000 and a fair market value of $7,000. How much gain should Allison recognize on this distribution?

A. $0
B. $1,000
C. $2,000
D. $7,000

3. The adjusted basis of Jeffrey's partnership interest is $10,000. He receives a distribution of $4,000 cash and a horse trailer that has an adjusted basis to the partnership of $9,000 and a fair market value of $12,000. This was not a liquidating distribution. What is Jeffrey's basis in the horse trailer?

A. $5,000
B. $6,000
C. $12,000
D. $16,000

4. Marty is permanently retiring from Sunnyside Partnership this year. His adjusted basis in the partnership is $50,000. He receives a distribution of $65,000 cash. How would Marty report this transaction on his personal income tax return?

A. $15,000 capital gain.
B. $50,000 capital gain.
C. $65,000 capital gain.
D. $65,000 ordinary income.

5. Nina, a partner in the Fairway Partnership, receives distributions of $1,000 of cash and property worth $2,000, in which Fairway has a basis of $1,500. Nina's outside basis at the time of the distributions is $20,000. Fairway Partnership has assets of $40,000 and no outstanding liabilities. The distributions are made at the end of the year, after partnership income (loss) has been recorded. How much gain should Nina recognize on the distributions, and what is her basis in the property received?

A. She recognizes a gain of $500 on the property received, and her basis in the property is $2,000.
B. She recognizes a gain of $1,500 on the property and cash received. Her basis in the property received is $3,500.
C. She recognizes no gain on the property received. Her basis in the property received is $1,500.
D. She recognizes a gain of $1,000. Her basis in the property received is $1,500.

6. Alfonso and Ellen are equal partners in the Bantam Partnership. In 2020, the partnership dissolves. Alfonso is insolvent, and Ellen becomes responsible for paying a portion of Alfonso's delinquent partnership debt. Which of the following statements is correct?

A. Ellen cannot take a bad debt deduction for any debt that the partnership incurred.
B. Alfonso is not responsible for paying any of his liabilities after dissolution.
C. Ellen can take a bad debt deduction for any amount that she must pay that is not her share of the partnership debt.
D. None of the above.

7. Laney is a 10% partner in Adamson Architects, LLP. In 2020, Laney sold her entire partnership interest for $45,000. Her adjusted basis at the time of the sale was $29,500, which includes her $12,500 share of partnership liabilities. When she initially invested in the partnership, she contributed $10,000 worth of equipment. There was no profit or loss at the partnership level that had not been credited at the time she sold her interest. Assuming the partnership holds no section 751 assets, what is the amount and nature of her income or loss from the sale of her partnership interest?

A. $7,500 ordinary loss.
B. $10,000 capital gain.
C. $12,500 ordinary income.
D. $28,000 capital gain.

8. The adjusted basis of Adrian's partnership interest is $17,500. He received a distribution of $9,000 cash and a piece of land with an adjusted basis of $2,500 to the partnership and a fair market value of $4,000. What is the gain to be recognized at the time of these distributions?

A. $0
B. $1,500
C. $4,500
D. $6,000

9. William owns a 75% capital interest in the Shanahan Partnership. William's wife, Veronica, is a 65% owner in the Gorlin Partnership. William and Veronica file separate tax returns and keep all their books and records separate. Shanahan Partnership sells Gorlin Partnership a factory machine for $7,600. Shanahan's basis in the machinery is $10,000. What is Shanahan Partnership's deductible loss?

A. $0
B. $2,400
C. $7,600
D. $10,000

Unit 11: Quiz Answers

1. The answer is C. Shannon must include ordinary income of **$30,000** on her individual income tax return for her tax year in which the partnership's tax year ends ($10,000 guaranteed payment + $20,000 [$200,000 × 10%], her distributive share). This example is modified from an example in IRS Publication 541, *Partnerships.*

2. The answer is A. Because the sum of cash and the adjusted basis of the property does not exceed the basis of her partnership interest, Allison does not recognize any gain on the distribution. Any gain on the machinery will be recognized when she sells it.

3. The answer is B. Jeffrey's basis for the trailer is limited to **$6,000** ($10,000 basis - $4,000, the cash he receives), equal to the remaining basis in his partnership interest after subtracting the cash received. After the distributions, his basis in the partnership interest is zero.

4. The answer is A. As he is a retiring partner, Marty must recognize **$15,000 of capital gain** on his personal tax return. This is the difference between his adjusted basis in the partnership and the amount of his distribution ($65,000 - $50,000). A retiring partner or the successor in interest of a deceased partner recognizes gain to the extent that any cash (and marketable securities treated as cash) distributed is more than the partner's adjusted basis in the partnership.

5. The answer is C. Nina recognizes no gain because the total of cash and the basis of property received does not exceed her basis in the partnership. She assumes the partnership's basis of $1,500 in the property received. She would only recognize gain or loss if she later sells the property.

6. The answer is C. Ellen is allowed to take a bad debt deduction for the liabilities she must pay that are in excess of her share of partnership liabilities. If a business partnership dissolves and one of the former partners is insolvent and cannot pay his share of the partnership's debts, other partners may have to pay more than their respective shares. If a partner pays any part of the insolvent partner's share of the debts, she can take a bad debt deduction for the amount paid.

7. The answer is D. When Laney sold her partnership interest, she was relieved of her $12,500 share of the partnership's liabilities, so the amount of liability relieved from Laney upon sale of her interest is treated as additional proceeds, so her gain will be **$28,000** ($45,000 + $12,500 - $29,500). As a partnership interest is normally a capital asset, any gain or loss recognized on the sale of the interest is typically treated as a capital gain or loss.

8. The answer is A. Because the total of cash does not exceed Adrian's adjusted basis of $17,500 in his partnership interest, he will recognize no gain as a result of the distribution. He assumes the partnership's adjusted basis of $2,500 in the property received, and will recognize gain or loss if he later sells this property.

9. The answer is A. Shanahan Partnership's loss of $2,400 is not deductible. A loss on the sale or exchange of property between related persons is not deductible. This applies to both direct and indirect transactions. The fact that William and Veronica file separate tax returns does not prevent them from being related parties for purposes of this transaction.

Unit 12: C Corporations in General

More Reading:

Publication 542, Corporations

Publication 544, Sales and Other Dispositions of Assets

Instructions for Form 1120, U.S. Corporation Income Tax Return

Publication 5292, How to Calculate Section 965 Amounts and Elections Available to Taxpayers

Most major companies are organized as C corporations, which are taxed under subchapter C of the Internal Revenue Code. A C corporation can own property in its own name, and it can be sued directly. The shareholders who own stock in a corporation do not own its individual assets. Individual shareholders are protected from legal liability, except in very unusual circumstances.

The IRS requires certain businesses to be taxed as corporations. The following businesses formed after 1996 are *automatically* treated as corporations:

- A business formed under a federal or state law that refers to it as a corporation
- A business formed under a state law that refers to it as a joint-stock company or joint-stock association
- Insurance companies and certain banks
- A business owned by a state or local government
- A business specifically required to be taxed as a corporation by the IRC (for example, certain publicly-traded partnerships)
- Certain foreign businesses
- Any other business that elects to be taxed as a corporation and files Form 8832, *Entity Classification Election*. For example, an LLC can *elect* to be treated as an association taxable as a corporation by filing Form 8832.

Basic Concepts

Basic concepts regarding C corporations include:

1. **Perpetual life and limited liability:** A C corporation enjoys perpetual life and limited liability.
2. **Double taxation:** Earnings of a C corporation may be taxed twice: first at the corporate level and again at the shareholder level if they are distributed as dividends. Shareholders of a C corporation cannot deduct corporate losses.
3. **Shareholder meetings:** A corporation must maintain a list of all its shareholders and generally must conduct at least one shareholder meeting per year.
4. **Organization:** A C corporation must file a charter, issue stock, and be overseen by a board of directors.
5. **Number of shareholders:** A C corporation may have a single owner-shareholder or an unlimited number of shareholders.

6. **Articles of incorporation:** A corporation's existence starts when articles of incorporation are filed with the state office that handles incorporations (usually the Secretary of State), along with any required filing fees.
7. **Liquidation:** If a C corporation liquidates, it will recognize gain or loss on the sale or distribution of its assets. Corporate shareholders then recognize gain or loss on the surrender of their stock to the corporation.
8. **Stock:** A C corporation may sell common and/or preferred stock with different voting rights.
9. **Tax-free fringe benefits:** A C corporation's shareholder-employees can receive tax-free employee fringe benefits that are deductible by the corporation as a business expense. This applies to employees who are owners of the company as well as other employees.

Filing Requirements for C Corporations

A domestic corporation in existence for any part of a tax year (including corporations in bankruptcy) must file an income tax return, regardless of its taxable income or activity. A C corporation files Form 1120, *U.S. Corporation Income Tax Return.*

There are some specialized forms for other types of corporations, such as foreign corporations, which must file Form 1120-F. Tax-exempt organizations organized as corporations file Form 990 rather than Form 1120. Electronic filing is mandatory for C corporations with $10 million or more in assets and/or at least 100 or more returns of any type, including information returns such as Forms W-2 or Forms 1099. [114]

A corporation must continue to file tax returns even if there is no business activity or profits. However, it does not have to file after it has formally dissolved.

A corporation must generally file by the fifteenth day of the fourth month after the end of its tax year. Thus, a calendar-year corporation must typically file its tax return by April 15 of the following year. The due date for calendar-year C corporations is April 15, 2021. C Corporations with fiscal years that end on June 30 will, until December 31, 2025, have a due date of September 15 (the fifteenth day of the *third* month after the end of the corporation's tax year).

Example: Sutherland Design, Inc. is a C corporation with a calendar year-end. It must file its 2020 Form 1120 by April 15, 2021. If Sutherland Design were to file an extension, their corporate return would be due on October 15, 2021.

The extended due date for calendar-year and fiscal-year corporate returns (except for June 30 fiscal year-end corporations) is six months after the original due date of the return. For calendar-year corporations, this results in an extended due date of October 15. June 30 fiscal year-end corporations receive a seven-month extension, putting their extended due date to April 15.

[114] The Taxpayer First Act (TFA) implemented an efile mandate for businesses that file information returns. Prior law prohibited any requirement that businesses that file more than 250 of information returns (of any type) during a calendar year are required to efile those forms. Under the TFA, the 250 return limit is reduced to 100 in calendar year 2021 (for 2020 tax filings), and down to 10 in 2022 (for 2021 tax filings).

Example: Standard Motors Inc. is a domestic C corporation with a fiscal year-end of June 30. Since the exception for June 30 fiscal-year corporations applies, the regular due date for the C corporation return (Form 1120) is September 15, which is the 15th day of the *third* month following the end of the company's taxable year.

Example: Kemmler Pharmaceuticals is a domestic C corporation. In 2020, Kemmler has $2 million in assets. Kemmler has 70 employees and will file 70 Form W-2 forms for the year. Kemmler also has 100 independent contractors that will receive a Form 1099-NEC from the company. For the purposes of the e-file mandate, Kemmler Pharmaceuticals is required to efile their information returns, because they have exceeded the 100 "information return limit."

A corporation must file Form 7004, *Automatic Extension of Time to File Certain Business Income Tax, Information, and Other Returns,* by the original due date to request an extension of time to file its income tax return. Form 7004 does not extend the time for paying the tax due on the return. Interest, and possibly penalties, will be charged on any part of the tax due and not paid. The interest is figured from the original due date of the return to the date of payment.

A penalty for late filing is assessed at 5% of any unpaid tax for each month the return is late, up to a maximum of 25% of the unpaid tax on the return. The late filing penalty is reduced by any late payment penalty for the same period.

In 2020, the minimum late *filing* penalty for Form 1120 has increased. If filed more than 60 days late, the penalty is $435 or the amount of tax owed, whichever is smaller. The penalty for late *payment* of corporate income tax is one-half of 1% of the unpaid tax for each month that the tax is not paid, up to a maximum of 25% of the unpaid tax.

Note: If the corporation is charged with both a penalty for late payment of tax and for late filing for the same period of time, the penalty for late filing is *reduced* by the amount of the penalty for late payment.

These penalties may not be imposed if the corporation shows reasonable cause for not paying or filing on time. A good example of "reasonable cause" would be a natural disaster, which would extend the filing deadline as well as extend the corporation's time to deposit its estimated taxes.

Example: Vision Management, Inc. is a fiscal-year C corporation doing business in Anchorage, Alaska. The fiscal-year year-end is January 31, and the due date for Vision Management to file their corporate return is May 15. However, on April 28, 2020, Vision Management incurred severe damage in its main office because of an earthquake. The affected area was later declared a federal disaster. Vision Management was unable to pay its quarterly taxes on time, and did not file its Form 1120 on time. Vision Management automatically qualifies for penalty abatement.

Estimated Tax Payments

Corporations are required to make estimated tax payments if they expect their tax due to be $500 or more during the taxable year. Corporations should use Form 1120-W, *Estimated Tax for Corporations,* to calculate their estimated payments. Late penalties apply if estimated tax payments are not made on time or at the required minimum amounts.

Corporations are required to use the Electronic Federal Tax Payment System, (also called EFTPS), to make all federal tax deposits, including estimated tax payments, payroll taxes, excise taxes, and corporate income tax installments are due on a quarterly basis, on the fifteenth day of the fourth, sixth, ninth, and twelfth months of the corporation's taxable year. This means that for a calendar year corporation, estimates are due:

April 15-First Estimate

June 15-Second Estimate

October 15-Third Estimate

December 15-Fourth Estimate

Note that this payment schedule is different from the payment schedule for individual taxpayers. An individual taxpayer's fourth-quarter estimated tax payment is due on January 15, not December 15.

Note: C Corporations cannot pay any income tax using a paper check; there are no federal deposit coupons or estimated payment vouchers for corporations. If a corporation owes a small balance when it files its annual return (under $500) then the corporation can pay using Direct Debit with the e-filed return. Otherwise, all payments must be made using EFTPS.

In general, each quarterly federal tax payment is 25% of the corporation's "required annual payment," which is the lesser of two amounts:

- **Current-year tax liability:** 100% of the federal income tax reported on the return for the current taxable year of the payment
- **Prior-year safe harbor:** 100% of a corporation's federal income tax reported on the return for the preceding year

If a corporation later determines that it needs to revise its estimated tax liability, they will be required to refigure the installment payments. In this scenario, an immediate catch-up payment should be made to reduce any penalty related to earlier installments.

There is no penalty for underpayment of estimated tax if the tax is less than $500, or if each quarterly estimated tax payment is at least 25% of the corporation's current-year tax. Penalties apply to corporate taxpayers who underpay their required quarterly payments. The penalty for underpayment is nondeductible.

There is also no underpayment penalty if each estimated tax installment is at least 25% of the income tax on the prior-year return. However, unlike individuals, corporations without a tax liability in the preceding year cannot use the 100% prior-year safe harbor amount to determine their required estimated tax payment. The safe harbor provision will also not apply in the following instances:

- If the prior tax year was a short year (less than 12 months)
- If the corporation did not file a return for the prior year
- If the corporation had at least $1 million of modified taxable income in any of the last three years

Example: CellStar Corporation had a net operating loss in the previous year, and therefore did not have a tax liability. Therefore, the safe harbor provision for estimated tax payments will not apply. CellStar Corporation must accurately estimate its federal income tax liability for the current year and pay 100% of the federal income tax due on the current year tax return.

Corporate Refunds and Amended Returns

Corporations may use Form 1139, *Corporate Application for Tentative Refund,* or Form 1120X, *Amended U.S. Corporation Income Tax Return,* to apply for a refund of overpaid tax. Generally, the corporation must file Form 1139 within 12 months of the end of the tax year in which an NOL, net capital loss, unused credit, or claim of right adjustment arose.

If a corporation does not file Form 1139, it must file Form 1120X to apply for a refund. Form 1120X must be filed within three years of the due date, including extensions, for filing the return for a year in which it sustains a loss.

If a corporation accidentally overpays its estimated tax, it may use Form 4466, *Corporation Application for Quick Refund of Overpayment of Estimated Tax,* to obtain a quick refund of its estimated tax payments. Form 4466 must be filed before the corporation files its tax return. Form 4466 may be used if a corporation's overpayment is at least 10% of its anticipated tax liability and at least $500.

Example: Segal Holdings, Inc. is a C corporation that reports its income and loss using the cash method. Segal Holdings made regular estimated payments throughout the year based on its current-year tax liability. On December 19, 2020, Segal Holdings suffers a financial loss when a fire destroys its main office building. After this catastrophic event, Segal Holdings expects to have a net operating loss for the year. The corporation files Form 4466 on January 10, 2021, to obtain a quick refund of the overpaid estimated tax that it paid in 2020. It does not have to wait until it files its Form 1120 in order to obtain a refund.

Corporate Taxation

Unlike a sole proprietorship, partnership, or an S corporation, a C corporation is not a pass-through entity. A C corporation pays tax on its earnings and can accumulate income. Corporations pay a flat tax of 21% on all their profits. The disadvantage that a C corporation has over other forms of business is that the earnings of a C corporation may be taxed twice–once at the corporate level and once at the shareholder level, through dividend distributions. A corporation does not receive a tax deduction for the distribution of dividends to its shareholders.

A C corporation's income does not retain its character when it is distributed to shareholders. A corporation can have revenue from many different sources, including sales of products, services, and investment income.

If, for example, a C corporation has rental income, it pays tax on this and any other sources of income at the corporate level. When the corporation's after-tax income is distributed to shareholders, this portion does not retain its character as rental income. It is distributed merely as a dividend.

This also applies if the corporation earns tax-exempt income. For example, a C corporation may earn tax-exempt income from investing in municipal bonds. If this income is used to make distributions to shareholders, its tax-exempt character is lost, and the distributions will be taxable dividends to the shareholders.

Example: Advanced Medical Devices, Inc. is a calendar-year C corporation with twenty shareholders. After deducting business expenses, Advanced Medical has $150,000 of taxable income. The corporation also earns $4,000 of nontaxable interest income from municipal bonds. The $4,000 of tax-exempt bond interest is excluded from the corporation's taxable income. On December 1, 2020, Advanced Medical Devices distributes $120,000 in dividends to its shareholders, based on their ownership stake. The company cannot take a tax deduction for the distribution. Each shareholder has an equal stake in the company, so each one receives $6,000 of dividend income ($120,000 ÷ 20 = $6,000). Each shareholder is required to recognize $6,000 of dividend income on their individual tax returns.

Example: Pepper Cutlery, Inc. is a C corporation that receives tax-exempt income from bonds. Pepper Cutlery subsequently distributes income to its shareholders as taxable dividends. Even though a portion of the income was tax-exempt to Pepper Cutlery, it does not retain its tax-exempt character when distributions are made to the shareholders. In contrast, in the case of an S corporation or a partnership, the income would have retained its character when it was passed through to the partners or S corporation shareholders.

Accumulated Earnings Tax

A corporation is allowed to accumulate a reasonable portion of its earnings for possible expansion or other bona fide business reasons. However, a corporation may be subject to the accumulated earnings tax if it does not distribute enough of its profits to shareholders. This tax was instituted to prevent corporations from hoarding income in order to avoid income tax on distributions for its shareholders.

Note: The **accumulated earnings tax** is levied at a rate of **20%** of the excess amount accumulated. It is not automatically applied; it is assessed only after an audit. A corporation would have the opportunity to try to justify the amount of its accumulated earnings during an IRS examination.

If the accumulated earnings tax applies, interest is also assessed from the date the corporate return was originally due, without extensions.

An accumulation of $250,000 or less is generally considered reasonable for most businesses. However, for personal service corporations, the limit is $150,000. "Reasonable needs" of the business include the following:

- Specific, definite, and feasible plans for the use of the earnings accumulation in the business. Specific examples include:
  - The expansion of the company to a new area or a new facility.
  - Acquiring another business through the purchase of stock or assets.
  - Providing for reasonable estimates of product liability losses.
- The amount necessary to redeem the corporation's stock included in a deceased shareholder's gross estate, if the amount does not exceed the reasonably anticipated total estate and inheritance taxes and funeral and administration expenses incurred by the shareholder's estate.

The absence of a bona fide business reason for a corporation's accumulated earnings may be indicated by many different circumstances, such as a lack of regular distributions to its shareholders or withdrawals by the shareholders classified as personal loans. Actions to expand the business generally qualify as a bona fide reason for the accumulated income.

The fact that a corporation has an unreasonable accumulation of earnings is sufficient to establish liability for the accumulated earnings tax unless the corporation can show the earnings were not accumulated to allow its shareholders to avoid income tax.

Alternative Minimum Tax Credit

The federal corporate AMT was permanently repealed in the Tax Cuts and Jobs Act. The AMT tax rate is currently zero. However, some corporations may have AMT credits from prior tax years, when the corporate AMT was still in effect.

Any AMT credits that the corporation had from a prior year are allowed to offset the regular tax liability.

Note: The CARES Act, signed in March 2020, allows C corporations to recover any remaining carryover AMT credits 50% in tax years 2018 and 50% in tax year 2019. Corporations may also elect to claim the entire credit in tax year 2018 by amending their 2018 corporate return. A corporation making this election must file a tentative refund application before December 31, 2020. The IRS would have 90 days to review the application and refund any overpayment.

Accounting Methods for Corporations

Like other entities, C corporations may generally use any permissible accounting method for keeping track of income and expenses. A corporation generally chooses its accounting method when it files its first tax return. A corporation can change its method of accounting at a later date, but the corporation must file Form 3115, *Application for Change in Accounting Method,* in order to request permission from the IRS to make the change.

Note: A corporation may use the cash method of accounting if it has average annual gross receipts less than $26 million in 2020. Once the corporation's average annual gross receipts exceeds this threshold, the business generally must use the accrual method. Tax shelters must always use the accrual method of accounting, regardless of their size.

The "nonaccrual experience method" is a method of accounting for bad debts. If a corporation uses the accrual method of accounting and qualifies to use the nonaccrual experience method for bad debts, it is not required to accrue service-related income that it expects to be uncollectible.

Accrual-method corporations are not required to maintain accruals for certain amounts from the performance of services that, on the basis of their experience, will not be collected, if:

- The services are in the fields of health, law, engineering, architecture, accounting, actuarial science, performing arts, or consulting (i.e., personal service corporations); or
- The corporation's average annual gross receipts for the three prior tax years do not exceed $26 million in 2020.

This provision does not apply if the corporation charges interest on late payments, or if it charges customers any penalty for failure to pay an amount timely. Further, a corporation cannot use this method for amounts owed from activities such as lending money, selling goods, or acquiring receivables.

Additional Form 1120 Schedules

Corporations may be required to submit certain additional schedules along with their Form 1120. These schedules are unique to C corporations, and are primarily used for reconciling "book" or accounting differences with the deductions that are allowable under current tax law.

Differences in accounting rules for financial reporting (also called "book income") and tax reporting can lead to differences in the amounts of income reported to shareholders and tax authorities. Preparation of a C corporation's income tax return includes a reconciliation of book income to taxable income. Schedule M-1 and Schedule M-3 are both used to reconcile book-to-tax differences. Schedule L includes balance sheets of the beginning and end of the year, based on the corporation's books and records. Small corporations are not required to complete Schedule L if both assets and gross receipts are below $250,000 for the taxable year.

Schedule M-1 is only required when the corporation's gross receipts or its total assets at the end of the year are greater than $250,000. Schedule M-3 is used for large corporations with assets that exceed $10 million. Very small corporations with **less than** $250,000 of gross receipts or total assets are not required to file Schedule M-1, or Schedule L.[115]

Example: Indigo Shoes, Inc. is a small C Corporation that reports income and loss on the cash basis. Indigo Shoes had $196,000 in gross receipts during the tax year. The corporation's total assets were $45,000 at the end of the year. Indigo Shoes, Inc. is not required to file a Schedule M-1, M-2, or a Schedule L.

Remember these filing thresholds for the exam:

Filing Requirements for Corporate Schedules	
No Schedule L, M-1, or M-3 required	Small corporations with < $250,000 in gross receipts **and** < $250,000 in assets.
Schedule L (Balance Sheet)	Required once gross receipts **or** total assets exceed $250,000
Schedule M-1 (Reconciliation of Income/Loss per Books With Income per Return)	Required once gross receipts **or** total assets exceed $250,000
Schedule M-3 (Net Income/loss Reconciliation for Corporations With Total Assets of $10 Million or More)	Required when total assets exceed $10 million.[116]

Remember, for small corporations with less than $10 million in assets, the differences in book income and taxable income are reconciled on Schedule M-1 of Form 1120. A large corporation with assets that exceed $10 million must use Schedule M-3. However, for corporations with more than $10 million in assets but less than $50 million in assets at the end

[115] The same threshold applies to small S corporations. A small S-corporation with less than $250,000 of gross receipts and assets does not have to file Schedule M-1.

[116] For corporations with more than $10 million in assets but less than $50 million in assets at the end of the year, the corporation generally has the option to complete only Part I of Schedule M-3 and Schedule M-1.

of the year, the corporation generally has the option to complete only Part I of Schedule M-3 and Schedule M-1.

Example: Caine Accounting, Inc. is a mid-sized CPA firm that reports income and loss on the accrual basis. Caine Accounting, Inc. has $7 million in gross receipts for the tax year. The company's total assets are $5 million. Caine Accounting is required to file Schedule M-1. The company is not required to file Schedule M-3.

Example: Allied Laboratories, Inc. is a large pharmaceutical company with $60 million in assets and $15 million in gross receipts for the year. Allied Laboratories must file Schedule L as well as Schedule M-3.

Example: Cadence Design, Inc. is a C Corporation that had $1 million in gross receipts and $8 million in assets. Cadence Design may use the simpler, shorter, Schedule M-1 to reconcile the difference between its book income and taxable income.

Note: You must be familiar with the filing requirements for Schedules L, M-1, M-2, and M-3 for the EA exam. Remember, small corporations with less than $10 million dollars in assets are not *required* to file Schedule M-3, but they can do so if they wish.

Schedule M-1 and Schedule M-3 are used to reconcile book and tax differences. Corporations (especially large corporations) have different objectives when they prepare financial statements and when they complete their tax return. The result of these differing objectives is a disparity between "book" income and taxable income. Examples of items that would be included in the reconciliation on Schedule M-1 or Schedule M-3, if applicable, are:

- Excess of capital losses over capital gains.
- Charitable contribution carryover (the amount of charitable contributions that are disallowed for tax purposes and must be carried over to the next taxable year).
- Travel, meal, and entertainment expenses in excess of the allowable 50% limit, or not allowed for tax purposes.
- Federal income taxes paid or accrued, which are deductible for accounting purposes but not for tax purposes.
- Other expenses recorded on the books but not deductible on the return.
- Advance rental income.
- Other taxable income that is not included in book income.
- Tax-exempt interest income.
- Other income included in the books but not subject to tax.
- Deductions on the return not charged against book income.

Example: Holloway Fixtures Inc. is a large manufacturer that has formal financial statements, prepared by an accounting firm. Holloway Fixtures has over $100 million in assets and is publicly traded on the New York Stock Exchange. In 2020, Holloway Inc. donates $275,000 to the American Cancer Society, a qualified 501(c)(3) charity. The entire donation is deducted on Holloway's financial statements, but only a portion of the donation is deductible for tax purposes. Holloway must file Schedule M-3 to reconcile the differences between its "book income" and taxable income.

Contributions of Capital to a Corporation

A corporation is initially formed by a transfer of money, property, or services by prospective shareholders in exchange for stock in the corporation. A transfer of assets may also take place when a business that previously operated as a partnership or sole proprietorship opts to become a corporation.

Contributions to the capital of a corporation are generally not taxable transactions to the corporation, whether or not they are made by the shareholders. A shareholder will not recognize gain when a cash contribution is made for stock. This is just like when a person purchases stock on the open market for cash. The shareholder's basis in the stock is the amount of cash contributed.

Example: Evie purchases 75 shares of Rock-Cola, Inc. stock in 2020. She is not a professional stockbroker or dealer. She purchases the stock through her online brokerage account, spending $6,525 to acquire the shares. Her basis in the shares is her cost ($6,525 total or $87 per share). Rock-Cola does not recognize income from this transaction, and it is not a taxable event to either party. Later, when Evie sells the shares, she may have to recognize a capital gain or loss. While Evie owns the shares, they are treated as a capital asset in her hands.

However, a transfer of property, rather than cash, to a corporation may have tax consequences to both the corporation and the shareholder. For example, if a shareholder contributes property to a corporation, the shareholder generally recognizes gain, and the basis of the contributed property to the corporation is the same as the basis that the shareholder had in the property, after an increase for any gain that the shareholder recognized in the exchange.

There is an exception, however, for situations in which property is contributed, and the shareholder controls the corporation immediately after the transfer. This is called a section 351 transfer, and is explained in the next section. The basis of property contributed to a corporation's capital by anyone other than a shareholder is zero.

Example: The city of Phoenix, Arizona, gives Ales Motors Corporation a plot of land as an enticement to locate its new manufacturing facility there. Ales Motors accounts for the property as a contribution to capital. The land has a zero basis since the property was contributed by a non-shareholder.

If stock is exchanged for services, the recipient of the stock recognizes taxable income based upon the fair market value of the services provided, and that amount is the taxpayer's basis in the stock.

Example: Rainier is a web designer who provides web design services to Property Solutions, Inc. He agrees to accept 300 shares of stock as payment instead of cash. The stock is valued at $5,000. Rainier must recognize ordinary income of $5,000 as payment for services he rendered to the corporation. His basis in the stock is $5,000. Several years later, the company becomes wildly successful, and Rainer is able to sell his 300 shares for $150,000. Rainer must report a $145,000 long-term capital gain on the sale of the stock ($150,000 -$5,000 basis).

Section 351: Nontaxable Corporate Transfers

If a taxpayer transfers property to a corporation in exchange for stock, and immediately afterward, the taxpayer controls the corporation, the exchange may not be taxable. This rule applies both to individuals and to entities that transfer property to a corporation. It also applies to whether the corporation is being formed or is already in operation.

The effect is to allow the investing shareholder to contribute assets to a corporation without immediate tax consequences and to defer recognition of taxable gain until the stock received is later disposed. This nonrecognition rule does not apply in the following situations:

- The corporation is an investment company.
- The taxpayer transfers the property in a bankruptcy proceeding in exchange for stock that is used to pay creditors.
- The stock is received in exchange for the corporation's debt (other than a security, such as a bond) or for interest on the corporation's debt (including a security) that accrued while the taxpayer held the debt.

In order to be considered "in control" of a corporation immediately after a section 351 exchange, the transferors must own at least 80% of the total voting power of all classes of stock entitled to vote and at least 80% of the outstanding shares of each class of nonvoting stock immediately after the transfer.

Example: Guinevere owns an office building that she rents out to commercial tenants. Her basis in the building is $380,000. She organizes a corporation when the building has a fair market value of $750,000. Guinevere transfers the building to the corporation for all its authorized capital stock. No gain is recognized by Guinevere or the corporation on the transfer.

Example: Barney transfers property with a basis of $100,000 to a corporation in exchange for stock with a fair market value of $300,000. This represents only 75% of each class of stock of the corporation. The other 25% was already issued to other persons. Barney must recognize a taxable gain of $200,000 on the transaction, because the transfer does not qualify for section 351 nonrecognition treatment. Instead, it is treated as a sale.

If, in an otherwise nontaxable exchange of property for stock, the shareholder receives "boot" (money or property) in exchange for the contribution of property, he would recognize gain to the extent of the money and the fair market value of property received (up to the amount of realized gain on the exchange).

Example: Claudia transfers farmland with a fair market value of $440,000 and an adjusted basis of $200,000 to a corporation in exchange for stock. Immediately after the transfer, Claudia owns 85% of the corporation's outstanding stock. Claudia receives stock with a fair market value of $200,000 and also receives $100,000 in cash. The total amount Claudia receives from the corporation is $300,000; ($200,000 in stock + $100,000 cash). The exchange still qualifies as a section 351 exchange, but Claudia must recognize the cash (the "boot") she received as a taxable gain. Claudia will increase her stock basis by the amount of her recognized gain on the exchange.

Assumption of a Shareholder's Liabilities

If the corporation assumes the shareholder's liabilities on the exchange, the assumption generally is not treated as if the shareholder received money or other property, unless:

- The liabilities the corporation assumes are more than the shareholder's adjusted basis in the property transferred, in which case gain is recognized by the shareholder up to the difference. However, if the liabilities assumed give rise to a deduction when paid, such as a trade account payable or interest, no gain is recognized.
- There is no good business reason for the corporation to assume the liabilities, or if the main purpose in the exchange is to avoid federal income tax.

The shareholder's basis in his stock must be reduced by the amount of the liabilities assumed by the corporation.

Example: Roche transfers farming machinery to a corporation in exchange for all of the corporation's outstanding stock. The machinery's FMV at the time of the transfer is $200,000. Roche's basis in the machinery is $80,000. The machinery is encumbered by an outstanding loan of $30,000, which the corporation assumes. In this example, the section 351 exchange is valid, and no gain or loss is recognized in the transaction. Roche's basis in the stock is $50,000 ($80,000 basis of property contributed minus the $30,000 loan that was assumed by the corporation).

Example: Aubert transfers a semi-truck to Cantrell Trucking, Inc. in exchange for 90% of the corporation's outstanding stock. Immediately after the transfer, Aubert controls the corporation. The corporation plans to use the truck in its shipping operations. Aubert also receives $10,000 in cash in the exchange. Aubert's adjusted basis in the transferred semi-truck is $20,000. The stock Aubert received has a fair market value (FMV) of $16,000. The corporation also assumes a $5,000 auto loan that is still outstanding on the semi-truck. Aubert was personally liable for the loan. Aubert's gain on the transfer is realized as follows:

FMV of stock received	$16,000
Cash received	10,000
Liability assumed by corporation	5,000
Total received	$31,000
Minus: Adjusted basis of property transferred	(20,000)
Realized gain	**$11,000**

The liability assumed by Cantrell Trucking is not treated as money or other property. The recognized gain is limited to $10,000, the cash received (example from Pub 542).

This nonrecognition rule does not apply to services that are rendered in exchange for stock. The value of stock received for services is income to the recipient.

Example: Charles is a licensed architect. In 2020, he transfers drafting equipment worth $35,000 and provides architectural design services valued at $4,000 to a corporation in exchange for stock valued at $39,000. Immediately after the exchange, Charles owns 85% of the outstanding stock. No gain is recognized on the exchange of the equipment. However, Charles must recognize ordinary income of $4,000 as payment for professional services he rendered to the corporation.

Both the corporation and certain stockholders involved in a nontaxable exchange of property for stock must attach to their income tax returns a complete statement of all facts pertinent to the exchange. This reporting requirement applies to stockholders who own 5% or more of a public company or 1% or more of a privately held company.[117]

Study Note: You must understand the concepts related to section 351 transfers as you may encounter multiple questions on this topic on the EA exam.

Exclusions from 351 Nonrecognition Treatment

This nonrecognition rule does not apply when the property transferred is of relatively small value when compared to the value of stock already owned, and the main purpose of the transfer is to qualify for the nonrecognition of gain or loss. Property transferred will not be considered to be of "small value" if its FMV is at least 10% of the FMV of the stock already owned or to be received by the transferor.

If a group of transferors exchanges property for corporate stock, each transferor may not receive stock in proportion to his interest in the property transferred. However, if a disproportionate transfer takes place, it may be treated as if the stock were first received in proportion to the interests in the property, and then portions were used to make gifts, pay compensation for services, or to satisfy the transferor's obligations.

If a corporation transfers its stock in satisfaction of indebtedness and the fair market value of its stock is less than the indebtedness, the corporation has to recognize income to the extent of the difference from the cancellation of indebtedness. For example, if the stock is given to an individual to pay for a debt that is owed to the individual, the transfer does not qualify for nonrecognition treatment.

Example: Kludge Motor Company is having some financial difficulties. The company owes its freelance web designer over $7,000 in delinquent invoices. The web designer threatens to shut down the company's web page, so Kludge Motors offers to give 400 shares of stock to the web designer in order to satisfy the debt. The designer accepts the deal, and Kludge Motors transfers 400 shares of stock with a FMV of $6,000 to the web designer. The transfer does not qualify for nonrecognition treatment. Kludge Motor Company is required to recognize $1,000 of taxable income from the transfer, because the corporation has a gain from the cancellation of indebtedness ($7,000 outstanding debt - $6,000 FMV of the stock).

Transfers of property to a foreign corporation generally do not qualify for nonrecognition treatment, regardless of the scenario or the value of the property transferred.

[117] The rules regarding section 351 exchanges also apply to S corporations. These rules are covered in IRS Publication 542, Corporations

International Information Reporting and Taxes

The Tax Cuts and Jobs Act included several major changes to existing U.S. international tax laws and radically changed the international tax system for corporations. In addition to lowering the corporate tax rate to 21% and providing some other benefits for domestic investment (such as bonus depreciation and the ability to immediately expense the purchase of equipment), the TCJA also substantially changed the international tax regime.[118]

Non-corporate taxpayers generally are not allowed indirect foreign tax credits or the GILTI deduction. In the next section, we will briefly cover these new international provisions.

BEAT (Base Erosion and Anti-Abuse Tax)

On December 2, 2019, the Treasury Department and the Internal Revenue Service issued final regulations regarding the Base Erosion and Anti-Abuse Tax (BEAT).

For decades, multinational corporations were motivated to shift profits overseas, thereby eroding the U.S. tax base, in order to reduce their overall tax burden. In an effort to limit this type of overseas "profit shifting," the Tax Cuts and Jobs Act enacted BEAT (base erosion and anti-abuse tax). BEAT targets mostly large U.S. corporations that make deductible payments such as interest, royalties, and certain service payments to related foreign parties. BEAT imposes a minimum tax on ordinary income plus certain payments to related foreign companies.

The BEAT is a minimum tax add-on to a corporation's regular tax. The BEAT rate is 10% in 2020 through 2025, and 12.5% percent in 2026 and thereafter.[119] A U.S. corporation calculates its *regular* U.S. tax at a 21% rate, and then recalculates its tax at a lower BEAT rate after adding back the deductible payments. The BEAT is calculated as follows:

BEAT TAX = (BEAT rate x modified taxable income) - adjusted regular tax liability

If the regular tax is lower than the BEAT, then the corporation will pay the regular tax plus the amount by which the BEAT exceeds the regular tax.

BEAT applies only to large corporations with average gross receipts of more than $500 million over the prior three years. It also applies only to a corporation that makes more than 3% of its total deductible payments to foreign affiliates (or 2% if the entity is a member of an affiliated group that includes a domestic bank or a registered securities dealer).

BEAT excludes payments that can be treated as cost of goods sold. For example, if a U.S. company properly accounts for interest or royalties as part of the cost of its inventory, the interest or royalties are not added back to the BEAT tax base.

GILTI (Global Intangible Low-Taxed Income)

On June 14, 2019, the Treasury Department and the Internal Revenue Service issued final and proposed regulations regarding Global Intangible Low-Tax Income (GILTI). The Tax Cuts and Jobs Act enacted this legislation in order to discourage U.S. companies from shifting income from intangible assets to low-tax foreign countries. To discourage this "profit shifting," Congress added a new 10.5% minimum tax on global intangible low-taxed income (GILTI). GILTI is

[118] *CRS Report Prepared for Members of Committees of Congress, Issues in International Corporate Taxation (P.L. 115-97).*
[119] The BEAT tax rate is 1% higher for entities that are members of an affiliated group that includes a bank or registered securities dealer.

intended to target, indirectly, profits earned from intangible property by foreign affiliates of US companies (intangible assets like trademarks, patents, brand names, software, and copyrights).

GILTI is intended to "approximate" the income from intangible assets such as patents, trademarks, and copyrights held in foreign countries. Since intangible assets are considered highly mobile, Congress sought to discourage US firms from shifting these assets offshore.

GILTI is calculated as the total active income earned by a US firm's foreign affiliates that exceeds 10% of the company's depreciable tangible property. A U.S. business must include GILTI in its gross income annually.

Under the TCJA, a U.S. person that owns at least 10% of the shares in a controlled foreign corporation (CFC) will be required to include its global intangible low-taxed income as currently taxable income, regardless of whether any amount is distributed to the shareholder. A "U.S. person" includes U.S. individuals, domestic corporations, partnerships, trusts, and estates.

A corporation can generally deduct 50% of the GILTI and claim a foreign tax credit for 80% of foreign taxes paid or accrued on GILTI. Therefore, if the foreign tax rate is zero, the effective U.S. tax rate on GILTI will be 10.5% or half of the regular 21% corporate rate due to the 50% deduction. If the foreign tax rate is 13.125% or higher, there will be no U.S. tax after the 80% credit for foreign taxes. These new reporting rules require the filing of Form 8992, *U.S. Shareholder Calculation of Global Intangible Low-Taxed Income,* to report this tax.

Section 965 Transition Tax (Mandatory Repatriation Tax)

As part of the TCJA's move to a quasi-territorial international taxation system, Section 965 required United States shareholders (including individuals, corporations, and other entities) to pay a one-time transition tax on the untaxed foreign earnings of certain specified foreign corporations as if those earnings had been "repatriated" to the United States. This one-time tax applied to certain foreign corporations in their tax year that began before January 1, 2018.[120]

Foreign earnings held in the form of cash and cash equivalents were taxed at a 15.5% rate, and the remaining earnings were taxed at an 8% rate. U.S. shareholders that may be affected include:

- Domestic C corporations,
- Other U.S. taxpayers, including; individuals, S corporations, partnerships, estate, trusts, cooperatives, REITs, RICs, and tax-exempt organizations.

Taxpayers could have elected to pay the transition tax in installments over an eight-year period, which includes 2020. The tax is includible in the U.S. shareholder's tax year in which or with which the foreign corporation's year ends. The tax is reported on Form 965, *Inclusion of Deferred Foreign Income Upon Transition to Participation Exemption System.*

[120] Although the Section 965 Transition Tax was a one-time tax on repatriated earnings, corporations that elected to pay the tax in installments would still be paying the tax in tax year 2020. The Section 965 Transition Tax is listed on the official Prometric EA exam test specifications for the current testing cycle.

Unit 12: Study Questions

(Please test yourself and check the correct answers at the end of this section.)

1. Seymour, a licensed CPA, transfers property worth $43,000 and renders accounting services valued at $6,000 to Cramer Industries Inc. in exchange for stock valued at $49,000. Right after the exchange, Seymour owns 90% of the outstanding corporate stock. How much income, if any, must Seymour recognize in this transaction?

A. $0
B. $3,000
C. $6,000
D. $49,000

2. Which of these domestic business entities will *not* be automatically taxed as a corporation?

A. A joint-stock company.
B. An insurance company.
C. A business owned by a state or local government.
D. A single-member limited liability company (LLC).

3. Shrill Media, Inc. has net "book" income of $3 million. What is its net *taxable* income if it also has the following activity?

Federal income tax expense	($1,500,000)
Business meal expenses	($200,000)
Tax-exempt interest income	$100,000
Capital losses from the sale of stock	($47,000)
Capital gains from the sale of cryptocurrency	$18,000

A. $1,529,000
B. $4,471,000
C. $4,529,000
D. $4,729,000

4. Nella transfers an office building with a basis of $200,000 and an FMV of $300,000 to Risky Solutions, Inc. in exchange for stock with a fair market value of $300,000. This represents 65% of the stock in Risky Solutions. Nella did not own any shares in the corporation prior to the contribution. How much gain is recognized by Nella on this transaction?

A. $0
B. $100,000
C. $200,000
D. $300,000

5. Mining Associates, Inc. has $1 million of gross receipts and $6 million of assets at the end of the year. Which of these schedules is the corporation required to file?

✓A. Schedule L.
B. Schedule L and Schedule M-1.
C. Schedule M-3.
D. Schedule L and Schedule M-3.

6. The accumulated earnings tax is levied at a rate of ______ on accumulated taxable income.

A. 5%
B. 15%
✓C. 20%
D. 50%

7. Lorraine and Marcus, a married couple, each transfer machinery with a basis of $10,000 to a corporation in exchange for stock with a fair market value of $30,000. The total stock received by them represents 75% of the corporation's stock. The other 25% of the corporation's stock is owned by Annie, an unrelated person. The taxable consequences are:

A. None, because it is a transfer of property for stock.
✓ B. Lorraine and Marcus each must recognize a gain of $20,000.
C. Lorraine and Marcus each must recognize a gain of $30,000.
D. 80% of the transaction is recognized as a taxable gain.

8. Vita Honey, Inc. is a small C corporation that produces organic honey and beeswax candles. In 2020, Vita Honey had $245,000 in gross receipts from the sale of their products. The company's total assets at the end of the year were $95,000. Which of these schedules is the Vita Honey required to file?

A. Schedule L and Schedule M-1.
B. Schedule L and Schedule M-2.
C. Only Schedule M-1.
✓D. None of these schedules.

9. Kirsten is trying to decide whether to form an S corporation or a C corporation for her business. What are some factors that may persuade her *against* using the C corporation structure?

A. C corporations can attract foreign investors and have foreign shareholders.
✓B. Shareholders of a C corporation cannot deduct corporate losses.
C. A corporation has limited liability.
D. C corporations can issue different classes of stock.

10. Acquisition Repo Services, Inc., is a cash-basis C corporation that operates on the calendar year. The company is required to make estimated tax payments during the year. What are the due dates for its estimated payments?

A. April 15, June 15, September 15, and December 15.
B. January 15, March 15, June 15, September 15, and December 15.
C. March 1, June 1, September 1, and December 1.
D. April 15, June 15, September 15, and January 15.

11. To be eligible for section 351 nonrecognition treatment, immediately after the exchange, a taxpayer must own at least ____ of the total combined voting power of all classes of stock entitled to vote and at least _____ of the outstanding shares of each class of nonvoting stock.

A. 50% and 50%
B. more than 50% and more than 50%
C. 80% and 80%
D. 100% and 100%

12. Superior Aviation, Inc. operates on a fiscal year that ends June 30. Not counting extensions, what is the due date for its corporate tax return (Form 1120)?

A. September 15.
B. April 15.
C. October 15.
D. January 15.

13. The accumulated earnings tax may be imposed on C corporations that accumulate earnings beyond the reasonable needs of their businesses. Which of the following reasons would not be an example of a reasonable accumulation?

A. The expansion of the company to a new area or a new facility.
B. Acquiring another business through the purchase of stock or other assets.
C. Allowing the shareholders to take bona fide loans from the corporation.
D. Providing for reasonable estimates of product liability losses.

Unit 12: Quiz Answers

1. The answer is C. Seymour recognizes ordinary income of **$6,000** as payment for accounting services he rendered to the corporation. Normally, the exchange of money or property for a controlling interest in a corporation is treated as a nontaxable exchange. However, the exchange of services for stock does not qualify for this treatment. The value of stock received in exchange for services is taxed as income to the recipient.

2. The answer is D. A single-member LLC owned by an individual will not automatically be taxed as a corporation. A single-member LLC will automatically be taxed as a disregarded entity (sole proprietorship) if the sole member is an individual, unless an election is made by filing Form 8832, *Entity Classification Election.* If a single-member LLC is owned by a C corporation, the LLC is treated as a division of the corporate shareholder for tax purposes – with the LLC's financial information included in the corporation's 1120 corporate tax return. The rest of the choices are automatically required to be taxed as corporations.

3. The answer is C. Shrill Media Corporation's net taxable income would be calculated as follows:

Net income for books	$3,000,000
PLUS federal income tax expense	$1,500,000
Adjustment for 50% of business meal expenses	$100,000
PLUS excess of capital losses over capital gains	$29,000
MINUS tax-exempt interest income	($100,000)
Taxable income	**$4,529,000**

A corporation must generally report on either Schedule M-1 or Schedule M-3 the items that reconcile from net income (loss) on their books to taxable income reported on the return. Specific examples may include:

- Excess of capital losses over capital gains.
- Charitable contribution carryover (the amount of charitable contributions that are disallowed and must be carried over to the next taxable year).
- Travel and entertainment in excess of the allowable 50% limit.
- Federal income taxes paid or accrued, which are deductible for accounting purposes but not for tax purposes.
- Advance rental income.
- Differences in book and tax depreciation.

4. The answer is B. Nella must recognize a taxable gain of **$100,000** ($300,000 FMV of the stock minus $200,000 basis in the property transferred) on the transaction. IRC section 351 provides that no gain or loss will be recognized if property is transferred to a corporation solely in exchange for stock if, immediately after the exchange, the shareholder is in control of the corporation. However, Nella did not control the corporation after the transfer. In order to be in control of a corporation, the transferor must own, immediately after the exchange, at least 80% of the total combined voting power of all classes of stock entitled to vote and at least 80% of the outstanding shares of each class of nonvoting stock. Since Nella owns only 65% of the shares, the exchange is taxable to her (i.e., it is treated as a sale).

5. The answer is B. Mining Associates, Inc. is required to file both, Schedule L, *Balance Sheets Per Books*, and Schedule M-1, *Reconciliation of Income (Loss) per Books with Income per Return*, along with its Form 1120. For small corporations with less than $10 million in assets, the differences in book and taxable income are reconciled in Schedule M-1 of Form 1120. Corporations with less than $250,000 of total receipts and total assets at the end of the year are not required to complete Schedules L, M-1, M-2, or M-3.

6. The answer is C. The accumulated earnings tax is levied at a rate of 20% of the excess amount of income that is accumulated by a corporation.

7. The answer is B. Lorraine and Marcus must each recognize a gain of **$20,000** ($30,000 FMV of stock - $10,000 basis). If a shareholder contributes property to a corporation, the shareholder generally recognizes gain. The basis of the contributed property to the corporation is the same as the basis that the shareholder had in the property, (after increasing the basis for any gain that the shareholder recognized in the exchange). There is an exception for situations in which property is contributed, and the shareholder controls the corporation immediately after the transfer. In order to be considered in control of a corporation immediately after the exchange, the transferors must own at least 80% of the total combined voting power of all classes of stock entitled to vote and at least 80% of the outstanding shares of each class of nonvoting stock. In this case, Lorraine and Marcus do not own at least 80% of the corporation immediately afterward, so the exception does not apply.

8. The answer is D. Vita Honey, Inc. is not required to file any of the listed schedules. Corporations with less than $250,000 of total receipts and total assets at the end of the year are not required to complete Schedules L, M-1, M-2, or M-3.

9. The answer is B. Shareholders of a C corporation cannot deduct corporate losses. It is a drawback of structuring a business as a C corporation, as opposed to an S corporation or a partnership, both of which are pass-through entities. One of the main benefits of a corporate structure, including C corporations, is the limited liability it affords directors, officers, shareholders, and employees, as well as the ability to attract foreign investors and raise capital through a stock sale.

10. The answer is A. Acquisition Repo Services, Inc. must make quarterly estimated tax payments. Installments for corporations are due by the fifteenth day of the fourth, sixth, ninth, and twelfth months of the year. For example, a calendar-year corporation would have estimated tax due dates of April 15, June 15, September 15, and December 15.

11. The answer is C. When a taxpayer transfers property to a corporation in exchange for stock and immediately afterward controls the corporation, the exchange may qualify for section 351 treatment. The exchange generally would not be taxable until the stock received is later disposed of. To be eligible as a section 351 nontaxable exchange, the taxpayer must own, immediately after the exchange, at least 80% of the total combined voting power of all classes of stock entitled to vote and at least 80% of the outstanding shares of each class of nonvoting stock.

12. The answer is A. The due date for Superior Aviation's income tax return is September 15. A corporation must normally file its income tax return by the fifteenth day of the fourth month after the end of its tax year. However, C Corporations with fiscal years ending on June 30, the due date for the C corporation return is September 15, the 15th day of the third month following the close of the fiscal year.

13. The answer is C. Allowing shareholders to draw personal loans from a corporation is not a valid reason for a corporation to accumulate earnings. In fact, this is one of the items the IRS looks for that may lead to imposing the accumulated earnings tax upon a corporation. Making loans to shareholders would allow them to access the corporation's earnings without taking taxable distributions.

Unit 13: Corporate Transactions

More Reading:
Publication 542, Corporations

The tax treatment of certain items is different for C corporations, as compared with individuals and other types of entities. C corporations are subject to their own tax rate schedule and they are taxed at a flat rate of 21%. C corporations are required to file returns and pay income tax on their profits. In some cases, a C corporation might provide more tax benefits than a pass-through entity such as a partnership or an S corporation.

Note: Among the drawbacks of the C corporation structure are double taxation; the inability of shareholders to deduct corporate losses; the absence of preferential capital gains tax rates; and the limitation on the deductibility of capital losses. A C corporation also has advantages that are unavailable to other business types. A C corporation has unlimited growth potential, because there is no limit to the number of shareholders a C Corporation can have. A C corporation can sell stock, either common or preferred, and can offer employees a stock option plan. Ownership of a C corporation is easily transferable through a stock sale.

Corporate Net Operating Losses (NOLs)

A C corporation figures and deducts a net operating loss (NOL) in a similar manner as an individual, an estate, or a trust. The CARES Act made significant changes to the treatment of net operating losses for 2020; these changes were retroactive, so they also affect prior years. Under the CARES Act, an NOL from a tax year beginning in 2018, 2019 or 2020 can be carried back five years. The CARES Act effectively *delays* the application of earlier TCJA amendments until January 1, 2021.[121] A corporation may elect to waive the carryback period and only carry their NOLs forward to future years, but only on a timely-filed return, filed by the due date of the tax year 2020 tax return.

See Chapter 6 for a full explanation of Net Operating Losses; these changes apply to C corporations, as well. A corporation cannot increase its current year NOL by carrybacks or carryovers from other years in which it has a loss. A prior-year NOL may be carried forward indefinitely.

Example: Engineering Dynamics Inc. is a C corporation that provides engineering services. The business incurs a $250,000 net operating loss in 2020. The company may choose to carryback its losses to each of the five taxable years preceding the taxable year in which the loss arises. This means that if Engineering Dynamics chooses to carryback its losses, it must carry them back to the earliest year within the carryback period in which the corporation has taxable income. The corporation had taxable income in 2015, so Engineering Dynamics must apply the NOL carryback to that year first. Engineering Dynamics Inc may also choose to waive the carryback period entirely by making an election on its 2020 tax return.

A corporation figures an NOL the same way it figures taxable income. It starts with gross income and subtracts its deductions. If its deductions are more than its gross income, the

[121] At the time of this book's printing, the five-year CARES Act NOL carryback provisions will expire in 2021.

corporation has an NOL. In general, the following items are not allowed when figuring a corporation's NOL.

- It cannot take any deduction for foreign-derived international income.
- The modified taxable income for any year cannot be less than zero.
- Capital losses in excess of capital gains.
- The section 1202 exclusion of the gain of qualified small business stock.
- Nonbusiness deductions in excess of nonbusiness income.

A corporation must figure its deduction for charitable contributions without considering any NOL carrybacks.

A corporation may file Form 1139, or an amended return (Form 1120X) to claim an NOL.[122] If a corporation carries forward its NOL, it enters the carryover on Form 1120, Schedule K, line 12. An NOL carryback or carryforward can *only* be used to reduce corporate income tax. If the corporation owes other taxes or penalties from a prior or in a future year, an NOL will not reduce the penalties.

Corporate Capital Gains and Losses

Unlike the favorable capital gains rates available to individuals, the capital gains of a C corporation are taxed at the same rate as its ordinary income. A corporation figures its capital gains and losses much like an individual. However, in the case of a C corporation, its capital losses are only deductible to the extent of its capital gains. A C corporation is not allowed to offset capital losses against its other income the way individuals can (up to a limit).

Note: In general, a C corporation's excess capital losses are carried to other years in the following order:

- Three years prior to the loss year
- Two years prior to the loss year
- One year prior to the loss year
- Any loss remaining is carried forward for five years (with few exceptions).

If, after carrying back a net capital loss three years and forward five years, any part of the capital loss still remains, it is lost forever, and the corporation cannot use the loss to offset any future capital gains.

If a corporation has an excess capital loss, it may carry the loss back or forward to other tax years and deduct it from any net capital gains that occurred in those years. The default election is for a corporation to carry back its capital losses to the earliest of the three preceding years in which it had net capital gains; any remaining losses may be carried forward a maximum of five years. A capital loss from another year cannot create or increase a net operating loss in the year to which it is carried. Further, capital losses can be carried only to years that would otherwise have had a net capital gain. In rare instances, longer carryback and carryforward periods may be allowed. Capital losses that are a result of foreign expropriation[123] may not be carried back, but

---

122 The CARES Act allows corporate taxpayers with a 2017/2018 NOL to file their tentative refund claim (Form 1139) no later than July 27, 2020.

123 This is when a foreign nation takes a U.S. corporation's assets for its own use.

may be carried forward for ten years. In the case of a regulated investment company (RIC), net capital losses may be carried forward eight years.

When a corporation carries back or carries forward a capital loss, the loss does not retain its character. All capital loss carryforwards and carrybacks are treated as short-term losses. A C corporation cannot carry back capital losses to any previous year when it was an S corporation.

Example: In 2020, Building Network, Inc., a calendar-year C corporation, has a capital gain of $3,000 and a capital loss of $9,000. The capital gain offsets some of the capital loss, leaving a net capital loss of $6,000 for 2020. Building Network treats this $6,000 as a short-term loss when carried back or forward. The corporation carries the $6,000 short-term loss back to the prior year (it had no capital gains in any other prior year). In the prior year (2019), Building Network had a short-term capital gain of $8,000 and a long-term capital gain of $5,000 (a total of $13,000 of capital gains in the prior year). It carries back the loss and subtracts the $6,000 short-term loss (carryback) first from the net short-term gain. This results in a net capital gain of $7,000 that consists of a net short-term capital gain of $2,000 ($8,000 - $6,000) and a net long-term capital gain of $5,000, which allows the corporation to receive a refund of the income tax it paid in the prior year.

Example: Hazlett Design, Inc. converted from an S corporation to a C Corporation on January 1, 2020. In 2020, Hazlett Design incurs $13,000 in long-term capital losses. All of the company's capital losses must be carried forward, because the corporation was an S corporation in the prior year. The losses that are carried forward will be treated as short-term losses, and will reduce capital gains in future years.

Corporate Charitable Contributions

Unlike other business entities, C corporations can deduct a certain amount of charitable contributions made to qualified organizations.

Note: Charitable donations of *property* are still generally subject to 10% of taxable income (with a 25% of taxable income limit for donations of food inventory in 2020). Under the CARES Act, a C corporation is generally entitled to deduct qualified contributions of up to 25% of its taxable income in 2020.[124] This increased limit applies to cash contributions only. However, under the *Taxpayer Certainty and Disaster Tax Relief Act of 2020* (TCDTRA of 2020), cash donations for relief efforts in qualified disaster areas can be made up to 100% of the corporation's taxable income. This does not include any disaster declaration related to COVID-19.

Donations in excess of these limits may be carried over and deducted in the following five years, subject to the same limitations. No carryback is allowed for charitable contributions. Any excess contributions not used within that five-year period are lost. A corporation figures its taxable income for this limit without regard to the following:

- The deduction for charitable contributions
- The dividends-received deduction

[124] The CAA-2021 extended this provision to 2021. This provision does not apply to contributions to a donor advised fund, or non-operating private foundations.

- The domestic production activities deduction (in the case of agricultural or horticultural cooperatives)
- Any net operating loss carryback to the tax year
- Any capital loss carryback (but not carryforward) to the tax year

If there is no taxable income, the corporation would not be able to deduct charitable contributions for that year.

Example: Staffing Solutions Inc., a calendar-year C corporation, makes a large charitable contribution in 2020. As a result, the corporation has a carryover of excess contributions and it does not use all the excess on its return. Staffing Solutions can carry the rest over to future tax years. After five years, it can no longer carry over the excess charitable contributions and the amounts are lost.

Example: Epic Design, Inc. donated $35,000 in cash in 2020 to the Sierra Wildlife Foundation, a qualified 501(c)(3) charity. Epic Design's taxable income before figuring its charitable contribution deduction is $95,000. The corporation's allowable charitable deduction is $23,750 ($95,000 x 25% = $23,750). The corporation will have a $11,250 charitable contribution carryover to use in future years ($35,000 actual contribution - $23,750 allowable amount = $11,250 carryover).

A corporation using the cash method can deduct charitable contributions in the year they are paid. A corporation using the accrual method can deduct unpaid contributions if the board of directors authorized the contributions during the year, and the corporation pays the contributions by the due date for filing the corporation's tax return (not including extensions).

A declaration with a statement that includes the date that the board of directors adopted the resolution must accompany the return.

Example: Strategy Programming, Inc. is a calendar-year, accrual-basis corporation. Strategy Programming's board of directors approves a charitable contribution of $5,000 to the Red Cross on December 15, 2020. Strategy Programming deducts the contribution on its 2020 corporate tax return. Strategy Programming, Inc. does not have to pay the contribution until April 15, 2021 (the due date for filing the corporation's tax return).

A corporation cannot deduct a carryover of excess contributions to the extent it increases a net operating loss carryover.

Example: Envision Management, Inc. has net income of $650,000 in 2020 before taking into account its charitable contributions. The corporation donated $125,000 in cash to a qualified charity in 2020. It also has a net operating loss carryover of $200,000 from a prior year. Therefore, the corporation's charitable deduction is limited to $112,500. The allowable contribution deduction is figured as follows:

($650,000 - $200,000 prior-year NOL = $400,000) × 25% = $112,500

The amount of the charitable contribution that is not allowed, $12,500 ($125,000 contribution - $112,500 allowable deduction) in the current tax year can be carried forward for up to five years. If Envision Management, Inc. does not use the remainder at the end of five years, the deduction is lost.

The rules regarding what qualifies as a charitable organization and required supporting documentation are the same for corporations as they are for individuals. Generally, no deduction is allowed for any charitable contribution of $250 or more unless the corporation obtains a contemporaneous written acknowledgment from the donee organization.

The written receipt or acknowledgment should show the amount of cash contributed or a description of the property contributed. The receipt or acknowledgment should also give a description and a good faith estimate of the value of any goods or services provided in return for the contribution, or state that no goods or services were provided in return for the contribution.

If a corporation (other than a closely held or personal service corporation) claims a deduction of more than $500 for contributions of property other than cash, a schedule describing the property and the method used to determine its fair market value must be attached to the corporation's return. In addition, the corporation should keep a record of:

- The approximate date and manner of acquisition of the donated property.
- The cost (or other basis) of the donated property held by the donor for less than 12 months prior to contribution.
- Any donation of a used vehicle, boat, or similar property if it takes a deduction larger than $500 for the donated vehicle.

If the deduction claimed for donated property exceeds $5,000, the corporation must complete Form 8283, *Noncash Charitable Contributions,* and attach it to its tax return. However, if the corporation is a personal service corporation or a closely held corporation, it must attach Form 8283 for a claimed non-cash charitable contribution of more than $500.

A corporation must obtain a qualified appraisal for all deductions of property claimed in excess of $5,000. A qualified appraisal is not required for the donation of cash, publicly-traded securities, or inventory.

Dividends-Received Deduction

A corporation can deduct a percentage of certain dividends received from other corporations in which it has an ownership interest. The dividends-received deduction (DRD) is designed to reduce the consequences of double taxation. Without this deduction, corporate profits could be taxed to the corporation that earned them, then to its corporate shareholders, and then again to the individual shareholders of the parent corporation.

The DRD complements the consolidated return regulations, which allow affiliated corporations to file a single consolidated return for U.S. federal income tax purposes. It is available to C corporations but not to LLCs, S corporations, partnerships, or individuals.

For corporations owning at least 20% of the dividend-paying company, the dividends-received deduction is normally 65% of the dividends. For corporations owning under 20%, the deduction is normally 50%. If the corporation receiving the dividends owns *more than* 80% of the distributing corporation, it is allowed to deduct 100% of the dividends it receives.

To summarize, the deduction for dividends received is based on the percentage of stock ownership in the distributing corporation:

Percentage of Stock Ownership	Dividends-Received Deduction
Less than 20%	50%
20 - 80%	65%
Greater than 80%	100%

The percentage of stock ownership is determined without regard to preferred stock.

Example: Lauder Management, Inc. owns 10% of Data Systems Corp. In 2020, Lauder Management has taxable income of $70,000 before taking into account its dividend income. During the year, Lauder Management received $50,000 of dividends from Data Systems Corp. Lauder Management is therefore allowed a 50% dividends-received deduction, figured as follows: $25,000 = ($50,000 × 50%). Lauder Management's taxable net income is $95,000 ($70,000 + [$50,000 - $25,000]).

Example: Excel Consulting, Inc. owns 95% of the outstanding stock in the Silgan Corporation. In 2020, Excel Consulting receives $250,000 of dividends from Silgan. Because Excel Consulting has over 80% ownership of Silgan, it can claim the 100% dividends-received deduction and the dividends are not taxable to Excel Consulting, Inc.

If a corporation is entitled to a 100% DRD, there is no taxable income limitation, and the corporation can deduct the full amount of the dividends received. However, if a corporation is entitled to a 65% DRD, it can deduct amounts only up to 65% of its taxable income. If a corporation is entitled to a 50% DRD, it can deduct amounts only up to 50% of its taxable income. In each case, the corporation would determine taxable income without the following items:

- The DRD
- The net operating loss (NOL) deduction
- Any adjustment due to the nontaxable part of an extraordinary dividend
- Any capital loss carryback to the tax year

If a corporation has an NOL for a tax year, the DRD is figured differently. The limit of 65% (or 50%) of modified taxable income (as detailed above) does not apply if the application of the unlimited DRD would result in a net operating loss for the receiving corporation.

Example: High Tech, Inc. has a $75,000 net operating loss in 2020 from its business operations. High Tech also receives $100,000 in dividends from a 20%-owned corporation. High Tech's taxable income is $25,000 ($100,000 dividends – $75,000 NOL) before the application of the deduction for dividends received. If High Tech claims the full dividends-received deduction of $65,000 ($100,000 × 65%) and combines it with its pre-DRD taxable income of $25,000, it will have an NOL of ($40,000). Therefore, the 65%-of-taxable-income limit does not apply. High Tech can deduct the full amount of the $65,000 dividends-received deduction.

Corporations *cannot* take a deduction for dividends received from the following entities:

- A real estate investment trust (REIT)
- A tax-exempt corporation
- A corporation whose common stock was held less than 46 days during the period that started 45 days before and ended 45 days after the ex-dividend date.
- A corporation whose preferred stock was held less than 91 days during the period that started 90 days before and ended 90 days after the ex-dividend date.
- Any corporation, if another corporation is under an obligation to make related payments for positions in substantially similar property

Dividends on deposits in domestic building and loan associations, credit unions, mutual savings banks, cooperative banks, and similar organizations are taxed as interest income—not dividends. They do not qualify for the DRD. Small business investment companies can deduct 100% of the dividends received from taxable domestic corporations. The deduction for dividends received is reported on Form 1120, Schedule C, *Dividends, Inclusions, and Special Deductions.*

Study Note: For the EA exam, you should take the time to understand how to calculate the dividends-received deduction and how it applies to a C corporation's taxable income and net operating losses.

Related Party Transactions

Strict rules apply to related party transactions. A corporation that uses the accrual method cannot deduct business expenses and interest owed to a related person or related entity who uses the cash method until the corporation makes the related payment and the amount is included in the related person's income. These rules also deny the deduction of a loss on the sale or trade of property (other than in the complete liquidation of a corporation) between related persons. For purposes of these rules, the following persons are considered "related" to a corporation:

- A corporation that is a member of the same controlled group.
- An individual who owns, directly or indirectly, *more than* 50% of the value of the outstanding stock of the corporation.
- A partnership, if the same persons own *more than* 50% of the value of the outstanding stock of the corporation and more than 50% of the partnership.
- An S corporation, if the same persons own *more than* 50% of the value of the outstanding stock of each corporation.
- A trust fiduciary, when the trust (or its grantor) owns, directly or indirectly, *more than* 50% of the value of the outstanding stock of the corporation.
- An employee-owner of a personal service corporation, regardless of the amount of stock owned.

In determining whether a person directly or indirectly owns any of the outstanding stock of a corporation, the following rules apply:

- Stock directly or indirectly owned by or for a corporation, partnership, estate, or trust is considered owned proportionately by or for its shareholders, partners, or beneficiaries.

- An individual is considered to own the stock that is directly or indirectly owned by or for his family. For the purposes of this rule, "family" includes only brothers and sisters (including half-brothers and half-sisters, but *not* step-siblings), a spouse, direct ancestors, and direct lineal descendants.[125] It does not include ex-spouses or in-laws.
- An individual owning any stock in a corporation is considered to own the stock that is directly or indirectly owned by his partner.

Example: Daniel is a 65% owner in Hotspur Properties, Inc. Daniel's wife, Lydia, is a 55% owner of Agilent Corporation. Daniel is considered a related person for the purposes of ownership in Agilent Corporation. Under the related-party transaction rules, Daniel is also considered a 55% owner in Agilent Corporation and Lydia is considered a 65% owner in Hotspur Properties, Inc. This would be true regardless of whether the spouses filed separate or joint returns.

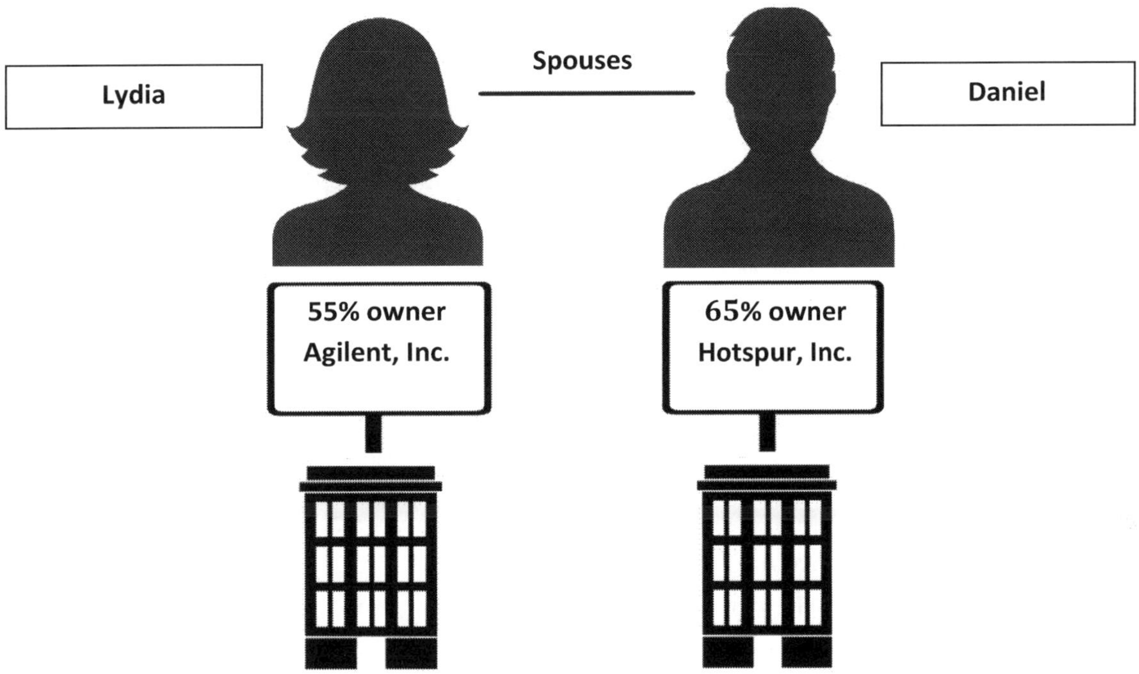

Closely-Held Corporations

A closely-held corporation, also referred to as a "closed corporation," generally has a small number of shareholders (often family members[126]) and no public market for its stock. Most small corporations in the United States are closely-held. Corporate ownership and management often overlap, and typically, management decisions are made by the shareholders. A corporation is considered to be "closely-held" if **both** of the following apply:

- It is not a personal service corporation (PSC).

[125] A "lineal descendant" is a person who is in direct line to the taxpayer, such as child, grandchild, or great-grandchild. For the purpose of this rule, family does *not* include cousins, step-siblings, uncles, aunts, or in-laws. It also does not include ex-spouses.

[126] Most closely-held corporations in the United States are also family-owned businesses, regardless of size.

- At any time during the last half of the tax year, more than 50% of the value of its outstanding stock is, directly or indirectly, owned by or *five or fewer* individuals. An "individual" in this case includes certain trusts and private foundations.

A closely-held corporation is subject to additional limitations in compensation paid to corporate officers and the tax treatment of items such as passive activity losses and at-risk rules. The at-risk rules for closely-held corporations are similar to those that apply to partners in a partnership. These rules dictate that a closely held corporation's losses are only deductible up to the amount at risk of financial loss in connection with an activity. The amount at risk generally equals:

- The money and the adjusted basis of property contributed by the taxpayer to the activity, and
- The money borrowed for the activity.

The at-risk amount also includes the FMV of property (adjusted for any liens or encumbered mortgages) that is pledged as security or collateral for the debts of the activity. The following items increase an entity's amount at risk:

1. A contribution of additional cash (or property) to the venture.
2. Any recourse loan for which the corporation is liable for repayment.

The amount at risk is decreased by the following items:

1. An investor's withdrawal of cash or property from the activity.
2. A nonrecourse loan where the corporation is not liable for repayment.

The amount at risk cannot be decreased below zero. If this occurs, suspended losses from prior years must be reduced.

Example: American Auto Corporation is a closely held C corporation with only two shareholders: a father and son. American Auto Corp. invests $20,000 cash in a business venture, and also pledges the value of a factory building as collateral for a $100,000 loan that is used in the business venture. American Auto's factory building has a fair market value of $150,000. American Auto's amount at risk in the business venture is only $70,000 [$20,000 cash investment plus the $50,000 ($150,000 - $100,000) equity in the building].

Controlled Groups

Under federal law, related companies and organizations are treated as a single, controlled group for certain tax purposes. A controlled group is a group of corporations that are related through common ownership, typically as either **parent-subsidiary** or **brother-sister.** Eligible affiliated corporations can elect to file a consolidated return.

Members of controlled groups are also subject to the rules regarding related party transactions that may require deferral of recognition for losses or expenses incurred by one party. A controlled group of corporations is entitled to only one $250,000 accumulated earnings tax credit, and only one section 179 deduction. In addition, the employees of those businesses are considered the same employee pool for certain qualified plan requirements.

Parent-Subsidiary Controlled Group

A **Parent-Subsidiary Controlled Group** involves a parent corporation that owns at least 80% of the voting power of at least one other corporation (with possible additional corporations that are at least 80% owned by either the common parent or one of the subsidiary entities); although a *foreign* corporation would not be considered a member of a controlled group.

Example #1: Express Corp. owns 80% of the outstanding shares of A&B, Inc. Express Corp. also owns 90% of the shares of C&D Inc. A controlled group exists with all three companies. In this scenario, Express Corp. is the "parent company" of the other two corporations. These companies can elect to file a consolidated corporate return.

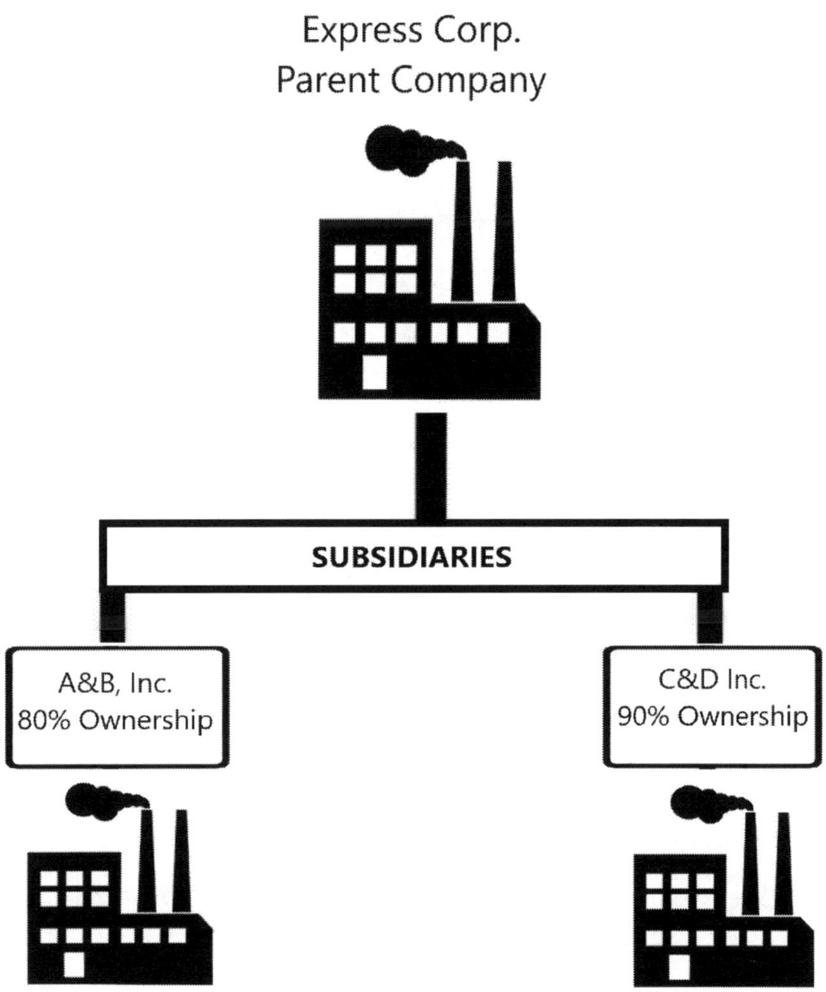

Parent-Subsidiary Controlled Group

Example#2 of a Parent-Subsidiary Controlled Group

Parasol Corporation owns:

- 90% of the stock of Arch Corporation
- 80% of the stock of Bawd Corporation
- 65% of the stock of Crain Corporation

Unrelated parties own the remaining percentage of stock not owned by Parasol Corporation. As Parasol Corporation owns 80% or more of the stock of Arch and Bawd Corporations, it is the common parent of a parent-subsidiary group consisting of the three corporations. Crain Corporation is not a member of the controlled group because Parasol Corporation's ownership is less than 80%.

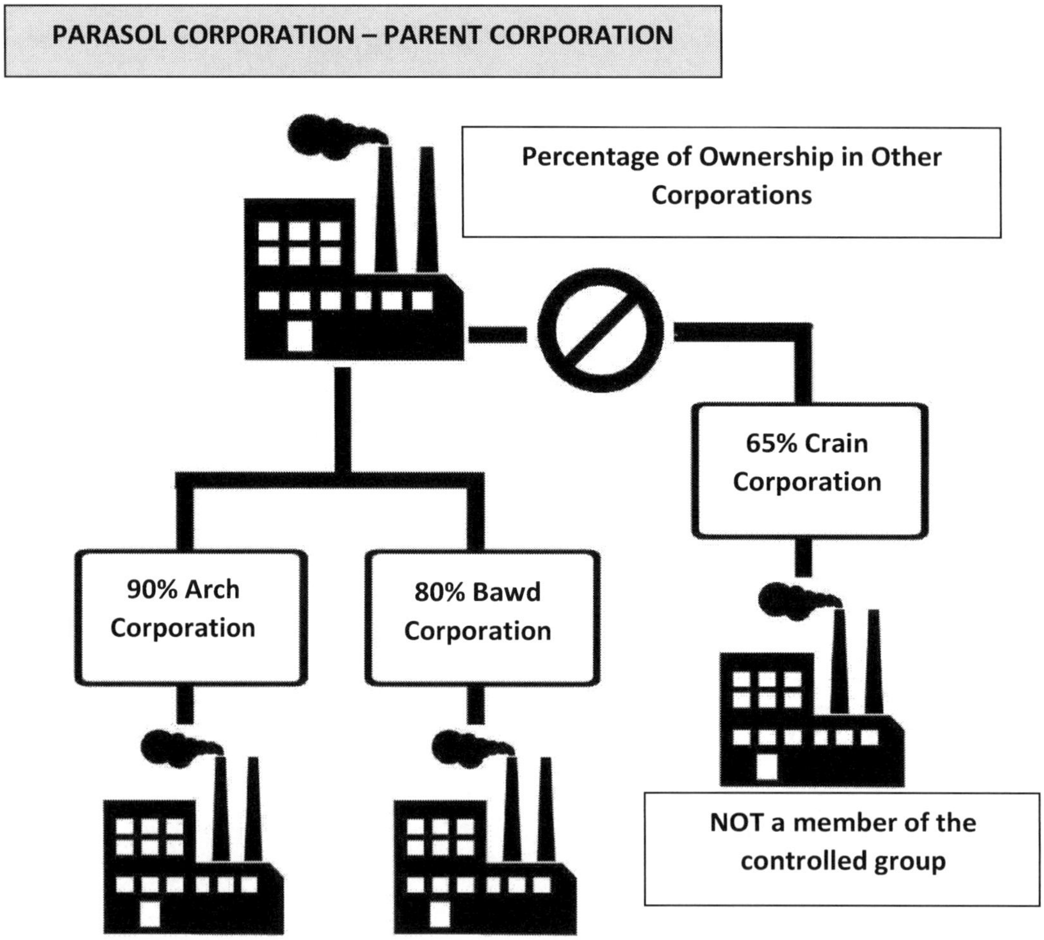

Brother-Sister Controlled Group

A **Brother-Sister Controlled Group** involves situations in which five or fewer individuals, estates, or trusts own 80% or more of the combined voting power for multiple corporations, and have identical common ownership within the individual corporations of at least 50%.

Unlike a parent-subsidiary controlled group, the focus in a brother-sister controlled group is on individual ownership. In other words, "effective control" requires collective ownership of more than 50% of the stock of each corporation, (but only to the extent such stock ownership is identical with respect to each corporation).

Example of a Brother-Sister Controlled Group

Innovation, Inc. and Keystone, Inc. are owned by three unrelated shareholders in the following percentages:

Shareholder	Innovation Inc.	Keystone Inc.
Elvin	70%	30%
Geary	10%	50%
Wayne	20%	20%
Total Ownership	**100%**	**100%**

The same five (or fewer) common owners must own more than 80% of the stock or some interest in all members of the controlled group. In this example, the three shareholders together own 100% of the stock of each corporation, so the first test is met. They also meet the second test of owning more than 50% of the stock of both corporations (the same three individuals, in aggregate, own at least 50% of both corporations), taking into account only the identical ownership in each corporation.

Shareholder	Identical Ownership Percentage in Both Corporations
Elvin	30%
Geary	10%
Wayne	20%
Total	**60%**

Unit 13: Study Questions

(Test yourself and then check the correct answers at the end of this section.)

1. During 2020, Abel Trucking Inc., a domestic C corporation, had the following income, expenses, and deductions:

Gross receipts	$95,000
Net capital gains	$10,000
Business expenses (not including charitable contributions)	$65,000
Cash charitable contributions	$20,000
NOL carryover from the prior year	$30,000

None of the contributions are qualified disaster contributions, but all the contributions were made to 501(c)3 charities. What is the amount of Abel Trucking's allowable charitable contribution deduction in 2020?

A. $1,000
B. $2,500
C. $4,000
D. $20,000

2. Belshaw Marketing, Inc. is a cash-basis C corporation. In 2020, Belshaw Marketing received $140,000 in dividends from a domestic corporation in which it owns 5% of the stock. Belshaw Marketing has taxable income of $180,000 during the year, before figuring the dividends-received-deduction. Based on this information, what is the allowable dividends-received-deduction for Belshaw Marketing?

A. $70,000
B. $98,000
C. $100,000
D. $126,000

3. Which of the following best describes a brother-sister controlled group?

A. Five or fewer individuals, estates, or trusts own 80% or more of the combined voting power for multiple corporations, and have identical common ownership within the individual corporations of at least 50%.
B. A parent corporation that owns at least 80% or more of the voting power of at least one other corporation, with at least two brothers and one sister or two sisters and one brother as owners.
C. A brother and sister each own 50% of a corporation, or a total of 100% of the corporation combined.
D. A corporation that controls at least two other corporations where a brother and sister are corporate officers of the different corporations.

4. Green Gardening Inc. is a calendar-year C corporation that uses the accrual method of accounting. What is the last day that the corporation can pay a charitable contribution and still deduct it on its 2020 tax return?

A. December 31, 2020.
B. January 15, 2021.
C. March 15, 2021.
D. April 15, 2021.

5. Seaside Capital, Inc. and Helena Mountain Coffee are both domestic C corporations. Seaside Capital, Inc. owns 25% of Helena Mountain Coffee. Seaside Capital's income from its business operations in 2020 is $500,000. In addition to its business income, Seaside Capital, Inc. received dividends from Helena Mountain Coffee of $145,000. What is Seaside Capital's dividends-received deduction?

A. $36,250
B. $94,250
C. $101,500
D. $145,000

6. In 2020, Reliable Motors Corporation made cash contributions totaling $20,000 to qualified charitable organizations. Due to income limitations, Reliable Motors could deduct only $15,000 of the contributions on its return. Which of the following correctly states the treatment of the excess $5,000 of charitable contributions?

A. The excess contributions can be carried back for 2 years and carried forward for 5 years.
B. The excess contributions can be carried forward indefinitely.
C. The excess contributions can be carried back for 3 years and carried forward for 10 years.
D. The excess contributions can be carried forward for 5 years. They cannot be carried back.

7. Pacific Holdings, Inc. is a cash-basis C corporation. In 2020, the corporation has a net short-term capital gain of $23,000 and a net long-term capital loss of ($29,000). How should these capital gains and losses be treated?

A. The corporation can deduct a $6,000 long-term capital loss on its current-year tax return.
B. The corporation can carry back the $29,000 long-term capital loss to a prior year, where it may only be deducted against long-term capital gains.
C. The corporation can carry back the $6,000 net capital loss to a prior year, where it may be deducted against short-term capital gains.
D. The corporation must carry forward the entire capital loss to the following tax year.

8. Which of the following statements is correct about a controlled group of corporations?

A. Members of a controlled group are entitled to only one accumulated earnings tax credit.
B. A parent corporation and its 80%-owned subsidiary would be members of a controlled group.
C. Members of controlled groups are subject to rules regarding related party transactions that may require deferral of recognition for losses or expenses incurred by one party.
D. All of the above.

9. Matrix Capital, Inc. owns 25% of Wilson Fine Foods, Inc. In 2020, Matrix Capital received $10,000 of dividends from Wilson's Fine Foods. Assuming no other limitations apply, Matrix Capital's dividends-received deduction is:

A. $2,000
B. $6,500
C. $8,000
D. $10,000

10. Banta Accounting, Inc. is a calendar-year C corporation. In 2020, it has $400,000 of taxable income before consideration of the following additional activities:

- Charitable cash contributions: $110,000.
- Dividends-received deduction: $70,000.

What portion of the charitable contributions is deductible?

A. $10,000
B. $82,500
C. $100,000
D. $110,000

11. Moulin Party Services, Inc. is a calendar-year C corporation. It is not a farming business. The company had an NOL of $3,000 in 2020. The corporation does not wish to carryback its losses, because the cost of filing the forms with the company's accountant would exceed the benefit. Which of the following statements is correct?

A. The corporation can forgo the carryback period and elect to carryforward the entire loss.
B. The corporation is required to carry back losses for two years and then forward for 15 years.
C. The corporation can carry back losses two years and carry them forward for 20 years.
D. The corporation cannot carry forward its losses. It can carry them back 5 years.

Unit 13: Quiz Answers

1. The answer is B. Abel Trucking is a C corporation, so it can deduct charitable contributions made to qualified organizations, up to 25% of taxable income (for cash contributions). Taxable income for this purpose is determined without regard to certain items, including the charitable contribution deduction itself and any net operating loss carryback (but not carryforward) to the tax year. Therefore, Abel Trucking's charitable contribution deduction would be determined as follows:

Gross receipts	$95,000
Expenses	($65,000)
Net capital gains	$10,000
NOL carryover from the prior year	($30,000)
Taxable income before contribution deduction	$10,000
Deduction limit at 25%	**$2,500**

2. The answer is A. Belshaw Marketing, Inc. has a DRD of **$70,000.** The DRD deduction for a corporation that owns less than 20% of the stock is 50% of the dividends received ($140,000 × 50% = 70,000). The DRD is limited to taxable income unless the corporation has an NOL after considering the deduction.

3. The answer is A. A brother-sister controlled group is when five or fewer individuals, estates, or trusts own 80% or more of the combined voting power for multiple corporations, and have identical common ownership within the individual corporations of at least 50%. Despite the name, the owners do not have to be related as siblings.

4. The answer is D. Green Gardening Inc. has until the due date of its tax return to pay the contribution (April 15). A corporation using the accrual method can choose to deduct unpaid contributions for the tax year if the board of directors authorizes the contribution during the tax year, and the corporation pays the contribution before the due date of the return.

5. The answer is B. Generally, if a corporation receives dividends from another corporation in which it owns an ownership stake of 20% to 80%, it is entitled to a deduction of 65% of the dividends received, subject to limitation based upon its taxable income without regard to the DRD and certain other items. Seaside Capital owns 25% of Helena Mountain Coffee, so its dividends-received deduction is **$94,250** ($145,000 × 65%).

6. The answer is D. Reliable Motors Corporation can carry over excess cash charitable contributions made during the year that result from the 25% limit on deductibility to each of the subsequent five years. Any excess charitable contributions that are not used in this five-year period are lost. A corporation cannot carry back excess charitable contributions.

7. The answer is C. Pacific Holdings, Inc. may carry back the $6,000 capital loss ($29,000 - $23,000) to the earliest of the three preceding years, where it may be deducted against capital gains. Any remaining losses can be carried forward for up to five years. The corporation treats this $6,000 as a short-term capital loss when carried back or carried forward, because capital loss carrybacks and carryforwards do not retain their original character.

8. The answer is D. A parent-subsidiary controlled group involves a parent corporation that owns at least 80% or more of the voting power of at least one other corporation. A controlled group is allowed a single set of graduated income tax brackets, and a single accumulated earnings credit of $250,000. Members of controlled groups are also subject to rules regarding related party transactions that may require deferral of recognition for losses or expenses incurred by one party.

9. The answer is B. If a corporation receiving dividends owns 20% or more of the corporation issuing the dividends, it generally qualifies for a dividends-received deduction equal to 65% of the dividends received. Therefore, Matrix Capital, Inc. can deduct amounts up to 65% of its taxable income, calculated without regard to the DRD itself and certain other items ($10,000 × 65% = **$6,500).**

10. The answer is C. Banta Accounting's deductible charitable contributions are limited to 25% of its taxable income, before consideration of the following items:

- The deduction for charitable contributions.
- The dividends-received deduction.
- The domestic production activities deduction.
- Any net operating loss carryback to the tax year.
- Any capital loss carryback to the tax year.

In this case, **$100,000** ($400,000 × 25%) would be deductible in the current year, and $10,000 would be carried over to the following year.

11. The answer is A. Moulin Party Services Inc. can elect to forgo the carryback period and carryforward its net operating loss on a timely filed return. Alternatively, the corporation may choose to carryback the loss five years. The CARES Act temporarily reinstated a 5-year carryback period for NOLs generated for tax years 2018, 2019, and 2020.

Unit 14: Corporate Distributions & Liquidations

More Reading:

Publication 542, Corporations

Corporate distributions, typically in the form of dividends, occur when cash, stock, or other property is distributed to shareholders based on the shareholders' ownership of the corporation's stock. When a corporation earns profits, it may retain the profits in the business (as retained earnings) or pay all or a portion of the profits as dividends to shareholders.

Corporations can issue their own stock to raise capital. Issuing stock has no impact on a corporation's net income. Alternatively, when a corporation later issues a dividend to its shareholders, the corporation cannot deduct the dividend payments as an expense. This is because if dividends were deductible by a corporation, the entity could effectively eliminate its tax liability every single year simply by distributing any taxable revenues to its shareholders.

Corporate Dividends

Dividends are most commonly paid in cash. However, a dividend can take the form of stock or other property. The most common kinds of corporate distributions are:

- Ordinary dividends (either in cash or in property)
- Capital gain distributions
- Nondividend distributions
- Distributions of stock or stock rights

The FMV of distributed property becomes the shareholder's basis in the property. A distribution may be reduced by the following liabilities:

- Any liability of the corporation the shareholder assumes
- Any liability applicable to distributed property, such as mortgage debt the shareholder assumes in connection with distribution of ownership in a building

It is important to note that the shareholder's basis in the property distributed to him remains at its FMV at the time of the distribution, even if the amount of the distribution is reduced by the amount of the liability attached to the property.

Reporting Requirements for Information Returns

A corporation must furnish Form 1099-DIV, *Dividends and Distributions,* to each shareholder who receives a dividend of $10 or more during a calendar year by January 31.

Note: Businesses (including corporations) must furnish Form 1099-MISC, and the new Form 1099-NEC to most recipients by January 31 (this date is pushed forward to February 1, 2021 for 2020 information returns, because January 31, 2021 is a Sunday).[127]

The corporation must also file copies of the Forms 1099-DIV with the IRS, along with Form 1096, *Annual Summary and Transmittal of U.S. Information Returns*. These forms are generally

[127] If a business is using Forms 1099-MISC to report amounts in box 8, *Substitute Payments in Lieu of Dividends or Interest,* or box 10, *Gross Proceeds Paid to An Attorney,* there is an exception to the normal due date. Those forms are due to recipients by February 16, 2021.

due by February 28 (March 31 if filing electronically)[128] of the year following the year of the distribution. The corporation is allowed to furnish Forms 1099-DIV to shareholders any time after April 30 of the year of the distributions if the corporation has made its final distributions for the calendar year.

Example: Fungible Capital, Inc. is an accrual-based corporation that operates on a fiscal year. The corporation issues a cash dividend to all its shareholders on February 10, 2020. Fungible Capital does not plan to issue any more dividends in 2020. Fungible Capital may choose to issue its 1099-DIV forms anytime after April 30, 2020 for the dividends that it has paid to its shareholders in 2020. In order to save time and reduce year-end workload, Fungible Capital files all its required 1099-DIV forms on May 30, 2020. The company has complied with its informational return reporting requirement for the year.

Distributions from Earnings and Profits

The amount of a C corporation's earnings and profits (E&P) determines the tax treatment of corporate distributions to shareholders. The starting point for determining corporate E&P is the corporation's taxable income. The following are the most common transactions that **increase** the amount of E&P:

- Long-term contracts reported on the completed contract method
- Intangible drilling costs deducted currently
- Mine exploration and development costs deducted currently
- Dividends-received deduction
- Nontaxable life insurance proceeds
- Federal income tax refunds
- Deferred gain on installment sales
- Tax-exempt income (i.e., interest income on state and local bonds)

The following are the most common transactions that **reduce** the amount of E&P:

- Corporate federal income taxes
- Life insurance policy premiums on a corporate officer
- Excess charitable contributions (over the allowable limit)
- Expenses relating to tax-exempt income
- Excess of capital losses over capital gains
- Corporate dividends and other distributions
- Fines and penalties
- Nondeductible lobbying expenses
- Nondeductible portion of meals and entertainment

[128] The IRS e-file deadline for information returns, such as most 1099-series Forms, is usually March 31; whereas if the corporation is filing these forms by paper, the deadline is February 28. However, the deadlines to provide the form to the recipient will vary. The federal government versions of Forms W-2 and 1099-NEC (forms showing nonemployee compensation) are due on or before January 31. In 2021, this filing deadline was pushed to Feb 1(for filing 2020 information returns) because January 31, 2021 is a Sunday.

Accumulated Earnings and Profits

Accumulated earnings and profits are earnings and profits (E&P) that the corporation accumulated in a prior year and has not distributed to its shareholders. If a corporation's current year E&P is less than the total distributions made during the year, part or all of each distribution is treated as a distribution of accumulated E&P.

Note: Any part of a distribution from current-year earnings and profits or accumulated earnings and profits is reported as dividend income to the shareholder and is generally taxable as ordinary income to the shareholder rather than as capital gains.

If a corporation's accumulated earnings and profits are reduced to zero, the remaining part of a distribution reduces the adjusted basis of the shareholder's stock. This is referred to as a "nondividend distribution," and it is not taxable to the shareholder until his basis in the stock is fully recovered.

This nontaxable portion is considered to be a *return of capital* that he had previously invested in the corporation. In other words, nondividend distributions mean that investors are getting back some of the money they originally invested in the company.

Definition: Return of capital refers to the return of some or all of an investor's investment in a company or partnership. Since it represents the recoupment of investment, the return of capital is not considered income, but instead decreases the net value and tax basis of their investment.

Example #1: Warden is the only shareholder of Green Ridge Corporation, a calendar-year corporation. During the year, Green Ridge Corporation makes four $1,000 dividend distributions to Warden. At the end of the year (before subtracting distributions made during the year), the corporation has $10,000 of current year earnings and profits. Since the corporation's current year E&P ($10,000) was more than the amount of the distributions it made during the year ($4,000), all of the distributions are treated as distributions of current-year E&P. The corporation must issue Form 1099-DIV to Warden by January 31 to report the $4,000 distributed to him as dividends. Green Ridge Corporation must use Form 1096**,** *Annual Summary and Transmittal of U.S. Information Returns*, to report this transaction to the IRS by February 28 (March 31 if filing electronically). The corporation is not allowed to deduct these dividends on its income tax return as a business expense.

Example #2: Nassim likes to invest in stock. On February 1, 2020, he purchased 1,000 shares of Frontier Motors Co. stock on the New York Stock exchange for $170,000. On November 1, 2020, Nassim receives a nondividend distribution of $9,000 from Frontier Motors, which is reported to him by the company on Form 1099-DIV (box 3). His cost basis will be adjusted downwards to $161,000 ($170,000 cost basis minus the $9,000 distribution). On February 5, 2021, Nassim sells all his shares in Frontier Motors for $180,000. His capital gain for tax purposes is $19,000 ($180,000 sales price minus his $161,000 adjusted stock basis). This amount will be taxed to Nassim as long-term capital gains, because he held the stock for **over one year.** He will report the stock sale on his individual return on Schedule D, Form 1040.

In most cases, the amount of a nondividend distribution will not exceed an investor's basis in his shares. However, if a corporation makes nondividend distributions to a shareholder that *exceed* the adjusted basis of his stock, the excess distribution is treated as a gain from the sale or exchange of property and is taxable to the shareholder as a capital gain.

Example: Fatima likes to invest in stock. Five years ago, she purchased 500 shares of Sachs Group Inc. for $8,000. On January 10, 2020, Sachs Group Inc. issues a nondividend distribution of $8,900 to Fatima. The first $8,000 of the distribution will reduce Fatima's stock basis to zero. Since her basis cannot be reduced below zero, the remaining $900 is taxable to Fatima as a long-term capital gain.

If nondividend distributions are made to shareholders, the *corporation* must report these distributions to the IRS on Form 5452, *Corporate Report of Nondividend Distributions.*

Distributions of Property

A sale or exchange of property by a corporation to a shareholder (that is not a corporation) may be treated as a distribution to the shareholder, to the extent the FMV of the property on the date of the sale or exchange exceeds the price he paid.

A distribution of property is also treated as if the corporation had sold the property to the shareholder. A corporation (either a C corporation or an S corporation) recognizes a gain on a distribution of property to a shareholder if the FMV of the property is more than its adjusted basis. This gain adds to the corporation's earnings & profits.

For this purpose, the FMV is considered to be the greater of the property's actual FMV or the amount of liabilities the shareholder assumes in connection with the distribution. If the distributed property was depreciable or amortizable, the corporation may have to treat all or a portion of the gain as ordinary income from depreciation recapture.

Example: Dynamics Ventures, Inc. distributes to an individual shareholder, Ulrich, $65,000 of cash, and an excavator with a $35,000 adjusted basis and a $50,000 FMV. The transaction is treated as a sale to Dynamics Ventures. Dynamics Ventures must recognize a $15,000 taxable gain on the distribution of property because its FMV is more than its adjusted basis ($50,000 - $35,000 = $15,000).

These transactions may be taxable to the shareholder at FMV and are reported to the IRS on Form 1099-DIV or Form 5452, *Corporate Report of Nondividend Distributions*. A corporation generally cannot recognize a loss on a distribution of property (i.e., where the property's FMV is less than the adjusted cost basis). However, a corporation is allowed to recognize losses when depreciated property is distributed to shareholders in complete liquidation (when the corporation ceases operations).

Stock Distributions

Stock distributions or stock dividends occur when a corporation issues additional shares of its own stock to shareholders, rather than paying a cash dividend or distributing property. Stock dividend distributions do not affect the market capitalization of a company, but a stock dividend generally reduces the per-share market price of the company's stock.

Stock rights, also known as "stock options," may be distributed by a corporation to some or all of its shareholders to allow them to purchase shares at a discount or at a stated fixed price.

Employee stock option plans are an extremely common type of fringe benefit. There are many different types of stock options, and below is just a simplified example.

Example: On January 1, 2020, Superior Electronics, Inc. issues employee stock options that allow Rachel, an employee, the right to buy 500 shares of company stock at a price of $8.00 per share. On April 20, 2020, Superior Electronics stock reaches $20.00 a share, and Rachel decides to exercise her employee stock options. Rachel decides to send $4,000 to her brokerage firm handling the options transaction and she receives 500 shares of Superior Electronics. She decides to keep the shares as an investment and not sell them.

Distributions by a corporation of its own stock or stock rights are tax-free to shareholders and not deductible by the corporation. However, they may be treated as taxable property distributions in rare situations, including when:

- The shareholder has the choice to receive cash instead of stock.
- The distribution gives cash or other property to some shareholders and an increase in the percentage interest in the corporation's assets or earnings and profits to other shareholders.
- The distribution is in convertible preferred stock.
- The distribution gives preferred stock to some shareholders and common stock to other shareholders.
- The distribution is paid based on ownership of preferred stock.

Expenses for Issuing Stock: A corporation must capitalize, rather than deduct, the expenses of issuing a stock dividend, such as printing, postage, and any fees for listing on stock exchanges. Typical costs associated with issuing stock include fees for attorneys, accountants, as well as underwriting costs. A corporation may not deduct or amortize costs incurred in connection with issuing its capital stock. A corporation may also not deduct any of the costs incurred in connection with the initial public offering of stock (also called an "IPO").

Instead, stock issuance costs are treated as a reduction in the proceeds of the stock sale. They are considered the equivalent of selling the stock at a discount; thus, they do not create an expense that could give rise to a deduction.

Note: An initial public offering (IPO) occurs when a private company issues stock to the public for the first time. This is also commonly referred to as "going public." The proceeds from the sale of stock shares in an initial public offering provide the issuing company with investment capital. The money that is received by the corporation from a stock sale is not taxable income. Consequently, the costs incurred by the corporation to issue stock are not deductible and must be capitalized. It is equivalent for income tax purposes to the sale of stock at a discount.[129]

Example: Choice Construction, Inc. issues a 2-for-1 stock dividend to all its existing shareholders in 2020. The corporation's stock is publicly listed on a national securities exchange. The legal fees and underwriting costs to issue the stock dividend totaled $145,000. This cost must be capitalized. It cannot be deducted as a current expense by the corporation.

[129] Internal Revenue Service, National Office Technical Advice Memorandum, TAM 200532048.

Constructive Distributions

A constructive distribution, also called a *constructive dividend*, may occur when a corporation confers a personal benefit upon a shareholder. Constructive distributions are treated the same as actual distributions. A transaction recorded by the corporation as an expense may be recategorized instead as a constructive distribution.

This would make the transaction nondeductible to the corporation and, in many instances, taxable to the shareholder. Consequently, constructive distributions have a very undesirable income tax impact. The probability of constructive distributions is greatest when a corporation is closely-held. Examples of constructive distributions include:

- **Payment of personal expenses:** If a corporation pays personal expenses on behalf of a shareholder, the amounts should be classified as a distribution rather than expenses of the corporation.
- **Unreasonable compensation:** If a corporation pays an employee-shareholder an unreasonably high salary considering the services actually performed, the excessive part of the salary may be treated as a distribution.
- **Unreasonable rents:** If a corporation rents property from a shareholder and the rent is unreasonably higher than the shareholder would charge an unrelated party for the use of the property, the excessive part of the rent may be treated as a distribution.
- **Cancellation of a shareholder's debt:** If a corporation cancels a shareholder's debt without repayment by the shareholder, the amount canceled may be treated as a distribution.
- **Property transfers for less than FMV:** If a corporation transfers or sells property to a shareholder for less than its FMV, the excess may be treated as a distribution.
- **Below market or interest-free loans**: If a corporation gives a loan to a shareholder on an interest-free basis or at a rate below the applicable federal rate, the uncharged interest may be treated as a distribution.

Example: Dennis is the sole shareholder and owner of the Powerpack Packaging, Inc., a C Corporation. Dennis hires his daughter, Melanie, who is 17 years old, to work as the shop's receptionist. Melanie works about 10 hours a week after school. Dennis pays his teenage daughter $500,000 as an annual salary. Later, the IRS audits the shop and determines that Dennis paid an unreasonably high salary to his daughter, considering the services actually performed. The excess salary is recharacterized as a constructive distribution, making it nondeductible to Powerpack Packaging, but still taxable to the recipient.

Example: Design Source, Inc. rents office space from a 75% shareholder, Timothy, who is the sole owner of the office building. The corporation pays Timothy $25,000 a month for its space. He charges other tenants $5,000 a month for offices with the same square footage. The excessive rent of $240,000 ($25,000 - $5,000 = $20,000 × 12 months) would likely be disallowed as an expense for Design Source and recharacterized as a constructive distribution to Timothy.

Stock Redemptions

A stock *redemption* occurs when a corporation buys back its *own stock* from a shareholder in exchange for cash or property. The stock acquired may then be canceled, retired, or held as Treasury stock. Common reasons why a corporation would redeem a shareholder's stock include:

- To make sure that ownership of the corporation remains with people that were chosen by current owners or by the original founders of the corporation;
- To go private by redeeming all publicly-traded shares
- To increase the market price of the stock through lowering the amount of outstanding shares;
- To eliminate hostile minority shareholders;
- To retire preferred stock to reduce or eliminate the dividend payments; or
- To avert a hostile takeover attempt

If a corporation buys back shares of its own stock from its shareholders, the transaction will either be treated as:

- A sale or exchange that results in a capital gain (or loss) for the shareholder; or
- As a dividend, depending on the facts of the transaction.

Stock redemptions are generally treated as dividends unless certain conditions are met. Non-dividend treatment includes situations where:

- The shareholder's proportionate interest and voting power in the corporation has been substantially reduced.
- There was a substantially disproportionate redemption of stock, meaning that the amount received by the shareholder is not in proportion to his stock ownership.
- The redemption was due to a complete termination of a shareholder's interest in the corporation.
- The redemption is of stock held by a non-corporate shareholder and was part of a partial liquidation.
- The distribution is received by an estate and does not exceed the sum of death taxes plus funeral and administration expenses to be paid by the estate.

If the corporation pays cash to redeem stock, there is no taxable effect to the corporation. However, if the corporation distributes *property* for a redemption (*instead* of cash), then it might have to recognize a gain, (but not a loss) as if the property were sold for the fair market value to the stockholder.[130] Corporate expenditures incurred in a stock redemption are not deductible by the corporation as a business expense.[131]

If a corporation distributes property in a stock redemption, the corporation must recognize income on the distribution of *depreciated* property to the extent of depreciation or the amount

---

[130] In this scenario, it would normally be advisable for the corporation to sell the property to an unrelated party, recognize a gain or a loss, and then use the cash *proceeds* from sale for redemption of the shareholder's stock.

[131] IRC section 162(k) specifically provides that no deduction is allowed for any amount paid or incurred by a corporation in connection with reacquisition of its own stock. The expenses of issuing or reselling stock are also not deductible

realized (whichever is less). The corporation may not recognize a loss on a stock redemption unless:

- The redemption occurs in a complete liquidation of the corporation, or
- The redemption occurs on stock held by an estate.

Qualified Stock Redemptions

In general, a "qualified" stock redemption must result in a substantial reduction in the shareholder's ownership. For example, when a shareholder retires or leaves the company permanently, and the other shareholders choose to "buy out" the retiring shareholder's interest.

Note: If a corporation buys back shares of its own stock from all of its shareholders proportionately, the transaction will normally be treated as a sale or exchange that results in a capital gain (or loss) for the *shareholder*.

A stock redemption by a C Corporation will generally not increase the basis of the stock owned by the remaining shareholders. In other words, a stock redemption generates no stock basis step-up for the other remaining owners. Instead, the corporation's E&P (earnings and profits) is reduced in a qualified stock redemption by the ratable share of E&P attributable to the stock redeemed.

By reducing the corporation's earnings and profits, this will also reduce the amount of income that would ultimately be taxable to the remaining shareholders.

Example: Micro Devices, Inc. has four unrelated shareholders: Donald, Sandy, Randall, and Jennifer. Randall, a 20% percent shareholder, has a disagreement with the other owners and quits the company. Randall's 20% stock interest has a fair market value of $400,000. Randall threatens to sell his company stock to an unrelated party. In order to avoid this scenario, Micro Devices, Inc. redeems all of Randall's stock on his departure for $400,000. For Randall, the stock redemption is treated as a sale, and he will either have a capital gain or loss, just as if he had sold his stock on the open market. The three remaining shareholders, Donald, Sandy, and Jennifer, now own all the outstanding stock. Their individual stock basis would remain the same, although the percentage of the stock ownership of the remaining shareholders would increase. Micro Devices, Inc. would reduce its E&P.

If a stock redemption is not a "qualified" stock redemption, it will be treated as a dividend distribution and not a sale. The following is an example of a stock redemption that is treated as a distribution and not a sale.

Example: Jiangyu is the sole shareholder of Analog Technologies, Inc. During the year, Analog Technologies redeems 50 of Jiangyu's 200 shares for $100,000 (the fair market value of the 50 shares redeemed). Because Jiangyu still owns the same percentage of shares in the company (100%) after the redemption, this will be treated as a dividend distribution to her (assuming sufficient earnings and profits of the corporation). In other words, the stock redemption is a *taxable dividend* to Jiangyu, (it is not treated as a sale of stock), because she is still a 100% owner (with no change in her ownership percentage) of the corporation after the redemption takes place.

Corporate Liquidations and Dissolutions

A corporate liquidation is considered at two levels, the *shareholder* level, and the *corporate* level. "Liquidating distributions" are distributions received by a shareholder during a complete or partial dissolution of a corporation. When a corporation dissolves, it redeems all of its stock in a series of distributions.

Complete liquidation occurs when the corporation ceases to be a going concern and its activities are merely for the purpose of winding up its affairs, paying its debts, and distributing any remaining balance to its shareholders.

In certain cases in which the buyer is a corporation in control of the distributing corporation, the distribution may not be taxable. A corporate dissolution or liquidation must be reported on Form 966, *Corporate Dissolution or Liquidation*, within 30 days after the resolution or plan is adopted to dissolve the corporation or liquidate any of its stock. Exempt entities are not required to file Form 966, even if they are organized as corporations.

When a corporation distributes property in a complete liquidation, the transaction is treated as if the corporation sold the distributed assets at their fair market value. The corporation recognizes gain or loss on the liquidation in an amount equal to the difference between the FMV and the adjusted basis of the assets distributed. A corporation is allowed to recognize losses during the liquidation, except for losses resulting from transactions with related parties.

Example: Harmon Corporation ceases all of its business operations in 2020. The company distributes a building to one of its shareholders as part of a complete liquidation. The adjusted basis of the building is $750,000, and its fair market price is $400,000. Harmon Corporation can recognize a loss of $350,000.

Amounts received by the shareholder in complete liquidation of a corporation are treated as full payment in exchange for the shareholder's stock. A liquidating distribution is considered a return of capital and is not taxable to the shareholder until the shareholder recovers all of his basis in the stock. After the basis of the stock has been reduced to zero, shareholders must report any additional amounts as a capital gain. A corporation is required to provide each shareholder a Form 1099-DIV showing the amount of the liquidating distribution.

Study Note: When a shareholder receives a series of distributions in a corporate liquidation, the *gain* is recognized once all of the shareholder's stock basis is recovered. A *loss*, however, will not be recognized until the final distribution is received.

Example: Babcock Motors, Inc. is dissolving and closing down its business operations. Zhavia is a 10% owner of the corporation and owns 2,000 shares. Her basis in the stock is $40,000. Babcock Motors, Inc. distributes $38,000 in two liquidating distributions to Zhavia. She receives $6,000 on November 5, 2020 and $32,000 on January 15, 2021. The corporation legally dissolves on January 30, 2021. Zhavia cannot take a loss on the liquidating distribution until the final distribution is received. Zhavia recovered $6,000 of her basis in 2020 and the remaining balance in 2021. Her loss is $2,000 ($38,000 total distributions minus her $40,000 basis). She may take a $2,000 capital loss in 2021, because the loss exceeds her basis in the stock. Zhavia should report her capital loss on Schedule D, Form 1040, in 2021.

If a dissolving corporation distributes property that is subject to a liability, the gain or loss is adjusted to reflect the assumption of the liability.

If the liability is greater than the FMV of the property, the amount of the liability is treated as the FMV of the property.

Example: Hubbell Growers, Inc. is going through a complete liquidation. Carter, a shareholder, receives a liquidating distribution of property (a tractor). Hubbell Growers' basis in the tractor is $3,000. The fair market value of the tractor is $13,000. However, the tractor is encumbered by a liability of $15,000 (an unpaid loan), which Carter personally assumes. Because the remaining loan amount is more than the FMV of the tractor, the amount of the liability is treated as the FMV. The corporation must recognize a $12,000 gain on the distribution ($15,000 loan - $3,000 basis), and Carter is treated as having received a liquidating distribution of $15,000.

A corporation must file an income tax return for the year it goes out of business, even if it has no income or business activity in that year. If the dissolution is effective on any day other than the last day of the corporation's tax year, the final tax return is due on the fifteenth day of the fourth month following the close of its short tax year.

Unit 14: Study Questions

(Test yourself and then check the correct answers at the end of this section.)

1. Ryan is a minority shareholder (1% shareholder) in Fluid Films Corporation with a basis of $20,000 in his stock. He also has an outstanding $10,000 loan that he owes to the corporation. Ryan has financial difficulties and defaults on the loan. Fluid Corporation tries to collect for a few years, but finally cancels Ryan's debt in 2020. How should this cancellation of debt be reported?

A. The debt cancellation is treated as a $10,000 distribution to Ryan.
B. The debt cancellation is considered a return of capital to Ryan.
C. The debt cancellation is a charitable contribution to Ryan.
D. The debt cancellation is a $10,000 capital gain to Ryan.

2. Equitable Funding Group, Inc. is a C corporation. The business is having financial trouble and formally dissolves on February 10. When is Equitable Funding's final tax return due (Form 1120)?

A. April 15.
B. June 15.
C. June 30.
D. September 15.

3. Trotter Corporation distributes to a shareholder $75,000 of cash and a delivery truck with a $40,000 adjusted basis and a $60,000 FMV. What gain or loss, if any, must Trotter Corporation recognize on this distribution?

A. $0 gain or loss.
B. $20,000 gain.
C. $40,000 gain.
D. $20,000 loss.

4. Geraldine owns 800 shares of Beckman Software Corporation. Geraldine purchased the shares five years ago, and her basis in the stock is $20,000. Beckman Software completely liquidates on November 30, 2020, and distributed $56,000 in two payments to Geraldine. She received $16,000 on December 5, 2020 and $40,000 on January 10, 2021. How much gain or loss does Geraldine recognize in 2020 and 2021?

A. $4,000 loss in 2020 and a $40,000 gain in 2021.
B. $4,000 loss in 2020 and a $44,000 gain in 2021.
C. No gain or loss in 2020 and a $40,000 gain in 2021.
D. No gain or loss in 2020 and a $36,000 gain in 2021.

5. Ten years ago, Mark purchased 100 shares of Rock Star, Inc. for $10 per share. In 2020 Rock Star completely liquidated and distributed $20,000 to Mark in exchange for all of his stock. Mark must report this distribution as:

A. $20,000 of long-term capital gain.
B. $19,000 of short-term capital loss.
C. $19,000 of long-term capital gain.
D. $19,000 of ordinary income.

6. All of the examples below are considered corporate distributions except:

A. Ordinary dividends to a shareholder.
B. Capital gain distributions to a shareholder.
C. Constructive distributions to an employee-shareholder.
D. Wage compensation to an employee-shareholder.

7. Distributions of stock rights or stock options are generally tax-free to shareholders. In which scenario would stock rights be taxable to the shareholder?

A. If a shareholder has a choice to receive cash instead of stock rights.
B. If the person receiving the stock rights is an employee of the company.
C. If the stock rights are in a domestic C corporation.
D. If the corporation shows a loss for the year.

8. Midwestern Grain, Inc. distributes an industrial compressor with an adjusted basis of $1,000 and a fair market value of $4,000 subject to a liability of $6,000 to Joseph, a shareholder. Joseph personally assumes the $6,000 loan. What is the gain or loss, if any, Midwestern Grain must recognize as a result of the distribution?

A. $0 gain or loss.
B. $1,000 loss.
C. $3,000 gain.
D. $5,000 gain.

9. Six years ago, Sabine purchased 100 shares of Vitality Vitamins, Inc. stock for $50 per share. In 2020, the corporation ceased operations and liquidated. After paying its outstanding liabilities, Vitality Vitamins distributed $10,000 of cash and appreciated property worth $90,000 to its shareholders. Sabine's portion of the distributed assets and cash was $12,000. What amount of taxable income must she report from this liquidating distribution in 2020?

A. $3,000 short-term gain.
B. $3,000 long-term capital gain.
C. $7,000 long-term capital gain.
D. $10,000 short-term capital gain.

10. When are stock distributions deductible by the corporation?

A. Stock distributions are deductible when the corporation's board of directors approves the dividend.
B. Stock distributions are deductible when distributed to shareholders.
C. Stock distributions are deductible by a corporation when they are issued.
D. Stock distributions are not deductible by the corporation.

11. American Builders, Inc. displays a collection of fine artwork in its corporate offices. When Donald, a 15% shareholder retires, he is presented with his choice from the art collection. Donald selects a painting with a fair market value of $250,000. American Builders' basis in the painting is $100,000, which is the price that the corporation paid for the painting over ten years ago. How should the transaction be reported on the American Builders' tax return?

A. $150,000 loss.
B. $150,000 distribution.
C. $150,000 taxable gain.
D. $250,000 taxable gain.

12. When using taxable income as a starting point, which of the following transactions *increases* the amount of a C corporation's earnings and profits?

A. Excess of capital losses over capital gains.
B. Dividends-received deduction.
C. Life insurance premiums on a corporate officer.
D. Excess charitable contributions.

13. Millerton Software, Inc. is a C corporation that was formed many years ago. At the beginning of 2020, Millerton Software had accumulated earnings and profits of $100,000. The company makes a $5,000 distribution to its 100% shareholder in the first month of each quarter (four distributions throughout the year). At the end of the year, Millerton Software had $150,000 of gross income and $140,000 of expenses from ordinary business operations. Millerton also received $5,000 in fully tax-exempt interest from state muni bonds. What part of the second quarter distribution is treated as a distribution of accumulated earnings and profits?

A. $1,250
B. $2,500
C. $3,750
D. $5,000

Unit 14: Quiz Answers

1. The answer is A. The debt cancellation is treated as a taxable distribution to Ryan. If a corporation cancels a shareholder's debt without repayment by the shareholder, the amount canceled is treated as a taxable distribution to the shareholder.

2. The answer is B. A corporation must file an income tax return for the year it goes out of business, even if it has no income or business activity in that year. This is called a "short year" return. In Equitable Funding's case, that date is June 15 (the 15th day of the fourth month *after* the month the corporation was officially dissolved).

3. The answer is B. Trotter Corporation will recognize a gain on the distribution of property to a shareholder if the FMV of the property is more than its adjusted basis ($60,000 FMV - $40,000 adjusted basis = **$20,000 gain**). This is the same treatment that would apply if the property were sold for its FMV.

4. The answer is D. The liquidating distribution is not taxable until the shareholder's stock basis ($20,000) has been recovered. Geraldine recovered $16,000 of her basis in 2020 and the remaining balance of $4,000 in 2021. Her recognized gain is $36,000 ($56,000 total distributions – her $20,000 basis). She will recognize no gain or loss in 2020, but must recognize **$36,000** of capital gain in 2021, because this amount exceeds her basis in the stock.

5. The answer is C. Mark has a **$19,000 long-term capital gain**. His basis in the stock was $1,000 (100 shares stock × $10), so his gain is figured as follows: ($20,000 distribution - $1,000 basis). Gain or loss recognized by shareholders on distributions in a corporate liquidation is generally determined by the difference between the total of the cash and property received by the shareholders and the basis of the stock they surrendered. The gain or loss will be long-term or short-term, depending on the length of time the stock was held. Since Mark purchased the shares many years ago, his holding period exceeds one year and is therefore recognized as a long-term capital gain on his personal income tax return.

6. The answer is D. Salaries or wages paid to an employee-shareholder are not considered a distribution. Instead, the wages would be treated as a business expense, just like wages for the corporation's other employees. The wages are deductible by the corporation as a business expense and taxable to the employee-shareholder.

7. The answer is A. If the shareholder has an option to receive cash instead of stock rights, the distributions of stock and stock rights are taxable.

8. The answer is D. A distribution of property to a shareholder is treated as if the corporation had sold the property to the shareholder. The corporation recognizes gain on the distribution if the FMV of the property is more than its adjusted basis. The FMV is considered to be the greater of the property's actual FMV or the amount of liability the shareholder assumes in connection with the distribution. In this case, the FMV is considered to be the liability of $6,000 assumed by Joseph, so Midwestern Grain must recognize a gain of **$5,000** ($6,000 – $1,000 adjusted basis).

9. The answer is C. The capital gain is calculated as follows: Sabine's basis in her stock is $5,000 ($50 × 100 shares). The excess of her portion of the distribution over her basis ($12,000 distribution - $5,000 basis) results in a $7,000 long-term capital gain on the liquidating distribution.

10. The answer is D. Generally, distributions of stock and stock rights are not taxable to shareholders and not deductible by the corporation.

11. The answer is C. American Builders, Inc. must recognize a gain for any appreciated property distributed that has an FMV higher than its adjusted basis. This is the same treatment the corporation would receive if the property were sold for its FMV. The answer is figured as follows:

FMV of distribution	$250,000
Subtract adjusted basis	($100,000)
Recognized gain	**$150,000**

It should be noted that the FMV of $250,000 is also reported as a distribution to the shareholder, and will be his basis in the painting.

12. The answer is B. The amount of a C corporation's earnings and profits determines the tax treatment of corporate distributions to shareholders. The starting point for determining corporate E&P is the corporation's taxable income. The following are the most common transactions that *increase* the amount of E&P:

- Long-term contracts reported on the completed contract method.
- Intangible drilling costs deducted currently.
- Mine exploration and development costs deducted currently.
- Dividends-received deduction.
- Interest income on state and local bonds.
- Nontaxable life insurance proceeds.
- Federal income tax refunds.
- Domestic production activities deduction.
- Deferred gain on installment sales.

The following are the most common transactions that *reduce* the amount of E&P:

- Corporate federal income taxes.
- Life insurance policy premiums on a corporate officer.
- Excess charitable contributions.
- Expenses relating to tax-exempt income.
- Excess of capital losses over capital gains.
- Corporate dividends and other distributions.
- Fines and penalties.
- Nondeductible lobbying expenses.
- Nondeductible portion of meals and entertainment.

13. The answer is A. Distributions from a C corporation are deducted first from current E&P, and then from accumulated E&P. Any part of a distribution from current-year E&P or accumulated E&P is reported as dividend income to the shareholder. If a corporation's current E&P is less than the total distributions made during the year, part or all of each distribution is treated as a distribution of accumulated E&P. Since Millerton's distributions during the year ($5,000 X 4 quarterly distributions = $20,000) were more than its current-year E&P of $15,000 ($150,000 gross income- $140,000 expenses + $5,000 interest), the amount of each distribution is treated as having been paid partially from current-year E&P in the ratio of current E&P for the year to total distributions for the year ([$15,000 ÷ $20,000] × $5,000) = $3,750. The remainder of each distribution ($5,000 - $3,750 = **$1,250**) is treated as having been paid from accumulated E&P.

Unit 15: S Corporations

More Reading:
Form 1120-S Instructions
Publication 538, Accounting Periods and Methods

Drawbacks and Benefits

The rules governing S corporations are found in subchapter S of the Internal Revenue Code. An S corporation has similarities to both a C corporation and a partnership. Like a partnership, an S corporation is a pass-through entity and is generally not taxed on its earnings. Instead, income and losses pass through to shareholders. Like a C corporation, an S corporation enjoys a level of liability protection that a general partnership does not.

Note: Shareholders of S corporations report the flow-through of income and losses on their personal tax returns and are assessed tax at their individual income tax rates. This allows S corporations to avoid double taxation on corporate income.

S corporations do have some drawbacks. They are less flexible than partnerships. For example, in a partnership, the partners can have different allocations for income and loss based on their partnership agreement.

However, with an S Corporation, profits and losses must be passed through to the shareholders based on their percentage of stock ownership. Shareholders can't make any special agreements or arrangements for allocating profits and losses in an imbalanced manner. Unlike C corporations, an S corporation can only have one class of stock (although differences in voting rights are permitted).

S corporations also have very strict limits on the number of shareholders and the type of shareholders that the company can have. A C Corporation does not have any shareholder restrictions. There are some instances in which an S corporation is forced to pay tax on its earnings, like a C corporation, although these instances are rare.

An S corporation generally may choose to use either the cash or the accrual method of accounting, but it does have a required tax year.

Electing S Corporation Status

To become an S corporation, a corporation (or other eligible entity) must file an election on Form 2553, *Election by a Small Business Corporation.* The filing must be made no later than 2.5 months after the start of its tax year for the election to be effective at the beginning of the year.

Example #1: (No prior tax year): Super Suds Laundry is a newly-formed corporation that was incorporated on April 7, 2020. In order to elect to be an S-Corporation beginning with its first tax year, Super Suds must file Form 2553 during the period that begins April 7, 2020, and ends July 21, 2020 (within 2.5 months after the start of its *first* tax year). Because the corporation had no prior tax year, and was not incorporated until April 7th, any election made *before* April 7 would not be valid.

Example #2 (Prior tax year): American Copiers, Inc. is a calendar-year C corporation that has been filing Form 1120 for the past five years. American Copiers wishes to convert to an S corporation, and make an S election for its next tax year beginning January 1, 2021. To be an S corporation beginning with its next tax year, the corporation must file Form 2553 *before* March 15, 2021 (2.5 months after the start of the year it wishes to become an S corporation) to be effective as of January 1, 2021. Because the corporation was already in existence and had been filing as a C corporation in the past, it can also make the election at any time during the prior tax year (2020) to make it effective for the following year (2021).

If the S election is made during the corporation's tax year for which it first takes effect, each individual shareholder who holds stock at any time during the part of that year before the election is made must also consent to the election. This is true even if the person may have sold or transferred his stock before the election is made.

Example: Reuben, Silvia, and Nicholas are all equal shareholders in a C corporation. On January 15, 2020, Nicholas decides to retire from the business. Nicholas sells all his shares in the C corporation to Martha, his cousin. On February 20, 2020, Reuben, Silvia, and Martha vote to elect S corporation status. All the current shareholders must agree to the election. Nicholas must also agree, even though he sold all his stock before the election was made. This is because Nicholas was still a shareholder at the beginning of the year that the corporation made the election.

Late Election Relief

An election made after the first 2.5 months of the tax year becomes effective on the first day of the following tax year, unless the corporation receives IRS approval to make the election retroactive to the beginning of the tax year. Based on updated guidelines, the IRS will generally accept a late S-election if the following requirements are met:

- The entity intended to be classified as an S corporation, is an eligible entity, and failed to qualify as an S corporation solely because the election was not timely,
- The entity has reasonable cause for its failure to make the election timely,
- The entity and all shareholders reported their income consistent with an S corporation election in effect for the year the election should have been made and all subsequent years, and
- Less than three years and 75 days have passed since the effective date of the election (unless certain additional conditions are met).

Also, if a late election is made by attaching Form 2553 to the corporation's Form 1120-S, the corporation must enter the following verbiage in the top margin of the first page of Form 1120-S:

"INCLUDES LATE ELECTION FILED PURSUANT TO REV. PROC. 2013-30."

Form 2553 can also be filed separately. If an entity does not qualify for relief under these guidelines, it may request relief through a private letter ruling.[132]

[132] Private letter rulings (PLRs) are written decisions by the Internal Revenue Service (IRS) in response to taxpayer requests for guidance. A private letter ruling is not free. The fee for obtaining a private letter ruling is $10,000 or more. We cover PLRs in more detail in Part 3, *Representation.*

Care should be exercised to ensure that the IRS receives the election. The IRS service center will notify the corporation if its election is accepted and when it will take effect. The corporation will also be notified if its S-election isn't accepted. The corporation should generally receive a determination within 60 days after it has filed Form 2553.

S Corporation Requirements

The main requirements for S corporation status are:

- It must be a domestic corporation.
- It cannot have more than 100 shareholders.
- Shareholders generally must be U.S. citizens or U.S. residents, (if individuals), or certain kinds of trusts, banks, estates,[133] or certain tax-exempt corporations. Corporate shareholders and partnerships are generally excluded. However, certain tax-exempt corporations, including 501(c)(3) corporations, may be S corporation shareholders. In contrast, an S corporation is allowed to own a partnership interest or own stock in a C corporation.
- Nonresident aliens cannot be direct shareholders in an S corporation.[134]
- A business must meet the definition of a small business corporation, per IRC section 1361.
- An S corporation can only have one class of stock, but that stock can have differences in voting rights. The difference in voting rights allows one group of shareholders to retain voting control, while allowing other shareholders to benefit from corporate earnings. However, all the stock of an S corporation must possess identical rights to distribution and liquidation proceeds.
- Profits and losses must be allocated to shareholders in proportion to each one's interest in the business.
- **All shareholders** of an S corporation must give **consent** for the S election.

Study Note: An S corporation must generally be owned *only* by individuals, trusts, or estates. S Corporations cannot be owned by another S corporation, a C corporation, or a partnership. Please note that an S corporation is allowed to have another S corporation as a wholly-owned subsidiary; this is called a qualified Subchapter S subsidiary, also referred to as "QSSS" or "Q-Sub." For example, if one S corporation acquires another S corporation, the acquired S corporation can be treated as a subsidiary by filing a proper election using Form 8869. The acquired S corporation is called the "subsidiary," while the purchasing corporation is called the "parent" corporation. If a proper Q-Sub election is *not filed,* then the acquired corporation will be treated as a C corporation for tax purposes.

Example: A husband and wife own 90% of an S corporation, and their son owns the remaining 10% of the stock. The son announces his marriage to a nonresident alien, and he promptly gives her one-half of his stock. The S corporation's status is revoked on the date of the stock transfer, or "disqualifying event," because a nonresident alien cannot hold stock ownership in an S corporation directly.

---

[133] Estates that qualify as shareholders include individuals' bankruptcy estates (Sec. 1361(c)(3)).

[134] The IRS generally prohibits nonresident aliens from being shareholders of S Corporations. However, nonresident aliens can now be *indirect* S corporation shareholders, but only through an ESBT, an electing small business trust. Nonresident aliens still cannot hold S corporation shares directly.

For the 100-shareholder limit, related persons can be considered one shareholder. Spouses are automatically treated as a single shareholder. A family, defined as a group of individuals descended from a common ancestor, plus spouses and former spouses of either the common ancestor or anyone lineally descended from that person, is considered a single shareholder as long as any family member elects such treatment.

When a shareholder dies, the deceased shareholder's spouse and the estate are still considered one shareholder for the shareholder limit.

However, a husband and wife cannot be considered a single shareholder if they divorce, or if the marriage is dissolved for any other reason than death. Therefore, a shareholder's divorce can potentially increase the number of shareholders to a number in excess of the 100-shareholder limit. If an S corporation fails to meet this restriction, the S election is considered terminated, and the S corporation ceases to be an S corporation and is instead taxed as a C corporation. The following entities cannot elect S corporation status:

- A bank or thrift institution that uses the reserve method of accounting for bad debts
- An insurance company
- A domestic international sales corporation (DISC)
- Any foreign entity

Filing Requirements for S Corporations

An S corporation files its tax return on Form 1120-S. Allocated amounts of income, deductions, and credits pass through to individual shareholders and are reported on Schedule K-1. The return must be signed and dated by an authorized corporate officer or, in certain instances, by a fiduciary, such as a receiver, trustee, or assignee, on behalf of the corporation.

An S corporation is always required to file a tax return, regardless of income or loss. The filing requirement ends only when the corporation is dissolved. In 2020, the IRS mandates electronic filing for S corporations with $10 million or more in assets that file 100 or more returns of *any* type (Forms W-2, Forms 1099, Schedules K-1) per year.

The tax return is due on the fifteenth day of the third month following the tax year-end. For a calendar-year S corporation, the tax return is due March 15. A corporation that has dissolved must generally file by the fifteenth day of the third month after the date it dissolved.

A six-month extension of time to file can be requested using Form 7004, *Automatic Extension of Time to File Certain Business Income Tax, Information, and Other Returns*. It must be filed with the IRS by the original due date to be effective.

Shareholders of an S corporation are potentially required to pay estimated taxes in connection with their own returns for their share of income derived from the S corporation.

In some rare situations, S corporations are required to pay corporate-level income tax on their earnings (covered later in this chapter). If an S corporation does owe income taxes, the S corporation is required to pay estimated taxes if the amount owed is $500 or more for the year.

Required Tax Year

Unlike a C corporation, an S corporation must have IRS permission to use a fiscal year. In general, S corporations must operate on a calendar year. An S corporation must use one of the following accounting periods:

- **A calendar year** (Jan 1-Dec 31)
- **A natural business year**: a "natural business year" is a 12-month fiscal year ending at a low point of a business's activities. For example, a ski resort may have a natural business year that ends after the close of the peak snowing season.
- **An "ownership" tax year:** the tax year that coincides with greater than 50% ownership of the corporation. Since most of the time, the shareholders of an S corporation are individual persons (rather than entities), then the S corporation must generally follow the calendar year.
- A fiscal year duly elected and approved by the IRS under section 444 (very rare).
- A 52-53 week year that ends with reference to any year listed above.

An S corporation may always use a calendar year, or any other tax year for which it establishes a *bona fide* business purpose. A new S corporation must use Form 2553, *Election by a Small Business Corporation*, to elect a tax year. An existing S corporation that wishes to change its existing tax year may use Form 1128, *Application to Adopt, Change, or Retain a Tax Year*. However, Form 8716, *Election to Have a Tax Year Other Than a Required Tax Year*, is used to apply for a tax year change under section 444.

S Corporation Income and Expenses

As with a partnership, all the income of an S corporation must be allocated to the shareholders, even if it is not distributed. Income, gains, losses, deductions, and credits are allocated to each shareholder on a pro-rata basis, according to the number of shares of stock held by the shareholder on each day of the corporation's tax year, and retain their character when they are passed through.

The shareholder then reports the items on his tax return. Some of the items that pass through to shareholders on a pro-rata basis and retain their character must be separately stated on an S corporation's tax return. These include:

- Net income or loss from rental real estate activity (rental income)
- Portfolio income or loss that includes:
    - Interest income
    - Dividend income
    - Royalty income
- Capital gains or losses
- Section 1231 gain or loss
- Charitable contributions
- Section 179 expense deduction
- Foreign taxes paid or accrued
- Any business credits,

- Investment interest expense
- Tax preference and adjustment items needed to figure a shareholder's AMT
- Nonbusiness bad debts

Unlike a C corporation, an S corporation is not eligible for a dividends-received deduction.

Example: Diamond Distributors, Inc. is an S corporation with a single shareholder named Noah. In 2020, Diamond Distributors has $100,000 of gross receipts; $40,000 wage expense to Noah, its shareholder; $15,000 of charitable contributions; $10,000 of rental losses; and $8,000 of capital gains. Its ordinary business income is $60,000 ($100,000 gross receipts minus $40,000 wages). The other items are all separately stated on Form 1120-S and are not used to determine the corporation's ordinary income or loss.

S Corporation Basis

To compute basis in the stock of an S corporation, a shareholder starts, just as for a C corporation, with his initial capital contribution or the initial cost of the stock purchased. However, his basis may vary based on how the stock was acquired (by purchase, gift, or inheritance). In general, a shareholder's basis in S corporation stock is determined as follows:

How Acquired	How Stock Basis is Determined
Stock purchase	If the S corporation shares were purchased outright, the initial basis is the cost of the shares.
S corporation capitalized	If the shares were received when the S corporation was formed under IRC §351, the basis in the stock is equal to cash invested and/or the basis of property transferred to the corporation, increased by any gain recognized on the transfer, and decreased by any boot received from the corporation (IRC §358).
Prior C corporation	The initial basis in S corporation stock is the basis in the C corporation stock at the time of conversion.
Gift	The recipient's basis in shares received by gift is generally the donor's basis (IRC §1015). Suspended passive activity losses can increase the basis of a gift (IRC §469).
Inheritance	The basis of inherited stock is its fair market value at the date of the former holder's death or, if elected, the alternate valuation date (IRC §1014).
Services rendered	Basis in stock received in exchange for services is measured by the stock's fair market value, rather than by the value of the services (Treas. Reg. §1.61-2).

Both the taxability of a distribution and the deductibility of a loss, are dependent on a shareholder's stock basis, and normally basis is adjusted annually, on the last day of the S corporation year, in the following order:

- *Increased* for income items and excess depletion
- *Decreased* for distributions
- *Decreased* for nondeductible, noncapital expenses
- *Decreased* for items of loss and deductions

S corporation shareholders must pay taxes on their share of the corporation's current year income, regardless of whether the amounts are distributed. The shareholder's Schedule K-1 reflects the income, loss, and deductions that are allocated to him, but does not state the taxable amount of a distribution. The taxable amount of each distribution is contingent upon a shareholder's stock basis, and it is the shareholder's responsibility to track his individual basis.

Distributions from an S corporation must be paid to all shareholders on the same date as pro-rata distributions based on the shareholders' individual ownership percentages.

S corporation distributions are generally not treated as dividends and not subject to income tax, except in cases where a corporation has accumulated E&P from years before it elected to become an S corporation.

Distributions from an S corporation with no accumulated earnings and profits are considered a return of capital and reduce the shareholder's basis in the stock of the corporation. Distributions that exceed the shareholder's adjusted stock basis are treated as capital gains and must be reported by the shareholder on Schedule D.

Example: Madeline is the sole shareholder of an S corporation. Her basis as of January 1, 2020, is $25,000. She receives a distribution of $28,000 on December 31, 2020, which reduces her shareholder basis to zero. She must report the excess $3,000 distribution as a capital gain.

The amount of an S corporation distribution is equal to the sum of cash and the fair market value of the property received by a shareholder. An S corporation can distribute property (as well as cash) to its shareholders. However, if an S corporation distributes *appreciated property*, the distribution is treated as a sale to the shareholder.

To the extent the FMV of the property exceeds the corporation's adjusted basis, the corporation would recognize gain. The gain passes through to the shareholders and increases the basis of their stock. No loss is recognized if the FMV of the distributed property is less than the corporation's basis. S corporation shareholders are required to compute both stock basis and debt basis. A shareholder's basis in S corporation stock can never be reduced below zero.

The amount of loss that is deductible on a shareholder's tax return is limited to the shareholder's at-risk basis, and is applied in the following order:

- Cash and the adjusted basis of property that the shareholder contributed to the S corporation, subject to annual adjustments as described above (adjusted stock basis), and
- Any loans the shareholder makes to the corporation or any amounts that are borrowed for use by the S corporation for which the shareholder is directly liable (debt basis).

If a shareholder has S corporation losses and deductions in excess of his adjusted stock basis and those losses and deductions are claimed based on debt basis, the debt basis of the shareholder will be reduced by the claimed losses and deductions. If an S corporation repays reduced basis debt to the shareholder, part or all of the repayment is taxable to the shareholder. The basis adjustment rules under IRC §1367 are similar to the partnership rules.

However, while a *partner* has a unitary basis in his partnership interest, the adjustments to the basis of stock of an S corporation are applied on a separate share basis. The following additional rules apply:

- Losses and deductions not allowable in the current year due to basis limitations are suspended. However, if nondeductible expenses exceed basis, they do not get carried forward.
- Suspended losses and deductions retain their character in subsequent years. They are carried forward indefinitely until basis is increased in subsequent years or until the shareholder permanently disposes of the stock.
- If stock is sold, suspended losses are lost. The sales price does not have an impact on the stock basis. A stock basis computation should be reviewed in the year stock is sold or disposed of.
- If the current year has different types of losses and deductions that exceed the shareholder's basis, the allowable losses and deductions must be allocated pro-rata based on the size of the particular loss and deduction items.
- In determining current year allowable losses, current year loss and deduction items are combined with the suspended losses and deductions carried over from the prior year, though the current year and suspended items should be separately stated.
- A shareholder only has debt basis to the extent he has personally lent money to the S corporation. A loan guarantee does not create debt basis.
- Part or all of the repayment of a reduced basis debt is taxable to the shareholder.

If an S corporation engages in a rental activity or has a shareholder who does not materially participate in S corporation activities, the passive activity loss rules apply to the individual shareholders. If the passive activity loss rules apply, the shareholders' at-risk amounts must be reduced by the full amounts allowable as current deductions. In contrast to the treatment applicable for a partnership, cancellation of debt income is applied at the entity level for corporations, including S corporations. The debtor is required to reduce specified tax attributes, including loss and credit carryforwards and the basis of assets.

Limited Taxation of S Corporations

S corporations generally are not subject to taxation since they are primarily pass-through entities. However, in certain cases, S corporations are subject to taxes. A subchapter S corporation may have to pay income tax due to:

1. **Excess net passive investment income**
2. **Built-in gains**
3. **Investment credit recapture**
4. **LIFO recapture**

Note: Except for the investment credit recapture provision, these taxes normally only apply to corporations which were once C corporations, and then converted to S corporations at a later date. If the corporation has always been an S corporation since its inception, these taxes generally will not apply.

None of these taxes are deductible as business expenses by the S corporation (except for the portion of any built-in gains tax allocable to ordinary income). An S corporation may also be responsible for other taxes, such as:

- Payroll taxes, (if it has employees),
- Excise taxes, (including excise taxes on: diesel fuel and gasoline, highway usage, indoor tanning, and wagering activities),
- Franchise taxes payable to state and local governments, and
- Penalties, such as late filing penalties.

Example: Bronze Beauty, Inc. is an indoor tanning salon organized as an S corporation. Bronze Beauty has two equal shareholders, Penny and Marjorie, who work full-time in the business. Although Bronze Beauty does not pay income tax on its earnings, it is required to pay payroll taxes on the wages paid to Penny and Marjorie. As an indoor tanning service provider, Bronze Beauty is also subject to the indoor tanning services excise tax. The company must file and pay quarterly excise taxes on Form 720, *Quarterly Federal Excise Tax Return*.

Excess Net Passive Income Tax

An S corporation that had been a C corporation previously and had accumulated E&P during that period may have to pay tax at the corporate level on excess net passive income (ENPI) if its passive investment income exceeds 25% of its gross receipts. The purpose of this requirement is to discourage a corporation with accumulated earnings and profits (E&P) from functioning as a holding company and gaining favorable tax treatment as an S corporation.

For this purpose, passive investment income includes interest, dividends, rents, and royalties. If income is generated in the ordinary course of business, it is non-passive, or active, income. The tax rate on excess net passive income is 21% (the highest corporate rate) and is applied against the lesser of:

- Excess net passive income (ENPI), or
- Taxable income figured as though the corporation were a C corporation.

If the corporation has accumulated E&P at the end of the tax year and has ENPI in excess of 25% of its gross receipts for three consecutive taxable years, the S election is terminated as of the beginning of the fourth year.

Example: Mercury Auto Parts, Inc. is an S corporation with accumulated E&P from earlier years when it was a C corporation. In 2020, Mercury Auto has gross receipts of $80,000, comprised as follows:

- Rental income from a residential rental: $25,000
- Interest income: $10,000
- Additional gross receipts from business operations: $45,000

Mercury's passive investment income for the year is $35,000, or 44% of its gross receipts. As this exceeds the 25% threshold, Mercury may be subject to the 21% excess net passive income tax on the lesser of its excess net passive income or its taxable income (calculated as if it were a C corporation).

Example: Laird Corporation, Inc. was a C Corporation in 2017. The company converted to an S corporation in 2018. For 2018, 2019, and 2020, Laird Corporation, a calendar-year S corporation, earned passive investment income in excess of 25% of its gross receipts. If Laird Corporation has accumulated E&P from earlier years in which it was a C corporation, its S election would be terminated as of January 1, 2021, and the corporation would be taxed as a C corporation as of January 1, 2021 (the beginning of the fourth year that it has ENPI in excess of 25% of its gross receipts).

Built-in Gains (BIG) Tax

When a C corporation elects to be taxed as an S corporation and has appreciated assets at that time, the appreciated gain in those assets can be taxed to the S corporation. These "unrealized" gains are called built-in gains. When these assets are later sold, the S corporation is forced to pay tax on the gains at the corporate tax rate of 21% in 2020.

This is why this tax is also referred to as the "BIG Tax." However, if the S corporation holds the assets long enough after the corporation has elected S-status, then the built-in gains tax does not apply. Instead, the gains would pass through to the shareholder and be taxed at the shareholder's normal capital gains rate. The built-in gains (BIG) tax *only applies* to the following S corporations:

- An S corporation that was a C corporation before it elected to be an S corporation.
- An S corporation that acquired an asset with a basis determined by reference to its basis (or the basis of any other property) in the hands of a C corporation (a transferred-basis acquisition).

The S corporation pays tax on the recognized built-in gain at the highest corporate rate. The tax is reported on Form 1120-S and is a deduction for the shareholders. The built-in gains tax applies only affects property dispositions during the five-year period beginning:

- On the first day of the first tax year in which the corporation is an S corporation, for an asset held when the S corporation was a C corporation, or
- On the date the asset was acquired by the S corporation, for an asset with a basis determined by reference to its basis in the hands of a C corporation.

Example: Exclusive Holdings, Inc. is a calendar-year C Corporation, and has been for five years. On May 1, 2020, Exclusive Holdings elects S-Corporation status. In the same year, on December 15, 2020, the corporation sells a plot of land that it had held as an investment for several years. The land had appreciated in value, and Exclusive Holdings recognizes a $10,000 long-term capital gain on the sale of the land. The entire capital gain is subject to tax, so there will be a $2,100 built-in gains tax ($10,000 gain X 21% BIG tax). If Exclusive Holdings had waited at least five more years to sell the land, then there would not have been any built-in gains tax applied to the sale.

Investment Credit Recapture

Business credit recapture is generally the responsibility of the entity that claims the credit. If a company is an S corporation when the credit originates, the credit passes through to the shareholders and they must report any subsequent recapture on Form 4255, *Recapture of*

Investment Credit. However, if a C corporation claims the general business credit and then converts to S status at a later date, the S corporation itself may be responsible for the recapture.

An example of when this might occur is if a company disposes of an asset that the company received an investment tax credit for, and then the corporation may have to forfeit part of the investment credit that it received in an earlier year. The Investment Credit is subject to recapture if the applicable property is disposed of within five years after the property is placed in service.

Example: In 2019, Construction Restoration, Inc. was a C corporation. In that same year, the company earned a $100,000 rehabilitation credit by restoring a certified historic structure. Construction Restoration used $60,000 of the rehabilitation credit to offset income tax in 2019 and carried forward $40,000 to offset tax in future years. On February 1, 2020, Construction Restoration sold the historic structure for a significant profit, triggering a credit recapture. On April 1, 2020, Construction Restoration elects to become an S corporation. The company must file Form 4255, *Recapture of Investment Credit*, to compute the recapture of the credit.

LIFO Recapture Tax

A corporation that accounts for inventory using the last in, first out (LIFO) method is subject to a LIFO recapture tax in its final year as a C corporation after making an S corporation election.

This tax is intended to address built-in gains in inventory that might not otherwise be recognized. The taxable LIFO recapture amount is the amount by which the amount of inventory assets calculated under the first in, first out (FIFO) method exceeds the amount under the LIFO method. If the LIFO value is higher than the FIFO value, no negative adjustment is allowed.

Inventory assets include stock in trade of the corporation, or other property of a kind that would properly be included in the inventory of the corporation if on hand at the close of the taxable year.

The LIFO recapture tax is paid in four equal installments, beginning on the due date of the final C corporation return. The three subsequent installments are payable on the due dates of the first three S corporation returns.

The Accumulated Adjustments Account (AAA)

If an existing C corporation elects to become an S corporation, it may have an accumulated adjustments account (AAA). The AAA is a corporate account that does not relate to individual shareholders. The S corporation maintains the account to track undistributed income that has been taxed during the period its S-election is in effect.

S corporations with accumulated E&P must maintain the AAA to determine the tax effect of distributions during S years and, if applicable, during the period after termination of an S election. It is not mandatory to track AAA if the S corporation does not have prior year C corporation E&P. Nevertheless, if an S corporation without accumulated E&P engages in certain transactions where an AAA account is required, such as a merger into an S corporation with accumulated E&P, the S corporation must be able to calculate its AAA at the time of the merger. Therefore, it is recommended that the AAA be maintained by all S corporations. The AAA may have a negative balance at year's end.

The ordering rules for distributions from an S corporation with accumulated E&P are as follows:

- First, from the AAA, tax-free to the shareholders and a reduction of each shareholder's basis.
- Second, from E&P, and taxable as dividends.
- Third, if applicable, from the corporation's Other Adjustments Account (OAA), which includes accumulated tax-exempt interest income that has not been distributed previously, and reduces basis in the stock.
- Additional distributions are considered a return of capital, up to the amount of each shareholder's basis in his stock.
- Distributions in excess of a shareholder's basis in his stock are considered capital gains from the sale of the property.

Note: An S corporation will *only* have accumulated E&P or an AAA if it was *previously* a C corporation (or it acquired the assets of another C corporation in a Section 351 transaction). An S corporation distribution from E&P is treated as a dividend.

Reasonable Compensation

An S corporation may wish to pay little or no salary or wages to employees or officers who are also shareholders, instead choosing to issue distributions of corporate profits instead. S corporation distributions are subject only to regular income tax. Unlike wages, distributions are not subject to withholding or payroll taxes.

However, the IRS wants companies to pay their fair share of payroll taxes, and therefore requires that S corporation shareholders who are also employees take adequate compensation for any services performed. This means that S corporations must pay employee-shareholders reasonable wages before making distributions.

If an S corporation is not paying "reasonable compensation" to a shareholder-employee, the IRS may reclassify distributions to the shareholder as wages, subject to employment taxes. Therefore, an S corporation will be at risk if it attempts to avoid paying employment taxes by having its officers treat their compensation as cash distributions, payments of personal expenses, or loans rather than as wages.

There are no specific guidelines in the IRC or in IRS regulations for what is considered "reasonable compensation." Factors considered by the courts in determining reasonable compensation for employees or officers of an S corporation include:

- Training and experience
- Duties and responsibilities
- Time and effort devoted to the business
- Dividend history
- Payments to non-shareholder employees
- Timing and manner of paying bonuses to key people
- Amounts that comparable businesses pay for similar services
- Compensation agreements
- The use of a formula to determine compensation

The regulations provide an exception for an officer of a corporation who does not perform any services or performs only minor services and receives no compensation. Such an officer would not be considered an employee for tax purposes.

Example: Lawrence was the sole shareholder and employee of an S corporation. He was an experienced accountant with a master's degree in business administration. His firm had annual revenues of $1.5 million. In 2020, Lawrence paid himself an annual salary of $24,000 and received distributions from the firm of $400,000. The IRS concluded Lawrence was deliberately paying himself a low salary to avoid employment taxes and required that $150,000 of the distributions be reclassified as salary. Additional employment taxes, penalties, and interest were assessed on the reclassified payments.

199A Qualified Business Income Deduction for S Corporations

With regards to the Section 199A Qualified Business Income deduction, "reasonable compensation" wages received by a shareholder-employee from an S corporation are excluded from the definition of "qualified business income," or QBI.[135]

The "reasonable compensation" rule does not extend to partners in a partnership (as partners do not receive wages from a partnership), although a similar restriction applies to guaranteed payments made to a partner in a partnership.

Employee-shareholders of S corporations are required to pay themselves reasonable wages. As stated above, the wages that are paid to an employee-shareholder are not included in the calculation of QBI.

Example: Judson is the sole shareholder of Spectrum Marketing, Inc., an S corporation. The company has $90,000 in ordinary income from business operations in 2020, *prior* to the payment of reasonable wages to Judson. Judson pays himself a reasonable salary of $50,000 leaving $40,000 of K-1 ordinary income, which qualifies for the QBI deduction. Judson is single, and he is below the pre-QBI taxable income limitation threshold for his filing status. Judson's tentative QBI deduction is 20% of QBI ($40,000), or $8,000.

Like other operating expenses, reasonable wages paid to an employee-shareholder is included in the QBI calculation of the corporation.

Health Insurance Premiums for Shareholders

Fringe benefits paid to employees who are *not* shareholders (or who have ownership of less than 2%) are generally deductible by the S corporation as a regular business expense. These benefits are also tax-free to the employees.

However, for shareholder-employees who have at least 2% ownership or more, health insurance premiums paid on their behalf are deductible by the S corporation as fringe benefits and are reportable as wages for income tax withholding purposes on the shareholder-employees' Forms W-2. The S corporation can exclude these health benefits from the wages subject to Social Security, Medicare, and FUTA taxes.

---

[135] IRC section 199A(c)(4)(A) states: "Qualified Business Income" shall not include reasonable compensation paid to the taxpayer by any qualified trade or business of the taxpayer for services rendered with respect to the trade or business.

A 2% shareholder-employee is eligible for an AGI deduction for amounts paid during the year for health insurance premiums if the health insurance coverage is established by the S corporation. If the coverage plan is in the name of the shareholder rather than the name of the S corporation, the coverage can still be considered to be established by the S corporation if:

- The S corporation either paid or reimbursed the shareholder for the premiums, and
- It reported the premium payment as wages on the shareholder's Form W-2.

Neither Schedule K-1 (Form 1120-S) nor Form 1099 can be used as an alternative to Form W-2 to report this additional compensation.

Example: Pulsar Consulting, Inc., an S corporation, provides health insurance coverage to its two owner-shareholders, Tucker and Cesar, as well as the health insurance premiums for their only employee, Dinah, who is a full-time secretary for the company. Pulsar Consulting paid $9,000 of health insurance premiums for Tucker and Caesar, and $3,900 for health insurance premiums for Dinah. The corporation treats the shareholders as having received the health insurance as additional compensation and reports the insurance premiums as Form W-2 wages. Dinah is not an owner/shareholder of the company, so her health insurance premiums are treated as a tax-free fringe benefit, and merely deducted as a business expense.

An S corporation cannot take a deduction for amounts incurred during periods in which the shareholder-employee is eligible to participate in any subsidized health plan maintained by another employer (or the spouse's employer).

Example: Franklin is the sole owner-shareholder in an S corporation. He pays the health insurance premiums for himself and his wife, Chrissy. Chrissy works full-time for an employer who has offered to provide family health coverage. Franklin and his wife declined the coverage because they did not want to switch doctors. Because Franklin had the option to participate in an employer plan through Chrissy's job, the health insurance premiums paid on his behalf by his S corporation are not deductible.

Termination of a Shareholder's Interest

If a shareholder sells or disposes of his stock interest in an S corporation, it is treated in the same manner as the sale of stock in a C corporation. The shareholder reports the sale of the stock on Schedule D. The gain or loss that is recognized by the shareholder is the difference between the shareholder's basis and the sale price of the stock.

If a shareholder in an S corporation terminates his interest in a corporation during the tax year, the corporation, with the consent of all affected shareholders (including those whose interest is terminated), may elect to allocate income and expenses as if the corporation's tax year consisted of *two separate* short tax years, the first of which ends on the date of the shareholder's termination.

To make this election, the corporation must attach a statement to a timely filed original or amended Form 1120-S for the tax year for which the election is made and state that it is electing to treat the tax year as if it consisted of two separate tax years. The statement must also explain how the shareholder's entire interest was terminated (e.g., sale or gift), and state that the corporation and each affected shareholder consented to the election.

A single statement may be filed for all terminating elections made for the tax year. If this election is made, **"SECTION 1377 (a)(2) ELECTION MADE"** should be written at the top of each affected shareholder's Schedule K-1.

Example: Sedgwick Realty, Inc. is an S corporation that operates on a calendar-year basis. Sedgewick Realty has two equal shareholders, Eldon and Kristof. In 2020, Sedgewick Realty has a $10,000 net operating loss for the first six months of the year (from January 1-June 30). On July 1, 2020, Eldon sells his entire stock interest in Sedgewick Realty to Wendy, an unrelated person. There are no more items of income or loss for the rest of the year. Sedgewick Realty makes a Section 1377(a)(2) election on its 2020 tax return. The $10,000 net operating loss would be allocated to the short taxable year ending June 30 (in other words, the first part of the year, when Eldon and Kristof were still shareholders). Eldon and Kristof would each be entitled to $5,000 of the NOL, which would be reported on their respective Schedules K-1. Since Sedgewick had no other activity for the rest of the year, Wendy would not have any income or loss allocated to her.

Termination or Revocation of an S Election

Once the S election is made, it stays in effect until terminated. In addition to the ways already discussed, the election will terminate automatically in any of the following cases:

- The corporation no longer qualifies as a small business corporation.[136]
- For each of three consecutive tax years, the corporation
    - Has accumulated earnings and profits,[137] and
    - Derives more than 25% of its gross receipts from passive investment income.
- The corporation creates a second class of stock (such as preferred stock and common stock).
- The shareholders willingly revoke the S election.

Absent an automatic termination due to failure to meet the requirements of its S status; an S election can be revoked only with the consent of the majority shareholders (those holding more than 50% of the corporation's stock, including nonvoting stock). The corporation must file a statement of revocation with the IRS that is signed by every shareholder who consents.

There is no specific form to revoke the S election. The corporation must submit a revocation statement to the IRS service center where it files its annual return. The statement must be signed by shareholders owning more than 50% of the stock, including nonvoting stock.

A shareholder revocation may specify an effective revocation date that is on or after the day the revocation is filed. If no date is specified and the revocation is made on or before the fifteenth day of the third month of that tax year, the revocation is effective at the start of a tax year. If no date is specified and the revocation is made after the fifteenth day of the third month of the tax

136 This termination of an election is effective as of the day the corporation no longer meets the definition of a small business corporation. A statement notifying the IRS of the termination and the date it occurred is attached to Form 1120-S for the final year of the S corporation.

137 This rule applies only to S corporations that were *previously* C corporations. An S corporation cannot accumulate earnings and profits as a C corporation can. However, it is possible for a C corporation to elect S corporation status and still have accumulated earnings and profits from prior years, at the time of the election.

year, the revocation is effective at the start of the next tax year. A revocation may be rescinded before it takes effect.

When an S election is terminated, two short tax years are created for the corporation. Income and loss must be allocated on a pro-rata basis between the period the corporation operated as an S corporation and the period as a C corporation that was created when the S election was terminated. The entity must file Form 1120-S for the S corporation's short year by the due date (including extensions) of the C corporation's short year return.

Example: Adventure Capitalist, Inc. is a calendar-year S corporation with three equal shareholders, Christopher, Elijah, and Meghan. Elijah and Meghan want to revoke the S election in order to become a C corporation, so they can broaden their investor base to include foreign shareholders. Christopher does not want to revoke the election. Together, Elijah and Meghan own more than 50% of the corporation's stock (they each own a third). Therefore, they can revoke the S election without Christopher's consent. Elijah and Meghan prepare and sign a formal revocation statement and mail it into the IRS, and their status as an S corporation will be revoked. After the revocation, the corporation will be treated as a C corporation.

Example: On May 1, 2020, Biomedical Corporation, a calendar-year S corporation, exceeded 100 shareholders. This will create two short tax years—one for the S corporation and one for the C corporation. Biomedical must file a Form 1120-S and a Form 1120. The due date for the 1120-S return, for the short year ending April 30, 2020, is July 15, 2020 (this would be the tax return for the S corporation that has terminated). The due date for the Form 1120 return, for the short year beginning May 1, 2020, and ending December 31, 2020, will be April 15, 2021 (this would be the tax return for the C corporation that is created upon the termination of the S corporation).

Inadvertent Terminations

Sometimes a corporation will inadvertently terminate its election. For an "inadvertent termination," a corporation's S-election terminates effective on the date that the company commits the act that triggers the ineligibility.

An S corporation election can be inadvertently terminated in several ways. For example, when a married couple divorces, and the two ex-spouses cause the shareholder limit to exceed 100. The date of the event would be the "termination date." Another common terminating event is when an S corporation makes disproportionate distributions—for example, distributing cash to some shareholders, but not to others. This could potentially be viewed as creating a second class of stock and terminating S status.

If the IRS deems that a revocation was inadvertent (that the shareholders did not mean to revoke their S election or that the revocation was accidental), the corporation may be allowed to correct the error and retain its S election status.

A terminating event will be considered inadvertent if the event was not within the control of the corporation, and the shareholders did not plan to terminate the election. Further, all of the following must occur:

- The S election must have involuntarily terminated either because:
    - The corporation no longer qualified as a small business corporation, or

    - It had accumulated earnings and profits from past C corporation activities.
- The IRS must agree that the termination was inadvertent.
- The corporation must take reasonable and immediate steps to correct the issue.
- The shareholders and the corporation must agree to any adjustments proposed by the IRS.
- The corporation must request a private letter ruling from the IRS for any inadvertent termination relief.

Example: Royal Consulting Inc., a calendar-year S corporation, inadvertently terminates its S status during the year. The S corporation shareholders immediately correct the problem and request a private letter ruling for termination relief. The IRS approves a request to have the termination status be reversed under the grounds that it was inadvertent. Therefore, the S corporation's "S status" is considered to have been continuously in effect, and no termination is deemed to have occurred. Only a single S corporation tax return will need to be filed for the tax year 2020.

Note: If the status of an S corporation is terminated, either because the shareholders elect to become a C corporation or because a terminating event has occurred, the S corporation normally cannot elect to become an S corporation again within the next five years (60 months). However, the IRS may choose to waive the five-year restriction.

Unit 15: Study Questions

(Test yourself and then check the correct answers at the end of this section.)

1. Westland Nursing, Inc. received its corporate charter and was officially formed on November 8, 2020. Westland Nursing would like to make an initial election to become an S corporation, effective from its incorporation date. What is the deadline for the company to file Form 2553?

A. December 31, 2020.
B. January 22, 2021.
C. March 15, 2021.
D. December 31, 2021.

2. First-Force Inc. is an S corporation with four shareholders. The corporation has 10,000 shares outstanding. The shareholders have the following ownership:

Shareholder	**Ownership**
Jordan	4,500 shares
Mai-Lin	2,000 shares
Simon	2,000 shares
Nora	1,500 shares
Total	**10,000 shares**

Nora and Jordan wish to terminate the S election, but Mai-Lin and Simon do not. Which of the following statements is correct?

A. Jordan can elect to terminate the corporation's S status on his own.
B. All of the shareholders must agree to terminate the election.
C. Nora and Jordan have enough stock ownership to terminate the election.
D. At least 75% of the shareholders with active ownership must agree to the termination.

3. Allred Consulting, Inc. is an S corporation with income from many different sources. What is the total amount of the separately stated income items on Allred Consulting's Form 1120-S?

Gross receipts from sales	$700,000
Rental real estate income	$300,000
Interest income	$25,000
Royalty income	$10,000
Section 1231 gain	$20,000

A. $345,000
B. $355,000
C. $700,000
D. $720,000

4. What is the tax rate on excess net passive income?

A. 10%
B. 15%
C. 20%
D. 21%

5. Which of the following will *not* terminate an S corporation's status?

A. The S corporation has 101 unrelated shareholders.
B. The S corporation, for each of three consecutive tax years, has accumulated earnings and profits, and derives more than 25% of its gross receipts from passive investment income.
C. The S corporation creates a second class of stock with different distribution rights.
D. The S corporation earns the majority of its revenue from passive activities for one year.

6. Close family members can be treated as a single shareholder for S corporation purposes. A family member in this instance includes:

A. A nonresident alien spouse.
B. A first cousin.
C. The estate of a shareholder's deceased spouse.
D. An ex-spouse.

7. Which of the following events would cause the immediate termination of an S corporation's status?

A. An S corporation that has an estate as a shareholder.
B. An S corporation that has a nonprofit corporation 501(c)(3) shareholder.
C. An S corporation that issues one share of stock to a C corporation.
D. An S corporation that owns one share of stock in a C corporation.

8. On January 1, 2020, Bodhi purchased 50% of the stock of Rancho Farms Inc., an S corporation, for $100,000, and also loaned the corporation $20,000. He did not own any stock prior to the January 1 stock acquisition. At the end of the year, Rancho Farms Inc. incurred an ordinary business loss of $180,000 from business operations. How much of the loss can Bodhi deduct on his personal income tax return for 2020?

A. $20,000
B. $90,000
C. $120,000
D. $180,000

9. A C corporation may not elect to become an S corporation if:

A. It has an estate as a shareholder.
B. It has voting and nonvoting stock.
C. It has two classes of stock.
D. It has common stock.

10. Silver Oak Architects, Inc. is an existing calendar-year C corporation that wishes to elect S corporation status for 2020. What is the latest date that Silver Oak Architects can elect S status for 2020?

A. March 15, 2020.
B. April 15, 2020.
C. December 31, 2020.
D. March 15, 2021.

11. In which circumstance is a C corporation unable to elect to become an S corporation?

A. The C corporation has 50 shareholders.
B. The C corporation is incorporated in Canada, operates in the U.S.
C. The C corporation has common stock with voting and nonvoting rights.
D. The C corporation is on a fiscal year with a legitimate business purpose.

12. An S corporation, regardless of when it became an S corporation, must use a "permitted" tax year. A permitted tax year is any of the following except:

A. The calendar year.
B. A tax year properly elected under section 444.
C. A fiscal tax year with a legitimate business purpose.
D. A short tax year.

13. Omar and Evelyn are shareholders in Centex Inc., an S corporation that has been in existence for three years. Omar owns 65% of the corporate stock, and Evelyn owns the remainder. Omar decides that he wants to convert Centex, Inc. to a C corporation. Which of the following statements is correct regarding the conversion?

A. Omar and Evelyn must both consent to the conversion to the C corporation.
B. The election to become a C corporation is taken on Form 1120-S.
C. Omar may choose to convert to a C corporation because he owns more than 50% of the stock. He does not need Evelyn's consent.
D. Centex cannot convert to a C corporation, because it must wait five years.

14. S corporations are generally not subject to taxation and are primarily pass-through entities. But in certain cases, S corporations are subject to taxes. Which of the following taxes do not apply to S corporations?

A. Excess net passive investment income tax.
B. Built-in gains tax.
C. Self-employment tax.
D. LIFO recapture tax.

15. On January 1, 2020, Gloria, Kristin, and Nancy are all equal shareholders in Fairview Heights Corporation, a calendar-year C corporation that has been in existence for four years. On February 1, 2020, Gloria sells her entire stock interest in the corporation to an unrelated party, Irving. Irving immediately wants to convert the corporation to an S corporation (retroactively) effective January 1, 2020. Whose consent is required for Fairview Heights to convert to S status?

A. Irving may convert the corporation to an S corporation if Kristin and Nancy consent.
B. Gloria must also consent to the election, along with Kristin and Nancy.
C. Irving may convert the corporation to an S corporation on his own.
D. The corporation cannot convert to S status until it has been in existence for five years.

16. Slate Consulting Inc. is a calendar-year S corporation operating on the accrual basis. The company has the following income items and expenses. What is Slate Consulting's ordinary business income, (not including the separately stated items)?

Gross receipts from business operations	$300,000
Interest income	$25,000
Royalty income	$10,000
Salary paid to a shareholder	($20,000)

A. $35,000
B. $280,000
C. $320,000
D. $345,000

17. Lydia transferred an office building to an S corporation for stock, and immediately after the transfer, she owned 90% of the corporation. She received stock with a fair market value of $155,000 plus a cash distribution of $60,000. The corporation also assumed an existing $30,000 mortgage on the property for which Lydia was personally liable. Her basis in the building was $175,000 immediately before the transfer. What amount of gain must Lydia recognize, if any?

A. $0
B. $30,000
C. $60,000
D. $70,000

Unit 15: Quiz Answers

1. The answer is B. Westland Nursing, Inc. has until January 22, 2021, to file Form 2553 (in order for the election to be considered timely). A newly-formed corporation that wishes to elect S-status must file an election within 2.5 months (75 days) of the date of formation for the election to take effect in the first tax year. In this example, the 2-month period ends January 7, and 15 days after that is January 22. Therefore, to be an S corporation beginning with its short tax year, the business must file Form 2553 during the period that begins November 8, 2020 and ends January 22, 2021. Because the corporation had no prior tax year, an election made before November 8 will not be valid (example modified from the Form 2553 instructions).

2. The answer is C. An S election may be revoked if shareholders holding more than 50% of the stock consent. Since Nora and Jordan together own 60% of the outstanding stock, they can elect to revoke the S election. Once they revoke the election, the S corporation ceases to be an S corporation, and becomes a C corporation.

3. The answer is B. All of the items, except for the gross receipts, must be separately stated on the S corporation's tax return. The answer is figured as follows:

Rental real estate income	$300,000
Interest income	$25,000
Royalty income	$10,000
Section 1231 gain	$20,000
Total separately stated items	**$355,000**

4. The answer is D. Excess net passive income earned by S corporations is taxed at a flat rate of 21%, because this is the flat income tax rate that applies to all corporations after the enactment of the Tax Cuts and Jobs Act.

5. The answer is D. An S corporation will not be terminated if it earns the majority of its revenue from passive activities for **one year.** All of the following actions will terminate an S election:

- When the corporation no longer qualifies as a small business corporation.
- For each of *three consecutive tax years*, the corporation:
- Has accumulated earnings and profits, and
- Derives more than 25% of its gross receipts from passive investment income.
- The S election is willingly revoked by the shareholders.
- If the corporation creates a second class of stock (such as common and preferred stock).

6. The answer is C. Spouses are automatically treated as a single shareholder, and when a shareholder dies, the deceased shareholder's spouse and the estate are still considered one shareholder for the purpose of the shareholder limit. A husband and wife cannot be considered a single shareholder if they divorce, or if the marriage is dissolved for any reason *other than* death. An S corporation cannot have a nonresident alien shareholder, so a nonresident alien spouse would not qualify.

7. The answer is C. An S corporation may own stock in a C corporation, but the same does not hold true in reverse. An S corporation *cannot* have a C corporation as a shareholder. S corporation shareholders must generally be U.S. citizens or U.S. residents, and must be physical entities (persons), so corporate shareholders and partnerships are excluded. Certain estates, trusts, and tax-exempt corporations, including 501(c)(3) corporations, are also permitted to be shareholders.

8. The answer is B. An S corporation shareholder can deduct his share of the corporation's losses only to the extent of his stock and debt basis. Before consideration of Rancho Farms Inc.'s business loss, Bodhi's stock basis and debt basis were $100,000 and $20,000, respectively, (his total is basis $120,000). Bodhi is a 50% shareholder in the company; therefore, he can deduct his entire 50% share of the company's ordinary loss ($180,000 ÷ 2 = **$90,000**). His losses are not limited.

9. The answer is C. A C corporation may not elect S corporation status if it has two classes of stock. A corporation may have both voting and nonvoting stock because they are not considered different classes of stock. Answer "A" is incorrect because an estate of a deceased taxpayer is a permitted shareholder of an S corporation.

10. The answer is A. An eligible corporation must make an S election within two months and 15 days from the *start* of its tax year (or within 2.5 months of its inception). Since Silver Oak Architects is a calendar-year corporation, its tax year begins January 1 and ends on December 31. It must make the election on or before **March 15, 2020**, in order for the election to be effective for 2020. (Note: although there is a procedure for late elections, the late election is not guaranteed—it has to be approved by the IRS).

11. The answer is B. Only domestic U.S. corporations are allowed to elect S status, so a Canadian corporation would not qualify. An S corporation can only have one class of stock, but differences in voting rights are allowed. An S corporation can have a fiscal year if it has a legitimate business purpose for doing so.

12. The answer is D. A short tax year is not considered a "permitted" tax year. A short tax year is only applicable when an S corporation is in its first year, or its S status is terminated.

13. The answer is C. All the shareholders must consent to an S election, but the same does not hold true in reverse. If an S corporation converts to a C corporation, only the consent of *more than* 50% of the shareholders is required. Since Omar owns more than 50% of the outstanding stock in Centex, he can revoke the S corporation's status and convert to a C corporation. He does not need Evelyn's consent to do so.

14. The answer is C. S corporations are not subject to self-employment tax. Self-employment tax applies only to individuals. The S corporation may have to pay tax due to:

- Excess net passive investment income.
- Built-in gains.
- Investment credit recapture.
- LIFO recapture.

15. The answer is B. In order for the election to be made, Gloria must also consent to the election, even though she has sold all of her shares to Irving. All the shareholders who were shareholders during the year must consent to the election. If the S election is made during the corporation's tax year for which it first takes effect, any individual shareholder who holds stock at any time during the part of that year before the election is made must also consent to the election, even though the person may have sold or transferred his stock before the election is made.

16. The answer is B. Slate Consulting's ordinary income is figured as follows: ($300,000 - $20,000 = **$280,000**). Ordinary income would reflect the gross receipts of $300,000 minus the salary expense to the shareholder of $20,000, or $280,000. Interest income and royalty income would be separately stated items on Form 1120-S, and would not be considered in determining ordinary income or loss.

17. The answer is C. Lydia receives a total of $245,000 ($155,000 stock + $60,000 cash + $30,000 debt relief) and has a $70,000 realized gain ($245,000 - $175,000 adjusted basis). As the liability assumed was less than Lydia's adjusted basis in the property and absent any indication the exchange was undertaken with the main purpose of avoiding federal income tax, the debt relief would not be considered in determining her recognized gain. Therefore, the **taxable gain is limited to <u>$60,000</u>** (the amount of the cash she received). In an otherwise nontaxable section 351 exchange, a shareholder might have to recognize gain if she receives money or property other than the corporation's stock. The gain is limited to the total of money, and the FMV of the other property received. If the corporation assumes the shareholder's liabilities, the assumption generally is not treated as if the shareholder received money or other property, unless:

- The liabilities the corporation assumes are more than the shareholder's adjusted basis in the property transferred, in which case gain is recognized up to the difference. However, if the liabilities assumed give rise to a deduction when paid, such as a trade account payable or interest, no gain is recognized.
- There is no good business reason for the corporation to assume the liabilities, or if the main purpose in the exchange is to avoid federal income tax.

Lydia's shareholder's basis in her stock must be reduced by the amount of the liabilities assumed by the corporation.

Unit 16: Farming Business

More Reading:

Publication 225, Farmer's Tax Guide

Farming businesses may be engaged in activities such as crop production, animal production, or forestry and logging. They may include stock, dairy, poultry, fish, fruit, and tree farms, as well as plantations, ranches, timber farms, and orchards. The entity type does not matter; a business will be classified as a "farming business" as long as the business cultivates, operates, or manages a farm (or fishery) for profit. There are many types of activities that qualify as "farms." Some examples include:

- **Agricultural farming:** a farm that cultivates and grows any type of agricultural crops, such as: grains, beans, hemp, cotton, flowers, vegetables, etc.
- **Dairy farming:** a class of farming for long-term production of milk and dairy products.
- **Fish farming (fisheries):** involves raising fish or shellfish commercially, usually for human consumption.
- **Silk farming:** the cultivation of silkworms to produce silk.
- **Fur farming:** a business that breeds and raises fur-bearing animals for their pelts.
- **Apiculture (Beekeeping):** a business that raises bees to collect products that the hive produces (honey, beeswax, etc.)
- **Snail Farming:** This is the business of raising land snails for human consumption.

A farming or fishing business operating as a sole proprietorship reports income and loss on Schedule F, *Profit or Loss from Farming*. A farmer is usually self-employed if he operates his own farm or rents farmland from others to engage in the business of farming. Self-employed farmers and fishermen must also complete Schedule SE.

Alternatively, a farming business may be organized as a partnership or a corporation. It is the nature of the activity that determines whether a business is classified as a "farming" business for tax purposes.

Not Classified as Farming Businesses

Certain associated businesses are not considered farming businesses and instead must file on Schedule C (if a sole proprietorship). Examples include:

- Veterinary businesses.
- Businesses that only supply farm labor or farming equipment.
- Businesses that only sell farm supplies, such as pesticides or herbicides.
- Businesses that are only in the business of breeding, including those that raise or breed dogs, cats, or other household pets.
- Businesses that provide agricultural services, such as soil preparation and fertilization, but do no actual farming of the land.

Not Classified as Farming Income: Certain types of income associated with farming businesses are not classified as farm income. Farm income does not include any of the following:

- Wages received as a farm employee.

- Income received under a contract for grain harvesting with workers and machines furnished by the taxpayer.
- Gains received from the sale of farmland and depreciable farm equipment.
- Gains from the sale of securities, regardless of who owns the securities.
- Passive rental income received from the rental of farmland where the owner of the land does not materially participate.

Farming Rents

If a farmer rents his farmland for someone else to use, the related revenue is generally classified as rental income, not farming income. This also applies to crop shares, when a tenant farmer pays a proportion of crop harvest proceeds to the landowner for the use of his farmland. This special type of rental activity is also commonly called "sharecropping" or "cropping." This passive activity income is reported on Form 4835, *Farm Rental Income and Expenses.*

On the other hand, if a farmer simply rents his pasture or other real property for a flat cash amount without providing services to the tenant, he will report the income as rent on Schedule E. If a farmer *materially participates* in farming operations on the land he owns, the rent is considered farm income and is reported on Schedule F.

Example: Harold is a farmer who owns 200 acres of pastureland in Wyoming. Harold rents out his pasture to someone else who owns cattle. Harold also takes care of the cattle for a fee. Since he is materially participating in the activity, as well as providing services by taking daily care of the livestock, the income is reported on his Schedule F as ordinary income.

Example: Norris also owns pastureland in Wyoming. Norris simply rents the pasture to other farmers for a flat cash amount. He does not provide any services or take care of the livestock in any way. Norris would report the income as rental income on Schedule E (Form 1040). The income would be passive activity income and not subject to self-employment tax.

Example: Anna owns a 90-acre farm in Montana. She generally rents out her land to a tenant farmer and does not do any of the planting herself. In 2020, Anna rents the land to a sharecropper who grows organic beets. Anna's contract with the tenant farmer requires the sharecropper to pay twenty-five percent of the crops harvested. Anna reports her share of the income from the crops on Form 4835, which is attached to her Form 1040. Anna's tenant farmer (the sharecropper) would be required to report *his* income on Schedule F as regular farming income, subject to self-employment tax.

Estimated Taxes for Farmers

Special rules apply to the payment of estimated tax by qualified self-employed farmers and fishermen. If at least two-thirds of the individual's or entity's gross income comes from farming or fishing activities, the following rules apply:

- The farmer does not have to pay estimated tax if he files his return and pays all the tax owed by **March 1**.
- If the farmer must pay estimated tax, he is required to make only one estimated tax payment, called the *required annual payment*, by **January 15.**

Example: Dustin grows wheat and sells his wheat to a local distributor. He files Schedule F to report his income and loss. He does not pay any estimated taxes in 2020. He files his individual tax return on March 1, 2021, paying all his tax owed for the prior tax year. He will not owe an estimated tax penalty, regardless of the amount owned, because of the special rules that apply to farmers regarding estimated taxes.

Example: Janelle is a beekeeper that raises honeybees and collects the honey for sale. She also gathers the beeswax and makes handmade creams and soaps. All of her income comes from her beekeeping activity, so she is a qualified farmer. Janelle doesn't plan to file her tax return until April, so she makes a single annual payment on January 15.

If a farmer does not receive more than two-thirds of his gross income from a qualified farming activity, the taxpayer is not eligible for this special treatment for estimated taxes. This rule also does not apply if the farming business is a C corporation.

Example: Angela grows fresh vegetables that she sells in a popular roadside shop. She is also a partner in a restaurant and receives substantial income from that activity as well. Angela files a Schedule F to report the income from her vegetable farm. She also files Schedule E to report her share of the partnership income from the restaurant activity. Her Schedule F shows $12,000 in net taxable income for the year. Her Schedule K-1 from the partnership shows $45,000 in distributable net income from her restaurant partnership. Even though Angela has a legitimate farming business, less than two-thirds of her income is from farming. So, she would not qualify for the special estimated tax payment provisions. Angela is required to make estimated payments throughout the year, or she will face an estimated tax penalty.

Accounting Methods for Farming

Farmers are allowed to use any accounting method that is available for other business types. In addition, there are a few special accounting methods that are applicable only to farming businesses. Farmers can use the following accounting methods:

- **Cash Method**
- **Accrual Method**
- **Combination (Hybrid) Method** (using two or more of the methods listed)
- **Special Methods, including the Crop Method**: The IRS allows a number of different special methods of accounting that apply to items such as depreciation, farm business expenses, or income. Among these is the crop method, which requires IRS approval and is allowed only for farming businesses. If crops are not harvested and disposed of in the same tax year they are planted, the farmer can capitalize the entire cost of producing the crop, including the expense of seed or young plants, and deduct them in the year income is realized.

In prior years, the accrual method of accounting generally was required when a business maintained an inventory, but small farmers were exempt from the usual requirements. As a result, most small farmers use the cash method. Inventory requirements also do not apply to most commonly grown crops.[138] Consequently, few farming operations are required to adopt the

[138] Generally, growing crops are not required to be included in inventory unless they have a pre-productive period of *more* than two years. Plants with a pre-productive period of less than two years include many common crops such as corn and

accrual method of accounting. However, the following farming businesses are required to use the accrual method of accounting:

- A farming corporation that had gross receipts of more than $26 million in 2020[139]
- A partnership with a corporate partner that exceeds the gross receipts threshold
- A tax shelter (of any size or income)

Example: Sherwood is a self-employed farmer who uses the **accrual** method (not the crop method or the cash method). He keeps his books on a calendar-year basis. Sherwood sells grain on December 3, 2020, but he is not paid until January 5, 2021. He must include the sale on his 2020 tax return. He can also deduct the costs accrued in producing the grain on his 2020 return, regardless of whether or not those costs have been paid.

Example: Theodore is also a self-employed farmer who uses the **cash** method. Theodore sells beef cattle on December 15, 2020, but he is not paid until January 5, 2021. Since Theodore uses the cash method and there was no constructive receipt of the sale proceeds in 2020, Theodore records the sale proceeds in income in 2021, the year he actually receives the payment.

Example: Lanie is a farmer that grows organic blueberries. She uses the cash method of accounting. Lanie requests permission to use the crop method of accounting. The IRS grants her request. Using the crop method, Lanie deducts the entire cost of producing the blueberry crop, including the expense of seed or young plants, in the year she realizes income from the crop.

Farming Inventory

Farm inventory includes all items that are held for sale, purchased for resale, and for use as feed or seed, such as the following:

- Eggs in the process of hatching.
- Harvested farm products held for sale to customers (i.e., such as grain, cotton, flowers, industrial hemp, corn, or tobacco).
- Supplies that become a physical part of an item held for sale, such as; containers, wrappers, or other packaging.
- Any livestock held primarily for sale or purchased for resale.
- Purchased farm products that are being held for seed or feed, such as hay, silage, concentrates, fodder, and pelleted feeds.

Livestock purchases for resale are deductible in the year of sale. Inventory includes the cost of freight charges for transporting the livestock to the farm. If livestock was purchased primarily for draft, breeding, sport, or dairy purposes, the farmer can choose to depreciate it, *or* include the livestock in inventory. All purchased livestock can also be treated as tangible personal property, and are therefore eligible for section 179 or bonus depreciation. Regardless of the method chosen, it must be consistent from year to year.

---

wheat. Plants with a pre-productive period of more than two years include many kinds of fruit and nut trees, and grape vineyards. Note that the Tax Cuts and Jobs Act also includes new provisions on the treatment of inventory, and these provisions apply to farmers too.

[139] These restrictions above do not apply to an S corporation or a business operating a nursery or sod farm, or the raising or harvesting of trees (other than fruit trees and nut trees).

Example: Jose is a qualified farmer. He specifically breeds rodeo cattle, which are primarily used for rodeo events such as team roping and steer wrestling. Jose chooses to depreciate his cattle the same way a business would depreciate equipment. As with other business assets, a farmer can claim depreciation on the purchase cost of their cattle, as long as the animals are held for draft, breeding, sport, or dairy purposes.

Example: Estelle owns a small hog farm. In 2020, Estelle purchases 100 weaned piglets that will be sold in 2021. She does not depreciate the piglets. Instead, she treats the piglets as inventory, because they are being raised to be sold. She deducts the cost of the pigs in 2021 as COGS when the mature hogs are finally sold.

Note: In 2020, a farming business may use the cash method of accounting if the entity's average annual gross receipts for the three preceding tax years is $26 million or less. This includes farming businesses that produce or maintain an inventory.

Farm "inventory" does not include real property, such as farmland or buildings, or depreciable equipment, such as tractors.

If a farming business is required to capitalize and track an inventory, the farmer may use the same inventory methods that are available to other businesses. However, there are two other inventory methods that are unique to farming businesses:

- **Farm-Price Method:** Under the farm-price method, each item, whether raised or purchased, is valued at its market price minus the costs of disposition. The costs of disposition include broker's commissions, freight, hauling to market, and other marketing costs. If a farming business chooses to use the farm-price method, it must use it for the entire inventory, except that livestock can be inventoried under the unit-livestock-price method.
- **Unit-Livestock-Price Method:** The unit-livestock-price method is an easier inventory method that allows farmers to group livestock together, rather than track the costs of each individual animal. A farmer may classify livestock according to type and age and use a unit price for each animal within a class. The unit price must reasonably approximate the costs incurred in producing the animal. If a farming business uses the unit-livestock-price method, it must include all raised livestock in inventory, regardless of whether they are held for sale or for draft, breeding, sport, or dairy purposes. This method accounts only for the costs incurred while raising an animal to maturity. It does not provide for any decrease in the animal's market value after it reaches maturity.

UNICAP for Farmers

In prior years, the uniform capitalization rules (UNICAP) required most mid-sized and large farming businesses to capitalize certain inventory costs. The Tax Cuts and Jobs Act significantly changes the rules for the capitalization of farming inventory. Because of the changes in the TCJA, most small and mid-sized farming businesses are now exempt from UNICAP.

Except for large farming businesses that have gross receipts exceeding $26 million in 2020, farming businesses are not required to apply the UNICAP rules. Large farming businesses (and tax shelters) are still required to capitalize direct labor and direct material costs, as well as certain allocable indirect costs, to inventory. These include the costs of:

- Raising plants for which the pre-productive period is two years *or less*
- Livestock that is treated as inventory
- Replanting certain plants that are lost or damaged due to casualty, bad weather, natural disasters, etc.

If a farmer's crop has a pre-productive period of *more than* two years, the farmer can generally elect not to have the UNICAP rules apply, unless the farmer is required to use the accrual method for other reasons.

For crops, the "pre-productive period costs" include the costs of irrigation, pruning, spraying, and harvesting. For livestock, pre-productive costs include the costs of feed, maintaining pasture or pen areas, breeding, veterinary services for the care of livestock, and bedding.

Example: Mulligan Farms, Inc. owns several peach orchards that produce an annual crop. The trees have a pre-productive period of more than two years. In other words, it takes a peach seedling at least 4-5 years before the tree produces edible fruit. Mulligan Farms has annual gross receipts of $35 million, so the company is required to use the accrual method of accounting, and it is subject to the UNICAP rules for capitalization of inventory. Mulligan Farms is required to capitalize the direct costs of the orchard and an allocable part of indirect costs incurred due to the production of the trees. However, Mulligan Farms, Inc. is not required to capitalize the costs of producing the annual peach crop because its pre-productive period is two years or more.

Sales of Farm Products and Farm Assets

When a self-employed farmer sells products or crops raised on a farm, his entire proceeds are reported on Schedule F, in a manner similar to any other taxpayer who sells inventory and reports the sales proceeds on Schedule C.

Gain on the sale of livestock inventory that is raised on a farm is generally the gross sales price reduced by any expenses of the sale, such as commissions or freight charges. The basis of the animal sold is zero if the costs of raising it were deducted during the years the animal was being raised.

Example: On January 3, 2019, twelve lambs were born on Lauren's farm. She correctly deducted the cost of feed and other expenses of raising the animals on her 2019 tax return. In 2020, the now-adult sheep were hauled to a nearby town for auction, where they sold for a total of $12,500, with $750 of sales expenses to the auction house. Lauren will report income of $11,750 on her 2020 Schedule F ($12,500 gross sales - $750 auction fees= $11,750).

When a farmer sells farm products bought for resale, his profit or loss is the difference between his basis in the item (usually cost) and any payment received for it.

Example: Two years ago, Josue bought 20 feeder calves for $6,000 for resale. The feeder calves are inventory. He sold them in 2020 for $22,000. Josue reports the $22,000 sales price, subtracts his $6,000 basis, and reports the resulting $16,000 gain on his Schedule F as business income.

Depreciation of Farm Assets

Farmers are allowed to use any depreciation methods available to other business types, but there are some unique rules for farmers with regard to depreciation. With regards to accelerated depreciation methods, farmers are allowed to use section 179 and bonus depreciation just like any other business. Qualified property for both section 179 and bonus depreciation may be *new* or *used*.

The Tax Cuts and Jobs Act modified the depreciation recovery period for *new* farm equipment and machinery placed into service during the year. The recovery period has been shortened from 7 years to 5 years.

Used machinery and equipment retains a seven-year class life under MACRS.[140] Farmers may use the 200% declining-balance method of MACRS depreciation for farming assets. In prior years, most farming property was depreciated using the 150% declining-balance method.[141]

Example: Avis owns a sheep farm. In 2020, he purchases 15 ewes to bring into his existing flock. Avis pays $250 per head. He plans to use the sheep to produce wool. He also purchases a used tractor during the year for use on the farm. The tractor costs $22,000. He can depreciate the cost of the sheep and the tractor using any depreciation method he chooses, including Bonus Depreciation or Section 179.

There are some differences in the property that qualifies for section 179 and bonus depreciation. In addition to machinery and equipment, farmers may use accelerated depreciation to immediately expense certain structures and land improvements.

Qualifying Depreciable Property for Farming Businesses	
Section 179 Must be acquired from an unrelated party	**Bonus Depreciation** Must be acquired from an unrelated party, unless the property is **new**
Business equipment, farming machinery and equipment	Tangible property with a MACRS recovery period of 20 years or less, including equipment
Livestock held for draft, breeding or dairy purposes[142]	Livestock held for draft, breeding or dairy purposes
Single-purpose agricultural or horticultural structures (i.e., milking parlors, piggeries, greenhouses)	Single-purpose agricultural or horticultural structures (i.e., milking parlors, piggeries, greenhouses)
Qualified nonresidential improvement property (alarms, fire protection, and security systems, HVAC, and roofing.)	Fruit and nut-bearing plants and trees, Qualified improvement property (QIP)[143]

[140] The shorter recovery period does not apply to grain bins, cotton ginning equipment, fences and other land improvements (whether new or used).

[141] This provision applies to 3, 5, 7, and 10-year property used in a farming business and placed in service in 2020. If the property is 15-year or 20-year property, the farmer should continue to use the 150% declining-balance method.

[142] This list does not include poultry.

[143] The CARES Act provided a retroactive technical correction in 2020, designating QIP property as 15-year asset class life, and thus eligible for bonus depreciation.

Disposition of Farm Assets

Income reported on Schedule F does not include gains or losses from sales or other dispositions of the following farm assets:

- Farmland
- Depreciable farm equipment
- Barns, stables, and other types of farm buildings
- Livestock held for draft, breeding, sport, or dairy purposes (unless held as inventory)

The sale of these assets is reported on Form 4797, *Sales of Business Property*, and may result in ordinary or capital gains or losses.

Like other businesses, when a farming business disposes of depreciable property (section 1245 property or section 1250 property) at a gain, the business may have to recognize ordinary income under the depreciation recapture rules. Any gain remaining after applying the depreciation recapture rules may be section 1231 gain, which may be taxed as capital gain. Capital gains can occur on buildings, machinery, and equipment when their values have appreciated over time.

Note: Equipment and machinery usually loses value as it gets older. So it is rare for equipment to actually *appreciate* in value over time, and sell at a gain. However, real estate, land, and buildings tend to appreciate in value over time, and thus, capital gains upon the disposition on these types of assets is commonplace.

Section 1245: Part or all of the gain of the sale of section 1245 property is treated as ordinary income under the rules of depreciation recapture. Buildings and structural components are not considered section 1245 assets. However, single purpose agricultural (livestock) or horticultural structures are section 1245 property. For example, a barn that houses different animals and is also used to store supplies would not be section 1245 property because it is not a single-purpose facility.

Note: A greenhouse that is used only to grow plants would be "single-purpose" and thus section 1245 property. If a cash register and a sales kiosk is installed in the greenhouse so that a farmer can sell plants in addition to growing them there, the greenhouse would no longer be section 1245 property because it is no longer "single-purpose" property.

Other examples of farming-related section 1245 property include a grain silo, fencing for the confinement of livestock, and wells for providing water to livestock.

Section 1231: Section 1231 assets include certain business (noncapital) assets that have been held for more than one year, as well as certain business and investment property disposed of in involuntary conversions. If the sold property was held for *less* than one year, the 1231 gain rules do not apply.

Note: Section 1231 assets receive special tax treatment. If a taxpayer has a net loss from all section 1231 transactions, the loss is treated as *ordinary loss*. If the section 1231 transactions result in a net gain, the gain is generally treated as capital gain, with the exceptions of (1) depreciation recapture and (2) recapture under the five-year "look-back" rule, which is taxed as ordinary income.

Example: Paul is a qualified farmer that raises farmed salmon for human consumption. Paul is also very good at fixing things. Five years ago, Paul purchased a leaky fishing boat for a bargain price of $3,200. He fixes up the boat and paints it nicely with his company logo, and then uses it daily in his business for the next five years. In 2020, he receives an offer from one of his friends to sell the boat for $13,000. Paul accepts the offer and sells the boat. He originally paid $3,200 for the boat and fully depreciated it, so the boat's basis is zero at the time of the sale. The first $3,200 of cost basis is considered Section 1245 recapture and is treated as ordinary income. The excess $9,800 gain is considered Section 1231 gain and will enjoy long-term capital gains treatment.

Gain or loss on the following farm-related transactions is subject to section 1231 treatment:

1. Sale or exchange of cattle or horses held for draft, breeding, dairy, or sporting purposes and held for 24 months or longer.
2. Sale or exchange of other livestock held for draft, breeding, dairy, or sporting purposes and held for 12 months or longer. Other livestock includes hogs, mules, sheep, and goats, but does not include poultry.
3. Sale or exchange of depreciable property used in the farming business and held for longer than one year. Examples include farm machinery, tractors, and trucks.
4. Sale or exchange of real estate used in the farming business and held for longer than one year. Examples are a farm or ranch, including barns and sheds.
5. Sale or exchange of unharvested crops.
6. Sale from cut timber.
7. The condemnation of business property held longer than one year. Condemnations of business property usually qualify for nonrecognition treatment if the replacement property is purchased within a certain time period, under the involuntary conversion rules.

Example: Claudia owns a livestock farm and reports her income and loss on Schedule F. She purchases a 1-year old stallion for $5,000 to use on the farm and also for breeding purposes. She takes Section 179 on the purchase of the horse, because it is being used for breeding purposes. The stallion is a Section 1231 asset. Two years after purchasing the horse, Claudia enters her stallion in a horse race on a whim. Surprisingly, her horse wins the race. She is immediately offered $18,000 for the stallion, which she accepts. Since she had depreciated the stallion using Section 179, her basis in the horse is zero. The $5,000 of her original cost basis is considered recapture and is taxed at ordinary income rates. The excess $13,000 gain is considered Section 1231 gain and will enjoy long-term capital gains treatment. The gains are also not subject to self-employment tax.

A Section 1231 gain treated as capital gain is excluded from the calculation of QBI, meaning that these capital gains are not eligible for the 20% deduction.

Postponing Gain Due to Weather Conditions

There are special rules for farmers regarding the postponement of gain due to weather conditions. If a farmer sells or exchanges more livestock (including poultry), than he normally would in a year because of a drought, flood, or other weather-related conditions, he may postpone reporting the income from the additional animals until the following year. The taxpayer must meet all the following conditions to qualify:

- The principal trade or business must be farming.
- The farmer must use the cash method of accounting.
- The farmer must be able to show that he would not have sold or exchanged the additional animals in that year except for the weather-related condition.
- The area must be designated as eligible for federal disaster assistance.

The livestock does not have to be raised or sold in the affected area. However, the sale must occur solely because the weather-related condition affected the water, grazing, or other requirements of the livestock. The farmer must figure the amount to be postponed separately for each generic class of animals, such as hogs, sheep, and cattle.

Example: Jeannie raises beef cattle. She is a calendar-year farmer, and she normally sells 100 head of beef cattle a year. As a result of a state-wide drought, Jeannie sells 135 head during 2020 and realizes $70,200 from the sale. On November 9, 2020, because of drought, the affected area is declared a disaster area eligible for federal assistance. The income Jeannie can postpone until 2021 is $18,200 ([$70,200 ÷ 135] × 35), which is the portion of the income attributed to the additional animals that she sold over her normal yearly amount.

To postpone gain, the farmer must attach a statement to his tax return for the year of the sale, providing specific information about the weather conditions and circumstances that led to the postponement of gain for each class of livestock.

A weather-related sale or exchange of livestock held for draft, breeding, or dairy purposes (but in this case, not including poultry) may also qualify as an involuntary conversion. For a sale that qualifies as an involuntary conversion, the farmer can file this statement at any time during the replacement period. The replacement period for an involuntary conversion generally ends two years after the end of the first tax year in which any part of the gain on the condemnation is realized. A three-year replacement period is allowed for real property that is held for business or investment, such as buildings or warehouses. The replacement period is four years for livestock that is involuntarily converted because of weather-related conditions. If the property is subject to an involuntary conversion in certain federally-declared disaster areas, the replacement period can be up to five years.

Example: Guillermo is a farmer who owns 8,000 head of beef cattle on two different farms. In 2020, his herd is struck by hoof-and-mouth disease, and he is forced to send 2,500 infected animals to slaughter. The infected animals cannot be used for human consumption, so his insurance reimburses his losses, and he promptly reinvests all the insurance proceeds into new livestock. This is treated as an involuntary conversion, and no gain or loss is recognized in the transaction.

Example: Kieran is a farmer that grows hydroponic lettuce. In 2020, a hurricane destroys one of his growing facilities. Kieran's basis in the structure is $230,000. He receives a check from his insurance company for $350,000, which was the fair market value of the property at the time of the disaster. He has at least three years to reinvest the funds into a new facility. If he reinvests all the insurance proceeds into a new growing facility, he does not have to recognize any of the gain from the insurance reimbursement. This is considered a 1033 exchange (an involuntary conversion).

Crop Insurance and Government Payments

Insurance proceeds, including government disaster payments, may be received as a result of destruction or damage to crops or the inability to plant crops because of drought, flood, or another natural disaster. These payments are generally taxable in the year they are received.

However, some farmers can elect to postpone reporting the income until the following year if he meets all of these conditions:

- The farming business must use the cash method of accounting.
- Crop insurance proceeds were received in the same tax year the crops were damaged.
- Under normal business practices, the farming business would have reported income from the damaged crops in any tax year *following* the year the damage occurred.

A statement must be attached to the tax return indicating the specific crops that were damaged and the total insurance payment received. To make this election to postpone income, the farmer must be able to prove that the crops would have been harvested or otherwise sold in the following year.

If a farmer forgoes the planting of crops altogether and receives agricultural program payments from the government, payments are reported on Schedule F, and the full amount of the payment is subject to self-employment tax.

Other Unique Tax Rules for Farmers

There are many special rules that apply only to farming businesses. Other examples of tax rules unique to farmers include the following:

Car and Truck Expenses: Farmers can claim 75% of the use of a car or light truck as business use without any records (such as a mileage log) if the vehicle is used most of the business day in a farming business.

Soil Conservation: Farmers can choose to deduct as a business expense land-related expenses for soil or water conservation or for the prevention of erosion. Examples include leveling, eradication of brush, removal of trees, or planting of windbreaks. Although farmland itself is not depreciable, land conservation expenses or other costs to improve the land for farming or growing crops are deductible as business expenses. For most other businesses, these types of land improvements would be considered nondeductible capital expenses and would have to be added to the basis of the land.

Excise Tax Credits: Farmers may be eligible to claim a credit or a refund of federal excise taxes on fuel used on a farm.

Farm Income Averaging: Certain farmers that operate as sole proprietorships or partnerships may use Schedule J, *Income Averaging for Farmers and Fishermen,* to average all or some of their current year's farm income by allocating it to the three prior years. This may lower a farmer's current year tax liability if the current year is high, and his taxable income from one or more of the three prior years was low. Income from the three previous years does not have to originate from farming or fishing activity.

Example: Erwin is a citrus farmer in Florida. In 2020, he has a record crop with gross income nearly double that of 2019 and 2018, when a cold frost had damaged a large percentage of his crop. Erwin elects to average his income by filing Schedule J. His taxable income for 2020 may be averaged with the corresponding amounts for the three previous years, which significantly reduces his tax liability in the current year.

Net Operating Losses for Farmers

In 2020, farming losses qualify for different carryback periods than other business types. The CARES Act provides a five-year carryback for losses earned in 2018, 2019, or 2020, which allows most businesses to amend tax returns up to five years prior to offset taxable income. An exception to the five-year carryback rule for farmers was implemented by the Consolidated Appropriations Act of 2021 in late December 2020. For farmers only, the CAA-2021 allows them to:

- Carry back a farm NOL five years, or
- Elect to carry back a farm NOL two years, or
- Waive the carryback entirely, and carryforward a 2018, 2019, or 2020 NOL.

Example: Sunshine Grass Farms, Inc. is a C corporation that grows and sells sod. In 2020, the business has a net operating loss of $12,000. This is the first NOL that the business has incurred, all prior years have been profitable. The business may choose a 2-year carryback, a 5-year carryback, or may elect to carry forward its losses indefinitely. Sunshine Grass Farms chooses to carry back its losses two years. In 2018, the business had $10,000 in taxable income. The loss is first applied to 2018, resulting in a refund. The remaining $2,000 in losses are applied to 2019, when the business had $14,000 in taxable income. Sunshine Grass Farms is a C corporation, so it uses Form 1139, Corporation Application for Tentative Refund, to apply for a quick refund of taxes due to the carryback of its NOL.

Unit 16: Study Questions

(Test yourself and then check the correct answers at the end of this section.)

1. All of the following are acceptable methods for valuation of farm inventory *except:*

A. Cost method.
B. Harvest discount method.
C. Farm-price method.
D. Unit-livestock-price method.

2. Which of the following would be an example of a potential Section 1231 asset for a farming business?

A. A tractor.
B. Inventory.
C. Livestock feed.
D. Fertilizer.

3. Joel is a qualified farmer who usually sells 500 beef cattle every year. However, because of a severe drought, he was forced to sell 800 beef cattle this year. Which of the following statements is correct?

A. Joel may choose to postpone all of the gain in this transaction.
B. Joel may choose to postpone a portion of his gain in this transaction.
C. Joel must use the accrual method in order to postpone gain.
D. Postponement of gain is not allowed.

4. All of the following should be included in farming inventory *except:*

A. Farming machinery.
B. Livestock held primarily for sale.
C. Farm feed or seed.
D. Supplies that become a physical part of items held for sale.

5. Which of the following statements about farmers is correct?

A. Gross income from farming includes capital gains from the sale of equipment.
B. An individual who grows a large garden can be considered a farmer for tax purposes.
C. A farmer does not have to report income from crop insurance payments.
D. A farmer who is a sole proprietor may use income averaging to reduce his tax liability.

6. All of the following would be considered section 1245 property *except:*

A. A single-purpose greenhouse.
B. A grain silo.
C. A wire chicken coop.
D. A barn that houses cows and horses, and also serves for the storage of supplies.

7. Rowan owns a dairy farming business and has income from the following sources:

Income from milk production	$50,000
Sale of old dairy cows no longer producing milk	$20,000
Sale of grain that was grown on the farm	$15,000
Sale of used farm machinery	$4,000

What amount of income should be reported on Rowan's Schedule F, *Profit or Loss from Farming?*

A. $50,000
B. $65,000
C. $74,000
D. $85,000

8. Oliver is a farmer who receives agricultural program payments after refraining from growing any crops in 2020. How should these payments be reported?

A. As "other income" on Oliver's individual Form 1040, Schedule 1.
B. On Schedule E, *Supplemental Income and Loss.*
C. As farm income on Schedule F, not subject to self-employment tax.
D. As farm income on Schedule F, subject to self-employment tax.

9. With regards to farmers, what is Schedule J used for?

A. Schedule J is used to report farm-related casualty losses.
B. Schedule J allows a farmer to use income-averaging.
C. Schedule J allows a farmer to deduct his home office.
D. Schedule J allows a farmer to report estimated payments.

10. The carryback period for farming losses in tax year 2020 is:

A. Two years or five years.
B. Two years or seven years.
C. Five years.
D. Seven years.

11. Holly grows organic heirloom tomatoes and also raises pedigreed goats on her 200-acre farm. She also rents a portion of her farmland to a sharecropper. Holly is an accrual-basis farmer who has the following income in the current year:

Rental of farmland in which she did not materially participate	$30,000
Sale of harvested tomatoes	$145,000
Gain from sale of goats held primarily for breeding	$85,000
Crop insurance payments	$115,000

What amount of *farming* income must Holly report on Schedule F?

A. $145,000
B. $260,000
C. $290,000
D. $345,000

12. Andy owns 150 acres of farmland that he rents to other farmers. His income from the rental is a crop-share, and based on the productivity of the tenant-farmer. He does not actively participate in any of the farming activity. How should the income from this activity be reported?

A. As ordinary income on Schedule C.
B. As farming income on Schedule F.
C. As rental income on Form 4835.
D. As passive income on Schedule E.

13. DeRose Farms, LLC is a qualified farming business that grows soybeans. In 2020, the company's entire soybean crop was destroyed by a flood. If the crop had not been destroyed, DeRose Farms would have harvested the soybeans in 2021. The business receives federal disaster payments in 2020. Which of the following statements is correct?

A. DeRose Farms can choose to postpone the income from this disaster payment until 2021.
B. Disaster payments are never taxable income.
C. DeRose Farms must report the federal disaster payments on its 2020 return.
D. DeRose Farms may delay recognition of the federal disaster payments for two years.

14. To be eligible as a "qualified farmer" and not have to pay quarterly estimated taxes during the year, what amount of a farmer's gross income must be from farming activities?

A. ½
B. ⅓
C. ⅔
D. ¾

15. What is the "Crop Method" of accounting?

A. The crop method of accounting allows farmers to delay expense recognition for crops that they sell in the year after they are sown.
B. The crop method of accounting allows farmers to delay expense recognition for at least three years after they harvest their crops.
C. The crop method of accounting is an accrual-basis accounting method.
D. The crop method of accounting does not exist.

16. Farm income averaging is computed on Schedule J, which may be filed:

A. For the current year, when a taxpayer files Schedule F showing a net operating loss.
B. For the current year, when a taxpayer files Schedule F showing net income from farming.
C. For the current year, along with Schedule C.
D. As an amended return showing the past three years of farming income.

17. What of the following conditions will force a farming business to use the accrual method?

A. A farming business that carries inventory, with gross receipts of $25 million.
B. A farming corporation that is also a tax shelter.
C. A farming business that files a Schedule F and has over $10 million in gross receipts.
D. A farming business that operates as a general partnership.

18. Which of the following business activities would not be considered a farming business?

A. A dairy.
B. A hog farm.
C. A vineyard.
D. A dog breeder.

Unit 16: Quiz Answers

1. The answer is B. The "harvest discount method" does not exist. All of the other inventory valuation methods listed are allowed for farming businesses.

2. The answer is A. A tractor would be considered a Section 1231 asset (if used for more than a year) because it is depreciable machinery used in a business. Examples of regular business expenses include fertilizer and livestock feed, which would be currently deductible as business expenses. Inventory is not a capital asset, because it is held for sale to customers.

3. The answer is B. Joel may postpone a portion of his gain to the following year. If a farmer sells or exchanges more livestock, including poultry, than he normally would in a year because of a drought, flood, or other weather-related condition, he may postpone reporting the gain from the additional animals until the next year. The farmer must use the cash method of accounting in order to postpone gain in this manner.

4. The answer is A. Farming machinery and equipment is a depreciable asset, and therefore not included in the calculation of inventory.

5. The answer is D. Certain farmers may average all or some of their current year's farm income by allocating it to the three prior years. This may lower a farmer's current year tax if the current year is high and his taxable income from one or more of the three prior years was low. Income averaging is only available to farmers and fishermen who operate as sole proprietors or partnerships. It is reported on Schedule J, *Income Averaging for Farmers and Fishermen*.

6. The answer is D. Section 1245 typically excludes buildings and other structural components. However, there is an exception for single-purpose agricultural or horticultural structures. A barn for cows and horses that also holds supplies is not a "single-purpose" agricultural structure, so it would not be considered section 1245 property.

7. The answer is B. Rowan's farming income reported is from milk production and sale of grain ($50,000 + $15,000 = **$65,000**). Gross income from farming activity is reported on Schedule F, and includes farm income, farm rental income, and gains from livestock that were raised specifically for sale on the farm, or purchased specifically for resale. The sale of old dairy cows and the sale of used machinery do not qualify. The sale of depreciable machinery and the sale of livestock used for dairy purposes are not reported on Schedule F. Instead, these amounts should be reported on Form 4797, *Sales of Business Property.*

8. The answer is D. Oliver must report the agricultural program payment on Schedule F, and the full amount of the payment is subject to self-employment tax.

9. The answer is B. Schedule J, *Income Averaging for Farmers and Fishermen,* allows a farmer to average income over the prior three years to lower current-year tax liability.

10. The answer is A. In 2020, the NOL carryback period for farming losses is either two years or five years. Farmers may elect either a two-year or five-year carryback due to changes in the CARES Act and the Consolidated Appropriations Act of 2021. Farmers may also elect to waive the carryback period entirely and carryforward their losses indefinitely.

11. The answer is B. Holly's farming income is **$260,000.** The answer is calculated as follows: $145,000 sale of harvested crops + $115,000 of crop insurance payments = $260,000. If a farmer rents her farmland for someone else to use, the related revenue is generally considered rental income, rather than farming income (this is also called a "sharecrop"). The gain from the sale of the livestock held for breeding would also not be reported on Schedule F. The insurance proceeds, (including government disaster payments), are generally taxable as ordinary income in the year they are received. A cash-basis farming business may elect to postpone reporting the income until the following year under certain conditions, but an accrual-basis business cannot. Income reported on Schedule F does not include gains or losses from sales or other dispositions of the following farm assets:

- Sale of land.
- Depreciable farm equipment.
- Buildings and structures.
- Livestock held for draft, breeding, sport, or dairy purposes (unless held as inventory).

The sale of these assets is reported on Form 4797, *Sales of Business Property*, and may result in ordinary income or capital gains or losses.

12. The answer is C. The rent received for the use or rental of farmland is generally rental income, not farm income. If the farmer does not materially participate in operating the farm and the rental income is based on the productivity of the tenant-farmer, the income is reported on Form 4835, *Farm Rental Income and Expenses*, and the income is not subject to self-employment tax. This is a special type of rental activity commonly called "sharecropping" or "cropping." If a farmer rents pasture or farmland out for a flat cash amount and does not provide any services to the tenant-farmer, then the rental income would be reported on Schedule E.

13. The answer is A. DeRose Farms can delay recognizing income on the federal disaster payments until the following tax year. Payments for disaster relief are taxable as ordinary income to farmers. These payments may be included in income in the tax year following the year in which they were awarded. In order to make this election, the business must be able to prove that the crops would have been harvested or otherwise sold in the following year.

14. The answer is C. An individual is a qualified farmer if at least two-thirds of his or her gross income from all sources was from farming. Note that these special rules only apply to self-employed farmers and do not apply to corporations.

15. The answer is A. Qualified farmers can, with the approval of the Internal Revenue Service, use the "crop method" of accounting to delay expense recognition for crops. Farmers who do not harvest and sell their crop in the same year it is planted can capitalize the costs of production and deduct the entire cost of planting and producing the crop in the year they realize the income.

16. The answer is B. Farm income averaging is computed on Schedule J for the current tax year. If a farmer or fisherman elects income averaging, he must file Schedule J along with a Schedule F showing his net farming income.

17. The answer is B. Most farmers can use the cash method. A farming business may use the cash method of accounting if the entity's average annual gross receipts for the three preceding tax years is $26 million or less in 2020. This includes farming businesses that produce or maintain an inventory. However, **all** tax shelters must use an accrual method of accounting, regardless of the type of business activity.

18. The answer is D. A business that sells or breeds household pets (like cats and dogs) would not be a qualified farming business. Certain associated businesses are not considered farming businesses and instead must file on Schedule C (if a sole proprietorship). Examples include:

- Veterinary businesses.
- Businesses that only supply farm labor or farming equipment.
- Businesses that only sell farm supplies, such as pesticides or herbicides.
- Businesses that are only in the business of breeding, including those that raise or breed dogs, cats, or other household pets.
- Businesses that provide agricultural services, such as soil preparation and fertilization, but do no actual farming of the land.

Unit 17: Nonprofit Organizations

More Reading:

Publication 4220, Applying for 501(c)(3) Tax-Exempt Status
Publication 557, Tax-Exempt Status for Your Organization
Publication 598, Tax on Unrelated Business Income of Exempt Organizations
Publication 1828, Tax Guide for Churches & Religious Organizations
Publication 1771, Charitable Contributions Substantiation and Disclosure Requirements
Publication 3833, Disaster Relief, Providing Assistance Through Charitable Orgs

The tax-exempt sector under section 501(c) of the Internal Revenue Code covers 1.5 million exempt entities of varying sizes and purposes. The U.S. Government Accountability Office estimates that spending in the tax-exempt sector represents about one-tenth of the U.S. economy, and the paid exempt workforce is comparable in size to some of the largest sectors of the U.S. civilian workforce, such as food and lodging.[144]

Charitable organizations usually rely on donor contributions to fund operations. Nonprofit organizations are generally exempt from income tax and receive other favorable treatment under the tax law; however, certain income of an exempt organization may be subject to tax, such as income from an unrelated business activity. Despite their exempt status, nonprofit organizations are still subject to many filing and recordkeeping requirements under federal tax law.

Exempt Entities and UBIT: Due to the Tax Cuts and Jobs Act, an exempt organization carrying on more than one "unrelated business activity" must now separately calculate UBTI for each activity. As a result, losses from one unrelated business activity cannot be used to offset income derived from another trade or business.

Exempt Entities in General

The majority of nonprofit organizations qualify for tax-exempt status under section 501(c)(3) of the Internal Revenue Code. In general, there are two types of exempt entities:

- 501(c) charities and
- Other 501(c) entities (this group includes *non-charities*, including: social clubs, labor unions, and nonprofit political organizations)

The 501(c)(3) designation is reserved for organizations that are *exclusively* charitable in nature. These organizations are exempt from paying income tax in connection with their charitable activities, and they are eligible to receive charitable contributions that are tax-deductible to the donor. To qualify for these benefits, an organization must file an application with the IRS and must meet the following requirements:

- **Organization:** It must be organized as a corporation, a trust, or an unincorporated association, and its purpose must be limited to a qualified exempt purpose, as described

[144] GAO report number (GAO-05-561T) *"Tax-Exempt Sector: Governance, Transparency, and Oversight Are Critical for Maintaining Public Trust"*

in section 501(c)(3). A nonprofit entity may not be organized as a partnership or sole proprietorship.

- **Exempt Purpose:** It must have one or more exempt purposes as listed under section 501(c)(3): charitable, educational, religious, scientific, literary, fostering national or international sports competition,[145] preventing cruelty to children or animals, or testing for public safety.
- **Operation:** A substantial portion of its activities must be related to its exempt purpose(s). Further, a 501(c)(3) organization must:
  - Refrain from participating in political campaigns of candidates
  - Restrict its lobbying activities to an "insubstantial" part of its total activities
  - Grants, donations, and activities may not assist any private election campaign or endorse any political candidates for public office.
  - Ensure that its earnings do not benefit any private shareholder or individual
  - Not operate for the benefit of private interests, such as those of its founder, the founder's family, or its shareholders
  - Not operate for the primary purpose of conducting a trade or business that is not related to its exempt purpose

Example: Harold McClellan is a wealthy business owner. He forms the McClellan Charitable Trust. When he fills out the exemption application, he states that the organization will provide college scholarships and grants to low-income college students. Harold McClellan then transfers $500,000 to the trust, taking a deduction for his donation. During the year, the McClellan Charitable Trust awarded several scholarships, but all of the scholarship "winners" were direct descendants and relatives of Harold McClellan, the organization's founder. The IRS audits the trust and retroactively revokes its tax-exempt status. The McClellan Trust will be required to pay income taxes on all its revenue, including any donations that it received, and donors will no longer be able to deduct contributions to the organization.

Applying for Tax-Exempt Status

Before applying for tax-exempt status, an organization must be created by preparing an organizing document. This is the first step, (even before requesting an EIN, or filing a formal application for exemption with the IRS).

The organization's "organizing document" must limit the organization's purposes to those set forth in section 501(c)(3) and must specify that the entity's assets will be permanently dedicated to the specified exempt purpose(s). The document should also contain a provision for distributing funds if the organization later dissolves.

To request exempt status under section 501(c)(3), an entity must use Form 1023, *Application for Recognition of Exemption*. Any organization (except for private foundations), with annual

[145] An example of a "sports-related" 501(c)(3) would be the Olympics and the Paralympic Games. They are usually qualified amateur sports organizations, youth sports organizations, or sports organizations for the disabled. Most youth sports organizations, such as Little League and Pee-Wee football leagues, also qualify for 501(c)(3) status.

gross receipts of no more than $5,000 is not required to file Form 1023 but must do so within 90 days of the tax year in which it exceeds this threshold.[146]

Beginning January 31, 2020, applications for recognition of exemption on Form 1023 must be submitted electronically online at *www.pay.gov.*

There is a user fee for filing this form. The user fee in 2020 for Form 1023 is $600. Form 1023-EZ is a simpler application form that is designed for small tax-exempt organizations. The application is only three pages long, compared to 26 pages for the traditional Form 1023. The user fee for Form 1023-EZ is less, $275. To qualify for the shorter form, an organization must have:

- Gross receipts of $50,000 or less in the three prior years, and
- Assets (based on fair market value) of $250,000 or less.

A 501(c)(3) must generally request an exemption from the IRS within 27 months after the end of the month in which it was formed in order to obtain exempt status as of the date of its formation. Other nonprofit groups must file a formal application within 15 months.

The IRS will review the organization's application and determine if it meets the requirements for exemption. If approved, the IRS will issue a letter recognizing the organization's exempt status and providing its public charity classification.

An organization that files its application before the deadline may be recognized as tax-exempt from the date of its creation. An organization that files an application after the deadline also may be recognized as tax-exempt from the date of the application by requesting exemption retroactive to the date of creation.

While an organization's application is pending approval, the organization may operate as if it were tax-exempt. Donor contributions made while an application is pending would qualify, assuming the IRS later approves its exempt status. If the application is not approved, these contributions will not qualify. The organization would also be liable for filing federal income tax returns unless its income is otherwise excluded from federal taxation.

Example: The Children's Soccer League was created five years ago by six founding members who wanted to create a youth sports league in their city. The organization did not exceed the $5,000 gross receipts test threshold until its fiscal year ended September 30, 2020. The Children's Soccer League must file Form 1023 to request formal tax exemption by December 29, 2020, 90 days after reaching the $5,000 threshold.

Example: The Anchorage Feline Rescue is a qualified 501(c)(3) organization that operates on the calendar year. The rescue organization officially formed on March 5, 2020. It has an official organizing document and an EIN that the organization's director requested from the IRS. At the end of 2020, the organization had collected a total of $12,000 in donations. Since this amount exceeds the threshold for the first tax year, the Anchorage Feline Rescue must apply for formal exemption within 90 days after the end of its first tax year.

[146] See IRS Publication 557, *Tax-Exempt Status for Your Organization*, under the section: Organizations Not Required to File Form 1023 or Form 1023-EZ.

Note: Churches and similar religious organizations are not required to request a formal exemption, regardless of their size or the amount of revenue or donations that the church receives.

Note: As noted above, a private foundation is *always* required to request formal tax exemption, regardless of the amount of its gross receipts.

Other Section 501(c) Organizations

Most organizations that do not qualify for exemption under section 501(c)(3) may qualify for tax-exempt status by filing Form 1024, *Application for Recognition of Exemption Under Section 501(a).* Organizations use this form to apply for recognition of exemption under section 501(a) or to receive a determination letter of IRS recognition of their exempt status. Remember, there are many types of organizations that qualify as nonprofit organizations, but not all exempt entities qualify to receive contributions that are deductible by the donor.

The PATH Act contained several provisions affecting tax-exempt organizations, specifically 501(c)(4) organizations, which include: civic leagues, local employees' associations, and social welfare organizations. The law requires all 501(c)(4) organizations to file a notice of registration with the IRS within 60 days of the organization's formation. Form 8976, *Notice of Intent to Operate Under Section 501(c)(4),* must be submitted electronically. There is no paper form.

Beginning January 5, 2021, the IRS made an electronic version of the Form 1024-A available, which is used by organizations seeking to be exempt under Section 501(c)(4). Qualifying organizations may submit the form online at Pay.gov. The IRS will provide a 90-day grace period during which it will continue to accept paper versions of Form 1024-A. However, after April 5, 2021, the Form 1024-A must be submitted electronically.

Note: Donor contributions to civic leagues or other section 501(c)(4) organizations generally are not deductible as charitable contributions for federal income tax purposes. A significant difference between charitable organizations and 501(c)(4) organizations is that 501(c)(4) organizations are permitted to engage in political campaign activity and lobbying.

Example: Sometimes, a large exempt organization will split its activities into two separate exempt entities in order to preserve their ability to lobby as well as accept tax-deductible donations. An example of this is the American Civil Liberties Union. The ACLU Foundation is a 501(c)(3) nonprofit charity that primarily conducts advocacy and public education. The ACLU is a 501(c)(4) that primarily lobbies for political policy. The ACLU Foundation may receive donations that are tax-deductible to the donor, but the ACLU cannot.

There are many types of organizations which fall under different exempt categories. This list is not comprehensive. Examples of "other" exempt organizations include the following:

- **501(c)(1):** These are exempt corporations that are organized under an Act of Congress, including Federal Credit Unions and National Farm Loan Associations.
- **501(c)(4):** Includes civic leagues and social welfare organizations. Examples include the American Civil Liberties Union (ACLU) and the National Rifle Association.

- **501(c)(5):** Includes labor unions, county fairs, agricultural cooperatives, and horticultural organizations. Examples include the United Steelworkers Union and the Texas Farm Bureau.
- **501(c)(6):** Includes business leagues, professional sporting leagues, and boards of trade. Examples include the American Medical Association, American Bar Association, the National Hockey League, and the PGA Tour.
- **501(c)(7):** Includes social and recreation clubs, college fraternities and sororities, athletics clubs, yacht clubs, and hobby clubs. Examples include the Boca West Country Club, the West Point Yacht Club, and the International Star Trek Fan Association.
- **501(c)(8)** and **501(c)10:** Includes and Fraternal beneficiary societies orders, or associations operating under the lodge system. 501(c)(8)s provide insurance benefits to the society's members, while 501(c)(10)s provide charitable benefits. Examples include the Knights of Columbus, Freemasons, and the Shriners.
- **501(c)(9):** These are voluntary employees' beneficiary associations (VEBA) that are organized to pay life, sick, accident, or similar benefits to members or their dependents. Employer contributions to a VEBA are tax-deductible. Examples include the AT&T Union Welfare Benefit Trust, and the United Auto Workers Retiree Medical Benefits Trust.
- **501(c)(12):** These are benevolent life insurance associations, exempt utility co-ops, and telephone and electric cooperatives.
- **501(c)(13):** These are nonprofit cemetery companies and crematoria. Individual contributions to 501(c)(13) entities are tax-deductible, but subject to a 30% of AGI limit for individuals.
- **501(c)(14):** These are state-chartered credit unions and other mutual financial organizations. Examples include the San Diego County Credit Union, and the California Credit Union.
- **501(c)(19):** These are veterans' organizations. In order to qualify for this exempt status, the group must originate in the U.S., and at least 75% of its membership must be current or prior members of the armed forces. Contributions to 501(c)(19) organizations are tax-deductible by the donor, but subject to a 30% of AGI limit for individuals. Examples include the National Guard Association of the United States, Veterans of Foreign Wars, and the American Legion Auxiliary.

Public Charity or Private Foundation

Every organization that qualifies for tax-exempt status under section 501(c)(3) is further classified as either a public charity or a private foundation. Tax-exempt entities are automatically *presumed* to be private foundations unless they fall into certain categories of organizations that are specifically excluded. Generally, churches, hospitals, medical research organizations, schools, colleges, and universities are automatically classified as public charities by default.

Note: All private foundations are 501(c)(3) organizations, but the same does not hold true in reverse.

The primary distinction between classification as a public charity or a private foundation is the organization's source of **financial support.** A public charity tends to have a broad base of support and accepts most of its donations from its members and the general public, while a private foundation has more limited sources of support. Generally, an exempt organization will not be considered a private foundation if it receives more than one-third of its annual support from governmental units and/or the general public.

Example: The Friedreich's Ataxia Research Alliance (FARA) is dedicated to finding a cure for a rare and disabling genetic disorder. The majority of its funding comes from individual donations from the public and various fundraising events that it sponsors, so FARA is classified as a 501(c)(3) public charity.

Example: The Johannes Educational Foundation supports charter schools, and 90% of its funding comes from wealthy members of the Johannes family, so it is classified as a 501(c)(3) private foundation.

The classification of public charity vs. private foundation is important because different tax rules apply: deductibility of contributions to a private foundation is more limited than the deductibility of contributions to a public charity. Further, there is an excise tax on the net investment income of domestic private foundations. This excise tax must be paid annually or, if the total tax for the year is $500 or more, in quarterly estimated tax payments.

Note: All private foundations must file Form 990-PF, *Return of Private Foundation*, every year, regardless of their income. All private foundations are required to file for formal exemption, regardless of their gross receipts, number of members, or their size.

Note: The Taxpayer First Act, passed on July 1, 2019, now requires tax exempt organizations to electronically file information returns and related forms. All exempt entities must file the return electronically for tax years beginning in 2020.

Exempt Entity Filing Requirements

Every exempt organization must file an annual information return with the IRS, generally on Form 990, *Return of Organization Exempt from Income Tax*, unless it is specifically exempt from the filing requirement. Only the following organizations are not required to file Form 990:

- Churches and their affiliated organizations
- Government agencies, as well as Section 501(c)(1) entities[147]
- Certain political organizations (special rules)

Tax-exempt organizations with gross receipts of $50,000 or less may file Form 990-N, *Electronic Notice for Tax-Exempt Organizations Not Required to File Form 990.* This form is also called an "e-postcard" because it is filed electronically and is short. Form 990-N *must* be completed and filed electronically. There is no paper form. A small tax-exempt organization may voluntarily choose to file a long form (Form 990) instead.

If an organization has gross receipts of less than $200,000 and total assets at the end of the year of less than $500,000, it can file Form 990-EZ.

[147] A section 501(c)(1) organization is a corporation organized under an Act of Congress that is an instrumentality of the United States, and exempt from federal income taxes. Examples include Federal Credit Unions.

Amended Returns: There is no separate form to file an amended exempt return, like there is with other entity types. Instead, the entity uses Form 990, and checks the box on the form, marking "X" for an amended return.

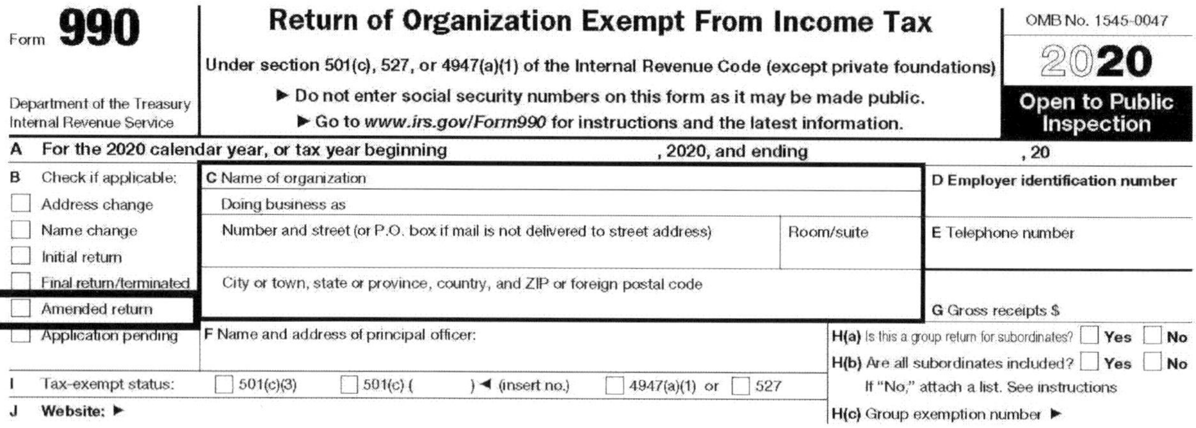

Form **990** | **Return of Organization Exempt From Income Tax** | OMB No. 1545-0047

Under section 501(c), 527, or 4947(a)(1) of the Internal Revenue Code (except private foundations)

2020

Department of the Treasury
Internal Revenue Service

▶ Do not enter social security numbers on this form as it may be made public.
▶ Go to *www.irs.gov/Form990* for instructions and the latest information.

Open to Public Inspection

A For the 2020 calendar year, or tax year beginning , 2020, and ending , 20

B Check if applicable:
☐ Address change
☐ Name change
☐ Initial return
☐ Final return/terminated
☐ Amended return
☐ Application pending

C Name of organization
Doing business as
Number and street (or P.O. box if mail is not delivered to street address) | Room/suite
City or town, state or province, country, and ZIP or foreign postal code

D Employer identification number
E Telephone number
G Gross receipts $

F Name and address of principal officer:

H(a) Is this a group return for subordinates? ☐ Yes ☐ No
H(b) Are all subordinates included? ☐ Yes ☐ No
If "No," attach a list. See instructions

I Tax-exempt status: ☐ 501(c)(3) ☐ 501(c) ( ) ◀ (insert no.) ☐ 4947(a)(1) or ☐ 527

J Website: ▶

H(c) Group exemption number ▶

Exempt Entity Filing Requirements	
Exempt Entities: Financial Activity[148]	**Annual Information Return Required**
Gross receipts normally ≤ $50,000	Form 990-N (e-postcard)
Gross receipts < $200,000, **and** total assets < $500,000	Form 990-EZ
Gross receipts ≥ $200,000, **or** Total assets ≥ $500,000	Form 990
Unrelated business income of $1,000 or more	Form 990-T
A private foundation (must file every year, regardless of financial activity)	Form 990-PF
Churches and similar religious organizations	No annual information return filing requirement, but may be required to file payroll returns if the entity has employees, and if the church owns an unrelated business, it also has to file Form 990-T

Example: Friends of the Oak Knoll Library is a 501(c)(3) organization that operates on the calendar year. At the end of each month, Friends of the Oak Knoll Library host a warehouse book sale, using donated books and books that have been discarded from local libraries. Funds raised support the programming and services of the library. The organization had gross receipts of $20,000 from its warehouse book sales in 2020. The organization must file Form 990-N, the e-postcard, by May 15, 2021.

---

[148] Table source: https://www.irs.gov/charities-non-profits/form-990-series-which-forms-do-exempt-organizations-file-filing-phase-in.

Example: Angelic Equine Rescue is a 501(c)(3) animal rescue organization. The organization receives $195,000 in donations from various fundraisers during the year. The entity's total assets are $700,000 because the organization owns several horse stables as well as pastureland to house its rescue animals. Angelic Equine Rescue is required to file Form 990 (the long form) because its total assets exceed $500,000. It cannot file Form 990-N or Form 990-EZ.

Example: As a religious organization, Calvary Methodist Church, is not required to file an application for exemption in order to be recognized as tax-exempt by the IRS. Calvary Church applies for an EIN as an exempt entity and begins regular worship. In the same year, Calvary Church hires three employees: a part-time pastor, a Sunday childcare worker, and a music leader. Although Calvary Church does not have to file Form 990, the church is still required to file employment tax returns and remit and collect employment taxes from its employees. In this way, an exempt organization is treated like every other employer.

An exempt entity may choose to file on a fiscal-year or a calendar-year basis. The applicable annual information return is due by the fifteenth day of the fifth month after the year ends. For a calendar-year entity, the due date is May 15. The extended due date for calendar-year exempt entities is November 15. Exempt entities may request a six-month extension of time to file by filing Form 8868, *Application for Extension of Time to File an Exempt Organization Return*.

If the organization has been dissolved and is no longer in operations, the final return is due by the fifteenth day of the fifth month after the dissolution.

A section 501(c)(3) organization must make its exempt application (Form 1023) and its three most recent annual returns (Form 990) available to the public. The IRS also makes these documents available for public inspection and copying.

Every tax-exempt entity must have an EIN, regardless of whether or not it has employees. Charitable organizations are required to provide a written disclosure to a donor who receives goods or services in exchange for a single payment in excess of $75.[149] Failure to make the required disclosure may result in a monetary penalty to the organization.

For example, if a donor gives a charity $100 and receives a concert ticket valued at $40, the donor has made a "quid pro quo" contribution. An organization may use any reasonable method to estimate the fair market value (FMV) of goods or services it provided to a donor, as long as it applies the method in good faith.

Example: The Montclair Fine Arts Museum holds a yearly fundraising dinner. Patrons of the museum pay $400 for a ticket to the dinner, which includes a catered meal as well as a live classical music performance. The FMV of the meal and entertainment is approximately $50. The museum gives each donor a written statement showing the value of the meal as well as the tax-deductible amount of their donation. In this case, $350 of the donation is tax-deductible to the donor, and $50 (the value of the meal and the entertainment) would not be tax-deductible.

[149] See Publication 1771, *Charitable Contributions Substantiation and Disclosure Requirements*.

Example: For a donation of $200, the Saratoga Museum provides an evening tour of the museum conducted by a famous artist. The artist does not provide tours on a commercial basis. Tours of the museum normally are free to the public. A good faith estimate of the FMV of the evening museum tour is $0 even though the artist conducts it. The Saratoga Museum is not required to issue a written disclosure to the donor, and the donor may fully deduct their donation, provided that they have a valid record or a receipt of the amount that they spent.

Penalties for Non-Filing

An exempt organization that fails to file a required return may be assessed a penalty for each day the return is late. The penalty applies on each day after the due date that the return isn't filed. The same penalty may apply if the organization provides incorrect information on the return.

In 2020, the late filing penalty is $20 a day, not to exceed the lesser of $10,500 or 5% of the gross receipts of the organization for the year, unless the organization shows that the late filing was due to reasonable cause. Organizations with annual gross receipts exceeding $1,084,000 are subject to a penalty of $105 for each day failure continues (with a maximum penalty for any one return of $54,000). The penalty applies on **each day** after the due date that the return isn't filed.

An organization's exempt status may also be revoked for a failure to file. Failure to file an annual information return for three years in a row will result in the automatic revocation of exempt status. In this case, the organization would be required to reapply for exemption. However, no penalty will be imposed if reasonable cause for failure to timely file can be shown.

If an organization's tax-exempt status was automatically revoked for failing to file a return or notice for three consecutive years, it must apply to have its tax-exempt status reinstated by filing either Form 1023 or Form 1024 and paying the appropriate fee.

An organization that has lost its tax-exempt status through automatic revocation may be required to file one of the following federal income tax returns and pay any applicable income taxes:

- Form 1120, U.S. Corporation Income Tax Return, or
- Form 1041, U.S. Income Tax Return for Estates and Trusts

In addition, a 501(c)(3) organization that loses its tax-exempt status cannot receive tax-deductible contributions and will not be identified by the IRS as eligible to receive tax-deductible contributions. To have its tax-exempt status reinstated, the organization must *reapply* for exemption. An organization may also request retroactive reinstatement as part of its application.

Note: Tax-exempt organizations that are required to file electronically, but do not, are deemed to have failed to file their return. This is true even if a paper return is submitted, unless the organization files by paper to report a name change. The use of a paid preparer does not relieve the organization of its responsibility to electronically file their return if required to do so by law.

Exempt Entities with Employees

Just like other businesses, exempt organizations are subject to the basic requirements for tax and wage reporting compliance, calculating withholding, making deposits, and keeping tax and reporting records.

Even though some organizations (such as churches or other religious organization) are not required to file Forms 990, any entity with employees must withhold and remit income and Social Security and Medicare taxes on its employees' wages, and some exempt organizations are also responsible for Federal Unemployment Tax (FUTA). The Tax Cuts and Jobs Act imposes an excise tax on exempt organization's executive compensation exceeding $1 million. The excise tax is 21% on executive compensation over $1 million. This is also called the excise tax on "excess executive pay". An employee will be treated as a "covered employee" if the employee is one of the entity's five highest-paid employees.

The excise tax is reported and paid using Form 4720. It is due on the 15th day of the fifth month after the end of the employer's taxable year.

Example: Ivy League University is an educational institution and an exempt 501(c)(3) organization. Ivy League University pays its football coach an annual salary of $1.5 million. The University is required to file Form 4720, reporting the "excess executive pay" and a 21% tax on the $500,000 in excess salary above the $1 million threshold.

Unrelated Business Income Tax (UBIT)

Although an exempt organization must be operated primarily for tax-exempt purposes, it may engage in income-producing activities that are unrelated to those purposes, so long as these activities are not a substantial part of the organization's regular activities. Income from unrelated business activities is subject to a federal tax called the *unrelated business income tax* (UBIT). For most organizations, an activity is considered an unrelated business activity and subject to UBIT if:

- It is a trade or business,[150]
- It is regularly carried on, and
- It is not substantially related to furthering the exempt purpose(s) of the organization.

Example: Artistic Pathways is a 501(c)(3) organization whose exempt purpose is to stimulate and foster public interest in the fine arts by promoting art exhibits and sponsoring cultural events. Artistic Pathways also leases studio apartments exclusively to artist tenants and operates a dining cafeteria primarily for these tenants. The leasing activity and the cafeteria activity do not contribute importantly to accomplishing the organization's exempt purpose. Therefore, they are unrelated trades or businesses.

An exempt organization that has $1,000 or more of gross income from an unrelated business must file Form 990–T by the fifteenth day of the fifth month after the tax year ends. An exempt organization must make quarterly payments of estimated tax on unrelated business income if it expects its tax for the year to be $500 or more. Any tax due with Form 990-T must be paid in full when the return is filed, but no later than the date the return is due (determined without extensions).

Under the TCJA, exempt entities are now required to calculate UBIT separately for each unrelated trade or business. As a result, losses from unrelated business activity cannot be used

[150] Any trade or business in which substantially all the work is performed for the organization by a volunteer workforce is not treated as an unrelated trade or business for tax purposes.

to offset income derived from another trade or business. Schedule M (Form 990-T), *Unrelated Business Taxable Income for Unrelated Trade or Business,* is used where there are two or more unrelated businesses.

Example: Hastings University enters into a multi-year contract with a company to be its exclusive provider of sports drinks for the athletic department and concessions. As part of the contract, the university agrees to perform various services for the company, such as guaranteeing that coaches make promotional appearances on behalf of the company. The university itself is a qualified nonprofit organization, but the income received from the exclusive contract is subject to UBIT. Hastings University is required to file Form 990-T.

Example: The Fresno Methodist Church is a qualified religious organization. The church owns a large building where it holds regular religious services. The building has four small offices on the second floor, which the church rents to commercial tenants. The church also owns a religious bookstore, where Bibles, religious books, and gifts can be purchased by the general public. The bookstore has two regular employees that work there full-time. Although the church is not required to file an annual information return (Form 990), the church is required to file employment tax returns for the employees of the bookstore, and the church is also required to file Form 990-T to report the rental income received from the office tenants. The church must also report the income that is generated by the bookstore on Form 990-T.

Example: Windsor State College is a qualified exempt organization. The school negotiates discounted rates for the food it purchases for its dorm residents in return for an exclusive provider arrangement. Generally, discounts are considered an adjustment to the purchase price and do not constitute gross income to the purchaser. Thus, the amount of the negotiated discount is not includable in UBIT. The college is not required to file Form 990-T.

Example: A volunteer fire association conducts weekly public dances as a fundraising activity. The fire association charges admission at the door. All of the work at the dances is performed by unpaid volunteers, so the activity is not treated as an unrelated trade or business.

Unit 17: Study Questions

(Please test yourself and check the correct answers at the end of this section.)

1. The Odessa Youth Softball League is a small nonprofit that was formed this year. Donations come from parents as well as members of the community. The league has gross donation receipts of $24,000 in 2020. The league's assets were $5,000, which consisted mostly of sports equipment. What form should the Odessa Youth Softball League use to apply for exemption?

A. Form 1023.
B. Form 1024.
C. Form 1023-EZ.
D. The organization is not required to apply for exemption.

2. The Immaculate Heart Church has two employees: Martha, who works as a secretary in the church rectory, and Albert, who is the church custodian. Which return(s) must the church file in order to fulfill its IRS reporting obligations?

A. Form 990.
B. Form 8300.
C. Form 941.
D. Form 990-PF.

3. An organization will have its tax-exempt status revoked if it fails to file required information returns for _______ years in a row.

A. Two.
B. Three.
C. Five.
D. Seven.

4. Child Rescue Inc. is a calendar-year nonprofit organization that helps prevent child abuse. It is required to file Form 990 in 2020. What is the due date of its tax return, not including extensions?

A. March 15.
B. May 15.
C. July 15.
D. November 15.

5. Every tax-exempt entity must have _______, regardless of whether it has employees.

A. An employer identification number.
B. A bank account.
C. A company officer.
D. A physical office.

6. Which of the following exempt organizations is *not* required to file an annual information return (Form 990)?

A. An exempt literary organization with $12,000 of gross receipts.
B. A Chamber of Commerce with $26,000 of gross receipts.
C. A church with gross donation receipts exceeding $1 million.
D. A private foundation with income of less than $6,000.

7. Most organizations seeking recognition of exemption from federal income tax must use specific application forms prescribed by the IRS. Which form must an animal rescue organization use in order to request recognition as a 501(c)(3) organization by the IRS?

A. Form 1023.
B. Form 1024.
C. Form 1040.
D. Form 990.

8. The Sanborn Youth Baseball League is a qualifying 501(c)(3) organization that operates on a fiscal year. The organization's tax year ends on January 31, 2020. Its annual gross receipts are less than $50,000. When is the organization's Form 990-N due?

A. March 15, 2020.
B. April 15, 2020.
C. May 15, 2020.
D. June 15, 2020.

9. Which of the following statements about churches is *correct?*

A. A church must always file for formal exemption.
B. A church is not required to file an annual information return.
C. A religious entity does not have to file payroll tax returns if it has employees.
D. A church may be organized as a partnership.

10. Christian Ministries, Inc. is a qualified religious association that is organized as a corporation under state law. The organization has $20,000 in unrelated business income in the current year from the rental of an office building. How should this income be reported?

A. Christian Ministries must file a Form 1120 to report the business income.
B. Christian Ministries is required to file Form 990-T to report the business income.
C. Christian Ministries will have its exempt status revoked.
D. Christian Ministries must file Form 990 to report the business income.

11. Which of the following organizations does not qualify for tax-exempt status?

A. A charitable organization.
B. A religious organization.
C. A private foundation.
D. An educational partnership.

12. All of the organizations listed below would qualify for tax-exempt status under the Internal Revenue Code except:

A. A Christian church with only ten members.
B. A political action committee.
C. A scholarship fund sponsored by a college alumni association.
D. A baseball league for children with disabilities.

13. Which kind of organization is allowed to file a Form 990-N, e-postcard?

A. A nonprofit with gross receipts of $50,000 or less.
B. A nonprofit with gross receipts of $75,000 or less.
C. A nonprofit with gross receipts of $100,000 or less.
D. A nonprofit with gross receipts of $250,000 or less.

14. Sierra Labrador Rescue is a calendar-year 501(c)(3) public charity that provides rescue and adoption services for abandoned and abused Labrador Retrievers. Sierra Labrador Rescue is required to file Form 990. The organization files a timely extension. What is the *extended* due date of its tax return?

A. November 15.
B. March 15.
C. May 15.
D. October 15.

Unit 17: Quiz Answers

1. The answer is C. The Odessa Youth Softball League should use Form 1023-EZ to apply for exemption. The Form 1023-EZ is designed for small tax-exempt organizations that have gross receipts of $50,000 or less and assets of $250,000 or less. This form is used to apply for formal federal income tax exemption from the IRS. However, it can choose to use Form 1023 if desired.

2. The answer is C. The Immaculate Heart Church must file employment tax returns (Form 941) for its employees. Exempt churches, their integrated auxiliaries, and conventions or associations of churches are not required to file information returns. However, every employer, including churches and religious organizations, are responsible for filing employment tax returns.

3. The answer is B. An organization's failure to file an annual information return for three years in a row will result in the automatic revocation of its exempt status. The organization would be required to reapply for exemption. The IRS has introduced new streamlined procedures for retroactive reinstatement of organizations eligible to file either Form 990-EZ or Form 990-N.

4. The answer is B. Since Child Rescue is on a calendar year, its tax return is due May 15. Each tax-exempt organization is required to file by the fifteenth day of the fifth month after its fiscal year ends.

5. The answer is A. Every tax-exempt entity must have an EIN, regardless of whether it has employees.

6. The answer is C. Only the church would not be required to file an annual tax return. Tax-exempt organizations generally must file a Form 990 or Form 990-N (e-postcard) unless specifically exempt (churches and religious organizations are exempt). Private foundations must file a Form 990-PF, regardless of income level.

7. The answer is A. The form required by the IRS to apply for 501(c)(3) status is Form 1023, *Application for Recognition of Exemption Under Section 501(c)(3) of the Internal Revenue Code*. Form 1023-EZ may also be used by some smaller tax-exempt organizations. The only organizations that are not required to request formal exemption are churches, affiliated religious entities, and government entities.

8. The answer is D. The Sanborn Youth Baseball League's Form 990-N is due **June 15, 2020**. Form 990-N must be filed by the 15th day of the fifth month after the end of the organization's accounting period. Since the organization's fiscal year-end is January 31, the 15th day of the fifth month after its year-end would be June 15.

9. The answer is B. A religious organization is not required to file an annual information return (From 990), nor is it required to apply for formal exemption. However, if a church has employees, it would still be required to file payroll tax returns.

10. The answer is B. An exempt organization that has $1,000 or more of gross income from unrelated business activity must file Form 990–T. The church does not have to file an annual return (Form 990). Corporations that are tax-exempt entities under section 501(c) do not file Form 1120, regardless of their charitable purpose.

11. The answer is D. A partnership does not qualify for exemption from income tax. A tax-exempt organization cannot be organized as a partnership or a sole proprietorship.

12. The answer is B. A political action committee (PAC) would not qualify. In general, if a substantial part of an organization's activities includes attempting to influence legislation, the organization's exemption from federal income tax will be denied.

13. The answer is A. A tax-exempt organization with gross receipts of $50,000 or less may file the short "e-postcard" Form 990-N, *Electronic Notice for Tax-Exempt Organizations Not Required to File Form 990*, instead of the longer information return, Form 990, if it so chooses.

14. The answer is A. Since Sierra Labrador Rescue is on a calendar year, its normal tax return is due May 15. However, the *extended* due date of the organization's return would be November 15, six months after the regular due date.

Unit 18: Retirement Plans for Businesses

More Reading:
Publication 560, Retirement Plans for Small Business
Publication 590-A, Contributions to Individual Retirement Arrangements
Publication 590-B, Distributions from Individual Retirement Arrangements
Publication 3398, Choosing a Retirement Solution for Your Small Business

Employers may establish retirement plans as fringe benefits for their employees. Self-employed taxpayers are also allowed to set up retirement plans for themselves. In this unit, we cover retirement plans from a business owner's perspective.

There are numerous forms of retirement plans that are available for small businesses: they include Simplified Employee Pension (SEP) plans, Savings Incentive Match Plan for Employees (SIMPLE) plans, and qualified plans, which include 401(k)s.

Note: The term "qualified plan" refers to certain IRS requirements that the plan and the employer must adhere to in order to obtain tax-favored status. SEP-IRAs and SIMPLE plans must also meet certain requirements, but the rules are much less complex than those that apply to most other retirement plans.

If retirement plans are structured and operated properly, businesses can deduct retirement contributions they make on behalf of their employees (or, if self-employed, themselves). Both the contributions and the earnings are generally tax-free until distribution. The rules vary depending on the type of business.

Business retirement plans do have their drawbacks. Pension plans are not free to administer. Even simple pension plans for small businesses can cost the employer thousands of dollars annually for administration, accounting, and insurance. In contrast, a traditional IRA or Roth IRA won't require pension plan administrative fees.

In the case of a sole proprietorship or partnership, if the owners of the business contribute to their own retirement accounts, they may take the deduction as an adjustment to income on Schedule 1 (Form 1040), but only if they have self-employment income. Any business, including a sole proprietorship or a partnership, can deduct retirement plan contributions made on behalf of employees, even if the business has a net operating loss for the year.

Example: Felicia is self-employed and reports her income from her catering business on Schedule C. She has a retirement account set up for herself and her five employees. In 2020, Felicia's catering business showed a loss from operations on her Schedule C, and Felicia has no other source of taxable income. She made regular contributions to her employees' retirement accounts in 2020, and she can deduct these contributions as a regular business expense. However, Felicia cannot make a retirement contribution for herself in 2020 because she has no self-employment income. Since her business showed a loss, she has no qualifying income for purposes of her own retirement plan contribution.

Self-employment income for the purpose of this deduction means net profits from Schedule C or Schedule F, or self-employment income from a partnership (less ½ deductible self-employment tax).

Since an S corporation is a pass-through entity, certain shareholder-employees in an S corporation are also required to report these deductions on their individual returns.[151] In the case of an S corporation shareholder-employee, retirement plan contributions can only be made from compensation (such as wages). Distributions received as a shareholder of an S corporation do not constitute "earned income" for retirement plan purposes.

A C corporation is not a pass-through entity, so the corporation may deduct the expense for retirement plan contributions on Form 1120, *U.S. Corporation Income Tax Return,* whether the contributions are made for employee-shareholders, officers, or other employees. This is true even if the corporation itself has a net operating loss for the year.

Retirement plans generally must adhere to certain nondiscrimination requirements intended to ensure they do not favor owners or executives of the sponsoring employer over other employees. Depending upon the type of plan, these requirements may include:

- Minimum coverage tests that limit elective deferral and employer contributions to highly compensated employees (HCEs) as percentages compared to the corresponding percentages for non-highly compensated employees.
- Prohibition of terms that favor HCEs' dollar amounts of contributions or benefits, or other rights.

Simplified Employee Pension (SEP-IRA) Plans

A SEP-IRA (also sometimes shortened to "SEP") provides the simplest and least expensive method for employers to make contributions to a retirement plan for themselves and their employees. Contributions to a SEP-IRA are treated similarly to contributions made to traditional IRAs and are subject to many of the same rules, although the contribution limits are significantly higher.

An employer may establish a SEP as late as the due date (including extensions) of its income tax return and have it be effective for that year. The employer must also make its contribution to the plan by the due date (including extensions).

Example: Grace is a sole proprietor with two full-time employees. She plans to file her 2020 tax return on the extended due date of October 15, 2021. She has until the extended due date of her tax return to establish and set up a SEP-IRA plan and make contributions for herself and her two employees.

With SEPs, there is no requirement for an official "plan document" such as those needed for qualified retirement plans. However, the employer must execute a written agreement[152] to provide benefits to all eligible employees under the SEP-IRA.

Except in certain circumstances, including when the employer also maintains a qualified plan, this can be done using Form 5305-SEP. Using this form will typically eliminate the need to file annual information returns with the IRS and the Department of Labor.

[151] This rule applies to employee-shareholders who own 2% or more of the S corporation stock.

[152] Employers can satisfy the "written agreement" requirement by adopting an IRS model SEP, using the simple Form 5305-SEP.

Contributions to a SEP-IRA can vary from year to year, so it is a very flexible option for small employers. A SEP-IRA can be set up for an individual person's business even if he participates in another employer's retirement plan.

> **Example:** Herman works full-time for the post office as a mail carrier, and also runs a profitable wedding photography business with his wife on the weekends. In 2020, they have $32,000 in self-employment income from their photo business. Herman may set up a SEP-IRA for himself and his wife through his photography business, even though he is already covered by a retirement plan through his job at the post office.

Under a SEP-IRA, employers make contributions to an individual retirement arrangement, which must be set up for each eligible employee. This is one of the drawbacks to a SEP-IRA arrangement. If an employer decides to set up a SEP-IRA for the business, all employees must also have a SEP-IRA set up for them. An employee cannot opt-out.

Like a traditional IRA plan, contributions to a SEP are generally 100% tax-deductible, and investment earnings in a SEP IRA grow tax-deferred. Employer contributions are pre-tax and not subject to income tax until later withdrawal.

Contributions to a SEP-IRA are immediately 100% vested. This means that the SEP-IRA is owned and controlled by the employee, and the employer makes contributions to the financial institution where the SEP-IRA is maintained.

> **Definition: "Vesting"** refers to a person's rights to receive some type of benefit, such as retirement benefits, or other employee benefits such as stock options. Some retirement plans allow vesting to occur on a gradual schedule, such as a certain percentage per year of employee service, or at a set time, such as five years after an employee has begun work for a company.

Unlike a traditional IRA or a Roth IRA, SEP-IRAs are funded exclusively by contributions from the employer. This means that only the *employer* may contribute to a SEP IRA, not employees. A SEP does not require employer contributions every year, but it cannot discriminate in favor of HCEs. An eligible employee for SEP-IRA purposes is one who meets all the following requirements:

- Is at least 21 years old
- Has worked for the employer in at least three of the last five years
- Has received at least $600 of compensation in 2020

An employer can use *less* restrictive participation requirements than those listed, but cannot use *more* restrictive ones. For example, an employer could choose to include all employees who are at least 18 years old, rather than at least 21 years old. The following employees can be excluded from coverage under a SEP-IRA:

- Employees already covered by a union agreement (union employees are also called "collective bargaining employees" in IRS Publication 560)
- Nonresident alien employees who have received no U.S. source income from the employer

Plan participants may be able to transfer or rollover certain property from another retirement plan account to a SEP-IRA. Each year an employer contributes to a SEP, it must contribute to the SEPs of *all* participants who had qualifying compensation.

Note: If an employer sets up a SEP, all eligible employees *must* participate in the plan, including part-time employees, seasonal employees, and employees who die or terminate employment during the year. This is true even if an employee does not want a retirement plan.

Example: Mountain Ski Resort decides to establish a SEP-IRA for its 50 employees. Mountain Resort has chosen a SEP-IRA because its industry is cyclical in nature. In good years, Mountain Resort can make larger contributions for its employees, and in down years, it can reduce or eliminate contributions. Mountain knows that under a SEP-IRA, the contribution rate (whether large or small) must be uniform for all employees. The financial institution that Mountain Resort identifies to be the trustee for its SEP-IRA has several investment funds for employees to choose from. Individual employees have the opportunity to divide their employer's contributions to their SEP-IRAs among these fund options.

Employee salary reduction contributions cannot be made. A SEP-IRA cannot be a Roth IRA. Employer contributions to a SEP do not affect the amount an individual can contribute to a Roth or traditional IRA. In other words, the IRS places no restrictions on contributing to both a SEP-IRA and a traditional IRA in the same year.

Example: Theodore is a full-time employee of Heusen Trucking Corp. He is not an owner of the company. Theodore has a SEP-IRA through Heusen Trucking. He also has a traditional IRA set up through his local credit union. Heusen Trucking contributes $4,000 to Theodore's SEP-IRA in 2020. Theodore may still contribute the maximum to his traditional IRA if he so chooses.

SEP-IRA Contribution Limits

Contributions to a SEP must be made in cash; participants cannot contribute property. Elective salary deferrals and catch-up contributions are not permitted in SEP plans. Employers cannot make contributions conditional, or require that any part of the contribution be kept in the employee's account after the business has made its contributions. SEPs generally are not required to file annual financial reports. SEP-IRA contributions are not reported on an employee's Form W-2. SEP-IRA contributions cannot exceed the *lesser* of:

- 25% of the employee's compensation, or
- $57,000 for 2020.

In 2020, annual compensation of more than $285,000 cannot be taken into consideration for determining eligible contributions. Unlike traditional IRAs and 401(k)s, SEP-IRAs do not offer any catch-up provisions.

Contributions to a SEP can be made for participants of any age. However, participants age 72 or over must still take required minimum distributions (although they are allowed to waive their RMD in 2020 only).

Note: The SECURE Act increased the age for required minimum distributions from tax-deferred IRAs (such as traditional and SEP IRAs) in 2020. Required minimum distributions must begin by April 1st following the year the individual turns age 72. However, the CARES Act waives required minimum distributions for 2020 for IRAs and retirement plans. This waiver includes RMDs for individuals who turned age 70 ½ in 2019 and took their first RMD in 2020. The waiver is temporary and only applies to tax year 2020.

Example: Computer Rescue Inc. offers a SEP-IRA to its ten employees. Computer Rescue's office manager, Karen, earned $21,000 for 2020. The maximum contribution that Computer Rescue can make to her SEP-IRA is $5,250 (25% x $21,000). Karen cannot contribute to the plan. Only Computer Rescue, the employer, is allowed to contribute to Karen's SEP-IRA.

SEP-IRA Distributions and Withdrawals

Employees have complete control over their own SEP-IRAs, so employers cannot prohibit distributions from a SEP-IRA. Similar to a traditional IRA, money withdrawn from a SEP-IRA (if not rolled over to another qualified retirement plan) is subject to income tax for the year in which a distribution is received.

Participants cannot take loans from their SEP-IRAs. However, participants can make withdrawals at any time. Withdrawals can also be rolled over tax-free to another SEP-IRA, to another traditional IRA, or to another qualified retirement plan.

If an employee withdraws money from a SEP-IRA before age 59½, a 10% additional tax may apply, unless the taxpayer qualifies for an exception.

SEP-IRA Basic Rules		
	Rules for Employers	**Rules for Employees**
Eligibility	Any business or self-employed individual may set up a SEP.	The SEP must be offered to all employees who are at least 21 years old, employed by the employer for 3 of the last five years, and had compensation of $600 for 2020.
Contributions	Vesting is immediate. Contributions to a SEP are not subject to a maximum age requirement.	Only employers and self-employed individuals can contribute to a SEP. Employees cannot contribute to a SEP.
Pros	Contributions can vary from year to year. Employers do not have to contribute to a SEP in a given year if they do not want to. Inexpensive to set up and administer.	Distributions from a SEP cannot be prohibited by an employer, because vesting is immediate.
Drawbacks	A SEP must cover all qualifying employees. Employees cannot opt out. Only employers can contribute to the plan.	Employees cannot contribute to their own plans. Elective salary deferrals and catch-up contributions are not permitted in SEP plans.

SIMPLE Plans (SIMPLE IRA and SIMPLE 401(k))

A SIMPLE (Savings Incentive Match Plan for Employees) plan provides another simplified way for a business and its employees to contribute toward retirement. Like SEPs, SIMPLE plans have lower start-up and annual costs than most other types of retirement plans. A SIMPLE plan can be structured in one of two ways:

- as a **SIMPLE IRA** or
- as a **SIMPLE 401(k)** plan.

If a business has 100 or *fewer* employees who received $5,000 (or more) of compensation during the preceding year, it can establish a SIMPLE plan.[153] The business cannot maintain another retirement plan unless the other plan is specifically for a union workforce.

The business must continue to meet the 100-employee limit each year. However, if a business maintains a SIMPLE plan and subsequently fails to meet the 100-employee limit, the business is allowed a two-year grace period to establish another retirement plan, with the business able to continue to maintain the SIMPLE plan during this 2-year grace period.

Another exception may apply if the business fails to meet the 100-employee limit as a result of an acquisition, disposition, or other similar transaction, so long as the coverage under the SIMPLE plan has not significantly changed during the grace period and the SIMPLE plan would have otherwise continued to qualify.

Example: Rapid Cash, Inc. is a check processing business with 90 employees. Rapid Cash offers a SIMPLE Plan to its entire staff. During the year, Rapid Cash acquires a lucrative outside contract. Rapid Cash is forced to hire twenty additional employees in order to deal with the increased work volume. Since Rapid Cash has exceeded the 100-employee limit (90 + 20 additional new hires = 110 employees), the company is required to establish another retirement plan. Rapid Cash has up to 2 years to establish a new retirement plan for its employees. The company is allowed to maintain its existing SIMPLE Plan during the 2-year grace period.

Employees can choose to make retirement plan contributions by allocating a portion of their salaries, and businesses can contribute matching or nonelective contributions. SIMPLE plans can only be maintained on a calendar-year basis.

SIMPLE IRAs

The SIMPLE IRA plan is less burdensome for an employer than other types of retirement plans. The employer has no requirement to make annual filings to the IRS.

Unlike a SEP-IRA, employees may contribute to their own SIMPLE IRA, so they can fund their own retirement. SIMPLE IRAs also require employer contributions. Contributions to each employee's SIMPLE IRA are made up of their own salary reduction contributions and employer contributions.

A SIMPLE IRA *must* be set up for each "eligible" employee. Eligible employees cannot decline. An eligible employee is generally one who received at least $5,000 of compensation during any

153 For purposes of the 100-employee limitation, all employees employed at any time during the year are taken into account, regardless of whether all of them are eligible to participate in the SIMPLE plan.

two years preceding the current calendar year and is reasonably expected to receive at least $5,000 in the current calendar year, except for:

- Employees covered by a union agreement.
- Nonresident alien employees who have received no U.S. source income.

Although an employer is not allowed to impose eligibility requirements that are more restrictive than the ones stated above, an employer may impose eligibility requirements that are less restrictive than the ones stated above.

Example: Halloween Supercenter Inc. is an S corporation with fifteen employees and one owner-shareholder. Halloween Supercenter establishes a SIMPLE IRA Plan for the owner and its employees. To participate in the company's SIMPLE IRA, an employee must have received at least $5,000 in compensation during any two years preceding 2020, and the employee must also be reasonably expected to receive at least $5,000 for 2021. Tracy is a part-time seasonal employee that has worked for the Halloween Supercenter for the last two years. She only works during the month of October, which is the company's busiest time of year. In 2019, Tracy earned $3,000 in wages working for Halloween Supercenter. In 2020, Tracy earned $3,900 in wages. Since Tracy has never earned at least $5,000 in wages during the year and is not expected to earn at least $5,000 in the future, Halloween Supercenter is not required to set up a SIMPLE IRA for Tracy.

Prior to an election period (generally 60 days) preceding the start of the calendar year, employees must receive formal notice of their rights to participate and make salary reduction contributions, and information regarding the employer's planned contributions.

Contributions to a SIMPLE IRA

The contribution limit for a SIMPLE IRA is 100% of compensation, up to $13,500 (for 2020). Participants who are at least age 50 by the end of the year may make an additional catch-up contribution of $3,000 (for a total contribution of $16,500 in 2020).

During the election period, an employee may execute or modify a salary reduction agreement to defer a portion of his salary. The employer cannot place restrictions on the contribution amount (such as limiting the employee's contribution percentage), except to comply with the annual contribution limit.

Each year, the employer must choose to make either matching contributions or nonelective contributions to the employee's retirement plan. In general, the employer must provide either:

- **Matching contributions:** A dollar-for-dollar "match" on payroll contributions up to 3% of compensation. This percentage can be reduced to as low as 1% in any 2 out of 5 yrs.
- **Nonelective Contributions:** The business may also choose to contribute a flat 2% of each eligible employee's compensation.

No more than $285,000 in employee compensation in 2020 can be taken into account when calculating matching and nonelective contributions.

If the employer chooses to make nonelective contributions, it must make them for *all* eligible employees, regardless of whether they choose to make salary reduction contributions or not. The employer must notify employees of its choice to make nonelective contributions within a specified period prior to the employees' annual period for making their own salary reduction contribution elections.

An eligible employee may choose not to make any salary reduction contributions for a given year. This means that an employee is not required to contribute to their own SIMPLE-IRA if they do not want to. In this case, the employee would accrue no employer **matching** contributions, but would receive a **nonelective** employer contribution if the employer elects to make this type of contribution for the year.

Example: Asher is 32 years old. He is a full-time employee of Standard Electronics Inc. Asher wants to contribute as much as possible to his SIMPLE IRA in order to build up his retirement fund. Standard Electronics must comply with Asher's request, as long as the amounts do not exceed his annual maximum contribution limits for his age. In 2020, the maximum that Asher can contribute to his own SIMPLE-IRA is $13,500.

The salary reduction contributions under a SIMPLE IRA plan are elective deferrals that count toward an overall annual limit on elective deferrals an employee may make to this and other plans permitting elective deferrals.

Example: Garnier Growers, LLC is a small farming business with 50 employees. Garnier Growers decided to establish a SIMPLE IRA plan for all of its employees and will match its employees' contributions dollar-for-dollar up to 3% of each employee's salary. Under this option, if an employee does not contribute to his or her SIMPLE IRA, the employee does not receive any matching employer contributions. Lolita works as a full-time bookkeeper for Garnier Growers. She has a yearly salary of $50,000 and decides to contribute 5% of her salary to her SIMPLE IRA. Lolita's yearly contribution is $2,500 (5% of $50,000). Garnier Growers' matching contribution is $1,500 (3% of $50,000). Therefore, the total contribution to Lolita's SIMPLE IRA that year is $4,000 (her $2,500 contribution plus the $1,500 contribution from her employer, Garnier Growers).

Example: Tenton Creamery, Inc. is a dairy processing business with 50 employees. The business has a SIMPLE-IRA plan for its employees. Tenton Creamery generally makes matching contributions of 3% of the employee's compensation. However, in 2020, the business does poorly, and revenues are down for the year. Tenton Creamery can reduce its matching contribution percentage down as low as 1% in order to conserve cash. This flexibility can help a business conserve cash flows in years when a business has a drop in revenues.

Example: Kathleen works for the All-Terrain Tire Company, a small business with 75 employees. All-Terrain decides to establish a SIMPLE IRA plan and will make a 2% nonelective contribution for each of its employees. Under this option, even if Kathleen does not contribute to her own SIMPLE IRA, she would still receive employer nonelective contributions to her SIMPLE IRA equal to 2% of her salary. Kathleen has a yearly salary of $40,000 and has decided not to make any contributions to her SIMPLE IRA this year. Even though she does not make a contribution, All-Terrain must make a nonelective contribution of $800 (2% of $40,000). The financial institution that All-Terrain uses for the SIMPLE IRA has several investment options from which Kathleen and the other plan participants can choose.

Employee and employer contributions in a SIMPLE IRA are 100% vested. This means that the money an employee has put aside, including employer contributions and net earnings from investments, cannot be forfeited. The employee has the right to withdraw funds at any time, but those withdrawals may be subject to tax.

Salary reduction contributions must be deposited with the applicable financial institution within 30 days after the end of the month in which they would otherwise have been paid to the employee. Matching or nonelective contributions must be made by the due date (including extensions) for filing the company's income tax return for the year.

An employer can set up a SIMPLE IRA plan effective on any date from January 1 through October 1 of a year, provided the employer did not previously maintain another SIMPLE IRA plan. A new employer may set up a SIMPLE IRA plan as soon as administratively feasible after the business comes into existence, if the business is established *after* October 1.

Example: American Pipeline, Inc. is a newly-formed business that was incorporated on November 1, 2020. Even though October 1 is the normal deadline for an employer to set up a SIMPLE IRA for the year, American Pipeline is still allowed to set up a SIMPLE IRA for 2020 because the business was formed after the October 1 deadline. American Pipeline sets up a SIMPLE IRA on November 10, 2020, for its employees, and starts making employer contributions immediately.

An employer can deduct SIMPLE IRA contributions for a particular tax year if they are made for that tax year and are made by the due date (including extensions) of the federal income tax return for that year.

Example: Matthew's Butcher Shop is a sole proprietorship with one employee. Matthew reports his business income on Schedule C. Matthew has one full-time employee, a shop assistant named Dineen. In 2020, Matthew sets up a SIMPLE IRA for himself and Dineen. Matthew deducts contributions to his own SIMPLE IRA as an adjustment to income on Schedule 1 of his Form 1040 (including contributions made for 2020 by April 15, 2021). The business's contributions to Dineen's SIMPLE IRA are deductible as a regular business expense on Schedule C.

A SIMPLE IRA plan may not require a participant to be employed on a specific date to receive an employer contribution. If a participant terminates employment during the year after making a salary reduction contribution, the employee would still be entitled to an employer contribution. The employer is *required* to make the contributions that were promised to the employees.

SIMPLE IRA contributions are not included in the "Wages, tips, other compensation" box of Form W-2, *Wage and Tax Statement*. However, salary reduction contributions must be included in the boxes for Social Security and Medicare wages.

Distributions from a SIMPLE IRA

Distributions are subject to income tax in the year they are received. If a participant takes a withdrawal from a SIMPLE IRA before age 59½, a penalty tax of 10% may apply. If the withdrawal occurs within two years of beginning participation in the SIMPLE IRA plan, the additional tax is increased to 25%.

SIMPLE IRA contributions and earnings may be rolled over tax-free from one SIMPLE IRA to another. A rollover may also be made from a SIMPLE IRA to another type of IRA, but it will be tax-free only if it is made after two years of participation in the SIMPLE IRA plan.

Distributions from SIMPLE IRAs must occur eventually. A participant in a SIMPLE IRA plan must begin receiving required minimum distributions by April 1 of the year following the year the participant reaches age 72. Participants in a SIMPLE IRA age 72 or over must still take required minimum distributions (although they are allowed to waive their RMD in 2020 only).

SIMPLE-IRA Basic Rules		
	Rules for Employers	**Rules for Employees**
Eligibility	Any employer with 100 or fewer employees who received at least $5,000 in the preceding year. The employer cannot maintain another retirement plan in addition to the SIMPLE IRA.	Any employee who has earned at least $5,000 in any two prior years and who is expected to earn at least $5,000 in the current year.
Contribution Thresholds	The plan generally must provide either (1) **match** on payroll contributions up to 3% of compensation or (2) a **nonelective** contribution equal to 2% of compensation.	An employee can contribute up to $13,500 of his salary in 2020 (or self-employment earnings, for a self-employed), plus an additional $3,000 if age 50 or older.
Pros	Employees can make contributions. Vesting is immediate.	Employees can make contributions. Vesting is immediate.
Drawbacks	Employer matching is mandatory.	Employees with higher salaries may prefer a retirement plan option that allows them to contribute more.

SIMPLE 401(k) Plans

A subset of the 401(k) plan is the SIMPLE 401(k) plan. The SIMPLE 401(k) plan is a combination of a SIMPLE IRA and a traditional 401(k) plan. A SIMPLE 401(k) offers some features of *both* plans. Unlike a traditional 401(k) plan, a SIMPLE 401(k) does not require annual nondiscrimination testing.[154]

Since nondiscrimination testing can be very expensive for the employer, this makes the SIMPLE 401(k) appealing to a small business owner who likes the features of a traditional 401(k) but can't afford the administration costs of nondiscrimination testing. Under a SIMPLE 401(k) plan, an employee can elect to defer some of their compensation into their retirement account. The employer is required to make either:

- A **matching** contribution, up to 3% of each employee's pay, or
- A **nonelective contribution** of 2% of each eligible employee's pay.

---

[154]"Nondiscrimination testing" is required to be completed by certain qualified plans and retirement plans, to ensure that plan benefits and retirement contributions do not discriminate in favor of highly compensated employees. Some retirement plans, notably small business plans like the SIMPLE 401(k) are exempt from this type of mandatory testing.

Note: The option to reduce matching contributions down to 1% is **not available** for SIMPLE 401(k)s. This is one of the major differences between a SIMPLE IRA and a SIMPLE 401(k).

No other contributions can be made. The employees are totally vested in any and all contributions. This means that the employee can withdraw from their SIMPLE 401(k) at any time. Unlike an IRA, participant loans are allowed from SIMPLE 401(k) plans. The loan feature can be offered to participants in both SIMPLE 401(k) plans and traditional 401(k) plans, but loans are never permitted from an IRA.[155]

In order to establish a SIMPLE 401(k) plan, the business:

- Must have 100 or fewer employees.
- Cannot have any other retirement plans.
- Needs to file a Form 5500 annually.

A SIMPLE 401(k) plan can be adopted if the business meets the 100-employee limit discussed above and does not maintain another qualified retirement plan.

An employee can elect to make salary reduction contributions as a percentage of his compensation, but not more than $13,500 for 2020. An employee age 50 or over can also make a catch-up contribution of up to $3,000 in 2020 (for a maximum contribution of $16,500). Elective deferrals for SIMPLE 401(k) plans are limited to the same contribution limits that apply to SIMPLE IRAs.

There are some notable differences between traditional 401(k)s and SIMPLE 401(k)s. Unlike a traditional 401(k), employee contributions SIMPLE 401(k) are fully vested. This is good for the employee, but not good for the employer offering the plan. With a traditional 401(k), employer contributions can be subject to a vesting schedule, and this may help reduce employee turnover. The other drawback to a SIMPLE 401(k) is that contribution limits for a SIMPLE 401(k) plan are lower than the limits for the traditional 401(k) plan.

SIMPLE 401(k) Basic Rules	
Pros	**Cons**
The plan is not subject to the discrimination rules that apply to traditional 401(k) plans.	No other retirement plans can be maintained if a business has a SIMPLE.
The plan may offer optional participant loans and hardship withdrawals to add flexibility for employees.	Withdrawal and loan flexibility adds an administrative burden for the employer.
Inexpensive to start.	Not available to larger employers with more than 100 employees.
Employees may contribute.	The plan must file Form 5500 annually.

155 While the law allows companies to offer 401(k) loans in their plans, companies are not required to do so.

SIMPLE Plan Terminations

SIMPLE retirement plans cannot be terminated mid-year and must run on a calendar-year basis. A business *cannot* suspend its employer matching contributions in the middle of the year. The business must maintain the plan for a full calendar year (except in the first year the business establishes the plan). This is regardless of whether or not the employer operates on a fiscal year basis.

Note: SIMPLE IRA and SIMPLE 401(k) plans cannot be terminated in the middle of the year. They can only be terminated at year-end and only if the employer gives timely written notice to all its employees. To terminate a SIMPLE plan effective the following year, an employer must notify its employees **prior to** November 2nd of that year. Employers do not need to notify the IRS that they have terminated a SIMPLE IRA plan, but they are required to notify all the employees.

Example: Grossman Golfing Inc. is having cash-flow difficulties. As a cost-saving measure, the company decides on October 30, 2020, to terminate its SIMPLE IRA plan. It quickly issues a notice to all its employees on November 1, 2020, that it won't sponsor a retirement plan in 2021. Since Grossman Golfing met the notification deadline, it can terminate its company retirement plan on January 1, 2021.

Example: Moneytree Brokerage Corporation decides on December 18, 2020, to terminate its SIMPLE IRA plan as soon as possible. Since Moneytree Brokerage Corporation missed the 2020 notification deadline (it would have been November 2, 2020), the earliest effective date for the termination of the company's SIMPLE Plan is January 1, 2022. Moneytree Brokerage must continue to maintain the plan during all of 2021, and the company is required to notify its employees before November 2, 2021, that it won't sponsor a SIMPLE IRA plan for 2022.

Qualified Retirement Plans

A "qualified" retirement plan is an employer benefit plan that meets specific Internal Revenue Code requirements. Most large employers offer some type of qualified plan to their employees. There are two basic kinds of "qualified" retirement plans:

- **Defined contribution plans** (examples include a traditional 401(k) or a 403(b)) and
- **Defined benefit plans** (often referred to as a pension plan or traditional pension)

Different rules apply to each. **Defined contribution** plans require the employee to fund their retirement account with their own money. A **defined benefit** plan is a type of retirement account for which the employer invests all the money and promises a set payout when the employee retires. Defined benefit plans are generally more desirable for the employee (as they are not dependent on the investment returns of the fund like in a defined contribution plan), but they cost more money to administer and maintain. For that reason, defined benefit plans have become uncommon, except for those who work in government or public service.

Each pension plan must have a pension plan administrator. This person or entity that is ultimately responsible for the oversight, management, and administration of the pension plan, and the administration and investment of the pension fund. In general, an employee's contributions to a qualified plan are not taxed until they withdraw money from the plan.

Example: Rupert worked as a custodian for the local public school district for over 25 years. The school district offers a traditional pension to all the employees who work for the district for at least two years. When Rupert retired in 2020 at age 65, he started receiving his monthly pension benefits. Rupert will receive lifetime monthly payments until his death. Rupert has a "**defined benefit**" plan.

Example: Nisha earns $36,000 in wages annually. She contributes $3,000 of her pay to her employer's traditional 401(k) plan on a pretax basis. As a result, her taxable income is now $33,000. She isn't taxed (for income tax purposes) on her contributions ($3,000), or any investment earnings, until she receives a distribution from the plan upon retirement. Her future benefits depend on the value of her retirement account. Nisha has a "**defined contribution**" plan.

All qualified plans are subject to federal regulation under the Employee Retirement Income Security Act (ERISA). The federal government does not require an employer to establish a retirement plan, but it provides minimum federal standards for qualified plans.

ERISA covers qualified retirement plans, as well as health and welfare benefit plans.[156] Among other requirements, ERISA specifies that individuals who manage plans (and other fiduciaries) meet certain standards of conduct. The law also contains detailed provisions for reporting to the government and for disclosure to participants. Further, there are provisions aimed at ensuring plan funds are protected, and participants receive their benefits. ERISA mandates minimum funding requirements to ensure that benefits will be available to employees when they retire. For defined benefit plans, it requires that plan funding be certified by an actuary.

ERISA also mandates that qualified plans meet specific requirements regarding eligibility, vesting, and communications with participants. The administrator of an employee benefit plan subject to ERISA must file an information return for the plan each year. Form 5500, *Annual Return/Report of Employee Benefit Plan*, must be filed by the last day of the seventh month after the plan year ends.

Distributions from Qualified Retirement Plans

Unlike a traditional IRA or a Roth IRA, which allow for withdrawals at any time, distributions from qualified plans are restricted. Generally, distributions cannot be made from a qualified plan until one of the following occurs:

- The employee retires, dies, becomes disabled, or otherwise terminates employment.
- The plan terminates (for example, when a business closes).[157]
- The employee reaches age 59½ or suffers financial hardship.

---

[156] "Health and welfare" benefit plans include plans that provide a variety of benefits to employees. This may include: medical and long-term health care insurance; severance benefits; life insurance; accidental death or dismemberment benefits, etc.

[157] A "plan termination" occurs most often when a business closes or dissolves. Generally, an employer is required to distribute assets from a terminated retirement plan as soon as it is administratively feasible, usually within one year after plan termination. Affected participants can generally roll over the distributed money to another qualified plan or IRA. All affected participants become fully vested in their account balances on the date of the plan termination, regardless of the plan's vesting schedule.

Unless a distribution is properly rolled over into another retirement plan or individual retirement account, it will be subject to income tax upon receipt. If a distribution is made to an employee before he reaches age 59½, the employee may have to pay a 10% additional tax on the distribution, unless the taxpayer qualifies for an exception. The additional 10% penalty may not apply in the following situations:

- Distributions are for the taxpayer's medical care, up to the amount allowed as a medical deduction.
- Disability or death.
- Distributions in the form of an annuity.
- Distributions are made because of an IRS levy on the plan.
- Distributions are made to a qualified reservist (an individual called up to active duty in the U.S. Armed Forces).
- Qualified birth and adoption distributions
- Qualified disaster distributions related to federal disaster areas[158]
- Qualified coronavirus distributions (in 2020)[159]

Even if these distributions are not subject to the additional 10% tax, they will be subject to tax at the taxpayer's applicable income tax rate. A distribution from a qualified plan must be reported on the employee's Form 1040.

Example: Leora, age 43, takes a $5,000 hardship distribution from her retirement account. She does not meet any of the exceptions to the 10% additional tax, so the $5,000 is treated as an early distribution. Leora must include the $5,000 in her gross income for the year the distribution is received and pay income tax on it. She must also pay an additional penalty of $500 (10% × $5,000).

Example: Joshua's employer is closing down the factory where he works. Joshua is 46 and has a traditional 401(k) through his job. He receives a check that provides a lump payment of the full amount that was in his retirement plan. Joshua transfers the entire amount into a traditional IRA account 30 days later. This is a qualified rollover, so Joshua will not owe any income tax or penalties on the distribution.

Required Minimum Distributions from Qualified Plans

Normally a participant in a qualified retirement plan must begin receiving distributions by April 1 of the first year following the later of:

- The calendar year in which the participant reaches age 72
- The calendar year in which the participant retires from employment with the employer maintaining the plan

158 A "qualified disaster distribution" is a special distribution of up to $100,000 from a qualified plan, such as a 401(K). These distributions are not subject to a 10% early withdrawal penalty, regardless of the participant's age, or 20% withholding that applies to most other early distributions.

159 A coronavirus-related distribution is a distribution that is made from an eligible retirement plan to a qualified individual from January 1, 2020 to December 30, 2020, up to an aggregate limit of $100,000. The 10% additional tax on early distributions does not apply to any coronavirus-related distribution.

Note: A defined benefit plan, most often known as a pension, is a retirement account in which the *employer* contributes all the money and promises a set payout upon retirement. A defined contribution plan, like a 401(k) or 403(b), requires the employee to fund the account (at least in part) with their own money.

Penalties apply to excess contributions. An excise tax of 6% applies to excess amounts contributed by employees and self-employed individuals if these amounts and related earnings are not withdrawn by the due date of their returns (with or without extensions, depending upon the type of plan). An excise tax of 10% applies to excess employer contributions.

Defined Contribution Plans

A defined contribution plan provides an individual account for each participant in the plan. The participant, the employer, or sometimes both, may contribute to the individual participant accounts. The value of the account will fluctuate due to the changes in the value of investments that have been made with the amounts contributed.

A participant's retirement benefits depend primarily on the amount of contributions made on his behalf, rather than upon his years of service with the employer or his earnings history. Examples of defined contribution plans include 401(k) plans, 403(b) plans, and 457 plans.

In 2020, employees can contribute up to $19,500 to their 401(k), 403(b), or 457 plan (an additional catch-up contribution of $6,500 is allowed for participants age 50 and over). Employers can contribute, too. There is a $57,000 limit on the *combined* employer and employee contributions for 2020. This limit increases to $63,500 if the taxpayer is age 50 or older and eligible for a catch-up contribution. Employer contributions to these plans are limited to **25%** of the employee's total compensation.

The most common type of defined contribution plan is a traditional 401(k) plan. Deferrals generally are made on a pretax basis, although some plans allow employees the option to make them on an after-tax basis. Pre-tax deferrals are not subject to income tax withholding, and they are not included in taxable wages on the employee's Form W-2. However, they are subject to Social Security, Medicare, and federal unemployment taxes.

Many financial institutions administer 401(k) plans, which can lessen the administrative burden on individual employers of establishing and maintaining these plans.

Example: Mission Bookkeeping, Inc. is an S Corporation with one shareholder-employee, Arlen, who is age 52. There are no other employees. The company has a traditional 401(k). Arlen earned $50,000 in W-2 wages from his S Corporation in 2020. He deferred $19,500 in regular elective deferrals plus $6,500 in catch-up contributions into the 401(k) plan, because he is over the age of 50. His corporation also contributed 25% of his compensation to the plan, $12,500 ($50,000 wages x 25%). Total employ<u>er</u> and employ<u>ee</u> contributions to Arlen's retirement plan for 2020 were $38,500. This is the maximum that can be contributed to his plan for 2020. These amounts grow tax-free for Arlen, until they are distributed, at which time they become taxable income.[160]

[160] Example source: https://www.irs.gov/retirement-plans/one-participant-401k-plans.

Defined Benefit Plans (Pension Plans)

A defined benefit plan (often called a "traditional pension" plan) promises a specified benefit amount or annuity after retirement. Most federal and state governments offer defined benefit plans to their employees. However, fewer and fewer private companies offer defined benefit plans because they are very costly to administer, inflexible, and with the uncertainties regarding life expectancies of employees as well as investment returns. The benefits in most defined benefit plans are partially protected by federal insurance.

Contributions to a defined benefit plan are not optional; a business is required to make them. They are typically based on actuarial calculations. Vesting can occur over time, according to plan terms, which may help reduce employee turnover.

Defined benefit plans for self-employed taxpayers do exist, but they are uncommon, usually due to high administration costs. Defined benefit plans are complicated to set up and costly to run. There are yearly administrative requirements, including annual actuarial calculations that must be done by a qualified professional. These administration costs can easily reach thousands of dollars per year.

The plan must file a yearly information return, so the costs will also include filing and tax preparation fees for Form 5500, *Annual Return/Report of Employee Benefit Plan.* The retirement plan trustee must apply for an EIN for the retirement plan's trust.

While this retirement option is more costly to implement and maintain, defined benefit plans allow for significantly larger contributions than other retirement plans. A defined benefit is also a superior legal choice because creditors cannot seize defined benefit plan assets. Plans that are not ERISA-qualified do not offer the same level of protection when it comes to creditors and bankruptcy protection.

Contributions to a defined benefit plan for self-employed taxpayers are limited to 100% of compensation. If a self-employed taxpayer does not have any taxable business income for the year, no contribution can be made.

The limitation on the annual benefit under a defined benefit plan in 2020 (i.e., a traditional pension) is the lower of: (1) $230,000 or (2) the average compensation of the employee in the three highest years. However, for government plans and a few private employer plans, the average of the three highest years potential limit does not apply. Usually, defined benefit plans are funded by the employer and generally do not require employee contributions. Defined benefit plans are also not limited to 25% of compensation like defined benefits plans are.

Note: Defined benefit plans are the most expensive to administer and maintain. For that reason, along with the uncertain amounts that are ultimately paid to the employee (given uncertain life expectancies and investment returns), defined benefit plans are becoming rarer in the marketplace. However, sometimes defined benefit plans are used by very high net worth individuals to legally shelter large amounts of income from tax. An example of when a defined benefit plan might be preferable might be a professional actor or famous musician with very large amounts of taxable income, but no other employees. Defined benefit plans also have the benefit of protection from creditors, even in the event of bankruptcy, in certain circumstances.

Prohibited Transactions

A "prohibited transaction" in an IRA is any improper use of an IRA account by the IRA owner, his or her beneficiary or any disqualified person. These rules were enacted by Congress to prevent misuse of IRA assets for personal gain. A disqualified person may include the following:

- A fiduciary of the plan (this might include accountants, financial advisors, attorneys, etc.)
- A person providing services to the plan
- An employer, any of whose employees are covered by the plan
- An employee organization, any of whose members are covered by the plan
- An indirect or direct owner of 50% or more of the applicable employer or employee organization
- A member of the family of anyone described in the bullet points above
- A corporation, partnership, trust, or estate of which any direct or indirect owner described in the bullet points above holds a 50% or more interest
- An officer, director, 10% or more shareholder, or highly compensated employee of the entity administering the plan

An initial 15% tax is applied on the amount involved in a prohibited transaction for each year (or part of a year) in a taxable period. If the transaction is not corrected within the taxable period, an additional tax of 100% of the amount involved is imposed. These taxes are payable by any disqualified person who takes part in a prohibited transaction. If more than one person takes part, each can be jointly and severally liable for the entire amount of tax. Disqualified persons or entities may not:

- Purchase, sell, or exchange assets with the IRA account. Disqualified persons may not rent or occupy the assets in the account (for example, if the IRA owns real estate, a disqualified person may not use it or occupy it for any reason).[161]
- Use any income or assets in the plan for personal benefit.
- Receive any kind of commission or fee for purchasing or exchanging plan assets.
- Take loans from the plan or keep plan earnings for themselves.

Example: Harold owns his own business as a sole-proprietor. He has a SIMPLE-IRA that he has set up for himself. Harold asks his daughter, who is a financial advisor, to manage his retirement plan assets for a reasonable fee, paid from the retirement plan. This is not permitted. Any compensation paid to the daughter would be a prohibited transaction and would immediately disqualify the plan, because children of an IRA owner are disqualified persons.

Example: Andrew has a self-directed IRA that owns two condos in a tourist area. These condos are rented throughout the year and Andrew does not use them himself. During the year, his sister, Marjorie, stays at one of the rentals for a week-long vacation. She pays the IRA fair market rent. This is not a prohibited transaction, because siblings are not considered disqualified persons for the purposes of the prohibited transaction rules.

[161] "Disqualified persons" include the IRA owner, the owner's fiduciary, and members of his or her immediate family (spouse, ancestor, lineal descendant, and any spouse of a lineal descendant.). It does not include siblings, step-siblings, step-children, uncles, aunts, nephews, nieces or cousins.

Example: Rebecca owns a retail shop. She has a SEP-IRA set up for herself and her employees. In 2020, she directs her IRA custodian to purchase a residential rental with her plan assets. She plans to use a management company to rent the house out to short-term tenants. An IRA is permitted to own real estate investments, so this is not a prohibited transaction. The rental is earning rental income for the IRA. However, later in the year, Rebecca's parents stay at the home, using it for a pleasure weekend. This is a prohibited transaction, even if Rebecca's parents pay fair market rent to the IRA, since disqualified persons have benefited from it. Rebecca or her family members cannot use the home while it is still owned by her IRA.

If a prohibited transaction is not corrected during the taxable period, the taxpayer usually has an additional 90 days after the day the IRS mails a notice of deficiency to correct the transaction.

Comparison of Defined Benefit and Defined Contribution Plans		
	Defined Benefit Plan (pensions)	**Defined Contribution Plan (like 401(k)s)**
Employer Contributions	Employer contributions are required based upon an actuarial calculation of amounts needed to fund specified plan benefits.	The employer may choose to match a portion of employee contributions or to contribute without employee contributions.
Employee Contributions	Employees usually do not contribute.	For many plans, employees are the primary contributors.
Investment earnings	The employer must ensure that contributions to the plan plus investment earnings will be enough to pay the promised benefits.	The employee often is responsible for managing the investment of his account. For some plans, the plan administrator is responsible for investing the plan's assets.
Calculation of Future Benefits	A promised benefit is based on a formula, often using a combination of the employee's age, years worked, and salary history. These plans typically pay the retiree monthly annuity payments that continue for life.	The future benefit depends on contributions made by the employee and/or the employer and investment earnings on the contributions.
Withdrawals, Loans & Payments	Payment of benefits after a specified event occurs (retirement, disability, plan termination, etc.). The plan may permit loans.	Withdrawals are permitted after a specified event occurs (retirement, disability, plan termination, etc.). The plan may permit loans and hardship withdrawals.
Vesting	May vest over time according to plan terms.	Employee salary reduction contributions are immediately 100% vested. Employer contributions may vest over time according to plan terms.
Guarantee	The government, through the Pension Benefit Guaranty Corporation (PBGC), may partially guarantee benefits.	No federal guarantee of benefits.

Unit 18: Study Questions

(Please test yourself and check the correct answers at the end of this section.)

1. What types of employers *cannot* establish a SEP-IRA?

A. A self-employed taxpayer without any employees.
B. A corporation with 90 employees.
C. A nonprofit entity with five employees.
D. All of the above can establish a SEP.

2. Jensen Biomedical, Inc. maintains a SIMPLE IRA for its employees and has elected to make 3% matching contributions. A former employee, Grace, quit her job on January 27, 2020, after the business had already deducted $75 from her wages based upon her election to contribute to its SIMPLE IRA plan. Grace had earned $2,000 of wages before she quit. How must Jensen Biomedical treat this $75 deduction from Grace's wages?

A. Jensen must return Grace's $75 salary reduction contribution.
B. Jensen must deposit Grace's salary reduction contribution in her SIMPLE IRA account. The company must also match Grace's salary reduction contributions up to 3% of her $2,000 compensation ($60).
C. Jensen must deposit Grace's salary reduction contribution in her SIMPLE IRA account. However, the company is not required to make a matching contribution for an employee who has terminated employment.
D. Jensen is required to remit the $75 to the U.S. Treasury.

3. "Prohibited transactions" are transactions between a retirement plan and a disqualified person. Which of the following is exempt from the prohibited transaction rules?

A. A fiduciary of the plan.
B. A person providing services to the plan.
C. An employer whose employees are covered by the plan.
D. A disqualified person who receives a benefit to which he is entitled as a plan participant.

4. Rudolph, age 45, is a self-employed farmer who reports income on Schedule F. He earned $180,000 in net self-employment income for 2020. What is the maximum that Rudolph can contribute to his SEP-IRA in 2020?

A. $7,000
B. $13,500
C. $45,000
D. $57,000

5. A traditional 401(k) is a type of:

A. Individual retirement account.
B. Government pension plan.
C. Defined contribution plan.
D. Defined benefit plan.

6. Huang Software, Inc. decides to establish a SEP-IRA for its ten employees. All of the following statements about Huang's retirement plan are correct *except*:

A. In good years, Huang Software can make larger contributions for its employees, and in down years, it can reduce the amount.
B. Individual employees have the opportunity to divide the employer's contributions to their SEP-IRAs among the funds made available to Huang employees.
C. Only employers and self-employed individuals can make contributions to SEPs.
D. Under a SEP, the contribution rate can be different for each employee, based on length of service.

7. Maura, age 26, began participating in her employer's SIMPLE IRA retirement account one year ago. She took an early distribution from the account on January 26, 2020. She does not qualify for any of the exceptions to the early withdrawal penalty. The distribution amount was $10,000. What is the penalty amount that Maura must pay on the early distribution?

A. $1,000
B. $1,500
C. $2,500
D. $3,000

8. Bing Accounting, LLP is operated as a partnership. The company has 150 employees. All of the following plans are available for Bing Accounting except:

A. A qualified plan.
B. A defined benefit plan.
C. A SIMPLE IRA.
D. Traditional 401(k) Plan.

9. Can a SIMPLE IRA plan be maintained on a fiscal-year basis?

A. Yes, if the business is on a fiscal year.
B. Yes, even if the business uses a calendar year.
C. Yes, but only if the business requests a 444 election.
D. No, a calendar year must be used.

10. The Azalea Partnership has fifteen employees and three general partners. The business contributes $3,000 to each employee's retirement account during the year. Identical contributions are made into each individual partner's retirement account. How is this transaction reported?

A. The business can take the deduction for the contribution to its employees' retirement accounts on Form 1065, *Partnership Income Tax Return*. Contributions made on behalf of the partners are passed through to each of them on Schedule K-1.
B. The partnership can deduct all the retirement contributions as an ordinary business expense directly on Form 1065.
C. The individual partners are allowed to deduct contributions to their employee retirement accounts on their individual returns.
D. Contributions made on behalf of the employees are deducted as regular wages on Form W-2. Contributions made on behalf of the partners are passed through to each of the partners on Schedule K-1.

11. All of the following are requirements of ERISA (the Employee Retirement Income Security Act) except:

A. ERISA requires that employers file an annual report on Form 5500 for their sponsored retirement plans.
B. ERISA requires large employers to set up retirement plans for their employees.
C. ERISA requires minimum funding standards for retirement plans.
D. ERISA requires certain communications with plan participants.

12. Leah is a sole proprietor who establishes a SEP-IRA for her small gift shop. The shop has two employees. After figuring her deductions for the year, Leah has a net loss operating in 2020 on her Schedule C. Which of the following statements is correct?

A. Because the business shows a loss, she is prohibited from contributing to her retirement account, as well as the retirement accounts of her employees.
B. Because the business shows a loss, she is prohibited from contributing to her retirement account, but she can contribute to the retirement accounts of her employees.
C. Leah can make a retirement contribution to her own retirement account, as well as the accounts of her employees.
D. Leah can make a retirement contribution to her own retirement account, but not to the retirement accounts of her employees.

13. Under the rules for prohibited transactions, all of the following would be considered disqualified persons except:

A. An entity administering the plan.
B. A fiduciary of the plan.
C. An employer whose employees are covered by the plan.
D. A cousin of the plan owner.

14. BBC Towing, Inc. is a small C corporation that maintains a SEP-IRA plan for its ten employees. Which of the following employees can be excluded from the retirement plan?

A. Stan, a 32-year-old part-time employee who has worked for the company for 5 years.
B. Aldo, a 42-year-old employee and U.S. resident alien who has worked for the company for 3 years.
C. Noel, an 18-year-old full-time employee who has worked for the company for 3 years.
D. Millie, a 35-year-old part-time employee who has worked for the company for 4 years.

15. Josie works full-time for the city of Las Vegas as a parking enforcement officer. She participates in the city's pension plan. She also has her own part-time bookkeeping business which she works in the evenings and weekends. She reports her bookkeeping income on Schedule C. Can Josie set up a SEP-IRA for her self-employment income, even though she is already participating in her employer's plan?

A. Yes, Josie can still set up a SEP-IRA for her Schedule C business.
B. No, Josie cannot set up a SEP-IRA because she is covered by an employer plan.
C. No, Josie cannot set up a SEP-IRA because she is a prohibited individual.
D. Josie can set up a SEP-IRA only if she incorporates. Sole-proprietorships cannot set up a SEP.

16. Which of the following statements regarding a SEP-IRA is correct?

A. Money can be withdrawn from a SEP-IRA by the employee at any time without tax or penalty.
B. Money can be withdrawn from a SEP-IRA by the employee at any time, but taxes may apply.
C. An employee must wait at least two years to withdraw money from a SEP-IRA.
D. An employee must wait at least three years to withdraw money from a SEP-IRA.

17. What are the initial penalties imposed on a disqualified person who takes part in a prohibited transaction?

A. 25% tax of the amount involved.
B. 50% tax of the amount involved.
C. An initial tax of 15% of the amount involved, and an additional tax of 100% if the transaction is not corrected within the taxable period.
D. An initial tax of 25% of the amount involved, and an additional tax of 100% if the transaction is not corrected within the taxable period.

18. What happens if an eligible employee entitled to a contribution is unwilling to set up a SIMPLE IRA?

A. Eligible employees may decline to participate in an employer's SIMPLE IRA.
B. Eligible employees may not opt-out of a SIMPLE IRA.
C. Eligible employees may choose to set up a ROTH IRA in lieu of a SIMPLE IRA.
D. Eligible employees may choose to set up a traditional IRA in lieu of a SIMPLE IRA.

19. The Ellsworth Company has started a SEP-IRA plan for its employees. The company currently has four employees. Which of the following employees is the company not required to cover under the SEP-IRA plan?

A. Faye, age 45, a full-time employee for the last five years.
B. Bruno, age 25, a part-time employee for the last three years.
C. Randolph, age 22, a full-time employee for the last three years.
D. Mack, age 42, a seasonal employee that has worked for the employer for one year.

20. If an employer makes an excess contribution to a defined contribution plan, an excise tax of ______ will apply:

A. 6%
B. 10%
C. 25%
D. 50%

Unit 18: Quiz Answers

1. The answer is D. Any employer or self-employed individual can establish a SEP-IRA. There is no employee limit with SEP-IRAs, but typically SEP-IRAs are used by very small businesses and self-employed persons.

2. The answer is B. Jensen Biomedical, Inc. must deposit Grace's salary reduction contribution in her SIMPLE IRA account. The company must also match Grace's salary reduction contributions at 3% of her $2,000 compensation ($60). An employer cannot return a salary reduction contribution after it has already deducted it from wages as a SIMPLE IRA plan contribution. A SIMPLE IRA plan may not require a participant to be employed on a specific date to receive an employer contribution. If a participant terminates service during the year after making a salary reduction contribution, she would still be entitled to an employer contribution, regardless of whether it is matching or nonelective.

3. The answer is D. It is not a prohibited transaction if a disqualified person receives a benefit to which he is entitled as a plan participant or beneficiary.

4. The answer is C. Rudolph can contribute a maximum of $45,000 in 2020. The maximum amount for contribution to a SEP-IRA plan in 2020 is the *lesser* of $57,000 (in 2020) or 25% of the participant's compensation. The answer is figured as follows: $180,000 x 25% =$45,000.

5. The answer is C. A traditional 401(k) is a very common type of defined contribution plan in which employees contribute to their own accounts on a pretax basis. Earnings grow tax-free until distribution.

6. The answer is D. Huang Software must give the same contribution rate to all employees. Under a SEP, the contribution rate must be uniform for all employees. Employers may potentially contribute a lower percentage to all employees when the employer has less income, but the plan *cannot discriminate* among employees.

7. The answer is C. Early withdrawals from an IRA generally are subject to an additional penalty tax of 10%. However, the additional tax is <u>increased</u> to 25% if funds are withdrawn within two years of beginning participation in a SIMPLE IRA. Maura will owe a penalty of **$2,500** ($10,000 × .25). The withdrawal would also be subject to income tax, in *addition* to the penalty.

8. The answer is C. Bing Accounting cannot set up a SIMPLE IRA for its employees, because the company exceeds the 100-employee threshold.

9. The answer is D. A SIMPLE IRA plan may only be maintained on a calendar-year basis.

10. The answer is A. The Azalea Partnership can deduct contributions to an employee's retirement plan, just as it would deduct any other ordinary business expense. However, the rules are different for contributions to the retirement accounts of the partners. Contributions made on behalf of the partners are passed through to each of them on Schedule K-1. The individual partners would make an adjustment for the retirement contributions on their individual Form(s) 1040.

11. The answer is B. The *Employee Retirement Income Security Act of 1974 (ERISA)* is a federal law that sets minimum standards for most pension and health plans. However, ERISA does not require that employers set up retirement plans for their employees. Retirement plans are always an optional benefit.

12. The answer is B. Leah is self-employed, so she must have qualifying compensation in order to contribute to her own retirement plan. However, she is not prohibited from contributing to her employees' retirement plan, even if the business has a loss.

13. The answer is D. A cousin would not be a disqualified person under the prohibited transaction rules.

14. The answer is C. Since Noel is under the age of 21, he may be excluded. The eligibility requirements under the SEP are: an employee must perform service in at least three of the immediately preceding five years, reach age 21 and earn the minimum amount of compensation during the current year. Also, nonresident aliens who do not have any U.S.-source income may be excluded. Answer B is incorrect because Aldo is a resident alien (not a *nonresident* alien), so he still qualifies to participate.

15. The answer is A. Josie can set up a SEP-IRA for her sole-proprietorship. A SEP can be established for a person's independent business activity even if she participates in another employer's retirement plan.

16. The answer is B. Although income tax may apply, including an additional 10% tax for withdrawals prior to age 59½, participants are allowed to withdraw money from a SEP-IRA at any time. Withdrawals can be rolled over tax-free to another SEP-IRA, to another traditional IRA, or to another employer's qualified retirement plan.

17. The answer is C. An initial 15% tax is applied on the amount involved in a prohibited transaction for each year in a taxable period. If the transaction is not corrected within the taxable period, an additional tax of 100% of the amount involved is imposed. These taxes are payable by any disqualified person who takes part in a prohibited transaction.

18. The answer is B. An eligible employee may not opt-out of participation. However, any eligible employee may choose not to make salary reduction contributions for a year. In that case, the employee would accrue no employer matching contributions for the year, but would still receive a nonelective employer contribution (if the plan provides for such contributions for the year).

19. The answer is D. Mack is not automatically eligible because he has only worked for the employer for one year. For purposes of a SEP-IRA, an eligible employee is an individual who meets all the following requirements:

- Has reached age 21.
- Has worked for the employer in at least three of the last five years.
- Has received at least $600 of compensation.

An employer can use *less* restrictive participation requirements than those listed (such as choosing to allow an employee younger than 21 to participate), but an employer cannot use more restrictive participation requirements.

20. The answer is B. An excise tax of 10% applies to excess employer contributions to a defined contribution plan. For employees and self-employed individuals, a penalty of 6% applies if excess contribution amounts and related earnings are not withdrawn by the due date of their returns (with or without extensions, depending upon the type of plan).

Unit 19: Trusts and Estates

More Reading:

Publication 559, Survivors, Executors, and Administrators

Publication 950, Introduction to Estate and Gift Taxes

Publication 536, Net Operating Losses (NOLs) for Individuals, Estates, and Trusts

Creation of an Estate or Trust

Estates and trusts are separate legal entities that are defined by the assets they hold. An estate is created when a taxpayer dies. A trust can be created while the taxpayer is alive, or by the taxpayer's death (by a taxpayer's last will and testament). The trust can be structured to distribute income during the taxpayer's lifetime or after the taxpayer's death. A trust can hold title to property for the benefit of one or more persons or entities. An estate or trust (if not a revocable grantor trust)[162] is required to obtain an employer identification number (EIN), just like any other entity.

Note: For Part 2 of the EA exam, you must understand how estates and trusts function at the entity level. This includes their reporting requirements, filing due dates, and exemption thresholds. Part 1 of the EA exam focuses more on estates from the standpoint of the beneficiary, as well as how the distributions affect an individual taxpayer's returns.

Estates and trusts generally terminate when all of their assets and income have been distributed, and all of their liabilities have been paid. If a trust or estate's existence is unnecessarily prolonged, the IRS can step in and terminate it after a reasonable period for completing the final administration. If an estate or trust has a loss in its final year, the loss can be passed through to the beneficiaries, allowing them potential deductions on their individual returns. Losses cannot be passed through to beneficiaries in a non-termination year.

Example: Johan died five years ago. He had two children, Teresa and Socorro, who are the only beneficiaries of his estate, which was worth $10 million at the time of his death. Teresa and Socorro immediately began to argue over the will and their late father's assets. While they are petitioning the court, Johan's estate continues to earn revenue from various assets (stocks, rentals, and other investments). In this situation, Johan's estate will not terminate until an agreement is made between the beneficiaries and the estate assets are distributed.

Estates in General

For federal tax purposes, an estate is a separate legal entity created when a taxpayer dies. American citizens are subject to U.S. estate taxation with respect to their worldwide assets. All the property the decedent owned at the time of death is included in the gross estate for estate tax purposes. Persons who inherit property directly from an estate (i.e., the beneficiaries of the estate) are generally not taxed on the transfer. Instead, the estate itself is responsible for paying any applicable taxes before the property is distributed.

[162] Revocable grantor trusts generally use the taxpayer's social security number as its tax ID number and do not file a 1041 tax return (all activity of the trust is reported on the grantor's 1040 tax return).

However, if the estate's assets are distributed to beneficiaries before the taxes are paid, the beneficiaries can be held liable for the tax debt, up to the value of the assets distributed. In 2020, an estate is allowed an exemption amount of $600 for *income* tax purposes and an exclusion amount of $11.58 million for *estate* tax purposes.

If a taxpayer dies, and the value of their assets at the time of death is less than $11.58 million, an estate tax return (Form 706) does not have to be filed (assuming no taxable gifts were made during the decedent's lifetime).

Beneficiaries must generally treat estate items the same way on their individual returns as they are treated on the estate's return. The executor of any estate required to file an estate tax return must furnish to the IRS (and to each person acquiring any interest in property included in the decedent's gross estate) a statement identifying:

- The value of each interest in that property as reported on the estate tax return, and
- Any other information about the interest that the IRS might require.

This separate statement is required to be furnished no later than 30 days following the due date (including extensions) of the return, or the actual filing of the return, whichever is earlier. This new reporting requirement is designed to combat inconsistent basis reporting of property inherited with a stepped-up basis when a sale of the property is later reported by the beneficiary.

Form 8971, *Information Regarding Beneficiaries Acquiring Property from a Decedent* is used to report the value of the property on an *estate* tax return. Executors who file estate tax returns will complete it and provide it to the IRS. Form 8971 includes a "Schedule A" which also must be filed with the IRS. Only Schedule A is provided to the beneficiary.

Example: Stefan is a U.S. citizen who lives in Spain. He owns several properties in Spain, as well as assets in the United States. On August 20, 2020, Stefan dies. At the time of his death, Stefan's assets in Spain included three vacation homes and a waterfront villa. The fair market value of these properties at the time of his death was $12 million. Stefan also owned U.S. investments and a vacation home in Miami, Florida. His U.S. assets totaled approximately $5 million at the time of his death. Stefan's estate has a filing requirement because his combined assets are worth more than $11.58 million. All the assets must be reported on the estate tax return (including any foreign assets) and any amount over the exclusion may potentially be subject to estate tax. His estate tax return and tax payment must be made on or before May 20, 2021 (within nine months of the decedent's date of death).

After a person dies, a personal representative, such as an executor named in the will or an administrator appointed by a court, will typically manage the estate and settle the decedent's financial affairs. Executors must provide documentation proving their status. Documentation will vary but may include documents such as a certified copy of the will or a court order designating the executor. A statement by the executor attesting to their status is insufficient.

The personal representative is also responsible for determining any estate tax liability before the estate's assets are distributed to beneficiaries. The personal representative is responsible for filing the final income tax return and the estate tax return, if required.

The personal representative and (if applicable) the paid preparer must sign the appropriate line of each of the following tax returns that may need to be filed:

- The final income tax return (Form 1040) for the decedent (for income received before death);
- Fiduciary income tax returns (Form 1041) for the estate for the period of its administration; and
- The estate tax return (Form 706).

Note: The Form 1041 is an annual *income* tax return, similar to the return an individual or business would file. Form 706 is different: it is not an income tax return. Instead, it is a tax form used to calculate *estate* taxes only. Depending on the value of an estate, and income that it generates, both forms may have to be filed (or, in the case of a small estate, neither form may have to be filed).

Executor fees are taxable to the recipient. In other words, the executor or "personal representative" must include fees paid to them from an estate in their own gross income. If the executor is not in the trade or business of being an executor (for instance, the executor is a friend or family member of the deceased), these fees are reported on the executor's individual tax return (Form 1040) as "other income" on Schedule 1 of their 1040. If the executor is in the "trade or business" of being an executor, they would report the fees received from the estate as self-employment income on their Schedule C.

Example: Prescott was unmarried when he died on April 20, 2020. His only daughter, Marcia, was named as the executor of his estate. Prescott earned $83,000 in wages during 2020 before his death, so a final tax return (Form 1040) is required for 2020. Marcia asks her accountant to help prepare her father's final Form 1040, which will include all the taxable income that Prescott received before his death. Marcia will sign her late father's return as the executor. The accountant also helps Marcia with the valuation of her father's estate. After determining the fair market value of all her father's assets, they conclude that Prescott's gross estate is valued at approximately $12 million. As this exceeds the exemption threshold of $11.58 million for 2020, an estate tax return (Form 706) is also required to be filed. As the estate's executor, Marcia is responsible for filing and signing both returns.

Example: Janice is a paralegal who is best friends with Loretta. In 2020, Loretta dies, leaving behind two sons, ages 18 and 22. Loretta's final will names Janice as the executor of her estate. Janice agrees to be the executor as a favor to her friend. Janice is not in the "trade or business" of being an executor and has never been the executor of any other estate in the past. Janice will file Loretta's final tax returns, as well as the tax return of the estate. She will also help distribute her deceased friend's assets to her beneficiaries (Loretta's two sons). Loretta's will stipulates that the executor of her estate is entitled to 2% of the income generated by the estate. The executor fees paid to Janice would be reported on her individual Form 1040 on Schedule 1, as "other income." The amounts would be subject to income tax, but not self-employment tax, because Janice is performing the duties of an executor only because she was a friend of the deceased.

Example: Eliezer is a professional estate tax attorney. One of his long-time wealthy clients, Caroline, dies in 2020 after a long battle with cancer. Caroline names her attorney, Eliezer, as the executor of her estate in her will. The sole beneficiary of Caroline's estate is her son, Benjamin, who is 17 and still a minor. By the terms outlined in the will, Eliezer will manage the affairs of the estate until Benjamin turns 21. By law, the executor has the right to charge a fee for managing an estate. Caroline's will stipulates that the executor of her estate is entitled to 5% of the income of the estate. The remaining income will go to provide Benjamin's ongoing support and pay for his schooling. As the attorney and executor, Eliezer would report the income that he earns as an executor on his Schedule C, subject to self-employment tax.

Final Income Tax Return (Form 1040)

The taxpayer's final income tax return is filed on the same form that would have been used if the taxpayer were still alive, but "deceased" is written after the taxpayer's name. The filing deadline is April 15 of the year following the taxpayer's death, the same deadline that applies for individual income tax returns.

The personal representative must file the final individual income tax return of the decedent for the year of death and any returns not filed for preceding years. If an individual died after the close of a tax year, but before the return for that year was filed, the return for that year will not normally be the final return. The return for that year will be a regular return, and the personal representative must file it.

Example: Evonne dies suddenly on March 2, 2021. At the time of her death, she had not yet filed her 2020 tax return. She earned $69,000 of wages in 2020. She also earned $18,000 of wages between January 1, 2021, and her death on March 2, 2021. Therefore, Evonne's 2020 *and* 2021 tax returns must be filed by her personal representative. The 2021 return would be her final individual tax return.

On a decedent's final tax return, the rules for deductions are the same as those that apply for any individual taxpayer. The full amount of any credits may be claimed on the final tax return, regardless of how long the taxpayer was alive during the year.

Income in Respect of a Decedent (IRD)

Income in respect of a decedent (IRD) is any taxable income that was earned but not received by the decedent by the time of death. IRD is not taxed on the final return of the deceased taxpayer. IRD is reported on the tax return of the person (or entity) that actually receives the income. This could be the estate, or it could be the surviving spouse or another beneficiary, such as a child.

IRD retains the same tax nature that would have applied if the deceased taxpayer were still alive. For example, if the income would have been a short-term capital gain, it is taxed the same way to the beneficiary. IRD can come from various sources, including:

- Unpaid salary, wages, or bonuses that was earned (but not received) before the taxpayer's death
- Distributions from traditional IRAs[163] and employer-provided retirement plans

[163] Because a traditional IRA is treated as IRD, both the estate tax and the income tax could be applicable upon the death of the IRA owner. Unless the IRA otherwise qualifies for the marital deduction (meaning, it would pass to a surviving spouse).

- Deferred compensation benefits
- Accrued but unpaid interest, dividends, and rent
- Accounts receivable of a sole proprietor who has died

Example: Howard was owed $5,000 of wages when he died. The check for these wages was not remitted by his employer until three weeks later and was received by his daughter and sole beneficiary, Gisele. The wages are considered IRD, and Gisele must recognize the $5,000 as ordinary income, the same tax treatment that would have applied for Howard.

Example: Evelyn died on April 30. At the time of her death, she was owed (but had not yet received) $1,500 of interest on bonds and $2,000 of rental income. Evelyn's beneficiary will include $3,500 of IRD in gross income when the interest and rent are received. The income retains its character as interest income and passive activity rental income.

If there is an estate tax return filing requirement, the IRD must be included in the decedent's estate and may be subject to estate tax. If it is received by a beneficiary and subject to income tax on the beneficiary's return, the beneficiary can claim a deduction for estate tax paid on the IRD.

Note: The estate tax IRD deduction is taken as a miscellaneous itemized deduction on Schedule A and is not subject to the 2% floor, so it is still available as an itemized deduction under the Tax Cuts and Jobs Act. Beneficiaries who do not itemize get no deduction.

Example: Salazar is age 55 when he dies on May 1, 2020. When he died, his estate was valued at $35 million, so an estate tax return must be filed. Salazar names his adult son, Quentin, as the sole beneficiary of his entire estate. Salazar also named Quentin as the beneficiary of his traditional IRA account. At the time of Salazar's death, his IRA was valued at $350,000. Quentin takes a lump-sum distribution of his late father's entire IRA on November 1, 2020. The estate tax attributable to the IRA is $120,000. Because the IRA is IRD, the distributed IRA funds are subject to estate tax. Quentin can effectively reduce his tax liability by claiming the IRD deduction for the federal estate taxes attributable to the IRA. Quentin would claim the deduction on his individual tax return in the year the income is reported (Schedule A, Form 1040).

Estate Income Tax Return (Form 1041)

Form 1041 is a fiduciary income tax return used to report the ongoing income for a domestic decedent's estate, a trust, or a bankruptcy estate:

- Current income and deductions, including gains and losses from the disposition of the entity's property and excluding certain items such as tax-exempt interest (collectively, *distributable net income* or DNI);
- A deduction for income that is either held for future distribution or distributed currently to the beneficiaries (income distribution deduction) that is limited to DNI; and
- Any income tax liability.

An estate will exist as a taxable legal entity until all of its assets have been distributed to the beneficiaries. A decedent's assets will often continue to earn revenue after a taxpayer has died, this income, such as rents, dividends, and interest, must be reported. The expenses of administering an estate can be deducted either from the estate's income on Form 1041, in determining its income tax, as well as from the gross estate on Form 706, in determining the estate tax liability. Schedule K-1 is used to report any income that is distributed or distributable to each beneficiary and is filed with Form 1041, with a copy also given to the beneficiary.

The due date for Form 1041 is the fifteenth day of the fourth month following the end of the entity's tax year, but a five-and-a-half month extension may be requested (not six months, as it is with other types of business extensions) if Form 7004 is filed by the original due date.

The tax year of an estate may be either a calendar or a fiscal year, subject to the election made at the time the first return is filed. An election will also be made on the first return as to method (cash, accrual, or other) to report an estate's income. Form 1041 must be filed for any domestic estate that has gross income for the tax year of $600 or more, or a beneficiary who is a nonresident alien (with any amount of income).

Example: Abelard died suddenly two years ago. He was a naturalized U.S. citizen. At the time of his death, he was unmarried and did not have a will. His estate had only one valuable asset: his primary residence in Los Angeles. Abelard also had cash in his personal bank account. The sole heir of his estate is his brother, Brock, who is a German citizen living in Germany. Brock is forced to hire an attorney and an accountant to help him navigate probate on his brother's estate. The estate is in its period of administration (Abelard's estate must go through formal probate in the courts, since he died without a will). In 2020, the residence in Los Angeles remains empty, so no income is generated by the home. However, Abelard's bank account generates a small amount of interest; $100. Normally, a Form 1041 would not need to be filed for the estate, because the income is less than $600. However, because the beneficiary of Abelard's estate is a nonresident alien (Brock, a German citizen who lives outside of the U.S.), a Form 1041 will need to be filed every year until the assets are dispersed, and the estate is closed.

Distributable Net Income

Taxable income earned by an estate or trust is taxable to either the entity or the beneficiaries, but not to both. Distributable net income (DNI) is income that is currently available for distribution. If the beneficiary receives a distribution in excess of DNI, only the DNI is taxed. Calculating distributable net income prevents double taxation of the money generated by an estate or trust. Distributable net income is the maximum taxable amount that can be received by a beneficiary.

The income distribution deduction (IDD) is allowed to trusts and estates for amounts that are paid, credited, or required to be distributed to beneficiaries. The income distribution deduction is calculated on Schedule B (Form 1041) and is limited to the lesser of distributions minus any tax-exempt income or DNI minus any tax-exempt income.

Example: The Harman Family Trust has the following income in 2020: $25,000 of taxable interest and dividends; $35,000 of capital gains; and $10,000 of tax-exempt interest. The trust also incurred fiduciary fees of $5,000. The trust document provides that capital gains are allocated to income, rather than the trust's corpus. The trust has distributable net income of $65,000 ($25,000 + $35,000 + $10,000 - $5,000). The trust makes distributions of $45,000 to three beneficiaries during the year. An income distribution deduction (IDD) of $35,000 may be claimed for the year. This amount represents the lesser of its DNI ($65,000) and its distributions ($45,000), minus its tax-exempt income.

Net Investment Income Tax (NIIT)

Estates and certain trusts are subject to the additional tax of 3.8% on net investment income. The provisions for this tax are generally similar to those for individuals, and it must be reported on Form 8960, *Net Investment Tax: Individuals, Estates, and Trusts.*

For trusts and estates, the tax applies to the lesser of undistributed net investment income or the excess of adjusted gross income over the threshold amount at which the highest tax bracket begins. The NIIT does not apply to tax-exempt trusts or to grantor trusts. Net investment income that is subject to the tax includes:

- Interest and dividends
- Capital gains
- Rental and royalty income
- Non-qualified annuities
- Income from businesses involved in trading of financial instruments or commodities
- Income from businesses that are passive activities for the taxpayer

Form 706: The Estate Tax Return

An estate tax return is filed using Form 706, *United States Estate (and Generation-Skipping Transfer) Tax Return.*[164] The estate tax applies to an individual's taxable estate, which is the gross estate, less certain deductions. After the taxable estate is computed, it is added to the value of taxable gifts made during the decedent's lifetime.

The applicable estate tax rate is applied to derive a tentative tax, from which any gift taxes paid or payable are subtracted to determine the gross estate tax. In 2020, each individual has the ability to transfer up to $11.58 million to others, either in lifetime gifting or at death. The maximum estate tax rate is 40% in 2020. All or a portion of the gross estate tax may be eliminated after consideration of the estate's available:

- **Basic Exclusion Amount:** This amount is adjusted for inflation each year and may be used to reduce or eliminate gift and/or estate taxes. For 2020, the basic estate tax exclusion amount is $11.58 million. Only estates valued in excess of the sum of these amounts need to file a return and pay estate tax (assuming no taxable gifts were made during the decedent's lifetime).
- **Deceased Spousal Unused Exclusion (DSUE):** This is the unused portion of the decedent's predeceased spouse's basic exclusion (the amount that was not used to offset gift or estate tax liabilities). A portability election must be made to claim the DSUE on behalf of the surviving spouse's estate. This election can be made automatically by timely completion[165] and filing of Form 706 for the estate of the predeceased spouse.

If an estate tax return is required to be filed, the due date for Form 706 is nine months after the decedent's date of death.[166] An automatic six-month extension may be requested by filing

---

164 Decedents who were neither U.S. citizens nor U.S. residents at the time of death must file Form 706-NA.

165 Revenue Procedure 2017-34 allows an executor up to two years to elect portability provided that no estate tax return is otherwise due.

166 The due date for the estate tax return is the day of the ninth calendar month after the date of the decedent's death. However, if there is no numerically corresponding day in the ninth month, the last day of the ninth month is the due date.

Form 4768, *Application for Extension of Time To File a Return and/or Pay U.S. Estate (and Generation-Skipping Transfer) Taxes.*

However, the tax is due by the due date and interest is accrued on any amounts owed that are not paid at that time. The assessment period for estate tax is three years after the due date for a timely filed estate tax return. The assessment period is four years for transfers from an estate.

Example: Chandra is unmarried. Chandra's only heir and beneficiary is her brother, Hamlin. She dies in 2020 and leaves an estate valued at $4 million. She had not previously used any of her basic exclusion amount to avoid paying gift taxes, so the entire $11.58 million exclusion is available to her estate. As the exclusion amount exceeds the entire estate's value, no estate tax is owed, and an estate tax return does not need to be filed. All of Chandra's assets may pass to her brother Hamlin, tax-free.

Example: Darrell and Hedda are married. Darrel dies on July 1, 2020. His estate is valued at $7 million at the time of his death, so an estate tax return is not required. However, Hedda files an estate tax return anyway, in order to elect the deceased spousal unused exclusion (DSUE). This will allow her to shield the assets that pass to her from Darrell's estate from federal estate tax liability, when she eventually passes herself.

A Form 706 *must* be timely filed by the executor of any estate who intends to transfer the DSUE to a decedent's surviving spouse, regardless of the amount of the gross estate.

Essentially, the DSUE allows a surviving spouse to use his or her unused estate exclusion amount, effectively increasing the amount that can be passed to the surviving spouses' family tax-free.

In 2020, this means that a surviving spouse's estate with value up to $23.16 million ($11.58 million × 2) of estate value could be excluded from taxation if both spouses died during 2020, neither spouse had used any of their basic exclusion amount to offset gift tax liabilities, all of the assets from the first deceased spouse passed to the surviving spouse, and the portability election for DSUE was properly made on Form 706 for the first spouse's estate.

Example: Jameson and Savannah are married and have one adult son, named Vance. On January 3, 2020, Jameson dies. His gross estate is valued at $8 million on the date of his death. All of Jameson's assets pass tax-free to his wife, Savannah, who is named the executor of her late husband's estate. Savannah doesn't bother to file an estate tax return for Jameson's estate, because the estate value is below the exclusion amount. On December 29, 2020, Savannah dies suddenly in a car accident. The value of her estate is now $13 million (which equals her combined assets as well as that of her late husband). Savannah and Jameson's only son, Vance, is named as the executor of his late mother's estate. Vance must file an estate tax return for his mother's estate. Since Savannah did not file a timely estate tax return to claim the DSUE for her late husband's assets, her estate is now subject to estate tax on the amount that exceeds the exclusion.

For example, if the decedent dies on July 31, 2020, the estate tax return and tax payment must be made on or before April 30, 2021.

Example: Ahearn dies on January 18, 2020, and leaves a gross estate valued at $10 million. All of his assets transfer to his wife, Darlene, and none are taxed because of the unlimited marital deduction. Thus, none of the $11.58 million basic exclusion amount available to Ahearn's estate is used (and none had been used to offset gift tax liabilities during his lifetime). Darlene dies six months later, on June 18, 2020. Form 706 was timely filed for Ahearn's estate, and Darlene had not used any of her basic exclusion amount, so Ahearn's unused basic exclusion is added to Darlene's basic exclusion, for a total exclusion amount of $23.16 million ($11.58 million × 2).

Applicable Credit (Unified Credit)

The gross estate tax described above is reduced by the *applicable credit*, also referred to as the *unified credit*, which is a tax credit amount that corresponds with the basic exclusion amount and, if applicable, the DSUE available to a surviving spouse. Each taxpayer is allowed a combined exclusion for lifetime gifts and estate tax. Very few taxpayers will pay a gift tax or an estate tax.

The dollar amounts and limitations on Form 706 are indexed for inflation. For decedents dying in 2020, the following amounts are applicable:

- The basic exclusion amount is **$11,580,000.**
- The applicable credit amount is **$4,577,800.**

Just as with the basic exclusion amount, any portion of the applicable credit amount used to avoid payment of gift taxes reduces the amount of credit available in later years that can be used to offset gift or estate taxes. For example, if someone had used the full applicable credit to avoid payment of gift taxes during his lifetime, he would have exhausted his entire basic exclusion. If he then died in 2020, his estate would be liable for tax on the taxable estate without further offset.

Example: Brannon, who is single, dies in 2020 and leaves an estate valued at $19 million. During his lifetime, he had used $1 million of his basic exclusion to offset payments of gift tax, for large gifts that he made to family and friends while he was alive. That reduces the amount his estate may exclude to $10.58 million (2020 basic exclusion $11,580,000 - $1 million), which is then subtracted from his $19 million taxable estate. That leaves a total taxable estate of $8.6 million.

The Gross Estate

The gross estate is based upon the fair market value of the decedent's property, which is not necessarily equal to his cost, and includes:

- The FMV of all tangible and intangible property owned by the decedent at the time of death.
- One-half of the full value of property held as joint tenants with the right of survivorship if the only other owner at the time of death was the decedent's spouse
- The decedent's share of the fair market value of property held as joint tenants with those *other than* a spouse. In this situation, the decedent's "share" is based on their share of the acquisition costs of the property.
- Life insurance proceeds payable to the estate, or payable to the heirs, for policies owned by the decedent.
- The value of certain annuities or survivor benefits payable to the heirs.

- The value of certain property that was transferred within three years before the decedent's death.

Example: Alexander died in 2020. He was 98 years old when he died. At the time of his death, Alexander owned hundreds of collectible baseball cards that he purchased during his childhood. The cards cost only pennies when he bought them, but now the cards are worth hundreds of thousands of dollars. For estate tax purposes, the baseball cards would be valued at their fair market value on the date of Alexander's death.

The gross estate does not include property owned solely by the decedent's spouse or other individuals. Lifetime gifts that are complete (so that no control over the gifts was retained) are not included in the decedent's gross estate. In order to qualify as a "lifetime gift," the transfer must be complete and irrevocable.

Deductions from the Gross Estate

Once the gross estate has been calculated, certain deductions (and in special circumstances, reductions to an asset's value) are allowed to determine the taxable estate. Deductions from the gross estate may include:

- Funeral expenses[167] paid out of the estate.
- Administration expenses for the estate (if not deducted on Form 1041).
- Debts owed at the time of death.
- The marital deduction (generally, the value of the property that passes from the estate to a surviving spouse who is a U.S. citizen).
- The charitable deduction (generally, the value of the property that passes from the estate to qualifying charities).
- The state death tax deduction (generally, any inheritance or estate taxes paid to any state. Some states impose a death tax, and some do not).

The following items are not deductible from the gross estate:

- Federal estate taxes paid.
- Alimony paid after the taxpayer's death. These payments would be treated as distributions to a beneficiary.

Property taxes are deductible only if they accrue under state law prior to the decedent's death.

Study Note: For both Parts 1 and 2 of the EA exam, you should be familiar with what is included in the gross estate and the taxable estate. You should also be familiar with the most common deductions that are available to an estate.

The Marital Deduction: Transfers from one spouse to the other are typically tax-free. The marital deduction allows spouses to transfer an unlimited amount of property to one another

[167] Funeral expenses are never deductible if they are paid by an individual taxpayer (whether living or dead). Funeral expenses are ONLY deductible if they are paid out of the funds of an estate. In this case, the funeral and burial expenses would be deductible on the estate tax return itself. They would not be deductible on the deceased taxpayer's individual return.

during their lifetimes or at death without being subject to estate or gift taxes if the spouse is a U.S. citizen.

If the surviving spouse is not a U.S. citizen, then the marital deduction is generally not allowed.[168] Note that the same does not hold true in reverse. The full marital deduction is available for transfers *from* a noncitizen spouse to a U.S. citizen spouse.

Note: For federal tax purposes, marriages of same-sex couples are treated the same as marriages of couples of the opposite sex. The term "spouse" includes an individual married to a person of the same sex. However, individuals who have entered into a registered domestic partnership, civil union, or other similar relationship are not considered "married" for federal tax purposes. Those unions are not eligible for the unlimited marital transfer or the DSUE.

Decedent's Medical Expenses: Debts that were not paid before death, including medical expenses subsequently paid on behalf of the decedent, are liabilities of the estate and can be deducted from the gross estate on the estate tax return. However, if medical expenses for the decedent are paid out of the estate during the one-year period beginning with the day after death, the personal representative can alternatively elect to treat all or part of the expenses as paid by the decedent at the time they were incurred and deduct them on the final tax return (1040) for the decedent.

The Basis of Estate Property

The basis of property inherited from a decedent is generally one of the following:

- The FMV of the property on the date of death.
- The FMV on an alternate valuation date (which is normally the FMV of assets six months after the date of death, except for assets distributed to an heir after death but prior to six months after death, in which case the basis will be the FMV as of the date of distribution), if elected by the personal representative.
- The value under a "special-use valuation" method for real property used in farming or another closely-held business, if elected by the personal representative.
- The decedent's adjusted basis in land to the extent of the value excluded from the taxable estate as a qualified conservation easement.

Example: Roger is unmarried. He dies on April 3, 2020. On the date of his death, Roger had a basis of $35,000 in his house in Los Angeles, which he bought in 1964 and lived in continuously since its purchase. Roger's only heir and beneficiary is his daughter, Mikaela, who is 26 years old. The house's FMV was $2,500,000, on the date of Roger's death. It was the only asset that he owned, so an estate tax return does not need to be filed. Mikaela inherited the house after Roger's death, and her basis would be $2,500,000. Mikaela sells the house two months later for $2,510,000. Her taxable gain would only be $10,000 (the amount of her stepped-up basis minus the sales price). Her gain would be reported on Schedule D and will be taxed at favorable long-term capital gains rates.

[168] An exception to this rule exists if a Qualified Domestic Trust (QDOT) is in place and an election is made. With a QDOT, the assets of the deceased spouse pass into the trust of a surviving noncitizen spouse. In order to make this election, the trustee of the QDOT must be a U.S. citizen.

Property that is jointly owned by a decedent and another person under *joint tenancy with a right of survivorship* or *tenancy in the entirety* (where the other co-owners of the property automatically inherit the property upon the death of the taxpayer) will be included, in full, in the decedent's gross estate unless it can be shown that the other person originally owned or otherwise contributed to the purchase price.

The surviving owner's new basis in property that was jointly owned under either of these two types of ownership is calculated by adding his original basis in the property to the value of the part of the property included in the decedent's estate. Any deductions for depreciation of the property allowed to the surviving owner are subtracted from the sum.

On the other hand, for properties owned with others as *tenants in common* (where the other co-owners do not automatically inherit the decedent's portion of the property upon their death), only the decedent's percentage ownership of the property will be included in their estate.

Example: Michael and Terrance are brothers. Several decades ago, they purchased a parcel of land together for $50,000. Michael contributed $12,500 to the purchase of the land, which was 25% of the purchase price. Terrance contributed $37,500, which was 75% of the purchase price. They held the property as tenants in common. On March 1, 2020, Terrance dies. He was unmarried. On the date of Terrance's death, the land is valued at $200,000. One-quarter of the value of the property is excluded from Terrance's gross estate, and three-quarters (75%) of the value would be included in his gross estate. Based on this scenario, the amount that would be included in Terrance's gross estate with respect to the value of the land would be $150,000 ($200,000 FMV on the date of death X 75%).

If property is jointly held between husband and wife as *tenants by the entirety* or *as joint tenants with the right of survivorship* (if they were the only joint tenants), one-half of the property's value is included in the gross estate, and there is a step-up in basis for that one-half. If the decedent holds property in a community property state, half of the value of the community property will be included in the gross estate of the decedent, but the entire value of the community property will receive a step-up in basis.

Trusts in General

A trust is an entity created under the laws of the state in which it is formed. A trust may be created during an individual's life (an inter-vivos trust) or at the time of death under a will (a testamentary trust). A trust is generally created to hold property for the benefit of other persons. The establishment of a trust creates a fiduciary relationship between three parties:

- **The Grantor:** The person who contributes property to the trust.
- **The Trustee (or Fiduciary):** The person or entity charged with the fiduciary duties associated with the trust.
- **The Beneficiary:** The person who is designated to receive the trust income or assets.

There are many types of trusts. A trust may be created for the benefit of a disabled individual, it can be created to benefit a charity, or it can be used to legally avoid certain taxes.

For example, a pension plan trust is a type of trust that holds assets for a qualified pension. A trustee administers the funds and invests the money, as well as distributes any pension benefits to retirees. A qualified disability trust is a type of trust set up exclusively for the benefit of a disabled individual.

While there are many different types of trusts, the two basic types are **revocable** and **irrevocable**.

A **"revocable trust"** allows the person who created the trust to retain control of the assets in the trust, and revoke or change the terms of the trust at any time. With an **"irrevocable trust"** the assets in the trust are no longer controlled by the grantor. For tax purposes, revocable trusts and some irrevocable trusts are treated as if they are still owned by the grantor, so all items related to the trust are reported on the grantor's 1040 returns. These are called "grantor" trusts (discussed later).

A living trust can be either "revocable" or "irrevocable." Upon the death of the grantor, a revocable trust automatically becomes irrevocable. A "testamentary" trust also becomes irrevocable upon the testator's death. A testamentary trust is a trust contained in a last will and testament of a decedent.

Example: Adelaide is having serious medical problems and decides to put her assets in a trust. She asks her attorney to create the trust, as well as manage the assets. The trust is structured so that it will pay Adelaide's living expenses, with the remainder of the assets going to her grandson after she dies. While Adelaide is alive, the trust is revocable, and Adelaide still controls the assets in the trust. Upon her death, her revocable trust automatically becomes irrevocable. In this scenario, Adelaide is the **grantor**, the lawyer is the **trustee**, and Adelaide and her grandson are both the **beneficiaries**.

Sometimes, a trust is used to transfer property in a controlled manner. For example, a parent may wish to transfer ownership of assets to his child, but does not want the child to waste the assets or spend them unwisely.

The assets could be transferred to a trust, with the parent as both the grantor and the trustee. The child would be the beneficiary. The parent still has control over the assets, and the child is prevented from using them all up.

The accounting period for a trust is generally the calendar year. The filing due date for a calendar-year trust is typically April 15. Form 1041, *U.S. Income Tax Return for Estates and Trusts,* is used by the fiduciary of a domestic trust to report:

- Income, deductions, gains, losses, etc. of the trust;
- Income that is either accumulated or held for future distribution or distributed currently to the beneficiaries, and
- The income tax liability of the trust.

A trust is required to file Form 1041, *U.S. Income Tax Return for Estates and Trusts,* if it has:

- Any taxable income for the year (after subtracting the allowable exemption amount),
- Gross income of $600 or more (regardless of whether the income is taxable or not), or
- Any beneficiary who is a nonresident alien.

Example: The Randall Family Trust has $200 of tax-exempt interest from municipal bonds during the year. There is no other income. Normally, the trust would not be required to file a tax return because the income earned by the trust is tax-exempt. However, the Randall Family Trust has a beneficiary who is a nonresident alien. Therefore, the trust is required to file Form 1041.

A trust calculates its gross income in a manner similar to an individual taxpayer. Trusts are allowed a small annual exemption, but the amount varies based on the type of trust. A trust that must distribute all of its income currently (a simple trust) is allowed an exemption of $300. Any other trust is allowed an exemption of $100 per year, with the exception of a qualified disability trust.[169]

A qualified disability trust is allowed a $4,300 exemption in 2020. This means that a qualified disability trust can retain $4,300 tax-free each year, creating a fund for a disabled beneficiary's future needs. A qualified disability trust may also distribute this amount tax-free to a disabled beneficiary. Income distributed from a qualified disability trust is also exempt from the kiddie tax.

Most deductions and credits allowed to individuals are also allowed to trusts. However, there is one major distinction: a trust is a potential pass-through entity that is allowed a deduction for its distributions to beneficiaries. The beneficiaries (and *not* the trust) pay income tax on their distributive share of income. Schedule K-1 (Form 1041) is used to report income that a trust distributes to beneficiaries. The income must then be reported on the beneficiaries' income tax returns.

Example: The Carson Disability Trust was set up for the sole benefit of Lyndsey Carson, who is the trust's sole beneficiary. Lyndsey Carson is permanently disabled. The Carson Disability Trust has an investment portfolio worth $350,000, which generates $25,000 in taxable dividend income. During the tax year, the trustee of the Carson Disability Trust paid for Lyndsey's educational expenses of $15,000 for special-needs tutoring and activities, as well as the cost of a summer day camp for disabled individuals. The trustee took reasonable compensation of $2,500 during the year for the administration of the trust. The Carson Disability Trust must file Form 1041, reporting the $25,000 in taxable investment income. The trust is allowed an exemption of $4,300 in 2020. The trustee fees of $2,500 will be deductible as administrative expenses, and Lyndsey's $15,000 in distributions will also be deducted. The trust will send a Schedule K-1 to Lyndsey showing her distributions, and she will be responsible for reporting $15,000 of taxable income (based on the amount of the distribution) on her personal Form 1040 tax return. Most of the income she receives will be shielded from tax, because Lyndsey will be allowed to claim a standard deduction of $12,400 on her 2020 personal income tax return. The amounts are not subject to the Kiddie tax, even if Lyndsey is claimed as a dependent on her parent's returns.

[169] The Tax Cuts and Jobs Act eliminated the personal exemption for individuals, but does not eliminate the exemption for trusts and estates. Qualified disability trusts are entitled to the same personal exemption that was allowed (before implementation of the TCJA) to all individual taxpayers when filing a tax return. Any income generated by the trust exceeding this exemption amount that is not distributed to or for the benefit of the beneficiary would be subject to income tax at the trust income tax rates.

Simple and Complex Trusts

With regard to income distribution, there are two types of trusts: a simple trust and a complex trust. The IRC defines a **simple trust** as a trust that:

- Must distribute all of its income currently (in other words, it cannot accumulate income from year to year),
- Makes no distributions of principal, and
- Makes no distributions to charity.

Any trust that is not a simple trust is automatically classified as a complex trust. Since simple trusts are required to distribute all their income currently, only complex trusts may accumulate income. A complex trust:

- Is allowed to accumulate income,
- Can make discretionary distributions of income,
- Can make mandatory (or discretionary) distributions of principal, and
- Can make distributions to charity.

A trust may be a simple trust one year, and a complex trust in the following year. For example, if a simple trust fails to distribute all its income in the current year, it becomes a complex trust. Unlike an estate or a simple trust, a complex trust reports its accounting income, (which may differ from its taxable income and its DNI and may be more or less than distributions for the year), on Form 1041.

Study Note: For Part 2 of the EA exam, you should understand the differences between a simple trust and a complex trust and know the rules for how each distributes income.

Grantor Trusts

A grantor trust is a valid legal entity under state law, but it is considered a disregarded entity for federal income tax purposes. A grantor creates the trust and retains control over the trust. Any taxable income or deduction earned by the trust will be taxed on the grantor's tax return. Therefore, in the eyes of the IRS, the grantor is the owner of the trust for income tax purposes. The grantor establishes the terms and provisions of the trust relationship between the grantor, the trustee, and the beneficiary. These will usually include the following:

- The rights, duties, and powers of the trustee,
- Distribution provisions,
- The ability of the grantor to amend, modify, revoke, or terminate the trust agreement,
- The designation of a trustee or successor trustees, and
- The designation of the state under which the trust agreement is to be governed.

Revocable trusts and some irrevocable trusts are grantor trusts in which the grantor retains the right to make changes or end the trust during his lifetime. The benefit of this type of trust is that the grantor retains control over the trust, and a separate trust income tax return is usually not required. The drawback is that trust assets are subject to estate tax upon the grantor's death. Many taxpayers use this type of trust instead of, or in addition to, a will.

Non-Grantor Trusts

A non-grantor trust is considered a separate legal entity from the individual or organization that created it, because the donor of the assets gives up all control. The trust itself is treated as a separate taxable entity. The trust's income and deductions are reported on Form 1041.

If a non-grantor trust makes distributions to a beneficiary, in general, those distributions are taxable income to the beneficiary. Examples include:

1. **Irrevocable Trusts**: An irrevocable trust is a trust that cannot be revoked after it is created. The transfer of assets into this type of trust is generally considered a "completed gift" subject to gift tax.
2. **Disability Trusts:** A qualified disability trust is a non-grantor trust created solely for the benefit of a disabled individual under age 65. A Qualified Disability Trust or QDT is allowed the same exemption as an individual ($4,3200 in 2020). This is a specific exception to the regular exemption amount that applies to most trusts. A Qualified Disability Trust is a complex trust, because it is designed to hold income and assets for the benefit of a disabled beneficiary.
3. **Charitable Trusts:** A charitable trust is a trust devoted to qualified charitable contribution purposes. Charitable trusts are irrevocable.

Example: Penelope Wells has severe autism. Penelope's wealthy grandfather set up a disability trust on her behalf before he passed away a few years ago. The Penelope Trust is a qualified disability trust, or QDT. In 2020, the trust had $19,000 of interest income and made $16,000 worth of distributions for Penelope's benefit. The money went directly to pay for Penelope's daily care. The $16,000 in distributions is taxed as interest income on Penelope's individual Form 1040. The amounts are not subject to kiddie tax, and Penelope can take the standard deduction to shield the majority of the income from tax. The remaining undistributed income ($3,000) would be reported on the trust's income tax return (Form 1041). Since the trust is a Qualified Disability Trust with a $4,300 exemption, there would be no income tax due on the $3,000 that was not distributed to the beneficiary (Penelope).

Example: Jacqueline Smith creates a charitable trust. The Smith Charitable Trust has a governing instrument that provides that her local Presbyterian Church (a qualified religious organization), and the SPCA (a 501(c)(3) charity) are each to receive 50% of the trust income for ten years. At the end of the ten-year period, the corpus will be distributed entirely to the Smithsonian Museum, also a 501(c)(3) organization. Jacqueline is allowed an income tax deduction for the value of the assets she places in the trust. The Smith Charitable Trust is irrevocable, which means that the trust cannot be modified or terminated without the permission of the beneficiary (in this case, the beneficiaries are the charitable organizations themselves).

Abusive Trust Arrangements

Certain trust arrangements purport to reduce or eliminate federal taxes in ways that are not permitted under the law. These abusive or fraudulent trust arrangements may be used to hide the true ownership of assets and income or to disguise the substance of transactions.

They frequently involve more than one trust, each holding different assets of the taxpayer (for example, the taxpayer's business, business equipment, home, automobile, etc.).

Some trusts may hold interests in other trusts, purport to involve charities, or be foreign trusts. Participants and promoters of abusive trust schemes may be subject to civil or criminal penalties. Abusive or fraudulent trust arrangements may promise such benefits as:

- Deductions for personal expenses paid by the trust
- Depreciation deductions for an owner's personal residence
- A stepped-up basis for property transferred to the trust
- The reduction or elimination of self-employment taxes
- The reduction or elimination of gift and estate taxes

Although these schemes give the appearance of separating responsibility and control from the benefits of ownership, as would be the case with legitimate trusts, the taxpayer, in fact, controls them. When trusts are used for legitimate business, family, or estate planning purposes, either the trust, the beneficiary, or the grantor will pay the tax on the income generated by the trust. Basically, someone has to pay the tax! If not, there is a chance that the trust is an abusive trust arrangement.

Trusts cannot be used to transform a taxpayer's personal, living, or educational expenses into deductible items. A taxpayer cannot use a trust to avoid tax liability by ignoring either the true ownership of income and assets or the true substance of transactions.

However, do not confuse an "abusive" trust with a legitimate trust that is used to pay the living expenses of a disabled individual. A qualified disability trust is a special type of trust that allows family members to plan for the future of a child with special needs. Even in the case of a qualified disability trust, the income generated by the trust is taxable (usually to the beneficiary), although the trust itself is allowed a higher exemption than other trust types.

Example: Kurtis transfers his family residence and its furnishings to a trust, which rents the residence back to Kurtis and his children. He deducts depreciation and the expenses of maintaining and operating the home, including landscaping, pool service, and utilities. Kurtis' second trust transfers assets to the Sham Charity Fund, which claims to be a charitable organization, but is in fact, not an IRS-qualified exempt organization. The trust pays for personal, education, and recreational expenses on behalf of Kurtis and his family. The trust then claims the deductions on its tax returns. Both trusts Kurtis created are fraudulent, and he would be subject to civil and criminal penalties.

Foreign Trusts

Foreign trusts are not always created to evade taxation. However, the IRS gives increased scrutiny to foreign trusts because of their growing popularity in foreign countries that provide financial secrecy and impose little or no tax on trusts. These are often in "tax haven" countries that are outside the jurisdiction of the U.S.

Example: Rosemary is a U.S. citizen with substantial business income. She forms an asset management company as a domestic trust, listing herself as the director and her son as the trustee. She then forms a business trust, very similar to the domestic trust, with both intended to show she is not managing her own business. Next, Rosemary forms a foreign trust in Bermuda, with the income from the business trust distributed to this foreign trust. Because the source of income is U.S.-based, and there is a U.S. trustee, this foreign trust has filing requirements (discussed next). Her next step is to form a second foreign trust. The first foreign trust funnels all of its income to this second foreign trust, which has a foreigner as the trustee. Since the trustee and sources of income are now "foreign," Rosemary claims there are no U.S. filing requirements. In actuality, she retains control of the income in this second foreign trust and has set up an elaborate scheme to evade U.S. tax laws. This is an abusive trust arrangement.

Typically, abusive foreign trust arrangements enable taxable funds to flow through several trusts or entities until the funds ultimately are distributed or made available to the original owner tax-free. Legally, however, the income from these arrangements is fully taxable. A trust is considered "foreign" unless a U.S. court supervises it, and a U.S. fiduciary controls all substantial decisions.

U.S. taxpayers are required to file Form 3520, *Creation of or Transfer to Certain Foreign Trusts*, Form 3520-A, *Annual Return of Foreign Trust with U.S. Beneficiaries*, and Form 926, *Return by a Transferor of Property to a Foreign Estate or Trust*, when contributing property to a foreign trust. These trusts are usually U.S. tax neutral and are treated as grantor trusts with income taxable to the grantor that should be included on Form 1040.

Foreign Accounts: Both individuals and entities, including trusts, may be required to report their foreign accounts to the IRS by filing an electronic Financial Crimes Enforcement Network (FinCEN), Form 114, *Report of Foreign Bank and Financial Accounts* (FBAR). The FBAR report must be e-filed by April 15 (with an applicable six-month extension, which is automatically granted without the need to request an extension) if:

- The taxpayer had a financial interest in, or signature authority over, at least one financial account located outside of the United States, and
- The aggregate value of all foreign financial accounts exceeded $10,000 at any time during the calendar year to be reported.

Certain exceptions apply to the filing requirement. For example, if the foreign financial accounts are owned by a governmental entity, international financial institution, participants, or beneficiaries of a qualified retirement plan, or IRA owners and beneficiaries, they are exempt from the FBAR filing requirements.

Unit 19: Study Questions

(Test yourself and then check the correct answers at the end of this section.)

1. Patricia died on May 3, 2020. The value of her assets at the time of her death was $1,500,000, which included investments and the value of her primary residence in San Diego. Patricia's estate had the following items of income during the year:

- Tax-exempt interest: $250
- Dividends: $170

Patricia's sole heir is her son, Ellery, who is a U.S. citizen. The estate made no distributions during 2020. In addition, Patricia had never made any taxable gifts during her lifetime. Based on the information provided, which of the following statements is correct?

A. The estate is not required to file an income tax return (Form 1041) but must file a Form 706.
B. The estate must file an income tax return (Form 1041) and an estate tax return (Form 706).
C. The estate is required to file a Form 706, but not a Form 1041.
D. The estate is not required to file an income tax return (Form 1041) or an estate tax return (Form 706).

2. All of the following are characteristics of a simple trust *except:*

A. The trust may distribute assets to charity.
B. The trust must distribute all its income currently.
C. The trust makes no distributions of principal.
D. The trust makes no distributions to charity.

3. The calculation of the gross estate includes all of the following except:

A. Life insurance proceeds payable to the decedent's heirs.
B. The value of certain annuities payable to the estate.
C. Property owned solely by the decedent's spouse.
D. The value of certain property transferred within three years before the taxpayer's death.

4. Dominique, an American citizen, has a trust in Monaco, where she regularly deposits funds and can withdraw funds at any time. Which of the following statements is correct regarding the trust?

A. Income deposited in the Monaco trust is shielded from all U.S. taxes.
B. Dominique is not subject to any filing requirements in connection with her foreign trust.
C. Dominique may have to pay gift taxes on funds distributed from the trust, but will not owe income tax.
D. All income in Dominique's foreign trust is fully taxable.

5. Who pays income tax on a trust's distributive share of income?

A. The trust.
B. The beneficiaries.
C. Income tax is split equally between the trust and its beneficiaries.
D. Income tax is not assessed on a trust's distributive share of income.

6. The Beaumont Estate is required to distribute all of its income currently. The estate has distributable net income (DNI) of $20,000 on its 2020 return. The only distribution the executor made during the year was $5,000, paid to the decedent's son, Carlton Beaumont. According to the terms of the will, Carlton is entitled to 50% of the estate's DNI, and his sister, Jasmine Beaumont, is entitled to the other 50% of the estate's distributable net income. Which of the following statements is correct?

A. Carlton must pay tax on $10,000.
B. Carlton must pay tax on $20,000.
C. Carlton is not required to pay tax on the distribution, since it is an inheritance.
D. Carlton must pay tax on $5,000.

7. The Mulcher Family Trust had the following in 2020:

- Taxable interest income: $4,000
- Capital gains income: $12,000
- Fiduciary fee: $2,000

At the end of 2020, the trust fiduciary distributes $4,000. The trust instrument allocates capital gains to income. What is the distributable net income (DNI) of Mulcher Trust for the year?

A. $12,000
B. $14,000
C. $16,000
D. $18,000

8. All of the following are examples of potentially abusive trusts except:

A. A taxpayer who claims charitable deductions from a charitable trust he has created, without receiving an IRS exemption letter.
B. A taxpayer who forms a grantor trust and retains the power to control or direct the trust's income or assets.
C. A taxpayer who forms a foreign trust in a "tax haven" country, so funds distributed will be outside the jurisdiction of the United States.
D. A taxpayer who transfers an ongoing business to a series of trusts to avoid taxation but continues to run the day-to-day activities of the business and control its income stream.

9. Patty died on February 2, 2020. A final paycheck was issued after the date of her death for work that Patty performed prior to her death. How is this income classified?

A. Nontaxable income.
B. Supplemental compensation.
C. Income in respect of a decedent.
D. Decedent's wages.

10. When Regina died, her estate included a large number of stock investments. The terms of Regina's final will require annual payments of $30,000 and $10,000 to her husband (her surviving spouse) and her son, respectively, out of her estate's income during each year of the administration. However, during the year, the value of her investments dropped, and the estate only has distributable net income (DNI) of $20,000. Since this amount is less than the required annual payments that were required by Regina's will, what are the amounts of income that will be reported by the estate to each beneficiary on their 2020 Forms K-1?

A. Husband: $10,000; Son: $10,000.
B. Husband: $15,000; Son: $5,000.
C. Husband: $20,000; Son: $0.
D. Husband: $0; Son: $0.

11. Parker, a single taxpayer, died on June 6, 2020. Based on the following information, determine the value of his gross estate:

FMV on the date of death	
Life insurance on Parker's life (payable to his estate, not his heirs)	$1,250,000
Parker's revocable grantor trust	$700,000
Debts owed by Parker when he died	($150,000)

A. $250,000
B. $800,000
C. $1,800,000
D. $1,950,000

12. Alvin Lewis died three years ago. Connie and her three brothers are equal beneficiaries of their late father's estate. In 2020, the Estate of Alvin Lewis has distributable net income of $12,000, consisting of $6,000 of rents, $4,000 of dividends, and $2,000 of taxable interest. The estate's executor, a family lawyer, distributes the income under the provisions of Alvin Lewis' final will, which includes a stipulation that allocates all the dividend income to Connie. How is the distribution to Connie characterized for tax purposes?

A. $0 rents; $3,000 dividends; $0 taxable interest.
B. $0 rents; $4,000 dividends; $0 taxable interest.
C. $2,000 rents; $1,333 dividends; $667 taxable interest.
D. $1,500 rents; $1,000 dividends, $1,000 taxable interest.

13. What is included in the gross estate?

A. The gross estate includes everything the taxpayer owns six months after the date of death.
B. The gross estate includes everything the taxpayer owns after the date of death.
C. The gross estate includes everything the decedent earned in the prior year, as well as income estimates for future years.
D. The gross estate includes everything the taxpayer owns at the date of death.

14. Georgiana died on March 1, 2020. The executor of her estate has elected to file the estate's income tax return on a calendar-year basis. No distributions have been made by the estate by the end of the year. Based on the following, what is the taxable income that will be reported on Form 1041 for the estate, for the tax year, before consideration of the estate's exemption amount?

Taxable interest	$2,000
Tax-exempt interest	$1,000
Capital gain	$3,000
Executor's fees	$300

A. $4,700
B. $5,100
C. $5,700
D. $6,000

Unit 19: Quiz Answers

1. The answer is D. An estate income tax return (Form 1041) must be filed for any domestic estate that has gross income of more than $600 for the tax year, or a beneficiary who is a nonresident alien, regardless of the estate's gross income. Since the gross income is below the $600 exemption amount, an income tax return is not required to be filed for 2020. Patricia's estate also does not have an estate tax return filing requirement, because the value of the estate assets does not exceed $11.58 million in 2020.

2. The answer is A. The IRC defines a simple trust as one that distributes all its income *currently*, makes no distributions of principal, and makes no distributions to charity. Any trust that is not a simple trust is automatically a complex trust. Only a complex trust can make charitable distributions.

3. The answer is C. The gross estate does not include property owned solely by the decedent's spouse or other individuals.

4. The answer is D. Although foreign trusts are often established in certain countries in an effort to evade taxation, the income from such arrangements is fully taxable under U.S. law. Dominique would also be subject to an annual filing requirement, Form 3520-A, *Annual Return of Foreign Trust with U.S. Beneficiaries.*

5. The answer is B. A trust is a partial pass-through entity that is allowed a deduction for its distributions to beneficiaries. The beneficiaries pay income tax on their distributive share of income that is distributed to them. Schedule K-1 (Form 1041) is used to report income that a trust distributes to beneficiaries. The income must then be reported on the beneficiaries' income tax returns.

6. The answer is A. Carlton must report and pay tax related to his entire share of DNI, $10,000, (which is 50% of the estate's DNI) rather than the portion he received in distributions during the year. The beneficiary of an estate required to distribute all its income currently must report his entire share of DNI, whether or not he actually received distributions for the full amount during his tax year.

7. The answer is B. The Mulcher Family Trust's distributable net income (DNI) is **$14,000** figured as follows:

Taxable interest	$4,000
Capital gains	$12,000
MINUS Fiduciary fees	($2,000)
Distributable net income	**$14,000**

By definition, "distributable net income" is income that is currently available for distribution.

8. The answer is B. A grantor trust is a legitimate form of trust. All of the other trusts described are potentially abusive. Trusts cannot be used to transform a taxpayer's personal, living, or educational expenses into deductible items. A taxpayer cannot use a trust to avoid tax liability by ignoring either the true ownership of income and assets or the true substance of transactions.

9. The answer is C. Patty's final paycheck would be considered IRD, because it was issued after her death. A paycheck issued after the date of death to a taxpayer for work performed prior to death is considered income in respect of a decedent (IRD).

10. The answer is B. The beneficiaries of an estate that is not required to distribute all its income currently must report all income required to be distributed to them currently (whether or not actually distributed), plus all other amounts paid, credited, or required to be distributed to them, up to their share of distributable net income. In this scenario, since the income of the estate (the DNI) is lower than the total amounts required to be distributed, it forms the limit on the amounts that must be reported as income to each beneficiary. DNI is allocated to each beneficiary in proportion to the required annual payments he received, thus 75% ($30,000/$40,000), or **$15,000,** to Regina's husband and 25% ($10,000/$40,000), or **$5,000,** to her son.

11. The answer is D. Parker's gross estate would be figured as follows: ($1,250,000 + $700,000 = **$1,950,000**). Life insurance payable to a trust and assets held in a grantor trust are included in a decedent's gross estate. Liabilities of the decedent are not included in the gross estate. However, they are an allowable deduction from the gross estate in determining the taxable estate.

12. The answer is B. Based upon the stipulation that allocates dividend income to Connie; the full amount of **dividends** included in distributable net income **($4,000)** is taxable to Connie.

13. The answer is D. The gross estate of the decedent includes everything the taxpayer owns at the date of death. Generally, assets are included in the gross estate at their fair market value on the date of the decedent's death.

14. The answer is A. Taxable income of $4,700 can be reported for Georgiana's estate, determined as follows: taxable interest of $2,000 plus capital gain of $3,000, minus the executor's fees of $300. The expenses of administering an estate can be deducted either from the estate's income on Form 1041 in determining its income tax or from the gross estate on Form 706 in determining the estate tax liability, but cannot be claimed for both purposes. The tax-exempt interest retains the character that would have applied if it had been reported by the decedent. The estate would be eligible for an exemption amount of $600 in determining its actual taxable income.

Index

A

B

C

D

E

F

G

H

I

J

K

L

M

N

O

P

Q

R

S

T

U

V

W

About the Authors

Joel Busch, CPA, JD

Joel Busch is a tax professor at San Jose State University, where he teaches courses at both the graduate and undergraduate levels. Previously, he was in charge of tax audits, research, and planning for one of the largest civil construction and mining companies in the United States. He received both a BS in Accounting and a MS in Taxation from SJSU and he has a JD from the Monterey College of Law. He is licensed in California as both a CPA and an attorney.

Christy Pinheiro, EA, ABA®

Christy Pinheiro is an Enrolled Agent and an Accredited Business Accountant. Christy was an accountant for two private CPA firms and for the State of California before going into private practice.

Kolleen Wells, EA

Kolleen Wells is an Enrolled Agent and a Certified Bookkeeper who specializes in tax preparation for individuals and small businesses. She has worked in the accounting field for many years, including positions at a CPA office and at the county assessor's office.

Thomas A. Gorczynski, EA, USTCP

Thomas A. Gorczynski is an Enrolled Agent, a Certified Tax Planner, and admitted to the bar of the United States Tax Court. Tom is also a nationally known tax educator and currently serves as editor-in-chief of EA Journal. He received the 2019 Excellence in Education Award from the National Association of Enrolled Agents. He earned a Master of Science in Taxation from Golden Gate University and a Certificate in Finance and Accounting from the Wharton School at the University of Pennsylvania.

Get more information, webinars, and practice exams on our official website:
www.PassKeyOnline.com

Made in the USA
Coppell, TX
24 January 2022

72148010R00249